The Lai

Yah's Nature Reve~~~ ~~~~ugh His Creation

Part Three -

The Language of God in History

A New Biblically Based Reinterpretation of History
That Traces The Ancient Religious Use of
God's Symbolic Language

Pillar of Enoch Ministry Books

Publisher's Cataloging-in-Publication data

Lehman, Helena.
The language of God in history / by Helena Lehman.
p. cm.
"Seventh Edition"
Series: The language of God -- Yah's nature revealed through His creation,
part three.
ISBN 978-0-9759131-2-3

1. Bible. O.T. Historiography. 2. Bible--History of Biblical events.
3. Bible. N.T.--Historiography. 4. Bible--Criticism, interpretation, etc. 5.
Symbolism in the Bible. 6. Cosmology, Ancient. 7. Great Pyramid (Egypt)--
Miscellanea. I. Title. II. Series.

BS1199 .L2 2008
221.95--dc22   2006901503

Dedication and Acknowledgements

This book is dedicated to the loving memory of my earthly father, John R. Lutz, Sr. (1926-2005), who did his best to be a good father, and who is sorely missed.

See you in Heaven, Dad!

Language of God Series Reader Endorsements:

"As an aspiring writer myself, I realize the amount of work that goes into writing a book such as you have so masterfully done in yours. The research that you have put into these works is incredible, and the fact that you can synthesize it all into a flowing, unique work is commendable." - Walter Rogoza, M. Div, Ontario, Canada

"Lehman has the ability to take heavy, deep facts and turn them into an enjoyable page turner. Anyone interested in the stars, in scripture, in history and in mysteries will delight in this fascinating book series." - Bruce Collins, Monster Radio Book Reviewer, and Big Finale Internet Radio Talk Show Host

"Helena displays an in-depth knowledge of the Bible, and has presented some very interesting and thoughtful insights evoked from her journey with God. If you are interested in Bible allegories and prophecy, this book series is well worth the read." - James Johnson, Ohio, USA

"I have read many books on subjects like the 7 Feasts, the Tabernacle, the Sabbath, Enoch, the Pyramids, the Zodiac, and the Nephilim, etc., but no author before you has ever tied them together, and then shown how they fit in YAH's Holy plan. Your books are truly inspired by the Holy Spirit." - Joyce Tapia, Texas USA

"Your books and contacts have helped get me through tough times. The scope and content of your books is truly amazing. I am sure you will bless many others, as you have me." - Nancy Shonkwiler, Indiana, USA

~ Author's Notes ~

In the Old Testament, whenever the expression "the LORD God" or "the LORD" is used, it actually says "Yahweh Elohim" or "Yahweh" in Hebrew. I have therefore chosen to use God's Name Yahweh instead of the generic term "LORD" and the title Elohim instead of "God" in the expression "LORD God" and have restored the phrase "Yahweh Elohim" to all Bible quotations where it appears in the original Hebrew. In addition, I have chosen to use Christ's Hebrew/Aramaic Name "Yahshua" instead of the Greek name Jesus, where the "Yah" in Yahshua is the contracted form of "Yahweh," as found in the expression "HalleluYAH!" A detailed explanation of my reasons for this is found at my web site: http://pillar-of-enoch.com.

All Scriptural quotations in this book (unless otherwise noted) are from the PC Study Bible using either the Holy Bible: New International Version ®, Copyright © 1973, 1978, 1984 by the International Bible Society; or the New King James Version of the Bible, Thomas Nelson, Inc. © 1982. The printed edition of the New International Version referred to in the Bibliography was also used. The origins of all quoted Scriptures from these two Bibles are identified with the abbreviation (NIV) for the New International Version and (NKJ) for the New King James Version. Due to copyright restrictions on these editions of the Bible, longer quotations of the Bible are abridged. To see the full content of each abbreviated passage, please utilize a full translation of the Bible. For the Book of 1 Enoch, the translation by R. H. Charles was used as listed in the bibliography, unless otherwise noted.

~ Table of Contents ~

The "Language of God" Book Series Summary

Author's Note: This book is the second in a series of four books that sprang from one book entitled: "The Language of God - Yah's Nature Revealed Through His Creation." Since the other books are frequently referred to in this book, the content of the entire series is summarized here, and it is highly recommended that this book be read in conjunction with the other books in the series.

All the books in the Language of God series are available for purchase from author Helena Lehman at the Pillar of Enoch Ministry web site at www.pillar-of-enoch.com, and through local bookstores, BarnesandNoble.com, Amazon.com, and Amazon.co.uk. You can also e-mail the author at helena@pillar-of-enoch.com, or write to: Pillar of Enoch Ministry, 1708 N. 77th Avenue, Elmwood Park, IL 60707-4107, USA, for more information about the "Language of God" Book Series.

Book One, "The Language of God in the Universe" takes a profound new look at Sacred Astronomy, the Gospel in the Stars, and their connection to the Bible. By understanding the allegorical Language that God utilizes to communicate to mankind, and applying it to the Zodiac and the Bible, both are shown to be filled with similar prophetic imagery. Many allegorical ties between the Bible, and the Gospel in the Stars are revealed, and once mysterious prophetic Scriptures suddenly make sense. The Universe, and the forty-eight constellations of the ancient Zodiac are like biblical parables on a giant scale. They tell a compelling story that fully agrees with the Bible, and the unfolding of biblical history. The Magi who found Christ likely knew this, and the book examines their possible use of Sacred Astronomy to locate His whereabouts in Bethlehem in 3 BC.

Secondly, the parable-like allegories found in our Solar System, upon the Earth, and in various elements of nature are explored. By seeking the Language of God apparent in every created thing, each layer of Yah's creation can reveal startling truths about our Creator, His love of mankind, and His desire to save us from our worst enemies: Satan and our fallen nature.

Book Two, "The Language of God in Humanity" explores what it means to be created in God's image, and how this reflects God's ultimate purpose for humanity. First, it shows how the dual witness of the Gospel in the Stars, and the Bible reveal God's allegorical Language of love to humanity. Then, using the knowledge of love revealed in these witnesses, Blood Covenant ceremonies like Communion are shown to symbolically communicate the correct basis for all human and divine social relationships.

Next, by comparing the familial relationships between God and His human children, this book shows how all people serve as living parables, and potential members of God's family. Using the Language of God as a key, the parables of Yahshua (Jesus), and biblically based festivals such as Passover, Chanukah, and Sukkot also take on far deeper meanings. This fervent look at Judeo-Christianity also deciphers the prophetic elements in biblically inspired religious buildings such as the Tabernacle, and rituals such as Communion, baptism, and blood sacrifice - and shows how vital and relevant their symbolic meanings still are today.

Book Three, "The Language of God in History" reinterprets history and archeology within a biblical framework. It does so by refuting the atheistic humanism behind modern archeological, scientific, and historical viewpoints. Then the evidence is examined through a biblical worldview, revealing how many ancient structures appear to have originally been designed not to honor Pagan deities, but the one true God. By deciphering the Language of God hidden in the sacred edifices of our ancestors, some startling conclusions are drawn concerning the spiritual teachings of the godly people before the Flood - especially the prophet Enoch.

Next, using facts found in the Bible and Ethiopian Book of Enoch, the scourge of the Nephilim on humanity, the possible causes of the Great Flood, and the swift Post-Flood devolution of mankind into sin are explored - as Noah and Shem's righteous witness were forgotten, and Yahweh's truths were perverted just as they had been prior to the Flood. Finally, the rise and fall of ancient Israel, the facts behind their migrations in the Diaspora, and the re-immergence of Israel in modern times are discussed in preparation for the study of biblical prophecy in the final book of this series.

Book Four, "The Language of God in Prophecy" is an explosive new exploration of the parable-like images used in biblical, and extra-biblical prophecies regarding the End Times. Prophecies in Ezekiel, Daniel, the Psalms, Revelation, Ethiopian Enoch, the Great Pyramid, the Great Sphinx, the Mayan Calendar, and the memoirs of George Washington are explored to disclose the End-Time roles of many nations, while dismantling the false doctrines behind British Israelism, and Anti-Semitism.

This book also examines the prophetic roles of the United States, the British Commonwealth, and modern Israel, and challenges many incorrect notions about God's vision for the End Times. In addition, the Great Pyramid and Great Sphinx are focused on, revealing their role as symbolic repositories of the complex scientific, spiritual, and prophetic knowledge of the godly antediluvian descendents of Seth. This study reveals that the Sethites had a keen knowledge of the coming Messiah revealed in the Gospel in the Stars, and a clear picture of End Time events - long before the Bible was written.

This startling view of End Time prophecy - with its urgent message that the Great Tribulation, and the end of Satan's reign on Earth may be imminent - will challenge many hardened Bible skeptics, and is sure to spur a renewed interest in God, His Son, the Gospel in the Stars, and biblical prophecy.

~ Author's Foreword ~

The Sinister Origins of the Nephilim Giants or Reptilians

The Language of God in History was written for two major reasons. First, it is an educated Christian response to the virulent anti-biblical attitudes among world secular academia, New Agers, and Neo-Pagans. Secondly, it is in response to the many alien conspiracy advocates and Darwinists who use author Zecharia Sitchin's corrupted research surrounding the Watchers (i.e. Sitchin's Anunnaki) and their Nephilim "offspring" to support Evolution, and to suggest that modern human beings, or Homo-Sapiens are the by-product of alien genetic manipulation.

This manipulation of apes or Neanderthals by the fallen angels (a.k.a. the Watchers, or Anunnaki) or their Nephilim offspring (a.k.a. Giants or Reptilians) supposedly resulted in the development of Homo sapiens, which Sitchin claims were created to be a quasi-intelligent slave race geared to serve the Watchers and Nephilim prior to the Great Flood. However, though humanity was subjugated by the Nephilim both before and after the Flood, the Bible teaches that mankind was created as a unique and fully developed animal species long before the Watchers came down to Earth. The fallen among the Watchers did, however, use genetic engineering to create the Pre-Flood Nephilim - some of whom somehow survived the Flood to produce the Post-Flood Anakim and Rephaim giants in an almost successful attempt to corrupt and destroy all life on Earth.

Some conspiracy theorists also believe in the Gap Theory, which supposes that another creation and destruction of the Earth by water occurred in an imagined gap of omission between the first two sentences of the Book of Genesis. The theory goes that the Watchers or Anunnaki were the first beings to inhabit the Earth, which was subsequently completely destroyed by a worldwide flood. This imagined flood would date to approximately 8,000 years before Noah's Flood in 2347 BC. This argument is often used by Evolution-touting Christians to support their belief in Darwin's theories, as the Gap Theory allows them to add as many imagined years as they want to biblical chronologies so that it will coincide with current evolutionary thinking.

Nonetheless, the Gap Theory is totally against the teaching of the Bible, and is misleading millions of people into believing falsehoods about the past that have absolutely no basis in fact. For example, many conspiracy theorists who accept the Gap Theory also believe that mankind is the product of genetic manipulation with Watcher and/or Nephilim genetic material. However, the Bible tells us that God created mankind in His image, not in the image of a subhuman ape or genetically-engineered Nephilim monster!

In fact, the writer of Genesis specifically stated that God saved Noah because he *"was perfect in his generations"* and *"the earth also was corrupt before God, and the earth was filled with violence"* (Genesis 6:9-11). He made this statement to clarify that both Noah and his sons were still perfectly human - with no Nephilim blood mixed in! In short, they were the only people who had not become genetically corrupted and violently unstable.

Humanity had sunken so low from genetic corruption by the time of Noah that they had inherited the Nephilim penchant for perpetual violence and bloodlust. As evidenced in the Book of 1 Enoch and the Book of Jasher, the Watchers succeeded in corrupting nearly all divinely-created life forms by mixing the genes of animals, birds and reptiles together in a multitude of ways to create a seemingly endless array of hybrid Nephilim monsters. Furthermore, these mutant creatures had no compulsion to follow God's laws and therefore became grossly wicked.

Sadly, because the Nephilim were cunning and powerful, mankind gradually succumbed to their evil ways, and became genetically corrupted with their genes through sexual unions that produced mutant hybrid children. The resultant mutant humanoid races were as disdainful of God's laws, and as evil and violent as their Nephilim forbears. This is why God grieved that He had created mankind, and why He wanted to destroy all life on Earth (Genesis 6:5-7). Thankfully, there were still some pure animals and plants among every species on Earth just before Noah's Flood or no animals would have been allowed to board the Ark.

Nonetheless, God's plan to completely destroy the Nephilim scourge in the Great Flood was somehow thwarted. This is why God chose Abraham and the Israelites. Yahweh wanted to raise up a purely human army of believers who would trust their one true Creator God for the help they needed to defeat their inhuman enemies. As will be shown in Chapter Eight of this book, the Israelites were chosen by God to kill all the Nephilim or Giants who had survived the Flood. They were ordered to do so because these evil alien beings had conquered the Sethites who originally lived in Canaan until shortly after Abraham's time. Furthermore, they had expressly done so to prevent Abraham's descendents from taking the Promised Land that God had promised to them through Abraham.

As explained in the Book of Jasher, Melchizedek the king of Salem was none other than Shem. As Noah's and God's favored son, Shem was the leading patriarch of the Shemite (i.e. Semitic) clans, and he resided in Canaan, which was to one day become known as Israel. Furthermore, the city of Salem that Melchizedek governed over was in the location of the future city of Jerusalem. This is why Melchizedek honored Abraham and vise versa. They both must have been divinely informed of God's plan for Abraham's offspring to one day inhabit Canaan forever. In addition, they both likely secretly knew that God had a plan to destroy the Giants, which required these mutants to invade and take over Canaan.

Per God's plan, the Nephilim were provoked by their hatred of God's chosen people to invade Canaan to annihilate and subjugate the human populace and then settle there - thus ensuring that most of the Giants would eventually be gathered into one place after the Flood. This made it much easier for Abraham's descendents to destroy the Nephilim and reclaim their stolen land for Yahweh. Assuming this explains partly why Shem didn't simply give the land to his eleventh generation grandson Abraham at the time that they were introduced to each other, since Abraham was the heir to God's promises to Shem.

The true conspiracy behind all the problems in the Middle East today is that this information is plainly recorded in the Bible and Book of 1 Enoch, but pastors have either been taught not to teach about this or refuse to do so. Yet this Nephilim conspiracy to destroy mankind is partly behind the hatred of the sons of Ishmael for the sons of Isaac. It is also exacerbated by the jealousy and sibling rivalry between Ishmael and Isaac, which has never been resolved.

To further complicate the situation, the Nephilim-tainted Philistines of ancient times have metamorphosed into the Palestinian people of today. Just as the Anakim, Amorites, Amalekites, and Philistines were Israel's bitterest enemies, their modern counterparts hate and desire to provoke and/or kill all the spiritual (i.e. Christian) and literal (i.e. Jewish) descendents of Abraham living in Israel and throughout the world.

Because ten of the twelve Israelite spies who were sent into Canaan to scout their defenses were afraid of these Nephilim giants, God forced the Israelites to wander in the Sinai for forty years (See Numbers, Ch. 13 & 14). This served as a blessing in disguise since - during their wilderness wanderings - the Israelites became physically fit, hardened warriors that were ready to fight their most fearsome enemies.

Subsequently, when the Israelites returned to Canaan, they had lost their slave mindset and - even more importantly - had learned to trust God. As a result of their new-found faith in Yahweh's power, they had virtually no trouble defeating most of the Philistines, Giants,

Anakim and Rephaim in Canaan and winning the Promised Land for Yahweh. As will be shown in this book and Book Four, however, the bloodline of the Nephilim was sadly not fully extinguished and can be associated with some of the aristocratic and noble bloodlines in Europe, Great Britain, Asia, and the Middle-East today.

This book - and the series it is a part of - was written to reveal many of the truths about the One True God and His Creation that the Nephilim, fallen angels, and the Pagans who followed them have mocked, perverted, hid, or otherwise tried to destroy since the dawn of time. For this reason, though this book has been written to stand alone, it is meant to be read in conjunction with the other books in the series, and is most beneficial when viewed as part of the set. However, if you do not have access to these other books, you can still gain much from this single volume in the series. As you continue to read, may Yahweh bless you on your spiritual journey into the secrets of the past.

- Helena Lehman,

March 17th, 2008

Chapter 1: The Importance of a Biblical Worldview

*"**The fool says in his heart, 'There is no God.'** They are corrupt, their deeds are vile; there is no one who does good. The LORD (Yahweh) looks down from heaven on the sons of men to see if there are any who understand, any who seek God. **All have turned aside, they have together become corrupt;** there is no one who does good, not even one." - Psalm 14:1-3 (NIV)*

The powerful Scripture quoted above is speaking to this current generation more so than to any other in history. Though there have been scoffers and atheists in every Age, this is the only one that has seen the rise of a completely atheistic worldview. This is a worldview governed by the concepts of Evolution and Secular Humanism, which are now being taught as a matter of course in schools around the world. However, both the theory of Evolution and the philosophy of Humanism are antagonistic to the biblical worldview presented to God's people in the Book of Genesis.

Because Genesis is as foundational to their faith as the Constitution is to the United States, Christians and Messianic Jews have an obligation to defend and understand the teachings of this important introductory book of the Bible. Sadly, however, few Christians and even fewer Jews believe the beginning chapters in Genesis need to be taken literally as well as allegorically. They instead relegate them to myth and view the stories of Yah's six-day Creation of the Universe, Adam and Eve, the Garden of Eden and the Serpent in the Garden as fables. As a result, few know how to defend the spiritual, historical and scientific points of view established in Genesis as the foundation for a belief in God and the need for redemption.

Due to this, many Jews and Christians have been beguiled into believing in Evolution and now assume that the biblical point of view set forth in Genesis is outdated. Sadly, they are succumbing to the recent flood of literature that denies the historical and scientific validity of the Bible's earliest chapters. As a result, many believers clandestinely ignore the fact that Evolution, which teaches a random origin for life, is anathema to God and denies a need for a Special Creation by one all-powerful Intelligent Designer.

In recent years, there has also been a series of seemingly authoritatively written books that totally deny or attempt to disprove the four hundred year sojourn of the Israelites in Egypt's region called Goshen. Some deny that a place called Goshen ever existed in Egypt, though it has been proven that there were several fertile, grassy plains in the Delta region of Lower Egypt that were heavily cultivated and provided excellent grazing for livestock through most of Egypt's history.

Still others deny that the Exodus occurred at all, or they say that it never occurred on as grand a scale as depicted in the Bible, where it records that hundreds of thousands of men fled Egypt, together with countless wives, children, friends and livestock. Though there is plenty of scholarly documentation showing that the historical information in the first few books of the Bible are absolutely true, many liberal Christians are unaware of this. As a result, they are easily swayed to think that the history recorded in Genesis, Exodus, Leviticus, Numbers and Deuteronomy are not factual accounts of the past, but legends with little basis in fact.

Despite the bad press that the Bible continually receives from skeptics, the assertion that the Bible is not a reliable source of history can be proven to be incorrect using clear logic. For example, we cannot know for certain what sort of artifacts would signify a Hebrew presence in Egypt. This is because none of the symbols ordinarily connected to the Israelites like the Star of David and seven-branched Menorah were a part of their theology prior to the time of Moses and the Exodus! Because the Exodus occurred over five hundred years *after* the time of Abraham, who was a Mesopotamian nobleman of Ur, Israelite artifacts also might not have any clear Mesopotamian relationship.

The descendents of Abraham were nomads for at least *one hundred years* prior to their sojourn in Egypt. Since they came into contact with many diverse cultures as they wandered about, their own culture would have been affected by the cultural practices of the many people groups they encountered during their travels. Similarly, after they had settled in Egypt, the culture of the Hebrews would have begun to reflect the culture of Egypt. After four hundred years, the influence of Egypt on Israelite artistic, religious and scientific ideas would also have been quite pronounced. Nonetheless, many archeologists and anthropologists assume that the Israelites utilized clearly Mesopotamian or Canaanite cultural characteristics and pottery styles. For the aforementioned reasons, however, this assumption is absurd!

Archeology, Geology and Anthropology were never meant to denounce or disprove the wisdom of our remotest ancestors, whose artifacts reveal that religion and ritual was of major importance everywhere in ancient times. Every ancient civilization believed in a Creator god or goddess and in a spirit world beyond our own. How is it, then, that many people today can blithely ignore the nearly universal ancient belief in and fear of a Creator god?

To put things into modern perspective, few people questioned the authority of the Bible as a source of history at the turn of the nineteenth century. Nor did they repudiate the historical information left to us by ancient writers such as Homer or Plato. In addition, most of them viewed Paganism as erroneous, but assumed that the historical information contained in ancient literature was mostly based on fact. Now, however, the Bible's historical information is being called into question, even though many scholars still believe in the historical veracity of Plato or Homer's writings. Yet these same intellectuals ignore the fact that our modern Bibles have literally been drawn from hundreds of manuscripts to prove their veracity, while only a few manuscripts that preserved the knowledge of Homer or Plato have survived.

Though many of our remotest ancestors may have been Pagans, there is no reason to believe that they were incapable of leaving essentially accurate records of the historical events in their time. Though our ancestors wrote their histories from their own unique and sometimes erroneous theological and scientific point of view, their writings should never be dismissed as pure fable. Though many Pagan religious texts were embellished with fables, there is often an underlying thread of truth underneath even the most outrageous myths.

As an example of how we have repudiated the wisdom of our ancestors, we must confront the theory of Evolution, which asserts that man evolved from apes. Despite the current popular belief in this theory, no ancient religion taught that men evolved from apes. Instead, even the most heinous Pagans had traditions that taught that a supreme deity of some sort created the Earth and the people and animals that inhabit it. Most of them also had myths indicating that a worldwide flood occurred - one so severe that it wiped out almost every living thing on the planet.

Now, if almost all our ancestors universally believed in the existence of a Creator god and a worldwide flood, how can any of us smugly assert that every one of them was wrong? Since we are thousands of years removed from any of the events our remotest ancestors wrote about, how could we believe that we have a more accurate view of the past than they did? Is the scientific method meant to be a total replacement for the wisdom of the ancients? My answer to that is a resounding "No!" even though many deceived people think it is!

Viewing the monumental and cultural achievements of our ancestors through the biased lens of modern archeology, scientists have been conditioned to assert that our ancestors weren't as capable of rational behavior and logical thought as we are today. Many of these so-called experts assume that our ancestors were not logical at all, but simple-minded fools who readily believed in fantasies such as a Creator god and a worldwide flood that was a punishment for mankind's spiritual transgressions. Furthermore, scientists often incorrectly assume that a particular aspect of culture did not exist simply because they have found no archeological evidence for it. For example, since no depictions of dancers have ever been found in archeological digs of the oldest civilization centers found at Sumer and Babylonia, many anthropologists assert that these people did not utilize dance as a form of expression! Nonetheless, every primitive culture thus far encountered has had some form of dance, and many ancient cultures left concrete evidence that they utilized dance in ritual and as a form of entertainment. In addition, there is a strong Middle Eastern tradition that the oldest forms of dance originated in Mesopotamia. Therefore, an absence of evidence is not evidence of absence!

Thankfully, some scholars are challenging the current academic propensity to dismiss logical deductions made from existing evidence as myths simply because they cannot be backed up with hard evidence. Nonetheless, especially where the Bible is concerned, there appears to be much archeological evidence verifying many events in the Bible that has simply been dated incorrectly. In other words, an enormous amount of archeological evidence that supports the historical events of the Bible has been ignored because it has been deliberately assigned to the wrong time periods. The sad truth is that many modern archeologists have misappropriated the evidence because they secretly either despise God or His chosen people the Jews!

Happily, there are a few exceptional scholars today who believe that the Bible is real history. In recent years, for example, the archeologist David Rohl has done much to prove the veracity of the Bible as a source of history with his New Chronology, which has significantly shortened the Ancient Mesopotamian and Egyptian timelines currently being touted as authoritative in textbooks. David Rohl views the history of the Bible as essentially true, and has provided much sound archeological evidence to prove it in his books, which are listed in the bibliography. For this reason, Rohl's books are highly recommended to those who want to see how Bible history can still be proven and upheld despite the atheistic mindset of current popular scholarship. Though I do not agree with all of Rohl's hypotheses, many of his ideas pepper this book, which focuses on how biblical characters like Enoch and Abraham understood and applied the Language of God in their respective cultural contexts.

In Book One, we explored the Gospel in the Stars and Sacred Astronomy and their place as the original heralds of the existence of the Language of God. We learned much about the allegories that God uses to communicate to us in every aspect of nature. In Book Two, the Language of God that is hidden in traditional family structures and the Blood Covenant rituals of Marriage and Communion were carefully revealed. Through the analysis of the rich symbolism in the heavens, in human nature, and in human rituals, we discovered more about ourselves while deepening our walk with Yahweh. As they are deciphered, each new layer of the Language of God also presents a profound wealth of knowledge surrounding the nature of our relationship with Christ. Our once seemingly simple faith is thereby enriched, with layer upon precious layer of beautiful and complex allegorical symbolism.

In this book, we will explore the reasoning behind the Biblical Chronology listed in the Appendix, which has been used as a foundation for assumptions made throughout this book series. From this chronology, this book constructs a biblical view of history that reconciles certain key archeological discoveries with the Bible's divinely inspired time scale. It also presents many extra biblical and biblical clues that the Language of God as found in the Gospel in the Stars (and fully discussed in Book One) was known to and utilized by Enoch, Noah, Shem, Abraham and Moses, who knew how to apply it spiritually.

In writing this abbreviated history, my goal is to help readers understand Yahweh and human history in the same ways that our righteous ancestors may have. Up until the time of Moses, there were few Scriptures to guide mankind and show them how to worship the Creator God. Outside of Enoch and Noah's writings, people learned about Yahweh and their place in His Universe through natural observations, mathematical computations, scientific discoveries, visions, dreams and direct contact with God's holy angels.

One example of the type of knowledge available to our antediluvian ancestors is the Great Pyramid or Pillar of Enoch. This pyramid contains astronomical, scientific, mathematical and spiritual knowledge that no mere dream or vision could reveal. In fact, as shown in this book and Book Four, the entire Giza pyramid complex reveals advanced celestial, spiritual and scientific knowledge, and likely served as a sacred pillar commemorating the Adamic Covenant made between God and mankind in Genesis 3:16, where it states:

> "So the LORD God (Yahweh Elohim) said to the serpent: 'you are cursed more than... every beast of the field; on your belly you shall go, and you shall eat dust... **And I will**

*put enmity between you and the woman, and between your seed and her Seed; he shall bruise your head, and you shall bruise His heel.' To the woman He said: 'I will greatly multiply your sorrow... in pain you shall bring forth children; your desire shall be for your husband, and he shall rule over you.' Then to Adam He said, 'Because you have... eaten from the tree... Cursed is the ground for your sake; in toil you shall... eat bread till you return to the ground... for dust you are, and to dust you shall return.' ...Also **for Adam and his wife the LORD God (Yahweh Elohim) made tunics of skin, and clothed them**." - Genesis 3:14-21 (NKJ)*

This is not only the first prophecy in the Bible about the coming Messiah or Seed of the Woman, but the final verse shows that it is connected to the foundational Blood Covenant from which all other Covenants are based! This is because, when Yahweh made skin tunics for Adam and Eve, He had to shed the blood of innocent animals to obtain the skins! God thereby performed the first animal sacrifice as a temporary covering for sin. **The idea of ritual sacrifice therefore originated with Yahweh God.**

The allegorical implications of Blood Covenant ceremonies that were explored in "The Language of God in Humanity" show that our righteous ancestors knew that their Creator God promised the coming of a Messiah who would vanquish the Devil and reverse the consequences of sin. In addition, as revealed in this book and "The Language of God in Prophecy," the hidden knowledge within the Great Pyramid shows that they learned much about this coming Savior from the allegorical messages locked into the starry heavens surrounding Earth. In fact, the entire Giza Pyramid Complex silently testifies that our remotest ancestors were spiritual giants and already knew many profound spiritual truths that traditionally are thought to originate from the Bible.

Though Nimrod and the priests of the false, polytheistic one world religion he set up turned the holy parables locked into Creation and the Star Gospel to evil ends and deified and worshipped created things like the constellations, Sun, Moon and planets, God's holy angels gave Sethite Wise Men or Magi like Enosh's son Cainan and Jared's son Enoch the knowledge of Sacred Astronomy long beforehand. Therefore, many truths are hidden behind the fables that comprise Mesopotamian, Greek, Celtic, Native American and Roman Mythology. In fact, though the starry symbols used within the Zodiac are found scattered throughout the myths of all these cultures, the stars were originally devised by God's own genius and have a purely divine purpose totally unrelated to false Pagan worship.

As shown in "The Language of God in the Universe," the original Star Gospel is a treasury of historical and prophetic knowledge. The Universe has an incredible spiritual story to tell us, and that is why this series was written - to educate the world about this hidden Gospel that fully agrees with the truths in the Bible and serves as the missing key needed to correctly decipher the architectural and cultural relics of our ancestors. In this book, it will be shown how important it is to view history through the divine perspective of the Language of God as revealed in both the Bible and the Star Gospel.

Before we determine what the antediluvians knew about Yahweh, His sacred Language of symbols, and Yah's Blood Covenant with us, however, we need to understand how antagonistic current secular theories about the age of the Earth and human origins are to the testimony of the Bible.

Creation or Evolution?

Now that we have a better understanding of why it is important to use a purely biblical chronology, and how one is created, let's tackle the subject of the origin of life. Current Evolutionary Theory tells us that the Universe may be the result of the Big Bang - a huge cosmic explosion. However, though this theory explains how the Universe may have evolved, it totally fails to explain how that one massive ball of light, matter, and energy that formed the Universe appeared in the nothingness that supposedly existed before it did. The Big Bang theory also fails to adequately address why this ball of matter exploded, or how it formed order out of the chaos that followed.

Ignoring the existence of God, secular scientists believe that the random process called Evolution combined with the structured Laws of Physics to transform lifeless matter into complex living things. Furthermore, they accept the random processes of Evolution as valid even though it supposedly occurred within highly structured celestial and terrestrial systems that show no real evidence of randomness, but are as regular and predictable as clockwork.

Evolution rests on the supposition the all life originated at random in the electronically charged cosmic soup that once filled the Earth's oceans. Evolutionary Theory also states that the Earth is billions of years old, and that it took millions of years for simple single-celled life to form in the "cosmic soup" that once filled the Earth's oceans. The Evolutionary model also tells us that it took many more millions of years for this simple life to evolve into more complex forms, and that this was supposedly accomplished through the processes of mutation and Natural Selection. The Evolutionary model of origins also assumes that reptilian life in the form of dinosaurs evolved on land first, but then this stage of evolution ended when some catastrophic event occurred. This catastrophe was so severe that it killed all the large dinosaurs, leaving only smaller ones to evolve into a more complex variety of life forms consisting of reptiles, birds, and mammals.

One major hole in the Evolutionary Theory is found in the fossil record. Though Evolutionists claim that life evolved through Natural Selection, also known as the "Survival of the Fittest," the fossil record tells us that animals were once far larger and more robust than the versions of them that exist today! There is no doubt that supposed Pleistocene Era animals like the giant (elephant-sized) Sloth, giant Condor, giant Beaver, giant Armadillo, Cave Bear, Saber-Toothed Tiger, Dire Wolf, giant Camel, giant Bison, Wooly Mammoth, and Mastodon skeletons shown in Museums are far larger and bigger-boned than any related versions of these creatures today. Many fossilized plant specimens also appear to be enormous in comparison to currently extant versions of these plants.

This begs us to ask the question: How can life be progressing forward if modern plant and animal life seems to have *devolved* in size and strength from those that existed in the past? Also, since modern apes are physically much stronger and more robust than human beings, how can Homo sapiens be a real improvement over them when taking Natural Selection into consideration? We are a species that is supposed to have evolved from apes to a higher state of being over a long period of time with relatively constant environmental conditions, which describes the theory known as Uniformitarianism. However, though humans are much smarter than apes, they appear to have lost their physical advantages. In addition, the Bible tells us that, with the exception of eight people, all humanity was destroyed in the Great Flood, and their civilizations were buried under many layers of mud and silt. This was a catastrophic event.

Not surprisingly, we find evidence for Catastrophism in the Archeological record, where distinctly thick layers of mud buried whole civilizations in Mesopotamia, and then show a gradual return of civilizations above the mud layer. In addition, rather than layers of dead animals being slowly and uniformly buried under a layer of dirt, the fossil record buried in many layers of geological strata could just as easily be the result of a massive sifting of animals and plants in layers after being violently churned up in water. Therefore, there is much evidence contrary to the idea that humanity and other life forms are evolving into superior forms of life, or that they did so over millions of years with consistently favorable living conditions.

Though Evolutionists believe that mass extinctions wiped out many Dinosaurs and Pleistocene era animals, they believe that these extinctions occurred gradually through isolated catastrophic events. However, according to Scripture, Dinosaurs and Pleistocene Era animals lived on Earth at the same time. Furthermore, the Bible records that only one major catastrophic event on the Earth could have caused such mass extinctions. This was the Great Flood, and it destroyed all life with the exception of the creatures on board the Ark or already living in the sea, not just isolated groups of living things.

For Christians, the biggest problem with the Evolutionary Theory should be that it ignores all the evidence of Intelligent Design in our Universe, and excludes the need for a Creator. Because it flies in the face of biblical teachings, the concept of Evolution has become the "religion" of Secular Humanists and Atheists, many of whom believe that mankind is the most superior form of animal life on Earth. The Bible and the fossil record, however, show that mankind and the world have digressed from a once perfect and immortal state to a sickly, mortal, and increasingly more chaotic and disorganized condition.

According to biblical chronology, the patriarchs routinely lived over 900 years prior to the Great Flood. Today, however, they rarely live even 100 years! Furthermore, the Bible teaches that all Creation is fallen due to sin, and this is the reason why our life spans have plummeted so much in the past 4000 years since the Flood. Like the rest of Creation, mankind was fatally flawed when sin entered the Universe. This is why there is so much biological evidence that all life is devolving; with greater incidences of cancer, disease and deformity occurring now than ever before, despite medical advances in treating them.

Another major theological problem with the Theory of Evolution is that its proponents claim that the Universe and the Earth have been around for much longer than biblical chronology allows for. This is a problem because many extra-biblical ancient religious texts like the Book of 1 Enoch and Epistle of Barnabus tell us that God provided a seven thousand year period for human history to unfold. These texts are quoted in Book Four on prophecy to show that our ancestors believed in the concept of a thousand-year Great Day, and that seven thousand years must pass between the Fall of Adam and Eve and the establishment of the New Heaven and New Earth described in the Book of Revelation. Numerous proofs using Sacred Astronomy attest to this seven thousand year time period, as carefully explained in Books One and Four of the "Language of God" book series.

In support of Special Creation over Evolution, the Bible contains accurate genealogical records that serve several important purposes. First of all, they show us how mankind descended from the first *human* couple Adam and Eve down to Noah, who was the tenth patriarchal ruler before the Flood. They also show how, after the Flood, all the different racial varieties of humans stemmed from Noah and his three sons Shem, Ham, and Japheth. These genealogical lists are very specific about the age of each patriarch when their eldest son was born, and when they died. If we assume that the Bible is the inerrant Word of God, these genealogies should be correct and complete. They therefore can be used to create a biblical chronology that shows the amount of time that passed between God's Creation of Adam and the birth of Christ.

In the Appendix, the abbreviated Biblical Chronological Time Chart used throughout this book series is provided. Furthermore, a detailed explanation for the dates given in this Biblical Chronology will be given in the next section, as it is highly relevant to the discussion of history. This section will show why you can rely on my Biblical Chronology with a fair degree of certainty.

Tracking the time span between each biblical patriarch's birthday to the time of Christ, my Biblical Chronology tells us that Creation and time began in 4003 BC. Though this date has been disputed due to purported scribal errors in the dates given in the Bible's genealogical records, many scholars have found good solutions to these problems. The methods used to compile my own Biblical Chronology are reflected in the next section. From my findings, I am confident that the 4003 BC beginning date of my chronology is accurate and can be relied on to date historical events up to the time of Christ.

In the Book of 1 Enoch, we have a record of the spiritual beliefs and perceptions of the people of Enoch's day. According to my Biblical Chronology, Enoch was born circa 3381 BC and was the seventh of the ten antediluvian patriarchs in the line of Seth. Using the same Biblical Chronology, we can also deduce that the Great Flood occurred in 2347 BC. Subtracting this date from 4003 BC, we can see that 1656 years passed between the Creation of Adam and the Great Flood, with an average of 165 years between each antediluvian generation. Biblical chronologies also show that human life devolved in lifespan after the Flood, with an average of 25 years between generations by the time of Christ. Furthermore, human life spans decreased from an average of 900 years prior to the Flood to around 125 years in the time of Abraham, which was only about 300 years after the Flood.

Now, if human history began sometime around 4003 BC, how can believers reconcile current archaeological and anthropological findings that claim that human civilization is much older than the Biblical record allows for? It is incredibly hard to hold fast to a truly biblical view of history because a plethora of information blatantly contradicting the Bible is being taught in every secular museum and school today. As a result, believers are being bombarded with ideas that openly suggest that Genesis' account of Creation and its explanation for the origin of mankind is a total fantasy.

Since few believers know how to reconcile the radical differences between current Evolutionary Theory and the Genesis account of Creation, they are being swayed to believe that the biblical view of the origin of life is nothing more than a fable! As a result, many believers now think that the Book of Genesis is almost entirely mythical in nature. Therefore, they do not see it as a reliable history. This is a terrible tragedy, however, since the teachings of the Book of Genesis were written to stand as a *foundation* to all the other teachings in the Bible. In fact, as shown conclusively in Book Two, the concept of sin, salvation, and the rite of the Blood Covenant are established in the first few chapters of Genesis. Furthermore, **without these foundational teachings about the origin of sin and the nature of atonement established in Genesis, all the biblical teachings about salvation from sin make no sense whatsoever!**

This book addresses the need among believers to re-examine the foundational teachings of their faith to see how these beliefs are weakened by the concept of Evolution. Believers must understand that believing in the concept of a Special Creation by our Creator isn't a matter of choice. Instead, **the roots of our faith are dependent on the concept of a perfect Creation that became tainted by sin, not an imperfect Creation that is evolving into a more perfect state.** Therefore, to reconcile their faith with scientific theory, believers must begin to carefully scrutinize, re-evaluate, and revise current geological, archeological, and anthropological ideas to harmonize with the history of humanity given in the biblical record.

In the following pages, we will reconsider currently accepted dates for historical events, and analyze where they should be placed in view of my Biblical Chronology. We will also examine why God created mankind and how our righteous ancestors perceived God. In the process, we will see how the terminology behind current Judeo-Christian religious beliefs is somewhat different from the way our ancestors expressed their understanding of God before the Bible was written. Nonetheless, though antediluvian spiritual expression was different than our own, it will be shown that their beliefs agreed with the Bible on all essential points of doctrine.

Disproving the Gap Theory

Though it is this author's conviction that the Book of Genesis does not leave anything out of its pages that is important to our knowledge of why we sin and are in need of salvation, some believers see it as incomplete. In fact, there are some who think that the Book of Genesis does not record the original Creation of the Earth, but its re-creation! This view is known as the Gap Theory, and those who espouse it believe that there is a gap of millions or billions of years hidden between the words of Genesis 1:1 and Genesis 1:2 that provides the time period necessary to support the Theory of Evolution.

However, in the Scripture in question, there is no proof whatsoever that the Gap Theory could be true. To understand why, let's take a close look at the opening sentences of Genesis:

> *"(1) In the beginning God created the heavens and the earth. (2) The earth was without form, and void; and darkness was on the face of the deep. And the Spirit of God was hovering over the face of the waters. (3) Then God said, 'Let there be light'; and there was light." - Genesis 1:1-3 (NKJ)*

Gap Theorists have a very unorthodox interpretation of Genesis 1:1 through 1:2. In fact, they insist on playing word games in this very first paragraph of Genesis that are totally unfounded. Furthermore, their theories supporting Evolution are unsupported in any other ancient manuscripts outside of the Bible, and - using God's Word alone - they can easily be refuted.

This Scripture begins with the verse: *"In the beginning God created the heavens and the earth."* In my book: "The Language of God in Prophecy" I show how this sentence is made up of seven words in Hebrew, with the middle word not pronounced, but representing the first and last letters of the Hebrew alphabet, Aleph and Tav (A-T). Furthermore, if the seven letters of this verse were placed over the lamps of a seven-branched Menorah, this Aleph-Bet combination would mark the fourth or center lamp. This lamp is known as the Servant Lamp, since it is used to light all the other lamps. As such, the letters connected to this lamp allegorically depict Christ as the Alpha and Omega or the First and the Last, and show that Christ is the Suffering Servant who came to be the Light of the World! Since the Servant Lamp lights all the other lamps, this designation of Christ as the Servant Lamp also suggests that He switched the Universe "on" in His Preincarnate state and filled it with the light of His and His Father's goodness.

In studying the Hebrew of the first half of the second verse of Genesis, where it says: *"The earth was without form, and void,"* **there is**

absolutely no indication of an implied gap of billions of years between this phrase and the next sentence, nor is there any support for this belief elsewhere in Scripture. In fact, this second verse of Genesis means exactly what it says: the existing matter that would serve to make up the Earth was without form or shape and it was void, meaning it had no life or structure. Nonetheless, Gap Theorists insist that the second verse actually says: "the Earth was desolate and laid waste," as if its original fully-formed surface features had recently been destroyed. Genesis 1:1, however, gives no indication that the Earth was partly destroyed before being mentioned as "without form and void" in Genesis 1:2.

In fact, in Mark 10:6, Yahshua said: *"But from the beginning of creation 'God made them male and female.'"* With these words, Yahshua was partly quoting this Scripture:

> *"So God created man in His own image; in the image of God He created him; **male and female He created them.**" - Genesis 1:27 (NKJ)*

This means that Yahshua was teaching that all the animals and Adam and Eve were created *"male and female"* in *"the beginning of creation,"* or immediately after the Earth had been fully formed at the end of the Fourth Creation Day. Only after this, on the Fifth Creation Day, did God begin to populate the Earth with animal life.

In Genesis, the Days of Creation are described as occurring over six indeterminate days consisting of darkness followed by light, which suggests something turning over from left to right or down to up - as in the turning of a Calendar Wheel or a planet making its orbit around the Sun. Since the Spring Equinox occurs in the same Zodiac sign for approximately two thousand years in each Precessional Cycle, a thousand years can be seen as the length of time it takes for one half of a Precessional regression through one sign of the Zodiac. Could this be the origin of the idea that God calculates one year as a thousand years, and that each Day in the Creation Week was a thousand years - just as the Apostle Peter suggested in his second letter?

> *"But, beloved, **do not forget this one thing,** that with the Lord one day is as a thousand years, and a thousand years as one day." - 2 Peter 3:8 (NKJ)*

Note here that Peter is drawing much attention to the great importance of this point by saying: *"do not forget this one thing."* Peter *emphasizes* that it is important to remember that a day to God is as a thousand years. This suggests that the time between the empty Earth and the creation of Adam and Eve could have amounted to 6000 years rather than 6 days, but could never have been billions of years! Also, the expression *"from the beginning of creation"* used by Christ rules out any "re-creation" or "second start" theories as taught by many Gap Theorists.

As the people at Answers in Genesis explain, the main reason that people try to place a gap between the first two verses of Genesis is to account for the billions of years they assign to Earth's age based on Evolutionary Theory. However, believers who do this are essentially placing more faith in the world's secular (i.e. without God) understanding than in God's infallible Word. They are also ignoring the fact that nearly every ancient society believed in a Special Creation by one or more gods. They also saw no gap of millions or billions of years between the world they inhabited or the world that many of them knew had been destroyed in a worldwide flood - a flood so devastatingly destructive that it could clearly account for the massive layers of fossils and oil and coal deposits found all over the Earth.

Yahshua made it plain that Adam and Eve have been around since the beginning of the finished Creation, which was - at best - only six thousand years old when they first inhabited it. For people to suggest otherwise clearly goes against God's Word and denies the inerrancy of the Bible record as well as the other ancient manuscripts deemed as canonical in the Ethiopian Church, which include the Book of Jubilees and the Ethiopian Book of Enoch.

The Waters Above and Below

In regard to the Gap Theory, this section presents several more sound refutations of Scripture-based arguments that Gap Theorists use to uphold their ideas. For example, to support their beliefs, Gap Theorists often point to the Appendix of the Companion Bible. In that Bible's Appendix, there are notes about the actual meaning of the phrase *"the foundation of the world,"* which occurs ten times in the King James Version of the Bible.

These notes suggest that the Greek word "katabole" used for "foundation" in this phrase should be translated "ruin," making the phrase read "ruin of the world," instead of *"foundation of the world."* However, according to Strong's concordance, the word "katabole" literally means "founded" or "conceived," and is derived from the word "kataballo," meaning to "cast down" or "lay." This is not referring to an act of destruction, but means "to lay down," as in laying down a firm foundation.

As already discussed, the Companion Bible contains notes regarding Genesis 1:1 and 1:2 that suggest that Genesis 1:2 speaks of a destroyed Earth, not an unfinished one. The notes also suggest that Peter taught that there were two destructions of the Earth by water. Here are Peter's words regarding his supposed reference to these two destructions:

> "For this they willfully forget: that by the word of God the heavens were of old, and the earth standing out of water and in the water, **by which the world that then existed perished,** being flooded with water." - 2 Peter 3:5-6 (NKJ)

In this passage, the Companion Bible suggests that the phrase "the world that then existed" is referring to the world of dinosaurs and giant animals that were supposedly destroyed prior to the creation of mankind and created the fossil record before the Six Days of Creation discussed in Genesis 1:3-27. However, this assumption suggests that the Great Flood was not violent enough to have caused the fossil record. Nonetheless, there is much evidence to the contrary all over the Earth, especially in the worldwide discovery of deep fissures and caverns that are filled with the ripped apart, churned together fossil remains of countless types of animals, birds, and fish that were much bigger but still recognizable as modern varieties that are smaller. These remains show clear evidence that many types of living creatures died horrible deaths in a massive flood that violently ripped these creatures apart, mixed them together, rapidly sifted their remains, and deposited them in layers. Yet Evolutionists completely ignore or refute this evidence!

In fact, Peter's words in 2 Peter 3:5-6 appear to support the conclusion that the Earth was destroyed by violent water action in the Great Flood. For example, Peter says that "the earth (was) standing out of water and in the water." In saying this, Peter may have been asserting that the world that Adam and Eve knew was surrounded by water in Outer Space and beneath the land they stood upon, and this world was subsequently destroyed by the violent action of these churning waters that came from above and below at the time of the Flood. In fact, Peter is likely referring to two conditions of the Earth that no longer exist to any great degree. These are revealed in Genesis, where it says:

> "In the six hundredth year of Noah's life, in the second month, the seventeenth day of the month, on that day **all the fountains of the great deep were broken up, and the windows of heaven were opened.** And the rain was on the earth forty days and forty nights." - Genesis 7:11-12 (NKJ)

Some godly scientists have postulated that a water canopy or ring of frozen water once surrounded our Earth, kept it uniformly warm, and protected it from harsh UV radiation. This water canopy may have contributed to mankind's much longer lifespan and the Greenhouse Effect that allowed the large stature of many plants and animals prior to the Flood. However, when the windows of heaven were opened (or removed), this water canopy slowly collapsed, partly causing the forty days of unrelenting rain that fell all over the Earth. The Book of Genesis also indicates that there was water underneath the surface of the Earth that watered the plants without the need for rain prior to the Flood. Interestingly, it does so in a paragraph that says it recaps *"the history of the heavens and the earth **when they were created.**"* Here, the word for "created" is the Hebrew word "bara," meaning "created," not "recreated":

> *"**This is the history of the heavens and the earth when they were created,** in the day... before any plant of the field was in the earth and before any herb of the field had grown. For the LORD God (Yahweh Elohim) had not caused it to rain on the earth, and there was no man to till the ground; but **a mist** (i.e. streams) **went up from the earth and watered the whole face of the ground.** And the LORD God (Yahweh Elohim) formed man of the dust of the ground, and breathed into his nostrils the breath of life; and man became a living being." - Genesis 2:4-7 (NKJ)*

In this passage, the streams that watered the ground likely had its source in the *"fountains of the great deep"* that broke up to flood the world in Genesis 7:11. In addition, note that the Earth was watered from below in order to fill it with the plant life that people and animals would need to eat in order to survive. Then, when the Earth was finally ready to support life, God created all animal life on the Fourth Day. Then, on the Fifth Day, *"God formed man of the dust of the ground."*

In conclusion, there is nothing in any of the Scriptures quoted here that suggest that the Earth in Genesis 1:1 had been created and destroyed before the rest of the Creation account in Genesis 1:2-27. In addition, there is no mention of this prior world in any other passages of the Bible, or in any other ancient Judeo-Christian manuscript. It is therefore an idea built on the flimsiest of evidence, and designed only to uphold the views of believers who support the Darwinian Theory of Evolution, or believe that the Earth was populated with aliens or angels for thousands or millions of years prior to the Genesis Creation account. Nonetheless, as will be shown in this book, these beliefs are contrary to the Bible's factual account of the Six-Day Creation ending with the

creation of mankind, the scourge of the fallen angels, the arrival of the
Nephilim, their ravaging of the Earth, the Great Flood that was sent to
destroy them, and the continuation of humanity and the Giants
afterward.

Creating a Purely Biblical Chronology

Throughout this book series, I refer to a historical timeline that
was created utilizing genealogical and historical information found in the
Bible. In this section, we will discuss these passages and how they were
applied to the Biblical Chronological Time Chart found in this book's
Appendix.

Many years ago, Archbishop James Ussher created a biblical
timeline that begins in 4004 BC and that is still widely used today. My
Biblical Chronology is similar to Ussher's, though mine begins one year
later. The main reason for this discrepancy of one year between these
timelines may be that Bishop Ussher attributed 100 years between
Abraham and Isaac's births, whereas I specify 99 years between them.
Following is a concise explanation of how I came to conclude that 4003
BC rather than 4004 BC is the starting point for human history.

First of all, a list factoring in the ages of the patriarchs at the time
of the birth of their heirs was created using the genealogies in Genesis,
Chapters 5, 10, and 11. The twenty-two patriarchs named in these
genealogies are sequentially listed as they appear in the Bible in my
Biblical Chronological Chart in the Appendix. Beginning with Adam's
age at the birth of Seth and ending with the age of Terah at Abraham's
birth, we can add up the ages of all the patriarchs at their son's births to
find out how many years passed from the creation of Adam to
Abraham's birth. This amounts to 1,948 years, placing Abraham's birth
in the year 2055 BC.

Interestingly, just as there were twenty-two patriarchs from
Adam to Abraham, there are twenty-two letters in the Hebrew Alphabet.
Now, as shown in Book Four, the number 22 indicates a complete
prophetic period of time. Even more intriguingly, the 1,948 years leading
to Abraham's birth matches the modern year 1948, which marks the
nation of Israel's phoenix-like rebirth. This might lead one to ask: "Are
these number connections a mere coincidence?" From what I have
learned about the spiritual meaning of symbols hidden throughout the
Bible, I don't think so. In fact, the hidden Mazzaroth references
discovered in the Bible as revealed in Books One, Two, Three and Four
and the hidden Bible Codes revealed in Book Four are good indicators

that the genealogies recorded in the opening chapters of Genesis were divinely inspired. As such, they can be fully relied upon to be an accurate reflection of the years that passed from Adam's fall until Abraham's birth.

Beyond the genealogies in Genesis Chapters 5, 10, and 11, other key references to genealogical time periods in the Bible can be found that help establish the number of years from the Creation of Adam and Eve until Yahshua was born, which may have been in September of 3 BC. The next key reference is to Abraham's age at Isaac's birth. When Abraham was 99 years old, God pronounced that Abraham would have a son by his wife Sarah, and Abraham had not reached his 100th year at Isaac's birth in 1956 BC (See Genesis 17:1 and 17:21). Since human gestation takes nine months, this accounts for 75 percent of one year.

Next, the Bible tells us that Isaac was 60 years old when Jacob and Esau were born, placing Jacob's birth to 1896 BC (Genesis 25:26). Therefore, patriarch Abraham's 99.8 years can be added to the 60 years of his son Isaac, showing a passage of 159.8 years.

Now, though Abraham's birth marked the beginning of God's first exclusive and unconditional Blood Covenant with a specific people group, the birth of Isaac's son Jacob marked the establishment of the bloodline that this special Covenant would ultimately be fulfilled through. After this momentous event, however, the Bible is strangely silent about the passage of time until we reach the story of Moses in the Book of Exodus. There, we are told the number of years from Jacob's birth to the time of the Israelite Exodus from Egypt:

> "Now the sojourn of the children of Israel who lived in Egypt was four hundred and thirty years." - Exodus 12:40 (NKJ)

Here, we are given a clue that another 430 years should be added to our Bible Chronology. However, this Scripture is not a clear-cut chronological marker because it does not specify whether 430 should be added to the year of Jacob's birth or to Jacob's age when he settled in Egypt. Surprisingly, this problem can be solved not with an Old Testament reference, but from a related statement attributed to the Apostle Paul in the New Testament:

> "Now to Abraham and his Seed were the promises made. He does not say, 'And to seeds,' as of many, but as of one, 'And to your Seed,' who is Christ. And this I say, that the law, which was four hundred and thirty years later, cannot annul the covenant that was confirmed before by God

in Christ, that it should make the promise of no effect." -
Galatians 3:16-17 (NKJ)

In this passage from the Book of Galatians, note that - although he was referring to Christ as the ultimate Seed of Abraham - the Apostle Paul was also alluding to the fact that God reconfirmed His original Covenant with Abraham a second time with his seed Isaac and a third time with Jacob, who was part of the seventy original Israelites that sojourned in Egypt (Genesis 46:26-27). Therefore, the time period from the birth of the promised seed called Jacob to the Exodus journey of the Israelites to Mount Sinai to receive the Law was 430 years. Now, since Jacob settled in the land of Goshen and was reunited with his beloved son Joseph at the age of 130 years (see Genesis 47:9), **the actual sojourn of the Israelites in Egypt was exactly 300 years**.

Next, there is a passage in the First Book of Kings that indicates the numbers of years between the Exodus and the laying of the foundations for the Temple of Solomon:

"...*in the four hundred and eightieth year after the children of Israel had come out of the land of Egypt, in the fourth year of Solomon's reign over Israel, in the month of Ziv, which is the second month, that he began to build the house of the LORD (Yahweh)." - 1 Kings 6:1 (NKJ)*

Thus, 480 years passed between the Exodus and the start of building the First Temple, which was in the fourth year of King Solomon's reign over Israel. In this passage, the month of Ziv corresponds to the Jewish Lunar month of Iyar, which can begin anywhere from early April to mid May on the Gregorian Solar calendar.

Now, to find the number of years between the building of the First Temple and the beginning of the seventy-year Israelite exile in Babylonia, the length of each King of Judah's reign was added up, beginning with King Solomon. Though King Saul and King David preceded Solomon as Kings of a united Israel, and David reigned for 40 years like his son, there is no reference point given during Saul or David's reigns, but only to Solomon's fourth year. Therefore, the King List on page 20 shows that exactly 430 years passed from the fourth year of Solomon's reign until the beginning of the Babylonian Exile. Incidentally, there were twenty-two kings of Judah from righteous King David to wicked King Zedekiah, just as there were twenty-two patriarchs from Adam to Abraham. Altogether though, twenty-three kings ruled over Judah.

List of 21 Kings of Judah from Solomon to Zedekiah

King of Judah	Length of Reign
Solomon (1 Kings 11:42)	**40 years**
Rehoboam (1 Kings 14:21)	**17 years**
Abiram (1 Kings 15:1-2)	**3 years**
Asa (1 Kings 15:9-10)	**41 years**
Jehoshaphat (1 Kings 22:42)	**25 years**
Jehoram (2 Kings 8:16-17)	**8 years**
Ahaziah (2 Kings 8:26)	**1 year**
Athaliah (2 Kings 11:2-3)	**6 years**
Jehoash (2 Kings 12:1)	**40 years**
Amaziah (2 Kings 14:1-2)	**29 years**
Azariah -Uzziah (2 Kings 15:1-2)	**52 years**
Jotham (2 Kings 15:32-33)	**16 years**
Ahaz (2 Kings 16:2)	**16 years**
Hezekiah (2 Kings 18:1-2)	**29 years**
Manasseh (2 Kings 21:1)	**55 years**
Amon (2 Kings 21:19)	**2 years**
Josiah (2 Kings 22:1)	**31 years**
Jehoahaz (2 Kings 23:31)	**.25 years***
Jehoiakim (2 Kings 23:36)	**11 years**
Jehoiachin (2 Kings 24:8)	**.25 years***
Zedekiah (2 Kings 24:18)	**11 years**
Subtract 4 years to align with Solomon's age at the building of the 1st Temple	**- 4 years**
Total:	**430 years**

The King List on this page reflects the fact that the years of Jewish kings were advanced on the 1st of Nisan (Abib) in the spring, not Tishri 1 in the autumn. However, the very brief lengths of reign marked ɔy an asterisk (*) in the King List indicate fractions of a year that were ɔounted as six months each by Israel's scribes, making these two short ·eigns that equal only six months of time artificially equal one year altogether. In the chronology I use, this extra half of a year coupled with Abraham's age at Isaac's birth of 99.8 years of age instead of 100 years ɔlaces Adam's creation to around the time of Rosh Hashanah on 4003 ЗC. This keeps the chronology from being artificially lengthened by one ⁄ear as Bishop Ussher's was, which set the beginning of his chronology :o the spring of 4004 BC instead of the autumn of 4003 BC.

Sadly, of the 23 kings of Judah, only two consistently displayed :he godly type of behavior that Yahweh required from all the kings of ˋsrael. These were David and Josiah. Only they will likely be spared the destruction prophesied by Enoch that is reserved for the rest of Israel's ancient kings and modern Prime Ministers, who will be consigned to the ˍake of Fire forever (1 Enoch 90:20-26). This prophecy is carefully deciphered and applied to Israel's history in Book Four, where it serves as a harsh reminder to all political leaders that their decisions should always be based on God's Will as reflected in the Ten Commandments and Two Commandments of Christ, and not on the will of people or nations.

Thus far, it has been carefully shown that the Bible contains all of :he information required to plot the number of years between Adam's ɔreation and the end of the Kingdom of Israel/Judah. So, despite the numerous scholars who argue that the Bible cannot be trusted to give a ɔomplete record of every year that humanity has been in existence up to and including the time of Christ, there apparently is no problem if we ɔelieve that the Bible is trustworthy and is lacking nothing that we need ˋo know to plot the times and seasons in God's Plan of Salvation.

The next reliable indicator of the passage of chronological time in :he Bible is found in the Book of the prophet Jeremiah concerning the ength of time that Yahweh would cause the Israelites to remain captives n Babylon, and allow Jerusalem and the Temple to lie in ruins:

"For thus says the LORD (Yahweh): **After seventy years are completed at Babylon,** *I will visit you and perform My good word toward you, and cause you to return to this place." - Jeremiah 29:10 (NKJ)*

This seventy-year length of the desolation of Jerusalem and the ˋsraelite captivity in Babylon was confirmed by the prophet Daniel (See Daniel 9:1). Because God softened the heart of the Persian king through he prophet Daniel, this captivity ended in the first year of Cyrus king of Persia in 486 BC. In that year, Cyrus allowed the Israelites to return to

Jerusalem and rebuild the city and the Temple to Yahweh (Ezra 1:1-2). Unfortunately, however, the majority of Israelites chose to stay in Babylon because they had prospered there despite persecution, and they did not want to forsake their established homes and businesses. Therefore, only about 50,000 people from the tribes of Judah, Levi, and Benjamin returned to Israel to rebuild Jerusalem and the Temple:

> *"Then the heads of the fathers' houses of Judah and Benjamin, and the priests and the Levites, with all whose spirits God had moved, arose to go up and build the house of the LORD (Yahweh) which is in Jerusalem." - Ezra 1:5 (NKJ)*

> *"The whole assembly together was forty-two thousand three hundred and sixty, besides their male and female servants, of whom there were seven thousand three hundred and thirty-seven; and they had two hundred men and women singers." - Ezra 2:64-65 (NKJ)*

Now, this is where Daniel's amazing Prophecy of the Seventy Weeks comes into play, indicating the number of years that would pass from Cyrus' command to rebuild Jerusalem until the birth of the Messiah and Deliverer that Yahweh had promised to send to Israel:

> *"Know therefore and understand, that from the going forth of the command to restore and build Jerusalem until Messiah the Prince, there shall be seven weeks and sixty-two weeks; the street shall be built again, and the wall, even in troublesome times." - Daniel 9:25 (NKJ)*

Altogether, this prophecy indicated that 69 weeks of years would pass until Yahshua Ha Mashiach (i.e. Jesus the Christ), and 69 X 7 = 483. Now, if we subtract 483 years from 486 BC, we arrive at 3 BC! Therefore, in order to fulfill Daniel's prophecy, Yahshua had to be born in 3 BC. Amazingly, as shown in Book One, there are biblical clues tied to Sacred Astronomy that indicate Yahshua was born in September of 3 BC. This was the last year in the Fourth Great Day of 1,000 years since Adam's creation.

Now, just as the Sun was created on the Fourth Creation Day, the Son of God arrived on the Fourth Great Day after Creation, which is symbolically tied to the Jewish Feast of Pentecost. Indeed, Yahshua's First Advent ministry, which included His death and resurrection during Passover Week, and His ascension and sending of the Holy Spirit on Pentecost fulfilled all the spring and summer Feasts of Israel, just as Christ's Second Coming will fulfill all of the autumn Feasts.

This concludes my explanation of how my Biblical Chronological Time Chart in the Appendix was derived, and why it can be relied upon for dating biblical events. This chronology was meticulously constructed using texts found mostly in the Old Testament, and reflects a high regard for God's Word as it has come down to us in our modern translations.

Adam and Eve: Apes or Humans?

Now that we have established a chronological framework for the unfolding of biblical history, let me show another example of why the Christian faith is incompatible with, and diametrically opposed to Darwin's Theory of Evolution. The Bible firmly declares that God created Adam and Eve as a fully-evolved human man and woman. How else could Adam have had the reasoning ability and insightfulness required to name all the animals in the Garden of Eden shortly after he was created?

> *"Out of the ground the LORD God (Yahweh Elohim) formed every beast of the field and every bird of the air, and brought them to Adam to see what he would call them. And whatever Adam called each living creature, that was its name. So Adam gave names to all cattle, to the birds of the air, and to every beast of the field. **But for Adam there was not found a helper comparable to him.**" - Genesis 2:19-20 (NKJ)*

This Scripture makes it clear that Adam named and remembered *every animal, bird, and reptile* that God created. Considering that there were many thousands of initial kinds of animal, reptile, and bird species on the Earth then, Adam must have had a far greater capacity to think and reason on his own than we do today! The Bible therefore attests to Adam's superb reasoning faculties even before Eve arrived on the scene and sought forbidden knowledge. This is important to know and understand because some people claim that the forbidden knowledge Eve sought was the ability to reason and think! The Bible, however, refutes the idea that Adam and Eve did not have the ability to reason prior to the Fall. It does so by giving us the distinct impression that, as Adam named the animals and saw how different each one was from himself, he became acutely aware of his true uniqueness in the animal world. Scripture therefore implies that no other creature - not even those among the monkeys and apes - could begin to compare to Adam in intelligence or appearance. Therefore, among all the beasts of the Earth - including the many varieties of monkeys and apes that God had created before Adam - no suitable partner for Adam was found!

Indeed, how could Eve have been tempted to seek the knowledge that Satan offered her if she had the simple sentience of an ape? She would have been too stupid to understand what she was missing, and generally uninterested in, as well as incapable of any form of higher learning! But the Bible makes it clear that Satan communicated some major sinful concepts to Eve such as suspicion and deceit, and Eve reflected her perfect understanding of them by coveting the supposed glory of godhood that could be gained with the knowledge of good and evil:

> *"Now the serpent was more cunning than any beast of the field which the LORD God (Yahweh Elohim) had made. And he said to the woman, 'Has God indeed said, "You shall not eat of every tree of the garden"?' And the woman said... 'We may eat the fruit of the trees of the garden, but of the fruit of the tree which is in the midst of the garden, God (Elohim) has said, "You shall not eat it, nor shall you touch it, lest you die".' Then the serpent said to the woman, 'You will not surely die. For God (Elohim) knows that in the day you eat of it your eyes will be opened, and you will be like God (Elohim), knowing good and evil.' So when the woman saw that the tree was good for food... was pleasant to the eyes, and... desirable to make one wise, she took of its fruit and ate." - Genesis 3:1-6 (NKJ)*

It's clear in this Scripture that the satanic Serpent and Eve used some method of intelligent communication that is unknown between people and reptiles of any kind today. Indeed, this Scripture tells us that Eve was bright enough to know how to speak to the Serpent in a language it understood, and vise versa. How could this be if Eve was an ape, since apes are incapable of clear speech, and cannot understand even the simplest words without concentrated drilling and repetition?

My point, of course, is that Eve was no idiot! Furthermore, this dialogue between Eve and the Serpent leaves no room to doubt that Satan exists or that he can speak to us in our own language. This is why Satan could communicate with Adam and Eve, who were fully formed humans when they were created. Indeed, both the Serpent and the two innocent humans he had set out to destroy were capable of speech, logic, and reasoning - traits that led to Satan and mankind's open rebellion against God - or what Christians call the Original Sin.

This is just one example of why many ungodly people are attacking, and trying to destroy any belief in the Book of Genesis' account of Creation. By doing so, they are ridiculing every major tenet of the Christian faith, which is dependent on the foundational teachings of

Genesis for its veracity. Indeed, in the first chapters of Genesis we are told that death and our imperfect world resulted from sin. Furthermore, we are told that we need redemption from sin to find the perfection and immortality that Adam and Eve had in abundance before they sinned.

Unfortunately for proponents of Darwin's theories, these foundational teachings in Genesis are in direct opposition to Evolutionist ideas. For example, if Evolution is true, death must always have been around rather than being a consequence of sin as the Bible says. In addition, if we are evolving from lower life forms to higher levels of perfection, then there could not have been a point in the past when we were already perfect and could not die - which is what the Book of Genesis clearly asserts!

This is the paradox of our faith: we cannot believe in the world's view of the past without losing site of the whole point of the Christian faith, which promises redemption and freedom from sin and death through *one* perfect, divine Savior. For a great review of the essential doctrines of the Christian faith, and how they are wholly dependent on our belief in Creation rather than Evolution, please see Mike Gascoigne's excellent book "Impossible Theology - The Christian Evolutionist Dilemma."

There Were Giants in Those Days - The Fossil Record

Go into any Natural History Museum on the planet, and you are likely to be confronted by a hall that showcases the gigantic remains of prehistoric animals, which are often shown in juxtaposition to their much smaller modern counterparts. What amazes me about these halls is that little attention is drawn to the fact that, other than their obvious decrease in size, modern day animals look almost exactly like their remote ancestors. The giant prehistoric sloth looks identical to a modern day sloth, the prehistoric moose looks like a giant version of the modern day moose, the saber-toothed tiger looks very similar to a female lion today, and the wooly mammoth looks remarkably like an African elephant.

In other words, there is little evidence of mutation or change among various animal species outside of their size over a supposed time period of 25 to 35 million years. And what of their curious decrease in size? Why isn't anyone asking the major question it presents, which is: "When and why did all these animals become so much smaller, and what does this decrease in size suggest?" In other words, based on the available evidence, have these animals devolved or evolved?

Though fossil evidence shows that many animals appear to have devolved rather than evolved, modern scientists cite animal adaptation to explain their devolution. They suppose that harsher living conditions during the Great Ice Age made many of these animals become extinct, while others adapted to it better by shrinking dramatically in size. The major reason touted for this decrease in the robustness and size of many prehistoric animals is that their food sources became less available, and the lush tropical and rain-forest vegetation they had known was replaced by advancing ice and encroaching grasslands and deserts where food was increasingly scarce.

Nonetheless, this seems like an odd way to explain their decrease in size, especially since some giant Ice Age animals like the Wooly Mammoth ate grass just like their modern day counterparts do, and there were huge swaths of our planet that were never frozen over during the Ice Age. So, unless the grass itself became smaller and/or less nutritious, there was plenty of grass on the Earth in various locations throughout the Ice Age, so there should not have been any appreciable change in the size or strength of the animals that lived in the more lush regions of the Earth nearer to the Equator.

A far more satisfactory answer to the problem of shrinking animal size can be deduced when a worldwide flood is supposed. If such a massive flood occurred, it would mean that the mass of the Earth may have increased dramatically, thereby increasing the gravitational pull of the Earth on all living things, and forcing them to decrease in size in order to be able to move under that stronger gravity. In addition, during the Flood, the land was inundated with salt water. Due to heavier than normal deposits of salt, and the probable washing away of once abundant trace minerals in the soils by the waters of the Great Deep, soils all over the Earth became incapable of supporting as much lush plant growth. In fact, only the hardiest of plants could have survived in this salty, nutrient-poor soil, and even they would have struggled to grow until the soil salinity was decreased by rain runoff.

This negative change in the soil would have logically led to a sizeable decrease in plant growth and animal health after the Flood. A reasonable consequence of this would be increasingly smaller and weaker animals, which were now forced to eat far less nutritious food than their Pre-Flood ancestors. In addition, the Post-Flood world had a far more inhospitable environment, suffering from the frequently severe weather and extreme highs and lows in temperature that we are familiar with today, but that would have been largely unknown to the people and animals aboard Noah's Ark who originated before the Great Flood.

We will discuss the physical and spiritual causes and affects of the Great Flood in greater detail in Chapter Five. Also, in Chapter Four, we will explore a revolutionary, little known view of the origins of dinosaurs prior to the Flood, and the possible spiritual reasons behind their complete extinction.

The Great Longevity of the Antediluvians

Before we explore human history after the Flood, let's take a close look at the claims made in the Bible about the great longevity of our antediluvian ancestors. In Genesis' Pre-Flood record, the patriarchs descended from Seth are said to have lived phenomenal lengths of time. For example, the Bible claims that Adam lived 930 years, and Jared lived 962 years. Likewise, Enoch's eldest son Methuselah lived 969 years, and was the longest-lived of all the antediluvian patriarchs discussed in the Bible. If this report of the long life of our ancestors is true, and today we only live to be about 75 years old on average, then it seems that we are not evolving as a species, but *devolving*.

Patriarchal Life Spans Before and After the Flood

Adam - 930 years (Gen. 5:5)

Cainan - 910 years (Gen. 5:14)

Jared - 962 years (Gen. 5:20)

Methuselah - 969 years (Gen. 5:27)

Lamech - 777 years (Gen. 5:31)

Noah - 600 years before, and 350 years

after the Flood, equaling 950 years (Gen. 9:29)

Shem - 100 years before, and 500 years

after the Flood, totaling 600 years (Gen. 11:10-11)

Eber - 464 years (Gen. 11:16-17)

Peleg - 239 years (Gen. 11:18-19)

Abraham - 175 years (Gen. 25:7)

Jacob - 147 years (Gen. 47:28)

Moses - 120 years (Deut. 34:7)

The list on page 27 features the names and ages at death of some Pre and Post-Flood patriarchs. It shows that our ancestors lived just shy of a thousand years prior to Noah's Flood. After that, however, there was a steady decline in the ages of the patriarchs. There are also biblical clues suggesting that later patriarchs decreased not only in age, but in relative size and strength. This makes sense because **the growth spurts associated with childhood and adolescence would decrease as the time between childhood and maturity dropped.** In fact, according to the Book of Jasher, the robustness of mankind dropped even more dramatically at the time of Peleg's brother Joktan, when some scholars such as myself believe that deadly bacteria and viruses may suddenly have been released into the world via some cataclysm (See Jasher 17:19-20 in Chapter Six, and its associated explanation).

Though it has slowed somewhat, this decrease in the longevity of humanity shows no signs of being reversed via any supposed evolutionary process. In fact, the average age of a human being today is 75, which is much lower than Abraham's age when he died over 4000 years ago at the age of 175! This suggests that men have been steadily devolving over the past 4000 years rather than evolving over millions of years.

Further contradicting the idea of life developing via a slow, random evolutionary process, the Bible and other Judeo-Christian religious texts suggest that the time allotted for mankind to exist in their current fallen state has been divinely limited to a set time period. Along with Psalm 90, the Book of Jubilees tells us a thousand years are reckoned as a day to Yahweh:

> "And at the close of the nineteenth jubilee, in the seventh week in the sixth year thereof, Adam died, and all his sons buried him in the land of his creation, and he was the first to be buried in the earth. And he lacked seventy years of one thousand years; for one thousand years are as one day in the testimony of the heavens and therefore was it written concerning the tree of knowledge: 'On the day that ye eat thereof ye shall die.' For this reason he did not complete the years of this day; for he died during it." - Jubilees 4:29-31

This passage of Jubilees explains that Adam died just shy of one thousand years because Yah stated that both Adam and Eve would die *in the same day that they ate of the forbidden fruit* (Genesis 2:17). Since we know that they did not die on that same 24-hour day, God must have meant a thousand-year long Great Day. Indeed, Adam died just 70 years shy of one thousand years old. Therefore, according to the truthful witness of the Bible and the Book of Jubilees, people today are much less robust than their Pre-Flood ancestors.

After the Great Flood, the lifetimes, and overall robustness of human beings and all other life on Earth gradually began to decline. Several ideas have already been suggested that would account for this great drop in life spans. Other possible causes include the destruction of a greater part of the ozone layer, which subjected living things to far more harmful levels of UV and X-Ray radiation from Outer Space. Another theory is that deadly forms of bacteria and viruses previously unknown on Earth were introduced when the waters above the heavens that helped cause the Great Flood precipitated into the Earth's atmosphere. Furthermore, as will be discussed in Chapter Five, the Earth may have been contaminated with deadly pestilences during the patriarch Joktan's generation when the Tower of Babel fell.

Another intriguing theory behind our much-shortened life-spans is that the reversal and weakening of the Earth's magnetic field, and the increased gravity caused by the Flood drastically affected the biological mechanisms that promote robustness and longevity in all living things. In fact, all of the above possibilities may have combined to create the great drop in mankind's life span from about 900 years prior to the Flood to about 120 years at the time of Moses.

Another cause for the decrease in mankind's longevity after the Flood could be some form of malnutrition. As alluded to in the existence of and purpose for the Tree of Life in the Garden of Eden, some key vitamins and nutrients that were needed to sustain life and health for long periods were removed from the Earth during the Flood. In addition, other plant foods necessary for optimum animal health may also have ceased to be available after the Great Flood. This plant food may have been essential for good health, but was not as beneficial as the fruit from the Tree of Life in the Garden of Eden, which the Bible tells us that Adam and Eve had to eat in order to live forever (Genesis 3:22-24). Therefore, when God removed all access to the Tree of Life because of sin, people and animals began to age, die, and eventually shrink in size. Sadly, the Tree of Life is now completely absent on Earth, and nutrients once available from that amazing tree and other highly nutritious plants that grew before the Flood are no longer available. As a result, all life has diminished in size and strength.

Unlike the Tree of the Knowledge of Good and Evil, the Tree of Life may have had to be eaten from periodically in order to reap the rewards of eating it. This is in keeping with the Messianic and Christian understanding of Christ, who is our Tree of Life. This means that Yahshua must constantly be in our thoughts via the Holy Spirit, and His loving actions must be reflected in our daily behavior if we are to live forever with Him. This is why we symbolically eat Yahshua's Body and Blood at every Passover and Communion service. We do it to commemorate Yahshua's atonement sacrifice for us on Calvary, and to remind ourselves that we are now a part of His Body via Adoption and Marriage, and must act accordingly.

Gloriously, when the Millennial Rule of Christ comes, the Tree of Life will be fully accessible again, and its leaves will be used for the healing of the nations:

"Along the bank of the river... will grow all kinds of trees used for food; their leaves will not wither, and their fruit will not fail. They will bear fruit every month, because their water flows from the sanctuary. Their fruit will be for food, and their leaves for medicine." - Ezekiel 47:12 (NKJ)

"In the middle of its street, and on either side of the river, was the tree of life, which bore twelve fruits, each tree yielding its fruit every month. The leaves of the tree were for the healing of the nations." - Rev. 22:2 (NKJ)

In Ezekiel's vision, many Trees of Life are growing along the bank of a river flowing from underneath a future Temple that will be built in Jerusalem one day. In the preceding quote from the Book of Revelation, however, there are two Trees of Life on either side of the river, and one in the midst of the street running through the New Jerusalem. In this holy city, all things will be made new, and there will be no more death or sickness. Nonetheless, the triple presence of this Tree of Life in the New Jerusalem will stand as a testimony to the healing benefits of fellowship with the one triune God whom Christ represents in the flesh.

Remember, the New Jerusalem is a perfect heavenly copy of the imperfect earthly Jerusalem that will exist during Christ's Millennial Kingdom on Earth - when healing will still be needed by many people. Thus, there is a high likelihood that some literal Trees of Life will be watered by the river flowing out of the Millennial Temple in Jerusalem, and that their year-round crops of fruit will be used to heal all sorts of sicknesses and diseases suffered by the mortal people and animals still living upon the Earth at that time.

Based on archeological and mythological evidence, it also seems that our ancestors were smarter than we are today, for they appear to have developed advanced technologies such as power tools and aircraft that did not rely on fossil fuels for power. One reason they didn't use fossil fuels is the likelihood that there wasn't any to be found on the

Earth before the Flood. This is because most of the crude oil and coal on the Earth today are most likely the remains of plants and animals buried and compressed during the cataclysmic events of the Great Flood.

Evolutionists tell us that the plant and animal matter that makes up the Earth's oil and coal deposits was buried over several millennia, and subjected to a gradual build up of pressure as each level of geological strata piled up on top of previous ones. The Bible, however, tells us that the source of this pressure was the heavy weight of the trillions of gallons of water that flooded the Earth during the Great Flood. As proof that this oil and coal could have formed in a very short period of time from cataclysmically ground up organic matter, a new process for creating high-quality fuel oil and fertilizer has been developed at a waste processing plant in the State of Michigan. It is done by collecting the remains of slaughtered pigs and chickens, grinding it up, and subjecting it to extremely high temperatures and pressure for only a few hours.

During the Great Flood, an immense amount of water covered the whole Earth to the tops of the highest mountains *for five months* (i.e. 150 days) (Genesis 7:24, 8:4). This provided plenty of time for every plant and animal outside the Ark to be torn apart, mixed together, flash buried, and then subjected to enormous pressure - creating the crude oil and coal reserves fueling our world today. In light of these facts, ***doesn't it seem ironic that all current world civilizations depend to varying degrees upon the remains of the dead for the energy they need to live and progress forward?***

Just one gallon of water weighs about eight pounds, and trillions of gallons of water were dumped on the Earth during the Great Flood. Can you imagine the pressure generated by billions upon billions of pounds of additional water on the Earth's surface? It would easily have crushed and shifted the entire crust of the Earth, which would have in turn caused numerous earthquakes and volcanic eruptions! This would have changed the Earth so much from its Pre-Flood conditions that most of its geological and geographical features would have changed. As a result, when Noah and his kin emerged from the Ark, the Earth likely appeared totally alien and virtually unrecognizable to them, and it may have even frightened them to see how vast the devastation of this planet truly was after God's Wrath had been poured out.

Make no mistake! The Earth will be as devastated by the Tribulation plagues and the Battle of Armageddon as it was from the waters of the Flood, and it will take a number of years under Christ's wise leadership to repair all the damage that it sustains, and to restore the Earth to a more pristine state. But restore it Christ will!

Josephus was a Jewish historian who witnessed the destruction of Jerusalem by the Romans in 70 AD. In his histories, Josephus reported that antediluvian people lived phenomenally longer than we do today, just as the Bible indicates. Here is his stance on this subject:

"...but let no one, upon comparing the lives of ancients with our lives, and with the few years in which we now live, think that what we have said of them is false or make the shortness of our lives at present an argument that neither did they attain to so long a duration of life; for those ancients were beloved of God and (lately) made by God Himself; and because their food was then fitter for the prolongation of life; might well live so great a number of years; and besides, God afforded them a longer time of life on account of their virtue and the good use they made of it in astronomical and geometrical discoveries; which would not have afforded the time of foretelling (the periods of the stars) unless they had lived six hundred years; for the Great Year is completed in that interval." – Josephus, The Antiquities of the Jews, 1.3.9

Here, Josephus refers to the 600-year time span it took for the Jewish Lunar Calendar to coincide exactly with the Solar Calendar. This Great Year was different than the prophetic thousand-year period the ancients knew as the Great Day, or "The Day of the Lord." Josephus also attributes the longevity of the antediluvians to their healthier food supply, thereby supporting my previous supposition about the Tree of Life and the extinction of key plants needed for the health of all terrestrial life.

The Language of God Shows the Meaning of Life

Now that we have explored the irreconcilable differences between the Evolutionary and Creation models of origins, we need to examine the reasons why God created man. To find out, we have to go to the very opening passages of God's Creation of mankind in Genesis. Here, Yahweh Elohim says that He created man to tend His earthly garden:

*"Then the LORD God (Yahweh Elohim) took the man and put him in the garden of Eden **to tend and keep it**." - Genesis 2:15 (NIV)*

The Hebrew words translated as *"to tend and keep it"* in the preceding passage could also be translated "to work and guard it" or "to care for and preserve it." We were therefore created to serve God as preservers of the Earth. We were **not**, however, created as slaves to toil and work in the garden until we die from neglect and overwork. We were instead made to have an affinity with and love for the Earth - almost as if we were married to it in a special bond. Since we were made from the soil of the Earth, we do in fact share an irrevocable physical bond with it. We were also meant to enjoy and find happiness from the fruit of our labors tending God's Creation on the Earth.

There is, however, another purpose for mankind. This is to serve as a perpetual dwelling place of the Holy Spirit and God's "Shekinah" or illuminating Glory. Simply put, the Shekinah Glory of God is the physical manifestation of God in our material Universe. Though the word "Shekinah" does not appear in the Bible, the concept clearly does.

The prophet Isaiah foretold the return of God's Glory to Israel when he wrote:

> *"Arise, shine; for your light has come! And the glory of the LORD (Yahweh) is risen upon you. For behold, the darkness shall cover the earth, and deep darkness the people; but the LORD (Yahweh) will arise over you, **and His glory will be seen upon you. The Gentiles shall come to your light,** and kings to the brightness of your rising." - Isaiah 60:1-3 (NKJ)*

Isaiah foresaw this return of Yah's Shekinah Glory to His chosen people at the time that their Redeemer Yahshua returns to conquer the wicked surrounding Jerusalem at the end of the Tribulation (Isaiah 59:19-21). At that time, believers will be clothed with God's light, and will be illuminated within by the Holy Spirit. However, now that Yahshua has won our salvation for us, His Spirit lives and reigns in all believers. Indeed, by believing in Christ, we communally become the spiritual children of Israel, and the Light of the World in Yahshua's absence (Matthew 5:14; John 8:12). We are therefore already touched with a small measure of that radiant light from within that will clothe us with God's Shekinah Glory when we are recreated with perfect resurrected bodies of immortal flesh and perfect spirit.

When we are Spirit-filled, it allows us to share love in a healthy manner, and to be in fellowship with Yahweh. Though all believers have a measure of the Holy Spirit that serves as a deposit guaranteeing their salvation (2 Cor. 1:22, 5:5; Ephesians 1:13-14), they will not be fully capable of fellowshipping with Yahweh until the Holy Spirit transforms them into immortal, incorruptible beings. Before Yahshua came as a Suffering Servant, God's presence or Glory dwelt over and inside the Israelite's Desert Tabernacle. Above the Mercy Seat of the Ark of the Covenant in the Holy of Holies, God's Glory appeared as a cloud that rabbinical literature suggests glowed with an internal, supernatural light that appeared as fire (Exodus 24:17, 25:21-22, 40:34-35; Leviticus 9:23-24, 16:2). This same cloud and fire of Glory also manifested itself above and inside the Temple built by Solomon (2 Chronicles 7:2-3).

The Shekinah Glory was seen not only in the Tabernacle and Temples of Yahweh, but on the faces, and on the bodies of living men. For example, when Moses came down from Mount Sinai with the Stone Tablets of the Testimony written by God's own finger, Moses' face glowed with the light of God's Shekinah Glory (Exodus 34:29-30,35). The Shekinah also manifested itself during the Transfiguration of Yahshua (Matthew 17:1-8). The Shekinah Glory can appear as wind, fire, light, and clouds of smoke (See 2 Samuel 22:11-13, where Yah manifests Himself in all four ways). In this way, the Shekinah Glory and the Holy Spirit manifest themselves identically (John 4:14, Acts 2:3; Revelation 10:1), and both have the same transforming power.

In these physical manifestations of His Glory, Yahweh is telling us something about His nature and character. They are visible symbols that speak to us in the allegorical Language of God. In the Language of metaphors, the fire, wind, water, and smoke tell us that only Yah can give true spiritual sustenance and enlightenment. Likewise, only Yah can transform and cleanse us. He does so with spiritual fire and water, which purifies and transforms us into holy spiritual beings. This book series is geared to sharing the power of these kinds of metaphorical symbols to instruct us spiritually. Book Two especially is a powerful exploration of the allegorical messages that God left for us in the symbols found throughout the Bible, our world and ourselves. Structures such as the Desert Tabernacle and Temple to Yahweh were filled with beautiful spiritual metaphors. Now, however, every human being who loves Yahshua will one day serve as a gleaming white allegorical stone in God's everlasting heavenly temple!

After Yahshua rose from the dead and sent His Holy Spirit to mankind, the Tabernacle and Temple were no longer needed to house God's Shekinah Glory. This is because all believers are now part of Yahweh's holy temple and are filled with His Holy Spirit:

> *"**For we are the temple of the living God.** As God has said: 'I will live with them and walk among them, and I will be their God, and they will be my people.' " - 2 Cor. 6:16 (NIV)*

In the above passage, what was Paul alluding to? He was implying that Spirit-filled Jews and Christians are like Adam and Eve were in the Garden of Eden, when Yahweh God walked among them. At that time, Adam and Eve were untainted by sin, and filled with the radiant Shekinah Glory of Yah's own Spirit. Paul is therefore saying that Yahweh God now walks among those who believe. He does so even before we obtain the perfection Yah has promised us in the resurrection to eternal life. For now, however, we form a rough-hewn stone monument to God's Glory. We believers are like the undressed, imperfect stone pillars that served as altars, memorial stones, and temples unto Yahweh in the past. More background on these sacred stone pillars will be given in Chapter Two. For now, however, picture a big heap of rough, undressed white stones and see it as an analogy for the church as it was *before* the coming of the Holy Spirit. In Book One of the "The Language of God" Book series, the nature and purpose of these ancient memorial pillars mentioned in the Bible is described.

In many places in the Old Testament, it is recorded that various patriarchs made heaps of stones, or erected enormous single unpolished stones to form pillars. These were used to memorialize people, places, and events that had spiritual significance. Sometimes, the blood and oil of sacrifices was poured upon them to honor a Covenant with Yahweh. These stone pillars used as layman's altars had to be made of undressed stones to be considered consecrated before Yahweh. The Patriarch Jacob made such a stone pillar at Bethel when Yahweh gave him the name Israel. This stone pillar marked the making of Yahweh's Blood Covenant with Jacob.

Now picture the beautiful Temple built by Solomon. It was constructed of fully dressed and decorated stone blocks and was cared for by the Levite priesthood. On the Last Day, after the Millennial Rule of Yahshua prophesied in Revelation (Revelation 20:2-6), all of Yahweh's faithful followers will become like the finely dressed stones of that temple. But this will be a symbolic temple built by God's chosen High Priest Yahshua with the power of His Holy Spirit. Our resurrected, spiritual bodies will be the perfect dwelling place of Yah's Spirit and Shekinah Glory - not temples made of stone or brick. We will be like perfectly dressed stones polished by Yahshua's own Spirit and consecrated by His holy blood. As such, each of us will become a perfect stone in the holy pillar that will be God's everlasting dwelling place. In the next chapter, how stone pillars were used in the past to honor and worship the living God Yahweh will be examined. This practice was very important among the descendants of Seth - both before, and after the Flood.

This allegorical picture of people serving as stones in a living temple devoted solely to Yahweh is a perfect example of how Yahweh communicates to us through His amazing metaphorical Language. We

believers are the stones that make up the temple of the living God. As
such, we shall have another glorious occupation that gives our existence
true meaning and purpose. This is to make a joyful noise before Yahweh
Elohim! In fact, our ultimate purpose as a living temple is to stand in
awe of Yahweh's mighty works, and to gladly worship and praise Him
for His greatness. This knowledge is alluded to repeatedly in the Psalms:

> *"I will exalt you, my God and King; I will praise your
> name forever and ever. Every day I will praise you and extol
> your name forever and ever. Great is the Lord (Yahweh) and
> most worthy of praise; his greatness no one can fathom. One
> generation will commend your works to another; they will tell
> of your mighty acts. They will speak of the glorious splendor
> of your majesty, and I will meditate on your wonderful works.
> They will tell of the power of your awesome works, and I will
> proclaim your great deeds. They will celebrate your abundant
> goodness and joyfully sing of your righteousness."* - Psalm
> 145:1-7 (NIV)

The above excerpt from the Psalms reveals that **praising and
worshipping God, and proclaiming His mighty works are the ultimate
reasons why people were created.** Our ancestors were aware of this
aspect of humanity's purpose, and therefore developed an extensive
sacred oral tradition that was passed down from one generation to the
next. This oral story tradition consisted of powerful word pictures
around which important events or ideas were recorded. Many ancient
records and myths appear to have underlying allegorical meanings, just
as the word pictures called Parables that Yahshua used do.

Entertaining and easy to remember, mythical stories from many
cultures still have the power to amuse, delight, and inspire people.
Because the ancients were familiar with the Language of God, many
ancient stories undeniably contain hidden spiritual messages, and had
the power to capture the imaginations of those who heard them. Perhaps
that is why these stories were once reverently recited whenever there
was a public gathering. The religious myths of many primitive cultures
are still remembered today due to this oral tradition.

In keeping with God's Language, storytellers from every past
age, region, and culture preserved religious myths and legends using
unforgettable word pictures - pictures that used the sacred Language of
allegory to tell others about the true God. Unfortunately, Satan's
followers eventually twisted the meanings of many of these ancient
stories, turning them from historical legends into bizarre myths.
However, some ancient religious myths still contain imagery and

meanings that are totally in agreement with Biblical ideas, and often reveal startling truths about Yahweh and His Creation.

For example, before the coming of the first European explorers, some of the native peoples of North America had a profound myth they fashioned to convey the glory of God's Creation of the Cosmos. Several tribes described their beginning in terms of a spider, which they lovingly called Grandmother Spider. They believed she spun a web in which to catch the stars. She is also said to have fashioned the Earth and created mankind. I found this myth a fascinating analogy. Why? Close your eyes and picture our own spiral-shaped Milky Way Galaxy. Isn't it uncanny that the bright central star cluster at the galactic core and the spiraling arms of stars extending from that core resemble the body of a spider? And I can almost picture the invisible web interwoven through it all, holding it together. How profound an allegory for a culture and people that Europeans viewed as primitive savages!

Nevertheless, because the Natives of North America began to worship many demon spirits over their Creator God, the great truths found in their religion became sadly distorted. Soon their basic knowledge of the one true God, and their insights about the nature of God were partially lost. In such revelations as that of Grandmother Spider, however, we see the underlying hand of Yahweh's truth. Unfortunately, the Native Americans forgot that the spider was simply an analogy for the action of Yahweh as Creator God, and instead deified the spider, thereby greatly diminishing and distorting the original truth found in the story.

Interestingly, many myths and legends from ancient times - as well as those still found among primitive people all over the world - talk of the Great Flood and other cataclysmic events that occurred in the remote past. When their meanings are compared and combined, these legends from places as diverse as Asia, India, Persia, Mesopotamia, Greece, Egypt, Europe, and North and South America relay the terrible destruction that occurred during one or more worldwide cataclysms. As shown in Book One, many of these myths and legends give an even more harrowing account than the Bible of the terrible destructive power that was unleashed upon the Earth at that time. They all speak of a horrendous natural disaster that utterly destroyed the remarkable world Noah had known before the Flood. Interestingly, many of these myths and legends make it clear that the Pre-Flood races were being annihilated for their disobedience and wickedness by the Supreme Being who created them - just as a the Bible indicates.

In this book, proof will be given that the antediluvians understood God's allegorical Language. The Bible records little of the world and culture before the Flood. However, there are several ancient manuscripts that shed considerable light on this dark time in history. One such book is the Ethiopian Book of Enoch, or 1 Enoch. It is called the Book of 1 Enoch to distinguish it from the Book of the Secrets of Enoch, which is also known as the Slavonic Book of Enoch, or the Book of 2 Enoch. Though considered Pseudepigraphical, both of these books have a legitimate claim to at least partial authenticity and spiritual veracity, and are therefore referred to often in this book series.

In the next chapter, the veracity of Enoch's writings will be examined, and we will explore what these ancient manuscripts say about Enoch and his vision of our spiritual past, present, and future.

Blood Sacrifice, Covenants, and the Noahide Law

Due to the long life spans of the antediluvians, Enoch's son Methuselah was alive during Noah's formative years. It is therefore likely that Noah received instruction about Yahweh Elohim, His Laws, and His promised Salvation from this great patriarch, and was shown the meaning of the Gospel in the Stars. However, due to the genetic impurity and spiritual degradation of most of humanity at the time of the Flood, Yahweh annihilated most of the people and the evil giants called Nephilim because they had violated the Earth with spilt blood and had polluted mankind's genetic picture. As a result, only Noah and his family were fully human and therefore fit to preserve a purely human and righteous bloodline for the Messiah to descend from.

In some respects, Yah's anger toward the antediluvian races may have been even greater than His anger toward the unrighteous people on the Earth today. The reason for this is that the antediluvians had access to superior spiritual knowledge - partly through their greater familiarity with the Language of God as taught by great prophets like Cainan, Enoch and Noah. In addition, the Gospel in the Stars, the Garden of Eden and the angelic overlords of the Earth called the Watchers were all in existence to bear witness to Yah's truth. For nearly a Millennium, Adam (who lived 930 years) was also there to testify about Yahweh's existence. As a result, the antediluvians had no excuse for their wickedness except their total disdain for Yahweh, His Star Gospel and His righteous Laws.

For these reasons, it is likely that the people before the Flood initially knew the truth about Yahweh, His Plan of Salvation, and His desire for us not to sin. But how much of God's Laws were the antediluvian races really aware of? From studying the behavior of the people mentioned in The Old Testament prior to Moses, it is evident that all people knew and followed a form of the Ten Commandments before the Flood. This spiritual code of conduct has been dubbed *the Noahide Law*. It included regulations regarding animal sacrifices and Blood Covenant ceremonies as well as laws prohibiting murder, lying, stealing, and the eating of blood as food.

This ethical code may have sprang up from the application of principles alluded to during sacred Blood Covenant ceremonies in particular. When Noah left the Ark, he offered burnt sacrifices to Yahweh. Deeply moved by Noah's sacrifices, Yahweh made a Covenant with Noah and all three of his sons. When Yah did, He provided the rainbow as a sign of His unconditional Covenant promise to all life, especially mankind (See Genesis 8:20-22, 9:1-17). Thereafter, the descendants of Noah through Shem (i.e.: the Semites), Ham, and Japheth used Covenant rites to legitimatize all weddings and treaties. *The rite of the sacred Blood Covenant was therefore universally understood at one time and was used to establish an ethical code of conduct to ensure that no one would break the Covenant.*

In Books One and Two of the Language of God series, we delved much further into the evidence showing that the antediluvians were well acquainted with the true God Yahweh Elohim, and the Covenant rite that Yahweh instated at the dawn of time. We explored how they knew Yahweh's universal scientific, mathematical, and spiritual Laws through the Language of God found in the heavens, and on the Earth. Furthermore, through their practice of the Blood Covenant ceremony, we saw that the antediluvians understood Yah's promise of a future Messiah who would provide total redemption from sin.

The knowledge of Yahweh's Plan of Salvation was openly established very early in human history - in a prehistoric age that supposedly came before the invention of writing. In fact, it was openly known about by the second generation from Adam and Eve. At that time, Adam's son Abel offered the first recorded burnt offering of fat portions of the firstborn from his flocks to Elohim. Unlike his brother Cain's offering of some of the fruit of his crops, Abel's sacrifice greatly pleased God.

Both the nature of the sacrifice and attitude of the person offering it affected Yahweh's choice. Abel sacrificed the first born of his flocks - young kids he could take no credit for growing or harvesting, but that he surely loved, and loathed having to kill. This suggests that Abel knew that he had nothing he could give Yahweh that would pay for his sins except his very own lifeblood. To find temporary atonement for his sins, and oneness with the Creator once more, Abel therefore sacrificed an animal innocent of his sins in his stead. Through Abel's actions, it was clear to Yahweh that Abel truly wished to have fellowship with Him, and cared deeply about whether or not God would accept his sacrifice:

> "Later she gave birth to his brother Abel. Now Abel kept flocks, and Cain worked the soil. In the course of time Cain brought some of the fruits of the soil as an offering to the LORD (Yahweh). But Abel brought fat portions from some of the firstborn of his flock." - Genesis 4:2-4 (NIV)

Cain's offering of some of the harvest of his crops seemed innocent enough on the surface, but the choice of offering reveals much when examined closely. When viewed critically, the fruits, vegetables and grains Cain likely offered to God were a boisterous statement to his skill and ingenuity as a farmer who knew how to produce good yields. Furthermore, plants do not have feelings that we can identify with and therefore we feel no great sorrow when a few fruits or grains are lost to us. **This is why Cain so displeased God. He felt no sorrow or suffering when he offered his sacrifice and he lost nothing of any great value** since he gave out of his plenty:

> "The LORD (Yahweh) looked with favor on Abel and his offering, but on Cain and his offering he did not look with favor. So Cain was very angry, and his face was downcast." - Genesis 4:4-5 (NIV)

Twisted by jealousy and selfishness, Cain was finally driven over a spiritual precipice into full-scale evil when he murdered Abel. Since there needed to be at least one righteous offspring of Adam from whom the Savior of God's people could descend, Seth was born and was deemed acceptable by God as a replacement for Abel. Since the Bible indicates that Seth was to replace Abel, it is likely that Seth and his descendants continued to follow in the righteous Abel's footsteps by practicing the same sacrificial system that he set up.

Much later in human history, Noah, Abraham, Job and many other patriarchal figures in the Bible practiced this same sacrificial rite (Genesis 8:20-21; Job 1:5). This blood sacrifice was the sign of the Blood Covenant (or cutting) between Yah and man. Yah Himself "cut" the deal or pact with Adam and Eve *twice*. He did so first when He gave Eve to Adam during the first Marriage Covenant ceremony. Then Yah did so again when He clothed Adam and Eve with animal skins after their Fall. In order to obtain the skins, Yah made the first blood sacrifices of animals to temporarily atone for the sins of His human children.

At the same time, Yah spoke of a specific Seed or offspring of Adam and Eve. This was the first promise God gave concerning the

Messiah to come. Through this Seed of the Woman, Yah promised to send them a perfect Savior who would achieve the lasting atonement and full freedom from Satan and sin that imperfect animals could never provide (Genesis 3:15). The first direct revelation of Yah that foretold the birth of Yahshua therefore came at the very dawn of human history!

Proof That Our Ancestors Awaited Spiritual Rebirth

Proof that prehistoric people had hope in a future spiritual rebirth can be found in many Pre-Dynastic burial sites found in Egypt, and in similar Stone-Age burials that have been found throughout the world. In these burials, the corpses were situated in the grave or tomb in a fetal position. In addition, their bodies were often interred naked and covered with red ochre. Furthermore, the bodies were buried in oval-shaped graves or pits in the ground, and their faces were positioned as if to face the rising Sun.

It is my belief that secular scholars have grossly misinterpreted the meanings of these burial customs, and the artifacts found in association with them, such as tiny carved figurines of faceless, chubby, seemingly pregnant women. The religion of these primitive Stone Age people is often cited by scholars as being polytheistic, as well as animistic - with a central mother goddess figure as their primary deity. Since there are no written records to convince them otherwise, secular scholars postulate that this mother goddess is likely a symbol for the Earth itself. They therefore assume that our ancestors worshiped the Earth, and other created things. However, could it be that their assumption is totally incorrect? Could they be misinterpreting the spiritual symbolism in these prehistoric artifacts and burials?

When seen through the eyes of the Holy Spirit, the symbolic aspects of these artifacts and burials can give a completely different impression. In fact, my Spirit-led impressions of these symbolic elements are diametrically opposed to the conventional hypotheses. For example, the oval shaped tombs and pregnant female figures often found inside them could signify the "womb" of the Holy Spirit, rather than an Earth goddess. In other words, the faceless carvings of a voluptuous pregnant woman that have been found all over the world may represent a symbolic mother and womb that people enter into to be born again spiritually. In fact, these carvings may represent the promise of the resurrection and everlasting life!

These burials may have also represented the allegorical spiritual message behind planting seeds. As discussed in Book One, our bodies can be viewed as seeds that must dry out or die before they are planted in the ground to sprout with new life. Therefore, the style of these simple primitive burials appear to prove that some of our ancestors knew the True God Yahweh, understood their need for a Savior, and longed to be spiritually reborn and physically resurrected.

If we view these burials from a Judeo-Christian perspective, then we can see many interesting parallels to the metaphorical symbols analyzed thus far in this book series. As already stated, the faceless female figurines could be a symbol for the Holy Spirit, our spiritual Mother who has no corporeal form, and is therefore faceless. As such, the statues would have visually portrayed the need for the deceased to enter into the Spirit's symbolic womb in order to be reborn and resurrected. Likewise, the red ochre may have symbolized the sacrificial animal blood spilled in atonement sacrifices to Yahweh that was required for this rebirth to occur one day. Abel and the righteous descendants of Seth knew that *Yah required this spilled innocent blood in order for men to have communion with Him in life as well as after death.* In fact, Yahshua died for our sins as a perfect atonement sacrifice so that blood sacrifices would no longer be needed, and so that we could live forever with Christ in the Resurrection.

Besides signifying the bloody fluid that covers a newborn baby, the red ochre covering all or part of the individuals in these Predynastic burials could also signify the shed blood of animals sacrificed in Blood Covenant rituals. With their covering of red ochre in death, these Stone-Age people could have been indicating that they had entered into Blood Covenant relationships with Yahweh, and that they were awaiting the eternal life promised through His coming Messiah.

When viewed through the Language of God, these ochre-covered bodies appear to clearly symbolize the perfect blood sacrifice for sins that was finally provided through the body and blood of Yahshua. Though these people may not have understood all of the implications of Yahshua's sacrifice, they nonetheless could have lived with the hope of salvation through the future Messiah promised in the Gospel in the Stars. They also could have died with the expectation that they would be included among the righteous like Noah and Abraham, who both entered into Blood Covenant relationships with Yahweh (Genesis 6:18, 9:11-13, 15:18, 17:2-4).

Though they never witnessed the First Advent of the "Seed of the Woman" promised in Scripture, and had no Bible to guide them, Noah and Abraham likely believed in their deliverance from sin through that coming Messiah. This is because the coming of their promised Deliverer was clearly foretold in the Gospel in the Stars. In fact, the ministry of this mighty Messiah was foretold throughout the forty-eight constellations in the ancient Zodiac, as shown in the outline with the sub heading "A Summary of the Gospel in the Mazzaroth" in Chapter Three. This outline shows how powerfully Christ is preached through the starry celestial symbols in the heavens. For a more detailed explanation, the full religious significance of the Gospel in the Stars and the spiritual meaning of Blood Covenant rituals are explored in Books One and Two of the "Language of God" Book Series.

If the hypothesis presented here is true - and the "Language of God" Book Series exhaustively proves that it is - then we can form a plausible reconstruction of what these prehistoric people actually believed spiritually. Could it be that some of our ancient ancestors understood that life on Earth was transitory, and that it would be followed by another existence in the spiritual realm? If so, then they likely knew that one had to be "reborn," or "recreated," in order to enter this blessed spiritual afterlife. Judging by the simplicity of these burials, the people who made them may also have known that the physical body and any other earthly goods accompanying it couldn't enter this afterlife, and would be totally unnecessary there. Therefore, the simple offerings of food and grain that were often left in these womb-like, oval-shaped graves may simply have been meant to be symbolic prayer offerings for the dead.

These primitive graves may have been seen as a fitting symbol for spiritual rebirth, and belief in a future physical resurrection from the dead. They may have symbolized the hope that these dead bodies would live again, just as seeds do when they are buried and sprout new life. That the dead were seen as symbolic seeds being planted might also explain why these burials often included grave offerings of grain. In addition, the fruits and vegetables buried with the bodies likely symbolized the good fruit these godly people had produced in their earthly lives, as well as the hope that they would live again and thereafter produce more good fruit. Incidentally, all fruits also contain seeds. In effect, the symbols placed in each grave could therefore easily be symbolic of the hope of the living in a future resurrection to eternal life. These Ark-like graves may have served as a powerful symbolic visual testimony that physical and spiritual death through sin is not final, and living a righteous life is never in vain.

Chapter 2: The Legacy of Enoch, Pre-Flood Prophet of God

> *"Enoch a righteous man, whose eyes were opened by God, saw the vision of the Holy One in the heavens, which the angels showed me, and from them **I heard everything, and from them I understood as I saw, but not for this generation, but for a remote one which is for to come**..."* - 1 Enoch 1:2-3

The Hebrew name Enoch (a.k.a. Henoch) means "initiated." It can also mean "narrow," which figuratively means to discipline or initiate into knowledge - just as a teacher might do by focusing on a subject in layers, revealing greater and greater detail with each lesson. This meaning also suggests the *"narrow road to life"* that Yahshua mentioned (Matthew 7:13-14). Enoch did as Yahshua calls us all to do. He followed a narrow spiritual and moral road - a road that he walked so faithfully with God that he was translated without seeing death (Gen. 5:22-24). Interestingly, because "Enoch" means both "initiated" and "narrow," it also suggests that being initiated into the knowledge that Enoch possessed is difficult to understand, and even harder to live by.

One of our most reliable sources of information about Enoch can be found in one ancient manuscript that bears his name: The Ethiopian Book of Enoch, or the Book of 1 Enoch. This manuscript clearly tells us what Enoch did, and what he believed. It also explicitly tells what happened in antediluvian times - during Enoch's lifetime. It tells us that, after Adam and Eve's Fall, our antediluvian ancestors sinned so deeply that Yahweh decided to destroy all living things with a flood. It therefore supports the Biblical account of the Great Flood. It also describes shadowy figures that few people today know anything about: the Nephilim and the fallen angels who spawned them in sin.

In this chapter's opening quote from 1 Enoch, we are told that **this manuscript was preserved for a generation that would exist far into the future.** I believe that future generation is this current one, and that we are in the final Age that Enoch foresaw, when God will put an end to wickedness on the Earth, and establish a Kingdom of righteousness that will have no end. But before this occurs, a time of trouble such as the world has never seen before is destined to come - a dreaded time known as the Great Tribulation, or the Apocalypse. With the exception of the Great Flood, no greater time of trouble has ever been experienced by the people of Earth, nor will they experience any greater one after it.

preteris premil view with definite extended times

For those who wish to avoid that horrible time of trouble, it would be wise to become reacquainted with Enoch's view of God, of righteousness, of angels and fallen angels, and of the genetic corruption the fallen angels spawned by creating the Nephilim, and also teaching mankind how to manipulate genes. This is because we are living in a time when men can again play God - when they can manipulate genes to create certain desired outcomes in people and plants that may appear beneficial to the world. Nonetheless, the long term affects of this tampering with God's sovereignty, and the Laws He set up to govern nature are unknown, and could potentially be disastrous.

Those who wish to avoid the terrible mistakes that humanity made in the past need to pay attention to Enoch's wisdom, and the future that Enoch foresaw. Enoch left a legacy of spiritual and historical knowledge that speaks to this current generation like no other. Will we be wise enough to listen to Enoch's messages to us, and to heed his warnings? Only time will tell. In the meantime, this book will reveal what Enoch's writings were always meant to tell the world. It will show that Enoch's words were meant to become a lamp, or beacon of light to this generation, and to help lead them out of spiritual darkness and ignorance.

Another clue that Enoch's writings were meant for this current generation is found in another prophecy recorded in the Book of 1 Enoch:

"And now I know this mystery, that sinners will alter and pervert the words of righteousness in many ways, and will speak wicked words, and lie, and practice great deceits, and write books concerning their words. **But when they write down truthfully all my words in their languages, and do not change or (de)minish ought from my words** but write them all down truthfully - all that I first testified concerning them. Then, I know another mystery, that **books will be given to the righteous and the wise to become a cause of joy and uprightness and much wisdom.** And to them shall the books be given, and they shall believe in them and rejoice over them, and then shall all the righteous who have learnt therefrom all the paths of uprightness be recompensed." - 1 Enoch 104:10-13

In effect, this passage of 1 Enoch tells us that his book would not be translated correctly until the time came for it to be known and understood. Furthermore, at that time, many correct translations of it would be made and dispersed throughout the world - even as other books that bring joy and knowledge to God's people would be revealed and made available to everyone. This prophecy began to come true within the last three hundred years. This began when the Book of 1 Enoch was discovered in Ethiopia by Scottish explorer James Bruce in 1773, and was finally translated into by English by scholar R. R. Charles in the late 1800's, and published in English by the Oxford University Press in 1912. Likewise, the Hebraic version of the Book of Jasher was rediscovered in 1829, then translated into English and published in 1887. Still later, the Book of Jubilees was translated into English and published in 1913.

Only within the last twenty years, however, has this prophecy been literally fulfilled. In fact, for the first time in history, the Book of 1 Enoch, Book of Jubilees, and Book of Jasher are both correctly translated and readily available to virtually anyone who can read, as new translations of these books into different languages have recently been made. In addition, versions of them are accessible in many libraries and in traditional and online bookstores throughout the Western world.

As Enoch's words are finally being correctly deciphered and applied, what was hidden until this Age is being made known again - just as Yahshua prophesied it would be:

> "And He said to them, 'Is a lamp brought to be put under a basket or under a bed? Is it not to be set on a lampstand? **For there is nothing hidden which will not be revealed, nor has anything been kept secret but that it should come to light.** If anyone has ears to hear, let him hear.'" - Mark 4:21-23 (NKJ)

Here, Yahshua was telling His disciples that there is indeed a hidden body of knowledge within Judeo-Christianity that He had come to reveal and would allow to come to light through Him at its appointed time. Besides the Book of Revelation, which was finally deciphered and correctly interpreted within the last one hundred years, the Books of 1 and 2 Enoch, the Book of Jasher, and the Book of Jubilees can help to reveal those hidden things that Scripture talks about. This is because they give much detail concerning the sins of our antediluvian ancestors, and their ill-fated involvement with the fallen angels and the Nephilim.

In fact, without these manuscripts, it is impossible to know what happened to mankind prior to the Great Flood with any detail, and it makes it difficult to understand why it should be important to us today. All we have left to go on is the abbreviated account of this time period given to us in the Bible's Book of Genesis, the histories of Josephus, and all the corruptions of the truth found in ancient legends and Pagan mythologies. Though Genesis and Josephus offer superb glimpses into the spiritual and historical past of the Sethites and Israelites, and Pagan myths and legends have their place in helping us to understand what occurred before recorded history, the four aforementioned non-biblical religious manuscripts have a stronger claim to veracity than any Pagan myth, and should be required reading in every theological school.

Which Ancient Texts Are the Most Reliable?

After seriously studying them for a number of years, I have come to the conclusion that the writings of Josephus, the Book of 1 Enoch, the Book of Jasher, and - to a more limited extent - the Book of Jubilees and 2 Enoch are authentic Semitic histories that preserve an accurate record of the spiritual beliefs that arose prior to and after the Great Flood. Therefore, they can be relied upon to fill in the huge voids left in the abbreviated Genesis account of antediluvian history.

Due to internal evidence and their harmonization with the Bible, it appears that the Book of Jubilees, Jasher, and 1 Enoch are either authentic histories, or compilations containing genuine historical information in a framework of later narrative. That is why these books are the basis for most of the suppositions in this book about what may have occurred prior to the Great Flood. However, unlike the Book of Jasher and Jubilees, the Book of 1 Enoch is also filled with divinely inspired prophecies. So, though it too is useful as a history, the Book of 1 Enoch is also a storehouse of extremely ancient, God-breathed prophetic knowledge. This makes 1 Enoch the oldest divinely sanctioned prophetic work available to mankind outside of the Gospel in the Stars.

When one ventures into religious literature for research purposes, it can be quite daunting to discover just how much extra-biblical literature is available in institutions of higher learning, or through specialty or Internet book stores. There is a wide range of material available to study, including many ancient texts that are considered to be Apocryphal or Pseudepigraphical in nature. That is, these texts are not considered to be canonical and are therefore unwisely looked down upon as completely unreliable, legendary, or fictitious in nature.

There are also the writings of Judaic scholarship to consider, including their copious amounts of written commentary on Scripture called the Midrash. In addition, there are compilations of material from the Apocrypha and Pseudepigrapha that are further commented on and explained in works such as Flavius Josephus' "Antiquities of the Jews," and Louis Ginzberg's "The Legends of the Jews." Though I always trust what the Bible says about origins and history over the Talmud, Midrash, Apocrypha, Pseudepigrapha, history, or compilation, these other sources are often helpful for filling in the blanks in areas that the Bible mentions but doesn't explain, and therefore invites questions about - such as the Giants, the Nephilim, and the Watchers that we will discuss at length in this book.

In this chapter, it will be shown that 1 Enoch is very valuable as a prophetic source - one that is comparable to some biblical prophetic books. Therefore, in addition to analyzing biblical and extra-biblical Judeo-Christian religious teachings about human history in this book, we will decipher what Enoch's prophecies were meant to show this final generation before Christ's Second Coming in Book Four.

Since the Book of 1 Enoch contains the best source of information about the Nephilim, it is quoted from extensively in this book. Many people, however, are not familiar with this ancient manuscript and may therefore wonder how reliable it is as an historical account of the past. This section will address these concerns regarding three ancient Judeo-Christian manuscripts which have given me the best source of information about our biblical past outside of Josephus: the Book of 1 Enoch, the Book of Jubilees, and the Book of Jasher. In the process, it will show that these books should be considered much more reliable than the many Pagan myths that non-Christian scholars often rely on to determine what happened in the far past.

Though some scholars believe that 1 Enoch or the Ethiopian Book of Enoch is a Jewish work conceived of no later than the third or fourth century before Christ, other scholars feel it may be much older. Originally, it was likely written in Hebrew, and many fragments of the book were found written in Hebrew among the Dead Sea Scrolls. It was also highly regarded among all the early Christian Church Fathers, but mysteriously vanished from Western liturgical usage after the establishment of the Roman Catholic Church. In Book Four, we will discuss Enoch's prophecies and the possibility that sinister efforts were made to suppress these prophecies. This may explain this manuscript's near total disappearance in the Dark Ages except in the commentaries and letters of the early Church Fathers.

In 1773, in Abyssinia - which is an archaic name for modern day Ethiopia - the English explorer James Bruce found the full manuscript of the Book of 1 Enoch to still be extant in the religious literature of the Ethiopian Christians, along with the Book of Jubilees. He brought back three copies of 1 Enoch recorded in Ethiopic script, and these effectively re-introduced Western scholars to Enoch's incredible record of antediluvian times. Today, the Book of 1 Enoch and the Book of Jubilees still hold a high place among the sacred books of the Ethiopian Christian Church. There, they are considered canonical, and they are used as references when Ethiopian Christians study God's Word. Unfortunately, they are still relatively unknown to many Christians in the West, who are often unaware of their spiritual and historical value.

Despite being regularly overlooked, the Book of 1 Enoch and the Book of Jubilees are considered to be authentic God-inspired scriptural documents by some Western scholars. Though most see Jubilees and 1 Enoch as compilations written by different people sometime during the post-exilic period of Jewish history, many scholars feel that 1 Enoch was written, at least in part, by Enoch and also possibly by Noah. If Enoch composed all or most of 1 Enoch, it would have been written sometime between Enoch's birth in 3381 BC and his translation in 3016 BC. If so, the historical information in 1 Enoch was recorded long before the Great Flood of 2347 BC.

In order to show how important the Book of 1 Enoch is as a Judeo-Christian reference work, it is important to establish who Enoch was, and - more importantly, why we should care about what he wrote in his manuscript. To find out, let's first look in the Book of Genesis. There, we are told that Enoch was the son of Jared, and the seventh patriarch in the line of Seth. We are also told that Enoch walked with God and never saw death:

"Enoch walked with God; then he was no more,
because God took him away." - Gen. 5:24 (NIV)

By saying that Enoch *"walked with God,"* the author of this section of Genesis was stating that Enoch had a very close personal relationship with Yahweh and, like Abraham, was considered righteous by his faith. Now, Enoch may have first been taught that the metaphorical Language of God was symbolically written into the Cosmos at the time of Creation by his great, great, great grandfather Cainan, who died at the age of 910, and lived for two hundred more years *after* the time that Enoch was translated.

As good students often do, Enoch sought to know more than his wise old ancestor Cainan, and drew so close to Yahweh and His holy angels that he understood the Language of God in the starry heavens better than anyone else of his era. Enoch called this celestial record the *"Heavenly Tablets,"* and said it contained the deeds of men and angels throughout time. As was shown in Book One, the celestial storybook we call the Zodiac also foretold the coming of the one future King, Priest, and Redeemer who would come to conquer the fallen angel Azazel (i.e. Satan), sin, and death forever.

Uncannily, Enoch's book often speaks of this coming Redeemer and King and His future reign of righteousness. For this reason, many skeptics have claimed that, after the time of Christ, Christians wrote over half of the Book of 1 Enoch found in Ethiopia, and that it was never part of the original book. However, there is no conclusive proof that this ever occurred. Furthermore, several of Enoch's most profound and earth-shaking prophecies about the future are found in the latter section of the book supposedly added long after Enoch was translated. Therefore, it would be safe to assume that only a great prophet of God like Enoch could have written these amazing prophecies.

Since Enoch had such great faith in Yahweh, he was chosen to reveal a great deal more of God's hidden testimony about Himself than Cainan. So, though the Language of God in the stars was probably initially revealed to Cainan, Enoch was likely the first man to discern its full implications. Though the Book of 1 Enoch was likely translated into Ethiopic from an Aramaic or Hebrew original, Enoch probably originally used some form of hieroglyphic writing to record this book. In addition, Enoch may have written other books which are now badly corrupted, such as the Book of the Secrets of Enoch, or 2 Enoch. There is also some reason to believe that Enoch - or one of his descendents or followers - carved the Dendera ceiling Zodiac and drew up the architectural plans for the Great Pyramid complex at Giza. This immense pillar of stone, which is so grand in scale that it has never been surpassed, is dedicated to Yahweh and appears to be connected to the messianic constellation of Orion, which has a very exalted place among the 48 constellations or chapters in the Gospel in the Stars.

Rather than being used for fortune telling, there is much evidence that the Zodiac was created to inform mankind of God's purpose for Creation, as well as His Plan of Salvation through Yahshua the Messiah (i.e. Jesus the Christ). This is why many people have come to believe that the Zodiac forms a divinely created Gospel in the Stars. In Book One of this book series, we examined all the marvelous spiritual truths that are found in the heavens, and the knowledge that Enoch may have known simply from studying the allegorical meaning of the stars with his spiritual eyes open. Then, in Book Two, we discussed how Christ and the prefigurations of Christ found in the lives of many Bible heroes are forever memorialized in the constellations of the Mazzaroth. Now, in this book, we will explore the history of mankind as it was, is, and has yet to be revealed in the heavens.

The written references that exist concerning Enoch portray him as a great king and spiritual teacher. They reveal that he served as a prophetic messenger between Yahweh, men, and angels, and that he recorded many prophecies in book form. His prophecies were about the coming destruction of the Earth, as well as the complete spiritual history of the world to the present. The Book of Jubilees mentions Enoch's prophetic visions and writings in a favorable light:

> *"And what was and what will be he saw in a vision of his sleep, as it will happen to the children of men throughout their generations until the day of judgment; he saw and understood everything, and wrote his testimony, and placed the testimony on earth for all the children of men and for their generations." – Jubilees 4:19-20*

The prophecies in the Book of 1 Enoch have proven to be incredibly accurate. In fact, much of 1 Enoch is prophetic in nature and full of the allegorical Language of God. In the metaphorical style of its prose, 1 Enoch is very similar to the Books of Daniel, Ezekiel, and Revelation in the Bible. We will closely analyze several of Enoch's prophecies in Book Four, "The Language of God in Prophecy." There, we will explore Enoch's prophecies of the One-Horned Ram, the Ten 700-year Ages of Men - or 7000 years, and the Prophecy of the Seventy Shepherds. In every respect, these prophetic visions have proven correct - even though, since Enoch likely lived between 3381 BC and 3016 BC, they may have been written *over five thousand years ago!*

In addition to using 1 Enoch as a historical and spiritual reference, this book relies on the history called the Book of Jasher or "The Upright Record," which is mentioned in the Old Testament twice (See Joshua 10:13 and 2 Samuel 1:18). Incidentally, "Jasher" isn't a person's name, but is the Hebrew word for "Upright." Like the Book of Jubilees, the Upright Record is a retelling of the Genesis story from a different person's perspective other than Moses'. It also contains a wealth of detail missing from Moses' abbreviated account. For those who wish to read the Book of Jasher, be forewarned that there are two books in circulation called "The Book of Jasher." The one that is purported to be a ninth century translation by Flaccus Albinus Alcuinus (the Abbot of Canterbury, and the religious tutor of Charlemagne) is an obvious forgery.

The books of Joshua and 2 Samuel in the Old Testament mention the Book of Jasher or Upright Record as a source of information for two historical events that the Bible covers briefly. These two stories are contained in the thirteenth century translation, but the incident in 2 Samuel is not covered in the ninth century edition at all. Furthermore, the thirteenth century translation appears to have been made from a Hebrew original.

Besides this important claim, the thirteenth century copy of the Book of Jasher has the feel of an authentic historical document written by someone with a Semitic background who actually witnessed some of the recorded events. This thirteenth century edition is far longer than the false ninth century edition, and contains too many authentic cultural descriptions of Near Eastern and Semitic life to have been invented. Furthermore, *none* of the more colorful historical and cultural recollections in the thirteenth century edition - the ones that give it such a ring of authenticity - appear in the supposedly older manuscript by Alcuinus.

Since the Book of Jasher isn't considered a religious document, but a historical narrative, some of its stories may have been embellished. In a few sections of the book, it appears that some tampering was done, but not enough to invalidate the entire book. Also, though the Book of Jasher's chronology for certain events differs from the abbreviated Genesis account of this time period in a few minor cases, I always trust that the sixty-six books of the Bible are more accurate.

Nevertheless, the Book of Jasher has great value as a history since it offers a wealth of details that the Genesis account by Moses lacks. In many ways, it can help us to understand difficult passages or situations recorded too briefly in the Bible. Still, it is currently impossible to prove whether or not the thirteenth century copy of the Book of Jasher available to us today is a full copy of the original Bible history - at least not until other authentic copies of it are found. In the meantime, I believe that there is enough internal evidence in the Book of Jasher to prove that it is genuine, and highly useful for study when read with the Holy Spirit's guidance.

What follows throughout this book are many suppositions about the past gleaned from studying these ancient manuscripts, the Bible, and countless secular history books. Since the history here is woven together from several little known ancient sources, the ideas in this book may sound very strange to people who have never delved very deeply into studying ancient history or ancient religions. However, the reader should carefully and prayerfully consider the ideas herein before rejecting them. If anyone fully researches these suppositions, they will see that they aren't far-fetched at all. Rather, they answer the many questions about the past that have been raised by adept non-Christian scholars such as Graham Hancock, Zecharia Sitchin, John Anthony West, Andrew Collins, and many others in recent times.

If anyone has read any books by the aforementioned scholars, they would realize that - though these gentlemen raise some very valid questions about the past - they aren't Christians. As a result, they challenge not only orthodox secular views of ancient history, but also biblical history. However, the same scholars have done us a great service by pointing out that orthodox views of history are not based on facts at all, but suppositions. Furthermore, they solidly point out that many in the academic communities around the world blithely ignore evidence that negates, or is contrary to their established ideas. If we are seekers of truth, the legitimate though conflicting data presented by scholars who question modern scientific orthodoxy should also lead us to question what we are being told about the past in schools, museums, books, and via audio-visual media.

It is time that we believers solidly addressed the findings of those who not only refute orthodox books on ancient history, but the Bible's record of what happened in the past. There are also many Christian scholars who question orthodox views in areas such as ancient history, anthropology, archeology, and geology. These include such godly men as Henry M. Morris - the founder of the Institute for Creation Research, and a prolific writer about the past.

This book is my attempt to reconstruct an accurate view of humanity's spiritual, historical, and intellectual past. This reconstruction is based on the findings of secular scholars, modern archeological research, Christian scholars, the Bible, mythology, ancient histories like those of Josephus and the Book of Jasher, and many ancient manuscripts that predate Christianity, especially 1 and 2 Enoch and Jubilees. By comparing and combining the facts found in these sources, sound Judeo-Christian answers can be given for the questions that are often raised regarding humanity's past and that are largely unanswerable in biblical terms without them.

Enoch as a Righteous Hermit, Messenger and Scribe of God

Now that we have explored the reasons for relying on the histories of Josephus, 1 and 2 Enoch, Jubilees, and the Book of Jasher in the process of making assumptions and forming conclusions about the past, let's see how much more they have to say about Enoch, the seventh antediluvian patriarch in Seth's line.

In the Book of 1 Enoch, Enoch is called the *"scribe of righteousness"* (1 Enoch 12:4; 15:2) who was able to read *"the heavenly tablets."* Some scholars believe that these Heavenly Tablets may refer to some invisible record that Enoch saw in the Heaven where God dwells, i.e. not the heavens surrounding our Earth. However, there is evidence that people before and after the Flood saw the heavens as a giant, divinely written picture book that tells a divinely authored story. This is found in the forty-eight constellations of the ancient Zodiac. In Book One, it was shown that the term Heavenly Tablets could be a reference to the Zodiac. Furthermore, it was shown that Enoch likely used picture symbols like hieroglyphics to record his knowledge of the picture story written in the vault of heaven.

In Arab legends, as well as in the Book of Jubilees, Enoch the Sethite is credited with the invention of writing:

> "...he (Jared) called his name Enoch. And he was the first among men that are born on earth who learnt writing and knowledge and wisdom and who wrote down the signs of heaven according to the order of their months in a book, that men might know the seasons of the years according to the order of their separate months. And he was the first to write a testimony and he testified to the sons of men among the generations of the earth..." - Jubilees 4:17-18

This quote from the Book of Jubilees clearly states that Enoch the Sethite invented writing. If Enoch did, Enoch's ancestor Cainan the Sethite probably learned hieroglyphic writing from Enoch, since the Book of Jasher tells us that Cainan wrote down his wisdom on stone tablets, ostensibly in a way that would make it possible for others to read it later on.

Referring to the above quote from Jubilees, it says that Enoch "wrote down the signs of heaven according to the order of their months in a book." It therefore clearly supports the idea that Enoch was the first to write down what he had seen in the twelve houses of the Mazzaroth or Zodiac and its 48 constellations. Indeed, in the Mazzaroth, the Sun, Moon, stars and planets serve as the allegorical "pens" that God uses to inscribe these Heavenly Tablets, and Enoch was an expert at interpreting the meaning of their movements. Furthermore, the pictorial symbols associated with the constellations serve as the theme markers for a 48 chapter story that God wrote in the heavens with His allegorical Language, and - as mentioned in Book One and later in this Chapter - the Dendera Zodiac is an indicator that Enoch fully understood the Star Gospel.

Fascinatingly, there are a few passages in the Old Testament Book of Ezekiel the Prophet that may be referring to Enoch in his role as a divine scribe that recorded all the deeds of mankind for God. In fact, in one of Ezekiel's early visions describing the coming destruction of the people of Judah and Jerusalem, a peculiar man with a writing kit is called to mark the foreheads of all those whom God will spare from death with the Hebrew letter "Tav:"

> *"And I saw six men... each with a deadly weapon in his hand.* **With them was a man clothed in linen who had a writing kit at his side.** *They... stood beside the bronze altar. Now the glory of the God of Israel went up from above the cherubim... and moved to the threshold of the temple.* **Then the LORD (Yahweh) called to the man clothed in linen who had the writing kit at his side and said to him, 'Go throughout the city of Jerusalem and put a mark on the foreheads of those who grieve** *and lament over all the detestable things that are done in it.' As I listened, he said to the others, 'Follow him through the city and kill, without showing pity or compassion. Slaughter old men, young men and maidens, women and children, but do not touch anyone who has the mark. Begin at my sanctuary.' So they began with the elders who were in front of the temple..."* **"Then the man in linen with the writing kit at his side brought back word, saying, 'I have done as you commanded.'"** *- Ezekiel 9:2-6, 11 (NIV)*

Interestingly, the ancient form of the Hebrew letter "Tav" or "T" was in the shape of an "X" or slanted cross, and is the likely origin of the English letter "T." Even more uncannily, Yahshua was given an honorary title as *"the Alpha and the Omega"* in the Book of Revelation, and the Hebrew equivalent of this title would be written as "the Aleph and the Tav." This means that the scribe identified the people who were to be spared with a mark that mimics the sign of the Cross! Likewise, believers are saved and spared from destruction by Christ's righteous blood that was shed on a T-shaped cross.

This scribe appears one other time in the Book of Ezekiel - in relation to the Cherubim, which are tied to the unfolding of history recorded in the Zodiac Gospel reflecting God's Plan of Redemption in every age:

> *"Then* **He spoke to the man clothed with linen, and said, 'Go in among the wheels, under the cherub,** *fill your hands with coals of fire from among the cherubim, and scatter them over the city (i.e. Jerusalem).' And he went in as I watched." "And the sound of the wings of the cherubim was heard even in the outer court, like the voice of Almighty God when He speaks. Then it happened... that he went in and stood beside the wheels.* **And the cherub stretched out his hand... to the fire that was among the cherubim, and... put it**

into the hands of the man clothed with linen..." - Ezekiel 10:2, 5-7 (NKJ)

In this abridged Scripture, it becomes apparent that this linen-clad scribe is acting in the messenger role of a holy angel, even though he is clearly called a man. Furthermore, he is intimately acquainted with the Cherubim, who govern the movements of the Universe with their wheels, who follow the unfolding of time with their wings, and who record the passage of time with their many eyes.

This scribe is clothed in linen, which is a white fabric that represents righteousness, purity and redemption in the Bible. It therefore signifies a righteous man who is gifted at remembering, recording, and recollecting events that occur on Earth even as they are reflected in the heavens. He also acts as an angel. For example, in his act of marking the foreheads of those to be spared and pouring out coals of heavenly fire onto Jerusalem in judgment, the linen-clad man with the writing kit can enact God's will, mercy, and wrath on the Earth. Furthermore, he does this service for none other than God Almighty. Shades of Thoth and Hermes aside, this scribe clothed in linen is therefore clearly Enoch's double!

Indeed, without mentioning Enoch by name but by character, the Bible's Book of Ezekiel fully supports and verifies what we are told about Enoch in the Books of 1 Enoch, Jubilees, and Jasher. In these books, Enoch is depicted as a very wise man that had a unique and privileged relationship with God, who could read the Heavenly Tablets, and who understood their connection to the Gospel in the Stars. In addition, Enoch is depicted as the inventor of writing, as well as a recluse who spent many hours praying, meditating, and conversing with angels.

In the Book of Jubilees, for example, we are told that Enoch spent most of his earthly lifetime in the company of the holy angels or Watchers who instructed Enoch in the ways of Yahweh. In addition, Enoch is described as a man who wasn't at all afraid to share what Yahweh had revealed to him in visions and dreams, as well as through his many discussions and journeys with angels.

The Book of Jasher describes Enoch as a very godly and spiritually aware man who wisely sought to find God in solitude for many years:

> *"And the soul of Enoch was wrapped up in the instruction of the Lord, in knowledge and in understanding;* **and he wisely retired from the sons of men, and secreted himself from them for many days.** *And it was at the expiration of many years, whilst he was serving the Lord, and praying*

before him in his house, that an angel of the Lord called to him from Heaven, and he said, 'Here am I.' And he (the angel) said, 'Rise, go forth from thy house and from the place where thou dost hide thyself, and appear to the sons of men, in order that thou mayest teach them the way in which they should go and the work which they must accomplish to enter in the ways of God.'" - Jasher 3:2-4

This voluntary time that Enoch spent in seclusion, prayer, worship and study reveals Enoch's deep reverence for and love of Yahweh. This is undoubtedly why Enoch's visions of Heaven and the fate of the blessed and the damned mirror the prophetic books of the Bible in virtually every respect. His writings are filled with much Bible-affirming historical agreement.

In the preceding quote from the Book of Jasher, it is also important to note that an angel appeared to Enoch and called him into God's service as a prophet and spiritual teacher. According to the Book of Jubilees and Book of 1 Enoch, this was not Enoch's only contact with an angel, but one of many such encounters:

"Before these things Enoch was hidden, and no one of the children of men knew where he was hidden, and where he abode, and what had become of him. **And his activities had to do with the Watchers, and his days were with the holy ones.***"* *- 1 Enoch 12:1-3*

Here, we are told that Enoch spent much time in the presence of the holy ones among the Watchers, who instructed him in all kinds of hidden wisdom. This is why, while he reigned over the kings of the Earth, Enoch never failed to repudiate evil, and he boldly rebuked the fallen Watchers when he served as a messenger between them and Yahweh God. The Book of Jubilees relays some information about this:

"And he was moreover with the angels of God these six jubilees of years, and they showed him everything which is on earth and in the heavens, the rule of the sun, and he wrote down everything. And he testified to the Watchers, who had sinned with the daughters of men; for these had begun to unite themselves, so as to be defiled, with the daughters of men, and Enoch testified against (them) all."

"And he was taken from amongst the children of men, and we conducted him into the Garden of Eden in majesty and honor, and observe there he writes down the condemnation and judgment of the world, and all the

wickedness of the children of men. And on account of it (God, i.e. Elohim) brought the waters of the flood upon all the land of Eden; for there he was set as a sign and that he should testify against all the children of men, that he should recount all the deeds of the generations until the day of condemnation." - Jubilees 4:21-25

The preceding passages from Jubilees tell us that Enoch spent many years studying with God's holy angels, and that he recorded everything that happened to him. These holy angels who were Enoch's mentors were the Watchers and Archangels who had not sinned, but who always remained faithful to Yahweh. The Book of Jubilees also teaches that Enoch testified of God's greatness to the Watchers who had sinned, and that Enoch was allowed to dwell in the Garden of Eden whenever he wished after his translation. There, Enoch was effectively isolated from the sinful world outside, and had access to the fruit of the Tree of Life. Indeed, it may be that Enoch is still eating from that same Tree of Life that has been preserved in Heaven, and he won't begin to age again until he returns to Earth during the Tribulation to serve as one of the Two Witnesses in Jerusalem.

But even before he entered the perfect peace and unspoiled perfection of the Garden of Eden, Enoch was one of the few people outside of Adam and Eve that was given the privilege of being taught personally by the holy Watchers. In addition, Enoch was taught how to record and write down all he learned. In this way, Enoch left a legacy of righteous instruction for his children. In fact, the Book of 2 Enoch tells us that Enoch wrote 366 books (2 Enoch 68:1-3). In this way, Enoch was allowed to teach mankind and preserve the righteousness that Adam failed to do after he followed Eve into sin. In upcoming sections of this book, we will discuss what the many books of Enoch may have consisted of, and where they could have disappeared to. Indeed, though only six of Enoch's books appear to have been found, as found in the Books of 1 and 2 Enoch combined, there may be an explanation for this that will be considered later in this book.

The Book of 1 Enoch gives far more information than either 2 Enoch or Jubilees about Enoch's testimony to the fallen angels. It tells us that, after Enoch foretold the destruction of the Nephilim, the fallen Watchers came to Enoch, and asked Enoch to intercede for them before God:

"The Watchers called me - Enoch the scribe - and said to me: 'Enoch, thou scribe of righteousness, **go, declare to the Watchers of the heaven who have left the high heaven,** *the*

holy eternal place, and have defiled themselves with women, and have done as the children of earth do, and have taken unto themselves wives: **'Ye have wrought great destruction on the earth: And ye shall have no peace nor forgiveness of sin:** *and inasmuch as they delight themselves in their children, The murder of their beloved ones shall they see, and over the destruction of their children shall they lament, and shall make supplication unto eternity, but mercy and peace shall ye not attain.'"* - *1 Enoch 12:4-6*

"And Enoch went and said: **'Azazel, thou shalt have no peace: a severe sentence has gone forth against thee to put thee in bonds:** *And thou shalt not have toleration nor request granted to thee, because of the unrighteousness which thou hast taught, and because of all the works of godlessness and unrighteousness and sin which thou hast shown to men.' Then I went and spoke to them all together, and they were all afraid, and fear and trembling seized them.* **And they besought me to draw up a petition for them that they might find forgiveness, and to read their petition in the presence of the Lord of heaven.** *For from thenceforward they could not speak (with Him) nor lift up their eyes to heaven for shame of their sins for which they had been condemned."* - *1 Enoch 13:1-6*

The preceding passages tells us that Enoch was a scribe, and was called the scribe of righteousness because he had an exalted place among men as a messenger to and scribe for God Almighty. Furthermore, Enoch had an exalted place among the holy angels. As a result, Enoch could converse with them as his friends, and go into God's holy presence like the angels - without fear of being destroyed.

What these passages do not tell us is the reason why God rejected the petition of the fallen angels who asked for forgiveness through Enoch (as an inferior substitute to Christ). But there is no real mystery here. It simply has to do with the fact that **the angels were not innocent when they were created**. They knew of good and evil like Yahweh, and were designed to serve both God and mankind with that greater knowledge. However, they rejected their position, and either desired to lord it over men and destroy mankind, or else to share in mankind's greater inheritance in an unlawful way.

Regardless of their initial reasons for joining Azazel in his rebellion, many of the fallen angels eventually felt shame for what they had done, and asked for forgiveness for themselves and their Nephilim offspring. However, the Giants are never recorded as personally asking for redemption anywhere in the Books of 1 Enoch, Jubilees, or Jasher. This suggests that the first races of Nephilim had no conscience - despite the apocrypha and Midrash to the contrary. How else could the Nephilim be transformed into evil spirits immediately upon death? Unlike the Nephilim, the later races of part-Nephilim giants may have been open to redemption. But the evidence of history suggests that most of them rejected the offer. The transformation of the Nephilim into evil spirits, and their rejection of salvation will be fully discussed in Chapters Four through Seven.

From the preceding excerpts in this book section alone, it should be clear that there is more history about the fallen angels and their evil influence on mankind in the Book of 1 Enoch than in any other ancient source. We are told herein that God sent Enoch, the scribe of righteousness to declare God's judgment against the fallen Watchers. The fallen angels, in turn, appeared to repent, and beseeched Enoch to ask God for their forgiveness. Nevertheless, their appeal for forgiveness was completely denied (1 Enoch 14:4-7). Enoch then issued a final warning about the coming doom of the fallen angels, as well as the impending destruction of their Nephilim children (1 Enoch 15:3-12).

Besides telling us about the behavior and judgment against the fallen Watchers and their evil Nephilim offspring, Enoch's writings describe the nature and activities of the good angels like Gabriel, Raphael, and Michael. Just as they are described in the Bible, these three benevolent messengers of Yah are depicted as extremely active in the affairs of both men and angels. Compare 1 Enoch 1:2, 6:2, 18:4, 19:1-2, 20:1-3, 22:3-5, 24:6, 27:2, 32:2,6, & 33:4 to Genesis 16:7-13; 18:1-3, 19:1-2, 32:1; Daniel 8:16, 9:21; Luke 1:19, 1:26, 2:9-14; Jude 1:9; and Revelation 12:7.

In addition to the previously referenced passages about major angelic visitations, there are countless other mentions of angels in both the Book of 1 Enoch and the Bible. However, the Book of 1 Enoch gives much more detail, and places much more emphasis on the affairs of angels and men, and the details of their affects on each other. The Book of 1 Enoch, therefore, sheds a much-needed light on angels in general, although it is especially concerned with the era of the antediluvian patriarchs and their dealings with both righteous and fallen angels, the unholy Nephilim offspring of the Watchers, and their unusual world.

Enoch's writings are heavily concerned with angels because, unlike current times, both holy and evil angelic beings were a visible, tangible, and powerful presence in Enoch's world. This is a bit how things will likely be during Yahshua's Millennial Rule on Earth, when mortal and immortal will dwell on the Earth together, and Yah's angels will be a visible presence on the Earth once more. Only this time, there will be no evil angels around to corrupt humanity until the end of the Millennial Kingdom, when the Book of Revelation tells us that Satan will be released again for a short time (Revelation 20:7-8). This will be done to deceive those who refuse to love the light and warmth of Yahweh, and who are destined to perish.

In the quote from the Book of Jubilees (Jubilees 4:21-22) earlier in this section, the writer tells us that **God's holy angels instructed Enoch for six Jubilees of fifty years each - or three hundred years!** Since Enoch only lived on Earth for 365 years, and Enoch's son Methuselah was born when Enoch was 65, Enoch spent the rest of his life being instructed by God's holy angels. Enoch would therefore have had wisdom and knowledge far beyond our own. Perhaps that is why all the prophecies recorded in 1 Enoch support and confirm the Old Testament prophetic books, especially the New Testament's Book of Revelation. This may also by why - as shown in Book Four - all of Enoch's prophecies have proven to be uncannily accurate. This prophetic accuracy suggests that Enoch was covered by the Holy Spirit's power. Not surprisingly, the Book of Jasher tells us that this was indeed the case:

> "And **the spirit of God was upon Enoch**, and he taught all his men the wisdom of God and his ways, and the sons of men served the Lord all the days of Enoch, and they came to hear his wisdom." - Jasher 3:8

Since the Holy Spirit inspired Enoch's words and - by extension - his writings, they should be considered Scriptural. In fact, Enoch's words were considered fully Scriptural at the time of Christ, and both the Apostle Peter and the brother of Yahshua called Jude referred to the teachings found in 1 Enoch:

> "For if God did not spare the angels who sinned, but cast them down to hell and delivered them into chains of darkness, to be reserved for judgment; and did not spare the ancient world, but saved Noah, one of eight people, a preacher of righteousness, bringing in the flood on the world of the ungodly..." - 2 Peter 2:4-5 (NKJ)

In the preceding Scripture, the Apostle Peter is referring to information about the fallen angels that is found in the Book of 1 Enoch. In the next Bible quote taken from the Epistle of Jude, Jude quotes directly from 1 Enoch 1:9-10, as shown here:

> "Enoch, the seventh from Adam, prophesied about these men: 'see, the Lord is coming with thousands upon thousands of his holy ones to judge everyone, and to convict

all the ungodly of all the ungodly acts they have done in the ungodly way, and of all the harsh words ungodly sinners have spoken against him.' " - Jude 1:14-15 (NIV)

Compare this to:

"And behold! He cometh with ten thousands of His holy ones To execute judgement upon all, and to destroy all the ungodly: And to convict all flesh of all the works of their ungodliness which they have ungodly committed, and of all the hard things which ungodly sinners have spoken against Him." - 1 Enoch 1:9-10

These references in Peter and Jude's letters make it clear that the apostles and early disciples of the church viewed the Book of 1 Enoch as a legitimate Scripture. For this reason and others that are presented in this book and in Book Four, the Book of 1 Enoch may deserve a place in the Old Testament equal to that of the Book of Revelation in the New Testament. In this regard, the Book of Jasher and Book of Jubilees are almost as valuable as the Book of 1 Enoch from a spiritual and historical standpoint, and - together - they can help us to understand the spiritual history in the Bible better and strengthen our walk with Yah.

A comparison of Enoch's portrayal in the Book of Jubilees, Jasher and 1 Enoch with Arab legends about him shows a remarkable correlation. In fact, these three Judeo-Christians sources fully agree with Arab legends about Enoch that tell us he was a wise and righteous man who ruled over men, invented writing, built great edifices, knew math and science, and served as God's messenger to mankind.

Unfortunately, though, these information sources about the prophet Enoch portray him in a way that correlates all too closely with the mythology surrounding the ancient Egyptian god of wisdom called Thoth, the deified ancient Egyptian architect Imhotep, and the Greco-Roman version of the god Thoth called Hermes or Mercury. This is unfortunate because the existing occult texts attributed to Thoth and Hermes are permeated with Paganistic lies and New Age half-truths that have nothing in common with the Bible and the other Judeo-Christian sources concerning Enoch discussed in this book. In contrast to occult hermetic writings and Egyptian mythological works, Judeo Christian sources depict Enoch as a fully righteous man who was as close to Yahweh as a fallen man can get short of being transformed in the coming resurrection to everlasting life.

Nonetheless, there appear to be so many similarities between Enoch and Thoth or Hermes that it can cause a discerning believer in Christ to assume that any reference to Enoch outside of the Bible should be avoided at any cost. Take, for example, the following: The ancient Egyptian god Thoth was the divine Scribe of the gods, just as Enoch was. As scribe to the gods, it was Thoth's job to keep and read heavenly records. He was also the messenger of the gods who relayed messages between gods and men. Thoth was also considered the god of wisdom who invented writing and kept records of the divine will of the gods.

In addition to these great feats, occult texts teach that Thoth/Hermes is a magician and alchemist that desires to show people how they can transcend their fleshly existence and become gods themselves by learning secret mysteries and applying them. In the process, hermetic teachings encourage people to utilize the hidden power of Astrology, magic spells, guided visualizations, and the aid of "spirit guides." However, these spirit beings are none other than demons disguised as angelic beings, and they promise to help people harness the power of demonic spiritual forces using occult knowledge and Magic. Sadly, many do not realize that they are also opening themselves up to becoming demonically possessed, and then luring others into utilizing Black Magic with promises of power, wisdom, riches, and freedom that serve only to enslave and corrupt those involved, and hurt innocent people. In addition, many people involved in the occult firmly believe that the material world is evil. As a result, they are highly interested in seeking secret knowledge in order to potentially save themselves from being forever imprisoned in a body of flesh.

Unfortunately, there are many Neo-Platonists, Satanists, Wiccans, New Agers, Neo-Pagans and supposed Christians who believe this same sort of false occult theology even today, just as they did within a decade of Christ's death, resurrection, and ascension into Heaven. The Christianized version of these heretical teachings is called Gnosticism, and - just as in ancient times - modern day Gnostics consistently deny that Yahshua came in the flesh. They also firmly deny that we are destined to exist in eternity in glorified bodies of flesh and bone, and that Yahshua had a body like this after His resurrection from the dead. Some of them even deny Yahshua's resurrection or need to die for our sins. In fact, they often completely deny that there is any absolute moral right and wrong. As such, all Gnostics are antichrists, and their teachings and beliefs should be avoided at all costs by anyone who wishes to inherit everlasting life.

Among the most damaging ancient documents associated with Judeo-Christian teaching ever found are the Nag Hammadi Gnostic texts that were unearthed in Egypt in December of 1945. This collection of ancient writings is dated to the Second Century AD, and has been spuriously labeled as Christian - despite the fact that this entire collection of codices emphasizes non-Christian ideas such as salvation by works and the attainment of secret knowledge through rational thought and manmade schools of wisdom rather than divine revelation from God. They also repeatedly deny the reality of sin and its consequences, ignore our need for atonement through the death and resurrection of Christ, and either claim that there will be no future resurrection into everlasting life in bodies of flesh and Spirit, or say that this is the fate of those condemned to Hell, because they view all flesh and every part of God's material Creation as evil. In fact, many Gnostics view Yahweh Elohim as Satan, and instead worship Satan as God!

Through occult influences, this is also what has happened to the person of Enoch. Instead of being depicted as a righteous lover of Yahweh, Enoch has been converted into a teacher of the false "Gnosis" or knowledge that originated with Satan instead of Yahweh. Even now, there is a demonic spirit that masquerades as the god Thoth, Hermes, or Mercury, and has invented this counterfeit composite figure to deceive people by claiming to be the source of all the spiritual, scientific and astronomical wisdom of the Sethite Magians Cainan and Enoch, as well as the inventor of all the occult teachings out there that are falsely attributed to them. Indeed, just as occultists see Thoth or Hermes as a great wise man, the Arabs and Jews knew of Enoch as the scribe of righteousness who wrote down every word of the Will of Yahweh that was recorded in the Heavenly Tablets. As a result, those who go seeking information about Enoch can easily get misled and deceived by the many false occult teachings concerning him.

Though there is no reason to believe that either Cainan or Enoch deified themselves, their Sethite ancestors very well could have done so when they fell into sin. However, there is another intriguing possibility for the source of these two opposing traditions about Enoch and Cainan besides human error and demonic influences. It could be that there really are two ancient opposing traditions or ideologies that originated before and after the Flood with two different individuals. In fact, the Bible hints at this in the very first chapters of Genesis, when we are told that Cain had a son that he named Enoch, and then, five generations later, the Sethite patriarch Jared named his own son Enoch.

Though some scholars have attempted to write the second, righteous Enoch in the line of Seth out of existence by claiming that there was only one line of kings before the Flood, this is a complete lie - as will be repeatedly shown in this book. Indeed, it is no accident that the line of Cain also had an "Enoch," or enlightened teacher among their ancestors. In fact, this book will conclusively show that this Cainite

Enoch is likely one of the main sources of all the occult knowledge that is falsely attributed to the righteous Sethite named Enoch. In addition, the Book of Jubilees speaks of a grandson of Shem named Cainan who was born after the Flood and may have misappropriated, misapplied or misinterpreted the spiritual truths found in Sacred Astronomy and the Gospel in the Stars that were known to the righteous Wise Men or Magi named Cainan and Enoch before the Flood.

Interestingly, the Egyptians called their hieroglyphic system of writing the "medew netjeru" or "the words of the gods." In keeping with the name they used to refer to writing, their highly symbolic system of writing has parallels to Yahweh God's unwritten symbolic Language that is found everywhere in His Creation, especially in the Star Gospel. Like God's unwritten Language, hieroglyphics use images of things rather than abstract letters to relay messages. Just as hieroglyphs use images as symbols for concepts, words and sounds, the antediluvians invented another system of communicating ideas that is hidden in Astronomy, geometry, science, and math, and in other symbolic associations with created things. It therefore relies on the divine language of allegory and a keen knowledge of higher learning to be deciphered.

This divine visual language of symbols is the real "Gnosis" or knowledge that the ancients desperately sought even while Satan has incessantly worked to corrupt it. Nonetheless, though many people gradually forgot or perverted the true meaning of this divine language after the Flood, it was still known among the righteous followers of Yahweh. This entire Language of God Book Series was written to reveal and restore this righteous knowledge and revive its use for God's Glory. In particular, this volume in the series will examine what this visual language was like, exactly how and why it was perverted, and how it can be reclaimed for Christ by understanding the Sethite view of it, and their desperate need to communicate it to us through their magnificent monuments in Egypt and elsewhere.

Enoch as a Leader of Men

Jubilees, the Book of Jasher, and 1 Enoch tell us that Enoch preached to all the rulers of the antediluvian world about the ways of Yahweh, and taught them the paths of righteousness. In addition, the Book of 1 Enoch contains carefully recorded written descriptions of many of the prophetic heavenly visions that Enoch saw. In fact, all of the above mentioned ancient sources record that, like Enosh's son Cainan before him, Enoch foretold the destruction of the world in a great flood:

"And at the ends of the earth I saw twelve portals open to all the quarters (of the heaven), from which the winds go forth and blow over the earth. Three of them are open on the face (i.e. the east) of the heavens, and three in the west, and three on the right (i.e. the south) of the heaven, and three on the left (i.e. the north)..." and *"Through four of these come winds of blessing and prosperity, and from those eight come hurtful wind... they bring destruction on all the earth and on the water upon it, and on all who dwell thereon, and on everything which is in the water and on the land."* - 1 Enoch 76:1-4*

"And all the cattle of that enclosure were gathered together until I saw how they sank and were swallowed up and perished in that water. **But that vessel floated on the water, while all the oxen and elephants and camels and asses sank to the bottom** *with all the animals, so that I could no longer see them,* **and they were not able to escape, (but) perished and sank into the depths.** *" - 1 Enoch 89:5-7*

The second reference above is from a prophetic vision that Enoch had, in which fallen angels, Nephilim, and people were depicted as different types of animals. Because this entire prophecy is full of End Time prophetic import, it is deeply analyzed in Book Four. However, it is being referred to here because it is a powerful example of the Language of God in action. In this section of that vision, Enoch describes the gruesome effects of the coming Great Flood, saying that all these allegorical animals *"perished and sank into the depths."*

In addition to receiving and recording many visions and dreams, Enoch became a "Tsadek," or teacher of righteousness after the birth of his son Methuselah. Now, according to the Book of Jubilees, Enoch married his first cousin Edna near the end of the twelfth Jubilee, or nearly 600 years after the Fall of Adam and Eve. Thereafter, just before the start of the thirteenth Jubilee, Enoch's firstborn son and heir Methuselah was born:

"And in the twelfth jubilee, in the seventh week thereof, he took to himself a wife, and her name was Edna, the daughter of Danel, the daughter of his father's brother, and in the sixth year in this week she bare him a son and he called his name Methuselah." - Jubilees 4:20

Due to his great spiritual and astronomical knowledge and wisdom, Enoch was greatly sought after as a teacher of righteousness, and was also called to serve mankind as a beloved leader of men:

> *"And Enoch rose up according to the word of the*
> *Lord, and... went to the sons of men and taught them the*
> *ways of the Lord... And he... proclaimed in all places where*
> *the sons of men dwelt, saying, 'Where is the man who wishes*
> *to know the ways of the Lord and good works? Let him come*
> *to Enoch.'* **And all the sons of men then assembled to him...**
> **and Enoch reigned over the sons of men** *according to the*
> *word of the Lord, and they came and bowed to him and they*
> *heard his word.*
>
> **And the spirit of God was upon Enoch, and he taught**
> **all his men the wisdom of God and his ways, and the sons of**
> **men served the Lord all the days of Enoch,** *and they came to*
> *hear his wisdom. And all the kings of the sons of men...*
> *together with their princes and judges, came to Enoch when*
> *they heard of his wisdom, and they bowed down to him, and*
> *they also required of Enoch to reign over them, to which he*
> *consented.*
>
> *And they assembled in all, one hundred and thirty*
> *kings and princes, and they made Enoch king over them and*
> *they were all under his power and command. And* **Enoch**
> **taught them wisdom, knowledge, and the ways of the Lord;**
> **and he made peace amongst them,** *and peace was throughout*
> *the earth during the life of Enoch." - Jasher 3:5-11*

The peacefulness of Enoch's reign on the Earth was a remarkable feat, considering the other factors working against any lasting peace. This was, after all, the Age when the fallen angels had settled among the children of Cain, and the murderous Nephilim offspring of the fallen Watchers began to raise havoc on the Earth. Despite their evil influence, Enoch managed to lead many men to live in peace and righteousness for the duration of his time on Earth, which was several hundred years longer than most men are given.

If we take the testimony of the Book of Jasher or Upright Record at its word, we can make several positive assumptions about Enoch's reign. First of all, the book indicates that Enoch made peace reign among 130 kings and princes ruling over their own kingdoms during Enoch's rule. This implies that - even at this early time in history - there were many kings and kingdoms in the world. In addition, it suggests that there already had been a time of war and unrest among the kings of the Earth prior to Enoch's reign. Since humanity appeared so enraptured by Enoch's spiritual teachings, this also implies that that many people who once appeared spiritually lost had begun to experience a deep hunger to know the true God more intimately. As a result, they clamored to hear the wisdom of this Wise Man or Magi who claimed to know Yahweh God better than anyone prior to him did - perhaps even better than Adam.

Due to the peace and wisdom of Enoch's reign, some scholars may be tempted to associate it with the supposedly thousand-year long "Zep Tepi" or the "First Time" that is mentioned in ancient Egyptian Mythology. According to the Egyptians, the First Time was associated with a time of peace, prosperity, and the giving of the gifts of civilization by the "gods." These "gods" were not gods at all, however, but should be identified as the Watchers or Anunnaki. The Watchers were sent to Earth by Yahweh in order to help mankind spiritually and technologically. However, some of these special angels rebelled against God and began to teach mankind useless and dangerous knowledge. While these evil angels began to corrupt all the men and women that they came into contact with, and to teach them ideologies and technologies that were against God's will, there is no doubt that the people who submitted to Enoch's reign also saw many benefits from the aid of the holy angels that remained loyal to Yahweh, and were Enoch's personal mentors.

When thinking about this remote period in history, it pays to keep in mind that there were both good and evil Watchers on the Earth prior to the Great Flood. As the Book of 1 Enoch communicates, the good Watchers did not leave when 200 among them decided to rebel against God and follow the wicked ways of the Archangel Azazel, who became Satan. In fact, judging by the way that they taught Enoch the Sethite the truth, the holy Watchers likely did everything in their power to thwart the plans of their evil counterparts. As part of their efforts, they taught Enoch the Sethite the truth, and - after instructing him in all their wisdom, the Watchers did as Yahweh wanted and sent Enoch to serve as a prophetic witness to mankind. For this reason, it is certain that Enoch taught humanity of the evil that lay in store for those who followed Satan and Cain into rebellion against God, and willfully perverted Sacred Astronomy and the Gospel in the Stars.

As will be shown repeatedly in this book, the Book of 1 Enoch is replete with references to the good Watchers or angels that conversed with Enoch, gave him visions, and took him on many incredible spiritual journeys through time and space in their efforts to show him the wonders of Creation, Sacred Astronomy, the beauty of the Universe, and God's Plan of Redemption.

Enoch as a Theologian and Messianic Prophet

The Ethiopian version of Enoch called the Book of 1 Enoch provides us with a wonderful record of how well the antediluvians knew the true God Yahweh - despite their lack of a Bible to study. Enoch's view of God and his prophetic knowledge of the Gospel message can be seen throughout the ancient manuscript that bears his name. Written long before the Bible, the Book of 1 Enoch probably served as the most authoritative written record of God's purpose and Will for *fifteen hundred years.* If so, it was likely relied on as a dependable source about God and His wisdom - especially after the knowledge about God and His Son locked into the Star Gospel was obliterated under an avalanche of Pagan myths and demonic fantasies.

The Book of 1 Enoch has five distinct sections that cover different topics. These five sections are:

1. **Chapters 1 thru 36, The Book of the Watchers**

2. **Chapters 37 thru 71, The Book of Parables**

3. **Chapters 72 thru 82, The Book of the Heavenly Luminaries**

4. **Chapters 83 thru 90, The Book of the Dream Visions**

5. **Chapters 91 thru 104, The Book of Blessings and Curses**

Due to these obvious divisions, it is possible that the Book of 1 Enoch was derived by grouping five shorter books that were written by Enoch together. These five books or sections have many different facets. Throughout them, for example, there are exhortations to the righteous who love God, descriptions of God's attributes, prophecies concerning the Last Days, and vivid descriptions of what will happen to the saved and the damned until God's final Judgment Day. In particular, the two middle sections or books in 1 Enoch include vivid accounts of Enoch's understanding of Astronomy in relation to the Earth and the keeping of time. In contrast, the last two sections or books in 1 Enoch deal with the prophetic visions that Enoch had, and the signs that he saw in the Heavenly Tablets that pertain to the far future. Some of the most powerful End Time prophecies found in 1 Enoch are discussed in Book 4, "The Language of God in Prophecy."

To understand Enoch's writings better, let's explore some of the terminology that Enoch used to talk about Yahweh. In the second section of 1 Enoch, called "The Book of Parables," Enoch repeatedly uses three distinct titles for God. These are the Head of Days, the Lord of Spirits, and the Son of Man. Even at first glance, it should be patently obvious to anyone that these three titles, or designations fit the Christian concept of God as a Trinity remarkably well. As such, these titles can be designated as follows:

The Head of Days, analogous to God the Father

The Lord of Spirits, analogous to God the Spirit, and

The Son of Man, analogous to God the Son

Following are four Chapters from the Book of Parables section in the Book of 1 Enoch that speak about the Head of Days, the Lord of Spirits, and the Son of Man in terms that are echoed in the Bible. To emphasize their agreement with biblical themes and ideas, Chapter 46 and 48 from 1 Enoch have been placed in a chart alongside complimentary quotes from the Bible. In these, note 1 Enoch's strong similarity in theme with biblical prophetic books, especially Daniel, Isaiah, and Revelation.

In addition, note that Verse 2 of Chapter 48 from the Book of 1 Enoch contains a prophecy about the Son of Man whom modern day believers know as Yahshua the Messiah, or Jesus the Christ. There, it says that Yahshua's earthly name was given to Him before He incarnated as a man. It also identifies the three Persons in our One Triune God Yahweh, as follows: *"And at that hour that Son of Man was named in the presence of the Lord of Spirits, and his name before the Head of Days"* (1 Enoch 48:2).

1 Enoch Chapter 46, Verses 1 thru 6

Ch. 46, 1 Enoch Verses 1 thru 6	Comparable Biblical Verses
*"And there I saw One who had a head of days, And His head was white like wool, **and with Him was another being whose countenance had the appearance of a man,** and his face was full of graciousness, like one of the holy angels."* *"And I asked the angel who went with me and showed me all the hidden things, concerning that Son of Man, who he was, and*	*"and in the midst of the seven lampstands One like the Son of Man, clothed with a garment down to the feet and girded about the chest with a golden band. His head and hair were white like wool, as white as snow, and His eyes like a flame of fire."* - Rev. 1:12-14 (NKJ) *"I was watching in the night visions, and behold,*

whence he was, (and) why he went with the Head of Days? And he answered and said unto me: "This is the son of Man who hath righteousness, with whom dwelleth righteousness, and who revealeth all the treasures of that which is hidden, because the Lord of Spirits hath chosen him, And whose lot hath the pre-eminence before the Lord of Spirits in uprightness for ever." "And this Son of Man whom thou hast seen shall raise up the kings and the mighty from their seats, [And the strong from their thrones] and shall loosen the reins of the strong, and break the teeth of the sinners." [And he shall put down the kings from their thrones and kingdoms] Because they do not extol and praise Him, nor humbly acknowledge whence the kingdom was bestowed upon them. And he shall put down the countenance of the strong, and shall fill them with shame."	One like the Son of Man, coming with the clouds of heaven! He came to the Ancient of Days, and they brought Him near before Him. Then to Him was given dominion and glory and a kingdom... His dominion is an everlasting dominion, which shall not pass away..." - Daniel 7:13-14 (NKJ) "And He... removes kings and raises up kings; he gives wisdom to the wise and knowledge to those who have understanding. He reveals deep and secret things; he knows what is in the darkness, and light dwells with Him." - Daniel 2:21-22 (NKJ) "It shall come to pass in that day that the LORD (Yahweh) will punish on high the host of exalted ones, and on the earth the kings of the earth." - Isaiah 24:21 (NKJ)

1 Enoch Chapter 48, Verses 1 thru 7

1 Enoch Ch. 48, Verses 1 thru 7	Comparable Biblical Verses
And in that place I saw the fountain of righteousness which was inexhaustible: and **around it were many fountains of wisdom: and all the thirsty drank of them,** and were filled with wisdom, and	"And He said to me, 'It is done! I am the Alpha and the Omega, the Beginning and the End. **I will give of the fountain of the water of life freely to him who thirsts.**'" -

their dwellings were with the righteous and holy and elect. **And at that hour that Son of Man was named in the presence of the Lord of Spirits, and his name before the Head of Days.**

Yea, before the sun and the signs were created, before the stars of the heaven were made, His name was named before the Lord of Spirits. He shall be a staff to the righteous whereon to stay themselves and not fall, and **he shall be the light of the Gentiles,** and the hope of those who are troubled of heart.

All who dwell on earth shall fall down and worship before him, and will praise and bless and celebrate with song the Lord of Spirits. And for this reason hath **he been chosen and hidden** before Him, before the creation of the world and for evermore.

And the wisdom of the Lord of Spirits hath revealed him to the holy and righteous; for he hath preserved the lot of the righteous, because they have hated and despised this world of unrighteousness, and have hated all its works and ways in the name of the Lord of Spirits: For **in his name they are saved,** and according to his good pleasure hath it been in regard to their life."

Revelation 21:6 (NKJ)

"For there are three that bear witness in heaven: the Father, the Word, and the Holy Spirit; and these three are one." - 1 John 5:7 (NKJ)

"Thus says God the LORD (Elohim Yahweh), who created the heavens and stretched them out... I, the LORD (Yahweh) have called You in righteousness, and... **I will keep You and give You as a covenant to the people, as a light to the Gentiles,** to open blind eyes, to bring out prisoners from the prison." - Isaiah 42:5-7 (NKJ)

"Kings shall see and arise, princes also shall worship, because of the LORD (Yahweh) who is faithful... and **He has chosen You."** - Isaiah 49:7 NKJ)

"Eye has not seen, nor ear heard... the things which God has prepared for those who love Him.' **But God has revealed them to us through His Spirit.**" - 1 Corinthians 2:9-10 (NKJ)

"Nor is there salvation in any other, for there is no other name under heaven given among men by which we must be saved." - Acts 4:12 (NKJ)

As chapters 46 and 48 show, the Messianic themes in 1 Enoch are quite strong and have an uncanny similarity to comparable passage in the Bible. This also holds true for chapters 62 and 63 of 1 Enoch. As you read through these chapters, note the similarities that they have to Chapters 46 and 48 of 1 Enoch, as well as to the Bible passages that are compared to those chapters. Also note the references to Yahshua as the Son of Man in these passages, which show that Enoch - and by extension his Sethite kin - knew this title for the Messiah long before it appeared in the accepted Old Testament writings.

1 Enoch, Chapter 62, Verses 1 thru 16:

"And thus the Lord commanded the kings and the mighty and the exalted, and those who dwell on the earth, and said: 'Open your eyes and lift up your horns if ye are able to recognize the Elect One.'

And the Lord of Spirits seated him on the throne of His glory, and the spirit of righteousness was poured out upon him, and the word of his mouth slays all the sinners, and all the unrighteous are destroyed from before his face.

And there shall stand up in that day all the kings and the mighty, and the exalted and those who hold the earth, and they shall see and recognize how he sits on the throne of his glory. And righteousness is judged before him, and no lying word is spoken before him.

Then shall pain come upon them as on a woman in travail, [And she has pain in bringing forth] When her child enters the mouth of the womb, And she has pain in bringing forth. And one portion of them shall look on the other, and they shall be terrified, and they shall be downcast of countenance, and pain shall seize them, When they see that Son of Man Sitting on the throne of his glory.

And the kings and the mighty and all who possess the earth shall bless and glorify and extol him who rules over all, who was hidden. **For from the beginning the Son of Man was hidden, And the Most High preserved him in the presence of His might, And revealed him to the elect.** *And the congregation of the elect and holy shall be sown, and all the elect shall stand before him on that day.*

And all the kings and the mighty and the exalted and those who rule the earth shall fall down before him on their faces, and worship and set their hope upon that Son of Man, and petition him and supplicate for mercy at his hands.

Nevertheless that Lord of Spirits will so press them that they shall hastily go forth from His presence, and their faces shall be filled with shame, And the darkness grow deeper on their faces. And He will deliver them to the angels for punishment, to execute vengeance on them because they have oppressed His children and His elect. And they shall be a spectacle for the righteous and for His elect: They shall rejoice over them, because **the wrath of the Lord of Spirits resteth upon them, and His sword is drunk with their blood.**

And the righteous and elect shall be saved on that day, and they shall never thenceforward see the face of the sinners and unrighteous. **And the Lord of Spirits will abide over them, and with that Son of Man shall they eat and lie down and rise up for ever and ever.** *And the righteous and elect shall have risen from the earth, and ceased to be of downcast countenance. And they shall have been clothed with garments of glory, and these shall be the garments of life from the Lord of Spirits..." - 1 Enoch 62:1-16*

1 Enoch, Chapter 63, Verses 2 thru 12:

"Blessed is the Lord of Spirits and the Lord of kings, and the Lord of the mighty and the Lord of the rich, and the Lord of glory and the Lord of wisdom. *And splendid in every secret thing is Thy power from generation to generation, and Thy glory for ever and ever:*

Deep are all Thy secrets and innumerable, and Thy righteousness is beyond reckoning. We have now learnt that **we should glorify and bless the Lord of kings and Him who is king over all kings.**

And they shall say: 'Would that we had rest to glorify and give thanks, and confess our faith before His glory! And now we long for a little rest but find it not: We follow hard upon and obtain (it) not: And light has vanished from before us, and darkness is our dwelling-place for ever and ever: **For we have not believed before Him, nor glorified the name of the Lord of Spirits, [nor glorified our Lord] But our hope was in the sceptre of our kingdom, and in our glory. And in the day of our suffering and tribulation He saves us not,** *and we find no respite for confession that our Lord is true in all His works, and in His judgements and His justice. And His judgements have no respect of persons. And we pass away*

*from before His face on account of our works, and all our sins
are reckoned up in righteousness.'*

*Now they shall say unto themselves: 'Our souls are
full of unrighteous gain, but it does not prevent us from
descending from the midst thereof into the burden of Sheol.'
And after that **their faces shall be filled with darkness and
shame before that Son of Man, and they shall be driven from
his presence,** and the sword shall abide before his face in their
midst."* - 1 Enoch 63:2-12

In all four of the chapters of 1 Enoch quoted, one thing should be
plainly evident. This is the fact that Enoch knew our triune God Yahweh
just as people who see God as a Trinity do today. In fact, he clearly
delineated between the Three Persons in the Godhead, calling them the
Head of Days, the Lord of Spirits, and the Son of Man just as we call
God the Father the Ancient of Days, Yahshua is known as the Son of
Man and the Son of God, and the Lord of the Spirits is known as the
Holy Spirit or Ruach Ha-Kodesh today.

In addition to his knowledge of the Trinity, Enoch was shown
many of the identical themes and events that are revealed in the Book of
Revelation - and Enoch saw it all 3,000 years before the Book of
Revelation was written! To prove this and to provide a convenient
reference, this book features a chart comparing complimentary verses
from the Book of 1 Enoch and the New Testament's apocalyptic Book of
Revelation beginning on this page. As you review this chart, it is helpful
to know that many fragments of 1 Enoch were found among the Dead
Sea Scrolls, including portions of Chapters 1 through 36 and Chapters 73
through 103.

Chart Comparing 1 Enoch and Revelation

Apocalyptic Passages From the Book of 1 Enoch	Corresponding Passages from the Book of Revelation
Note: Here, Enoch describes seven mountains that resemble an enormous seven-branched Menorah. This represents God's Throne in the New Jerusalem, and, just as present-day Jerusalem sits on seven hills, the New Jerusalem will allegorically sit on the Seven	Note: Revelation's Seven Churches and Seven Lampstands correspond closely with 1 Enoch's Seven Mountains: *"I was in the Spirit on the Lord's Day, and I heard behind me a loud voice, as of a trumpet,*

Churches, which correspond to Enoch's Seven Mountains:

"And I... saw seven magnificent mountains... and the stones (thereof) were... of glorious appearance and fair exterior: three towards the east, one founded on the other, and three towards the south, one upon the other... And the seventh mountain was in the midst of these, and it excelled them in height, resembling the seat of a throne..." - 1 Enoch 90:24

Note: Here, Enoch sees the righteous saints who were killed for their faith beseeching God the Father to avenge their deaths:

"And in those days shall have ascended the prayer of the righteous,
And the blood of the righteous from the earth before the Lord of Spirits. In those days the holy ones who dwell above in the heavens shall unite with one voice and supplicate and pray [and praise, and give thanks and bless the name of the Lord of Spirits on behalf of the blood of the righteous which has been shed, and that the prayer of the righteous may not be in vain before the Lord of Spirits, that judgement may be done unto them, and that they may not have to suffer for ever." - 1 Enoch 47:1-2

saying, 'I am the Alpha and the Omega, the First and the Last,' and, *'What you see, write in a book and send it to the seven churches...'*

And having turned I saw seven golden lampstands, and in the midst of the seven lampstands One like the Son of Man... He had in His right hand seven stars, out of His mouth went a sharp two-edged sword, and His countenance was like the sun shining in its strength..." - Rev. 1:1-16 (NKJ)

Note: Revelation also vividly describes the voices of the martyrs rising up to God and asking for justice to be done on their behalf:

"When He opened the fifth seal, I saw under the altar the souls of those who had been slain for the word of God and for the testimony which they held. And they cried with a loud voice, saying, 'How long, O Lord, holy and true, until You judge and avenge our blood on those who dwell on the earth?' Then a white robe was given to each of them; and it was said to them that they should rest a little while longer, until both the number of their fellow servants and their brethren, who would be killed as they were, was completed." - Rev. 6:9-11 (NKJ)

Note: Here, Enoch is shown the judgment of the wicked and their final fate in a fiery abyss (i.e. lake of fire):

"And the judgement was held first over the stars, and they were judged and found guilty, and went to the place of condemnation, and they were cast into an abyss, full of fire and flaming, and full of pillars of fire. And those seventy shepherds were judged and found guilty, and they were cast into that fiery abyss. And I saw at that time how a like abyss was opened in the midst of the earth, full of fire, and they brought those blinded sheep, and they were all judged and found guilty and cast into this fiery abyss, and they burned..." - 1 Enoch 90:25-27

"In those days I saw the Head of Days when He seated himself upon the throne of His glory,
And the books of the living were opened before Him:
And all His host which is in heaven above and His counselors stood before Him..." - 1 Enoch 90:25-27

Note: Here, Enoch is describing the throne of God in the New Jerusalem and the Tree of Life that will perpetually bloom there:

Note: Revelation's account of the judgment of the wicked and the Last Judgment is described in very similar terms to 1 Enoch:

"Then the beast was captured, and with him the false prophet who worked signs in his presence, by which he deceived those who received the mark of the beast and those who worshiped his image. These two were cast alive into the lake of fire burning with brimstone."

"The devil, who deceived them, was cast into the lake of fire and brimstone where the beast and the false prophet are. And they will be tormented day and night forever and ever. Then I saw a great white throne and Him who sat on it... And I saw the dead, small and great, standing before God, and books were opened. And another book was opened, which is the Book of Life. And the dead were judged according to their works, by the things which were written in the books."

"Then Death and Hades were cast into the lake of fire. This is the second death. And anyone not found written in the Book of Life was cast into the lake of fire." - Rev. 19:20, Rev. 20:10-12, 14-15

Note: Like 1 Enoch, Revelation also describes the New Jerusalem, God's Throne, and the Tree of Life:

"...and fragrant trees encircled the throne. And amongst them was a tree... it had a fragrance beyond all fragrance, and its leaves and blooms and wood wither not for ever: and its fruit... resembles the dates of a palm. Then I said: 'How beautiful is this tree, and fragrant, and its... blooms very delightful in appearance.' Then answered Michael (the archangel)...

'This high mountain which thou hast seen, whose summit is like the throne of God, is His throne, where... the Lord of Glory, the Eternal King, will sit, when He shall come down to visit the earth with goodness. And as for this fragrant tree no mortal is permitted to touch it till the great judgement, when He shall take vengeance on all and bring (everything) to its consummation for ever. It shall then be given to the righteous and holy. Its fruit shall be for food to the elect: it shall be transplanted to the holy place, to the temple of the Lord, the Eternal King.'" - 1 Enoch 24:2-6, 25:1-6

Then I, John, saw the holy city, New Jerusalem, coming down out of heaven from God, prepared as a bride adorned for her husband...

And I heard a loud voice from heaven saying, 'Behold, the tabernacle of God is with men, and He will dwell with them, and they shall be His people. God Himself will be with them and be their God.'" - Rev. 21:2-3

"Then one of the seven angels... talked with me, saying, 'Come, I will show you the bride, the Lamb's wife.' And he carried me away in the Spirit to a great and high mountain, and showed me the great city, the holy Jerusalem, descending out of heaven from God." - Rev. 21:9-10 (NKJ)

"And he showed me a pure river of water of life, clear as crystal, proceeding from the throne of God and of the Lamb... and on either side of the river, was the tree of life, which bore twelve fruits... The leaves of the tree were for the healing of the nations. And there shall be no more curse, but the throne of God and of the Lamb shall be in it... And they shall reign forever and ever." - Rev. 22:1-5 (NKJ)

Curiously, the section of 1 Enoch known as "The Book of Parables," which consists of chapters 37 through 71, has thus far not been found among the Dead Sea Scrolls, and this section contains the most messianic themes found in 1 Enoch. In fact, "The Book of Parables" has been found only in the Ethiopic version of 1 Enoch, which was copied in 1773 from a manuscript that could not have been older than the Renaissance era due to the deterioration of manuscripts and the need to recopy and replace them every 100 to 150 years or so. In my opinion, the absence of these chapters in the Dead Sea Scrolls seems extremely significant since there was only a very small group of scholars and scientists who have been allowed to examine, preserve and translate the scroll fragments, and initially not one of them was a Christian.

In other words, it is possible - even probable - that the existence of Qumran fragments of these chapters in 1 Enoch may have been covered up and destroyed by those who want no evidence that would support Christianity's claims about Yahshua. Of course, it takes many years of painstaking labor to piece together and translate each scroll, and - as a result - not all of the Qumran texts have apparently been translated as of 2008. As a result, fragments of the missing chapters of 1 Enoch could yet turn up in the next few years as new translations of the texts emerge - though I wouldn't count on it at this late hour! Eschatologically-speaking, we are already in the Last Day, and the seven-year Tribulation that must occur before Christ's Second Coming is imminent. This means that the Antichrist of antichrists is probably alive and well at this time, and it is likely that he already has some political, economic and military power to utilize toward achieving his destructive and diabolical aims.

Enoch: the First Magi to Fully Decipher the Heavenly Tablets

Unfortunately, many wonderful records of Yahweh's greatness were almost completely lost due to satanic corruption and destruction before and after the Flood. One of these magnificent records is found in the night sky - in the constellations of the Zodiac. There is ample evidence in the Book of 1 Enoch that the Language of God found in the Mazzaroth or Zodiac was known and understood prior to the Great Flood. Let's examine this book for clues as to the extent of this knowledge.

As mentioned earlier, 1 Enoch contains a section called "The Book of the Heavenly Luminaries." This section of Enoch's book contains a great deal of astronomical observations and facts, and discusses the way he was shown how to track both the movements of the Sun and Moon using an outdoor construction known as a henge. We will discuss various aspects of this celestial section of 1 Enoch in the remainder of this chapter.

In his writings, Enoch mentions a special record that he had access to, and that he called *"the heavenly tablets."* Furthermore, Enoch mentioned a testimony that Yahweh God had placed in Heaven. Could this heavenly testimony and the Heavenly Tablets be the same thing? As explained in Book One, it is fairly certain that Enoch called the band of symbolic stars that we call the Zodiac, as well as the thirty-six decan signs associated with them the Heavenly Tablets. In addition, the Dendera Zodiac may represent the 360 other books Enoch purportedly wrote before being taken up to Heaven. If so, this carved Zodiac would be a pictorial record of everything that Enoch saw in God's Heavenly Tablets, and would be much older than the Greco-Roman era temple it was found in that is dated to around 400 BC.

Could Enoch have carved the Dendera Zodiac prior to the Great Flood? Later, could it have been re-appropriated by the ancient Egyptians and placed in the Chapel to Osiris that was built on the roof of the Temple to Hathor at Dendera? Though it is an intriguing possibility, there really is no way of proving this for certain. But there are clues, for this carving appears to show advanced weathering and more messianic symbols for the constellations than the Egyptians used for the same star signs in the Temple to Hathor below the Chapel.

Zodiac Relief in Chapel to Osiris

Relief in Temple to Hathor

Another clue often overlooked by archeologists is the fact that the Dendera Zodiac features a more difficult raised style of relief carving than the inferior incised type of reliefs used on the walls of the New Kingdom era temple it was found above. This raised style of relief carving is associated with the Old Kingdom (i.e. Pre-Flood) dynastic period and early Middle Kingdom period of ancient Egypt. It is a very difficult technique that requires the background around images to be fully carved away. This makes the images appear to be rising up out of the stone without noticeable borders made around them to create an illusion of depth. This is very different from the inferior reliefs in the Temple to Hathor, which feature deep incisions around the otherwise shallowly carved images. This makes the images appear to have depth, but in actuality they don't rise up higher than the flat stone base they are carved into. This can be seen in the illustrations on page 81, which show both styles of relief carving.

An Illustration of the Dendera Zodiac Ceiling

Copyright 2008 By Helena Lehman

Even more compelling as a clue to its advanced age, the Dendera Zodiac depicts the night sky in a much earlier era. Instead of the sky in

400 BC or even 1500 BC, it shows the sky as it would have appeared in 4000 BC! This fact alone suggests a much earlier date for its creation. Interestingly, that was the era when Adam was created. The Dendera Zodiac may therefore depict the primeval night sky as initially viewed by Adam, the first human being.

Though Enoch is the most likely candidate to have carved the Dendera Zodiac, there are a few others who could have manufactured this Zodiac. One candidate is mentioned in the Book of Jasher, where Job is identified as an advisor to the Pharaoh of the Exodus. Another is found in Josephus' histories, where we are told that Abraham taught the Egyptians the science of Astronomy.

Center Detail of the Dendera Zodiac

The Dendera Zodiac

Copyright © 2008
By Helena Lehman

ILLUSTRATION KEY:
48 constellation figures -
12 Zodiac signs with 3 decans each

Figures numbered 1-36 represent 36 decans as 10-degree divisions of the 360-degree Solar Year

As I explored this vein of thought, it dawned on me that the patriarch Joseph also could have ordered the carving of the circular Dendera Zodiac while he served as the Vizier of all Egypt. After all, in one of his prophetic dreams, Jacob's son Joseph saw the Sun, Moon and eleven stars as his father, mother and brothers, and they were bowing down to his star. This dream strongly suggests that Joseph and his family were already familiar with their allegorical connection to the stars in the heavens (Genesis 37:6-11).

These facts briefly made me wonder: "Could Abraham be the source of the Dendera Zodiac? Or could Job or Joseph have commissioned its manufacture while they served as advisors to the Pharaoh?" Though these questions intrigued me for a while when I contemplated the feasibility of the hypothesis that the Israelites could have built the Great Pyramid under Joseph's direction, the weathering and carving style of the Dendera Zodiac strongly suggest that it had a Pre-Flood origin, which firmly rules out Abraham, Job and Joseph as its creators. Yet, no matter who carved the Dendera Zodiac, the great depth of meaning that is so expertly displayed in it, and the precise way it was carved and polished suggest that someone spent a great deal of time planning and executing it for posterity for an extremely important reason.

As shown in the illustrations on pages 82 and 83, the Dendera Zodiac is a carved circular Zodiac showing allegorical images associated with the 48 constellations of the ancient Zodiac. These are encircled by a procession of figures depicting the 36 decan signs of the Zodiac. In Book One, each one of these symbols is meticulously analyzed. Archeologists speculate that the Zodiac was depicted this way to show that the ancient Egyptians used a 10-day sacred week to keep their years, and each 10-day week was marked by one of the 36 decan signs of the Zodiac, of which there are 3 assigned to each of the twelve Zodiac signs. To keep their year in sync with the Solar Year, the Egyptians then supposedly added five days at the end of every 360-day year cycle.

In the course of my research, it became apparent to me that this traditional interpretation of the Egyptian calendar may be incorrect. In fact, it seems far more likely that the Egyptians initially measured their year in 36 ten-degree increments that followed the movement of the decan signs. In other words, as discussed in Book One, the creators of the Dendera Zodiac likely marked out each Solar Year in 360 degree circles of the Zodiac along the Ecliptic rather than by the number of days that had passed.

If they measured each year by the movements of the Zodiac in degrees rather than in the hourly increments reserved for dividing the day, they wouldn't need to add any days to the end of the year since a celestial circle of 360 degrees measures the full length of the Solar Year. However, perhaps during one of the periods of chaos between ruling dynastic periods in Egypt, the infrastructure needed to carefully observe and record the movements of the heavens was lost. If so, the Egyptians may have switched to a more primitive method of keeping time. In that regard, simply adding 5 days to a 360-day year doesn't require particularly careful astronomical calculations.

Due to the use of the term "Heavenly Tablets" to refer to the Mazzaroth or Zodiac in the Book of 1 Enoch and the Book of Jubilees, it is likely that Enoch and his Sethite descendents collectively called the forty-eight ancient constellations depicted in the Dendera Zodiac by this name. In 1 Enoch, we are told that these tablets instructed men and angels - ostensibly through the major star clusters in the night sky. In the following visionary journey, Enoch is caught up to an other-worldly place of fiery torment for sinners where he asks one of the holy angels accompanying him to explain what he is seeing:

> *"And wait ye indeed till sin has passed away, for their names shall be blotted out of the book of life and out of the holy books, and their seed shall be destroyed for ever, and their spirits shall be slain, and they shall cry and make lamentation in a place that is a chaotic wilderness, and in the fire shall they burn; for there is no earth there. And I saw there something like an invisible cloud; for by reason of its depth I could not look over, and I saw a flame of fire blazing brightly, and things like shining mountains circling and sweeping to and fro.*
>
> *And I asked one of the holy angels who was with me and said unto him: 'What is this shining thing? for it is not a heaven but only the flame of a blazing fire, and the voice of weeping and crying and lamentation and strong pain.' And he said unto me: 'This place which thou seest - here are cast the spirits of sinners and blasphemers, and of those who work wickedness, and of those who pervert everything that the Lord hath spoken through the mouth of the prophets - (even) the things that shall be. **For some of them are written and inscribed above in the heaven, in order that the angels may read them and know that which shall befall the sinners, and the spirits of the humble,** and of those who have afflicted their bodies, and been recompensed.'" - 1 Enoch 108:3-7*

As the angel and Enoch view this hellish place that appears to be separate from the Earth, the angel proceeds to tell Enoch that some of the past, present and future deeds of both good and evil people are written or recorded in the heavens by some mysterious method. Furthermore, the angel also testifies that he and his fellow angels have been instructed on how to read these records.

Now, since Yahweh is actively involved in righteous people's affairs, it follows that the Will of God is also recorded in these same heavens and that both good and fallen angels could perceive God's Will there. Unfortunately, since the fallen angels had access to these same records, they eventually attempted to alter the future and tamper with God's recorded will for humanity. Thankfully, however, the angels were not privy to all of God's secrets, but only the Holy Spirit, who knows the hearts of men and angels and can withhold vital information from them whenever necessary. Otherwise, if Satan and his minions had known how efficacious Yahshua's death and resurrection would be for humanity, Yahshua would never have been crucified! Nonetheless, as shown in Chapter Three, the nature and location of Yahshua's crucifixion and the merciful result of His sacrificial death for mankind are clearly revealed in the heavens and can be perceived by those whom the Holy Spirit has chosen to reveal them to. Here is an astronomer's glimpse of the starry heavens surrounding the Zodiac signs of Gemini and Taurus - where the record of Yahshua's crucifixion and the purpose of His death was recorded by Yahweh for all time:

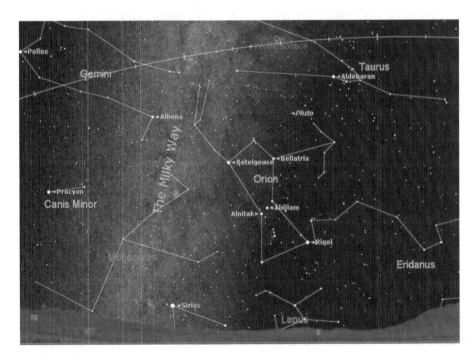

That the heavens serve as a divine record of mankind's deeds and God's Will over time makes sense spiritually. This is because the Sun signifies God's power, and the stars allegorically represent God's holy angels (1 Enoch 86:1-4) as well as the natural and spiritual offspring of Abraham (Genesis 15:5; Deut. 1:10, 10:22). The natural descendents of Abraham include the people descended from Ishmael's twelve sons, the Twelve Tribes of Israel, and the children Abraham fathered with his second wife Keturah, whom Abraham married after Sarah died. In addition, the redeemed are adopted into both Abraham's and Yahweh's Family through the rites of Blood Covenanting, Adoption, and Marriage (See Book Two for more on these important subjects). In this way, all those who love Yahshua are seen as His intimate blood relations, and can share in all of God's promises to Abraham, Israel and Joseph.

In the Book of 1 Enoch, Enoch deems it important enough to remind his audience several times that he was given the ability to read these Heavenly Tablets, and that - once he understood them - he realized that they tell a story like books:

"And he said unto me: '**Observe, Enoch, these heavenly tablets, And read what is written hereon,** And mark every individual fact.' And I observed the heavenly tablets, and read everything which was written (thereon) and understood everything, and read the book of all the deeds of mankind, and of all the children of flesh." - 1 Enoch 81:1-2

"Yea, I Enoch will declare (them) unto you, my sons: According to that which appeared to me in the heavenly vision, and **which I have known through the word of the holy angels, and have learnt from the heavenly tablets.**" - 1 Enoch 93:1-2

"I know a mystery and **have read the heavenly tablets,** and have seen the holy books..." - 1 Enoch 103:1

"And after that there shall be still more unrighteousness than that which was first consummated on the Earth; for I know the mysteries of the holy ones; for He, the Lord, has showed me and informed me, and **I have read (them) in the heavenly tablets.**" "**And I saw written on them that generation upon generation shall transgress,** till a generation of righteousness arises, and transgression is destroyed and sin passes away from the Earth..." - 1 Enoch 106:18 thru 107:1

Though we do not ordinarily think in metaphorical terms, Enoch's generation did. That is why Enoch's references to reading

Heavenly Tablets that he described as holy books seems strange to us.
We find it hard to picture a material artifact such as a written record or
book in a spiritual place such as Heaven. But, since it is written in the
heavens, this record cannot be an ordinary book, which is composed
using a specific language and alphabet. In fact, any mental picture of a
heavenly book seems nonsensical until we regard it as using allegorical
pictures to convey spiritual truth instead of words.

When the Heavenly Tablets are thought of as an allegorical
record, it makes sense to suppose that Enoch was talking about a series
of symbols that were somehow transcribed onto the vault of the physical
heavens. It also seems reasonable to assume that this record is easily
observable both to angels in their heavenly realms, and by people
residing on Earth. These assumptions make sense because Enoch clearly
indicated that these Heavenly Tablets tell a story *"of all the deeds of
mankind,"* and that they were initially created for the angels by God.
They are therefore not just technical explanations of how the heavens are
structured, or lists of universal facts. Instead, these Heavenly Tablets tell
a story about the deeds of men, and they can be read like a book.

As he read the Heavenly Tablets, Enoch tells us that: *"I saw
written on them that generation upon generation shall transgress, till a
generation of righteousness arises."* This means that Enoch saw the
entire future of mankind - from the Creation and Fall of Adam and Eve
to the New Heaven and Earth - written in the Heavenly Tablets. As
discussed in my book: "The Language of God in the Universe," it is my
contention that the forty-eight constellations of the Ancient Zodiac may
represent the Heavenly Tablets that Enoch discovered.

In the next chapter, the review of all forty-eight constellations
shows what Enoch and his Sethite kin may have understood concerning
the Gospel in the Stars. In fact, it clearly shows that the ancient Zodiac
was always meant to be an eternal record of Yahweh's unchanging Will,
mankind's disastrous choices, and the amazing forgiveness, salvation,
Grace and Spirit that Christ offers to all who love Him.

Enoch's Four Corners and Eighteen Part Day

The Book of 1 Enoch has thus far been shown to be a storehouse
of knowledge about the triune nature of God, as well as a prophetic
powerhouse announcing the coming of the Son of Man or Messiah - just
as the Gospel in the Stars found in the Heavenly Tablets does. But it is
so much more than that! In fact, because the Sethite Enoch no doubt
wrote 1 Enoch, it can serve as a proof text showing that the Sethites

were indeed the inventors of Astronomy, just as the 1st century historian Josephus recorded.

For example, 1 Enoch can help us to understand some terms used often in the Bible that relate to Astronomy, time and direction. These are *"the four winds of heaven"* or *"the four winds,"* and *"the four corners of the earth"* or *"the (four) ends of the earth."* Four is the number of Creation - it being the one thing as a whole that was created by the Three Persons of the Trinity working together, and 3 + 1 = 4. As such, the number four figures prominently in most calendrical systems used for telling time. In the Bible, the number four is used to identify God's physical creation in time and space. This is shown in these key Scriptures:

> *"He will set up a banner for the nations, and will assemble the outcasts of Israel, and gather together the dispersed of Judah* **from the four corners of the earth.**" - Isaiah 11:12 (NKJ)

> *"Then He said to me, 'Prophesy to the breath, prophesy, son of man, and say to the breath, "Thus says the Lord GOD:* **'Come from the four winds, O breath, and breathe on these slain, that they may live.'"** - Ezekiel 37:9 (NKJ)

> *"And He will send His angels with a great sound of a trumpet, and* **they will gather together His elect from the four winds,** *from one end of heaven to the other."* - Matthew 24:31(NKJ)

> *"I saw* **four angels standing at the four corners of the earth, holding the four winds of the earth,** *that the wind should not blow on the earth, on the sea, or on any tree."* - Rev. 7:1 (NKJ)

The four corners or ends of the Earth are mentioned in the Bible to indicate that the whole Earth is being referred to, and that God has control over every part of it. The four corners of the Earth are connected to the directions north, south, east and west, as well as the fixed signs of the Zodiac associated with these directions, which are Scorpio, Taurus, Leo and Aquarius. There are also four Cherubim before God's Throne that are tied to the four fixed Zodiac signs and represent all of God's heavenly Creation. These four corners are also tied to the four elements: earth (Taurus), air (Aquarius), water (Scorpio) and fire (Leo); the four seasons (circa 4000 BC): spring (Taurus), summer (Leo), autumn (Scorpio), and winter (Aquarius); the four phases of the moon (full, waxing, waning, and new), the four divisions of the day (dusk, midnight, dawn, and noon), and the four major phases of the Sun found at the two equinoxes and solstices every year.

The four corners may have had physical locations along the Earth's equator that were known and utilized as spiritual and geographical markers before the Great Flood. It is also likely that Noah and his sons utilized an already established border found with Sacred Astronomy to divide the world into four quarters after the Flood. We will discuss these ideas further in Chapter Six.

In the following passage, Enoch tells us that the four archangels assigned to these four corners or directions are Michael, Raphael, Gabriel and Phanuel:

> "**And on the four sides of the Lord of Spirits I saw four presences...** and I learnt their names: for the angel that went with me made known to me their names, and showed me all the hidden things. And **I heard the voices of those four presences as they uttered praises** before the Lord of glory..."
> "After that I asked the angel of peace who went with me, who showed me everything that is hidden: 'Who are these four presences which I have seen and whose words I have heard and written down?' And he said to me: '**This first is Michael, the merciful and long-suffering: and the second, who is set over all the diseases and all the wounds of the children of men, is Raphael: and the third, who is set over all the powers, is Gabriel: and the fourth, who is set over the repentance unto hope of those who inherit eternal life is named Phanuel** (NOTE: Phanuel encourages people to repent to gain eternal life, but does not offer salvation. Only Christ can do that). And these are the four angels of the Lord of Spirits and the four voices I heard in those days." - 1 Enoch 40:2-3, 8-11

The four angels are on the four sides of the Lord of Spirits, who corresponds in function to the Holy Spirit. The sides around the Lord of Spirits are analogous with the sides of the outer court of the Tabernacle and Temple, which housed the Ark of the Covenant. Now the earthly Tabernacle and Temple served as a literal, but temporary dwelling place of the Holy Spirit through the Ark. The four angels are therefore tied to the sides and the corners formed by the sides of that Ark, as well as the heavenly Ark in the heavenly Temple. These are most likely the four angels in Revelation that control the four corners and four winds (Rev. 7:1). The connection of the four angels with the four sides and corners of the heavenly Tabernacle or Temple can be seen in 1 Enoch 71:5, 8-9, which speaks of the Heavenly Temple as a structure built of crystals:

> *"And he translated my spirit into the heaven of heavens, and I saw there as it were a structure built of crystals, and between those crystals tongues of living fire."* *"And **Michael, and Raphael, and Gabriel, and Phanuel, and the holy angels who are above the heavens, go in and out of that house. And they came forth from that house,** and Michael and Gabriel, Raphael and Phanuel, and many holy angels without number." - 1 Enoch 71:5, 8-9*

These same four angels going in and out of that heavenly Temple may govern *"the four winds"* mentioned in the Bible. These winds are intimately connected to Astronomy, because they describe the entire expanse of heaven, which is the realm of the atmosphere, as well as Outer Space. It is also used in Scripture to describe the Spirit of God moving through specific time periods, and specific places in heaven. This is because three dimensions in the physical world - height, depth, and width - are tied to size, place, or location. But when a specific speed, direction of travel, or time period is being alluded to within creation, the fourth dimension called time must be added.

Hence, the four winds are a description of the four dimensions: height, depth, width, *and time, with time being intimately connected to velocity.* In addition, the four winds are related to the four rivers in the Garden of Eden, which in turn are tied to this idea of four dimensions. This is because rivers, like wind, continually flow through time and space, and only the infinite being called Yahweh can navigate the endless rivers of time, and steer the eternal winds governing motion in space.

Interestingly, four is often used in the Bible to show completeness or wholeness on a spiritual level as well as a physical level. There are, for example, four Hebrew letters in God's Name, which correspond to YHWH in English. There are also four cups at the Passover Seder, which may correspond to the four corners of the altar used in the Tabernacle and Temple. Interestingly, the Third Cup of the Seder is the Cup of Redemption that Yahshua connected to His saving blood that was shed for us on the Cross. There are also four corners on the ritual garment called the "tallit," or prayer shawl, which has a blue thread included in the four long strands knotted to each corner of it that represents the Messiah.

As the Messiah, Yahshua certainly wore a prayer shawl or tallit, from which the woman with the issue of blood was healed when she touched the fringes on its edge (Mat. 9:20-22). In addition, the four canonical Gospels can be seen as four symbolic pillars connected to the four corners of the world and the four corner tassels on the tallit.

During the Feast of Tabernacles, or Sukkot, four species of plants are gathered together for the ritual bundle used to decorate festival booths called "sukkahs." This bundle is made from the branches from four symbolic trees: the citron, the date palm, the myrtle, and the willow. Four poles are also needed to hold up the special wedding canopies known as "chuppahs" used at Jewish weddings, suggesting that a wedding represents the melding of the four corners of the earth and the four winds of heaven into one creation. This is, in all probability, why the Bible speaks of Yahshua marrying His Bride, the True Church. Jews also see four ways of interpreting the Torah. These are by finding the plain meaning, the allegorical meaning, the interpretive meaning, and the mystical meaning. All Bible prophecies and all of Yahshua's Parables should be interpreted in all four ways in order to not lose any of their allegorical and literal meaning.

In the section called "The Book of the Heavenly Luminaries" in chapters 72 through 76 of the Book of 1 Enoch, Enoch speaks at length about his astronomical observations made with the help of an angel named Uriel, who was a Watcher who never sinned, and therefore still had access to the Third Heaven beyond our Universe where God dwells. To see what truths 1 Enoch reveals about Enoch's Pre-Flood calendar, we must systematically examine these four chapters in which Uriel unselfishly shares much special celestial and spiritual knowledge with Enoch.

Let's start with Chapter 72 of the Book of 1 Enoch, where a mysterious 18-part day is used to mark the varying length of the ratio between day and night. Some scholars have speculated that this means Enoch's day was only 18 hours long compared to our 24-hour day, and they assume that there was some cataclysmic change since Enoch's day that caused our day to be longer than his.

However, since Enoch lived in a far different Age than our own, it makes no sense to suppose that the divisions of the day Enoch used were even remotely similar to ours! There is, rather, a far better explanation for this 18-part day that fits right in with the Sacred Astronomy Enoch knew. Since Enoch likely viewed the circle of a year as a division of twelve Zodiac signs with three decan subdivisions each, he probably also viewed the length of a day on a circle with divisions based on the numbers 12, and 36 (3 X 12 = 36). If so, each part of Enoch's 18-part day would consist of the space allotted to 2 decans on the Zodiac circle, and would form the basis for dividing up the sections of the circular Enochian Time Clock.

To imagine Enoch's clock, picture a Zodiac diagram with 12 main divisions in the topmost circle depicting 12 Solar months, and below it an inner circle of 36 divisions each measuring 10 degrees of the 360 degree Zodiac circle. Now, below the inner circle, envision a still smaller circle of 18 divisions reflecting an Enochian hour, with each space covering 20 degrees of a circle. Fascinatingly, when added up, the three parts of this clock - 12, 36, and 18 - equal 66, which is the number of books in the Protestant Bible!

The illustration on page 94 shows what this Enochian Clock may have looked like if conceptualized in a circle with the 36 decan divisions of 10 degrees each as time markers around its circumference. If envisioned this way, Enoch's clock could have had 18 "hour" markers, and 36 "half-hour" markers. In addition, each set of three decans under each Zodiac sign totals 30 degrees - with each degree closely reflecting the day of the month.

If this Enochian Clock were mechanized, the beginning of the nighttime portion of the 18-part day shown in the inner circle would be marked with a clock hand ending with a Moon symbol pointer, while a Sunburst symbol pointer would mark dawn or the beginning of the daylight hours. Meanwhile, the Zodiac and Decan divisions would turn to align with their real position at any of those 18 given times of day. Finally, a clock hand with an arrow tip would point to the part or hour of the day. By the location of the Sun and Moon symbol hands in relation to the Zodiac decans, a person viewing the clock would know exactly what month and day it was, how many daylight hours were in each day, and - per the arrow symbol clock hand - the hour of the day.

Now, in his book, Enoch said that he could read all the deeds of men and angels in the "Heavenly Tablets," which is most likely a reference to the Zodiac. Since Enoch could read *"all the deeds of mankind"* at any moment in time, the idea that the Zodiac depicts the entire scope of human history all at once makes sense. Since the Jews believed that six thousand years would pass during which mankind would be judged, and there are 36 times 10 on the Zodiacal Wheel, we can divide 6000 years by 36, which equals the repeating decimal 166.666..., and assigns approximately 166.5 years of human history to every ten degrees on the Zodiacal Wheel.

However, understanding time through a series of infinitely repeating decimals is awkward at best, and highly confusing. In addition, Enoch wrote a prophecy filled with allegorical imagery that covers the entire span of human history as occurring in 10 times 700 years, or 7000 years (1 Enoch 89:1 through 91:17). This fascinating, parable-style prophecy is fully interpreted in my book "The Language of God in Prophecy" as it pertains to the End Times. Because this prophecy spans 7000 years, Enoch was including the Millennial Rule of Christ with the six-thousand years allotted to mankind, which covers the period from the creation of Adam in 4003 BC to the end of the Sixth Great (1000-year) Day in 1999 AD.

Illustration Depicting an Enochian Solar Clock

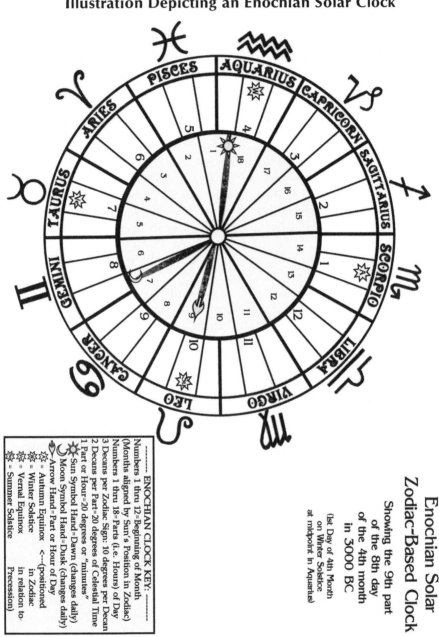

Enochian Solar Zodiac-Based Clock

Showing the 9th part of the 8th day of the 4th month in 3000 BC

(1st Day of 4th Month on Winter Solstice at midpoint in Aquarius)

------- ENOCHIAN CLOCK KEY: -------
Numbers 1 thru 12=Beginning of Month
(Months aligned by Sun's Position in Zodiac)
Numbers 1 thru 18=Parts (i.e. Hours) of Day
3 Decans per Zodiac Sign: 10 degrees per Decan
2 Decans per Part=20 degrees of Celestial Time
1 Part or Hour=20 degrees or "minutes"
☼ Sun Symbol Hand=Dawn (changes daily)
☽ Moon Symbol Hand=Dusk (changes daily)
☞ Arrow Hand=Part or Hour of Day
✵ = Autumn Equinox <--(positioned
✵ = Winter Solstice   in Zodiac
✵ = Vernal Equinox   in relation to
✵ = Summer Solstice   Precession)

The Eighteen Parts of the Enochian Year

Month Number	Portal Number	Days in Month	Length of Day	Length of Night
1	4	30	10 parts	8 parts
2	5	30	11 parts	7 parts
3	6	31	12 parts	6 parts
Summer	Solstice	in third	month	of year
4	6	30	11 parts	7 parts
5	5	30	10 parts	8 parts
6	4	31	9 parts	9 parts
Autumn	Equinox	in sixth	month	of year
7	1	30	8 parts	10 parts
8	2	30	7 parts	11 parts
9	3	31	6 parts	12 parts
Winter	Solstice	in ninth	month	of year
10	3	30	7 parts	11 parts
11	2	30	8 parts	10 parts
12	1	31	9 parts	9 parts
Spring	Equinox	in twelfth	month	of year

The table above reflects each month of the 364-day Pre-Flood year exactly as given in 1 Enoch, Chapter 72. Enoch divided one day from dusk to dusk into eighteen parts or "hours," and then indicated how many parts occurred in daylight and how many in darkness as the year progressed. **The Four Quarters or Seasons were determined by the Equinoxes and Solstices, with the Spring Equinox ending the year and marking the beginning of the first month of the New Year.** Each month was 30 days with an extra day at each Equinox and Solstice, giving the last month per Quarter 31 days. On the Enochian Clock, the Sun and Moon hands would **not** advance for 2 full days in order to "count" the 30th & 31st day. Each part or "hour" covered 2 decans of 10 degrees or 20 degrees (i.e. "minutes") on the Zodiacal Wheel.

Currently, even though we are in the millennial period when Yahshua's Kingdom should have already been established, it has been delayed so that there would be no question about God's ability to show mercy and compassion above and beyond the allotted time He gave for mankind to repent. See Book Four for a deeper explanation of why Yahshua's Millennial Rule didn't begin in 1999 or 2000 AD, and what humanity can expect when they enter the seven-year Tribulation period - or the time when mankind's works will be judged, and when the imperfection and sinfulness of their works outside of God's leadership will be fully exposed.

Zodiacal Wheel Depicting 10 Times 700 Years

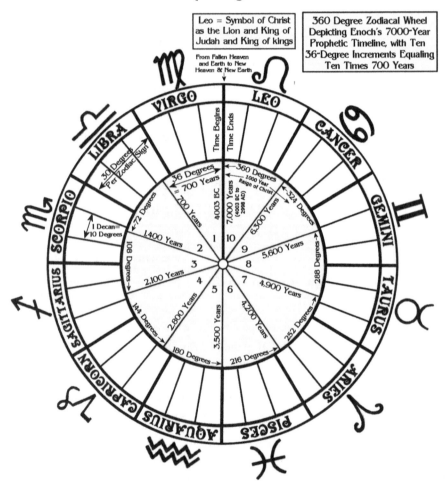

Now, since Enoch envisioned human history over ten 700-year periods, it strongly suggests that Enoch saw the Zodiacal Wheel not as 36 divisions of 10 degrees, but as 10 divisions of 36 degrees. It also suggests that archeologists have seriously bungled the interpretation of the Egyptian Calendar, which may depict the 10 Enochian Ages rather than ten 36-degree weeks. However, there is no way to evenly divide 700 years into 36 unless we start thinking outside the box.

With thinking outside the box in mind, let's do a little math. First, let's assume that Enoch divided the Zodiacal Wheel into 360-degrees, which can easily be divided into ten sections of 36. Now, since each year of those 7000 years can be measured by a 360-degree circle, let's multiply 7000 years by 360 degrees. This equals 2,520,000 degrees, which - when divided by 10 - equals 252,000. If we then divide 252,000 by 360, it equals 700 years. This means that each 36-degree piece of a circle divided into 10 equal sections can represent 36 X 7,000 degrees, or 700 years! Using this calculation, then, the Zodiacal Wheel can represent 10 Ages of 700 years - beginning this time with the Autumn Equinox sunrise in the Sign of Virgo (where the Sun was located when Adam was created) and ending it with the last sunrise of the summer quarter in Leo during Christ's Millennial rule. How fitting that the sign representing the Tribe and King of Judah would also spiritually depict the Millennial Kingdom of God on Earth! The Lion of Judah's reign over that final millennium before the New Heaven and Earth is shown in the Zodiacal Wheel on page 96.

Enoch's Knowledge of Heaven and Henges

As cited in my first book about the Gospel in the Stars, the Book of 1 Enoch explains the science involved in the construction of henges such as Stonehenge. A henge is a circular earthwork in which stone menhirs or wooden posts have been aligned to mark astronomical events on the surrounding horizon. Enoch's description of how to construct a henge is found in 1 Enoch's "Book of the Heavenly Luminaries," where Enoch identifies the source of his information as Uriel, one of seven holy archangels who will always remain faithful to Yahweh. In 1 Enoch, these seven holy angels of Yahweh are identified as those *"who watch,"* meaning that they are Watchers:

> *"And these are the names of the holy angels who watch. **Uriel**, one of the holy angels, who is over the world and over Tartarus. **Raphael**, one of the holy angels, who is over the spirits of men. **Raguel**, one of the holy angels who takes vengeance on the world of the luminaries. **Michael**, one*

of the holy angels, to wit, he that is set over the best part of
mankind and over chaos. **Saraqael,** *one of the holy angels,*
who is set over the spirits, who sin in the spirit. **Gabriel,** *one*
of the holy angels, who is over Paradise and the serpents and
the Cherubim. **Remiel,** *one of the holy angels, whom God set*
over those who rise." - 1 Enoch 20:1-8

This Scripture shows that the seven holy angels that are also
Watchers are Uriel, Raphael, Raguel, Michael, Saraqael, Gabriel, and
Remiel. Like Michael and Gabriel, the other five likely serve as
archangels as well. These seven obey Yahweh and fulfill His Will in the
heavens and on Earth. Interestingly, three of these seven angels -
Raphael, Michael, and Gabriel - also serve as three of the four angels
governing the four corners and four winds of the Earth - with Phanuel
being one of the four angels that is not listed among the seven. In
addition to governing Earth's four corners, these seven angels appear to
oversee divinely decreed events throughout the seven thousand years, or
Seven Great Days from the Fall of Adam and Eve until the New Heaven
and Earth. They may also be connected to the seven most spiritually
significant celestial bodies in our Solar System, which are Mercury,
Venus, Earth, the Moon, Mars, Jupiter, and Saturn.

Among these seven Watcher angels was Uriel, who is cited often
in Enoch's book as a personal mentor to Enoch. Over a period of time,
Uriel instructs Enoch concerning the movements of the celestial bodies in
the heavens. For example, Uriel tells Enoch about the movements of the
Sun and Moon through twelve windows along Earth's horizon - with six
on the eastern horizon, and six in the west. Enoch's instructions from
Uriel concerning these windows begin in Chapter 72 of 1 Enoch:

"The book of the courses of the luminaries of the
heaven, the relations of each, according to their classes, their
dominion and their seasons, according to their names and
places of origin, and according to their months, which Uriel,
the holy angel, who was with me, who is their guide, showed
me; and he showed me all their laws exactly as they are, and
how it is with regard to all the years of the world and unto
eternity, till the new creation is accomplished which endureth
till eternity."

"And this is the first law of the luminaries: the
luminary the Sun has its rising in the eastern portals of the
heaven, and its setting in the western portals of the heaven.
And I saw six portals in which the sun rises, and six portals in
which the sun sets and the moon rises and sets in these
portals, and the leaders of the stars and those whom they

lead: six in the east and six in the west, and all following each
other in accurately corresponding order: also many windows
to the right and left of these portals. - 1 Enoch 72:1-4

1 Enoch, Chapter 72 goes on to meticulously explain how the Sun rises in six imaginary portals on the eastern horizon, and sets in its corresponding portal on the western horizon. These portals correspond to the perceived northward and southward movements of the Sun on the horizon during the course of one 364-day Enochian year. Enoch's year began at the Fall Equinox, which closely corresponds to the first Lunar month of the Jewish Civil Year, or the seventh Lunar month of their Religious Year.

As shown in the illustration on page 101, Enoch's style of henge had six portals in the east and six in the west that marked the rising and setting Sun. In addition, there were forty-eight smaller divisions called windows in between the six portals on either side that marked the waning and waxing of the year between the Winter and Summer Solstices. Thus, the design of Enoch's solar henge with its 12 overall portals and 48 windows per side mimicked the divine design of the Zodiac, which God divided into 12 houses with 4 constellations each, or 48 constellations that mark the Sun's path.

The windows in the portals were used to accurately measure the changes in position of the Sun, Moon, and stars in the course of one year. For this purpose, there were twelve windows in the fourth or great portal on the northeast side of the post marking the Equinox sunrise, and also twelve windows in portal 4 on the northwest side of the post marking the equinox sunset (1 Enoch 72:7). There were also twelve windows in portal 3 on either side. From there, the amount of windows in the portals decreased as they approached the sunrise and sunset Solstice positions on either side of the henge, with 8 windows in portals 2 and 5 and only four windows each in portals 1 and 6 bordering the Solstice sunrise and sunset posts.

The reason for this marked decrease in the number of windows as the Sun approaches the Solstice points is that the Sun's movements along the horizon speeds up and then slows down like the movement of a giant pendulum. During the course of one year, the Sun moves a set number of degrees north or south of true east at the Winter and Summer Solstices, with the Sun's path swinging like a pendulum between Solstices. The closer the Sun is to the Equinoxes, the faster it moves. Then, as it moves away from the Equinoxes, the Sun gradually slows down, then stops momentarily at the Solstices before it retraces its swing in the opposite direction. Near to the Equator, the Sun's pendulum swing between Solstices is almost nonexistent, while the further the latitude north or south of the Equator in which one lives, the larger it becomes. As the sunrise's position moves along the eastern horizon, sunset occurs in a corresponding portal in the west. Therefore, if the Sun rises in the sixth portal marking either the late spring or early summer of the year, it sets in the corresponding sixth portal in the west.

Judging by the very short number of daylight hours that Enoch observed at the Winter Solstice, when only 6 of the eighteen parts of the Enochian day were during daylight, the henge Enoch described was most likely located between 45 and 55 degrees north or south latitude. Incidentally, the remarkable Stonehenge and Avebury henges in Wiltshire near London, England are just over 51 degrees north latitude, making earlier versions of either one of them prime candidates for the henge described in 1 Enoch.

The illustration shows that the style of henge that Enoch described is very similar to other Neolithic henges that have been found all over the world, especially in Great Britain and Northwestern Europe. In fact, henges with 12 or more posts or stones in a circle or semicircle have been found nearly everywhere that human civilizations have developed. Like Stonehenge, the earliest stages of these henges were likely built prior to the Great Flood, when both good and evil Watchers were influencing the spiritual beliefs and technological advancements of humanity all across the globe. However, though the Watchers may have built a henge or two like Stonehenge to instruct mankind, it is highly likely that many other henges were built by men, and at times only loosely styled after those the angels built. In other words, people innovatively adjusted the design and function of henges to suit their needs as time passed, making many henges according to their own purely human design.

By definition, a true henge has earthwork enclosures surrounding the entire circumference of the site. In addition many of these earthwork enclosure walls appear to have formed areas where rain water or channeled water could be pooled, thereby making the henge appear as if it were rising up out of the water. Though various hypotheses have been proposed for these water-filled earthworks, few seem to touch upon the fact that the water-filled areas around these henges may have served as reflecting pools for comfortably observing the stars on a clear dark night, just as the patriarch Joseph studied the stars and had a divining cup that he very likely used for studying the signs in the stars while he was the Vizier of Egypt (Genesis 44:2-5; Jasher 53:17-21).

Illustration of an Enochian Style Henge Layout

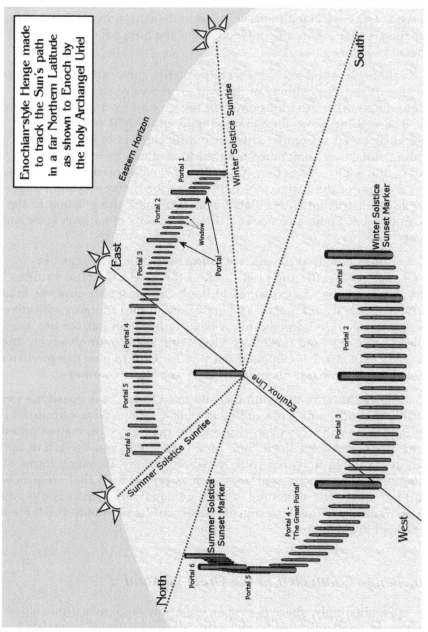

Enochian-style Henge made to track the Sun's path in a far Northern Latitude as shown to Enoch by the holy Archangel Uriel

Eastern Horizon

Winter Solstice Sunrise

South

Portal 1

Portal 2

Window

Portal

East

Portal 3

Winter Solstice Sunset Marker

Portal 1

Portal 4

Portal 2

Portal 5

Equinox Line

Portal 6

Portal 3

Summer Solstice Sunrise

West

Summer Solstice Sunset Marker

Portal 4 - "The Great Portal"

Portal 6

Portal 5

North

Though earthworks mark a true henge, stone and wooden circles that do not have an earthwork enclosure appear to have been used for astronomical observation, and have been associated with megalithic religious rituals as well. In addition to their ritual uses, all henges appear to have been constructed to serve as accurate astronomical time-keeping mechanisms that follow the movements of the Sun, Moon, various planets, and stars.

Stone or wooden circles were primarily constructed to mark the sunrise and sunset positions of the Sun. These were sighted on the surrounding horizon to plot points on the ground over a period of one year. These points were then marked with an upright wooden rod or stone pillar called a menhir. These resulting clusters of menhirs or standing stones are sometimes referred to as dolmens today. Some clusters of upright stones may have once served as markers for tombs. As in the case of the henge that Enoch described, many extant henges were also constructed with pillars or posts to mark the position of the Sun and Moon. Some also marked the movements of various stars and planets.

Could it be that the ancient cultures that built henges like Stonehenge used reflecting pools around these celestial observatories like giant divining cups? As explained in Book One, Joseph's cup was made of silver, which would make any liquid poured into it highly reflective. It was also likely wide-brimmed like a bowl rather than narrow like a chalice so that it would make a good viewing surface for observing the stars, and may also have opened the way for God to give Joseph visions to help him understand his own dreams, and those of others.

Since this sort of divining is still used today, it is possible - even probable that different types of highly polished cups were once used for divining God's will. However, this ancient method of divination relied on the actual positions of the Sun, Moon, and stars and the gift of Spirit-given discernment to work properly, whereas there are many forms of divination using reflective surfaces such as crystal balls that are purely occult in nature. These methods utilize demonic rather than godly power to work, and therefore have no connection to the Gospel in the Bible or the Gospel in the Stars.

Stonehenge Connected to the Great Pyramid

Fascinatingly, there is evidence that the large megalithic stone structure in England called Stonehenge is a sophisticated celestial observatory. In fact, it bears a few similarities to the henge where the holy Watcher Uriel taught Enoch the basics of Astronomy, which starts with a working knowledge of the movements of the Sun and Moon over any given year. For a better understanding of Astronomy, however, one also has to know how the "wandering stars" or planets move over their magnificent background of stars, and it is likely that Enoch also learned this at some point or he would not have known how to read the Gospel in the Stars, which he most certainly knew how to do if he was the designer of the Great Pyramid.

Stonehenge as it appears today:

Fascinatingly, there also appears to be a real design connection between Stonehenge in Wiltshire, England and the Great Pyramid at Giza near Cairo, Egypt. For one thing, both structures were constructed of giant megalithic stone blocks that took much energy to carve out, transport and maneuver into position. As shown in the illustrations on the next two pages, both structures feature the peculiar design angle of 51 degrees, 51 minutes, and also share marked connections to the Summer Solstice sunrise. For example, the main avenue at Stonehenge is aligned with the Summer Solstice sunrise at 51 degrees, 51 minutes south of north - just as the long causeway leading to the base of the Great Pyramid points directly at the Summer Solstice sunrise as it appears at that latitude. Incidentally, the Great Pyramid also has a side slope of 51 degrees, 51 minutes, which exactly mimics the angle formed between true north and the direction of the Sumer Solstice at Stonehenge.

Stonehenge Site Plan Angles Pointing to Great Pyramid

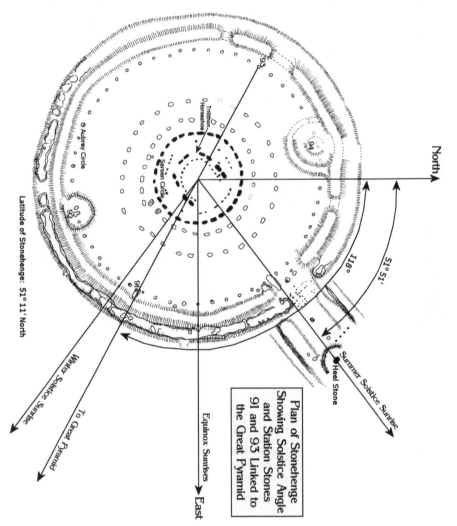

Plan of Stonehenge
Showing Solstice Angle
and Station Stones
91 and 93 Linked to
the Great Pyramid

        Though some may see the design connections between these two
structures that are separated by thousands of miles and widely disparate
cultures as coincidental, the reality of Sacred Astronomy and the
knowledge of the Language of God found in the design of both
monuments suggests otherwise. For example, if we look to the allegorical
implications of the Language of God for answers, we find that the
Summer Solstice marks the longest day of the year - when night and
darkness are at their shortest. This implies that Stonehenge and the
Great Pyramid were intended to reveal the sovereign will of the only

Being of Light who can conquer the darkness of sin and the coldness of death forever: Yahweh Elohim - in partnership with His Son Yahshua.

Stonehenge and the Great Pyramid's Design Connection

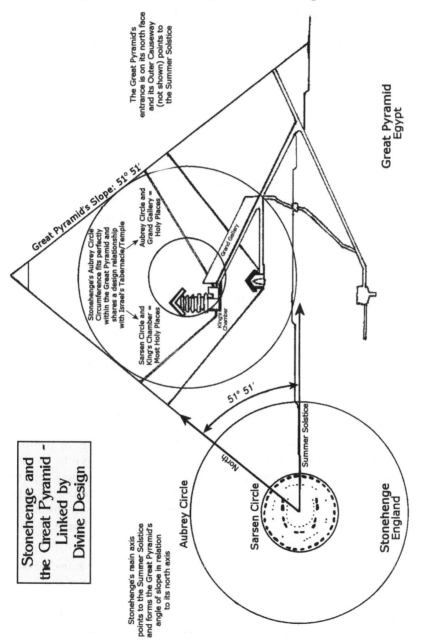

Stonehenge and the Great Pyramid - Linked by Divine Design

The Great Pyramid's entrance is on its north face and its Outer Causeway (not shown) points to the Summer Solstice

Great Pyramid
Egypt

Great Pyramid's Slope: 51° 51'

Stonehenge's Aubrey Circle Circumference fits perfectly within the Great Pyramid and shares a design relationship with Israel's Tabernacle/Temple

Aubrey Circle and Grand Gallery = Holy Places

Sarsen Circle and King's Chamber = Most Holy Places

Grand Gallery

King's Chamber

51° 51'

North

Summer Solstice

Aubrey Circle

Sarsen Circle

Stonehenge
England

Stonehenge's main axis points to the Summer Solstice and forms the Great Pyramid's angle of slope in relation to its north axis

In addition to their connection to the Summer Solstice, the Great Pyramid and Stonehenge share a common design in overall proportion (as shown in the illustration on page 105), with the outer circular border of Stonehenge fitting neatly into the triangle outlining one side of the Great Pyramid. When this is done, it can be seen that Stonehenge's inner and outer circular areas may originally have been intended to serve as two circular sanctuaries that mimic the Great Pyramid's shared design elements with the Desert Tabernacle built by Moses (as shown in Book Four). In fact, Stonehenge's inner circle of large standing stones called the Sarsen Circle bears a close relationship to the King's Chamber in the Great Pyramid and the Most Holy Place in the Desert Tabernacle, and Stonehenge's Aubrey Circle appears to be connected to the Grand Gallery in the Great Pyramid and the Holy Place in the Tabernacle.

Finally, just as Stonehenge is designed as a series of circles within circles, the Great Pyramid represents one hemisphere of the Earth. Furthermore, the Great Pyramid's inner chambers and shafts signify the relationship of the spherical Sun, Moon and stars with the circular sphere of the Earth. In particular, this common design element between Stonehenge and the Great Pyramid may explain why a line drawn between Station Stone 91 to Station Stone 93 at Stonehenge appears to point to the Great Pyramid. In fact, if an imaginary line connecting Station Stones 91 and 93 together is extended outward on a globe of the Earth, it would eventually slice directly through the Great Pyramid at Giza.

Enoch's Solar System: Geocentric or Heliocentric?

Currently, some Christians are proposing a geocentric model of the Universe that supposes the Earth is at the center of the Universe, and the planets and the Sun revolve around it. In this strict geocentric model, the Earth is seen as stationary, and not as rotating, or orbiting anything. This means that the Sun and planets would have to be orbiting around the Earth. In addition, with this geocentric view, the Earth would have to rock back and forth like an old lady in a rocking chair to explain the celestial phenomena we see in the heavens through astronomical observations. However, the only time Scripture sees the Earth as rocking is as a result of punishment! Note the following passage:

> *"And it shall be that he who flees from the noise of the*
> *fear shall fall into the pit, and he who comes up from the*
> *midst of the pit shall be caught in the snare; for the windows*
> *from on high are open, and the foundations of the earth are*
> *shaken. The earth is violently broken, the earth is split open,*

the earth is shaken exceedingly. **The earth shall reel to and fro like a drunkard, and shall totter like a hut; its transgression shall be heavy upon it, and it will fall, and not rise again.** *It shall come to pass in that day that the LORD (Yahweh) will punish on high the host of exalted ones..." "Then the moon will be disgraced and the sun ashamed; for the LORD of hosts (Yahweh Tsavout) will reign on Mount Zion..." - Isaiah 24:18-23*

Now, verse 20 says: *"The earth shall reel to and fro like a drunkard, and shall totter like a hut; its transgression shall be heavy upon it, and it will fall, and not rise again."* This is a future judgment on the Earth that says it will *"reel to and fro like a drunkard"* as a punishment for the iniquity of the wicked people living on it, but not that it does so now! Furthermore, Isaiah has this to say about this future judgment of the Earth:

"Therefore I will shake the heavens, and the earth will move out of her place, in the wrath of the LORD of hosts (Yahweh Tsavout) and in the day of His fierce anger." - Isaiah 13:13

Here, the prophet Isaiah tells us that the Earth will be moved out of its place when God's wrath is poured out on it during the Great Tribulation. This suggests that the Earth is now fixed with a particular orbit, rotation, and axial tilt, but that its orbit, rotation, and tilt will be changed during the Great Tribulation, most likely when the Earth is bombarded with the asteroid-like mountain of fire, and a comet-like star called Wormwood:

"Then the second angel sounded: And something like a great mountain burning with fire was thrown into the sea, and a third of the sea became blood. And a third of the living creatures in the sea died, and a third of the ships were destroyed. Then the third angel sounded: And a great star fell from heaven, burning like a torch, and... a third of the waters became wormwood, and many men died." - Rev. 8:8-11

It is interesting to note that the Roman Catholic Church once upheld a geocentric view of the Solar System, as did almost all the Pagan cultures of Classical times. Also interesting to note is the fact that the same Church officials that supported the geocentric view of the Universe also attempted to destroy all extant copies of the Book of 1 Enoch because the Roman Catholic Church was being singled out as evil in Enoch's Prophecy of the Ten Times Seven Hundred Years, as shown in Book Four on Prophecy.

The Roman Catholic Church likely held this dogmatic geocentric view of the Earth partly because it had a very over-inflated view of mankind's importance in God's Creation. This was because the leaders of the Catholic Church felt (and still feel) that they could set up God's Kingdom on Earth *on their own*, with their own flawed views of righteousness, and without any need for Christ to return. In effect, they deny any need for the coming Millennial Rule of Christ, and place the Sun of Righteousness, which represents Christ, in a subordinate position to humanity and the Church itself! Smacks of pride, don't you think?

Another major problem with the geocentric view of the Solar System is that it does not agree with the Language of God as revealed in Scripture. For example, the Bible ties God the Father, and the Son of God to the Sun in the heavens in the following passages, and many others that refer to light as a symbol of righteousness:

> "God be merciful to us and bless us, and cause His face to shine upon us. Selah." - Psalm 67:1 (NKJ)

> "For the LORD God (Yahweh Elohim) is a sun and shield; the LORD (Yahweh) will give grace and glory; no good thing will He withhold from those who walk uprightly." - Psalm 84:11 (NKJ)

> "But the path of the just is like the shining sun, that shines ever brighter unto the perfect day." - Prov. 4:18 (NKJ)

> "The people who walked in darkness have seen a great light; those who dwelt in the land of the shadow of death, upon them a light has shined." - Isaiah 9:2 (NKJ)

> "Indeed He says, 'It is too small a thing that You should be My Servant to raise up the tribes of Jacob, and to restore the preserved ones of Israel; I will also give You as a light to the Gentiles, that You should be My salvation to the ends of the earth.'" - Isaiah 49:6 (NKJ)

> "Arise, shine; for your light has come! And the glory of the LORD (Yahweh) is risen upon you." - Isaiah 60:1 (NKJ)

> "But to you who fear My name the Sun of Righteousness shall arise with healing in His wings; and you shall go out and grow fat like stall-fed calves." - Malachi 4:2

In Malachi, the Sun of Righteousness is a clear reference to Christ, as is Isaiah's pronouncement that Yahweh would give His Servant Yahshua as a light to the Gentiles. This and the other passages quoted make it fairly clear that God the Father and God the Son - who are greater than any earthly man or material source of light - are the true source of all spiritual light and righteousness in the Universe. Therefore, since our Sun represents this righteousness of God for us, it should not be in a subordinate position to the Earth. The allegorical Language of God, which shows God's truth in symbolism, completely contradicts the geocentric view!

Many who want to give the Earth more importance than it was ever meant to have like to cite Bible passages stating that the Earth will stand forever, such as:

> *"Generations come and generations go, but the earth remains forever." - Eccles. 1:4 (NIV)*

> *"You who laid the foundations of the earth, so that it should not be moved forever, You covered it with the deep as with a garment; the waters stood above the mountains. At Your rebuke they fled; at the voice of Your thunder they hastened away. They went up over the mountains; they went down into the valleys, to the place which You founded for them. You have set a boundary that they may not pass over, that they may not return to cover the earth." - Psalm 104:5-9 (NKJ)*

Now, note that Psalm 104 refers to the foundations of the Earth, which is not a reference to the surface of the Earth, but *its inner core*. This is shown by the fact that it states the foundations of the Earth should not be moved forever, but in the next verses speaks of the Great Flood, when the Earth was covered with water like a garment, and its surface was moved, crushed, and shaken up. This passage therefore only suggests that the basic core of the Earth may survive forever, but not its surface!

To understand these passages even better, we have to understand what is meant by the term "forever." Because of other passages in the Bible, which clearly teach that the Earth we live on will one day be completely destroyed and replaced with a New Earth, this term must mean "forever" in the sense of "for as long as God ordained the current Earth to exist." In that regard, consider the following passages, which all say that the current Earth we live on is finite, and will not last forever in the sense of eternity:

> *"Of old You laid the foundation of the earth, and the heavens are the work of Your hands. **They will perish, but You will endure; yes, they will all grow old like a garment;** like a cloak You will change them, and they will be changed." - Psalm 102:25-26 (NKJ)*

"Heaven and earth will pass away, but My words will by no means pass away." - Matthew 24:35 (NKJ)

*"But the day of the Lord will come as a thief in the night, in which the heavens will pass away with a great noise, and the elements will melt with fervent heat; **both the earth and the works that are in it will be burned up**." - 2 Peter 3:10 (NKJ)*

*"Then I saw a great white throne and Him who sat on it, from whose face **the earth and the heaven fled away. And there was found no place for them**." - Rev. 20:11 (NKJ)*

These Scriptures make it clear that believers should abandon any notion that the Earth is everlasting in its current state, or that it is the center of the Universe or the Solar System. Even though God the Father - as the source of all life and energy - is best represented by the Sun, it is the Holy Spirit - as our shield and strength - that is best represented by the Earth's atmosphere. Furthermore, the Body of Christ - as our everlasting home - is best represented by the Earth's land and ocean. Indeed, all of these celestial objects in our Solar System are finite examples of an infinite triune God. They have a beginning and an end, and they will one day be replaced by a better and more perfect Creation.

Since our future home and bodies in eternity will be brand new, we should keep our eyes focused on the divine Creator of all these things, and remember that He alone is the center of all things - including this present Creation.

The Language of God Supports a Heliocentric View

If the preceding section did not offer enough evidence, there are other biblical proofs that the heliocentric model that Astronomers use today is just as viable as the geocentric model, and - in many respects - is superior to it. As an example, let's examine the following Scripture:

"One generation passes away, and another generation comes; but the earth abides forever. The sun also rises, and the sun goes down, and hastens to the place where it arose. The wind goes toward the south, and turns around to the north; the wind whirls about continually, and comes again on its circuit. All the rivers run into the sea, yet the sea is not full; to the place from which the rivers come, there they return again." - Ecclesiastes 1:4-7

Most geocentrists point to the specific verses of the Bible just quoted as biblical proof that their geocentric theory of the Solar System is correct. They claim that this passage views the Earth as stationary, and says the Sun and planets are moving in relation to it. However, their interpretation of this passage is too limited. To explain how, let's focus on the first sentence of this passage, which says: *"One generation passes away, and another generation comes; but the earth abides forever."* Here, Solomon is telling us that generations of human beings rise and fall on the Earth in a circular fashion, just like the four seasonal changes on the Earth. As shown in Book One, each spring is reflective of new life replacing and hiding the decay of death, and therefore can be associated with infancy and childhood.

Likewise, the activity and warmth of summer is a reflection of our youth and young adulthood, while the autumn is akin to old age and feebleness. Finally, winter is connected to death and decay, and so on. Like the generations of men, the seasonal cycles on the Earth have and will continue on forever, or until their appointed replacement. In fact, just as all righteous people will experience a physical and spiritual resurrection into immortality, the Universe will pass away and then be resurrected in a perfect, pristine form when the New Heaven and New Earth are created.

As previously shown in Books One and Two, the fact that the heavens and the Earth are going to be re-created as perfect just as we will be suggests that Yahshua's death not only redeemed mankind, but the entire Earth and the Universe at large as well. This is evidenced in the fact that the Tabernacle and Temples of Israel were small-scale representations of the heavenly Tabernacle/Temple where God dwells. Since blood sacrifices for sin were carried out in these structures that represented both humanity at large and the Universe as a whole, it stands to follow that the blood shed in them was meant to redeem not only the Israelites, but also all of God's Creation and all life within that creation.

Now let's look at Ecclesiastes 1:5, which says: *"The sun also rises, and the sun goes down, and hastens to the place where it arose."* Geocentrists believe that this brief statement is irrefutable proof that the Sun is moving in space around the stationary Earth, and not vise versa. However, they are ignoring the fact that, in our observation of the Sun from Earth, it does indeed appear to move as it rises and sets. Modern Science has determined that the Sun appears to move in the sky due to the rotation of the Earth on its own axis, and that this axial rotation is responsible for the high and low pressure systems, or four winds of Enoch that rotate in opposition to one another in the Earth's Northern and Southern Hemispheres. However, Solomon may also have been suggesting that the Sun is indeed moving in a much bigger circle than we can see, since it is in one of the spiral arms of the Milky Way Galaxy, which looks like a giant, rotating pinwheel!

This is just as the wheels within wheels of Ezekiel's Cherubim suggest:

> "Now as I looked at the living creatures, behold, **a wheel was on the earth beside each living creature** with its four faces. The appearance of the wheels and their workings was like the color of beryl, and all four had the same likeness. The appearance of their workings was, as it were, **a wheel in the middle of a wheel**. When they went, they went toward any one of four directions; they did not turn aside when they went. As for their rims, they were so high they were awesome; and their rims were full of eyes, all around the four of them." - Ezekiel 1:15-18 (NKJ)

As shown in Book One and Four, the Cherubim represent the movements of the Mazzaroth, which signifies the Universe. In addition, the awesomely high wheels within wheels covered with eyes that Ezekiel saw alongside the Cherubim represent the relative motions of the various stars and galactic components of the Universe. In fact, the only stationary part of this series of wheels within wheels might be the Universal center where God's Throne may be located, though this too may revolve on its own axis! If our own galaxy is revolving, and our Solar System is revolving within it, and our planet is revolving around the Sun, this suggests that all the stars rise and set in a giant galactic cycle. In other words, **the Sun and all the stars may wax and wane in their orbit within the Milky Way, and around the even greater circle they form around the center of the Universe**.

In addition to this, Solomon was stating the obvious fact that, relative to our position on the Earth, the Sun does rise and set. In fact, all Earth-centered observations of the Cosmos are necessarily geocentric in relation to us, and this won't change unless we are observing the Universe without an Earth-based perspective - which can only happen from Outer Space. In this case, the true position of the Earth in relation the Sun, planets, and Universe at large would be apparent. Also, since Yahweh always chooses to speak to us with expressions we can understand, it makes sense for Him to refer to the Universe around us from our perspective rather than His own.

Now let's examine Ecclesiastes 1:6-7, where it says: *"the wind whirls about continually, and comes again on its circuit. All the rivers run into the sea, yet the sea is not full; to the place from which the rivers come, there they return again.* "As already stated in the last paragraph, the four winds Solomon speaks of are related to the high and low currents that are opposite to each other on either hemisphere. These four currents are connected to the four winds mentioned elsewhere in the Bible (Jeremiah 49:36; Daniel 7:1; Revelation 7:2). They are also described in Enoch's book:

> *"And I saw the corner-stone of the earth: I saw the four winds which bear [the earth and] the firmament of the heaven. And I saw how the winds stretch out the vaults of heaven, and have their station between heaven and earth: these are the pillars of the heaven. I saw the winds of heaven which turn and bring the circumference of the sun and all the stars to their setting. I saw the winds on the earth carrying the clouds: I saw the paths of the angels." - 1 Enoch 18:2-6*

When Enoch spoke of the cornerstone of the Earth in verse 2 of the preceding passage, he was likely referring to the pyramidion shape that is formed when cubing a sphere - as evidenced in the design of the Great Pyramid.

Now, just as the four winds of the Earth rotate in opposition to each other to create various wind patterns, there are also currents in the oceans and seas of the world that flow in opposition to one another in circular or figure eight patterns around the continents. In fact, these same ocean and sea currents also flow underneath the Earth's crust, just as they ebb and flow as ground water on the surface.

When everything is viewed as a series of circles within circles, there is no real contradiction between Enoch and Solomon's supposed geocentric view of the world, and the heliocentric model we use today. Of course, we must always keep in mind that no scientific principle is carved in stone. They are in a state of flux, and are often based on assumptions that are subject to change. Though the heliocentric model best explains the current set of observable facts Astronomers and Astronauts can see, a better theory that may be neither heliocentric nor geocentric may dominate our future view of the Universe in the Millennial Kingdom. At that time, just as Solomon shared his human wisdom in Ecclesiastes, Yahshua will be able to directly share His incredible divine wisdom with all who thirst for righteousness as well as knowledge. Then, and only then, will we who desire to know finally know the truth of the matter.

Chapter 3: Sethite Astronomy - Heaven and Earth Entwined

> *"Now this Seth, when he was brought up, and came to those years in which he could discern what was good, became a virtuous man; and as he was himself of an excellent character, so did he leave children behind him who imitated his virtues. All these proved to be of good dispositions. They also inhabited the same country without dissensions, and in a happy condition, without any misfortunes falling upon them, till they died. **They also were the inventors of that peculiar sort of wisdom which is concerned with the heavenly bodies, and their order.**" – Josephus, The Antiquities of the Jews, 1.2.3, Verses 68-69*

This reference from outside of the Bible sheds light on the subject of what the Heavenly Tablets were. In his "Antiquities of the Jews," Josephus makes it clear that he believed that the descendants of Seth invented the science of astronomy prior to the Flood. Interestingly, the prophet Enoch was the patriarch of the seventh generation from Seth. As already shown, the Book of 1 Enoch shows advanced astronomical knowledge. It is therefore likely that Enoch was among those who helped develop the science of astronomy. Could he also have been the first to record the meanings of the constellations in the signs of the Zodiac? Ancient Arab legends suggest that this was the case, as does the Book of Jubilees, Jasher, and 1 Enoch.

Though none of these ancient records contain Enoch's written account of the symbols used in the pictorial Zodiac that formed the Heavenly Tablets, they tell us Enoch was a hermit who spent more time in the presence of angels than with men. Furthermore, we are told, these angels fully instructed Enoch about the meaning and purpose of the Heavenly Tablets (1 Enoch 33:2-4, 93:1-2; Jubilees 4:21-22; Jasher 3:2). In addition, Enoch may have borrowed some of this knowledge from his ancestors Seth and Cainan, and then developed it much further using what the angels had taught him about the divine, allegorical Language of God. The Book of 1 Enoch records that he passed down his books to his son Methuselah for safekeeping and dissemination:

> *"And now, my son Methuselah, all these things I am recounting to thee and writing down for thee! and I have revealed to thee everything, and given thee books concerning all these: so preserve, my son Methuselah, the books from thy fathers hand, and (see) that thou deliver them to the*

generations of the world. I have given Wisdom to thee and to thy children, And thy children that shall be to thee, That they may give it to their children for generations, this wisdom (namely) that passeth their thought. **And those who understand it shall not sleep,** *but shall listen with the ear that they may learn this wisdom, and it shall please those that eat thereof better than good food." - 1 Enoch 82:1-3*

In the above passage, Enoch says that during a time when people would be able to fully understand his wisdom, they would not sleep. This suggests two things. First of all, it could imply that anyone who understands Enoch's wisdom will receive everlasting life. Secondly, this passage in 1 Enoch seems related to the following Scripture from the Bible:

"Behold, I tell you a mystery: We shall not all sleep, but we shall all be changed -- in a moment, in the twinkling of an eye, at the last trumpet." - 1 Corinth. 15:51-52(NKJ)

By saying: *"those who understand it shall not sleep,"* Enoch therefore may be implying that some among the last generation will finally understand his books, and will be among those taken up to Heaven in the event known as the Rapture. The Language of God Book Series is likely one part of the fulfillment of that prophecy, as it goes further than any previous study in proving that 1 Enoch should be included in our modern Bibles as an aid in understanding God's Plan of Salvation, the Book of Revelation, and all the other books of the Bible dealing with End Time prophecies.

Interestingly, the Book of the Secrets of Enoch records that Enoch wrote 366 books. Here are two excerpts from 2 Enoch about this, with the second quote containing the account of Enoch's translation into Heaven:

"And Pravuil told me: All the things that I have told you, we have written. Sit and write all the souls of mankind, however many of them are born, and the places prepared for them to eternity; for all souls are prepared to eternity, before the formation of the world. And all double thirty days and thirty nights, and **I wrote out all things exactly, and wrote three hundred and sixty-six books.***" - 2 Enoch 23:2-3*

"Enoch was born on the sixth day of the month Tsivan, and lived three hundred and sixty-five years. *He was taken up to heaven on the first day of the month Tsivan and remained in heaven sixty days. He wrote all these signs of all* *creation, which the Lord created, and wrote three hundred and sixty-six books, and handed them over to his sons and remained on earth thirty days,* **and (Enoch) was again taken up to heaven on the sixth day of the month Tsivan, on the very day and hour when he was born.** *As every man's nature in this life is dark, so are also his conception, birth, and departure from this life. At what hour he was conceived, at that hour he was born, and at that hour too he died.* **Methosalam (i.e. Methuselah) and his brethren, all the sons of Enoch, made haste, and erected an altar at that place called Achuzan, whence and where Enoch had been taken up to heaven."**

"And they took sacrificial oxen and summoned all people and sacrificed the sacrifice before the Lord's face. All people, the elders of the people and the whole assembly came to the feast and brought gifts to the sons of Enoch. And they made a great feast, rejoicing and making merry three days, praising God, who had given them such a sign through Enoch, who had found favour with him, and that they should hand it on to their sons from generation to generation, from age to age." - 2 Enoch 68:1-9

Fascinatingly, the first two highlighted passages in the second excerpt from the Book of the Secrets of Enoch tells us that Enoch was born and translated on the sixth day of the month Tsivan, or Sivan, which is the third lunar month of the Jewish religious year. Sivan usually coincides with the modern month of June, in which the Feast of Weeks or Pentecost is most often held. After they had finished building the altar to God where Enoch was taken up, Enoch's family made sacrifices and had a celebration there, which they promised to perpetually observe. This suggests that Pentecost was considered a Holy Day among the Sethites long before the advent of the Israelites and the giving of the Law on Mount Sinai. Incidentally, tradition maintains that both Enoch and Elijah were translated or taken up to Heaven on Pentecost.

This section of 2 Enoch also reveals that Enoch's family made their sacrifices *"before the Lord's face."* As explained in Book Two, the phrase *"before the LORD"* in Leviticus 1:11 is mistranslated in the Bible and should say *"against Yahweh",* or *"in opposition to Yahweh."* This is because the Levite priests sacrificed animals on the north side of the altar, in the shadows where the light of the Sun, which allegorically represents God the Father, did not reach.

This is also where the satanic signs of the Zodiac prevail around the North Star: Polaris. There, we find the Christ figure Hercules crushing the head of Draco the Dragon, which is a symbol for Satan. Meanwhile, near to Hercules and Draco in the sky, Serpens the satanic Serpent is being wrestled into submission by Ophiuchus - another Messiah figure representing Christ as a sin offering. Just below Ophiuchus is another Satan figure called Scorpio the Scorpion, whose head is being crushed by Ophiuchus' foot in mimicry of the very first messianic prophecy in Genesis 3:15.

Now, as shown in Books One and Two, Orion and Taurus are in the far south, on the opposite side of the Zodiac to Scorpio, which is figuratively as far away from the sin being displayed in the northern sky as is feasible in four dimensions. In Book Two, it was also shown how the signs of Taurus and Aries form an immense allegorical altar in the heavens, and this is why there was one horn on each corner of the great horned altar in front of the Temple to Yahweh in Israel. These represented the two horns of the bulls sacrificed daily for atonement, and the two horns of the goats or rams sacrificed daily in thanks. On the southern side of the altar, it is interesting to note that there was a ramp leading up to two piles of wood where the daily sacrifices were burned, with a special fire in the southeast corner of the altar that consumed the morning sacrifices, while the southwest fire consumed the evening sacrifices.

Now, the third highlighted passage from 2 Enoch reveals that Enoch's son Methuselah (i.e. Methosalam), and all his Sethite kin built an altar in the exact spot where Enoch had been taken up to Heaven, and this place was called Achuzan. Some scholars think "Achuzan" refers to the Temple Mount in Jerusalem. However, Andrei Orlov, a Theology Professor at Marquette University in Wisconsin, has identified Achuzan as "the center of the world."

Now, the term "center of the world" is related to the ancient concepts of *"the center of the earth,"* and *"the Navel of the World."* Though modern mystics think Cuzco in Peru, Easter Island, or the Temple Mount in Jerusalem could be the illusive "center of the world," there is no greater physical candidate for this honor than the Giza plateau. As will be fully explained in subsequent sections, the unique geographical location of the Great Pyramid may mark the Giza Plateau as the true Navel of the World, or Center of the Earth. Consequently, could the altar that the Sethites built in the place called Achuzan, or the center of the world in 2 Enoch 68:6 be referring to the Great Pyramid or the Giza Pyramid Complex as a whole? We will explore this very real possibility throughout this chapter.

Interestingly, this Navel of the World may correspond to one of four places on the Earth where Yahweh physically manifested Himself to the children of Adam and Eve. This is revealed in the Book of Jubilees, where we are told that Enoch burned incense to Yahweh on Mount Sinai, which was one of God's four special places on the Earth:

> *"And he (Enoch) burnt the incense of the sanctuary, (even) sweet spices acceptable before the Lord (Yahweh) on the Mount. For the Lord (Yahweh) has four places on the earth, the Garden of Eden, and the Mount of the East, and this mountain on which you are this day, Mount Sinai, and Mount Zion (which) will be sanctified in the new creation for a sanctification of the earth; through it will the earth be sanctified from all (its) guilt and its uncleanness throughout the generations of the world."* - Jubilees 4:25-27

These four places may correspond to four physical locations on the Earth today. The most current scholarship has located Mount Sinai not on the Sinai Peninsula, but with a more appropriately fire-blackened mountain called Jabal Al-Lawz in northwest Saudi Arabia. In addition, the Garden of Eden may have been near modern Eritrea or Kuwait, and the Mount of the East was either the Temple Mount in Jerusalem or the Mount of the Transfiguration. This would leave Mount Zion as a possible reference to the Great Pyramid on the Giza Plateau. Though Old Testament references to Zion seem to pertain more to a spiritual realm than an earthly one, the Book of Jubilees identifies Zion with a physical place - albeit a very spiritual one. In addition, the Giza Complex does directly connect to a heavenly place in the constellation of Orion! Therefore, is it possible that Mount Zion on Earth is the Great Pyramid, while Mount Zion in Heaven is the star called Al Nitak?

Not surprisingly - as shown in Books One and Two - the constellation of Orion is a symbol for Christ as both the Suffering Servant and conquering King of kings that the Bible also prophesies about. Since the Gospel in the Stars is God's Gospel to the angels and mankind, could it be that Enoch designed the man-made mountain at Giza called the Great Pyramid using a divinely given blue print? Furthermore, could it reflect the vast foreknowledge that Enoch had about Yahshua, the Coming Messiah repeatedly prophesied about in the heavens before the Bible was written? We will explore this possibility a bit later.

Besides mentioning that four holy places are special to God, the Book of Jubilees further identifies Mount Zion as *"the center of the Navel of the Earth"* (Jubilees 8:14). Though Zion is often considered to be a reference to the Temple Mount, it is possible that Zion is referring to the

Great Pyramid or Pillar of Enoch. Fascinatingly, if the Giza site where the Great Pyramid was built is used as the center of an equal projection map, then Giza falls at the midpoint between the Eastern and Western Hemispheres of the Earth. In addition, a line drawn through the 30th North Parallel where the Great Pyramid is located cuts through less water and more land mass than at any other point on the globe, making Giza the geographical "Navel of the World."

Incidentally, when a line is drawn between three of the sites I have identified among the four special places to God on the same equal projection map, these three high places form a triangle surrounding some of the land area that will be allotted to Israel during Christ's Millennial Kingdom, which includes southern Israel and all of the Sinai Peninsula.

The Book of 1 Enoch explains that Enoch received the knowledge that he put into his books when the fallen angels married and mated with women. It also briefly states what subject matter these books contained:

"And it shall come to pass in those days that elect and holy children will descend from the high heaven, and their seed will become one with the children of men. And in those days Enoch received books of zeal and wrath, and books of disquiet and expulsion." - 1 Enoch 39:1-2

Since these books were "received," it implies that they were divinely inspired, which is highly likely considering the evidence proving it in this book and Book Four. Now, there are five sections to the Ethiopian Enoch, though some scholars assert that it contains only four distinct Enochian books that have been spliced together. In addition, the Book of the Secrets of Enoch can be counted as another book or two. Now, let's suppose that the Ethiopian and Slavonic manuscripts attributed to Enoch account for six of the 366 books that Enoch wrote. If they do, this would mean that 360 books are supposedly missing. But, **what if these 360 books were not written with sentences filled with words, but in images representing strings of stars as strings of words?** If so, then the stars and images governing each degree on the 360-degree Zodiacal wheel could have formed a hidden book.

Could Enoch have memorialized these images in some tangible form other than as words on a scroll? It is my supposition that Enoch did so twice. He did so the first time when he carved what is known as the Dendera Ceiling Zodiac, which was thoroughly explored in Book One. This Zodiac depiction is circular to evoke the idea that its displays a full circle of 360 degrees of historical time. If each degree is envisioned as a book written in starry symbols, then Enoch wrote 360 books when he carved this Zodiac on a giant stone tablet that was made to last throughout the ages.

The second time Enoch may have left a symbolic 360-book record was when he designed the Great Pyramid, which has a base perimeter of 365.242 Sacred Cubits of 25 Pyramid Inches each (1 Pyramid Inch = 1.001 British Inches). This number is close to 366, and measures the Sun's complete circuit through the Zodiac, and hence through 360 degrees or one full circle of space and time. It also indicates the length of Enoch's 365-year terrestrial life from beginning to end, suggesting that the Great Pyramid represents the beginning and end of the Zodiac, the beginning and end of Enoch's terrestrial life, and the beginning and end of time.

There are many intertwined meanings associated with the 48 constellations in the ancient Mazzaroth, and - along with the brief description of each sign and decan found later in this chapter, there is a chart from Book One showing the meanings of the Twelve Signs of the Zodiac in the Appendix. In Book One, the fact that there are 4 X 12 constellations in the Mazzaroth was briefly touched upon. As mentioned there, each of these four groups of twelve signs can represent a group of twelve key people or people groups in God's Plan of Salvation and their righteous ancestors. The first twelve may signify the first twelve patriarchs from Adam to Arphaxad, the second twelve represent the Twelve Tribes of Israel, the third twelve may depict the Twelve Apostles, and the fourth twelve are likely connected to the 12 X 12,000, or 144,000 Witnesses of the Tribulation.

These four groups of twelve can also be seen as a depiction of four Dispensational Ages covering a 7000-year period consisting of the Age of the Blood Covenant and Star Gospel (4003 BC to 2003 BC), the Age of the Law and the Prophets (2003 BC to 3 BC), the Age of the New Covenant of Grace (3 BC to 1998 AD), and the 1,000-year Millennial Kingdom Age, which was slated to begin on Rosh Hashanah in 1999 AD on the Gregorian Calendar, but has been purposely delayed to allow mankind more time to repent before God's Wrath is poured out during the Great Tribulation. As explained in Books One and Four, the Millennial Age will be ushered in immediately after the Great Tribulation. This means that the 144,000 Witnesses are likely alive on the Earth today.

Josephus ascribes the descendents of Seth with the invention of Sacred Astronomy, and Enoch's books record that Enoch was the first man to know what a henge is, and to know how to decipher the Heavenly Tablets or Gospel in the Stars. This meant that Enoch was called to be a teacher and prophet and to guide his fellow human beings into greater degrees of righteousness. It is therefore likely that, in addition to being the greatest prophet of that past Age, Enoch was the greatest astronomer and prophet at any time before the Flood. In fact, judging from the incredible celestial-related spiritual wisdom locked inside the Book of 1 Enoch, it is likely that Enoch was the greatest astronomer and prophet ever born outside of Christ, who created the Mazzaroth, and whose miraculous birth was announced in the stars that He alone named!

The Spiritual Legacy of Enosh, Enoch, and Cainan

Before the New Covenant, Scripture makes it fairly clear that Yahweh Elohim revealed Himself in visions and dreams to all those who sincerely honored and worshipped Him as the Creator. He also chose to reveal Himself via prophets, of which there were two *before* the Great Flood. As already mentioned, Cainan and Enoch the Sethite were the two most highly regarded prophets of Yahweh prior to the Flood. The Bible indicates that men began to call upon the name of Yahweh in the antediluvian patriarch Seth's lifetime - after the birth of his son Enosh:

> *"Seth also had a son, and he named him Enosh. **At that time men began to call on the name of the LORD (Yahweh).**" - Genesis 4:25-26 (NIV)*

The highlighted statement in the Scripture above makes it clear that people - from the dawn of history onward - knew that the name "Yahweh" or "Yah" was the sacred Name of God. From this we can deduce that these prehistoric men knew of the Creator, His sacred Language, and His plan of redemption. Just how much Bible characters such as Cain, Abel, and Enosh knew about these things was already explored in Books One and Two, where the Gospel in the Stars and God's allegorical messages to us hidden in Blood Covenants, the Noahide and Mosaic Laws, and Tabernacle and Temple design and ritual were explored as vehicles of spiritual knowledge.

Due to the statement in Genesis that Enosh's peers called on the name of Yahweh, it is likely that Enosh or his son Cainan was one of the first prophets of God. In the Book of Jasher, the first great prophet and wise man identified is Cainan, the son of Enosh. According to Biblical Chronology, Cainan was born around 3600 BC. Cainan is said to have written his wisdom on tablets of stone and *"hid them among his treasures."* This treasure trove may have been an ancient mastabah-type tomb or monument. A great profusion of these mastabahs were built in ancient Egypt and many have survived to modern times, though the majority of them were found empty of the material and spiritual treasures they once likely contained.

Before Enosh died, Cainan may have built monuments for his father and himself that were not necessarily tombs, but vaults to store other treasures such as the divine knowledge given to Enosh and Cainan by Yahweh. These monuments could be the Red and Bent Pyramids found at Dahshur. Based on circumstantial evidence alone, these two pyramids are attributed to one Pharaoh named Sneferu. However, unlike most ancient Egyptian tombs, they were found empty and undecorated - just like the Great Pyramid and its two sister pyramids at Giza.

Uncannily, if the Nile is viewed as the Milky Way, the two Old Kingdom pyramids at Dahshur mimic the position of two prominent stars in the Zodiac sign of Taurus, and only at one specific time period in the far past. This was in 2500 BC - at the exact time that the three Old Kingdom pyramids at Giza mimicked the position of the belt stars of Orion, which is a decan constellation of Taurus. As was shown in Book One, the sign of Taurus the Bull represents Yahshua coming again in wrath to judge the wicked. However, Taurus also represents the righteous line of Seth, as well as Seth's descendents through Abraham and Israel's son Joseph. In complimentary fashion, Taurus' decan constellation Orion represents Yahshua as both the crucified and resurrected Messiah and the conquering King of kings. More about these startling correlations and their possible meanings will be disclosed as we probe deeper into this study of God's allegorical language.

Here is what the Book of Jasher says regarding Cainan and his father Enosh:

> *"And Enosh lived ninety years and he begat Cainan; And Cainan grew up and he was forty years old, and he became wise and had knowledge and skill in all wisdom, and he reigned over all the sons of men, and he led the sons of men to wisdom and knowledge; for* **Cainan was a very wise man and had understanding in all wisdom, and with his wisdom he ruled over spirits and demons;**

> *And Cainan knew by his wisdom that God would destroy the sons of men for having sinned upon earth, and that the Lord would in the latter days bring upon them the waters of the flood.* **And in those days Cainan wrote upon tablets of stone, what was to take place in time to come, and he put them in his treasures.** *And Cainan reigned over the whole earth,* **and he turned some of the sons of men to the service of God.** *- Jasher 2:10-14*

By saying that Cainan ruled over spirits and demons, the Book of Jasher is telling us that Cainan became the world's first healer and exorcist! Despite his righteous abilities, however, we are told that Cainan only turned some men to God's service, implying that Cainan lived during a time of great spiritual apostasy. Jasher 2:2-9, which was quoted earlier, tells us that the sons of men first began to worship false gods at this time. This is why Moses recorded that Enosh called upon Yahweh by name (Genesis 4:26). He was not sinning by calling upon Yah as some Jews erroneously teach, but upholding the righteous faith of his father Seth and exercising authority over demons in the Name of Yahweh! The name Enosh means "mortal" and implies weakness. Therefore, it suggests that - since Enosh was acutely aware of his mortality and frailness - he called upon the Name of Yahweh for protection and help in that early time of great apostasy.

Though Cainan managed to convince some people to serve Yahweh, he knew that future generations would not remember what he had taught them. He had the foresight to see the affects of sin on mankind's perception of their origins, and felt compelled to record the truth for future generations. This is likely why Cainan inscribed symbolic truths *"on tablets of stone."* Though the text is translated to suggest that Cainan placed these tablets in a hidden treasure trove somewhere, is it possible that these stone tablets *actually formed the place* where Cainan stored his treasures?

Egypt's Old Kingdom Pyramids: Tombs or Storybooks?

Can these inscribed stones actually be found in the interior and exterior construction and dimensions of the two biggest pyramids at Dahshur called the Red and the Bent Pyramids? Could the vehicle of expression that Cainan used to record his knowledge have been Sacred Geometry, which incorporates the precise geometric formulas that underlie the structure of all created and living things? Could Cainan also have applied his knowledge of Sacred Astronomy to these pyramids, making them precise markers showing the passage of time, as well as the godly path Cainan followed?

Uncannily, this may indeed be the case. For example, the interior spaces of the two large stone pyramids at Dahshur have similarities to those in the Great Pyramid. They are precisely engineered of solid stone blocks, and are both totally devoid of ancient interior surface carvings or inscriptions. In addition, both the Bent and Red Pyramid each have three corbelled chambers that share definite structural similarities to the Grand Gallery in the Great Pyramid. Therefore, just as the Grand Gallery contains hidden allegorical knowledge, these unusual corbelled chambers in the pyramids at Dahshur may also.

As shown in Book Four, the Grand Gallery has 36 stone ceiling slabs that allegorically suggest the 36 decans of the Zodiac, or the full circle of human history, and seven massive corbels that appear to reflect the passage of seven thousand years of human history, which includes the Millennial Rule of Christ, and is followed by the Last Judgment and creation of the New Heaven and Earth. It also contains 28 sets of niches at the base of the bottom corbel, which correspond to the 28 Mansions of the Moon. In addition, they may mark the 28-degree arc on the horizon (14 degrees each north and south of east) at Giza that reflect the ever-changing position of sunrise between solstices and equinoxes.

This sort of allegorical language is also evident in the corbelled chambers in the Red and Bent Pyramids at Dahshur. In the Bent Pyramid, for example, a small 4-corbelled chamber leads into a higher chamber with 12 corbels reaching upward to a ceiling height of 41.5 feet (12.6 meters). Next, there is a higher chamber with 14 corbels in its ceiling that reaches to a height of 54 feet (16.5 meters). Since these corbels are part of a ceiling, and the ceilings in all of the Great Pyramid's chambers reflect celestial knowledge, it would seem logical to conclude that the numbers of corbels in the Bent Pyramid's chambers correspond to the passage of millenniums - just like they do in the Grand Gallery. If so, the twelve-corbelled chamber suggests the 12,000 years that will elapse from God's first act of Creation to the beginning of Christ's Millennial Rule, which is the thirteenth and final Great Day of this current Creation. In direct relation to this, the 14-corbelled chamber would therefore logically suggest the end of Christ's Millennial Rule, which will mark the formation of the New Heaven and New Earth in eternity.

Taking this information into consideration, I was struck with the revelation that the Bent Pyramid may not be bent due to the poor architectural skills of its builders, as archeologists have long supposed. Instead, it may be bent to allegorically reflect the fact that its larger and steeper foundation represents God's perfect creations over a 6,000 year period, while the 6,000 years of mankind's imperfect works are signified by the lower and smaller top half of the structure. Indeed, this makes far more sense when viewing this pyramid with the Language of God in mind than the traditional explanation, and there is now no doubt in my mind that this amazing structure is indeed a religious monument dedicated to mirroring God's Will in Heaven on the Earth.

Not surprisingly, the Red Pyramid's corbels also seem to mark the beginning and end of Christ's Millennial Rule, though they exclude the Six Great Days of Creation that are represented in the Bent Pyramid. For example, there are two ground level chambers in this pyramid that both have seven corbels each. Uncannily, these corbels correspond to the 7,000 years of human history that will elapse from the creation of Adam and Eve until the creation of the New Heaven and Earth. These chambers lead to another chamber that is set much higher inside the pyramid. This chamber has another magnificent corbelled ceiling that reaches 50 feet (15.24 meters) up into the pyramid's solid stone masonry, and has eight corbels. These eight corbels appear to target the end of Christ's Millennial Rule after 7,000 years have past, for this is when the New and perfect Heaven and Earth will be created to last for eternity! This makes the allegorical message of the eighth corbel quite fitting, since - when turned on its side - the number 8 represents eternity.

Interestingly, the Bent Pyramid allegorically corresponds to the star marking Taurus' left horn at the top of the "V" shaped Hyades star cluster in the face of Taurus - as shown in the illustration below. Meanwhile, the Red Pyramid corresponds to the Red Giant star named "Al Debaran" or "The Leader" in the Hyades that is connected to the right horn of Taurus. The allegorical connection of these stars with the horns of this heavenly bull has much hidden spiritual meaning that we will delve into later.

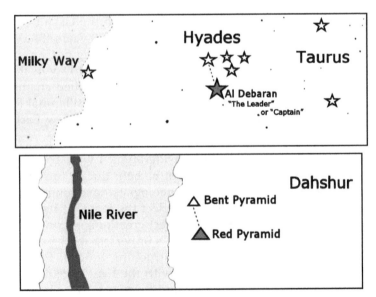

If my interpretation of the allegorical knowledge hidden in the Red and Bent Pyramids is correct, then this encoded information seems to have greatly influenced the seventh patriarch Enoch's religious ideas, as well as his subsequent design of the Great Pyramid and its two sister pyramids, which he likely designed with the help of the Holy Spirit and God's holy angels. As superior reflections of Cainan's knowledge, the pyramids at Giza formed a more perfect testimony of what Enoch and Cainan understood about Yahweh God and His Creation. Because the spiritual and scientific knowledge recorded in these monuments is written in the allegorical Language of God, however, it is only obvious to those who have the Holy Spirit within them, and - through that same Spirit - have the ability to look beyond the surface of things to correctly determine their underlying truth.

A pyramid is a geometric shape that has five sides and, as shown in Book Four on prophecy, the Great Pyramid has five interior divisions that seem to correspond in some way to its five-sided construction. The number five appears repeatedly in the mathematical and geometric principles reflected in the Great Pyramid's design. This has allegorical import in that the Great Pyramid represents one hemisphere of the Earth, which was fully formed and ready to support all kinds of life on the Fifth Creation Day. This pyramid also conveys five distinct sets of allegorical and spiritual messages about the Earth and its position and purpose in the Universe that are fully explained in Book Four.

Interestingly, since Cainan lived over nine hundred years, he would likely have known Enoch, who was born when Cainan was 297 years old. Since Enoch was translated when he was 365 years old, and Cainan lived for 910 years, Cainan could have known Enoch over his entire lifetime. As a brilliant Wise Man himself, Cainan could also easily have shared his knowledge freely with Enoch - just as Enoch likely would have shared his in return. Therefore, Cainan could have learned writing from Enoch and composed his own written testimony long before he died, though no one knows what became of Cainan's writings.

As already suggested in discussing the two pyramids at Dahshur, it is possible that Cainan did not write anything in the traditional sense, but rather built the Red and Bent Pyramids to testify about what he knew of God and prophecy. If so, Cainan used the Language of God via architectural design, measurements, geometry, and numbers rather than words constructed from an alphabet to convey his spiritual and scientific knowledge to posterity. So, though we have not found conclusive evidence of Cainan's Pre-Flood written inscriptions or books that might compliment those written by Enoch, it is possible that we still have access to allegorical messages from both godly patriarchs that have been preserved in five pyramids dated to Egypt's Old Kingdom.

Since Cainan was born hundreds of years before Enoch, the monuments at Dahshur might predate the Great Pyramid complex at Giza, which was likely built using Enoch's own design many years later.

Nonetheless, since both of these pyramid sites are tied to the Gospel in the Stars and the passage of time, they were likely meant to utilize the Language of God in the same way to communicate spiritual, scientific, mathematical and celestial truths.

Cainan may have been the first to utilize many of the concepts that underlie the Language of God to create earthly sacred architecture, and could have inspired Enoch's relatives to do the same thing after Enoch was translated. On the other hand, Cainan may have organized the building of the two biggest pyramids at Dahshur right after Enoch's translation. If so, Cainan's relations would likely have worked at the Dahshur site at the same time that Enoch's relations worked at the Giza site, and the two work parties may also have supported and helped each other to complete their respective sacred tasks.

Though the Bible does not record it, the Book of 1 Enoch teaches that Enoch was taken up to heaven on several occasions, after which he returned to Earth until his final ascent at his translation, which may have been at Pentecost. During his visionary trips into heavenly realms, Enoch communicated with and gained much of his wisdom from the holy angelic Watchers. Afterward, Enoch may then have recorded all that he learned from Yahweh and the angels by carving the Dendera Zodiac, designing the Giza pyramid complex, and also recording many books in written form.

Furthermore, Enoch also appears to have dwelled in the Garden of Eden at some point after he was translated, for the Book of 1 Enoch relates that Enoch's son Methuselah found Enoch there when he sought to find out if the infant Noah was part Nephilim or not (1 Enoch 106:8-15). More on this later!

If, as the Book of Jasher indicates, Enosh's son Cainan did have great spiritual wisdom, Enoch likely utilized some of Cainan's astronomical and spiritual knowledge when writing the apocryphal book that bears his name. Furthermore, with the help of the holy Watchers, Enoch appears to have developed a much more complex architectural application for the divine Language of God than Cainan did. This is evident in the superiority and far greater complexity of the Great Pyramid and its associated pyramids at Giza when compared with those at Dahshur.

Like the builder of the two biggest pyramids at Dahshur, the builders of the Great Pyramid and the entire Giza Pyramid Complex did not use symbols from a verbal language to convey ideas. Instead, they revealed prophetic and spiritual truths within a complex series of structures built to relay a wealth of scientific, geometric, and mathematical concepts without the use of one written word.

Based on ancient Arab legends about Enoch, the testimony about him found in the Book of Jasher and the Book of 1 Enoch, and from the facts regarding the Giza pyramid complex that will be disclosed here and in Book Four, it is highly likely that the true designer of the Great Pyramid was not really Enoch or his son Methuselah, who was the guardian of Enoch's prophetic writings, but God Almighty. In fact, it may be that - just as God inspired Moses to build the Tabernacle and Ark of the Covenant - Yahweh inspired Enoch to design the Great Pyramid with its empty coffers and allegorically-charged passages and chambers, and guided Enoch in drawing up the plans for the entire Giza Pyramid Complex. It is then possible that Yahweh sent His holy angels to help Enoch's Sethite kin to build the plans in the exact location where Enoch was translated.

If - as mentioned in the Book of Jasher - Cainan's *"tablets of stone"* are indeed the Red and Bent Pyramids at Dahshur, many more secrets may be hidden in the design of these two pyramids than just their correlation with two prominent stars in the Hyades star cluster in Taurus. In fact, these pyramids likely draw on the allegorical associations of the Gospel in the Stars, and have much to do with the application of Sacred Astronomy and prophetic time-keeping. We will explore these connections in upcoming sections of this chapter.

Deciphering Who Built the Great Pyramid

Josephus indicates that the antediluvian ancestors of Seth built two pillars - one of stone and the other of brick - that would record all their knowledge of the heavens:

> *"...And that their inventions might not be lost before they were sufficiently known, upon Adam's prediction that the world was to be destroyed at one time by the force of fire, and at another time by the violence and quantity of water,* **they made two pillars, the one of brick, the other of stone:** *they inscribed their discoveries on them both, that in case the pillar of brick should be destroyed by the flood, the pillar of stone might remain, and exhibit those discoveries to mankind; and also inform them that there was another pillar of brick erected by them.* **Now this remains in the land of Siriad to this day.** *"* - Josephus, The Antiquities of the Jews, 1.2.3, Verse 70

In the preceding passage, Josephus claims that the Sethites built one stone and one brick "pillar" in a place called Siriad, and that these two pillars still existed when Josephus wrote his histories in the 1st Century AD. Siriad is an ancient name for Egypt, so we can logically conclude that these monuments were built there. Furthermore, as we have already seen in previous sections of this book, there are several pyramid-shaped stone pillars in Egypt that conclusively show advanced astronomical knowledge. These are five pyramids attributed to the rulers of the Old Kingdom's Fourth Dynasty. In addition, due to its complimentary astronomical meaning, the Great Sphinx is likely to be a Sethite construction.

The Fourth Dynasty in ancient Egypt is estimated to have been between 2650 and 2480 BC. This was very early in Egypt's history. If my Biblical Chronology is followed with the creation (or Fall) of Adam and Eve in 4003 BC and the Great Flood in 2347 BC, *these five Old Kingdom pyramids and the Great Sphinx were built hundreds of years before the Great Flood.* However, these structures may be even older. This would especially be true if Cainan built the pyramids at Dahshur before Enoch's translation, or both Cainan and Enoch's Sethite kin built the pyramids at Giza and Dahshur in honor of Enoch and his teachings from Sacred Astronomy and the Star Gospel, as the Book of 2 Enoch suggests. This is because, according to my Biblical Chronology, Enoch was born in 3381 BC, and translated in 3016 BC - exactly 365 years after he was born. Therefore, unless the Great Pyramid was built sometime during Enoch's patriarchal rule, it would likely have been built within one hundred years of his translation.

The three biggest pyramids at Giza, and their two enigmatic companions to the south at Dahshur were built entirely of stone blocks, while the Great Sphinx's rear section was partly constructed of fired bricks. Badly damaged, these bricks have since been covered over with a veneer of stone in subsequent ancient and modern repairs. Near the Sphinx is the Great Pyramid, which is the only one of the Seven Ancient Wonders of the World still standing.

The building of the Great Pyramid is attributed to the Old Kingdom Pharaoh Khufu, whose reign is currently dated between 2589 and 2566 BC. Khufu was the second Pharaoh of Egypt's Fourth Dynasty, which is traditionally dated to between 2650 and 2480 BC. In addition, the second largest pyramid at Giza and the Great Sphinx are attributed to one of his successors named Khafre, whose reign is often dated from 2558 to 2532 BC. However, ancient stellas erected between the paws of the Great Sphinx and in the Sphinx Temple suggest that Khufu and

Khafre only repaired the Sphinx and pyramids, which were already ancient in their time.

As shown in Book Four, the star shafts in the Great Pyramid target the night sky in 2500 BC, which would place its possible construction in the Old Kingdom era at about 200 years before the Flood. Since my Biblical Chronology places the reign of Khufu in the era when Noah was the leading patriarch of the Sethites, it may be that the star shafts target 2500 BC to identify Noah as their builder. Or it could just be meant to identify when to begin reading the dateline hidden in the lengths of the interior passages, which appears to begin in 2500 BC. However, though it is possible that Noah was Khufu, or that he or his son Shem built the Great Pyramid instead of Khufu, the Giza pyramid complex could be much older than Khufu's reign. If so, Noah and Shem would not have built the Great Pyramid, though they certainly may have overseen finishing the Giza site before the Flood, or repairing it after the Flood.

As shown in Book Four, there are 4,510 Pyramid Inches measuring from the doorway into the Antechamber, down the Grand Gallery, down the Ascending Passage, and up through the first half of the descending passage to the entrance of the Great Pyramid. If we assume that every Pyramid Inch in the Great Pyramid is equal to one year of time, and if we subtract 2,500 from 4,510, this leaves 2,010 inches to add to 1 AD, provided we subtract 1 year to account for the missing zero date between BC and AD. This leads us to the year 2010 AD, which is a very important prophetic year discussed in Book Four. Noah, who lived to be 950 years old, would have been 447 years old in 2500 BC.

Evidence that the Great Pyramid was built in two stages is suggested by the fact that the stone blocks used to construct its foundation are far larger and more expertly worked than the blocks in the upper stages of the pyramid's visible exterior masonry. Nonetheless, immense and expertly worked blocks were also used to construct some hidden interior features high up in the Great Pyramid's extensive interior passage system, as well as the ceilings of the King's and Queen's Chambers. This suggests that most of the foundation, interior passages and chambers of the Great Pyramid were constructed with the same level of skill *before the Great Flood,* and that only the upper masonry layers may have been added or reconstructed sometime after the Flood.

As to the Great Pyramid's true age, there is an odd salty layer encrusted inside the passageways in the lower thirty-five courses of the Great Pyramid that suggests that it was once filled with sea water that seeped inside from the supposed air shafts in the pyramid, and then the ocean water trapped inside eventually dried up, leaving the salt behind.

Some scholars think this is good evidence of the Great Pyramid's existence prior to the Great Flood, which occurred in 2347 BC.

Not surprisingly, many design elements of the Great Pyramid have meaning, and this salt also has an allegorical spiritual significance as a Covenant symbol. In addition, there is speculation that the four narrow shafts leading into the pyramid were completely closed to the outside at one time, which means no sea water may have been able to pour in through these passages. However, though it is not certain that the Flood waters added their own spiritual significance to the wisdom already hidden within the Great Pyramid, the salt layer inside the Queen's Chamber and Jubilee Passage leading into it suggest that the Great Pyramid was built before the Flood and at least one shaft in the Queen's Chamber was open to the outside.

The Great Pyramid is made of an estimated 2.5 million massive stone blocks - with most of them weighing around two tons. Some of the blocks used in the interior of the Great Pyramid, however, weigh between forty and *seventy* tons! Could this pyramid be part of one of the two "pillars," or sacred sites that the antediluvian descendents of Seth built before the Flood? This seems highly likely, as some form of advanced technology that was unavailable to the Egyptians after the Great Flood appears to have been used in the construction of the pyramids at Dahshur and Giza.

In particular, the Great Pyramid at Giza shows advanced technological, astronomical, and mathematical knowledge that the ancient Egyptians simply did not have for most of their history – mathematical knowledge such as the value of Pi (π), and astronomical knowledge such as the position of the Earth in relation the Sun, Moon and constellations. This suggests that **some culture other than that of the ancient Egyptians built the Great Pyramid in the remote past.**

Certain Arab legends indicate that it was the godly antediluvian patriarch Enoch who built the Great Pyramid. These legends also indicate that the Great Pyramid was built to record the scientific, mathematical, and prophetic knowledge of a lost civilization. In Book Four, an entire section has been devoted to showing that this Arab legend is absolutely true. The Great Pyramid is a veritable encyclopedia of arcane knowledge about the Universe, our Solar System, and our Earth. It may also have been meant to record the date of the Universe's creation, the year of the birth of Christ, and the date of the world's probable demise at the end of time - when the New Heaven and the New Earth will be created.

Based on the quotation by the historian Josephus about the antediluvian descendants of Seth building two monuments in Siriad, they may have built the biggest pyramids at Giza including the Great Pyramid and the Great Sphinx, as well as the two Old Kingdom pyramids at Dahshur in Egypt, since Cainan was also a Sethite. However, though the Sethites are the likely builders of these monuments in Egypt, it is my contention that God inspired Enoch when he designed the layout of the Giza Pyramid Complex. Subsequently, Enoch likely gave the plans for the Giza Pyramid Complex to his son Methuselah so that he could organize the building of it after his father was translated. Of course, this does not rule out the fact that the Sethites may have received some help from the godly Watchers who never sinned when they built these monuments, though it was primarily meant to be a human undertaking done for God's glory, and not for the glorification of some despotic pharaoh.

As mentioned earlier, Adam's great grandson Cainan the Sethite was ascribed with knowing and recording much wisdom on stone tablets, and - like Enoch - he likely was a priest and king in the order of Melchizedek. Therefore, some of Cainan's wisdom may have served as the foundation for Enoch's own understanding of God and the Gospel in the Stars. However, Enoch was the first prophet of Yah to understand the full spiritual and prophetic implications of all forty-eight ancient Zodiac signs, as well as the allegorical meaning of the major stars and planets.

Even more so than Cainan, Enoch the Sethite was imminently qualified to be a priest and a king in the order of Melchizedek. Pleased with Enoch's great love for Him, Yahweh may soon have commissioned Enoch to record all his spiritual knowledge for the future posterity of mankind. Inspired by God, Enoch then may have designed the Giza Pyramid Complex and Great Pyramid to serve as a mathematically, scientifically and allegorically discerned altar, as well as a Gospel in Stone.

The Book of 1 Enoch reveals that great spiritual and astronomical knowledge was given to Enoch in visions. Enoch could therefore have been given visions showing what his kin were to build at Giza. This may have been how Enoch was shown that the three stars in Orion's belt signified the Messiah that Enoch knew as the Son of Man. As surviving copies of the Book of Enoch attest, Enoch then readily wrote down and shared what he had been shown so others could benefit from his wisdom.

Judging from what is said about him in the Book of 1 Enoch, Book of Jubilees and Book of Jasher, Enoch certainly would have had the prophetic vision and astronomical knowledge needed to draw up the plans to build the Great Pyramid to fit the astronomical signs in any Age. Enoch is therefore the most likely candidate to have designed the Great Pyramid as a sacred pillar dedicated to Yahweh and His Son Yahshua. *This is why I call the Great Pyramid the "Pillar of Enoch," and why my web site was named "Pillar of Enoch Ministry," or POEM.*

The ingenious design of the Great Pyramid and Great Sphinx put all of Enoch's divinely given spiritual and scientific knowledge into a form that was both universal in its message and not easily destroyed. Designing such an incredibly complex and meaningful structure would uniquely qualify Enoch for the title *"scribe of righteousness."*

The holy Watchers could also have shown Enoch how to fill the Great Pyramid or "Pillar of Enoch" with much more scientific and prophetic knowledge than any other pyramid, pillar or altar to Yahweh was designed to reveal prior to, or after that. Using the knowledge that Yahweh and His angels gave him, Enoch could easily have drawn up the plans for the Giza pyramids and Sphinx. However, as the Book of 2 Enoch asserts, Enoch's Sethite kin likely undertook the gargantuan task of building what God and Enoch had envisioned after Enoch's translation.

As demonstrated in Book Four: "The Language of God in Prophecy," the three pyramidal-shaped stone pillars and sphinx built at Giza may be one of the two pillars that Josephus attributes to the Sethites, assuming that Josephus counted the separate pyramids at Dahshur and Giza as two separate "pillars." On the other hand, Josephus did not identify Cainan or Enoch as the designers or builders of any pyramids in Egypt, and we can't be sure which monuments Josephus was referring to in Siriad.

In any case, it is clear from my findings in Book Four that the Great Pyramid contains an amazing amount of astronomical and religious knowledge that could only have belonged to a technologically and spiritually advanced person or society. By divine revelation, Enoch (or someone who had to be very much like him) appears to have known exactly how to depict the movements of the constellation of Orion through the pyramids at Giza. As shown via the detailed study of the Gospel in the Stars in Book One and later in this chapter, Orion can repeatedly be associated with Yahweh's promised Messiah and his sacrifice for sin on the Cross. This is likely why Enoch was directed to show the triune nature of this Messiah by depicting Him via three pyramids linked to the three belt stars in Orion.

Though Enoch likely designed the Great Pyramid, Enoch's son Methuselah would have overseen building it using blueprints that Enoch either left behind before he was translated, or delivered to Methuselah later via one of the holy Watchers. Methuselah could then have overseen one of the most ambitious building projects ever devised by men outside of the legendary Tower of Babel.

Despite the evidence that points to a Pre-Flood construction for the Great Pyramid, a few scholars believe that Noah's Flood was so violent that nothing could have withstood its ferocity. They therefore think that every building constructed by human beings prior to the Great Flood was completely destroyed. I have problems with this theory for several reasons. First of all, they ignore the fact that the Great Pyramid remains the most massive and expertly constructed stone building in the world *to this day*. No other building in stone or metal was ever as well constructed as the Great Pyramid, which has withstood severe earthquakes and storms for thousands of years. Secondly, *Josephus claims that two structures in Siriad that were still standing in his day were built by the Sethites prior to the Flood*. Finally, my Biblical Chronology dates the Great Flood to 2347 BC. Since the Great Pyramid was likely built on or before 2500 BC as per the dating of the four star shafts in the Great Pyramid, it would have been standing for at least 200 years prior to then.

Nevertheless, Noah and Shem may have been caretakers of the Pyramid Complex at Giza after its construction. For instance, there is some evidence that the top courses of the Great Pyramid from the King's Chamber up were added to the structure later - perhaps in an effort to hide and preserve the internal chambers of the pyramid before the Great Flood. Noah and his son Shem are also likely to have watched over and repaired the Great Pyramid until Nimrod overthrew their dominion over Giza, as will be discussed in Chapter Seven.

There are some scholars that cite the patriarch Joseph and his Israelite brethren as the builders of the Great Pyramid after the Flood. They also speculate that the Israelites could have built or repaired the Great Pyramid under the leadership of Joseph after he became the Pharaoh's Vizier, and before the Israelites became slaves in Egypt. To prove this, many cite Josephus' claim that the ancient Egyptians had no knowledge of Astronomy before Abraham taught Sacred Astronomy to them sometime after he was born in 2055 BC. However, though both Abraham *and* Joseph could have taught the Egyptians Sacred Astronomy, and Joseph and the Israelites could have built the Great Pyramid, it is far more likely that those godly patriarchs taught the

Egyptians what the Great Pyramid's geographical orientation and interior chambers meant spiritually.

In addition to imparting his God-given wisdom to the ancient Egyptians, the patriarch Joseph would have eventually known that the Zodiac sign Taurus the Bull represented him and his offspring, and that Orion partly signified his own rise to power as Vizier of all Egypt. Joseph therefore may have repaired, expanded and added to the sacred pyramid complexes built by his ancestors at Giza and Dahshur as an act of respect to his forefathers, as well as an act of worship to God. He may also have added to them to serve as a memorial to the material promises of power and prosperity made to Joseph by his father Jacob on his death bed. Indeed, this great man's dying words were prophetic utterances inspired by the Holy Spirit. As such, they not only tie the Twelve Tribes of Israel to the Zodiac, but also accurately foretell that all twelve tribes would exist and have a purpose to fulfill in the Last Days.

Uncannily, there is an astounding connection between portions of the journey of the dead recorded in the Egyptian Book of the Dead and the layout of the interior passages of the Great Pyramid. It is therefore an intriguing possibility that this book contains knowledge that was given to the Egyptians by at least one well-educated Semite. After all, as Semitic patriarchs descended from Seth and Enoch, both Abraham and Joseph would have been familiar with the amazing secrets of Sacred Astronomy and the Heavenly Tablets. Indeed, the Book of Jasher indicates that Joseph and Benjamin learned Sacred Astronomy from their father Jacob (See Jasher 53:18-21, quoted on pages 411 and 412).

However, due to the advanced scientific and spiritual information hidden inside the Great Pyramid, the Egyptians likely had nothing to do with building it. This is because - as will be shown in future chapters - the Egyptians eventually became gross idolaters and followers of magicians and soothsayers. For this reason, the Pillar of Enoch was likely built by the Sethites before the Post-Flood civilization of Egypt came into being - just as Josephus claims. It is also likely that the Sethites had an understanding of Sacred Astronomy that exceeded Abraham's own. We will address Abraham's place in this scenario a bit later.

After the Great Flood, it is likely that only a select few initiates had any deep knowledge of Sacred Astronomy. This knowledge was likely kept hidden because Noah and others were afraid that it would be corrupted or used toward evil ends if given to ungodly people, just as had already been done prior to the Great Flood. Noah therefore would only have revealed the deeper secrets related to Sacred Astronomy to carefully selected believers in Yahweh that were hungry for a deeper relationship with and understanding of God.

After Noah's Ark landed on the mountains of Ararat, which are found in present day Turkey and Armenia, Noah and his sons founded many new civilization centers in Mesopotamia. In fact, due to a very thick layer of artifact-free mud that has been found between civilization layers, many Post-Flood cities were likely built over the ruins of Pre-Flood civilization centers in Mesopotamia.

Since Shem was the son of Noah chosen by God to receive God's promises, Noah would likely have taught the knowledge of Sacred Astronomy to Shem alone. This means that the descendents of Ham who settled in Egypt after the Great Flood would have had no knowledge of Sacred Astronomy. They also would not have known the true purpose of the already ancient pyramid complexes at Giza and Dahshur until Abraham reintroduced this knowledge in Egypt, and the patriarch Joseph reinforced Abraham's teachings with his own celestial knowledge (Jasher 53:17-21).

As already discussed, the Book of Jubilees records that Shem's grandson Cainan learned Sacred Astronomy from ancient writings carved into stone that originated with the Watchers. We are not informed whether or not this was the same knowledge that the antediluvian Sethites understood, or if it was the bastardized version of it that is known as Astrology today. Whichever the case, however, **Cainan later taught this celestial knowledge to those who did not deserve to know it. Furthermore, these unworthy initiates adopted the idolatry and Sorcery associated with Astrology and celestial fortune-telling.**

Though Josephus identifies the Aramaic-speaking Chaldeans as the source of the science of Astronomy that Abraham knew, the Chaldeans actually inherited this science from the earlier Babylonians and Sumerians, who were also Semites. However, their incorporation of Sorcery, fortune-telling, and star worship into Sacred Astronomy effectively obliterated the true purpose of the Gospel in the Stars, which was a sacred science. For this reason, Shem and Abraham likely taught its secrets only to the wisest and most godly men of Mesopotamia, Canaan, and Egypt. It is also likely that they did so before the cultures of the world degenerated into Paganistic societies with the many false gods that increased mankind's ignorance of the one true God Yahweh. This occurred at the time when Nimrod - as the world's first dictator - ruled Mesopotamia *and many other places.* This is also when Nimrod - in an effort to destroy the power of the Gospel in the Stars - introduced Pagan idolatry and star worship.

As shown later in this chapter, the Book of Jasher records that Shem was the biblical King of Salem, and the priest of God Most High known as Melchizedek. Furthermore, Salem was the arcane name for

Jerusalem, which places Shem as the ruler in southern Canaan or Palestine after the Flood. Meanwhile, Ham was the patriarch who is believed to have settled in Egypt. Shem was therefore the king of a city hundreds of miles away from Shem's brother Ham's territory. Since most Bible historians agree that Ham's descendents ruled Egypt, Shem's descendents would have had no direct authority to build anything there - that is, unless they did rule over Upper Egypt at some point after the Flood because it was an administrative center shared by all three of Noah's sons. There are several intriguing reasons for believing that this was possible, and these are discussed in Chapter Six.

Many scholars are coming forth with various theories showing that the ancients apparently understood a complex form of Astronomy. Yet even before this current knowledge came to light, other books were available that disclosed the amazing mathematical and scientific knowledge that is contained in the structure of the Great Pyramid. Many have also shown that the interior passages of the pyramid are literally *a prophecy in stone*. The Great Pyramid's internal passages, when measured in Pyramid Inches, may show the date when Christ died, and the date immediately prior to the Tribulation. In addition, the layouts of the passages contain clear metaphorical messages that show the entire spiritual walk of mankind through the Ages. See Book Four for more about this.

Miracles Falsely Attributed to Alien Technology

Sadly, despite the Great Pyramid's message to the world that God the Father and His coming Son were known to and loved by some of our righteous ancestors, Satan has done all he can to delude people into thinking that this Pillar of Enoch was built by aliens, Nephilim, or fallen angels. These suppositions, however, are a clear demonic attempt to misappropriate a monument erected to testify of the greatness of the God of the Bible.

Along with these theories, there are many others floating around that are clearly demonic in origin. Take, for instance, those who suppose that the Nephilim knew how to shape and levitate stone blocks in minutes, and that they wanted to build sophisticated stone monuments to record their spiritual beliefs. Though this could have been done by the holy Watchers and the fallen angels, it never would have been done by the monstrous killing and eating machines that Enoch describes as the Nephilim offspring of the fallen angels!

Indeed, as shown in Chapter Four, there is no likelihood that these insatiable monsters had anything else on their mind except where their next sexual encounter or meal was coming from. These creatures were totally controlled by their ravenous hunger, fleshly lusts, and sexual desires, and they had no compunction to share wisdom or impart knowledge unless it served to fulfill their desire for more sex, blood and/or meat!

Nonetheless, there is the possibility that the fallen angels might have built stone monuments to serve their own evil purposes. In fact, building projects that may be attributed to the Watchers may be found in, or may have been inspired by many bizarre and sophisticated religious monuments now standing in Asia, India, the Middle East and the Americas. Some ruins that may have been built by the holy Watchers or the fallen among them include the foundation platform for the large religious temple complex at Baalbek in Lebanon, the plans for the many temples that appear to map out the position of the stars in the constellation Draco the Dragon in Angkor, Cambodia, and the foundation structures at Tiahuanaco and Machu Picchu in Peru. We'll discuss these edifices more thoroughly in future sections of this book.

Now, though the fallen angels certainly could have built some Pre-Flood monuments that were restored by the Post-Flood demon worshippers that controlled nearly everything during Nimrod's world dictatorship, it is foolhardy to assume that every technologically amazing archeological site is an evil product of the fallen angels or their Nephilim children. In fact, as shown repeatedly in this book and Book Four, the Great Pyramid has absolutely nothing to do with evil, and everything to do with good. Furthermore, it appears that this may also be true of the Sphinx and other big pyramids at Giza, the pyramids at Dahshur, the huge monoliths at Stonehenge in England, and the hundreds of enigmatic stone statues everywhere on Easter Island.

Despite the overwhelming facts showing that the Great Pyramid is a godly edifice designed to tell us about Yahweh and His Plan of Salvation through Yahshua, however, there are people who speculate that the Great Pyramid was built by the fallen Watchers or Nephilim as a magical doorway between the material and spiritual worlds. Others believe that the ancients used some sort of power inside the Great Pyramid to beam people's spirits up into the realm of the dead in the stars. Their false conclusions are partly based upon the magical incantations found in the Pyramid Texts attributed to several Old Kingdom Pharaohs. These speak of transporting the soul of the Pharaoh to the stars in the celestial realms, where the Egyptian god king Osiris and all past Egyptian pharaohs supposedly were guaranteed eternal life and perpetual kingship.

In addition to the Pyramid Texts, the Egyptian Book of the Dead utilizes allegorical references to the interior passages of the Great Pyramid to map out a deceased person's perilous journey to the Judgment Seat of Osiris. From there - if they were righteous enough to pass judgment - the dead were granted entrance into the joyful Kingdom of the Dead presided over by Osiris, where a perpetual banquet was supposedly always going on.

If these places and events in the Book of the Dead sound suspiciously similar to Christian concepts like the Judgment Seat of Christ, the Last Judgment, Paradise, and the Wedding Supper of the Lamb, they are. In fact, it is my supposition that the Egyptian Book of the Dead was the closest thing to a Bible that many Egyptians had access to, and some of its contents may have been non-Egyptian. In fact, the Book of the Dead may have been inspired by the teachings of Abraham or Joseph, who were likely considered to be great Wise Men in the eyes of certain Egyptians. If so, their ideas would likely have been incorporated into the existing Pagan beliefs of the Egyptians, which were sadly mired in Magic and Sorcery. See the end of Chapter Six for more about this.

Rather than serving as an idolatrous portal into Heaven, though, the true godly function of the Great Pyramid is to serve as an altar and monument conveying the nature of God the Father and the purpose of His Son to mankind. In an effort to succeed at this, the Great Pyramid points to a specific star located in Orion's belt, and also allegorically points to the Gospel in the Stars surrounding Taurus and Orion. In addition, the internal structure of the Pillar of Enoch reveals cleverly encoded truths that allude to our salvation, resurrection, and ascent into Heaven after death. Nonetheless, it was never intended to be a mystical teleportation device for dead spirits to find their way to Heaven! It is instead a symbol of things that God has and will accomplish without any need of technology.

Indeed, if Yahweh wanted to translate anyone from Earth to Heaven, He could do it without the need of a building at any time - just as He did in Enoch and Elijah's case, and also did for Christ. If He wants to, God can even move our unregenerated, mortal human bodies from one geographical location to another instantly. This is intimated in Acts 8:39-40, where Phillip was physically and rapidly moved from one place to another in a supernatural manner in order to serve God and His children better. The First Resurrection will also occur *"in the twinkling of an eye"* or fraction of a second (1 Corinth. 15:52).

Nevertheless, some people believe that God used a spaceship to take Enoch and Elijah to Heaven. However, there is no reason to believe that the fiery horses and chariots that transported these godly men to Heaven were technological marvels! If they were, then are we to assume that the white horses of believers who accompany Yahshua when He returns to Earth at the end of the Great Tribulation are spaceships too? On the contrary, based on how Paul describes the translation of believers as a miraculous spiritual event, it seems nonsensical that these same glorified believers would need earthly technology to return to Earth!

The Bible clearly teaches that Elijah performed miracles that did not need technology to be accomplished, as did Moses, Yahshua, and His first apostles and disciples. Nonetheless, some alien enthusiasts still have a persistent desire to attribute almost every biblical miracle to aliens or natural phenomena, or to use the miracles as evidence for some physical form of advanced technology. Furthermore, many of them believe that God is a superior but limited alien life form, and nothing we know in this world is from a supernatural and infinite God who created it all. Instead, they insist that mankind was created to serve as slaves for some superior alien race that genetically engineered Homo sapiens by mixing alien and ape or Neanderthal genes.

Unfortunately for alien lovers, however, the only aliens in our midst today are likely to be demonic spiritual entities that have a legendary satanic ability to twist the facts surrounding everything godly in order to make it appear evil! We will discuss the evil origins and satanic objectives of all fallen angels, demons and Nephilim in Chapter Four.

Despite the beliefs of the misguided, there is no reason why the invisible and immaterial Creator God of the Bible can't be a truly infinite supernatural entity that does not need any form of technology to accomplish His will on Earth. Also, as spiritual beings that can materialize in a physical form, God's holy angels do not need technology of any kind. Furthermore, when they die, people are spirits, and go to God as spirits. So they would not need any form of technological device to get to Heaven!

In an old 1995 fiction manuscript that I wrote about the Age of Enoch prior to the Great Flood (and plan to re-write and publish in 2009), I fantasized that Enoch's antediluvian peers had space ships and other forms of advanced technology that was taught to them by the Watchers. I also believed that the fallen angels needed the technology taught to us, but that their space ships were far superior to our own. I also thought that the fallen Watchers turned their technology against us when people began to use powerful technologies of holy Watcher origin in an attempt to destroy the Nephilim. However, I had no proof that any of it was true until I started reading Jewish legends, which teach that the fallen angels lost their supernatural abilities when they sinned, and therefore needed technology to travel through this dimension of time and space.

However, though our antediluvian ancestors may well have had advanced technology at their disposal that they developed with help from the Watchers, there is absolutely no truth to the idea that the holy angels were dependent on technology. As long as they didn't sin, the angels had supernatural abilities like God and did not need spaceships to go anywhere. Yet alien enthusiasts are probably correct in believing that the fallen Watchers and their Nephilim offspring needed Watcher technology, just as human beings did to rapidly travel through Earth's air space.

Nonetheless, it is a shame that many people are beginning to believe the nonsense that God and His angels need spaceships to travel through space and are seriously beginning to doubt the existence of a real, supernatural God. Indeed, the only purpose of this lie may be to delude people into accepting and trusting Azazel, the fallen angels, and the descendents of the Nephilim that will control the Earth with the Antichrist during the Tribulation.

I do not doubt that both holy and fallen Watchers could have shown men how to use technology to ease our workload and aid in our defense or destruction. However, this does not mean that God Almighty or His angels ever needed the technology they know how to utilize. As an immortal, immaterial being, God doesn't need technology now and *never did* - nor do His angels! Nonetheless, Nephilim and humans certainly needed advanced technology for swift air travel - just as the fallen angels probably did.

Why the Sethites Chose To Bring Heaven to Earth at Giza

Thus far, we have established that the Giza Pyramid Complex and Dahshur pyramids in Egypt may have originally served as encoded records containing the scientific and spiritual knowledge of a lost civilization. Furthermore, we have determined who may and may not have built the five massive stone pyramids at these sites. Since Book Four deals with the scientific and prophetic information encoded into the Great Pyramid, this book will deal with the spiritual information hidden at Dahshur and Giza.

Illustration of Old Kingdom Pyramid Star Correlations

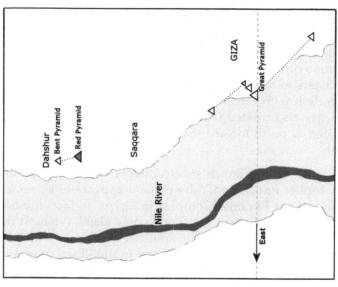

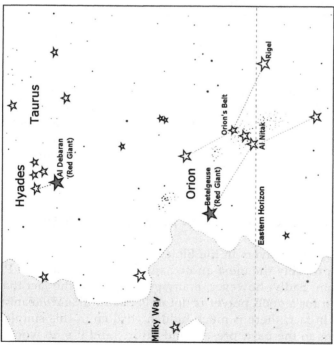

When Sacred Astronomy is applied to the constellations surrounding our Earth, it involves interpreting what modern scholars have dubbed "The Gospel in the Stars." I believe that Enoch the Sethite was an expert at deciphering the messages hidden in the Star Gospel, which he called the Heavenly Tablets. It is also reasonable to assume that Enoch wanted to share his knowledge of the heavens in a way that could not be misconstrued. Therefore, Enoch sought divine inspiration to plan a monument that would withstand the Great Flood and all other natural disasters to the end of time. Furthermore, Enoch sought divine help to encode it with celestial, mathematical, spiritual and scientific knowledge. He also trusted God to choose a place on Earth that was ideally aligned to point toward the most important information in the Star Gospel.

The place where Enoch's descendents built that monument to honor the prophet Enoch and Yahweh God appears to be none other than the entire Giza Pyramid Complex in Egypt. In fact, the Sethites that were descended from Cainan and Enoch may also have built the two pyramids at Dahshur - a site to the southwest of Giza, which is near modern day Cairo, Egypt. As can be seen in the illustration on page 143, the Giza and Dahshur Pyramid Complexes correspond almost perfectly with prominent stars in the Zodiac sign of Taurus and its decan sign called Orion.

As shown extensively in Book Four, the Great Pyramid may be a sacred Covenant pillar or altar built to honor Yahweh. As such, it may also reveal a great deal of divinely inspired prophetic and scientific knowledge that mankind was unable to fully understand prior to the 20th Century. In my book on Prophecy, it is suggested that Moses was aware of the Great Pyramid's true purpose, and that he was inspired by God to use its divinely given design when he laid out the plans for the Desert Tabernacle, just as God may have inspired the patriarch Enoch the Sethite to design the Pyramid Complex at Giza.

"On Earth as it is in Heaven" - Mirroring God's Will

Of all the prayers in the Bible, the one known as "The Lord's Prayer" is probably the most quoted and memorized in all of Protestant Christendom. Sadly, however, many people ignore the fact that this prescription for a good prayer is not only beautiful and meaningful, but prophetic. In fact, there is much hidden wisdom in this simple prayer that pertains to the past, present and future, and it's no wonder since it was uttered by Christ Himself! So, though some of the literal and symbolic meanings of this divinely suggested blueprint for prayer were discussed in Book Two, we will discuss another prophetic aspect of it here that is contained in the following verses:

> "Your kingdom come. Your will be done **on earth as it is in heaven**." - Matthew 6:10 (NKJ)

Amazingly, this passage suggests a couple of things that are extremely relevant to this section of the book. First of all, it intimates that the Kingdom of God in Heaven should be manifested on Earth through the prayers of intercession offered up by believers working under the authority given to them in Christ. Secondly, it suggests that - since God's Will is already visibly displayed in the heavens - it can be visibly displayed on the Earth as an act of prayer and worship. Therefore, Yahshua was literally telling his disciples that - in anticipation of its fulfillment - God's Will can and should be displayed or mirrored on Earth just as it is in Heaven. Therefore, in addition to praying for God's Kingdom to come and for His Will to be done on Earth as it is already done in Heaven, Yahshua was also suggesting that *God's past, present and future Will has been literally mirrored on Earth just as it is already displayed in Heaven*.

This is precisely what this chapter is endeavoring to show: that God's righteous antediluvian followers knew God's past, present and future Will and mirrored it on Earth for the benefit of helping future generations to remember it, and to joyfully await its fulfillment. Indeed, even the numbering of this verse in Matthew that calls for God's Will to be done on Earth and in Heaven tells us when God's Will would be accomplished, with the chapter number 6 signifying the Six Great Days that must pass before the final Great Day signified by the verse number - 10 - which can be reduced to 1 to indicate the Millennial Rule of Christ!

In this book, we have already ascertained that part of God's Will displayed in the heavens was mirrored on Earth at Giza and Dahshur. That in itself is an amazing feat, but it is not the end of this story! Indeed there is far more to tell, for it appears that the whole Earth may have been purposefully aligned with the constellations at one moment in history. In other words, many cities, towns and religious monuments on Earth may be aligned with prominent stars in our night skies as they appeared in a particular time period. Among these celestial configurations that align with particular times and places in history, several were prominently displayed on Earth like those at Giza, Dahshur, and Easter Island. Others were far more subtly pointed to, however, though they are no less amazing in their implications. Take, for example, the following:

During my study of the Star Gospel, I began to wonder if there might be terrestrial counterparts to other prominent stars besides those already found in Egypt - especially Sirius, which is the brightest star in Earth's night sky. My speculations eventually led me to discover that there is a temple complex called Angkor Thom in Cambodia with many different structures including the temple known as Angkor Wat that are aligned with the stars in the constellation Draco the Dragon. Furthermore, these buildings depict Draco as it appeared in the sky in 10,500 BC, which is one of the same time periods that the Giza Complex targets.

As I pondered whether or not there might be more structures like this on the Earth, I started looking for correlations nearest to the Giza Complex in Egypt by comparing a star map to a geographical map of Egypt and Israel. On this map, I had drawn the miraculous Christ Angle that - as shown in Book Four - begins at the Great Pyramid and intersects Bethlehem. This is when I saw that the star Sirius appears to be aligned with one place in Israel! This is none other than Bethlehem - the town where Yahshua the Messiah was born on one blessed night in 3 BC! In fact, the angles and distance between the Great Pyramid at Giza and Bethlehem correspond exactly with the celestial position and relative distance between the stars Al Nitak and Sirius!

First, as shown on page 147, a section of a star map had to be reversed to make it correspond to the way the pyramids at Giza are laid out on the Earth in a mirror fashion. Next, a transparency of Al Nitak and Sirius was transposed over the Christ Angle of approximately 28 degrees, 18 minutes, and 9 seconds that was drawn onto the geographical map on page 148. Amazingly, this showed a perfect correlation between Sirius and Bethlehem, and Al Nitak and the Great Pyramid!

In the illustration on page 148, note the reversed star names indicating the dot for the star Al Nitak overlaid over the Great Pyramid and the dot for the star Sirius overlaid over the location of Bethlehem. This shows the uncanny correlation between the stars Al Nitak and Sirius with Giza and Bethlehem along the Christ Angle. See Book Four for the explanation of how this amazing angle can be found inside the Great Pyramid using geometric principles.

After making this amazing discovery, I recalled that the star Sirius is in the constellation Canis Major, and that it is the brightest star in our night sky. Furthermore, the largest known star in our Universe - VY-Canis Majoris - is located in Canis Major. To get an idea of just how big this star is - if we were to put VY-Canis Majoris in our Solar System in the place of our Sun, its circumference would swallow the Sun,

Mercury, Venus, Earth, the Moon, Mars, Jupiter, and far beyond it. In fact, it would reach all the way to the distant orbit of the planet Saturn!

Reversed Star Chart Showing Al Nitak and Sirius

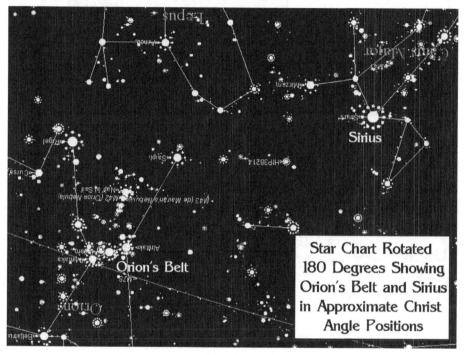

Star Chart Rotated 180 Degrees Showing Orion's Belt and Sirius in Approximate Christ Angle Positions

If the constellation Canis Major is actually connected to the physical location of the Promised Land, which it appears to be, the fact that both the largest and brightest stars in our Galaxy are located there is certainly no accident! This is because, just as VY-Canis Majoris is the largest star in the sky, and Sirius is the brightest, Bethlehem is the one shining place on this Earth where Yahshua chose to be born, and its neighboring city Jerusalem is the one place where Yahshua compassionately chose to die for the sins of the whole world, and where He will one day set up His throne.

Adding to this astounding physical correlation, incredible messianic imagery is attached to Canis Major, which is a decan of the Zodiac sign of Gemini. Here is an excerpt from "The Language of God in the Universe," which explains just how special Canis Major and Sirius actually are:

The Sirius/Bethlehem and Giza/Great Pyramid Correlation

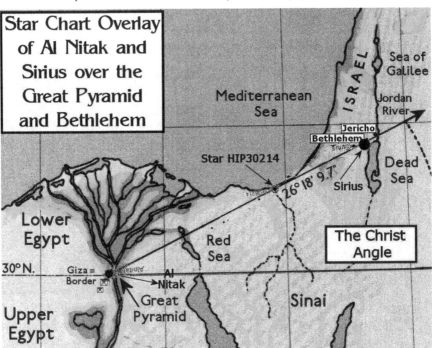

Start of Excerpt 1 from "The Language of God in the Universe:"

In the Dendera Zodiac, Canis Major is called "Apis," meaning "the Head Commanding," or "Swiftly Coming Down in Victory," and is pictured as a double-crowned hawk, or eagle standing triumphantly atop what appears to be the fanned out head of a papyrus stalk capping a papyrus bundle. If viewed with the Language of God, this symbol may represent the whole land of Egypt. This is because there is a strong physical similarity between the shape of the delta region called Lower Egypt from the air, and a lotus blossom, or papyrus head. Similarly, Upper Egypt along the Nile resembles a bent lotus stem, or papyrus stalk from the air...

The eagle or hawk is the natural enemy and destroyer of the serpent, as depicted in the neighboring decan sign of Lepus. In the Dendera Zodiac, the hawk shown for Canis Major is labeled separately as "Naz Seir" and represents the star Sirius in Canis Major. In Egyptian, "Naz" means "Caused to Come Forth," or "Sent," while "Seir" means "Prince," or "Chief." Therefore, the title "Naz Seir" can mean "Sent Prince." Since "Naz" and "Zar" both mean "Prince" in Hebrew, Naz Seir could also mean "Prince of princes," a fitting epithet for Yahshua as King of kings!

There is, however, another symbol for both Sirius and Canis Major in the Zodiac of Dendera showing their tremendous spiritual importance. It is found in the symbol of a large bull riding in a solar boat. This reclining bull represents the sign of Taurus, and it has a star symbol between its tall, upright horns that signifies the star Sirius and the Great Prince it symbolizes: Yahshua the Messiah! Meanwhile, Taurus the Bull signifies the faithful Gentile followers of Yahshua, while the solar boat is the Egyptian symbol for Argo, the most important ship sailing in heaven. Since Canis Major is depicted as a bull, it is also connected to the bulls that served as atonement sacrifices in ancient Israel.

Brightest Star: Latin, "Sirius;" Ancient Egyptian, "Naz-Seir." The star name "Sirius" is derived from the Egyptian word "Seir" and the Hebrew word "Zar," and both "Seir" and "Zar" mean "Prince." Sirius is the brightest star in the night sky, and is actually part of a binary star system. Sirius A is the bright star we can see. However, circling around Sirius A is a white dwarf star that is invisible to the naked eye. Scientists have labeled it Sirius B. It has an orbit around Sirius A that takes fifty Earth years to complete.

Fifty is the number of years it takes to arrive at a biblical Jubilee year. This was a year when all captives in Israel had to be set free, fields were to lie fallow, and all debts were to be cancelled. When Yahshua died on the Cross for our sins, all who accepted Him as Savior and King were automatically given access to an eternal year of Jubilee when their debts were fully paid *for all time*. Sirius A therefore appears to represent Yahshua as a Great Prince and future King of kings accompanied by His Bride, the True Church, which is signified by the white dwarf star called Sirius B.

End of Excerpt 1 from "The Language of God in the Universe."

This excerpt clearly shows why Yahshua was called the "Nazarene." It was not just because His hometown was Nazareth, but also because He is the "Naz Seir" or "Prince of princes," and the town of Nazareth only hinted at the glory of Christ's purpose as it was mapped out in the heavens! In fact, Scripture specifically refers to Yahshua as the Prince of princes in Daniel 8:25, who will supernaturally overcome the fierce king who is the Antichrist. In addition, "Nazar" means "Branch" in Hebrew, and Scripture exclusively refers to Yahshua as the Branch, or Branch of the Lord (Isaiah 4:2; Zech. 3:8, 6:12).

This excerpt also explains that the bright star Sirius A is a double star system with a virtually invisible neighboring white dwarf star called Sirius B rotating around it over a period of 50 years. Now, every 50 years was a Jubilee year in ancient Israel - when all captives and slaves were set free and all debts were cancelled. Furthermore, Sirius A is allegorically tied to Yahshua as the King of kings, while Sirius B is tied to His redeemed Bride - the True Church. Uncannily, this same truth is also reflected in the sign of Gemini - of which Canis Major is a decan.

Now, Bethlehem is a small suburb of Jerusalem - and Jerusalem is one of the most high profile cities in the world. In fact, these places are arguably the most important pieces of Real Estate to God than anywhere else on the planet! Jerusalem and Bethlehem are intimately connected to the birth of Christianity, Messianic Judaism, and the formation of the True Church because Christ was born in Bethlehem - and died and rose from the dead just outside of Jerusalem. In the process, Christ paid for the sins of the world, and all our spiritual debts are cancelled through His sacrifice. Now, since there appears to be a correlation of Sirius A with Christ and Sirius B with His Church, and because Bethlehem is right next door to Jerusalem, this double star system may also be meant to represent these two physical locations in Israel! In fact, it is likely that Sirius B - with its 50-year Jubilee-marking orbit around Sirius A - represents Jerusalem, while Bethlehem remains the city tied to the bright star Sirius A, which means it may be the true Star of Bethlehem that perpetually marks the miraculous moment when God first became a man and dwelt among us!

If this were not enough, there is another correlation between the heavens and the Earth that is just as astounding, and highly illuminating of God's Will concerning the Law of Moses and the Age of Grace. This correlation was found after I learned about a new proposed site for Mount Sinai, which is also called Mount Horeb in the Bible. If this new site is the true Mount Sinai, it is not in the Sinai wilderness at all, but in present day Saudi Arabia. In fact, the once elusive Mount Sinai may be a mountain called Jabal Al Lawz, which is Arabic for "Mountain of Almonds." We will further discuss this proposed site of the mountain where Moses received the Law from God in Chapter Six. For now, however, let me show you that the heavens certainly confirm that this mountain could be the real Mount Sinai!

After much study, it became apparent to me that Jabal Al Lawz has more surface and geographical features that match the biblical narrative than any other proposed site for Mount Sinai, including Jabal Al Musa in the Sinai. So, after discovering the Sirius-Bethlehem correlation, I noted that the star Procyon in Canis Minor looked remarkably close to matching the geographical location of Jabal Al Lawz.

Now, using the same star to land ratio as was used to match Bethlehem with Sirius, I attempted to align Procyon exactly over Jabal Al Lawz. Though this was not possible, however, another amazing correlation immediately showed itself, as is shown in the illustration on this page. Even though the star circle signifying Procyon is placed just off the left border of the drawing, a line connecting it and the star Al Nitak, which is situated over the Great Pyramid shows that it exactly crosses over the site of Jabal Al Lawz:

Mount Sinai Correlation with Procyon in Canis Minor

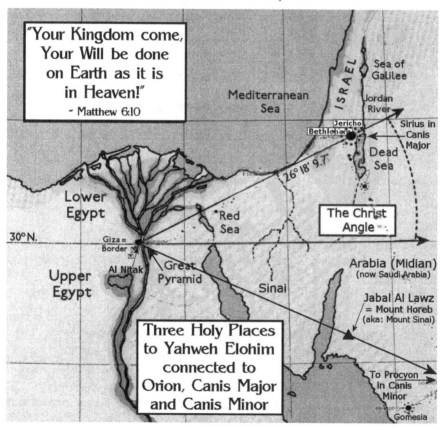

As per the Language of God, this appears to be no accident, but may be meant to show the connection of Jabal Al Lawz with the meaning of both Procyon and the constellation Canis Minor. Here is a brief excerpt from Book One explaining the allegorical meaning of Canis Minor and its stars Gomesia and Procyon:

Start of Excerpt 2 from "The Language of God in the Universe:"

In the Dendera Zodiac, Canis Minor is represented by a human figure with a hawk's head named "Sobek," meaning "Conquering," or "Victorious." As seen in previous examples, this hawk's head is a symbol for Yahshua and His victory over the serpent figures in the Zodiac that depict Satan.

Description: Canis Minor is seen as a small dog or wolf that is chasing after Orion, the hunter and following the lead of the bigger canine depicted by Canis Major. Though this sign is depicted as a small dog or wolf today, it was not always seen this way. Its brightest star names reveal what this sign truly stood for.

Bright Stars: "Procyon," "The Redeemer;" "Al Gomesia," "Bearing for Others." From these revealing star names, it is obvious that this sign represented Yahshua in His role as the Redeeming sacrifice that bore our sins on the Cross. The Dendera Zodiac supports this fact. There, Canis Minor is shown as a hawk-headed man carrying a staff. This hawk-man represents the man who will claim the ultimate victory over the serpent who is Satan forever.

After comparing Canis Minor with Canis Major and Gemini, it became clear to me that ***Gemini is one of the most Messianic signs in the Zodiac.*** This is because (as has been shown) Canis Major represents Christ and His followers as the Prince and His royal court, while Canis Minor represents Christ and His followers as the Redeemer and the redeemed. Furthermore, these two decan signs are clearly connected with the Gemini twins, since Castor signifies Christ the Ruler, or Prince, and Pollux depicts Christ as the "one who comes to labor, and is afflicted" (i.e. the Redeemer). Therefore, more than any other sign, Gemini shows Yahshua's dual calling, and suggests His dual coming."

End of Excerpt 2 from "The Language of God in the Universe."

This description of Canis Minor from my first book offers some interesting information, such as the Messianic names of the stars Procyon and Gomesia that refer to Christ's role as the Suffering Servant. It also explains that Canis Major depicts Christ the King and His Israelite court, while Canis Minor depicts His Cross. However, it doesn't note that Canis Minor's stars are not as bright as those of Canis Major. In light of the correlation of Jabal Al Lawz and Midian in Arabia with Canis Minor, this is a significant fact. Indeed, it suggests that - though the light of God that was known and revealed to Moses in the land of

Midian was great - as is attested to in the Old Testament - the Torah was only half as bright as the radiance of the glorious revelations given to us by the Messiah when He came in human flesh and dwelt among us.

Pyramids, Bethlehem, Mount Sinai Tied to Star Gospel

Al Cyone: "The Center" of the Universe, & Yahweh's Symbolic Throne?

Plelades

Mercy to and Judgment of the Gentiles

2 Dahshur Pyramids Depict the Hyades

Hyades

Could the Giza and Dahsur Pyramids be the Pillars that the Sethites built in Mizraim (Egypt)?

Zourak

The Gospel in the Stars Surrounding Taurus & Gemini

Rigel - marks the Foot of Orion (Christ) "that Crushes" the Serpent (Satan)

El Nath

TAURUS

ORION

ERIDANUS

Cursa

LEPUS

Taurus (Bread): Christ's Body Orion (Cup): Christ's Blood

Bellatrix

Christ and His Bride (The Church)

Betelgeuse

Orion's Belt = 3 Pyramids at Giza = 3 Crosses on Calvary

Rigel

Saiph

GEMINI

Mebsuta

Al Henah

MILKY WAY

"The Wounded One" - Christ (Great Pyramid)

CANIS MAJOR

Sirius

CANIS MINOR

Castor

Pullox

Wedding Supper of the Lamb

Al Gomesia

Procyon

Mount Horeb/Sinai tied to Procyon, "the Redeemer" in Canis Minor

Sirius - "Naz Sier" The Prince (Christ) Nazar (The Branch) Christ, the Nazarene!

Bethlehem tied to Sirius - Israel Tied to Canis Major

Since Canis Major houses the brightest and largest stars in our Universe, there is much more glory hidden in this constellation than in

Canis Minor. Sadly, this may upset a few people - especially Messianic Jews that continue to observe and enforce all the Mosaic Laws in the Torah. However, this cannot change the fact that the revelation given on Mount Sinai consisted of limited spiritual and moral wisdom with temporary forgiveness, while the fulfillment of total wisdom and everlasting forgiveness is found in Christ and His indwelling Spirit. Furthermore, the glory of Christ's Palace and Temple in the Millennial Kingdom will far outshine the tent of Moses and the Desert Tabernacle, just as Sirius far outshines Procyon in glory.

During His entire earthly ministry, Christ amended to and improved upon the Mosaic Law by adding love, grace and mercy to every aspect of it. In the process, Yahshua's Law of Love transcended the partial redemption and fellowship that was offered to the Israelites. Indeed, Yahshua offered nothing less than total forgiveness and oneness with God through His Spirit. This oneness was permanently made possible by Christ's atoning blood that was shed on the Cross, and was fully offered to all believers on the Pentecost after His resurrection - just as it will be forevermore.

The giving of the Holy Spirit on the Pentecost that followed Christ's Ascension into Heaven ended the curse of not being able to keep the whole Law by the instatement of the abiding gift of Grace, and opened the way for direct communication with God through visions, dreams and words of knowledge. Today, these same revelatory gifts are still continually being made available to everyone who accepts their need for Christ's redeeming sacrifice, their need to emulate Him in all things, and their need to humbly ask the Holy Spirit to make it so.

What is even more amazing about the spiritual messages cleverly hidden away in Canis Major and Canis Minor is the fact that they show the awesome power of our Almighty God! In fact, combined with the meaning of Taurus and Orion, the meaning of Gemini and its decans offer one of the most complete pictures of the coming Messiah than any other constellations in the night sky! Indeed, the most amazing thing about these star/ground correlations is that they are tied to the Star Gospel.

The reality that the heavens were indeed mirrored on Earth in the far past by a vastly intelligent group of people, and that the section of the sky that they chose to mirror is ripe with messages from the Gospel in the Stars is captured in the detailed star chart on page 153. This illustration conclusively reveals that this area of the sky has many layers of biblical symbolism pertaining to Christ in His role as the Messiah, the Suffering Servant, the Great High Priest, and the conquering King of kings who will come again at the end of the Great Tribulation.

Adding to this amazing Gospel story that is locked into the symbolism of Gemini and Taurus and their decans is the possibility that the center of the visible Universe may be located somewhere in the area of Taurus - around the star called "Al Cyone" or "The Center" in the Pleiades. Even if the Universe has no center as some claim, however, could it be that the ancients saw this star cluster near the junction of Taurus and Aries as the allegorical seat of God's throne in the Third Heaven where God dwells? Interestingly, though, no structures in the desert southwest of Giza have yet been found that correspond to Al Cyone or the Pleiades, these may be buried underneath the shifting sands of the desert - waiting to be found. Since the Pleiades symbolize six of the Seven Churches of Revelation, Al Cyone may also signify the Church of Smyrna, the only one of the six directly tied to the enormous congregation of martyrs that are seen beneath the altar in Heaven that is signified by Taurus and Aries (Rev. 2:8-11, 6:9).

Based on the Star Gospel message of Taurus and Orion revealed here, it is clear that God directed someone in the distant past to carefully mirror these two constellations on the Earth for our benefit. What's even more miraculous is the fact that - long before Israel became a nation, and before Egypt, Bethlehem, Jerusalem, or Mount Sinai even existed, the Preincarnate Yahshua created a star map within that heavenly Gospel message to show us that He always knew exactly where on Earth He would deliver the Law to Moses, where He would be born, where He would die, where He would be resurrected, and where His throne would be forever established. Furthermore, He named the stars connected to this star map to further verify His Plan of Salvation, His hand in creating it all, and His destiny as its total and absolute fulfillment. Isn't that miraculous? In my humble opinion - it certainly is!

The Pillar of Enoch as an Altar to Yah

In addition to charting the course of the Sun, Moon, planets, and stars to determine the length of the year, the antediluvians likely used the Mazzaroth or Zodiac to measure greater lengths of time. When dealing with very long lengths of time, stars alone were probably used to mark the desired reference dates. This practice is evident in the star shafts, and in the overall ground plan for the pyramid complex at Giza.

Interestingly, the star shafts and entrance of the Great Pyramid point to the year 2500 BC as a significant year. This suggests that the

Great Pyramid may have been built on or around that year. Now, Josephus tells us that Abraham taught the science of Astronomy to the ancient Egyptians, and this would have been around 2000 BC. Furthermore, since the Egyptians were descendants of one of Ham's sons born after the Flood, it follows that the Egyptians could *not* have built the Giza Pyramid Complex. Because the ancient Egyptian culture that Abraham knew originated after the Great Flood of 2347 BC, the Pillar of Enoch's construction belongs to a culture that inhabited the area around Giza prior to the Flood. Furthermore, there is no reason why this culture could not have belonged to the righteous Sethite clan, of which Enoch was the seventh patriarch.

Though it existed before the Bible was written, the Great Pyramid conceals the Path to Salvation that is laid out in the Bible very well. In addition, scholars have sought to locate some confirmation of the Great Pyramid's purpose in the Bible. Amazingly, they found this confirmation in the Book of Isaiah:

> *"In that day there will be an altar to the LORD (Yahweh) in the midst of the land of Egypt, and a pillar (Hebrew: mastabah) to the LORD (Yahweh) at its border. And it will be for a sign and for a witness to the LORD of hosts (Yahweh Tsavout) in the land of Egypt; for they will cry to the LORD (Yahweh) because of the oppressors, and He will send them a Savior and a Mighty One, and He will deliver them."* - Isaiah 19:19-20 (NKJ)

Though some believe that this prophecy could have applied to Moses as the savior of the oppressed Israelites, Isaiah was born long after Moses died. This prophecy is therefore speaking of a future time in Egypt's history. In this case, Egypt figuratively represents the Gentile nations where the Ten Lost Tribes of Israel have been scattered. Judging from the context of this Scripture, their Savior and Mighty One will be Yahshua Ha Mashiach at the moment He returns to Earth to set up His Millennial Rule.

At this time, Yahshua will come to free the spiritual Israelites trapped in the figurative place of sin called "Egypt." Thus, Egypt is a synonym for the sinful nations all over the world that will side with the Antichrist. After Yahshua conquers the Antichrist and the wicked nations that the Antichrist controls, an altar to Yahweh will be recognized **that is both in the midst (i.e. center) of the physical land of Egypt, and at its border.** There is only one spot in all of Egypt that fulfills both requirements. This is at Giza, the location of the Great Pyramid. Let's examine why.

The word "Giza" is an Arabic word that means "border." In ancient times, Egypt was divided into two sections called Upper Egypt in the south, and Lower Egypt in the northern Delta region. The dividing line between them was located at Giza. The Great Pyramid at Giza and its two smaller companions therefore may have served as a visual marker dividing the two halves of Egypt. As far as arable land area, Giza is also in the heart of Egypt.

Giza has another peculiarity in relation to the whole Earth. When viewed on an equal surface projection map, Giza lies in the geographical middle between the Eastern Hemisphere, or Orient, and the Western Hemisphere, or Occident. In addition, the Great Pyramid's north-south longitudinal meridian is nearly 30 degrees east of Greenwich, and it also on the 30th north parallel. This gives the site of the Great Pyramid another important distinction. The meridian and parallel at Giza dissect more land, and less water than any other positions on Earth. Giza is therefore the true geographical center of the world's landmasses. *That is why Giza was once known as the "Navel of the World." It is the natural Zero Meridian of the Earth* - far better than the Zero Meridian currently in use, which is Greenwich. This is probably why some ancient maps used the vicinity of Cairo, Egypt as the center point for their cartographic drawings of the Earth's geographical features.

By truly being in the *"the heart of Egypt, at its border,"* the Great Pyramid fulfills one condition of Isaiah's prophecy. The prophecy of Isaiah also says that this place must serve as an altar. As already shown, there is compelling evidence that the Great Pyramid was designed to serve a more sacred function than any other pyramid built on Earth. In fact, it likely served as a sacred Covenant Pillar or mastabah, as is explained in the next section.

The Sacred Pillars of the Melchizedek Priesthood

In Old Testament times, various patriarchs made heaps of stones, or erected enormous, unpolished stones to form solitary pillars as part of Blood Covenant ceremonies. These were used to memorialize sacred pacts between people that had spiritual significance. Sometimes, blood or oil was poured upon these single standing stones, or heaps of stones. This was done either in sacrifice to Yahweh, or to honor a Covenant with God.

To be considered consecrated before Yahweh, these stone pillars that formed layman's altars were *required* to be constructed of rough, undressed stones. The Patriarch Jacob made such a stone pillar at Bethel

- when Yahweh gave him the name Israel. The stone pillar that Jacob erected there marked the renewal of Yahweh's Blood Covenant with Jacob's grandfather, Abraham. As such, **no blood other than that already shed through the rite of circumcision had to be shed to seal this renewed Covenant:**

> *"And God said..., 'Your name is Jacob; your name shall not be called Jacob anymore, but Israel...' Also God said to him: 'I am God Almighty (El Shaddai)...; The land which I gave Abraham and Isaac I give to you; and to your descendants after you...'* **So Jacob set up a pillar (mastabah) in the place where He talked with him, a pillar (mastabah) of stone; and he poured a drink offering on it, and he poured oil on it.** *And Jacob called the name of the place where God spoke with him, Bethel." - Genesis 35:10-15 (NKJ)*

As shown in the Scripture above, a sacred stone heap was called a "mastabah" in Hebrew. "Mastabah" is most often translated in the Bible as "pillar." These sacred pillars were made of either one large, upright, undressed stone, or a pile of such stones. The stones had to be unpolished due to a prohibition Yahweh made against using dressed stones. This appears in the Mosaic Law: *"If you make an altar of stones for me, do not build it with dressed stones"* (Exodus 20:25). This law may have been made so that the altar pillars would reflect the imperfect people making the sacrifices.

Not all mastabahs were used as altars. Some were used as tomb markers, such as the one Jacob built over Rachel's Tomb:

> *"So Rachel died and was buried on the way to Ephrath (that is, Bethlehem).* **And Jacob set a pillar (mastabah) on her grave, which is the pillar of Rachel's grave to this day."** - *Genesis 35:19-20 (NKJ)*

Rachel's Tomb still exists today on the outskirts of Bethlehem, and underneath the domed building that was built around it many years ago is the original tomb, which is topped by a pile of eleven large, uncut stones - one for every son of Jacob living at the time of Rachel's death in childbirth.

In Isaiah's prophecy mentioned before, I have shown in the quotation that the Hebrew word "mastabah" also identifies the altar to Yahweh that is to be found in Egypt. The Great Pyramid, which technically is a beautifully constructed pile of stones, could definitely qualify as a "mastabah." Though its exterior casing was once constructed of outwardly dressed stones that were perfectly fitted together, the core masonry of the Great Pyramid consists of uniformly sized, though *roughly hewn* stone blocks. In their rough appearance, these core masonry blocks therefore resemble the stone "pillars," "menhirs," or groups of menhirs called dolmens that were erected by the ancients all over the world. Before we make a decision about whether or not the Great Pyramid could have served as an altar, however, let's explore the concept of altars in the Old Testament a bit further.

There was another type of altar mentioned in the Bible that was either horned on its four corners, or contained pillars that served as horns. To have horns, these altars had to be made of some worked material such as stone or metal. Horned, finely worked altars consecrated to Yahweh appeared during Mosaic times, when the crude stone altars of laymen that were made to Yahweh were finally outlawed because of the idolatrous abuses often associated with them. However, this was not always the case.

Prior to the Flood, the Bible records that all the patriarchs from the line of Seth acted as, and were considered to be priests as well as leaders and judges for the people they governed. As such, they would have commissioned their people to build altars and to set up Covenant Pillars of undressed stones that served as boundary markers, as well as memorials recognizing agreements between God and various people groups.

According to Genesis, Abel acted as the first patriarchal priest who served Elohim, and, as Abel's divinely ordained replacement, Seth continued this priesthood. This antediluvian priesthood was of the order of Melchizedek, which Christ fulfilled as *"a priest forever, in the order of Melchizedek"* (Psalm 110:4; Hebrews 5:5-6). Therefore, though Moses appointed his Levite brother Aaron as the first High Priest of the Aaronic priesthood, **this was not the only priesthood ordained by God. The Melchizedek priesthood came before the Aaronic, and was superior to it** - just as the Abrahamic Covenant was superior to the one made under the Mosaic Law. Furthermore, since Scripture implies that anyone who served as a priest in the order of Melchizedek was a priest *forever*, it suggests that this priesthood is everlasting, while the time and place for the Aaronic priesthood ended with Christ's First Advent.

There is compelling evidence that all the Pre-Flood patriarchs were regarded as inheritors of this everlasting priesthood. In the Book of Jasher, for example, **Melchizedek - who was the King of Salem and High Priest of "El Elyon" or "God Most High" - is identified as Shem, the son of Noah.** Melchizedek is translated as Adonizedek in the Book of Jasher, though these names are virtually interchangeable, and both mean "King (or Lord) of Righteousness" in Hebrew.

The fact that the Aaronic priesthood was hereditarily passed down suggests that this was also true of the Melchizedek priesthood. Yahshua was called a priest forever in the order of Melchizedek, suggesting that Yahshua inherited that priesthood from Melchizedek and all the hereditary priests who came before him. Yahshua therefore would have inherited this role from an unbroken bloodline of priests that included the patriarchs Seth, Enosh, Cainan, Enoch, Methuselah, Noah, Shem, Abraham, Isaac, Jacob, Moses, and David. Abel, Job, and Jethro (i.e. Reuel) are also notable examples of priest-kings in the order of Melchizedek that were not reckoned in the bloodline of Christ.

Since Christ inherited and fulfilled both the Melchizedek and Aaronic priesthoods in a way that no man before Him ever could, it implies that the Aaronic priesthood did not do away with the Melchizedek priesthood, and that the Melchizedek priesthood continued so that Yahshua could inherit an active and everlasting priestly office. In fact, there is evidence that each tribal leader in Israel acted as a priest and prince/king in the order of Melchizedek until the dedication of the Desert Tabernacle was completed. This is suggested in the Book of Numbers, where each leader of the Twelve Tribes of Israel offered grain, burnt, sin, and peace offerings before Yahweh during the Tabernacle's official dedication as a place of worship and sacrifice (Numbers 7:10-84).

Interestingly, the leader of the Tribe of Judah named Amminadab (meaning "people who give freely") was the first among the leaders of the Tribes of Israel to offer these dedicatory sacrifices in the Tabernacle. Like Amminadab, Yahshua was of the same Royal Tribe, and a priest in the order of Melchizedek. This suggests that the Melchizedek priesthood continued via the patriarchs who led the Tribe of Judah from the time of David up until the time of Christ. This is supported by the fact that King David (2 Samuel 6:17, 24:25), his rebel sons Absalom and Adonijah (2 Samuel 15:12, 1 Kings 1:9), and his son King Solomon acted as priests before Yahweh (1 Kings 3:3, 4, 15). Later, King Josiah of the Tribe of Judah also acted as a priest when he made a Covenant with Yahweh (2 Chronicles 34:30-31).

Though an altar isn't mentioned in the Genesis story of Cain and Abel, both brothers were acting as if they had a right to act as priests before Yahweh. In fact, it may be that their choice of offering was a divinely given test to see which son was truly worthy to carry on the hereditary priesthood that began with their father, Adam. Therefore, when Yahweh rejected Cain's sacrifice, it meant that Abel's bloodline and priesthood were chosen over Cain's to be the source of the Promised Seed, whereas Cain's seed would bring forth the Seed of the Serpent. As will be revealed in later chapters, the Cainites certainly lived up to their notorious legacy.

Now, the reason Abel's sacrifice was acceptable over Cain's is because it required the shedding of innocent blood - a key requirement in the process of redemption, and in cutting a Covenant with God. After the Flood, Noah offered a sacrifice to Yahweh on an altar designated by the Hebrew term "mizbayak" (Genesis 8:20). This same word was used to identify the altar that Isaiah foresaw being revealed in Egypt (Isaiah 19:19), as well as the bronze altar for incense and the altar for burnt offerings used in the Desert Tabernacle. In Tabernacle and Temple times, the bronze altar for burnt offerings was constructed to include four horns on top of the junction of all four sides:

> "You shall make an altar of acacia wood, five cubits long and five cubits wide -- the altar shall be square -- and its height shall be three cubits. **You shall make its horns on its four corners; its horns shall be of one piece with it.** And you shall overlay it with bronze." - Exodus 27:1-2 (NKJ)

These horns were smeared with blood from the animal sacrifices offered upon the altar, and they were made to be one piece with the altar. Could the three pyramids that represent Orion's Belt - coupled with the Great Sphinx - be symbolic of the four horns on the altar to Yahweh described in Exodus? Given the amazing prophetic power of these structures, this seems likely. The Great Pyramid can, therefore, be viewed as part of an immense stone altar constructed of partially dressed and undressed stones. If this is true, then not just the Great Pyramid, but the Giza Plateau as a whole was meant to serve as an altar to Yahweh. If so, the structures built at Giza are part of an immense, immovably imbedded altar stone that also serves as the Navel of the World.

Proof that the Giza Plateau was originally considered to be part of a four-horned altar dedicated to Yahweh is found in the grotto underneath the Great Pyramid, where there is a conspicuous stone abutment in the shape of a lamb's head that, as shown earlier, allegorically represents the Lamb of God! In addition, the stone head and forelegs of the Great Sphinx were formed from an unusual natural stone formation that once jutted high up out of the relatively smooth-surfaced Giza plateau. In addition, each one of the three big pyramids at Giza are built on rises carved into the bedrock of the plateau. They were, therefore, made to be an integral part of the plateau, just as the bronze altar's horns were one piece with it.

Taurus, Aries and Orion: A Temple with Two Altars

As already shown, the constellation of Orion is a symbol for Yahshua's Second Coming in wrath and triumph, and the pyramids at Giza represent Orion's Belt. In Book One, it was also shown that Orion is another symbol for Yahshua in His Role as a conquering King, and the Great Sphinx is a symbol for Yahshua as the Alpha and Omega. Furthermore, in Book Two, it was shown how the sign of Taurus signifies the unleavened bread of Passover, as well as the shed Body of Christ, while the hourglass shape of Orion depicts a giant chalice or cup signifying the third Passover Cup of Redemption, as well as the shed Blood of Christ. In addition, it was shown that the Zodiac signs Taurus and Aries face opposite to each other to serve as a symbolic four-horned altar to Yahweh in Heaven! Therefore, it is fitting that the Giza Plateau - and the Great Pyramid in particular - appear to have been built as an altar dedicated to Yahshua, who served as our Creator God *"in the beginning,"* was our Kinsmen Redeemer and Passover Lamb in 31 AD, and will be our Avenger of Blood and Deliverer at the end of the Tribulation.

Indeed, just as Israel had two calendars - a spiritual one and a civil one - the Zodiac may have two beginning and ending points. Indeed, Aries often houses the Sun when the spiritual calendar of Israel begins, while Virgo often houses the Sun when the Jewish civil calendar begins. Meanwhile, Aquarius signifying Reuben (which Taurus signifying Joseph supplanted) often houses the Sun at the end of the spiritual calendar, while Leo the Lion often houses the Sun at the end of the civil year. As such, both pairs of Zodiac signs serve to illustrate the purpose and ministry of *"the Beginning and the End"* - who is Christ!

This truth is mutely attested to in the symbol of the Great Sphinx, which depicts Yahshua as the Creator and King (Leo), the Seed of the Woman and Desired Son (Virgo/Coma), and the Living Water, which saves us from sin (Aquarius). Just as Leo and Virgo began and ended the Ancient Zodiac, this duality to Christ is seen in the Bible's Book of Revelation where it says: *"I AM the Alpha and the Omega, the Beginning and the End, and the First and the Last"* (Rev. 22:13). Interestingly, this passage of Scripture is numbered 22:13, and both of these numbers are connected to Yahshua's Millennial Rule. After all, The Millennial Kingdom of God is the 13th Great Day, or the Last Day - just as the last letter of the Hebrew alphabet is the 22nd letter.

Based on the fact that the Giza Plateau may be meant to serve as part of a huge earthly Altar to Yahweh that is mirrored in heaven in the Zodiac signs of Taurus and Aries, is it also possible that the constellation of Orion served as another giant altar near this celestial altar? For example, if the four bright stars marking Orion's shoulders and feet are seen as markers for the four horns of a huge altar, then the belt stars of Orion would be in the exact center of that immense altar, and would symbolically represent an atonement sacrifice for sin.

Likewise, if the tips of the four horns belonging to Taurus and Aries are seen as altar horns, then the Pleiades and Hyades appear to represent two atonement sacrifices in the center of this crucially important altar in heaven, which may correspond to the Temple's Altar of Incense and courtyard Altar of Sacrifice! In fact, it may be that the Pleiades depict the lambs sacrificed daily and on Passover, as well as the people who are saved by the blood of the Lamb of God, while the Hyades depict the Bull sacrificed daily outside the camp of Israel, as well as the many people who are now redeemed by Christ's blood. It could also be that the Hyades and Pleiades are connected to the two goats sacrificed in ancient Israel on the Day of Atonement, with the Azazel Goat being led into the desert wilderness to die, while the other goat was sacrificed on the Altar to Yahweh as an atonement sacrifice for all Israel.

It seems fitting that the heavenly altar formed by Taurus and Aries represents the horned Altar of Incense and courtyard Altar of Sacrifice dedicated to Yahweh, while Orion depicts the Altar of Sacrifice outside the Camp of Israel, just as *"the place called Calvary" was outside the walls of Jerusalem.* Indeed, Orion's Belt depicts the Cross of Christ flanked by two other crosses, and serves as the heavenly counterpart to the following Scripture:

> *"And when they had come to the place called Calvary, there they crucified Him, and the criminals, one on the right hand and the other on the left." - Luke 23:33 (NKJ)*

Uncannily, **as seen from the air, each one of the Pyramids at Giza have the geometric appearance of a cross within a square**. These three aligned pyramids could therefore represent the three crosses that were raised on Calvary or Golgotha: the Cross of Christ which corresponds with the middle Pyramid of Khafre, the cross of the repentant robber which corresponds with the Great Pyramid, and the cross for the unrepentant, scornful robber, which corresponds with Menkaure's Pyramid. In addition, the four arms on each cross may depict the four corners of the heavens, and hence all of God's fallen Creation. This symbolism recalls the truth that Christ's blood atonement paid for the sins of the righteous and the unrighteous in every age.

The star names for the three belt stars of Orion fully support this idea. "Al Nitak," meaning "The Wounded One," corresponds with the Great Pyramid, and is the brightest star in Orion's Belt. The middle star in Orion's Belt was named "Al Rai" or "Al Nilam," meaning "Bruised" in Arabic, and corresponds to Khafre's Pyramid. Most significantly, the smallest of the three stars in Orion's Belt that corresponds with the pyramid of Menkaure is named "Mintaka," which means "Divided," or "Cut in Half," as in a Covenant sacrifice. ***Could this be why Orion's three belt stars appear to mimic the Crucifixion of Christ, where two other crosses flanked Christ's Cross?***

Fascinatingly, just as the three pyramids at Giza with their massive stone foundation were located outside of the old city of Mennefer (a.k.a. Memphis, which is now represented by modern Cairo), Christ and the two robbers crucified on either side of Him died on a rocky outcrop outside the old city of Jerusalem. There, Yahshua signed and sealed a New Covenant with His own sacred blood on Calvary, which was the greatest gift to mankind ever given by God the Father. Anyone who accepts this unconditional Covenant by repenting and believing in Christ's miraculous birth, painful sacrificial death for our sins and resurrection into everlasting life are to be forever freed from sin and death, and will take part in the First Resurrection.

In addition, the New Covenant sealed by the Blood of Christ allows all who believe in Yahshua to act with the same authority as He did. This means that anyone who fully believes in Christ and trusts Him to help them can pray in Christ's name or character to thwart Satan's schemes and destroy his evil hold on mankind. Indeed, having supremacy over the Devil and his demons in all ways, Yahshua won back the authority and dominion that Adam and Eve lost. Afterward, Yahshua gave that authority to His saints, thereby negating the effects of the powerlessness that Adam and Eve discovered when they sinned against God and foolishly allowed Satan to usurp their authority.

A powerful symbol of the New Covenant made by Yahshua with mankind was hidden away inside the Desert Tabernacle and Solomon's Temple. It was called the Ark of the Covenant, and the Mercy Seat atop that Ark symbolized the very throne of God that inhabits a place as vast and wide and seemingly infinite as the starry heavens surrounding our Earth. It also symbolized both the literal body of Christ that was sacrificed for sin and the Body of His Bride, the True Church that was saved by His blood. Similarly, the constellation of Orion depicts the sacrificed body of Christ on the Cross, as well as the resurrected Christ at His Second Coming. Therefore, Orion may be a type of heavenly Ark of the Covenant.

Illustration of the Temple and Ark in Heaven

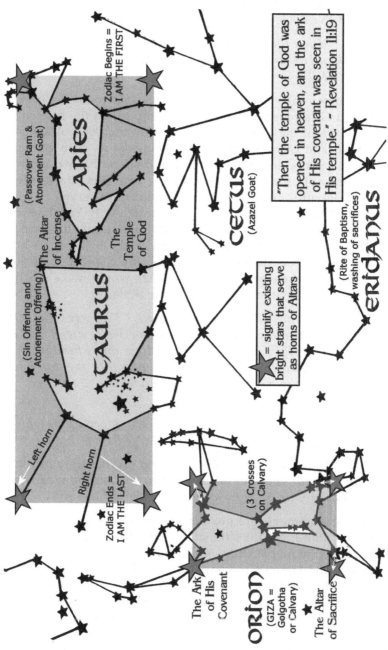

The idea that there is an eternal heavenly counterpart to the Temple of Yahweh in Jerusalem and a heavenly Ark of the Covenant is supported in the Book of Revelation, where it says:

"Then the temple of God was opened in heaven, and the ark of His covenant was seen in His temple." - Revelation 11:19 (NKJ)

As shown in the illustration on page 165, could the pyramids at Dahshur and Giza represent earthly counterparts to the heavenly Temple of God and Ark of the Covenant spoken of in the Book of Revelation? Could Taurus and Orion be heavenly symbols of an even greater heavenly reality in a dimension of time and space that we cannot see? Furthermore, could the connection of these heavenly altars to those five pyramids in Egypt indicate that the pyramids once served as temples and altars to Yahweh before the Flood? Though only Yahshua fully knows the answer to these questions, there are simply too many compelling clues pointing in that direction, and which beg us not to ignore that hypothesis. Indeed, if it is true, the connection of these pyramids to God's heavenly Temple and Ark would make much sense of the following three statements made in the Bible:

"Go and tell My servant David, "Thus says the LORD (Yahweh): Would you build a house for Me to dwell in? For I have not dwelt in a house since the time that I brought the children of Israel up from Egypt, even to this day, but have moved about in a tent and in a tabernacle.'" - 2 Samuel 7:5-6 (NKJ)

"Blessed be the LORD (Yahweh) out of Zion, who dwells in Jerusalem!" - Psalm 135:21 (NKJ)

"But I am the LORD your God (Yahweh your Elohim), [who brought you] out of Egypt. You shall acknowledge no God but me, no Savior except me." - Hosea 13:4 (NIV)

These statements are puzzling because they all indicate that Yahweh God identifies Himself as the God who came out from a symbolic home He had already established in Egypt, and allowed the Israelites to build Him a temporary home in the Desert Tabernacle. Note, for example, that Psalm 135 hints that Yahweh came out of Zion, which most certainly is a reference to the Great Pyramid and the Giza Pyramid Complex as a whole. Note especially the words in parentheses that were added to Hosea 13:4 even though there are no Hebrew words there that would support this translation of the text. In other words, the passage literally says: ***"I am the LORD your God out of Egypt."*** It does not say that God brought the Israelites out of Egypt, but that *the Shekinah Glory of God came out of Egypt!*

Due to these references, there is a possibility that the Great Pyramid served as a type of Ark of the Covenant where God's presence dwelt in Egypt until it left with the Israelites. In fact, if true, *this would clearly explain why the Coffer in the King's Chamber of the Great Pyramid is exactly the same dimensions as the Ark of the Covenant.* It would also explain why - as carefully shown in Book Four - the chambers inside the Great Pyramid are tied in design and meaning to various parts of the Desert Tabernacle and Temple to Yahweh.

Since the Great Pyramid and neighboring pyramids at Giza and Dahshur may represent a horned altar dedicated to Yahweh and His Son Yahshua, or alternatively served as a temple complex in which God's Shekinah Glory was symbolically housed before the Israelites built the Tabernacle and Ark of the Covenant, religious rites were likely performed there after the Great Pyramid's construction, and may have continued until its true purpose was forgotten. As such, patriarchs and priests in the eternal order of Melchizedek would have been the main officiates at any ceremonies or rituals carried out near the Great Pyramid prior to the Flood.

If the Great Pyramid complex is part of the altar built to Yahweh in Egypt that is mentioned in Isaiah (and I firmly believe that it is), then it is Yahshua Himself who will re-consecrate this holy altar and pillar to Yahweh during His Millennial rule on Earth. This is when Christ, our great High Priest, will show the world all the secrets that the Great Pyramid and Giza Complex were designed to hold and reveal. In addition, Yahshua will reveal the full meaning of the Red and Bent Pyramids at Dahshur, and will also disclose who their builders were.

Nonetheless, though Yahshua has not yet returned to illuminate the past to us, the meaning of the pyramids at Dahshur do not have to remain a mystery to us. Just as the Great Pyramid, Jerusalem and Bethlehem, and Mount Horeb are tied to constellations in the night sky that are loaded with deep messianic meanings, the pyramids at Dahshur serve to bring the Star Gospel surrounding Taurus the Bull and its' two horns down to Earth in an effort to reveal God's will to mankind. As such, the two Dahshur pyramids were likely built by the same righteous line of Sethites that built the Giza Complex.

As already shown, the Dahshur Pyramids were aligned with the two most prominent stars in the Hyades star cluster, which define the face of the heavenly bull called Taurus. As shown in the other books in the Language of God Series, the sign of Taurus has a dual meaning. This is derived from its two horns, which are tied to two different congregations that carry opposing spiritual and material ideologies.

These two congregations are alluded to in the two prominent star clusters in Taurus: the Hyades and the Pleiades. In fact, these two congregations can be accurately defined by studying the allegorical meanings of these two star clusters. For example, just as the Hyades star cluster defines the eyes and mind of Taurus, which represents Christ coming in judgment, so too the people signified by the Hyades are people who think as Christ does, and do His Will. On the other hand, the Pleiades that are sitting on Taurus' back appear to be enjoying the fruits of calling themselves Christians, but tend to live outside of God's Will. These are those many lazy or backslidden Christians who are enjoying Christ's material blessings without having any spiritual strength. In other words, they will not die to and come out of the world in order to live for Christ as the people signified by the Hyades have done.

Because of this, though the Pleiades may represent the Tribulation Saints from the Tribulation churches that are riding to victory in Christ, they may also signify the Apostate Church riding on the back of the Beast from the Sea. The Harlot riding this Red Bull or Beast signifies the Apostate Church that worships the Beast, and it is chillingly mimicked in the symbol of the European Union, which happens to be the Greek noblewoman Europa being abducted on the back of a leaping bull signifying the Pagan god Zeus. Sadly, if this analogy is indeed accurate, then the apostate members of the Tribulation churches will likely die as a representation of the Azazel goat, or scapegoat on the Day of Atonement. Meanwhile, the martyred saints of Christ in the Great Tribulation will signify the goat that was killed as an atonement sacrifice on the Altar to Yahweh on the Day of Atonement, or Yom Kippur in ancient Israel.

Interestingly, the Pleiades star cluster contains a super bright star known as Al Cyone, meaning "the Center." Some Scientists say that the center of the known Universe may be in the vicinity of the Pleiades, though the most current research indicates that our ever-expanding Universe may not have a central point or nucleus. If this is true, then perhaps Al Cyone is symbolically pointing not to the center of the Universe, but to the vicinity of God's heavenly Throne Room, where Christ now sits at the right hand of His Father, and from where He will judge all unrepentant sinners at the Last Judgment. In this case, Al Cyone's name may represent the center of the conflict between God and Satan, good and evil, and light and darkness. For now, however, only God and His holy angels truly know the meaning of this star's name.

Sirius or Jupiter as the Star of Bethlehem?

In Book One, a considerable amount of time was spent showing that there need not have been a supernatural phenomenon associated with the Star of Bethlehem, and that it most likely was the unusual behavior and alignments of the Messiah planet Jupiter that served as that miraculous star over a two year period. However, that was before I learned that the stars Sirius A and B appear to be directly associated with the town of Bethlehem and the city of Jerusalem. Considering this new information, it appears quite clear that Sirius is, and always has been the Star of Bethlehem in the truest sense of the word.

On September 11th, 3 BC, a sign appeared in the heavens that announced Christ's imminent birth. This sign perfectly mimicked the sign in heaven prophesied about in Revelation 12:1-2. This was of the Woman clothed with the Sun - a sign made up of the Zodiac signs Virgo and Leo, the Sun, Moon and Jupiter in the early morning sky due east over Bethlehem (See Book One for all the pertinent facts surrounding this sign).

At 12:24 a.m. the next day, the star Sirius rose on the horizon in the southeast. Over the next few months, when viewed at midnight, Sirius gradually appeared higher and higher in the southern sky. Then, at midnight on December 25th, 2 BC - when the Magi may have first met Yahshua - Sirius appeared at midpoint high in the southern sky. At the same time, Jupiter, the Messiah planet rose in the east in the upper torso portion of the sign of Virgo the Virgin, which allegorically represented the toddler Messiah (Jupiter) feeding at His mother Miriam's breast (Virgo).

The suburban town of Bethlehem is about 5 miles south of Jerusalem, and shortly after midnight on December 25th, Sirius could be seen in Jerusalem's sky in the direction of the town of Bethlehem. Thus, if Sirius B had been in its Supernova stage at that time - and depending on how bright the debris cloud around it was - it may have served as an incredibly luminous and beautiful beacon over Bethlehem that the Magi could not have missed.

In my studies of the mysteries surrounding the Star of Bethlehem over the years, some have speculated that the star that led the Magi to Yahshua's birthplace may have been in the Supernova stage, which means it was a star that had reached the end of its time as a Red Giant and was beginning to collapse into itself to form a white dwarf. At this time, stars are thought to emit a cloud of gas and debris as they implode. This cloud is called a Supernova, and these can remain visible for several weeks, months or years before fading from view.

Given that Sirius B is a small white dwarf star today, the fact that it may once have been an old Red Giant star that later formed a Supernova seems to be a very real possibility. In fact, it is possible that the Supernova formed by Sirius B in the past could have occurred at the time that Christ was about to be born in Bethlehem, and that it remained visible until the Magi found Him there as a toddler in His mother Miriam's loving arms.

Interestingly, if Sirius B's Supernova stage became visible on Earth at the time of Christ's birth, it would not only have served as a sign that Christ had been born, but that Jerusalem was no longer the guiding spiritual light of the world. Instead, Yahshua the Messiah - the living Word of God who is the true Light of the World - had finally arrived. Indeed - as intimated by Sirius A's Bethlehem association - Yahshua is, was and always will be the guiding light of not only the world, but the entire Universe.

One intriguing bit of evidence for Sirius B having gone Supernova around the time of Christ's birth is found in the fact that Sirius was described as a reddish-hued (i.e. Red Giant) star in ancient times, while today it is unquestionably a brilliant blue-white star. Of course, since there is no specific reference to any Supernova in any surviving records from that time in history, we can only speculate if Sirius B's Supernova stage had become visible at the time of Yahshua's birth. In addition, even if it could be proven that Sirius B was visible as a Supernova at that time, there is no doubt that Jupiter's position and behavior from September 3 BC through the end of 2 BC was extraordinary in connection with the sign of the Woman clothed with the Sun.

The Heavenly Promise and the Earthly Reality

In the last few chapters, we have spent much time focusing on the symbolic meanings of the material realities surrounding our Earth. In the process, this study has shown how much of the written Gospel in the Bible was already known to our remotest righteous ancestors through the auspices of the Star Gospel. Yet, despite all the incredible knowledge hidden in the stars that populate the Mazzaroth, and all we can learn from studying the interrelationships of the constellations with the Bible, neither one of these spiritual revelations that were so graciously given to us by God will last forever in their present form.

This is because every prophecy, priest, king, and ritual of the Bible, and every prophecy and character in the Star Gospel has found their ultimate fulfillment and realization in Yahshua the Messiah - the Word of God made flesh. Indeed, the Bible makes it abundantly and repeatedly clear that every symbol and ritual introduced in the Law and the Prophets were fulfilled through Christ's perfect, sinless life and ministry, and His sacrificial death on the Cross. Furthermore, every aspect of these heavenly and biblical prophecies will soon be fulfilled on another level by Christ during His Millennial Rule on Earth. For confirmation of this, we need to study the Old Testament rituals and sacrifices that looked forward to the day when their purpose would be fulfilled in Christ. One of the most important of these rituals fell on the Day of Atonement.

On the very first Day of Atonement, Moses' older brother Aaron - as the high priest of all Israel - performed the rites necessary for the atonement sacrifice that extended temporary forgiveness to the people for another year. His duties on that day are vividly described in the Book of Leviticus, Chapter 16. There, it says:

> "Thus Aaron shall come into the Holy Place: with the blood of a young bull as a sin offering, and of a ram as a burnt offering." - Leviticus 16:3 (NKJ)

Now, though this was on the Day of Atonement, this bull and ram that Aaron was instructed to offer up were part of the daily ritual sacrifices performed every single day to temporarily secure God's forgiveness of the Israelites. On this particular day, however, they were especially important because they sanctified Aaron so that he could function as High Priest, and they also sanctified the altar so that it was ready to bear the atonement sacrifice. These sacrifices temporarily covered Aaron's sins so that he could go into the Most Holy Place without being struck dead before the Ark of the Covenant. Once there, Aaron would sprinkle the blood of the bull and a male goat on the Mercy Seat of the Ark to temporarily guarantee the atonement of the people whose names were written in the Book of Life for another year (Daniel 7:10, 12:1).

After ritually washing, dressing in special white linen robes and being sanctified by the sacrifices of the bull and ram, Aaron did the following:

> "And he shall take from the congregation... **two kids of the goats as a sin offering, and one ram as a burnt offering. Aaron is to offer the bull**... to make atonement for himself and his household. Then he is to take the two goats and present them before the LORD (Yahweh) at the entrance to the Tent of Meeting. He is to cast lots for the two goats -- one lot for the

LORD (Yahweh) and the other for the scapegoat. Aaron shall bring the goat whose lot falls to the LORD (Yahweh) and sacrifice it for a sin offering. But the goat chosen by lot as the scapegoat shall be... used for making atonement by sending it into the desert..." - Leviticus 16:5-10

Note that on that holy day, Aaron had to sacrifice a bull, a ram, and a goat as atonement sacrifices, just as is intimated by the altar in heaven symbolized by the adjacent Zodiac signs of Taurus and Aries. Uncannily, the symbol for Aries in the Square Zodiac of Dendera found in the Temple to Hathor shows a male ram with two different sets of horns: a male ram's curved horns and a male goat's straight horns. This is just one more sign that the two depictions of the Zodiac carved in the Temple complex at Dendera were not the product of Pagans, but of godly people familiar with the ritual need for Blood Atonement, and the symbolic spiritual meaning of sheep and goats. How sad that Satan nearly succeeded in obliterating their godly origins in ancient times just as he is succeeding in destroying and attacking every tenant of Christianity in the world today.

After sacrificing the bull, ram, and one goat, Aaron took the blood of the bull and goat and sprinkled it on the four horns of the Altar of Sacrifice:

*"No one is to be in the Tent of Meeting from the time Aaron goes in to make atonement in the Most Holy Place until he comes out, having made atonement for himself, his household and the whole community of Israel. Then he shall come out to the altar that is before the LORD (Yahweh) and make atonement for it. **He shall take some of the bull's blood and some of the goat's blood and put it on all the horns of the altar. He shall sprinkle some of the blood on it with his finger seven times** to cleanse it and to consecrate it from the uncleanness of the Israelites." - Leviticus 16:17-19*

From this passage, it can be seen that these altar horns unquestionably represented the four horns of the sacrificed bull and goat or ram, which in turn represent the four corners of the Earth. In addition, their sprinkled blood represented the blood of Yahshua that was shed in Jerusalem even before He was crucified. Yahshua's cruel bloodletting began when our loving Savior Yahshua was falsely accused, heartlessly sentenced, mocked and beaten bloody by Jewish members of the Sanhedrin (Matthew 26:67-68). After that, while they mocked Him, a crown of long, needle-sharp thorns was literally beaten into Yahshua's skull with a reed by Roman solders (Matthew 27:29-30). Immediately after that, the soldiers flogged, mocked Yahshua again and beat Him bloody with their fists (Matthew 27:27-31; John 19:1-3). In the end, as the movie "The Passion of the Christ" graphically conveyed, Yahshua's tortured body and the ground beneath Him were liberally sprinkled with His blood, just as the horns of the altar in Jerusalem were liberally sprinkled with innocent blood. How awful that our perfect and innocent Savior had to suffer so terribly to secure our salvation!

Bull, Goat and Scapegoat Depicted at Giza and Golgotha

As the Gospels clearly convey, Yahshua was not alone when He was crucified at Golgotha. He shared His agonizing death with two other men - one on His right and the other on His left - just as the spiritual sheep and goats are to be divided on the Last Day (Matthew 25:33). As discussed in Book Two, these robbers may have been two of Yahshua's key disciples: James and John, the Sons of Zebedee. But, regardless of who they were, they were called robbers to teach this important spiritual lesson: *all sinners are divinely viewed as thieves and robbers that must rely on dead animals and self-directed good works for their potential atonement until they are saved and receive Christ's free gift of Grace!*

To understand this better, let's closely look at the robbers who took part in Christ's crucifixion (Mark 15:27). Now, the Scriptures say that one robber believed that Yahshua was the Messiah, but the other one cruelly mocked and rejected Yahshua:

> *"Then one of the criminals who were hanged blasphemed Him, saying, 'If You are the Christ, save Yourself and us.' But the other, answering, rebuked him, saying, 'Do you not even fear God, seeing you are under the same condemnation? And... we receive the due reward of our deeds; but this Man has done nothing wrong.' Then he said to Jesus, 'Lord (Adonai), remember me when You come into Your kingdom.' And Jesus said to him, 'Assuredly, I say to you, today you will be with Me in Paradise.'"* - Luke 23:39-43 (NKJ)

By studying the nature of the robbers, as well as the nature of the crucifixion utilizing the Language of God, a hidden spiritual message to mankind is revealed. First of all, the robber who believed in Yahshua allegorically signifies all the spiritual sheep that lovingly follow their Messiah, while the robber who rejected Yahshua represents all the spiritual goats that will rebel against and reject His salvation. In addition, these two robbers represent the two goats that were chosen on the Day of Atonement. This can easily be seen by studying the allegorical meaning of the Giza Pyramids, as shown in the illustration on this page:

Sacred Meaning Behind the Giza Pyramid Complex

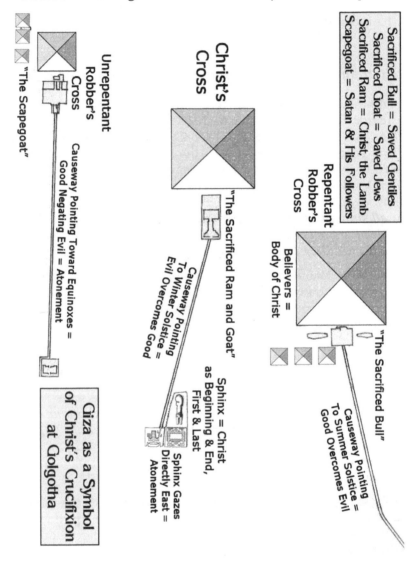

When looking at Giza from the air, the Great Pyramid or Pillar of Enoch is to the east or right of the middle pyramid associated with the Great Sphinx, while the smaller pyramid connected to Menkaure is to the left of the middle pyramid. Now, since Yahshua was crucified between the two robbers, the middle pyramid should represent His Cross. Though this pyramid is not as large as the Great Pyramid, it is very close to it in size, suggesting the greatness of the man it is connected to.

In verification of its connection to the Cross of Yahshua, this pyramid's causeway leads to the Great Sphinx, which symbolizes the message behind the Zodiac signs of Leo, Aquarius, and Virgo. Virgo (Eve and the Garden of Eden) and Leo (Christ as King) are the beginning and ending themes of the Zodiac, which represents the entire history of mankind's salvation. Indeed, Christ is the First and the Last dispenser of salvation, and the Beginning and the End of all Creation. In addition, Leo signifies Christ's role as an Avenger of Blood for all those martyred for their faith, and Aquarius represents the inexhaustible flow of the Holy Spirit on humanity during the Millennial Kingdom.

Other allegorical spiritual messages are hidden in the middle pyramid's causeway, which points to the Winter Solstice sunrise but ends with the Sphinx gazing at the Equinox sunrises. These two solar positions on the horizon convey truths about Yahshua's two-fold purpose. For example, the Winter Solstice - when the darkness signifying evil is at its fullest - represents the punishment for sin, which is death and separation from God. Yahshua suffered this punishment for all mankind when He died on the Cross. In connection to the animals sacrificed on the Day of Atonement, the middle pyramid at Giza is connected to the sacrificial ram offered up on that day along with a bull. These both signify Christ's role as the Lamb of God who takes away the sins of the world - just as depicted in Taurus and Aries. To make atonement for us, Christ became sin for us. This was represented by the goat sacrificed on the altar on the Day of Atonement.

At the moment He died, Yahshua - the Light of the World - was extinguished under the crushing weight and total darkness of humanity's sins. Yet, Yahshua was also first recognized as the King of kings by the Magi - who visited Him near to the Winter Solstice, and during the Feast of Chanukah, or Jewish Festival of Lights. As the Light above all the other lights of the World that follow Him, Yahshua will one day obliterate every dark place in the Universe! Meanwhile, the Equinoxes signify the concept of atonement, which is the negation of evil with good. Negation implies more than destruction. Rather, it calls for the complete removal of all evil.

Christ's perfect righteousness provided our everlasting atonement, and His blood perfectly covers over and washes away our sins. In other words, Christ's perfect blood sacrifice promises believers that the evil within them will be fully negated in the First Resurrection, and we will be made fully perfect in Him.

Now, the robber who believed in Yahshua's ministry (Luke 23:40-43), accepted His sacrifice, and was promised a place in paradise with Him immediately after death is signified by the Great Pyramid, which stands to the right of the middle pyramid, and signifies the sheep who follow the Good Shepherd Yahshua. In addition, the Great Pyramid represents the goat sacrificed on the altar on the Day of Atonement. Remember that this goat was offered up not just for one redeemed sinner, but for millions upon millions of forgiven, glorified saints that make up the pyramidal Body of Christ as depicted by Taurus the Bull, which signifies Gentile believers, and Aries the Ram, which signifies Jewish believers. Furthermore, Christ's coming kingship over His Body, the Church is signified by the missing capstone of the Great Pyramid (Psalm 118:22; Mark 12:10), and the causeway of the Pillar of Enoch points directly to the Summer Solstice - when darkness is allegorically overcome with light. This signifies that Christ's followers will completely triumph over evil one day soon.

Intriguingly, there are several boat pits at the foot of the Pillar of Enoch that may all contain large, dismantled high-prowed wooden sea-faring vessels in the Egyptian style. One certainly did when it was excavated and re-assembled in recent years, and it is now housed in a special building near to the pyramid that is open to tourists. In light of the enormous hidden meaning behind this pyramid, there is no doubt that these boat pits have allegorical meaning as well. Let's explore that meaning.

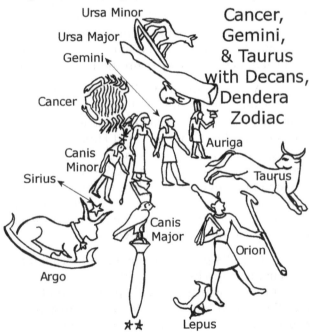

In the Dendera Zodiac, the star Sirius of Canis Major is depicted between the horns of a great bull that is reclining in exactly the same type of high-prowed boat that was buried at Giza. The bull signifies the sign of Taurus and the boat represents the constellation Argo the Ship, which in recent years was renamed and divided into four different constellations that signify different parts of a ship. Since Argo is far in the southern sky below Canis Major, Sirius, the belts stars of Orion, and the bright stars in Taurus could be seen as allegorical passengers on board, which is likely why the ancient Mage who carved the Dendera Zodiac created this particular symbol that combines these three different constellations.

Fascinatingly, Argo the ship can be viewed as sailing along the heavenly river named Eridanus, which is the celestial counterpart of the Jordan River. Therefore, it can represent a heavenly ship of salvation that is sailing toward the New Jerusalem! In ancient times, ships often had the connotation of being like water going serpents and were often depicted with a serpent-like form. As such, ships represent the transforming of something evil (the serpent) into something good (an ark or safe haven in inhospitable territory). It therefore signifies the overcoming of evil with good! Could this be why some legends state that the benevolent "god" Quetzalcoatl came to the New World on a ship covered with serpent skins? We will discuss Quetzalcoatl's connection to both Noah and Shem in the last chapter.

Returning to analyzing the meaning of the Giza Complex, the smaller pyramid to the left of the middle pyramid signifying Christ's Cross stands for the crucified robber that was angry at Christ and mocked Him (Mat. 27:44; Luke 23:39). This unrepentant robber was spiritually stubborn like a goat, and he and those who are like him may potentially perish for rejecting Christ's atonement sacrifice. Satan - who was represented by the scapegoat on the Day of Atonement - certainly will perish, along with many of his followers. When Yahshua died, however, He took the place of unruly (i.e. sinful) goats and paid their death penalty - whether they accept it or not. Indeed, because this small pyramid's causeway points toward the Equinoxes, which represent Christ's perfect atonement, it suggests that unrepentant sinners are covered by Yahshua's sacrifice until the very end, and will be spared at the Last Judgment if they are finally willing to repent and seek God's mercy and forgiveness. As verification, this is clearly implied in the Parable of the Workers (See Matthew 20:1-16). Though some believers may balk at this, it nonetheless underlines the suggestion that God takes no pleasure in seeing anyone perish, and His mercy truly is great - but only if even the worst of sinners can sincerely repent and humbly ask for forgiveness (2 Peter 3:9).

Now, go back and take a look at the illustrations of Stonehenge on pages 104 and 105, and compare them with the illustration of the Giza Pyramid Complex on page 174. As you do, remember that Stonehenge's main axis points to the Summer Solstice - just as the Great Pyramid's causeway does. Could this be another indicator that the center circle of monoliths called the Sarsen Circle is indeed meant to represent the Most Holy Place? Could it also be that Stonehenge is a visual metaphor for the very Throne room of Almighty God as described in the Book of Revelation? In addition, could the Aubrey Circle represent the Holy Place where the redeemed saints will gather to worship and glorify God after the Rapture, and where they will partake in the Wedding of the Lamb?

Could Stonehenge have been built by the righteous human followers of Yahweh with the aid of holy Watchers like Uriel, and was it made to instruct mankind about their ultimate purpose? This is certainly possible and would explain why it exhibits knowledge that the common people of that time era were generally ignorant of. If so, it is just as likely that the Pillar of Enoch in Egypt was built by the Sethites with the aid of the Watchers to preserve their knowledge of the coming Messiah for future generations. In addition, this mighty pyramid may stand as a symbol for the ultimate place of the righteous in Christ's everlasting Kingdom. Indeed, the truth that the Great Pyramid represents the Kingdom of God seems to be encoded in Scripture since Mount Zion appears to refer to the Great Pyramid and its heavenly counterpart:

> *"Then I looked, and behold, a Lamb standing on Mount Zion, and with Him one hundred and forty-four thousand, having His Father's name written on their foreheads." - Revelation 14:1 (NKJ)*

Could it be that - on one fateful day during the Great Tribulation - Christ will literally stand atop the Great Pyramid with His 144,000 Witnesses just as Revelation 14:1 intimates? If so, will Christ cap and complete that unfinished pyramid at that time? It certainly is possible that Christ and His Witnesses will repair and finish this artificial mountain that was built in Christ's honor by our righteous ancestors. At that time, they may also reconsecrate that magnificent ancient altar to God. After that, Christ may send His Witnesses to preach in the four corners of the Earth - corners that are appropriately signified by the Great Pyramid's four corners.

In direct contrast to this, the small Pyramid at Giza attributed to Pharaoh Menkaure signifies the robber that rejected Christ on Calvary and the scapegoat on the Day of Atonement. This goat was also known as the Azazel goat signifying the fallen Watcher Azazel (i.e. Satan):

> *When Aaron has finished making atonement for the Most Holy Place, the Tent of Meeting and the altar, he shall bring forward the live goat. He is to lay both hands on the*

head of the live goat and confess over it all the wickedness and rebellion of the Israelites... and put them on the goat's head. He shall send the goat away into the desert... The goat will carry on itself all their sins to a solitary place; and the man shall release it in the desert." - Leviticus 16:20-22

The ritual of total abandonment described in the preceding Scripture graphically portrays what Hell will be like for Satan and all those who follow him in rebellion against God. Like the scapegoat, all unrepentant sinners will be abandoned forever in a barren, lifeless place of unending heat, thirst and everlasting torment. And like the scapegoat, they will forever remain spirits whose mortal resurrected bodies will perish in the heat of the Lake of Fire, and whose spirits will never be able to escape from it. This is the horrible fate that awaits all the angels and people who rebel against God without remorse. Indeed, there will be no escape for anyone who refuses to worship the Lamb or humbly accept His sacrifice for their sins. How tragic that so many currently seem destined to dwell in Hell forever. May Yahweh help them all!

Another fact of the crucifixion represented at Giza is that the whole grisly event occurred just outside the walls of the old city of Jerusalem. Likewise, Giza is just outside of the much greater area that the New Jerusalem will one day encompass, which will include all of the Sinai Wilderness to Egypt's eastern desert border, and all of the land north of modern Israel up to the borders of the Euphrates River as per Revelation 21:16: *"The city is laid out as a square; its length is as great as its breadth. And he measured the city with the reed: twelve thousand furlongs (or stadia). Its length, breadth, and height are equal."*

Note that the New Jerusalem is described as having an enormous square base, with each side of the city being 12,000 furlongs or stadia in length. Now, one stadium is 600 feet long, meaning that the New Jerusalem will have an incredible side length of 7,200,000 feet! Since there are 5,280 feet in a statute mile, the New Jerusalem will measure 1,363.63 miles per side, and its height will equal that length! So, though this could be envisioned as a giant cube-shaped city, it is more likely that the New Jerusalem will mimic the aesthetically beautiful shape of the Great Pyramid - only on a much grander scale! If so, the Great Pyramid may be a small representation of the New Jerusalem. Also known as the City of God, the New Jerusalem will be the everlasting home of Christ's Bride, the True Church. It will cover all the territory once belonging to the ancient Kingdom of Israel, stretching all the way to Egypt in the south and Turkey in the north. Like old Jerusalem, the Great Pyramid, Great Sphinx and the Sphinx Temple may also receive a makeover in eternity so that they can forever commemorate Christ's death and resurrection outside of the New Jerusalem's sacred walls.

Uncannily, there are other secrets hidden in this region that will one day serve as the foundation of the New Jerusalem. One of them is found in the shape of the Kingdom of Ancient Israel, which covered about the same amount of land as the New Jerusalem will one day. As shown in the first illustration on page 181, this land area is roughly in the shape of a Shofar, or trumpet made from a Ram's Horn, as shown in the illustration inset. Why hasn't anyone seemed to notice this, or comment on the fact that this Shofar appears to follow the same path as the great highway that will reach from Egypt to Assyria during the Millennial Rule of Christ? In addition, it may trace the path that the 144,000 Witnesses will take after meeting Yahshua on Mount Zion during the Great Tribulation, and the path that Yahshua will take when He comes to save Israel in the Battle of Armageddon.

Intriguingly, several Scriptures connected to the Day of the Lord mention the sounding of a great trumpet, a highway stretching from Egypt to Assyria, the city of Jerusalem, and the Lord (Yahweh) coming out of Zion to rescue Jacob or Israel:

> *"In that day there will be a highway from Egypt to Assyria, and the Assyrian will come into Egypt and the Egyptian into Assyria, and the Egyptians will serve with the Assyrians." - Isaiah 19:23 (NKJ)*

> *"In that day the LORD (Yahweh) will thresh from the flowing Euphrates to... Egypt, and you, O Israelites, will be gathered up... And in that day a great trumpet will sound. Those who were perishing in Assyria and those who were exiled in Egypt will come and worship the LORD (Yahweh) on the holy mountain in Jerusalem." - Isaiah 27:12-13 (NIV)*

> *"Oh, that the salvation of Israel would come out of Zion! When the LORD (Yahweh) brings back the captivity of His people, let Jacob rejoice and Israel be glad." - Psalm 14:7 (NKJ)*

> *"Blow the trumpet in Zion, and sound an alarm in My holy mountain! Let all the inhabitants of the land tremble; for the day of the LORD (Yahweh) is coming, for it is at hand: A day of darkness and gloominess, a day of clouds and thick darkness..." - Joel 2:1-2 (NKJ)*

Israel, Yahshua's Shofar or Ram's Horn

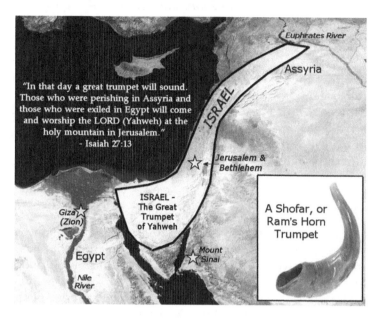

Sacred Places Tied to Christ, the One-Horned Ram

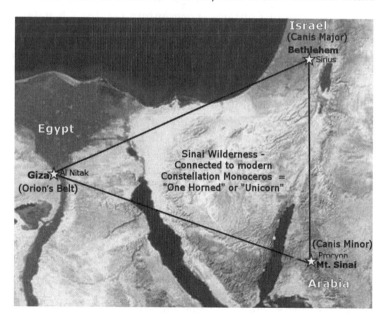

*"And so all Israel will be saved, as it is written: **'The Deliverer will come out of Zion**, and He will turn away ungodliness from Jacob; For this is My covenant with them, when I take away their sins.'" - Romans 11:26-27 (NKJ) (also see Isaiah 59:20-21)*

Note that the first of the five Scriptures just quoted appears shortly after Isaiah's prophetic reference to the Great Pyramid as the Altar to Yahweh *"in the midst of the land of Egypt"* (Isaiah 19:19). These Scriptures make it fairly clear that Zion, Egypt, Israel, Jerusalem, and Assyria are all connected to the trumpet imagery of the Bible surrounding the coming of the Day of the Lord, or the Millennial Rule of Christ. As such, they all may collectively be seen as a part of Zion, though the Pillar of Enoch seems to have been the first place on Earth labeled that way.

Another hidden meaning related to Israel as a symbolic ram's horn trumpet is found in looking at a new constellation that has been added to the sky between Canis Major, Canis Minor, and Orion. This constellation happens to be called Monoceros, and - as shown in the second illustration on page 181 - it is within the boundaries of the triangle formed by connecting Al Nitak, Sirius and Procyon with lines. Monoceros means "One Horned" as found in a unicorn, and - as shown in Book Four - a unicorn can serve both as a symbol for Christ - and the Antichrist. It can also represent the right horn of Taurus, which is connected to the Tribe of Ephraim representing Gentile Christianity.

Now, if Monoceros were to be depicted on the Earth, its stars would signify various locales within the triangle-shaped Sinai Wilderness between Israel and Egypt. In other words, in the recent past, God saw to it that what I am revealing here would be verified and divinely acknowledged by the creation of a new constellation called "One Horned" in the bowl portion of a symbolic horn or trumpet formed by Israel's old borders! This suggests that Yahshua, the One-Horned Ram foreseen by Enoch - as opposed to the One-Horned Goat belonging to the Antichrist seen by Daniel - will come from Zion (i.e. the Great Pyramid) with an army of saints and angels, will go into Israel from that direction, and then will go as far as Assyria to conquer the Antichrist's armies and re-establish the old boundaries of Israel under King David.

All of this horn and trumpet symbolism that is tied to Israel is also connected to the animal horns blown on Rosh Hashanah, or the Feast of Trumpets, and the animals sacrificed on the Day of Atonement, or Yom Kippur. Ideally, animals sacrificed as sin and atonement offerings sported horns. Though Yahshua did not have literal horns on His head like rams or goats, John the Baptist called our Messiah *"the*

Lamb of God who takes away the sins of the world" (John 1:29). Indeed, even the very shape of the land of Israel from the air recognizes Yahshua's symbolic role as the One Horned Ram of Yahweh who died for our sins. In addition, the sounding of trumpets is mentioned repeatedly in connection with the Rapture of the True Church, which will likely occur before Yahshua's Second Coming (Mat. 24:31; 1 Cor. 15:52; 1 Thess. 4:16; Rev. 4:1).

Heavenly Animals as Symbols of Blood Atonement

The place of Christ's crucifixion, which was outside of old Jerusalem's ancient walls, was graphically represented on the Day of Atonement or Yom Kippur, which is and always was the holiest day of the Israelite liturgical year. On Yom Kippur, even modern non-religious Jews still find the time to go to their neighborhood synagogue and pray for God's forgiveness.

Early in Israel's history, Aaron became the first to offer the special blood sacrifices prescribed by God on the Day of Atonement. On that day, a ram was burned on the Tabernacle's altar inside the camp, and a bull and goat were burned whole on an altar outside the Israelite camp:

> *"The bull for the sin offering and the goat for the sin offering, whose blood was brought in to make atonement in the Holy Place, shall be carried outside the camp. And they shall burn in the fire their skins, their flesh, and their offal. For on that day the priest shall make atonement for you... for the Holy Sanctuary... for the tabernacle of meeting and for the altar, and he shall make atonement for the priests and for all the people of the assembly." - Leviticus 16:27-29, 33 (NKJ)*

Per Yahweh's orders, the bodies of the bull and goat were to be burned whole and together on the same makeshift altar outside the camp. Likewise, when Yahshua died on the Cross, none of His bones were broken. He was sacrificed outside the walls of Jerusalem with two robbers, and His bones were not broken because He died quickly and there was no need to break His legs to speed His death. Now, since this and so many other allegorical messages that are found in the Giza Pyramid Complex are connected to the crucifixion of Christ, it is more than possible that this sacred place has a holy and divine purpose. In fact, there should be no doubt in any believer's mind that it is indeed a holy altar unto Yahweh built to mimic the altar in Heaven that it mirrors - just as was quoted from Revelation 11:19 earlier. Indeed, the Great

Pyramid, Tabernacle and Temple to Yahweh all have heavenly counterparts, just as these Scriptures proclaim:

> "But Christ came as High Priest of the good things to come, with the greater and more perfect tabernacle not made with hands, that is, not of this creation. Not with the blood of goats and calves, but with His own blood He entered the Most Holy Place once for all, having obtained eternal redemption." - Hebrews 9:11-12 (NKJ)

> "After these things I looked, and behold, the temple of the tabernacle of the testimony in heaven was opened. And out of the temple came the seven angels having the seven plagues, clothed in pure bright linen, and having their chests girded with golden bands." - Revelation 15:5-6 (NKJ)

In the preceding Scripture from the Book of Hebrews, the author's point is that the need for all the blood sacrifices offered on the horned altars in Jerusalem was completely done away with when Christ shed His holy blood and died for our sins on Calvary, and then sprinkled His own blood on the horned altar in Heaven as a perfect propitiation for our sins. As Scripture declares:

> "The Holy Spirit was showing by this that the way into the Most Holy Place had not yet been disclosed as long as the first tabernacle was still standing... the gifts and sacrifices being offered were only... external regulations applying until the time of the new order. When Christ came as high priest... he went through the greater and more perfect tabernacle that is... not a part of this creation. He did not enter by means of the blood of goats and calves; but... by his own blood, having obtained eternal redemption. The blood of goats and bulls... sprinkled on those who are ceremonially unclean sanctify them... outwardly... How much more, then, will the blood of Christ... cleanse our consciences from acts that lead to death, so that we may serve the living God! For this reason Christ is the mediator of a new covenant... now that he has died as a ransom to set them free from the sins committed under the first covenant." - Hebrews 9:8-15 (NIV)

In this same way, the heavenly altar formed by the constellation of Orion symbolically represents the sacrifice of one perfect man for our sins - a perfect sacrifice that completely did away with the need for the animal sacrifices memorialized by the heavenly horned altar seen in the signs of Taurus and Aries. In addition, the star Al Nitak in Orion's Belt is a heavenly symbol for the New Jerusalem that will come down out of Heaven someday to be forever situated on the New Earth!

Likewise, the old conditional Covenant made with the Israelites at Mount Sinai and symbolized in Canis Minor was replaced with a better unconditional Covenant. It was promised at Christ's birth in Bethlehem and was fulfilled just outside of the walls of Jerusalem when Christ died - just as is depicted by the stars Sirius A and B in the constellation Canis Major.

Yet, though the old Covenant made at Mount Sinai was only given to the Israelites, the New Covenant instituted in Israel by Christ has been made with all mankind, and is symbolically portrayed in the heavens by the star Sirius. Once our entrance into the New Covenant is sealed with the Holy Spirit dwelling inside of us, it does not require the keeping of man-made laws to be fulfilled. Instead of bondage, Yahshua's Covenant with mankind offers people real freedom from all ritualized religious observances and social customs.

In the Book of Hebrews, the relationship between Christ and the heavenly Mount Sinai, Mount Zion, and Jerusalem are emphasized and contrasted with the earthly ones. Indeed, the heavenly counterparts to the earthly realities are spoken of in a way that shows the freedom that all born-again believers in Yahshua possess from the moment that they are saved:

> "You have not come to a mountain that can be touched and that is burning with fire (i.e. Mount Sinai); to darkness, gloom and storm... **But you have come to Mount Zion, to the heavenly Jerusalem, the city of the living God... You have come to God, the judge of all men, to the spirits of righteous men made perfect, to Jesus the mediator of a new covenant..."**

> "At that time his voice shook the earth, but now he has promised, 'Once more I will shake not only the earth but also the heavens.' The words 'once more' indicate the removing of what can be shaken -- that is, created things -- so that what cannot be shaken may remain. Therefore, since we are receiving a kingdom that cannot be shaken, let us be thankful, and so worship God acceptably with reverence and awe, for our 'God is a consuming fire.'" - Hebrews 12:18-29 (NKJ)

Interestingly, the preceding Scripture directly pertains to the heavenly Tabernacle that is found in the Signs of Taurus and Aries. Indeed, the heavenly symbols found in Gemini, Taurus, and Aries and their decans convey the same message that was given to the earthly

Mount Sinai in Arabia, Mount Zion in Egypt, and Mount Moriah in Jerusalem. Together, these three mountains symbolically stand for Christ's selfless love and desire for intimacy with His chosen people Israel, His work on the Cross for their salvation, and His love, acceptance and forgiveness of all people who acknowledge Him as their Savior, Priest, Husband, and King.

In my Orion Code PowerPoint Presentation, which is based on the knowledge surrounding the constellation of Orion that has been revealed to me and the world little by little via my Language of God books, I show how the heavenly Tabernacle revealed in the constellation of Orion reflects the idea that the earthly Tabernacle and Temple and its sacrifices were only a shadow of the reality found in Christ, who died once and for all time so that we would find Grace and deliverance from the curse of sin and the Law.

Nonetheless, though the old Mosaic Law and all its rituals, Sabbaths, and sacrifices were nailed to Christ's Cross in fulfillment, some still strive to keep the same Feasts and Sabbaths as observant Jews do today. They also choose to keep the customs surrounding the Jewish Feasts. These include fasting from leaven during Passover and the Feast of Unleavened Bread and general fasting during the month of Elul and the Days of Awe before the Day of Atonement. Though none of these observances are necessary any longer for born-again believers, they have such a beautiful ritual significance and allegorical meaning that they are a real joy to keep when one is a believer in Yahshua as the Messiah!

However, though some believers feel motivated to fast and perform rituals to draw nearer to God as an act of love and devotion, others have become so dogmatic and legalistic about keeping these shadows and types that they ignore the fact that religious observances and daily sacrifices in the Tabernacle and Temple under the old Mosaic Law were only pale reflections of the glorious reality that came later, which is found fully in knowing Christ and His Spirit personally.

Yahshua is the mediator of a new and better Covenant that does not rely on strict observance of feasts, fasts, dietary restrictions or temple rites, but on the baptism of the Holy Spirit. As we develop an intimate relationship with Yahweh and His Son through prayer, reflection, and Bible study, the Spirit of God teaches us the deeper things of God. In drawing us near to Christ, the Spirit does not lead us to keep the old Law, or to enter the old Temple or Tabernacle, but shows us how the divine laws surrounding these symbols were perfectly fulfilled in Christ. Indeed, the Holy Spirit goes beyond these outward symbols to the substance behind them. Therefore, within the tabernacles of their own hearts, true born-again believers commune with the Spirit of

God and are gradually shown all the fullness found in Christ (Ephesians 3:11-14).

In this way, the Holy Spirit helps believers to be freed from the restrictions, rituals and fasts imposed by men who seek false humility. Once they are freed from keeping the Law through faith in Yahshua's salvation, believers can develop true righteousness by seeking a deep personal relationship with the living God. Through Christ's atonement sacrifice, and their desire to be like Christ, all believers will one day become everlasting, fully purified temples of the Living God (1 Corinthians 3:16-17; Ephesians 2:19-22).

As believers in Yahshua who are baptized fully with His Spirit, today's living saints can go to Him at any time within themselves, and without restrictions or limits. Because of Christ's sacrifice, there is no longer any need for fasts, but only a deep love for Yahshua and His Spirit in baptism, which leads to deep repentance and withdrawal from worldly wants, a desire to seek Christ in deep contemplation and prayer, and the ability to know the living God personally through His Son and Spirit.

A Summary of the Gospel in the Mazzaroth

NOTE: Over the years since writing my first book: "The Language of God in the Universe" back in 2004, my understanding of the Mazzaroth or Zodiac and the Gospel in the Stars has grown exponentially. To give an overview of my ideas, I have produced this summary, which incorporates all my newest findings concerning the forty-eight constellations of the Zodiac, some of which are now also in the 2008 revised edition of my first book.

1. **Virgo the Virgin** - A young maiden holding a leafy branch and/or a small sheaf of grain - this represents the first prophecy in the Bible of the woman (Eve and Miriam) who gives birth to the promised Seed (Seth and Yahshua), who is also the Branch of Jesse and David (Isaiah 11:1, Jeremiah 23:5, 33:15). Coupled with Leo, this also signifies Yahshua as the First (Virgo) and the Last (Leo) - as signified by the Great Sphinx in Egypt with its woman's face and lion's body (Isaiah 44:6; Revelation 1:11, 22:13). **Virgo's 3 decans are:**

- **Coma the Desired Son** - a seated woman with an infant child on her lap - the promised Seed of the Woman of Genesis 3:15, Yahshua the Messiah being held in his virgin mother Miriam's arms. This signifies the promised coming of the Messiah from a virgin (Isaiah 7:14; Matthew 1:22-23).

- **Centaurus the Centaur** - usually seen as a centaur, which is a half man and half cloven-hoofed sacrificial animal somewhat like a rider on a horse. Often seen holding a spear that is piercing a victim, though he can also be seen holding a bow with an arrow ready to fly. This signifies Christ as a sin offering and atonement sacrifice (Psalm 22; Matthew 27; Hebrews 9).

- **Bootes the Coming One** - Once named after its brightest star, Arcturus, Bootes is most often depicted as a combination shepherd and harvester carrying a shepherd's crook and a sickle. Since Bootes appears to be lying prostrate at Virgo's feet, this decan signifies the first shepherd Abel lying at his mother Eve's feet after being murdered by the first farmer Cain, who likely used his sickle to kill Abel. It also represents Yahshua as the Good Shepherd of the flock of sheep represented by nearby Ursa Major, as well as the wrathful Judge of the unfaithful flock signified by Ursa Minor (Matthew 23:34-36).

2. **Libra the Scales, or Altar** - shows Yahshua as the balancer of the Scales of Justice who makes all those who love Him appear perfect even though they are not yet so. To balance these scales for all people, and negate our evil with His good, Yahshua became the sacrificial offering that brings reconciliation and atonement. In addition, Libra signifies Revelation's Rider on a Black Horse, which brings famine and death in judgment. (1 Timothy 2:5-6; Hebrews 9:14-15, 12:24; Rev. 6:5). **Libra's 3 decans are:**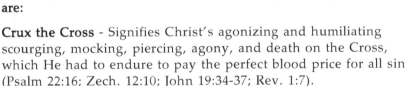

Libra

- **Crux the Cross** - Signifies Christ's agonizing and humiliating scourging, mocking, piercing, agony, and death on the Cross, which He had to endure to pay the perfect blood price for all sin (Psalm 22:16; Zech. 12:10; John 19:34-37; Rev. 1:7).

- **Victima the Victim, a.k.a. Lupus the Wolf** - The object of Centaurus' spear thrust, this wolf is a symbol for Christ, who freely offered Himself up and was pierced unto death to pay for our sins (see references for Crux). In addition, this sign signifies the countless saints who have been (and still are being) ruthlessly martyred for their faith in Christ (Rev. 6:9-11).

- **Corona Borealis the Northern Crown** - This crown signifies Christ's kingship and authority over all of creation, and also the authority over the Earth given to mankind that was wrestled away via sin and Satan, but that Christ won back for us by His blood (2 Corinthians 5:17-21).

3. Scorpio the Scorpion - represents Satan as our enemy, with claws to entrap us, as well as to seemingly thwart Christ. Satan sought to fatally sting Christ's heel through the crucifixion - not realizing that he had just sealed his own defeat. Indeed, Satan's folly allowed Christ and all who follow Him to put Satan under their feet, or authority. Scorpio signifies the fulfillment of Genesis

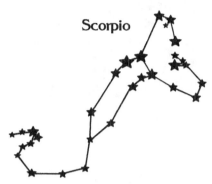

Scorpio

3:15, when the Seed of the Woman who is Christ will triumph over the seed of the Serpent - the Antichrist (See also Matthew 13:38). In addition, Scorpio signifies Revelation's Pale Horse that is ridden by Ophiuchus in judgment. **Scorpio's 3 decans are:**

- **Serpens the Serpent** - the original Serpent who beguiled Eve with lies is caught in the Christ figure Ophiuchus' mighty grasp, where he has no chance of winning even though he still tries to snatch Christ's crown - as found in the Corona Borealis constellation near Serpens' head. This serpent also signifies all those in that "brood of vipers" that hates Christ and follows their evil spiritual father: Satan (Matthew 3:7, 12:34-35; John 8:44: Rev. 12:9).

- **Ophiuchus the Serpent Holder** - this big constellation hovering over Scorpio represents a mighty man that is wrestling with and subduing Serpens, which represents Satan. This mighty man is Christ and His foot is over Scorpio's head just as Hercules' foot is over Draco's - in mimicry of the feet of Christ that will one day crush Satan and all who follow Satan. In addition, Ophiuchus is Revelation's Rider on a Pale Horse, which is depicted by Scorpio (Genesis 3:14-15; Rev. 6:8).

- **Hercules the Mighty Man** - Like Ophiuchus, this Mighty Man is Christ as a victorious warrior holding a club as he raises his foot to crush the head of Draco the Dragon, which represents Satan in his most beguiling and malevolent form (Genesis 3:15; Romans 16:20).

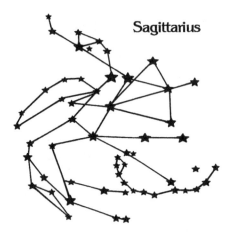

Sagittarius

4. Sagittarius the Archer - Here we see Christ depicted as a half man, half sacrificial animal just as in Centaurus - a composite image that can also be viewed as Christ victoriously riding his white horse Pegasus - as he aims his bow and arrow at the heart of the enemy seen in adjacent Scorpio. In addition, Sagittarius is Revelation's Rider on the White Horse, which depicts the Gospel being preached during the seven-year Tribulation (Zechariah 9:12-14; Revelation 6:2). **Sagittarius' 3** decans are:

- **Lyra the Lyre or Harp -** This harp carved to look like an eagle represents the exaltation, thanks, and praise due to Christ as the Eagle who destroys the Serpent. The saints Raptured before the worst part of the 7-year Tribulation will sing Yahshua's praises - as will the Ephraimite saints in the USA and elsewhere when they are caught up to receive everlasting life at the end of the Great Tribulation (Rev. 7:9-12, 19:5-6).

- **Ara the Altar -** An upside down altar set ablaze with unclean sacrifices. This represents the Lake of Fire that the Dragon - who is Satan and the spirit of the Antichrist - and all the unrepentant wicked are to be cast into in two waves: once at the end of the Great Tribulation, and once at the end of the world (Revelation 19:20, 20:10-15).

- **Draco the Dragon -** This destroying Dragon representing Satan and the Antichrist is coiled around the imperiled sinners represented by Ursa Minor in the circumpolar region of the sky that never sets. Surrounding him are the constellations Cepheus and Cassiopeia signifying the true King and Queen of the Universe: Yahshua and His Bride, the True Church - who together will vanquish Satan and cast him into the Lake of Fire (Revelation 12:9, 20:2, 10).

5. Capricorn the Goat-fish - A creature that is partly a dying goat signifying the sinful people and the Nephilim that perished in the Flood, and

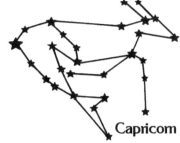

Capricorn

partly a lively fish signifying the eight righteous people who escaped judgment on Noah's Ark. As such, Capricorn represents both judgment and mercy. Just as humanity was saved from the Great Flood via the Ark, all future humanity will be saved by Christ, who is represented by Noah's Ark as well as the Ark of the Covenant (Matthew 4:18-20). **Capricorn's 3 decans are:**

- **Sagitta the Arrow** - Per Zechariah, Judah is God's bow, and Ephraim is His arrow, and together they will aid Christ when He comes to destroy His earthly enemies at the Battle of Armageddon (Zechariah 9:13-15).

- **Aquila the Eagle** - A flying eagle that is wounded and falling toward the ground with Sagitta the arrow clutched in its claws. This Eagle is the King of the birds and it is wounded to signify Christ as the King who was wounded for our transgressions, and who delivered a fatal blow to the enemy when He died and then was resurrected, for by His stripes, we are healed (Isaiah 53:5-7). This Eagle also represents the United States of America, and its End Time role in history as a beleaguered nation of new saints at war with the Antichrist and his armies.

- **Delphinus the Dolphin** - A dolphin vigorously leaping upward symbolizing deliverance from evil and the resurrection of the dead. This fish is tied to the Sign of Jonah that Christ gave, for just as Jonah was dying in the belly of the fish for three days and nights, so Christ was dead in the tomb for three days and nights before He rose up from the dead (Matthew 12:39-42; 16:1-4; Luke 11:29-32).

6. Aquarius the Water Bearer - This man pouring water out of an urn into the mouth of a big fish signifies Yahshua as the Living Water pouring out His Holy Spirit like a river to all of God's people, just as Moses delivered water to the Israelites out of a split rock (Numbers 20:8-11; Joel 2:28-29; Acts 2:14-17; John 4:10-11, 7:38). It also signifies

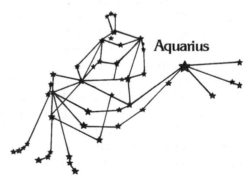

Noah's and his family's' deliverance from the Great Flood (Genesis 6:18, 7:7).

- **Piscis Australis the Southern Fish** - This fish signifies the Ark of Noah that delivered eight people from utter destruction. It also represents the everlasting refuge from death and deliverance from destruction that all repentant sinners can find in Yahshua, who gave the Sign of Jonah (Matthew 12:39-42; 16:1-4; Luke 11:29-32)

- **Pegasus the Winged Horse** - The White Horse that Christ will ride when He returns, which is like the white horses of His saints who will be following Him out of Heaven (Revelation 19:11-14).

- **Cygnus the Swan, or the Northern Cross** - With the North America Nebula near to Deneb, the brightest star in this constellation, it signifies the pure and soaring heights that Christianity once reached in America, and the evangelistic and missionary nature of the Christians in the USA. By extension, this white bird or cross also depicts everyone who is baptized and born again by the Holy Spirit, faithfully follows their Redeemer, and honors His sacrifice for all their sins on the Cross (Mat. 10:38, 16:34; John 3:3, 12:26; 1 Peter 1:22-23).

7. **Pisces the Fishes** - two fishes bound to Cetus the Sea Monster by ropes tied to their tails, making it impossible for them to flee. However, the fishes are protected by the restraining influence of Aries, the Ram that signifies Christ as the Redeemer. Through Christ's Spirit, believers receive freedom from bondage to sin and unity with

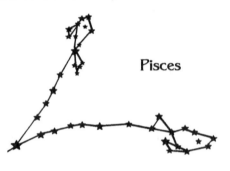

Pisces

Christ. The fish near to Andromeda signifies Jews (i.e. Judah) and legalistic Christians who remain bound to the Mosaic Law, while the fish swimming along the path of the Sun and hovering over the back of the heavenly horse called Pegasus represents the Gentile Church (i.e. Ephraim) that will be Raptured. In addition, the fish that signifies Judah represents Messianic Jews united in love with the fish signifying the Gentile Church during the Millennium. Pisces therefore dually signifies the division that now exists between those under the Law and under Grace, and the eventual unity of this Two-House Church of Judah and Ephraim in Christ (2 Fishes and 5 Loaves: Matthew 14:16-20; Sign of Jonah: Mat. 12:39-42; 16:1-4; Luke 11:29-32). **Pisces' 3 decans are:**

- **The Band** - this band or rope binds the fishes of Pisces to Cetus the Sea Monster, and represents the bondage of all humanity to Satan and sin and the captivity of God's people who were never taught to be noble and fierce warriors in the Kingdom of God, as the constellation Cassiopeia under Aries suggests we must be in order to be victorious in Christ (Eccles. 7:20; Romans 3:22-23; 1 John 1:8).

- **Andromeda the Chained Woman** - Andromeda was a princess who was bound to a stone to be eaten by Cetus the Sea Monster (a decan of Aries) in sacrifice. She signifies the Israelites who were first enslaved in Egypt. Then they were made captive by the curse of the Law because they feared God instead of loving Him, and eventually rebelled against Him, turning to false gods and being held captive by sin and a weak prayer life. Sadly, many apostates in the Church and outside of it have done this (Deuteronomy 6:21-25; Ezra 9:9-13; Roman 3:19-26; Galatians 3:10-13, 4:8-11).

- **Cepheus the Crowned King** - Cepheus the king is paired with Cassiopeia his Queen (a decan of Aries) in the northern sky. This king signifies Christ as the King of kings, who is ruling alongside His Bride the True Church during His Millennial Kingdom on Earth. Alongside Him is the forbidding sign of Draco the Dragon, who will be bound in the abyss throughout Christ's Millennial Kingdom until the end, when he will be released for a little while (Rev. 17:14, 19:11-16, 20:1-3).

    8. Aries the Ram - a ram whose front hooves are resting over the band that binds the Pisces fishes to Cetus, recalling the prophecy in Genesis 3:15. This sacrificial male lamb represents Christ as the Lamb of God, who died for our sins. In the process, Christ allows us to break the binds of sin, fear, terror and death that Satan holds us by. When we are covered by the Blood of Christ, we can claim His authority over demons, sickness, oppression, and death. Sadly, however, 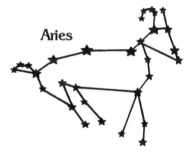 very few exercise that authority. Thus, they are like Andromeda - made powerless by her enslaved relatives (i.e. false teachers) and held captive by Satan. Finally, along with Taurus, Aries forms a heavenly four-horned altar with the ram being a symbol of the lambs sacrificed daily as sin offerings in ancient Israel (Genesis 3:15; Exodus 12:21, 29:38-39; John 1:29: Rev. 5:6-13, 7:9-10, 21:22-23). **Aries' 3 decans are:**

- **Cassiopeia the Enthroned Woman** - this is Christ's Queen, the True Church sitting enthroned in the sky above Andromeda, her enslaved counterpart. This beautiful woman has been given liberty (i.e. freedom) by Christ to reign with Him and act with the same authority. Those who follow Christ are not captives, but are freed via the Holy Spirit, and can help Yahweh fight spiritual battles with praise, worship and constant authoritative prayer in Christ's Name (Rev. 5:8-10, 20:6; 2 Cor. 3:17; Gal. 4:6-7, 5:1).

- **Cetus the Sea Monster** - this giant sea monster or leviathan signifies Satan as the Dragon in Revelation, who is threatening to eat the fishes of Pisces that represent the Two-House Church consisting of those still enslaved by the Law and those saved under Grace via the Blood of Christ. One fish or part of this Church is still bound by false teachers who deny Christ, His Holy Spirit, and the authority Christ gives to His saints. Sadly, however, only those who have learned to exercise Christ's authority without fear can be saved from Cetus' (i.e. Satan's) evil grasp (Leviathan: Psalm 74:14; Isaiah 27:1; Dragon: Rev. 12:4, 17).

- **Perseus the Breaker** - is a Mighty Man that breaks the binds holding Andromeda - just as Christ can break Satan's hold when Christ's saints exercise His authority. When they look to Christ's blood for their authority, God's people can help in the spiritual war to bind Satan and his followers, and to free all those still being held captive. Like Cetus, Satan attempts to destroy God's people with a constant flood of evil, which can only be stopped by born-again Israelites (i.e. Christ's Messianic and Gentile saints), who are victorious in Yahshua and are not afraid to use His authority to protect themselves. This is why Perseus' foot rests above the Pleiades, which signifies six of the Seven Churches of Revelation. Perseus is a warning sign that many apostates who think they are Christians will be left behind, with some siding with, and being destroyed by the Antichrist, while many others will find faith and strength in suffering during the Tribulation (Jeremiah 51:19-24; Daniel 2:44-45, 8:25; Micah 2:12-13; 1 Cor. 3:13-15; Phillip. 1:27-29).

9. **Taurus the Bull** - this raging or excited red bull charging forward with its two horns lowered in self-defense is a dual sign that signifies the great material blessing, power, and forgiveness given to those who love Christ, as well as Christ's coming in judgment against those who hate Him and despise His blessings. These two opposing groups are depicted by Taurus' two horns, and the two star clusters that are a part of its body. Both

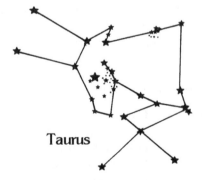

Taurus

of these groups of people profess to be loved by God, but have little else in common. The Pleiades are connected to Taurus' left or wayward horn, while the Hyades are connected to its right, or righteous horn. The symbol of the unicorn represents the righteous horn of Taurus. In addition, Perseus is Revelation's Rider on the Red Horse, the bringer of war and judgment that is depicted by Taurus. Finally, along with Aries, Taurus forms a heavenly four-horned altar with the bull being a symbol of the bulls sacrificed outside the camp as sin offerings in ancient Israel, just as Christ was sacrificed as a sin offering outside of Jerusalem's walls (Exodus 29:36-37; Lev. 4:4-12; Deut. 33:17; Mat. 27:33-37; Rev. 6:4). **Taurus' 3 decans are:**

- **Orion the Hunter or Brilliant** - envisioned as a Mighty Man striding forward with his sword raised in battle, this large, bright constellation that looks like an hour-glass or wine cup is very easy to spot in the sky for a reason. It is one of the most important constellations in the Star Gospel, with many layers of meaning and startling End Time applications. Besides signifying the Patriarch Joseph as a prince of Egypt, Orion symbolizes Christ's wine cup at the Last Supper, and also memorializes His sacrificial death on the Cross. In fact, Orion can be seen as a heavenly Ark of the New Covenant sealed with Christ's blood, and housed near the heavenly altar and temple formed by Taurus and Aries. As such, Orion signifies Yahshua's triumph over death and the Devil. It also marks His return as a resurrected, conquering Prince wielding His double-edged sword while crushing the Serpent's head and trampling Satan's followers under His feet. This sign's meaning is also tied directly to Mount Zion and the Great Pyramid complex in Egypt, which signifies Orion's Belt stars, and the altar of Isaiah 19 (Genesis 3:15, 49:26; Isaiah 19:19; Mat. 26:27-28; 1 Cor. 15:25-28; Rev. 11:19).

- **Eridanus the River** - This fiery river flowing downward from Orion's foot is the heavenly counterpart to the Jordan River in Israel, and as such it signifies that those who are baptized with the Holy Spirit will be spared from judgment and condemnation. So, though it is a fiery river of judgment akin to the Lake of Fire, this river has a far gentler side tied to the fact that Orion depicts the crucifixion of Christ, which established Yahshua's New Covenant of Grace, mercy and forgiveness with all mankind (Mat. 3:5-6, 3:13-17, 26:28; Rev. 19:20, 20:10-15).

- **Auriga the Goatherd** - when drawing a star diagram of this constellation, I envisioned it as a shepherd holding a pregnant goat in his arms. As such, it depicts Christ gently caring for the unruly goats in His flocks even though they are not gentle and kind like His obedient sheep. In this way, this sign cleverly portrays the mercy and forgiveness that Christ will extend to His wayward flocks now, and during the Tribulation - at the moment that these spiritual goats realize their folly, repent and fully turn to Him for help, and thereby avoid the hellish fate of the goats who refuse to repent (Psalm 28:8-9; Mat. 25:31-41; Heb. 9:13-14).

10. Gemini the Twins - The twin stars Pollux and Castor mark two people being united either in a Marriage or Adoption Covenant. Biblically, they signify warring brothers who will eventually reconcile through Christ. These include Isaac and Ishmael, Jacob and Esau, and the Two-House Church of Judah and Ephraim as a Gentile bride and Jewish groom. United in love, some from among all of these fighting pairs will learn to love and forgive one another through Christ, which will give them the right to attend the glorious Wedding of the Lion of Judah and His Jewish brothers with His Gentile Bride, the Church (Ezekiel 37:16-19; Zech. 9:13; Malachi 1:1-4: Romans 11:17-24). **Gemini's 3 decans are:**

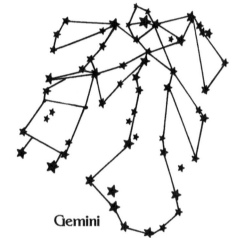

Gemini

- **Lepus the Hare or Enemy** - Lepus is not a hare at all, but a Serpent signifying Satan whose head is beneath Orion's foot as a symbol of Christ crushing the Devil's head. Furthermore, the river Eridanus begins where that foot and head meet, signifying the Lake of Fire that Satan will one day be cast into (Exodus 15:6; Mat. 13;39; Luke 10:19; 1 Cor. 15:25-28).

- **Canis Minor the Lesser Dog** - though seen as a small hunting dog trailing behind Orion the Hunter, this constellation's brightest star Procyon is tied directly to the real Mount Sinai, which is the mountain called Jabal Al Lawz in modern Saudi Arabia. It signifies the Law of Moses, which was fulfilled by Christ via the New Covenant sealed with Christ's Blood, and will be fully realized in the Kingdom of God (Exodus 24:16-18; 1 Kings 2:3; Hebrews 8:8-13; Romans 14:16-18).

- **Canis Major the Greater Dog** - though seen as a large hunting dog trailing behind Orion the Hunter, this constellation's bright double star system consisting of Sirius A and B is tied directly to the town of Bethlehem and the City of Jerusalem, of which Bethlehem is a suburb. The true meaning of this constellation therefore has little to do with dogs or hunting, but signifies the land of Israel, where the birth, ministry, death and resurrection of Christ as the "Naz Seir," "Chief Prince," or Prince of princes occurred. Because Christ has paid the price for all sin with the New Covenant sealed in His blood, He will one day sit on David's throne as the King of kings (Daniel 8:23-25; Jeremiah 33:15-17; Luke 1:32-33, 2:4-7; John 19:17-18; 1 Cor. 11:25; Rev. 17:14).

11. Cancer the Crab - actually signifies the gathering of God's people Israel into one sheep pen, corral or family whose Shepherd is the ultimate King of Judah: Yahshua the Messiah. This interpretation is derived from the Beehive Cluster in Cancer, which is seen as the manger for two

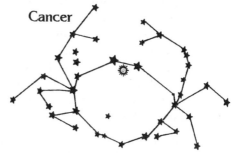

Cancer

donkeys represented by two bright stars on either side of the cluster. This beehive or manger signifies Christ as the Bread of Life, while the two donkeys that Christ rode into Jerusalem before He died symbolically signify the Messianic Jewish and Gentile Christian branches of the True Church (Genesis 49:10-11; Psalm 23:1-3, 80:1-2; Ezekiel 37:11-28).
Cancer's 3 decans are:

- **Ursa Minor the Little Bear or Dipper** - this sign is seen as a little bear today, though in ancient times it was seen as a sheep pen with sheep going in and out of it. Along with Ursa Major, it represents Christ's Parable of the Sheep and the Goats, and the final harvest of humanity into groups of good sheep and evil goats at the end of the ages. In this case, Ursa Minor signifies a flock of unruly goats, which signify rebellious people with sinful hearts, some of whom will just barely escape Hell when they finally repent at the last moment (Matthew 7:22-23, 25:41-46; 1 Cor. 3:15; Jude 1:21-23).

- **Ursa Major the Big Bear or Dipper** - this sign is seen as a big bear today, though in ancient times it was seen as a sheep pen with sheep going into it. This signifies a spiritual sheep pen or congregation of good sheep that follow Christ, the Good Shepherd and Lamb of God. It signifies the heavenly pasture where Christ is gathering his faithful flock. It also signifies the good sheep that will be gathered into a large fold to inherit everlasting life in paradise (Matthew 25:31-40; Luke 12:32; John 10:16, 21:17: 1 Peter 5:2-4).

- **Argo the Ship (i.e. Carina)** - this big constellation that symbolized a large sailing ship has recently been divided up into four smaller constellations that name various parts of a ship. Argo once included the bright star Canopus and the star cluster called the southern Pleiades, which are now part of the constellation Carina near Canis Major in the Southern Hemisphere. Argo signifies the fishing boats of Christ's apostles, who were fishers of men. As such, those who follow in their footsteps are still catching many schools full of faithful fish - even though Satan still seeks to sink this ship so that everyone aboard will perish. The many saints who work with Christ to defeat Satan are represented by Pisces and Piscis Australis. These heavenly fishes signify the cargo of Argo - huge schools of fishes that will ultimately surrender themselves to Christ in worship (Matthew 4:17-20; Mark 6:38-45; Luke 5:10-11).

12. Leo the Lion - a reclining or pouncing male lion with the king star Regulus at the top of his forelegs - This lion signifies Christ as the victorious Kings of kings, and the conquering Lion of the Tribe of Judah. Yahshua is the Seed of the Woman and the King of kings (or Prince of princes). Yahshua is also 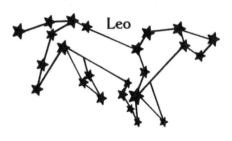 the First and the Last to defeat the Serpent's Seed by crushing its head with His foot. The lion's body of the Great Sphinx in Egypt signifies this sign, while its human head signifies both Virgo and Aquarius (Genesis 3:15; Daniel 8:25; 1 Timothy 6:14-15; Rev. 1:11, 17:14, 22:13). **Leo's 3 decans are:**

- **Hydra the Serpent** - this serpent signifies the evil hearts and deeds of men who worship Satan, and follow the Antichrist and his armies. All of them will be torn to pieces and cast into Hell by the Lion of Judah at the beginning and end of His Millennial Rule (Rev. 12:9, 14-15, 20:2-10).

- **Crater the Cup** - this is the Cup of God's Wrath that will be poured out on all wicked apostates during the Great Tribulation. This cup also represents the shed Blood of Christ that God the Father, in His role as His Son's "Avenger of Blood" seeks vengeance for (Numbers 35:19, 21; Romans 12:19; Rev. 14:10, 16:19, 18:6). It also represents the blood-filled cup in the hand of the Harlot of Babylon who rides the Scarlet Beast, and who the Lion of Judah will soon vanquish forever. The blood in this cup belongs to the many martyrs who died because of their faith in God the Father and His Son (Rev. 17:4-6).

- **Corvus the Crow** - this sign signifies the birds of prey that will devour the flesh of the Antichrist's armies, which will be slain when they fight against Yahshua and His angels and saints at His Second Coming (Rev. 19:17-21).

For a highly detailed and extensively illustrated examination of God's love letter to us in the heavens, please see my book: "The Language of God in the Universe," ISBN # 978-09759131-0-9 - the most up-to-date and comprehensive study of Sacred Astronomy and the Gospel in the Stars available today.

Sacred Astronomy, the Divine Science Known to Abraham

In previous sections of this book, we discussed the wisdom that Cainan and Enoch had, and the great current value of the ancient book that bears Enoch's name. In this section, we will explore whether or not Abraham understood Sacred Astronomy, how this divine science was corrupted into Pagan Astrology, and how both philosophies survived despite the Great Flood.

In countless Hollywood movies and religious plays, the patriarch Abraham is invariably depicted as a simple shepherd who lived a poor nomadic existence and - at best - had a rudimentary education. However, as I learned more about the past, this picture of Abraham really began to bother me. In fact, if one judges Abraham's lifestyle by the luxury and ostentation exhibited by past desert sheiks living in conditions that parallel Abraham's, nothing could likely be further from the truth. However, though we will touch upon the fact that Abraham was not poor here, the objective of this section is to explore Abraham's knowledge of God and the heavens. We will therefore carefully explore Abraham's origins and material status in Chapter Eight.

Popular misconceptions aside, the Bible tells us that Abraham was a resident of Ur of the Chaldeans before he became a nomadic wanderer. Furthermore, the historian Josephus tells us that Astronomy was both a Sethite and a Chaldean specialty. This, in turn, suggests that Abraham was educated in the wisdom of the Chaldeans, and may have been intimately acquainted with the symbols, star names, and allegorical meanings of all 48 constellations in the ancient Mazzaroth. This assumption is supported by Josephus' assertion that Abraham was able to authoritatively teach Astronomy to the ancient Egyptians:

> "For whereas the Egyptians were formerly addicted to different customs, and despised one another's sacred and accustomed rites, and were very angry one with another on that account, Abram conferred with each of them, and, confuting the reasonings they made use of, every one for their own practices, demonstrated that such reasonings were vain and void of truth: whereupon he was admired by them in those conferences as a very wise man, and one of great sagacity, when he discoursed on any subject he undertook; and this not only in understanding it, but in persuading other men also to assent to him. **He communicated to them arithmetic, and delivered to them the science of astronomy; for before Abram came into Egypt they were unacquainted with those parts of learning;** for that science came from the Chaldeans into Egypt, and from thence to the Greeks also." - Josephus, Antiquities of the Jews, 1.8.2

Since Josephus was a fairly reliable ancient historian, his claim that Abraham taught the Egyptians the science of Astronomy beckons us to investigate this assertion further. First of all, let's determine if the Bible hints at when Abraham might have shared his knowledge of the heavens with the leaders of Egypt.

Unfortunately, there is only one mention of Abraham visiting Egypt in the Bible, and it is recorded in Chapter Twelve of the Book of Genesis. At that time, there was a famine in Canaan, and Abraham and his wandering clan of warriors, craftsmen, merchants, and shepherds were compelled to go to Egypt to find sustenance, just as Jacob's sons would have to do over one hundred years later. However, Abraham was afraid for his life at the hands of the Egyptians due to the great beauty of Sarah, his wife and cousin. Apparently, Abraham was afraid of this because powerful men were known to kill the husbands of lovely women in order to procure the women for their harems. So, in order to escape possible assassination, Abraham asked Sarah to hide their marriage while in Egypt, and to misrepresent their biological relationship.

Now, possibly as a punishment for their lack of trust, God may have brought about the very thing that Abraham and Sarah feared. Thus, Sarah was indeed taken to Pharaoh's court as a concubine. Nonetheless, the Bible tells us that God protected Sarah from being violated by afflicting the Pharaoh and his entire household with plagues:

"He (i.e. Pharaoh) treated Abram well for her sake. He had sheep, oxen, male donkeys, male and female servants, female donkeys, and camels. But the LORD (Yahweh) plagued Pharaoh and his house with great plagues because of Sarai, Abram's wife." - Genesis 12:16-17 (NKJ)

Fortunately, this story is also recounted in the Book of Jasher, where we are given a much fuller account of the events that occurred after Sarah and Abraham entered Egypt, and Sarah became an unwilling servant in the Pharaoh's household:

"And the Lord hearkened to the voice of Sarai, and the Lord sent an angel to deliver Sarai from the power of Pharaoh. And the king came and sat before Sarai and behold an angel of the Lord was standing over them, and he appeared to Sarai and said to her, Do not fear, for the Lord has heard thy prayer.

And the king approached Sarai and said to her, 'What is that man to thee who brought thee hither?' and she said, 'He is my brother.' And the king said, 'It is incumbent upon us to make him great, to elevate him and to do unto him all the good which thou shalt command us;' and at that time the king sent to Abram silver and gold and precious stones in abundance, together with cattle, men servants and maid servants; and the king ordered Abram to be brought, and he sat in the court of the king's house, and the king greatly exalted Abram on that night.

And the king approached to speak to Sarai, and he reached out his hand to touch her, when the angel smote him heavily, and he was terrified and he refrained from reaching to her. And when the king came near to Sarai, the angel smote him to the ground, and acted thus to him the whole night, and the king was terrified.

And the angel on that night smote heavily all the servants of the king, and his whole household, on account of Sarai, and there was a great lamentation that night amongst the people of Pharaoh's house. And Pharaoh, seeing the evil that befell him, said, 'Surely on account of this woman has this thing happened to me,' and he removed himself at some distance from her and spoke pleasing words to her.

And the king said to Sarai, 'Tell me I pray thee concerning the man with whom thou camest here;' and Sarai said, 'This man is my husband, and I said to thee that he was my brother for I was afraid, lest thou shouldst put him to death through wickedness.' And the king kept away from Sarai, and the plagues of the angel of the Lord ceased from him and his household; and Pharaoh knew that he was smitten on account of Sarai, and the king was greatly astonished at this.

And in the morning the king called for Abram and said to him, 'What is this thou hast done to me? Why didst thou say, She is my sister, owing to which I took her unto me for a wife, and this heavy plague has therefore come upon me and my household. Now therefore here is thy wife, take her and go from our land lest we all die on her account.' And Pharaoh took more cattle, men servants and maid servants, and silver and gold, to give to Abram, and he returned unto him Sarai his wife.

And the king took a maiden whom he begat by his concubines, and he gave her to Sarai for a handmaid. And the king said to his daughter, 'It is better for thee my daughter to be a handmaid in this man's house than to be mistress in my house, after we have beheld the evil that befell us on account of this woman.'" - Jasher 15:19-32

Through this story, we are told that Sarah's Egyptian maidservant Hagar, the mother of Ishmael was the privileged daughter of one of Pharaoh's concubines. Since she was chosen to be a servant, it is probable that Hagar was quite young when she was sent to live with Sarah and Abraham. This would have made it easier for her to adjust to the differing customs and way of life that she would discover in her new foreign household. In addition, we are told that the Pharaoh gave Abraham gold, silver, and other riches as gifts, and there is no indication that Pharaoh took them back when Sarah was returned. In fact, in order not to further anger the offended deity protecting Abraham, the Pharaoh likely would not have asked for their return. This story therefore conveys the knowledge that, even if Abraham was materially wanting before he entered Egypt, he was rich when he left!

This interesting story also has a spiritual message. Indeed, even though Abraham and Sarah did not trust God enough to protect them from harm in Egypt, they ultimately were given more riches and status as a result of their reliance on God after their deception led to the misfortune of others. This is meant to show us that even a righteous man like Abraham who trusts in Yahweh can make poor choices because of misplaced fear or timidity that can cause others to suffer needless injury. However, the story is also meant to strongly convey that Yahweh can and will intervene when we make poor choices, bringing great good out of an otherwise bad situation if we trust Him to do so.

Now, just before the story about Abraham and Sarah in Egypt, the Book of Jasher recounts the story of a wise man named Rikayon who leaves Shinar (i.e. Mesopotamia) and goes to Egypt seeking his fortune. There, he charms the people and encounters the reigning pharaoh, whose name is remarkably similar to the god king of Egypt known as Osiris. Even more remarkably, his father is identified as Anom. Could Anom be a corruption of Amon or Amun - names associated with a powerful false deity in Egypt?

> *"And he resolved to go to Egypt, to Oswiris the son of Anom king of Egypt, to show the king his wisdom; for perhaps he might find grace in his sight, to raise him up and give him maintenance; and Rikayon did so." - Jasher 14:2*

Though Rikayon is an interesting character, the fact that he visits Egypt during the time of Abraham, and the reigning king there is known as Oswiris the son of Anom is even more interesting. Indeed, the Book of Jasher also informs us that - in the same year that Rikayon beguiled Oswiris - there was a famine in Canaan whereby Abraham came to Egypt. Not long after, the king of Egypt was subsequently charmed and cursed by his attraction to Abraham's ravishingly beautiful wife Sarah (Jasher 15:1). This means that Sarah was the one time object of Oswiris' lust. Eerily, the name "Oswiris" is quite close to "Osiris," and - as will be shown in Chapter Seven - "Osiris" was likely not a name, but a ruling title for the man named Cush, who was the son of Noah's son Ham and the father of Nimrod. Since Oswiris was a king of Egypt and the Egyptians worshipped their Pharaohs as gods, this suggests that Cush not only ruled or co-ruled Egypt at one time, but that he probably saw himself as a god and demanded worship.

Now, though Abraham was born over 250 years after Cush, Cush was born much closer to the Flood and therefore likely lived at least 400 years. If so, Ham's son Cush could have been alive and either ruling or co-ruling a portion of Egypt with his brother Mizraim when Abraham visited there to avoid starvation. Furthermore, though Cush would have been over 200 years old at the time that Jasher's Oswiris narrative was referring to, he would have only been equivalent in age to a modern middle-aged man. Therefore, Oswiris could have been just as interested in women as he was in his youth. So there is no reason to doubt that Cush could have desired Sarah, especially since she was very beautiful.

If Cush was indeed the Pharaoh of the portion of Egypt that Abraham visited (which was most likely in the north and close to the pyramids at Giza), and Abraham was a legitimate Semitic Chaldean prince from Ur of the Chaldees who had acquired some wealth of his own in Nimrod's court, he likely entered Egypt with considerable enough pomp to attract Cush's interest and hospitality. Abraham therefore could easily have gained ample opportunities to share his knowledge of Sacred Astronomy with the ruling elite and the priests of the biggest deities worshipped there while he waited for the famine to end.

In further support of Josephus' claim that Abraham shared his knowledge of Sacred Astronomy with the Egyptians, the Book of Jasher tells us that Abraham was raised and educated by Noah and Shem, who would no doubt have taught Abraham all about Sacred Astronomy and the Star Gospel before he left their tutelage to forge his own divinely ordained destiny:

> *"**And Abram was in Noah's house thirty-nine years,** and Abram knew the Lord from three years old, and he went in the ways of the Lord until the day of his death, as Noah and his son Shem had taught him; **and all the sons of the earth in those days greatly transgressed against the Lord,** and they rebelled against him and they served other gods, and they forgot the Lord who had created them in the earth; and the inhabitants of the earth made unto themselves, at that time, every man his god; gods of wood and stone which could neither speak, hear, nor deliver, and the sons of men served them and they became their gods."* - Jasher 9:6

The Book of Jasher explains that, despite the terrible apostasy and idolatry of *"all the sons of the earth,"* Abraham was a righteous man from the time he was a toddler until death due to the upright instruction he received from Noah and Shem. This kept Abraham from practicing the idolatry and open rebellion against God that was so heavily encouraged in Nimrod's despotic Hamite dictatorship - a dictatorship no doubt partly supported by his father Cush, who sat on Egypt's throne!

As explained earlier, there is absolutely no doubt that Noah and Shem knew the Gospel in the Stars. After all, they were Sethite leaders whose ancestors had built the spiritually-inspired pyramids at Dahshur and Giza. Through the power of the Holy Spirit, these godly patriarchs would have been made aware of the Zodiac's spiritual message, and would have been shown how to utilize the symbolic messages found in the heavens to convey truth on Earth. To aid their understanding of God's symbolic Language, these godly patriarchs would also have been given Spirit-led visions and dreams that showed them the Path to Salvation that would one day be fulfilled by Christ. Through their belief in Yahweh Elohim and His promised Messiah, Noah and Shem no doubt received forgiveness for their sins, and were given the promise of the resurrection to everlasting life. This is why Yahshua could declare that the God of Abraham, Isaac, and Jacob is the God of the Living!

By the time Abram arrived on the world scene in 2055 BC, or 292 years after the Great Flood, Noah was likely a greatly revered old man, while Shem was biologically in his early middle age. Due to their longevity and great wisdom, it is highly likely that Noah and Shem had acquired much wealth, and were viewed as almost god-like by the local populace. At Abram's birth, Noah would have been 892 years old. Since he lived to the age of 950, Noah was alive until Abram was 48 years old. In addition, Shem - who lived 600 years - was a sprightly 392 years old when Abram was born. Indeed, according to my Biblical Chronology, *Shem actually outlived Abraham, and would have been alive to see the births of Abraham's sons Ishmael and Isaac, and Isaac's sons Esau and Jacob - who was renamed Israel!*

The account of Abraham's upbringing by Noah and Shem in the Book of Jasher also shows us that Noah and Shem were not idolaters. They worshipped one God, and only one God. Furthermore, contrary to popular belief, other sources show that they knew God's name as Yah, or E-Yah (i.e. Ea), and also addressed God as Elohim or El Elyon, which means God Most High. In fact, Yahweh Elohim has been worshipped since the beginning of time as the one true God. However, for a long time in the ancient past, Yahweh was considered merely a nature deity, or storm god worshipped by disparate Semitic tribes throughout Ancient Mesopotamia and the Middle East. This shows how quickly mankind fell into sin and idolatry after the Great Flood. Nonetheless, *the Name and Title Yahweh Elohim appears in the Bible thousands of times. Each time this Name is mentioned, it bears witness to the fact that the ancient Israelites who read these Scriptures knew Yahweh's true Name.*

Tragically, however, God's personal, holy Name has been poorly translated throughout the Bible with the impersonal words: "the LORD God." Translated this way, the personal Name and title "Yahweh Elohim" loses its true meaning and power to transform lives. There were, however, those who followed the one true God Yahweh even in those dark days of idolatrous cultures like Ancient Rome, Greece, Babylon, Phoenicia, Egypt, India and Assyria. These righteous people had a personal relationship with Yahweh and knew the power of Yahweh's Name when uttered in faithful prayer. Furthermore, they shared a Blood Covenant of fealty and unity with Yahweh, their one and only Elohim.

Abraham and his wife Sarah were two such followers of Yahweh. Using the meaning of their names as a guide, Abram and Sarai were also likely to be people of some note in their society. Abram means "high father" and Sarai means "head person," "chief," or "noble" in Hebrew. Furthermore, the Book of Jasher indicates that Abram's father Terah was a trusted advisor and prince in the court of Nimrod. It is therefore likely that both Abram and Sarai were members of the Babylonian nobility.

We will further discuss Abraham's noble status and his important role in God's Plan of Salvation in Chapter Eight. To make better sense of the next few chapters, however, it is important to realize that Abraham was a Sethite-style Magi and Chaldean Prince of Ur rather than a poor, Bedouin-style shepherd. As such, Abraham was well-versed in the science of Sacred Astronomy, and knew of the coming of the Messiah Yahshua long before He was born. Indeed, Abraham also knew of Yahshua's coming sacrifice, resurrection, and everlasting Kingdom. Otherwise, as mentioned in Hebrews 11:8-10, how could Abraham have longed to live in the City of God within that future Kingdom, which will be the habitation for all Christ's followers in eternity?

Now, since Abraham was likely a master Astronomer, the fact that God's Covenant promises to Abraham mention the starry heavens should not be dismissed as a coincidence. In fact, it is highly likely that Yahweh directed Abraham to gaze at certain portions of the Gospel in the Stars to show his place in it, and all that pertained to Abraham's Seed or offspring. This idea is implied in Genesis 15:5-6, where the words "count" and "number" could have been translated "declare" or "reckon:"

> "Then He brought him outside and said, 'Look now toward heaven, and count (i.e. declare) the stars if you are able to number (i.e. reckon) them.' And He said to him, 'so shall your descendants be.' And he believed in the LORD (Yahweh), and He accounted it to him for righteousness." - Genesis 15:5-6 (NKJ)

This starry promise to Abraham is just one more example in the Bible where Yahweh was dropping a pointed hint about the source of Abraham's spiritual wisdom and faith. Indeed, though Abraham no doubt knew God through the intellectual and spiritual lessons inherent in the ritual of Blood Covenanting, he was also likely filled with the Holy Spirit - especially because of his strong devotion to and faith in God the Father. This meant that Abraham likely not only knew Yahweh via words of knowledge, visions and dreams, but that he could consult God directly to discern His will, and thereby accurately interpret and teach the Gospel in the Stars.

Beware of Enoch's Occult Twin!

Unfortunately, as many readers may be aware, practitioners of modern Freemasonry, as well as Pagans and New Agers often cite the Great Pyramid as a source of esoteric and occult knowledge, as well as a mechanism once used in Pagan religious ceremonies surrounding the dead.

One of the worst groups promulgating spiritual falsehoods concerning the Great Pyramid are the Freemasons - a very old, once decidedly Christian men's organization that has slipped further and further into gross spiritual error over the past 150 years. As an example of their spiritual waywardness, two Freemasons recently wrote a book entitled "Uriel's Machine," in which they convincingly tie ancient henges found all over the world with a henge described in the Book of 1 Enoch. Unfortunately, however, they also attempt to prove that these henges were meant to convey New Age style, demonically inspired esoteric knowledge rather than godly astronomical knowledge.

In an ominous twist to the information supplied by Josephus about the two memorial pillars built by the descendents of Seth, these occult practitioners have attributed the building of the two Pre-Flood pillars built by the Sethites to the descendents of Cain, not Seth. To show this, the authors of "Uriel's Machine" quote from two obscure sources called the "Indigo Jones Manuscript," and the "Wood Manuscript." Here is a large section from the Indigo Jones manuscript, which is highly regarded by some Masons:

> "...before... NOAH's Flood, there was a Man called LAMECH... who had two Wives, the One called ADA, the other ZILLA; BY ADA, he begat two SONS, JABAL and JUBAL, by ZILLA, he had One SON called TUB ALL and a Daughter called Naamab: These four Children found the beginning of all crafts in the World: JABAL found out GEOMETRY, and he Divided Flocks of Sheep, He first built a House of Stone and Timber. HIS Brother JUBAL found the ART of MUSICK He was the Father of all such as Handle the Harp and Organ, TUBAL-CAIN was the Instructer of Every Artificer in Brass and Iron, And the Daughter found out the ART of Weaving. THESE Children knew well that GOD would take Vengeance for SIN either by Fire or Water; Wherefore they Wrote their SCIENCES that they had found in Two Pillars, that they might be found after in Two Pillars, that they might be found after NOAH's Flood."

"ONE of the Pillars was Marble, for that will not Burn with any Fire, And the other stone was Laternes for that will not drown with any Water... next is to Tell you Truly, how... these STONES were found whereon these SCIENCES were Written. THE Great HERMES (Surnamed TRISMAGISTUS, or three times Great) Being both King, Priest and Philosopher, (in EGYPT) he found One of them, and Lived in the Year of the World Two Thousand and Seventy Six (2076 BC), in the Reign of NINUS, and some think him to be Grandson to CUSH, which was Grandson to NOAH, he was the first that began to Learn of Astrology, To Admire the other Wonders of Nature; He proved, there was but One GOD, Creator of all Things, He Divided the Day into Twelve Hours. He is also thought to be the first who Divided the ZODIACK into Twelve Signes, He was scribe to OSYRIS King of EGYPT; And is said to have invented Ordinary Writing, and Hierogliphiks, the first (Anno Mundi. MDCCCX.) Laws of the Egyptians; And Divers Sciences, and Taught them unto other Men."

This excerpt from the manuscript shows that - rather than the Sethites - its author attributed the descendents of Cain and Lamech with building two stone pillars in Egypt, and also believed that the Cainites were far more creative and talented than the Sethites. Furthermore, the author believed that the monuments the Cainites supposedly built preserved four specific types of knowledge: geometry, music, metal working, and weaving. They also believe these structures were built during the reign of the legendary god/king of Egypt called Osiris. However, according to the Book of Jasher, the god/king Osiris lived during the time of Abraham, which was long after the Flood.

As proof that the Indigo Jones manuscript is a sloppy forgery full of false history, the pyramids at Giza and Dahshur do not encode any direct knowledge of music, metal-working, or weaving. However, these pyramids do display a major knowledge of geometry that includes complex mathematics, physics, and highly sophisticated astronomical and Star-Gospel knowledge, which the Indigo Jones manuscript says absolutely nothing about. We can therefore assume that the Cainites were not more creative than the Sethites. Rather, we can confidently assert that the Sethites were highly creative mathematicians and skilled master scientists in their own right.

Despite its glaring flaws, the Indigo Jones manuscript is touted as fact by those who hate the truth of the Bible and wish to discredit all that it says. That is why this forgery boldly yet falsely asserts that the Cainites, who followed the false teachings of the fallen Watchers, supposedly built the structures that Josephus correctly assigned to the godly Sethites before the Flood.

Though it is obvious that the Indigo Jones manuscript attempts to mislead people into thinking that the Cainites built the pyramids at Giza, however, there could be some truth to the manuscripts' claims that the Cainites created some record of their beliefs. In fact, the Cainites may have been the builders of the small, largely ruined pyramids attributed to the Old Kingdom Pharaohs Unas and Pepi I.

Now, as will be shown later, the Cainites were easily influenced by the fallen angels and their Nephilim offspring long before the Sethites fell under their spell. It is therefore quite possible that these two inscribed pillars in Egypt attributed to Unas and Pepi - who lived before the Flood - may contain the oldest written record of Cainite religious beliefs. These consist of occult incantations, which were meant to be recited to sway deities to overlook the sinfulness of each person uttering them. Therefore, could the Pyramid Texts be part of the teachings of the fallen Watchers, which Cainan the son of Arphaxad supposedly copied and hid from Noah? Or did Cainan find the Dendera Zodiac and subsequently become the first person to pervert the purpose of the Star Gospel, just as ignorant people twist our written Scriptures today? It is certainly possible that one or both occurred in the case of Cainan, though we won't know for sure until Yahshua comes.

Due to its disagreement with the Bible, Book of 1 Enoch, and Book of Jubilees, the Indigo Jones Manuscript seems to have been created to support the false idea that there was only one patriarch named Enoch prior to the Great Flood, and this Enoch was not of the godly line of Seth, but of Cain. This lie has been promulgated by several scholars (unfortunately including David Rohl) who believe that there was only one line of patriarchal kings prior to the Great Flood instead of the two listed in the Book of Genesis.

Nonetheless, the idea that the two men named Enoch found in the Pre-Flood bloodlines of both Seth and Cain were the same man is an outright heresy meant to obscure the fact that there are two very real, very powerful, and very opposed spiritual and intellectual philosophies in the world today - and these warring ideologies have been around since Eve listened to the Serpent in the Garden. These opposing ideologies have always been at odds with one another, and clashes between people groups who follow one or the other ideology are the source of all wars, including those surrounding the Middle East Crisis and the War on Terrorism. In one ideology, it is mankind, angels and/or demons that are deified and worshipped. Meanwhile, the other ideology worships the one true God of love and light called Yahweh, who is completely just, totally good, and incapable of evil. We will discuss these warring ideologies much more in future sections of this book.

The Indigo Jones Manuscript states that the deified Hermes Trismegistus found the writings of the Cainites and then invented Astrology, which is a gross perversion of the Sacred Astronomy that the Sethites developed. This partly identifies Hermes with Cainan, who was not a grandson of Cush, but of Shem. Therefore, the grandson of Cush mentioned here is likely none other than Nimrod, who was deified as the gods Tammuz and Bacchus (i.e. "Bar Cush," or Son of Cush), among others. Could Nimrod, like Cainan, have found and perverted Pre-Flood teachings? Or could Nimrod have coaxed or coerced Cainan to share what he had learned? Either eventuality is certainly possible.

Incidentally, since the Book of Jubilees attributes Cainan with being able to read these Pre-Flood writings of the Watchers, it precludes the fact that he understood the meanings of the symbols used to record them. Therefore, some form of symbolic writing obviously existed prior to the Great Flood. If so, writing and record keeping were *not* invented after the Flood by Hermes/Cush or anyone else - only revived, altered, and/or restored from pre-existing writings.

As will be shown in Chapter Seven, the mythical god/king of Egypt called Osiris may have been none other than Cush or Hermes. Though Hermes was supposedly the father of Ninus in the Indigo Jones manuscript, Ninus could well be a perversion of "Nimrod," the name of the evil emperor of Babylon who rose to power after the Flood, created a false religion centered on Astrology and the worship of mankind and demons, and formed a world empire symbolized by the doomed Tower of Babel. It is therefore likely that Shem's grandson Cainan found some of the secret teachings of the Watchers regarding Astronomy and the Star Gospel, and then foolishly shared it with Nimrod. However, this knowledge was only meant to be revealed to extremely wise men with great powers of discernment, and - as the Bible and the Book of Jasher suggest - Nimrod was a mighty man of valor, but he was also in rebellion against God, and therefore did not have godly spiritual discernment.

Before we move on to other topics, it is vitally important here to remember that the Indigo Jones manuscript attributes the knowledge of writing, time-keeping, record-keeping, and astronomy to Hermes Trismegistus - a.k.a. Nimrod - who was falsely painted as a supposed scion of the ancient Wise Men called Magi. This teaching is in direct opposition to the record of the Jewish historians Josephus and the Semitic writers of the Book of Jasher and Jubilees, which testify that the righteous descendents of Seth rather than Cain invented writing, developed Astronomy, and built two stone pillars to preserve their knowledge before the Great Flood. The Book of Jasher also records that Abraham taught the ancient Egyptians Astronomy, which means they likely did not study the stars or refer to them much in their religious myths until after Abraham's visit to Egypt.

Sadly - to their eternal peril - those who currently promote the false teachings of the Pre-Flood Cainites are doing as Nimrod and Arphaxad's son Cainan did after the Flood. These deceived people idolize mankind and demons, experiment with Astrological "magic," worship false gods, practice idolatry and Sorcery, and grossly misuse Sacred Astronomy - thereby turning it into a demonic religion and means of fortune-telling. They are the damned modern torchbearers of a great spiritual deception - one that many biblical prophets foresaw.

If you have not already read the Author's Foreword of this book, you may want to do so now to whet your appetite for the material in the following chapters. The Author's Foreword contains a succinct overview of the source and inspiration behind the two opposing ideologies in this world today. For this reason, it will help readers to understand the purpose of this book better, and it may also inspire them to raise some important questions. It is my hope that these questions will be adequately answered in the remainder of this book.

Chapter 4: Watchers and Nephilim - A Legacy of Evil

"I saw in the visions of my head while on my bed, **and there was a watcher (i.e. "eer" or "ire"), a holy one (i.e. "kadeesh" or "saint"), coming down from heaven.** *He cried aloud and said thus: 'Chop down the tree and cut off its branches, strip off its leaves and scatter its fruit. Let the beasts get out from under it, and the birds from its branches... Let his heart be changed from that of a man, let him be given the heart of a beast, and let seven times pass over him.* **This decision is by the decree of the watchers (i.e. "irene"), and the sentence by the word of the holy ones (i.e. "kadeesh"),** *in order that the living may know that the Most High rules in the kingdom of men, gives it to whomever He will, and sets over it the lowest of men." - Daniel 4:14-17 (NKJ)*

In the above Scripture, King Nebuchadnezzar of Babylon was relaying a dream to the prophet Daniel for interpretation. King Nebuchadnezzar re-named Daniel as Belteshazzar after the chief male deity of Babylon, and called Daniel *"the chief of the magicians"* (Daniel 4:8-9). This meant that Daniel was the chief court Magi, or Wise Man. This places Daniel as leader over the same learned class of men as those who followed the Star of Bethlehem to find Yahshua. Incidentally, this may be why the Wise Men who sought Yahshua awaited His Coming! They may have been entrusted to do so by Daniel himself, who was given the Prophecy of the Seventy Weeks to pinpoint the exact year of Yahshua's birth. See Book One for a detailed explanation of the celestial signs at Yahshua's birth in 3 BC that Daniel's Seventy Weeks Prophecy pointed toward.

After Jerusalem fell, the Israelite captive Daniel, who was a young noble of the Tribe of Judah, was chosen to serve King Nebuchadnezzar in Babylon because he was attractive and intelligent. This earned Daniel the right to live in the king's palace, where he was educated in the language and literature of the Chaldeans (Daniel 1:3-6). It was here that Daniel probably showed an unusual aptitude for applying Sacred Astronomy, which was a Chaldean specialty that the Babylonians, Persians, and Parthians inherited, and that Abraham and the Magi who found Yahshua in Bethlehem were fully acquainted with. In fact, the Magi may have been Zoroastrian priests or Jews who came from Parthia - the land that once belonged to the Chaldeans. Some even speculate that Daniel may have been the man who inspired the prophet

Zoroaster to form the Zoroastrian religion in Persia - a religion that closely parallels Judaism and Christianity.

Like the Magi who found Christ, Daniel was a Mage, and as such he was completely familiar with the Language of God and the Gospel in the Stars. Incidentally, *there is not one word in the Bible passages concerning Daniel or the Magi that condemns them as Sorcerers or evildoers!* What this clearly conveys is that not all stargazing in ancient times was the fortune-telling variety known as Astrology, which is condemned in the Bible because it is a form of Sorcery. Instead, as has been maintained throughout this book series, Sacred Astronomy is a holy and divinely sanctioned science whose practitioners seek to determine God's Will as it is revealed in the heavens, and then seek to act in keeping with it. For example, the Magi who came to honor Christ as a toddler with gifts definitely acted in keeping with God's revealed Will by pointing the world to the divine Author of their existence and salvation. Meanwhile, Herod acted as a Sorcerer by trying to *change* God's revealed will!

Not only did Daniel have a keen ability to understand the language of symbolism in the Star Gospel, but he was also very good at interpreting dreams, which is a gift that his remarkable ancestral cousin Joseph shared. Now, following Nebuchadnezzar's recollection of his strange dream of a mighty tree that gets cut down, Daniel was reluctant to tell the king what the dream meant. This is because the angels called Watchers - acting on Yahweh's behalf - had decreed that the king would be plagued with madness for seven "times," or years, and would lose his position as king until his sanity was miraculously restored.

Interestingly, this passage in Daniel is the only one in the Bible that definitively mentions the Watchers, which translates as "Irene" in Hebrew, and may be the root word that inspired the name for the country of Ireland, which was once part of one big continent - along with North America, England and Europe before the Great Flood. As was shown in the previous chapter, the truth that I have uncovered about Stonehenge certainly suggests that the name "Ireland" could have been chosen for that land because many of the "Irene" or Watchers who inhabited Earth along with men at one time settled in what we now call the British Isles and helped and educated the people who shared the land with them. Whether they were good or evil Watchers is open to debate, but my guess is that they were all initially good. Eventually, however, some of them sinned and left "Ireland" to cohabitate with women, and those that sinned chose Mount Hermon in modern day Lebanon as their new abode because it was likely near to Cainite held land.

Without other spiritual resources to refer to, any reader that stumbles upon the elusive references to the Watchers in the Bible is left to wonder who the Watchers were, or why they had the ability to issue decrees over men on God's behalf. Thankfully, the Book of Jubilees, 1 Enoch, and Jewish commentaries expounding upon God's Word preserve many more details about the Watchers. Jews and Christians should therefore see these works as having much more veracity concerning the Watchers than Pagan legends. From the Book of Jubilees, for example, we learn that the Watchers are angelic beings that were originally sent by Yahweh to watch over and instruct mankind in the ways of righteousness, and to bring some aspects of higher civilization to them:

> *"...and he called his name Jared, for in his days **the angels of the Lord descended on the earth, those who are named the Watchers,** that they should instruct the children of men, and that they should do judgment and uprightness on the earth." - Jubilees 4:15-16*

In essence, then, during the Sethite Enoch's father Jared's lifetime, the Watchers were sent to Earth to be mankind's guardian angels. They had a holy purpose, and were meant to be the teachers and benefactors of God's human children and to aid them in tending to and caring for the Earth. Unfortunately, when Satan discovered God's plan to help mankind via the Watchers, he was no doubt furiously angry, and quickly devised a way to thwart God's Will by attempting to corrupt the Watchers.

In the Book of 1 Enoch, Lucifer or Satan was called Azazel, and he was the first angel to fall. Later, Azazel led other angels to rebel against God. Subsequently, Azazel taught mankind their two worst vices: the deceit of vanity and the selfishness of covetousness that leads to war. For being the first to fall and the most wicked among the fallen angels that sinned against God and conspired to destroy mankind, Azazel was ascribed with all of the guilt of the damned (1 Enoch 10:8-9). Thereafter, Azazel was bound and buried alive to await judgment in a dark, barren wasteland that may be somewhere beneath the surface of the Earth (1 Enoch 10:4-6).

At first glance, this seems to contradict the Bible, which indicates that Satan is still able to roam about in Heaven and on the Earth quite freely (Job 1:7; Zech. 3:1). However, just as the Apostle Paul mentions that traveling "out of the body" or astral projection is possible for humans to do, there is no doubt that angels can also travel this way (2 Cor. 12:2-3). They could even be masquerading as the Avatars or Ascended Masters so revered by Hindus, Buddhists, and New Agers today. Therefore, though Satan is still bound and entombed in darkness, he has been traveling about the Earth in spirit form, and will continue to do so until God sends an angel to physically release him and many other fallen angels and demons from the bottomless pit inside the Earth for a short time during the Great Tribulation (Rev. 9:1-11). Though it is often described as a fiery place of punishment, the bottomless pit or abyss is not the same as the Lake of Fire, which is a place of everlasting torment that will be completely removed from the Earth after the New Heaven and New Earth are created.

According to 1 Enoch, the same fate that befell Azazel also visited the other fallen angels, though their place of imprisonment is described as a barren wasteland filled with columns of fire rather than the total darkness of Azazel's place in that prison:

> "And I saw a deep abyss, with columns of heavenly fire, and **among them I saw columns of fire** fall... And beyond that abyss I saw a place which had no firmament of the heaven above, and no firmly founded earth beneath it: there was no water upon it, and no birds, but it was a waste and horrible place. I saw there seven stars like great burning mountains, and to me, when I inquired regarding them, the angel said: 'This place is the end of heaven and earth: **this has become a prison for the stars and the host of heaven**... And the stars which roll over the fire are they which have transgressed the commandment of the Lord in the beginning... And **He was wroth with them, and bound them till the time when their guilt should be consummated (even) for ten thousand years.**
>
> And Uriel said to me: 'Here shall stand the angels who have connected themselves with women, and their spirits assuming many different forms are defiling mankind and shall lead them astray into sacrificing to demons as gods, (here shall they stand,) till the day of the great judgement in which they shall be judged..." - 1 Enoch 18:11-14, 19:1-2

In the first preceding paragraph quoted from 1 Enoch, Enoch was shown that the *"hosts of heaven"* or the fallen angels who sinned with Azazel at the very beginning of human history as well as the fallen Watchers that *"connected themselves with women"* were punished by being bound in a fiery pit together for ten thousand years. Now, since the time allotted for the consummation of mankind's salvation is a period of seven thousand years, this ten thousand years must be a figurative number referring to the ten increments of 700 years in Enoch's Prophecy of the 7,000 Years (a.k.a. the Apocalypse of Weeks), which includes the Millennial Rule of Christ (1 Enoch 93:1-10, 91:12-17). In this prophecy, which is discussed in detail in Book Four, Enoch foresaw the future of mankind in ten "weeks" of 700 years each.

Beginning with 1 Enoch 19:1, the preceding quote also tells us that - even after the fallen angels were cast into the fiery abyss (a.k.a. bottomless pit) to await judgment - the "spirits" or spiritual essence of the fallen Watchers could still assume many different forms. This suggests that the fallen angels were not only capable of traveling outside of the body, but that their spirits can assume many different shapes in this out-of-body state. Interestingly, the Nephilim children of the fallen angels were imbued with the evil spiritual essence of the fallen angels who fathered them instead of God's essence. This is likely why the spirits of the Nephilim were doomed to roam the Earth as spirits after their physical bodies died, and these demon spirits can also assume hideous forms.

If the evil angels imbued their Giant Nephilim offspring with a portion of their divine and immortal spiritual essence, this explains the fact that, though the Nephilim could be killed, their spirits could not be. As quoted later in this chapter, the Book of 1 Enoch states that the spirits of all dead Nephilim were destined to become the demons that plague mankind today (1 Enoch 15:6-12). Even after the Flood, the Nephilim who perished still existed as demons and were able to possess people and lead mankind into sin and rebellion against Yahweh all over again, just as the spirits of the fallen angels in prison can use astral projection to wander about the Earth and deceive humanity by pretending to be the Avatars or Ascended Masters so revered by proponents of Eastern mysticism and the New Age Movement.

Thankfully, the deception of the fallen angels will be forever stopped when Satan and the fallen angels are cast into the Lake of Fire (Rev. 20:7-10). When this occurs, the fallen angels will likely be bound with impenetrable chains that will never be removed again, as is indicated by following section of the Book of 1 Enoch. The Lake of Fire is likely deep inside the Earth, but may eventually exist in a separate part of God's New Creation. Enoch's vision of the judgment of the fallen angels at the end of human history was recorded in the following verses:

> *"And I looked and turned to another part of the earth, and saw there a deep valley with burning fire. And they brought the kings and the mighty, and began to cast them into this deep valley. And there mine eyes saw how they made these their instruments, iron chains of immeasurable weight. And I asked the angel of peace who went with me, saying:* **'For whom are these chains being prepared?' And he said**

unto me: 'These are being prepared for the hosts of Azazel, so
that they may take them and cast them into the abyss of
complete condemnation, *and they shall cover their jaws with*
rough stones as the Lord of Spirits commanded. And Michael,
and Gabriel, and Raphael, and Phanuel shall take hold of
them on that great day, and cast them on that day into the
burning furnace, that the Lord of Spirits may take vengeance
on them for their unrighteousness in becoming subject to
Satan and leading astray those who dwell on the earth.'" - 1
Enoch 54:1-6

This passage calls the Lake of Fire *"the burning furnace,"* which
is located in a *"deep valley."* It also explains that the four holy
archangels that govern the four corners and winds of the Earth -
Michael, Gabriel, Raphael, and Phanuel - will also be given the final
privilege of casting Satan and his evil angels into the Lake of Fire, where
their torment will never end (Rev. 14:11).

Myths: Evidence of Watchers in Human Affairs

After reading about the Watchers in 1 Enoch, Jubilees, and the
Bible, many are compelled to ask: "What archeological and historical
evidence exists that supports the past presence of these Watchers on the
Earth?" According to traditional views of the past, there is no compelling
physical or intellectual evidence to support the idea that a race of angelic
beings once inhabited the Earth and intervened in the affairs of men.
Most archeologists tell us that nothing unusual happened in the past that
would support the presence of a superior race of beings that interfered
with humanity's physical, intellectual, and spiritual development.
However, if we view all the available evidence from a more objective
perspective, this supposition can be proven false.

Some of the biggest proofs of the past existence of the Watchers
and Nephilim and their activity in human affairs are found in the many
Pagan mythologies of the world. In every Pagan belief system, there is a
hierarchy of gods and goddesses who exercised control over the Earth
and human affairs, demanded worship, food, and gifts in return for their
protection, and exacted retribution and meted out punishment when
they were displeased or angry with their human subjects. Even more
disturbingly, their male deities often lusted after women and had sexual
relations with them, thereby producing hybrid children such as
Hercules, who was supposedly the son of the god Zeus and a mortal
woman named Alcmene.

Unfortunately, though the study of Classical Mythology is considered to be a fine literary and philosophical pursuit and an acceptable form of entertainment, modern-day scholars in the West have routinely scoffed at these myths as pure fiction, thereby silently proclaiming that our human ancestors were superstitious and irrational - even if their myths did reflect a great deal about people's intellectual character and emotional tendencies. By doing so, they have also silently compelled the rest of humanity to accept these myths as pure fantasies. And so, to satisfy the establishment, people often dismiss all of these complex mythologies with their colorful and devious deities as entertaining fairy tales.

However, if one discards the theory of Evolution and maintains a biblical worldview instead, then we have no right to assume that the ancient Greeks, Romans, Persians, Asians, Indians, Ethiopians, Egyptians and a host of other people groups were any less intelligent than we are today, or that they were mentally inferior to us. In fact, their intellectual, scientific and technological achievements and the many pieces of their high civilization that are littering the shelves of virtually every museum on Earth tell us the exact opposite story.

The massive profusion of finely crafted jewelry, weapons, vases, mosaics, frescoes, household items, idols, ruins, and funerary goods left by our ancient ancestors on every continent shows that they were not Stone Age simpletons living in caves, but immensely creative and rational intellectuals that developed and maintained all the elements of higher civilization that we utilize today. Furthermore, once we see through their Pagan worldview, their historical records contain accurate details about major political events, personages, and happenings in their civilizations as a source of knowledge for their descendents.

Since most academic people appreciate and admire the rationality and intelligence displayed in the historical records, mathematics, science, geometry, literature, accounting, and technology of our ancestors that are necessary for a higher civilization to flourish, **then it follows that they should appreciate their theology as being just as rational and intelligent.** But because they do not, this becomes a vexing problem for anyone trying to uncover the truth.

If we do accept ancient mythologies as sober attempts at history by fairly rational and sane human beings, then we would have no cause to doubt the fact that *they were describing a very real state of affairs,* and we would be forced to re-examine what we think we know about the past in a new light. That said, we have to be careful not to assign more importance to these ancient Pagan histories and myths than to ancient Judeo-Christian literature. We therefore should take the events and characters discussed in Pagan myths, and compare them to what we are told in the Bible, 1 Enoch, Jubilees, and the Book of Jasher, and leave the lesser Pseudepigraphical or Apocryphal works out of the picture unless they help to clarify something that these more reliable records do not elaborate on.

Other reasonably good sources of biblically related information are the histories of Josephus, Louis Ginzberg's "The Legends of the Jews," which is a compilation of legends from the Talmud and Midrash, the Talmud and Midrash themselves, the Testaments of the Twelve Patriarchs, 1 and 2 Maccabees, 1 and 2 Esdras, 2 Enoch (to a limited extent), the Epistle of Barnabus, and Baruch, Chapter 6. The reason for my omission of many other lesser religious works is simple: many of them contain corruptions and additions to the historical data in them. Even the somewhat reliable Judeo-Christian resources mentioned in this paragraph contain errors. Therefore, their value must be weighed against Scripture and used with caution.

Not surprisingly, when we examine these ancient Judeo-Christian sources of history, it becomes clear that some of the Watchers or fallen angels behaved much like the false deities expounded about in Classical Myth that lusted after mankind and toyed with them at every opportunity. According to many of these ancient mythologies, the gods dwelled on Earth on top of a mountain so high that it was always swathed in clouds.

Among the few mountains on Earth today that are high enough to be continually cloaked in clouds, however, the mountain identified as Mount Olympus in Greece is not one of them. In addition, it is a barren and inhospitable place today - certainly not a location that would serve as a good dwelling place and base of operations by human standards. It is therefore highly unlikely that the Watchers ever dwelled atop the Mount Olympus located in Greece. However, as will be shown in Chapter Nine, this fabled mountain of the gods likely did exist - though it is not anywhere near Greece.

Now, as shown in Chapter Two - and in agreement with Pagan myths - the Book of 1 Enoch, Jasher, and Jubilees explain that Enoch spent much time apart from men while he was being instructed by God's holy angels. It is therefore likely that these holy Watchers did not reside where men ordinarily dwelt. In fact, it is highly likely that they sought remote and inaccessible places to reside such as high mountains or valleys cut off from civilization centers by ridges of extremely high mountains similar to the Alps, Himalayas, Rockies, or Andes Mountains.

According to the Book of 1 Enoch, the first prideful and jealous angel to rebel against God was the Archangel Azazel or Satan. Later, Azazel was followed by two hundred rebellious Watchers that left the extremely remote abode of their sinless peers and found a new base of operations for their nefarious activities on top of Mount Hermon in modern day Lebanon (1 Enoch 6:6). Unlike the distant home of the good Watchers, these evil angels settled atop a mountain situated right in the middle of the heavily populated area of the Earth that we call the Fertile Crescent today. However, from the preponderance of Pagan myths telling us that the Earth was filled with many gods, goddesses, and partly divine heroes at one time that lusted after and exercised dominion over mankind, it is likely that the fallen Watchers and their Nephilim children did not stay close to Mount Hermon. In fact, they appear to have spread out all over the Earth to rule over men.

Therefore, despite God's desire that the Watchers should remain separate from and subservient to mankind, two hundred of the Watchers sinned by leaving their set-apart (i.e. holy) dwelling places. In an evil attempt to put mankind in a wrongfully submissive position, these fallen angels decided to proclaim themselves as gods, and to demand worship.

Though men probably initially saw these angelic beings as their teachers and friends, the objective of these fallen Watchers was far from benevolent. Since they were jealous of mankind's place as the potential spiritual and literal brethren of Yahshua the Messiah, these rebellious angels were determined to destroy what Yah had so carefully created. Therefore, as 1 Enoch records, the fallen angels used their advanced knowledge of biology, science and technology to destroy, pervert, and defile every living thing.

In a similar evil fashion, the Nephilim offspring of the Watchers also likely saw themselves as superior to men. In fact, some legends preserved in Jewish religious records suggest that the Nephilim eventually sought to destroy every last human being in a massive genocidal war. As will be shown in upcoming portions of this book, however, the Nephilim proved to be so uncontrollably violent that - in addition to killing many men and animals - they also destroyed many of their own kind. Likewise, men also became very violent in order to protect themselves.

Due to the anarchy and lawlessness among most of the people at that time, the entire Earth soon became hopelessly corrupt and incessantly violent. The Book of Jasher describes the Pre-Flood breakdown of civilization in this way:

*"And all the sons of men departed from the ways of the Lord in those days as they multiplied upon the face of the earth with sons and daughters, and they taught one another their evil practices and they continued sinning against the Lord. **And every man made unto himself a god, and they robbed and plundered every man his neighbor as well as his relative, and they corrupted the earth, and the earth was filled with violence.**" - Jasher 4:16-17*

The passage above that says *"every man made unto himself a god"* suggests that men eventually rejected the angels and Nephilim as their gods and instead made themselves gods by virtue of their oppressive tyranny and power over one another. In other words, they mimicked their fallen Watcher overlords, and sought to wield demonic power and dominion over one another instead of fostering God's righteousness, love, and mercy. In fact, as will be shown quite clearly in Chapter Seven, many human leaders were celebrated so much by their subjects that they were eventually seen as deities themselves, and worshipped as such.

Did Extraterrestrials Visit Earth Before the Flood?

Finding sentient life anywhere else in our Universe other than Earth is a burning desire of many who wish to think we are not alone in the vast reaches of the Universe. Perhaps as a result of that desire or fear, many Sci-Fi movies and television series explore this idea, with the most notable among them being the Star Wars movies and the Star Trek series, which both featured many alien races that supposedly developed parallel to mankind along different evolutionary pathways. Some of these beings were benevolent, while others were hostile toward mankind.

In addition to our fascination with the possibility that fantastic creatures and intelligent beings besides ourselves can be found elsewhere in the Universe, millions of people believe that extraterrestrial beings have visited Earth on numerous occasions. Some believe this because they have seen UFO's, or know people who say they have seen them. Even more fantastically, some people claim to have been abducted by these aliens and experimented with. Some women even claim to have had fetuses planted inside or harvested out of their wombs by these alien beings. As this chapter will reveal, this fetus-harvesting may be a chilling echo of the past.

Others believe in aliens because of the books that have been written that attempt to identify the deities of ancient times as intelligent alien beings from another world. Still others claim that the United States and other countries have found the wreckage of crashed alien space craft that were reverse engineered in recent times to develop modern military and commercial jet liners, microchip technology used in computers, visual media and communication devices, laser technology, and digital satellite and microwave communications.

Despite the current belief among many intellectuals that the knowledge humanity possesses has an extraterrestrial origin, however, almost all human technological advancements over the last one hundred and fifty years can be seen as logical developments after the discovery of electricity, the light bulb, the internal combustion engine, the telephone, and television - all of which show no signs of having been developed by aliens of any kind. Nonetheless, due to the remarkable progress mankind has made in technology, medicine, and science in the past fifty years, an unsettling mania that all human civilizations rose and fell in tandem with extraterrestrial visitations is increasing. It is as if mankind were collectively being prepared to face a very real (but far less benevolent) "close encounter of the third kind" at some point in the future. As a result, anyone who suspects a dark side to all this is often compelled to ask, "Who or what could be causing this UFO mania, and what are we possibly being prepared for?"

Interestingly, many reported alien abductions and UFO sightings have a paranormal quality to them. People often report being taken to a spaceship in the middle of the night or seeing someone else being taken. The aliens that abduct these people are nearly always described as short, slight gray-colored humanoids with huge black eyes. This would suggest that the agencies causing these phenomena aren't extraterrestrial visitations from Outer Space at all, but clear signs of the existence of demons and at least one race of humanoid Nephilim that were intelligent enough to understand and utilize technological knowledge.

One little known but important fact about alien abductions that ties the aliens in these cases to demons and demonic activity is that there have been over fifty reported cases of alien abductions in progress that were instantly stopped when the potential abductees uttered the name of Yahshua or Jesus in a plea for supernatural aid. This shows that these alien beings are demons or Nephilim whose spirits become demons, for the Bible states that demons are subject to anyone who loves Yahshua and shares in His authority by using His Name in prayer:

> *"Then the seventy returned with joy, saying, 'Lord,*
> *even the demons are subject to us in Your name.' And He*

*said to them, 'I saw Satan fall like lightning from heaven.
Behold, I give you the authority to trample on serpents and
scorpions, and over all the power of the enemy, and nothing
shall by any means hurt you. Nevertheless do not rejoice in
this, that the spirits are subject to you, but rather rejoice
because your names are written in heaven.'" - Luke 10:17-20
(NKJ)*

In this wonderful Scripture, Yahshua is telling His disciples that
their joy over being able to cast out demons in His Name should pale in
comparison to the fact that their names are written in Heaven in the
Book of Life, and that they now have authority over all the creatures of
the Earth, not just demons. Therefore the poison of snakes and
scorpions can no longer hurt them anymore than a demon could -
provided they trust in Yahshua and utter His Name in faith (Luke 10:19;
Mark 16:18; Acts 28:3-6). For this reason, Yahshua proclaimed that the
deepest joy of the disciples should stem from the knowledge of their
salvation rather than from the authority in His Name that they have over
demons, which is nonetheless also a good reason to celebrate.

Significantly, this is also when Yahshua informed His disciples
that He was there when Satan fell *"like lightning from heaven."* This
statement must have made the disciples pause and wonder how Yahshua
could have seen Satan fall. Even though they already knew Yahshua was
far more than a righteous human teacher, they likely did not yet suspect
that He was also claiming to be their God in fleshly form.

In this passage, it is likely that Yahshua was referring to Satan
being cast down to Earth to cause mischief after he and his angels lost a
war that broke out with God's holy angels over the control of heaven in
the distant past. However, this may also be referring to the moment
when the Preincarnate Yahshua watched the archangel Michael cast
Azazel into a prison inside the Earth where he has been bound to await
judgment, but still can cause mischief using astral projection and
spiritual possession.

According to 1 Enoch, demons do indeed exist and they are the
spirits of physically dead Nephilim. Furthermore, all of these evil spirits
have an all-consuming burning desire to hurt, deceive, and destroy
humanity. These wicked entities are also the source of many lies
concerning human origins. By far their biggest and most successful lies
to date are the lie of Evolution and the deception of Intelligent Design,
which does not stipulate that God Almighty had to be the designer. In
short, there are ungodly top scientists and intellectuals that are being
controlled by these demons that want us to believe that Homo sapiens
are just one end product of angelic genetic experiments.

Though there is some truth to the idea that the fallen angels tampered with God's creation using their knowledge of genetics, however, they did not create mankind! Instead, as the Book of 1 Enoch teaches, they created the Nephilim or Giants of old. Rather than appearing human, many of these violent superhuman beings did not resemble mankind at all, but assumed gargantuan proportions and hideous forms. As the Book of Jasher indicates, their appearance was largely generated by the types of genes that were mixed together to form them. In fact, only the Nephilim that were naturally conceived likely resembled mankind closely. The rest were far more beastly composite creatures that lacked compassion, intellect, and creativity. In short, they were little more than cunning and giant brutes that soon developed an insatiable taste for all animal flesh and blood - especially that of humans.

Unlike the naturally born half-breed children of the Watchers, the rest of the Nephilim that were genetically manipulated were likely implanted in the wombs of the human women that the fallen angels had chosen to serve as surrogate mothers. These woman likely served only as slaves, and the inhuman creatures they gave birth to likely did not look humanoid at all. It is even horrifically possible that the women so chosen to incubate these genetically modified fetuses were later killed or eaten by the very creatures they gave birth to - a terrifying idea that was recently explored in the classic Sci-Fi movie "Aliens." We will discuss the probable way these evil creations of the fallen angels looked in upcoming sections.

The Affects of the Watchers on Human Culture

There is much evidence in ancient Egypt and Mesopotamia that there was an unusual surge in technological and scientific knowledge around 3400 BC. Cultures throughout the Fertile Crescent apparently went from Stone Age tribal shepherding and farming communities to advanced civilizations seemingly *overnight*, with little or no developmental stages evident in any of the archeological strata. An interesting but misguided book on the subject is "Fingerprints of the Gods" by Graham Hancock. In it, Hancock points to the astounding abruptness at which this tremendous cultural flowering occurred in the far past. Advanced societies like our own, complete with a sophisticated government, refined religious mythology, and many artistic developments in writing, the arts, and the sciences seem to have appeared fully developed at the very onset of these civilizations.

The same is true, to some extent, for the sophisticated societies that appeared in Mexico and Central and South America. Despite archeological claims that the oldest of these sites are from around 1500 BC, there is reason to believe that some of these cultures, especially that of the Olmecs, are considerably older. The Olmec civilization predated the Mayan culture and is considered to be the oldest native civilization in the Americas. Though the Olmec culture is dated to no earlier than 1500 BC, the beginning date of the Olmec and Mayan Long-Count calendar is curiously set to August 13th, 3114 BC. This fact almost begs us to ask the question: "Why would the Olmecs begin keeping time at a date so remote into the past from their own? Wouldn't it be more logical to start their calendar when the founder of their civilization was born?" Interestingly, according to the Biblical Chronology in the Appendix, Enoch was 267 years old in 3114 BC and could very well have invented the Long Count calendar that was so carefully preserved in Mesoamerica. In addition, the ninth Sethite patriarch Lamech - who was the father of Noah - was 15 years old in 3114 BC.

Another burning question that once often came to my mind when contemplating the past was: "What could have caused the tremendous surge in culture, science and creativity around 3400 BC?" In search of answers to this question, some scholars have entertained the idea that aliens from another world have visited Earth and tampered with our normal evolutionary development. Some have even heretically claimed that these powerful beings genetically altered apes or Neanderthals to be more creative and intelligent, thus creating modern Homo sapiens.

Some even speculate that these alien beings introduced fully developed forms of agriculture, science, mathematics, and astronomy to humans who had previously been living as predominantly nomadic Stone Age hunter-gatherers. In other words, they believe that mankind originated from the genetic mixture of these aliens with Neanderthals. Some alien enthusiasts with an atheistic bent also believe these aliens were so much more powerful than mankind that they had much to do with the development of the religious mythologies around the world, which are based on superstition and mankind's gullibility in seeing these aliens as deities. Sadly, these atheists are partly correct, and therein lies considerable danger to traditional Judeo-Christian beliefs. For this reason, the information in this chapter is vitally important for people to know and understand before they make any foolish decisions that may adversely affect their eternal destinies.

For example, according to Anti-Christian scholars like Zecharia Sitchin and Andrew Collins, archeological and literary evidence supposedly suggests that mankind is nothing more than one variety of an endless array of races created by alien genetic tampering. They claim that the ancients had technological abilities that were equal to and even superior to modern humanity's at one time, and that this technology was inherited from a superior alien race that saw mankind as their slaves. They also claim that many of the greatest advancements in human knowledge did not originate with mankind, but with these aliens from another realm that the Babylonians called the Anunnaki. Are these scholars right? Could aliens from elsewhere in our Universe have invaded Earth, become our "gods", and forever changed our history?

These are intriguing questions. However, though something very unusual appears to have occurred in the past to speed up humanity's knowledge in some of the arts and sciences, this was not true in every area of knowledge. Indeed, contrary to modern thought, there is evidence that our Stone Age ancestors developed the rudiments of civilization quite rapidly, and without any outside intervention. In fact, the Bible makes it clear that *human beings alone were farmers like Cain, or keepers of domesticated animals like Abel by the second generation from Adam and Eve*. Furthermore, people were not only living in towns and settlements, but in permanent cities within the third generation, and long before the Watchers arrived at the time of Enoch's father Jared (Gen. 4:17). This indicates that *the first humans were intelligent enough to work out many aspects of higher civilization all on their own, and within a hundred years or so of their creation*.

The Book of Jasher cites Cainan, the son of Enosh and only a third generation Sethite as a great spiritual wise man whose father was the first to call on the Name of Yahweh in supplication and prayer. This means that humanity already had a developed monotheistic form of religion that was not without its prophets and knowledge of God from the Gospel in the Stars even at that remote epoch in history.

Nonetheless, there does seem to be a point when these civilizations took a giant developmental leap forward. In short, our ancestors went from living in simple towns and cities constructed of wood, reed, and mud-brick to building heavily fortified cities with fired bricks and finely worked stone almost overnight. In the same way, simple shrines and chieftain's huts gave way to palaces and temples, monotheism was rejected in favor of polytheism, and tribal cultures took on a feudal aspect as one civilization center after another vied for supremacy over all the others. At the same time, the common people were often subjected to harsh control and taxation, and eventually reduced to servitude. Doesn't this sound familiar? Now what could have caused this unusual upsurge in government, art, science, war, and technology? Furthermore, what caused such moral and religious degradation, which developed into Paganism, and reduced most of humanity into the abject slaves of the "gods"?

The Real Aliens Who Came From Heaven to Earth

As mentioned earlier, a group of powerful alien beings that did not originate on Earth did settle on our planet prior to the Great Flood of Noah's time. In fact, the Book of 1 Enoch tells us that Yahweh appointed special angels to *watch over* the Earth during the patriarchal reign of Enoch's father Jared. This is why the antediluvian patriarch and prophet Enoch called them the Watchers in his writings. These Watchers came to mentor mankind around 3400 BC, or about twenty years before Enoch was born in 3381 BC. Intriguingly, this is also the epoch where the archeological record shows that a giant developmental leap forward occurred among many different civilization centers.

This suggests that the Watchers were at least partly responsible for humanity's cultural and spiritual flowering in Mesopotamia and the Middle East. Unfortunately, however, Enoch also tells us that some of the Watchers rebelled against God and became fallen angels. As a result, they began to undo the good work of the holy Watchers by corrupting humanity with forbidden, useless or counterfeit knowledge, and turning them away from righteousness.

Though not all of the holy Watchers chose evil over good, the Book of 1 Enoch tells us that two hundred Watchers led by the fallen angel Semyaza fell into grievous sin by marrying and fornicating with women (1 Enoch 6:1-6, 9:6-10). The most depraved angel to come to Earth and sin, however, was the fallen angel Azazel, who was identified as the ringleader that coerced the other fallen angels to sin, and who was to be ascribed all the blame for their fall (1 Enoch 10:4-9, 54:4, 55:4). This suggests that Azazel is Satan, who tempted Eve in the Garden of Eden.

According to 1 Enoch, Azazel was not alone when he fell, and other fallen angels aided him in his efforts to teach humanity the most horrible of vices - including open rebellion against God, vanity, covetousness and the use of sex, violence and war to obtain power. But the full sexual and genetic corruption of mankind did not begin until about 600 years later - during the lifetime of Enoch's father Jared.

Yet Enoch also makes it clear that there were Watchers who did not fall into sin, and did their best to teach mankind godly approaches to science, technology, and Astronomy. For example, the Book of 1 Enoch speaks of the holy Watchers that guided Enoch in the ways of righteousness, and also instructed him with geographical and astronomical knowledge. In addition, they were experts at interpreting the Gospel in the Stars, and would have encouraged Enoch and the rest of mankind to follow God's righteous paths as laid out in the Stars and in Blood Covenant ceremonies. So, even though there were fallen angels causing trouble early in human history, the holy Watchers were there to try and offset their evil influence.

Indeed, the holy Watchers likely offered their light to mankind for as long as people were open to receiving it - as is evidenced by those Watchers that Enoch knew, and was instructed by. However, the sinful ways of the fallen angels were seductive and powerful. They taught men to aspire to vanity, sensuality, sexual perversion, and the love of self, and then introduced the deadly art of war. After this, it did not take humanity long to succumb to the venomous charms of vice, and to become lost in sinful lusts and violent behavior.

Sadly, the fallen angels taught humanity useless knowledge that was not aimed at understanding and loving God, but in manipulating science, technology, geology and biology in ways that were contrary to Yahweh's Will, and antagonistic to the message that God proclaimed to mankind through the Gospel in the Stars in the Mazzaroth or Zodiac. As a result, people who were born mostly innocent and peaceful were gradually led into sin with the false and/or forbidden knowledge given to them by the fallen Watchers who sinned.

Enoch reveals what this false knowledge was. It began with the evil wisdom that the fallen angel Azazel/Satan gave to humanity. Azazel's methods of polluting mankind with sin included teaching them to aspire to vanity, selfishness, greed, and the use of cosmetics, gaudy jewelry and brightly hued clothing to manipulate and seduce others into moral and sexual sin. According to the Book of Jasher, this promiscuity coupled with a completely selfish desire to remain beautiful at all costs eventually led to abortion on demand, just as it has in today's fallen world (Jasher 2:20-22). In addition, Azazel taught mankind how to make war and weapons of war when he introduced the concept of acquisition and conquest through war, which is a form of covetousness and theft:

> "And Azazel taught men to make swords, and knives, and shields, and breastplates, and made known to them the metals of the earth and the art of working them, and bracelets, and ornaments, and the use of antimony, and the beautifying of the eyelids, and all kinds of costly stones, and all colouring tinctures. And there arose much godlessness, and they committed fornication, and they were led astray, and became corrupt in all their ways." - 1 Enoch 8:1-3

In regard to the art of beautification, it was not the use of cosmetics and ornaments but their overemphasis and deployment in encouraging emotional manipulation, sexual sins and promiscuity that are evil in the sight of Yahweh, as is the overweening pride and vanity that Satan encourages in all those who follow him. As for the dark art of war, God views the shedding of human blood and the violent taking of another human life as the most heinous sins mankind has ever engaged in. But war is not just about killing. It is about coveting your neighbor's possessions, taking the land and animals by force, and then raping and enslaving the people for selfish gain.

In addition to these sins, Enoch states that Azazel taught mankind forbidden heavenly secrets that they had already been seeking to know and understand:

> *"Thou seest what Azazel hath done, who hath taught all unrighteousness on earth and revealed the eternal secrets which were (preserved) in heaven, which men were striving to learn."* - 1 Enoch 9:6-7

At first, I assumed that this passage meant that Azazel had taught the corrupted science behind Astrology and the reading of omens in the Sun, Moon and stars to mankind. However, a half-dozen other fallen angels are described as having done this:

> *"Baraqijal (taught) astrology, Kokabel the constellations, Ezeqeel the knowledge of the clouds, Araqiel the signs of the earth, Shamsiel the signs of the sun, and Sariel the course of the moon."* - 1 Enoch 8:3

It is therefore far more likely that the *"eternal secrets which men were striving to learn"* had much more to do with understanding the laws of Physics and harnessing atomic and other forms of technological and scientific power rather than star-gazing in an effort to find omens. As Azazel no doubt saw it, this type of knowledge would make it easier for men to kill themselves and destroy the Earth, and that was his goal, after all. Remember, Satan hates us all and will never repent. This is also true for the other fallen angels and their Nephilim offspring - though some Pseudepigraphical works erroneously suggest otherwise.

Being made of strange flesh, and opposed to everything godly, the Nephilim were not included in Yahshua's order for His human brethren to love one another. Instead, Yahweh rose up the Israelites as a righteous people to fight against the physical and magical might of the Anakim descendants of the Nephilim. As we will discuss in more depth in Chapter Eight, God called the Israelites not only to subdue, but to murder every last Anakim-tainted people group living in Canaan with swords, arrows and spears. By doing so, our God of Love was making a pointed statement: **anyone who willingly unites with and desires the strange flesh of the Nephilim or Anakim will perish!** In addition, anyone who lusts after strange flesh and does not repent will never be forgiven. We will discuss the spiritual reasons for this in a future section.

Initially, the wars and aggression that sprang up between different people-groups because of the meddling of the fallen angels made living in heavily fortified cities essential. Prior to that, archeological findings show that men lived in small cities and villages and enjoyed relative peace with their neighbors. As will be shown in the next chapter, however, some people began to view raiding and pillaging others to acquire what they needed as a virtue. As a result, those who sought protection from theft, murder and rape needed the protection of walled cities. In that regard, it is possible that the fallen angels, who at first acted as benevolent "gods," initially helped men to build their first fortified cities. In addition, it is likely that the holy Watchers who had not rebelled against God stepped in to help and protect the beleaguered and oppressed people who remained righteous followers of Yahweh.

Unfortunately, even as humanity quickly embraced and excelled at the arts of higher civilization taught to them by the angels, the fallen angels likely played at war along with their human worshippers, sending armies against cities controlled by other fallen angels in heated bids for absolute power. To achieve supremacy, however, they also had to make war against civilization centers governed by godly people being guided by the holy Watchers and Yahweh God's Spirit.

Consequently, if the more godly societies were following the so-called Noahide Laws, which included not murdering people or being cruel to animals (just as Judaism and Christianity do today), they would have been forbidden to fight back by any normal means. Therefore, their only correct recourse to protect themselves and still remain faithful to God's laws would have been to find some remote place to hide to avoid slaughter, which is exactly what some were ordered to do - as will be shown in Noah's case in Chapter Five.

According to Enoch, the false teachings of Azazel/Satan were so bad that God ascribed him with all sin, even though he was not the only fallen angel to engage in teaching humanity false wisdom. For example, Enoch identifies the fallen angel Semyaza as the Watcher who led some of his peers to sexually abuse women and genetically corrupt mankind through their giant offspring.

For a time, antediluvian people were content to be governed by their Watcher and Nephilim overlords. They worshipped and adored these powerful beings for their seemingly benevolent dissemination of forbidden or useless knowledge that made life appear more carefree and enjoyable. But when humanity gradually began to be oppressed, enslaved, and slaughtered at the hands of their false gods, humanity no longer felt adulation for them, but fear and hatred. Indeed, in place of worship and adoration, many human beings became angered at their superhuman overlords, and they began to rebel against them. Soon, their rebellion led to a state of total anarchy and barbarism, and the world was filled with constant hatred and merciless violence.

It was at this point that Yahweh again intervened in human affairs, calling Noah to separate himself from the rest of humanity in order to be free to build the Ark as the world erupted into a continual state of war and rumors of war. These were not ordinary wars over territorial rights or political, religious or economic dominion, however. Instead these attacks were often genocidal in nature. Not only were the fallen angels fighting amongst themselves, but the three races of Nephilim whom they had created were pitted against each other in battles to the death. In addition, various human cultural groups were also warring with one another, and both mankind and the Nephilim were battling each other to the death! With both sides bent on the total extermination of one or the other, one can only imagine how terribly violent and bloody that time in history really was. So it was not just the genetic corruption that grieved God so much, but the unrestrained, merciless violence being engaged in that sickened and saddened Him.

In fact, it was this state of total violence and depravity that led our heavenly Father to desire to annihilate all life on Earth except for Noah and his kin, and the animal life that God chose. Indeed, so outraged was Yahweh over the violence of that time in history that He even blotted out mankind's clear memory of it until now, since we are currently approaching the same level of violence and anarchy that there was prior to the Great Flood due to spiritual rebellion and strong demonic influences.

This is why the Book of 1 Enoch, the Book of Jasher and the Book of Jubilees have finally become readily available. The knowledge contained in them is vitally needed to reach this final generation that will witness Yahshua's return. Unfortunately, however, many unsaved people are already misquoting and misinterpreting these books (especially Freemasons and New Agers), making the need for an apologetic book like the one you are now reading absolutely necessary as the Tribulation approaches.

UFOs: Alien or Advanced Human Technology?

Interestingly, many UFO sightings have been attributed to the Nephilim or Fallen Watchers in recent times. For example, people reported sighting strange, bright lights and "V" or triangle shaped aircraft in the sky at night over Arizona and New Mexico in 2008. These sightings, which have been dubbed the Phoenix Incident, had several natural causes. For example, some were supposedly elaborate hoaxes, or were said to have been caused by airborne flares used by the military in training exercises, which would seem to explain the US Military's lack of concern over these reported UFO sightings in American air space.

Having served in the military, I can offer some enlightenment about their apparent lack of concern regarding UFO sightings in US air space. In fact, while serving in the US Air Force in Hawaii, I learned firsthand that many of these reports of strange lights and "V" or triangle shaped UFOs are *real*. I also learned that they are not being caused by alien aircraft from Outer Space at all, but by advanced, top-secret military aircraft.

Unlike the majority of conspiracy theorists and alien enthusiasts, I don't believe that most of these secret military aircraft have their roots in alien technology. In fact, there is much documented proof that mankind entered the space age on their own merits through the massive amounts of military and civilian scientific research that was done in the 20th Century, especially in the USA, Russia, and Asia.

As a result of all that concentrated research into electronic and computer technology, we humans are now collectively smart enough to devise and develop many wondrous hi-tech gadgets all on our own such as microcomputer technology, nanotechnology, mobile technology, and laser and microwave technology. Unfortunately, however, all of this sophisticated electronics gear has not only improved civilian lifestyles, but has allowed modern industrialized nations to develop the most lethal, efficient and technologically sophisticated armies, navies, and air forces that the world has ever known.

Nonetheless, as will be discussed further in Chapter Five, ancient artifacts and records suggest that various forms of alien technology existed, and some of it may have been uncovered via archeologists or miners. When I say alien, however, I do not mean little green men from Mars or any other planet. Instead, I am referring to angels - specifically the fallen angels who have been called Watchers, Anunnaki, Grays and Nephilim - though the evil, half-human offspring of the fallen angels were the real Nephilim. The Watchers or Anunnaki were not half-human like Nephilim, but immortal angels. These angels are mentioned in the Bible as the "sons of God" or "Beni Elohim" spoken of in Genesis 6:4.

In the Bible, messenger angels looked like men in appearance whenever they materialized in front of human beings, so it is likely that the Anunnaki/Watchers also took the form of extraordinarily handsome and robustly healthy men. However, the humanoid alien beings known as Grays among Science Fiction and Alien enthusiasts do not look like humans. Therefore, they are either a type of living Nephilim or a Nephilim-inspired demonic delusion - though the spacecraft that these aliens supposedly fly around in may not be delusional. In fact, I have no doubt that technologically amazing aircraft are currently in top-secret use around the world. This is partly because I accidentally saw some huge, highly sophisticated aircraft when I was an airman that definitely had to have belonged to the US Military.

I will never forget my sighting of several of these advanced alien-type aircraft early in 1981, while I was living on Hickam Air Force Base in Hawaii. I had been having trouble sleeping one night, so I pulled on some clothes and went outside to sit on the front step of my duplex home in the enlisted personnel housing section of the air base. It was a mild evening, and I had just lit up a cigarette and settled in to listen to the night sounds when the air around me suddenly changed. It was as if the air was being sucked up and away from me somehow.

Then, as the air temperature dropped slightly, the star-filled sky suddenly began to turn pitch black. At this point, the hair on my neck and arms stood on end in a bad case of goose bumps as I realized that the sky hadn't turned black at all, but that the clear skies above me had suddenly been filled with an immense, hovering black aircraft of some type that looked as if it had come right out of a Science Fiction movie.

Slowly, it dawned on me that I was looking at a gigantic, triangular, non-reflective black-hulled aircraft with tail-end extensions that gave it a somewhat V-shape. Then, as I watched the aircraft slowly fill up the sky directly overhead, I realized that it was accompanied by two other identical aircraft traveling in a "V" formation with it. Because I could see the shadowed hills and valleys of the black-hued hulls of these ships, it looked as if they were hovering just above the base housetops. However, these aircraft were so massive that they may only have appeared to be nearer to the ground than they actually were.

To explain what I mean, picture a Boeing 747 aircraft on the runway at the airport. On the ground, it looks fairly massive. But, if this same aircraft is seen flying at 30,000 feet up, it looks tiny and insignificant when being viewed from the ground. So, to fill the sky the way these aircraft did, **each one would have had to be the size of several football fields** if they were flying at about 10,000 feet up. I therefore don't think they were that high up.

As I watched these three massive airships move slowly to the east, and then out of sight over the military base housing and palm trees on the horizon, I was stunned at how unbelievably silent they were despite their incredible mass. In fact, these aircraft became very difficult to see or hear at all at a distance since their visible fuselage was black and non-reflective, no outside running lights were illuminated on them anywhere, their virtually silent engines could not be heard at all from my position, and they left no exhaust trails that I could see.

After these giant aircraft disappeared from view, I went inside and attempted to tell my sleepy husband - who was an Air Force Sergeant - about what I had just seen. Nonetheless, he wouldn't believe me - no matter how hard I tried to emphasis that I was not attempting to fool him. But, upon discussing it that day with several other people that I worked with on base, one of them told me that they had seen the same aircraft not only last night, but on one other occasion at the same base.

Now, keep in mind that - when I saw these strange, seemingly alien aircraft - I was sitting inside the grounds of a US Air Force Base, and yet no alarm was sounded and no truthful report was given later as to the nature or purpose of these aircraft, which I was not alone in seeing that night. Instead of being told the truth, those of us who saw these UFOs were all told that we had witnessed a top-secret military training exercise using specially camouflaged but unremarkable cargo planes with their running lights shut off, and we were not to discuss this exercise with anyone off-base. Nonetheless, though base personnel who had not seen the aircraft were satisfied with that explanation, those of us who had seen them did not buy this story. We knew what we saw, and these aircraft weren't ordinary cargo planes!

My guess is that these triangular UFOs with their "V" shaped tail sections are in use at many US Military bases, and that is why similarly described aircraft have reportedly been seen in several parts of the US mainland at different times over the past few years. It is therefore highly likely that these advanced transport-type aircraft were devised by the US Military. Just why these particular airships are being kept so top-secret, however, is anyone's guess. Perhaps one reason for this is that they do partly utilize so-called "alien" technology that was given to us by the Watchers who were sent by God to help mankind.

Unfortunately, according to 1 Enoch and other ancient manuscripts, some of these Watcher angels sinned like Satan before them. Therefore, instead of helping mankind, some Watchers became resentful of God's purpose for mankind. Still others wanted to procreate like mankind and began to lust after women, which was contrary to God's will for them. As a result of their sinful desires, some of the Watchers disobeyed God, took human wives, had sexual relations with them, and taught them various forms of Sorcery in order to tamper with God's Creation in ways He never intended. This led to the birth of the Nephilim, who eventually joined Azazel in his desire to destroy humanity because of mankind's privileged place in Yah's Creation.

Was The Original Sin A Sexual One?

Among the apocryphal literature and Jewish Midrash that have survived to modern times, there are a few Judeo-Christian writings that suggest that Eve did not eat a literal fruit when she sinned, but transgressed against God and Adam by engaging in forbidden sexual encounters with the "Serpent" guise of the fallen angel Azazel or Satan in the Garden of Eden. As a result, there is a growing body of people who believe that Eve sinned by having unauthorized sex with the Serpent. Even more oddly, some people believe that this serpent was a reptilian humanoid that either was Azazel's true form, or that this reptilian was possessed by the spirit of the fallen angel Azazel, also known as Lucifer or the Devil. Finally, some people think that this reptilian being was the biological father of Eve's firstborn son Cain. Therefore, by this warped hypothesis, Eve became the first human woman to sleep with a fallen angel and also the first to be transformed into an evil demoness or Siren that is known today by the name of Lilith.

By this reasoning, Eve's son Cain would not have been fully human but a hybrid Nephilim monster that hated mankind as much as his father the Devil! In this way, Eve supposedly gave birth to the literal "seed of the Serpent" mentioned in Genesis 3:15 - the one that God promised would eventually be defeated by the Seed of the "Woman" or Holy Spirit, whose "Seed" is Yahshua. However, though a Nephilim seed of the Serpent was eventually born by a human woman, it was not by an innocent and sweet maiden named Eve. Instead, as will be shown in Chapter Five of this book, the first woman to literally sleep with Satan was most likely a brazen, fallen temptress named Naamah, the gorgeous but evil daughter of Lamech the Cainite!

Now, before we begin destroying the erroneous premise that Satan fathered Cain via Eve, let me make it clear that, though allegorical meanings are frequently implied in Scripture, their literal meaning must also be taken into consideration and understood so that any allegorical messages hidden there are not misconstrued. The story of Adam and Eve in the Garden is one such case, and since Genesis literally forms the foundation of the Judeo-Christian faith, we must be extra careful not to read anything into it that is not meant!

Depiction of Eve's Temptation by the Serpent

(Preliminary Sketch Drawn in College, finished by Author 32 years later in 2009)

Though the Garden of Eden was a real garden that was filled with literal fruit-bearing trees, they have an allegorical meaning that is defined by Scripture. Therefore, the allegorical meanings are not simply to be interpreted in any way by our imaginations. For example, the Tree of Life was a literal tree that also has a scriptural connection to Yahshua as our spiritual sustenance and the Giver of everlasting life. This is also conveyed by the rite of Communion, where Yahshua is pictured as the Bread of Life, the True Vine, the New Wine, and the Living Water.

The Tree of Life is also a symbol of the Cross of Christ, whereby a dead man hung on a dead tree secured the promise of everlasting life for all living things and became the source of new life and redemption for all Creation! Therefore, the Tree of Life ideally represents one's deep and abiding love for Yahweh God, His Son and His Spirit as well as one's obedience to God.

Thirdly, like the Tree of Life, the Tree of the Knowledge of Good and Evil was a literal tree that bore fruit that was pleasing to the eye. But just as the Tree of Life signified one's love for and obedience to God, the Tree of Knowledge signified the rebellion against God epitomized in the person of Satan, who spiritually twisted and then physically possessed a once wise and beautiful Serpent in order to deceive Eve. Therefore, the Tree of Knowledge could not offer light or wisdom but only darkness, error and death through the act of rebellion against God.

Now, scholars that argue that Eve became Lilith and slept with the Devil argue that the "fruit" in the Garden of Eden was supposed to be an allegorical reference to sexual acts, and the "trees" allegorically represented people. But if this is the true allegorical meaning, then when Eve said she could eat the fruit from almost any tree in the Garden of Eden, she was indicating that she could have sex with anyone she wanted! But could God truly have meant this? Since one of the Ten Commandments is *"do not commit adultery,"* it is logical to assume that God meant no such thing! Let's read the passages in question here:

> *"Now the serpent was more cunning than any beast of the field which the LORD God (Yahweh Elohim) had made. And he said to the woman, 'Has God indeed said, "You shall not eat of every tree of the garden?"' And the woman said to the serpent, 'We may eat the fruit of the trees of the garden; but of the fruit of the tree which is in the midst of the garden, God has said, "You shall not eat it, nor shall you touch it, lest you die."' Then the serpent said to the woman, 'You will not surely die. For God knows that in the day you eat of it your eyes will be opened, and you will be like God, knowing good and evil.' So when the woman saw that the tree was good for*

food... and a tree desirable to make one wise, she took of its fruit and ate. She also gave to her husband with her, and he ate. Then the eyes of both of them were opened, and they knew that they were naked...'" - Genesis 3:1-7 (NKJ)

Now, if these passages are interpreted the way proponents of the Eve as Lilith hypothesis maintain, they would be suggesting that Eve could promiscuously have sex with anyone she wanted to have it with *except the crafty Serpent, who was represented by the Tree of Knowledge!* Furthermore, since the Tree of Life in the Garden allegorically represented Christ, and Eve could eat from that tree, then this passage would be saying that Eve could have sex with Yahshua too, and this is not only heretical, but ludicrous!

In addition, since Adam ate from the same fruit as Eve and that fruit was supposedly the act of sex, this line of reasoning can only lead to one totally absurd conclusion: that Adam also had sex with the Serpent when he ate the forbidden fruit! Unfortunately, this conclusion is so far-fetched that it doesn't even bear consideration - especially since it can be rationally concluded and scripturally proven that Adam was desperately in love with Eve, was originally sinless and like Yahshua in character, and was not deceived like Eve. Furthermore, thinking that the Original Sin was sexual in nature is patently heretical, since it attempts to discredit the idea that *any* transgression against God is sinful.

The idea that Eve sinned sexually with the fallen angel Azazel in the guise of a Serpent and had Cain by him is not only reprehensible, but seems illogical when examined rationally. First of all, Adam and Eve were perfectly innocent before they fell into sin. As a result, neither Eve nor Adam struggled with feelings of lust. Furthermore, if Eve had sinned in such a way toward Adam, his righteous anger toward her would have been reason enough for him to reject her! This also makes no sense since it is likely that Adam only ate the fruit Eve ate because he could not bear to be separated from her for eternity. This could not have been the case, however, if Adam was consumed by anger over Eve's betrayal.

Remember that the Apostle Paul declared that Adam was not deceived, but only Eve (1 Timothy 2:14). This means that - before biting the forbidden fruit - Adam unquestionably knew that Azazel had lied to Eve, but he loved Eve too much to spend eternity without her! So Adam ate the fruit out of a desire not to lose Eve. Indeed, Adam loved Eve so much that he was completely willing to suffer and die for her, and hence it was the first Adam who set the pattern for the Messiah who was to come and reverse Adam's folly! This is why Yahshua was called the *"Second Man"* and the *"Last Adam"* by the Apostle Paul:

*"And so it is written, 'The first man Adam became a
living being.' The last Adam became a life-giving spirit.
However, the spiritual is not first, but the natural, and
afterward the spiritual. The first man was of the earth, made
of dust; the second Man is the Lord from heaven." - 1
Corinthians 15:45-47 (NKJ)*

This Scripture teaches us that, though Adam's love for Eve
caused him to sin against God and bring death and despair into the
world, Yahshua's love for us caused Him to glorify God the Father, obey
Him, and bring abundant life and hope into the world:

*"The thief does not come except to steal, and to kill,
and to destroy. I have come that they may have life, and that
they may have it more abundantly." - John 10:10 (NKJ)*

In the preceding Scripture, Azazel or Lucifer is the thief who
brought us the agony of death through his desire to kill us all, while
Yahshua is the life-giver who gives life so abundantly when we love Him
that it springs up into resurrection and everlasting life:

*"Jesus (Yahshua) answered and said to her, 'Whoever
drinks of this water will thirst again, but whoever drinks of
the water that I shall give him will never thirst. But the water
that I shall give him will become in him a fountain of water
springing up into everlasting life.'" - John 4:14 (NKJ)*

Besides showing us how Christ came to undo the damage that
Adam had done by loving Eve more than he loved God the Father or His
Preincarnate Son and Spirit, Scripture makes it perfectly clear that Adam
was the biological father of Cain:

*"Now **Adam knew Eve his wife, and she conceived
and bore Cain**, and said, 'I have acquired **a man** from the
LORD (Yahweh).'" - Genesis 4:1 (NKJ)*

Thus, the Bible confirms that Cain was *"a man,"* not a Nephilim
or reptilian, and Adam was Cain's true father. However, many cite the
fact that Cain behaved differently than Adam did by killing Abel as proof
that Azazel fathered Cain - thus turning Cain into a Nephilim! However,
they are too blind to see that **Adam brought death to all mankind
through his foolishness.** Nonetheless, just as Adam was manipulated by
Satan's cunning when he chose to follow Eve into rebellion rather than
lose her, Cain's jealousy allowed Satan to manipulate him into killing
Abel. However, to be fair to Adam, we need to remember that Eve
literally shared Adam's flesh, bone and spirit. Therefore, **due to Azazel's
overwhelming hatred of Adam and Eve and all their future children, no**

other human couple has even known the perfect love and intimacy that this first married couple only had a brief chance to share.

In reality, the suggestion that Eve could so easily be tempted into sinning against Adam completely defies the nature of how perfectly matched Adam and Eve were. You see, *Eve was Adam's perfect soul mate.* As soul mates, their bond of intimacy and love was stronger than anything we can possibly imagine in our fallen condition. In fact, anyone who professes to have a soul mate could not know what this truly means unless they were Adam or Eve, who were sinless in the beginning and likewise shared the radiant Shekinah Glory of God. Indeed, because Eve was formed from Adam's rib, they even shared almost identical DNA!

Though some might argue that Eve did not have the baptism of the Spirit to give her the ability to resist temptation, there is good reason to believe that Adam and Eve were both indwelled by God's Spirit before they fell. However, their initial covering with the Spirit of God which clothed them with the Shekinah Glory or Light of God in the Garden of Eden was conditional on their good behavior. They needed to remain obedient to God to keep that Spirit covering of light and truth to do the good works that God ordained for them to do. In contrast, *humanity's New Covenant with Christ offers unconditional salvation and communion with God and an irrevocable baptism with the Holy Spirit to anyone who loves and accepts Christ, asks for His mercy and forgiveness, and sincerely asks and wants to become like Him.*

Adam and Eve's possession of the Holy Spirit before their fall into sin is inferred because the first human couple were unaware of their nakedness before they sinned, but clearly could see that they were naked after they sinned. Now, many argue that this was a sign that Eve's disobedience gave mankind intelligence and the ability to reason. However, *if Adam and Eve were created in God's image, they would already have had God's sentience, wisdom and Spirit!* As a result, there was nothing good that they did not already possess. They knew God's total goodness and perfection and shared in it because they were filled with His Spirit and clothed with His Shekinah at the moment that they were created! They did not need to earn the right to share in God's Glory or dominion over all Creation as we do, but they nonetheless could lose it as a consequence of disobedience to God.

Sadly, when Adam and Eve sinned by being disobedient, later events in the Book of Genesis make it clear that they and all their descendents lost the perfect knowledge and discernment that God had given them through His Spirit. At the moment Adam and Eve fell, they lost the Shekinah that had clothed them with beautiful, radiant light. As a result, they quickly discovered the unpleasant emotions associated with nakedness, shame, and guilt. Indeed, Eve would have seen Adam's shock at her nakedness as she offered him the fruit, and she would have soon known that what Satan had given her was not the truth or the uplifting and empowering knowledge of godhood, but a terrible lie. Eve thus gained the horrible knowledge of sin and its destructive spiritual, emotional, and physical consequences.

How sad it is that so many of Eve's progeny still seek the godhood that she could never achieve without Yah's miraculous intervention. Yet, therein lies the reason why the Two-House Church of Judah and Ephraim are to marry Yahshua as His Bride! Through Christ, all born-again believers shall finally gain Eve's desire to be like God - but through obedience rather than rebellion!

Based on these reasons, it is highly likely that Eve actually did eat the fruit of a real tree when she sinned, just as the Bible states, and no allegorical meaning was intended. Though Eve may have been mesmerized by the beauty of the Tree of the Knowledge of Good and Evil, and by the persuasiveness of the Serpent's speech, her overwhelming love for Adam and her emotional connection to him would have been strong enough to keep her from entering into any sexual sin with someone else - angelic or not.

Nonetheless, Satan was extremely cunning and knew exactly how to cajole Eve into sin. First, from the biblical narrative, it is apparent that the Serpent approached Eve when Adam was not nearby. There is, however, no suggestion that Adam and Eve were angry at each other, and this was highly unlikely anyway because they were so perfectly matched and totally sinless at the time. So, while Eve worked in the garden that God had given the first human couple to tend, a clever Serpent approached Eve that she never had reason to fear before. This Serpent, who knew how to communicate with Eve (possibly on a telepathic level), was no doubt possessed by Azazel or Satan. Hidden in this guise, Azazel began to fill Eve's mind with enormous doubt and suspicion against her heavenly Father, and made it clear that the only way she would be able to satisfy her curiosity and find out if God had lied to her would be to disobey God.

Note that the Serpent did not beguile Eve with promises of sensual pleasure as would be expected if he was attempting to have sex with her. Instead, **Azazel used the Serpent to tempt Eve by fomenting a greedy desire within her for knowledge and godhood:**

> "The serpent said to the woman, 'You will not surely
> die. For God knows that in the day you eat of it your eyes will

be opened, and you will be like God, knowing good and evil.'" - Gen. 3:4-5 (NKJ)

It was therefore not sexual desire, but Eve's curiosity, pride and greed for greatness that caused her to sin, and to thereby lose her Shekinah Glory covering. Incidentally, pride and greed are also what caused Lucifer or Azazel to sin against Yahweh, so he was merely reutilizing the same arguments with Eve that he had used to rationalize his own decision to rebel against God in the first place!

When Adam saw the terrible result of Eve's folly through her nakedness, he realized that Eve was now mortal and sinful, and because light and darkness cannot dwell together, they would be separated forever unless he chose to follow her into sin. Adam also knew that the moment he took a bite of that fruit, he would suffer the same fate as Eve, and would lose the Shekinah that had clothed him and Eve with light. But he chose to do it anyway out of love for Eve. Thus, **they both lost the Holy Spirit and the Shekinah that covered them at the moment they sinned, and they suddenly knew the pain of evil emotions like guilt, shame, fear, loss, and blame for the first time** - not to mention the physical pain that would come when they were expelled from the Garden.

After her fall from grace, Eve likely no longer felt kindly toward the Serpent, but extreme loathing. Perhaps she even felt hatred toward another living thing for the first time in her life. Indeed, Adam and Eve would have known soon enough that Azazel was the real culprit behind the Serpent's cunning, and they both likely communicated their enormous anger toward the Serpent for allowing Azazel to deceive them when they sinfully passed their own blame onto him for their fall.

For the preceding reasons, it is likely that Eve was smitten by the beguiling Serpent's overwhelming charm, scintillating erudition, and mesmerizing speech to take a bite of a real fruit she should not have eaten, and then was subsequently ashamed and repentant. After all, Eve would have known immediately after losing her Shekinah Glory covering that the Serpent had lied to her, and this would have become even more apparent when Adam and Eve were expelled from the Garden of Eden and were forced to toil and labor for their food in a suddenly hostile environment.

Nonetheless, because they were totally cut off from God's guidance after being cast out of Eden, Adam and Eve continued to sin and - whether or not they desired it - they were both eventually worshipped as deities - as will be shown later in this book. As a result, the Serpent's prediction that Eve would be like God when she discovered evil proved true - but only in the most twisted and basest sense. As the first father and mother of all the living, Adam and Eve were unique among human beings, and even though it was sinful to worship them or turn them into idols, they were eventually seen as deities whether they liked it or not.

The Origin of the First Race of Nephilim

One of the reasons why some people believe that Eve had sexual relations with the Devil is the fact that Cain was so unrighteous that he murdered his own brother in cold blood - a sinful behavior people readily equate with Satan. However, the Bible makes it clear that Adam and Eve were fallen and sinful from the moment they rebelled against God. In fact they even lied to God and blamed one another and the Serpent when they were confronted by God with their sin. These actions were clearly unrighteous, and there is no reason to think that Cain and Abel were born with any less of a propensity to sin than their parents! In fact, the whole concept that mankind is essentially born innocent and good is erroneous. As a parent, I have seen the evidence of sin in my own sweet daughter before she was even a toddler, and the Word clearly teaches that: *"no one is good but One,"* and *"for all have sinned and fall short of the glory of God"* (Luke 18:19; Romans 3:23).

Another reason some people see Cain as the progeny of Lucifer surrounds the first prophecy in the Bible that was extensively discussed in Book Two. Found in Genesis 3:15, this prophecy suggests the existence of two bloodlines - one related to the Woman (i.e. the Holy Spirit), and the other related to the Serpent (i.e. Satan or Azazel):

> *"And I will put enmity between you and the woman,*
> *and between your seed and her Seed; he shall bruise your*
> *head, and you shall bruise His heel." - Genesis 3:15 (NKJ)*

This prophecy indicates that **a messiah would come one day that was the Seed of the Woman, but not of the man**. This prophecy was perfectly fulfilled when the Holy Spirit caused a godly virgin named Miriam to become pregnant with Christ. Remember, Yahshua was the literal son of Miriam, a.k.a. Mary, but was not genetically related to Joseph! In addition, though Yahshua shared Miriam's DNA, He nonetheless also shared the perfection of His spiritual and intellectual Mother, the Holy Spirit! In fact, the genealogy of Christ from Adam to Miriam's father Yoseph in Matthew points to this fact (Matthew 1:1-17). There, in Matthew 1:16, Aramaic translations of the Bible most often have "Yoseph the guardian (or father) of Miryam" instead of "Joseph the husband of Mary" as it is translated in most English translations.

This makes sense of Matthew 1:17, where Matthew insists that there were fourteen generations from the Babylonian Captivity to Christ. However, if the Joseph mentioned in Matthew 1:16 is seen as Mary's husband, there are only thirteen generations listed, not fourteen because Miriam's name can no longer be counted in Christ's genealogy. Yet it was Miriam's DNA alone that Christ shared, not Joseph's! In addition to Yahshua's physical body being tied to the bloodline of the woman Miriam, the Holy Spirit who conceived Yahshua in Miriam's womb is feminine, not masculine in nature. This made Yahshua the Seed of the Woman at both His divine and human level.

Nonetheless, the prophecy also indicates that the Serpent would bring forth his own evil seed that would fight the righteous Seed of the Woman. Unfortunately, the prophesied arrival of this "seed of the Serpent" has also led to the idea that Cain was the product of Eve's unlawful sexual relations with the Serpent, as is erroneously suggested in one text found in the Jewish Midrash. Even though Cain was a son of the Devil spiritually, the Bible is clear that the origin of Satan's physical "seed" or bloodline should not be traced directly to Cain, who was merely a man and not a Giant humanoid or reptilian Nephilim (Gen. 4:1).

However, as will be shown in Chapter Five, Cain's connection to the seed of the Serpent came through the bloodline of his direct female descendents. In effect, the first woman to marry and have sexual relations with the "sons of God" or fallen angels spoken of in the Book of Genesis was named Naamah, and she was the daughter of the Cainite patriarch Lamech. Furthermore, many other women of Cain's line eventually joined in her lust after strange flesh:

> "Now it came to pass, when men began to multiply on the face of the earth, and daughters were born to them, that the sons of God (i.e. the "Beni Elohim") saw the daughters of men, that they were beautiful; and they took wives for themselves of all whom they chose." - Genesis 6:1-2 (NKJ)

These unlawful sexual unions produced the first hybrid race of Nephilim or Giants that were also known as the "mighty men of old" and "men of renown" (Gen. 6:4). In fact, the Bible and 1 Enoch tell us that it was the supernatural addition of the DNA of the fallen angels into the human gene pool through base sexual relations with human women that created the first races of Nephilim giants.

As this chapter will show, the fallen angels not only introduced Paganism and Sorcery to mankind before the Great Flood, taught men how to make war, gave them the advanced technology they needed to kill one another more effectively, and took human wives to pollute mankind's bloodline, but also began to engage in sinful genetic experiments. In short, the fallen angels wanted to destroy God's Plan of Salvation by attempting to make it impossible for the purely human Messiah foretold in the Star Gospel to be born from a righteous human family. In fact, they eventually attempted to utterly destroy all terrestrial life on Earth.

In an almost successful attempt to thwart the arrival of the Messiah and only begotten Son of God, the fallen Watchers took human wives and had unlawful sex with them, which resulted in the birth of the first race of Giants. The Greeks called this first race of Giants the Titans (though the Greeks also depicted righteous Sethites as Titans to demonize them - as shown in Chapter Seven). However, the fallen angels were not satisfied with this level of perversion, and wanted to increase the genetic corruption going on in the world. They therefore began to splice mankind's genes together with those of birds and other animals, thereby creating inhuman hybrid races of beings that were very cunning and violent. These genetically mixed species - which God did not design - acted contrary to natural laws. This is why they eventually had a desire to kill and destroy all that Yah had created.

The monstrous, bloodthirsty Giants that resulted from the sexual promiscuity of the fallen angels with women as well as their genetic experiments were called by many names in the Bible, including "Nephilim," "Anakim" or simply "Giants." Keep in mind, however, that - in the Bible - only the Pre-Flood Giants are called Nephilim. Those born after the Flood were called Anakim because they were descended from Nephilim males and human females, meaning that they were more human genetically than they were related to the Watchers. As a result, the Anakim were smaller, less powerful, and less long lived than their Nephilim forbears.

Most people do not know that the Nephilim or Anakim ever existed, or that God caused the Great Flood to destroy all the Nephilim and end the massive amounts of violence and blood-letting that had been initially started by them. Somehow, however, the Bible makes it clear that some of these Nephilim survived the Flood. Furthermore, their desire to destroy mankind and all other life on this planet has never left them. In short, since these Nephilim had no hope of everlasting life, they wanted to take everyone and everything with them to Hell.

The Book of 1 Enoch clearly teaches that the Nephilim born before the Flood were the seed of the Serpent because they were the literal seed of the fallen angels, who shared their spiritual father Azazel's fallen nature. In addition, like the fallen angels that created them, the Nephilim were tainted by their same sinful nature, and so they automatically rebelled against Yahweh. Even more grievously, Old Testament narratives suggest that - like their fallen Watcher sires - the Nephilim took human wives and had forbidden sexual relations with them, which tragically led to the birth of more varieties of Nephilim that were less gigantic and increasingly more human in appearance.

The Watchers were the *"sons of God"* who married the daughters of men in Genesis 6:4-5. Through their forbidden sexual unions with women, these fallen Watchers fathered another alien race of beings that were gigantic in stature, and fiercely evil in appetites. The biblical account of the Nephilim is short, mysterious, and tantalizing - thereby inviting further inquiry:

> *"There were giants (i.e. "Nephilim") on the earth in those days, and also afterward, when the sons of God (i.e. the "Beni Elohim") came in to the daughters of men and they bore children to them. Those were the mighty men (i.e. "gibborim", a.k.a. giants) who were of old, men of renown (Eesha Ha Shem). Then the LORD (Yahweh) saw that the wickedness of man was great in the earth, and that every intent of the thoughts of his heart was only evil continually." - Genesis 6:4-5 (NKJ)*

What one discovers upon further study is that the *"sons of God,"* or the *"Beni Elohim"* in the above passage were the fallen Watchers of 1 Enoch who conspired to beget children with human females as partners. As proof of this, Job 1:6 and 2:1 clearly identify the *"sons of God"* as angelic beings in the King James Version of the Bible. Furthermore, **though the Bible does label godly men as "sons of God," the application of the term to humans appears only in the New Testament - never in the Hebrew and Aramaic renditions of the Old Testament**. In other words, only born-again Christians and Messianic Jews can rightly be called sons of God due to their kinship with Christ, who is above all the angels in glory!

The children brought forth from these unholy unions were called *"Nephilim"* in Hebrew, which means "to fall" or "fallen," but is most-often translated as "Giants" in English versions of the Bible. The word "Nephilim" therefore implies that these giants were *fallen in character*, i.e.: evil by nature. The Nephilim children of the fallen angels are also described as *"Mighty Men"* or *"Gibborim."* Interestingly, the word

"Nephilim" used here for "Giant" is distinct from the words "Rephaim" or "Anakim" that are used more often in the instances where these giant races are mentioned in the Bible.

The Giants that resulted from the unholy marital unions between the sons of God and the daughters of men were called *"Mighty Men"* to show us two things: first, that they were extremely strong, and second, that *none of them were female.* As a result, the Nephilim would have needed to mate with human women to father their own children, and this would have subsequently resulted in the gradual genetic corruption of mankind.

The Book of 1 Enoch concurs with the Bible in teaching that some of the Watcher angels sinned against God and mankind by mating with human women and creating this race of demonic humanoid Giants:

> *"And the angels, the children of heaven, saw and lusted after them, and said to one another: 'Come, let us choose wives from among the children of men and beget us children.'" - 1 Enoch 6:2-3*

The Book of 1 Enoch summarizes the sad state of affairs that resulted from the sexual interactions between the fallen angels and human females, and eventually bathed the Earth with human and Nephilim blood. These unholy unions are clearly defined as sexual in nature, since the Watchers were said to have taken human women as wives and had children by them. As further proof of this, Enoch relates a dream vision in which the Watchers - which are called "stars" in the vision - are shown to have *"huge privy members"* (See verse 4 in the following quote). These "privy members" are a clear allegorical allusion to the sexual organs of these fallen angels or "stars." Furthermore, we are told that these angels *"covered the cows,"* which explicitly implies that these fallen angels were sexually united with human females. Thereafter these same females (described as cows) gave birth to three distinct races of inhuman beings that were totally unlike them. This is implied the by the description of the Nephilim as elephants, camels and asses – three classes of animals that look very different from cows:

> *"And again I saw in the vision, and looked towards the heaven, and behold I saw many stars (fallen angels) descend and cast themselves down from heaven to that first star (Satan), and they became bulls amongst those cattle (men) and pastured with them [amongst them]. And I looked at them and saw, and behold they all let out their privy members, like horses, and began to cover the cows (women) of the oxen (men), and they all became pregnant and bare*

elephants, camels, and asses (three different varieties of
Nephilim). And all the oxen (men) feared them and were
affrighted at them, and began to bite with their teeth and to
devour, and to gore with their horns. And they (the Nephilim)
began, moreover, to devour those oxen (people); and behold
all the children of the earth began to tremble and quake before
them and to flee from them." - 1 Enoch 86:3-6

In the preceding passages, the associations shown in
parentheses are my own, and were added to show how Enoch's
prophetic words should be interpreted using the allegorical Language of
God. Applying the Language of God to express Himself, Yah showed
that the big elephant and camel-sized creatures in this vision resulted
from the unholy union of the fallen Watchers, or "stars" with human
women. Furthermore, through the language of allegory, God showed
that these creatures were much larger than any bull-sized fallen angel or
oxen-sized human being. In addition, these unholy offspring of the
"stars" or fallen angels began to devour the "oxen," which allegorically
means that the Nephilim began to eat the human beings who were
descended from Adam and Seth. Since the Nephilim were so much
bigger, people were relatively easy prey for them to overtake and kill,
and this potentially made the Nephilim desire to claim dominion over
Yah's creation by destroying mankind possible.

The Book of 1 Enoch tells us that the Nephilim and their
genetically mutated offspring were veritable giants that towered over
humans and had voracious appetites. Furthermore, they were inherently
evil and began to cause untold violence as they devoured vegetation,
animals, humans, and each other without remorse:

"And they (the human women) became pregnant, **and**
they bare great giants, whose height was three thousand ells:
Who consumed all the acquisitions of men (i.e.: cultivated
plants). And when men could no longer sustain them, the
giants turned against them and devoured mankind. **And they**
began to sin against birds, and beasts, and reptiles, and fish,
and to devour one another's flesh, and drink the blood. *Then*
the earth laid accusation against the lawless ones." - 1 Enoch
7:3-6

The preceding passage indicates that the first monstrous
Nephilim were conceived in the wombs of their biologically human
mothers. However, there are suggestions in several extra-biblical texts
that that some of the women who married the fallen angels served as
surrogates who were implanted with the mixed genetic material of birds,
reptiles, and other living things. In either case, the monstrous children

born to these women were nothing like them. For one thing, they grew to enormous sizes, and - as a result - they were far more powerful than the humans, mammals, reptiles, and birds they were derived from. In addition, due to the fact that their life force was inherited from the fallen angels rather than God, the Nephilim displayed some of the supernatural strength and longevity of the Watchers who sired them.

Though most Pre-Flood era land animals that scientists place in the purely hypothetical Miocene, Pliocene and Pleistocene geological epochs were much larger than their modern counterparts, 1 Enoch tells us that the Nephilim giants of old reached the unlikely height or length of 3000 ells. In ancient times, a European measurement called an "ell" existed that ranged in length from 45 inches in England to the Flemish ell of 27 inches, which was close to the Egyptian sacred cubit of 25.25 inches. However, even if we assume the smallest measure of an ell at approximately 2 feet, this would indicate that the Nephilim either stood around 6,000 feet high, or were that length from their heads to the tips of their tails!

Nonetheless, such a massive size for the Nephilim is completely impossible. First of all, due to gravitational forces on the Earth today, a creature that enormous would be unable to move, much less hurt any other living thing! Secondly, these creatures would require so much land and food to survive at that size that they would soon have stripped the Earth of all vegetation and animal life, and they would have subsequently perished. It has therefore been suggested that a scribal error was made with this measurement, and Enoch's description of the Nephilim should read 30 ells in height if they were bipedal, or in length if they were quadrupeds. Using 30 ells, then, the Nephilim would be 60 feet (or 18 meters) in height or length using the 27 inch ell or 120 feet (or 36 meters) using the 45 inch ell.

Due to the size of the biggest dinosaurs so far found, it is likely that the 45 inch ell was being referred to in 1 Enoch. Though 120 feet is still a staggeringly large size, it is far more conceivable based on the gravitational forces that are exerted upon all life on Earth today. However, *there is a strong probability that all life was larger prior to the Flood because Earth's gravitational pull was much smaller*, but increased greatly after billions of tons of water mass was added to Earth after the Flood.

Though 1 Enoch could suggest that the inhuman creatures called Nephilim were bigger than many modern day skyscrapers, the Nephilim could probably never have achieved such an enormous size. As an example of how impossibly enormous some these giants might have been if they were 300 ells tall, picture the Sears Tower in Chicago. It is one of the tallest buildings in the world, with a structural height of 1,451 feet and a base that spans an entire city block. On a clear day in Chicago, this massive black commercial building dominates the skyline - towering over other nearby skyscrapers.

Nonetheless, the only reason Sears Tower can withstand Earth's gravity without collapsing is the fact that it is built of thick steel beams covered by heavy sheets of glass. Due to the incredible weight of the steel in the Sears Tower alone, anyone that desired to move the tower's entire bulk at once would soon learn that it is impossible for mankind to do. There is simply no known human mechanism that could move such a massive building in one piece! This is why picturing a ravenous living creature of flesh and bone that is even one half as massive as this huge tower seems incredibly absurd. Even though the Nephilim were as spiritually dark as Sears Tower is physically, their muscles could not have moved them even one inch if they were as massive as Sears Tower! Nonetheless, even at the more "diminutive" height of 120 feet, the Nephilim must have been specially constructed to withstand Earth's gravity. We will explore the special attributes that the Nephilim may have possessed in a moment.

The Three Races of Nephilim Seen in Myths

Adding to their fearsome appearance, the inhuman Nephilim monsters fathered by the fallen angels needed much fresh food to survive. Indeed, several extra-biblical sources suggest that the Nephilim ravaged whole farms by devouring all their crops, and then resorted to killing all the livestock and the people caring for the farms and animals when the plants the Nephilim initially preferred to eat were in short supply. They also further showed their vile and debased character by drinking the blood of their victims, and resorting to cannibalism within their own ranks!

In parallel to the Genesis account of the Nephilim who inspired God's desire to destroy the world, the Book of Jubilees adds some much-needed detail lacking from the Genesis account. For example, Jubilees concurs with 1 Enoch and Genesis regarding the violent nature of the Nephilim:

> "Noah began to enjoin upon his sons' sons the
> ordinances and commandments, and all the judgments that he
> knew, and he exhorted his sons to observe righteousness, and
> to cover the shame of their flesh, and to bless their Creator,
> and honour father and mother, and love their neighbour, and

guard their souls from fornication and uncleanness and all iniquity. For owing to these three things came the flood upon the earth, namely, owing to the fornication wherein **the Watchers against the law of their ordinances went a whoring after the daughters of men, and took themselves wives** *of all which they chose: and they made the beginning of uncleanness. And* **they begat sons the Naphidim, and they were all unlike, and they devoured one another: and the Giants slew the Naphil, and the Naphil slew the Eljo, and the Eljo mankind, and one man another.** *And every one sold himself to work iniquity and to shed much blood, and the earth was filled with iniquity. And after this they sinned against the beasts and birds, and all that moves and walks on the earth: and much blood was shed on the earth, and every imagination and desire of men imagined vanity and evil continually." - Jubilees 7:21-25*

Besides speaking of the Nephilim propensity for violence, the preceding passage from the Book of Jubilees tells us that there were many diverse kinds of Nephilim, and these were all unrepentant cannibals and killers. It also clearly indicates that there were three different kinds of Nephilim that were preying upon one another, and ultimately upon human beings - who soon became as violent as the Nephilim that preyed upon them. **These three types of Nephilim were:**

1. **The Giants, a.k.a. Naphidim, Gibborim or Mighty Men**

2. **The Nephil, or Nephilim, and**

3. **The Eljo, a.k.a. the Eliud**

These three classes of Nephilim - the Mighty Men or humanoid Giants, the Nephilim, and the Eliud or Eljo - were all descended in some way from the fallen angels called Watchers. By the totally violent actions of these new races, it also soon became apparent to the besieged Noah and his sons that these alien beings were created by the Watchers in a perverted attempt to thwart Yahweh's lofty plans for mankind. As a result, Noah did his best to educate his children in the ways of righteousness (Jasher 5:18-19).

Interestingly, each of these races of Nephilim ties in fairly well with worldwide myths pertaining to three basic types of mythical creatures: giants or ogres, chimeras like harpies and mermaids, and the elfin races that were once said to dwell upon the Earth. So there is no doubt some truth behind the many oral and written accounts about these supposedly mythical creatures that are recorded throughout the world.

In reference to chimeras, however, it is possible that some of them were not Nephilim at all, but Cherubim or Seraphim.

Those chimeras that most likely were Cherubim include the centaurs, griffins, and fauns of folklore. These creatures bore a striking resemblance to the biblical Cherubim, which had the bodies of bulls, tails of lions, wings of eagles, and the heads and hands of men to tie in with the four fixed signs of the Zodiac. After all, the Garden of Eden was still on the Earth at that time, and there were two Cherubim guarding the entrance to that Garden that no doubt looked just as the prophet Ezekiel described them! See Book One for a detailed account of the purpose and nature of Cherubim.

Now, in Enoch's vision, the first race of Nephilim were seen as elephants and camels, with the elephant being the largest and the camel being one of the tallest land mammals known today. Therefore, these creatures were likely very large and/or tall in stature, and some likely had long necks like the camel. These would correspond most closely to the Ogres and Giants of myth. In addition, since Enoch allegorically envisioned humans as oxen or cattle, and the Eljo as smaller mammals about the size of asses, the Eljo were likely smaller in size than human beings.

If the Eljo were smaller than men, but were god-like as the use of the term "El" in their name implies, could these humanoid creatures have been equivalent to the elves of myth? In addition, could the Eljo, as the most diminutive Nephilim in size, also have been the most beautiful race of Nephilim? Is it possible that the elfin folk of human myth and legend have an actual basis in fact? Could the Nephilim race called the Eljo have been the seemingly immortal, supposedly magic-wielding, enchanted woodland beings mythically called elves?

Whether the giants, ogres, dragons, mermaids, and elves of myth are memories of the three classes of Nephilim introduced in Jubilees is open to debate. However, the huge amount of mythic literature that speaks of these other races of beings on the Earth suggests that these alien creatures actually existed at one time or another. However, despite the often endearing depictions of these mythical creatures in popular fantasy movies, the Book of Jubilees tells us that the chimeras and the elfin races were apparently just as evil as the brut giants or ogres who came before them. In fact, since elves are depicted as having many magical powers in myths, it is likely that the Eljo practiced Magic and Sorcery and used violence to subjugate or terrorize humans whenever they were unfortunate enough to encroach upon Eliud-held territory.

The Book of 1 Enoch and Jubilees tells us that these three types of Nephilim: the Naphidim (the Gibborim, or Giants), the Nephilim (Fallen Ones), and the Eljo (or Eliud meaning "godlike men") were so violent that they often hunted and killed one another, as well as all other creatures - including mankind. Similarly, the Book of 1 Enoch tells us that the first race of these Nephilim creatures towered over men. Enoch also tells us that the first Nephilim were totally immoral in their eating habits, had voracious appetites, eventually devoured all living things, and drank the blood of both animals and humans in an unrestrained blood bath of murder.

Since humanity coexisted with these vile and violent Nephilim, it is likely that most people were terrified of them as a whole, or resorted to armed combat with them - thereby creating even more violence. Aware of their violent strength and power, people the world over likely either saw the three races of Nephilim as pernicious gods that had to be appeased through worship, offerings, and blood sacrifices, or else that had to be destroyed at any cost as the superhuman yet mortal monsters that they were.

For those humans who refused to worship the Nephilim, life must have been very harsh. Imagine bands of frightened, homeless humans whose villages and crops have been destroyed by the Nephilim. Imagine these terrified people hiding in caves among the rocks, or under the earth in an effort to avoid the horrid fate of being devoured alive. For those without a good place to hide, their lives would have soon been forfeit. Consequently, the need for heavily fortified cities and lethal weapons likely arose rapidly, and only the most bloodthirsty warrior societies among men likely survived the ravages of Nephilim attacks.

If the Watchers (i.e. fallen angels) and Nephilim aided their human subjects in finding better protection, as some myths suggest, they likely did so with the goal of creating even more bloodshed. The fallen angels, in an effort to provide enough food for their beloved Nephilim children, could suddenly have begun to demand the need for human sacrifice in exchange for their supernatural aid. These sacrificed humans then may have become food for the Nephilim. Traces of this vile method of "feeding" bloodthirsty Nephilim "gods" can be found in the evidence of human sacrifice that has been found all over the world, especially among the ancient Mesoamericans. We will focus on their propensity to human sacrifice - and what it clearly suggests - in the final chapter.

The practice of exposing the dead on mountaintops (or elsewhere) so carrion birds can feast on their flesh may also be connected to ancient methods of appeasing Nephilim bloodlust. This method of disposing of the dead is still practiced in India - as it has been for thousands of years. It was also the favored method for disposing of corpses at Catal Huyuk. This supposedly prehistoric settlement was unearthed in Turkey, and is purported to be one of the earliest known human civilizations. Incidentally, this culture used bull and vulture imagery in their religious rituals – uncannily similar imagery to that used in the *concurrent* culture that flourished in Predynastic Egypt.

Since there is supposedly little trace of the Nephilim in the archeological findings from Mesopotamia and Egypt, many people might balk at the existence of these violent giants among men. However, they fail to take into account that skeletons of giant humanoids, though rare, have been found all over the world. They also tend to ignore that there have been documented giants throughout history, with over a dozen cases reported in the last thousand years or so. They also tend to dismiss all the colossal statues of various Pharaohs and gods found in ancient ruins. These statues were often carved with much smaller representations of humans around them.

Could it be that these statues represented the literal Nephilim giants who ruled over mankind in the remote past? *It is my firm belief that some of these monstrous statues were carved to scale, showing the actual size difference between these giant rulers and their human subjects*. Still other colossal statues and carvings, though they exaggerated these size differences between humans and Nephilim, still depicted the actual state of affairs when true Nephilim giants ruled as kings over human subjects.

In addition to the colossal statues that have been found in South America, Mexico, Mesopotamia, and Egypt, many ruins of ancient buildings in Egypt and elsewhere display doorways that are overwhelmingly large and imposing. However, several of these doorways were subsequently bricked up to form smaller doorways in later eras. Some archeologists believe these doorways were initially made so large to allow priests carrying the arks of the gods into and out of the temples. However, these enormous doorways were far higher than the fifteen or twenty feet height they needed to reach in order to accommodate the arks of the gods or the Pharaoh. In fact, some doorways were in excess of forty feet high! Why were these doors so big? My contention is that *these immense doorways would have suited the tremendous heights of the Nephilim* who either built some of these monuments, or coerced humans to build them and resided in some of them when they were worshipped as gods.

When looking for evidence of the Watchers and Nephilim in human affairs, it is helpful to know when Biblical Chronology places their existence on Earth. Since the Watchers entered into human affairs sometime around 3400 BC, their Nephilim offspring originated sometime after that. Enoch was translated sometime in 3016 BC, and if we assume Enoch wrote the book we know as 1 Enoch before that time, than many of the vile affects of the Watchers and Nephilim on Earth must have begun to occur *before* that time. Otherwise Enoch would not have been able to record all of it before his translation.

Since the Book of 1 Enoch contains a fairly comprehensive record of this dark time in human history, it is certain that much of what became the scourge of the Nephilim began during Enoch's time on Earth. The only one who may have added anything to Enoch's testimony was Noah. As the patriarch who preserved Enoch's writings, Noah apparently added his own words to Enoch's book after Enoch was translated. This is why portions of the Book of 1 Enoch are assigned to Noah, as evidenced in 1 Enoch, Chapters 60 and 70 and 1 Enoch, Chapters 106 through 108.

Myth VS Reality: Gibborim as Ogres and Eliud as Elves

In addition to the monstrous and unholy Nephilim giants, more part-human hybrids of the Nephilim soon appeared on the Earth. These were called the "Eliud," or God-Men. Among the three races of Nephilim mentioned in the Book of Jubilees, this Eliud race may have resembled angels and humans more than any of the other Nephilim. Is it possible that we know the Eliud today in the fabric of fairytales? Could they be those mythical beings called elves?

Based on myths surrounding Giants and Elves, the first race of Nephilim known as the Gibborim or Mighty Men and the Eliud may have been blonde-haired and fair-skinned, but widely different in size. While the first race of Nephilim were of monstrous, gigantic proportions, the Eliud were likely smaller in stature than men like the elves they may have resembled. According to Enoch, they were also so long-lived that they appeared to be as immortal as the fallen angels they descended from. In comparison, their human subjects aged and died relatively quickly, even though they lived ten times longer than most of us do today! In addition, these two races of Nephilim likely had magical powers and supernatural abilities, just as they are often depicted.

As direct descendants of the fallen angels with human mothers, the Gibborim and Eliud no doubt followed in the steps of their angelic forebears and claimed their status as gods and leaders among men. In this way, both Gibborim and Eliud became *"the heroes of old"* and *"men of great renown"* that the Bible tells us existed both before and after the Flood. Furthermore, though some of the Eliud may not have sought to be gods or to hurt or control humans initially, they would have eventually despised humanity for the same reasons that the fallen angels despised them. However, for a time, there were likely Eliud and other types of Nephilim that set themselves apart and tried to live their lives peacefully and without causing harm to others.

The Gibborim or Giants and the Eliud or Elves who wanted power were so terrifyingly strong and godlike compared to humankind that they were likely readily elevated to the status of gods. In fact, the Gibborim and Eliud could have made such a great impression on humanity that they evoked fear and held enormous power - so much so that the true worship of Yahweh was soon forgotten. Sadly, even long after the various varieties of Pre-Flood Nephilim died, Pagan mythologies attest to the fact that they were still revered and worshipped as the fathers of the gods along with their Watcher fathers. As such, the fallen angels and Nephilim were the primary inventors and promulgators of all idolatrous, polytheistic religions and the proponents of Sorcery and Astrology both before and after the Flood.

Nephilim: Product of Evil Genetic Experiments?

Thus far, we have discussed the mythological connections of the first and third races of Nephilim, but not the second race that were specifically called Nephilim. Is it possible that this second race of Nephilim were not produced in the same way as the Gibborim and Eliud? Is there evidence that would point to the fact that the second category of Nephilim were far different in appearance and behavior than the other two races of Nephilim, and less intelligent?

The Book of 1 Enoch leaves us no doubt that the fallen angels and their unholy Nephilim offspring found great pleasure in disrupting God's Creation by freely engaging in various sexual perversions, genetic manipulation, and war. Furthermore, 1 Enoch hints at the fact that the fallen angels taught the unholy skill of genetic splicing to their human wives, likely as a type of sport. The enigmatic phrase *"cutting of roots"* in 1 Enoch clearly suggests that certain fallen angels taught the women they married the science of genetic splicing:

> *"And all the others together with them took unto themselves wives, and each chose for himself one, and they began to go in unto them and to defile themselves with them,* **and they taught them charms and enchantments, and the**

cutting of roots, and made them acquainted with plants." - 1
Enoch 7:1-2

Though this phrase is most often interpreted to mean the use of
particular plant roots as ingredients in magical potions, the *"cutting of
roots"* in the above passage could be describing unholy genetic splicing
experiments. The roots being referred to in this case would be the
entwined, root-like strands of DNA within each living cell. Adding
support to this idea, Semyaza is identified as the Watcher that showed
humans how to perform horrible genetic experiments that produced
diverse kinds of Nephilim.

Indeed, in 1 Enoch 8:3, it specifically states that *"Semjaza taught
enchantments, and **root-cuttings,** "*meaning that the same fallen angel
that first led some of the Watchers to fornicate with women also likely
introduced the first abominations in the animal world known as
chimeras. If this *"cutting of roots"* or *"root-cutting"* was indeed a
euphemism for DNA splicing, it would explain why many of the
resultant Nephilim offspring were unlike either their human or angelic
"parents" in appearance, and were also often physically unlike each
other.

As suggested in the Book of 1 Enoch, the idea that some of the
Nephilim were genetically engineered monsters is supported in the Book
of Jasher and Book of Jubilees. First, let's look at the relevant verses
from the Book of Jubilees:

> *"And it came to pass when the children of men began
> to multiply on the face of the earth and daughters were born
> unto them, that the angels of God saw them... that they were
> beautiful to look upon; and they took themselves wives of all
> whom they chose, and they bare unto them sons and **they
> were giants**. And... **all flesh corrupted its way, alike men and
> cattle and beasts and birds and everything that walks on the
> earth - all of them corrupted their ways and their orders**, and
> they began to devour each other, and lawlessness increased
> on the earth and every imagination of the thoughts of all men
> (was) thus evil continually."* – Jubilees 5:1-3

> *"And after this **they sinned against the beasts and
> birds,** and all that moves and walks on the earth: **and much
> blood was shed on the earth,** and every imagination and
> desire of men imagined vanity and evil continually."* - Jubilees
> 7:24-25

Just as the Bible intimates, the Book of Jubilees records that the
unholy unions of the fallen angels and human woman gave birth to the

Nephilim giants. Then, following this, the flesh of all animals and men *"corrupted their ways and their orders."* In these days of gene splicing, passages in ancient texts like this suddenly appear in a different light and seem to take on a far more ominous tone. Could it be that this corruption of the animals resulted in the creatures called chimeras today? Could the second race or category of Nephilim have been far more monstrous, violent, and bloodthirsty than either the Gibborim or the Eliud?

Like the Book of Jubilees, the Book of Jasher specifically tells us that the Nephilim were fashioned in part from the genetic material of birds. The following quote from the Book of Jasher makes it clear that the genes of birds were spliced into the genes of other animals to form the offspring of the Nephilim. Furthermore, it suggests that the Watchers *and the Nephilim* took human wives:

> *"And their judges and rulers (i.e. the Watchers and the Nephilim) went to the daughters of men and took their wives by force from their husbands according to their choice, and the sons of men in those days took from the cattle of the earth, the beasts of the field and the fowls of the air, and taught the mixture of animals of one species with the other, in order therewith to provoke the Lord; and God saw the whole earth and it was corrupt, for all flesh had corrupted its ways upon earth, all men and all animals."* - Jasher 4:18

Though many may balk at the idea that our remote ancestors had knowledge and abilities approaching our own today, there is simply no way to mix animals like a *"fowl of the air"* or bird and a *"cattle of the earth"* or cow except through genetic splicing! This therefore cannot be referring to the making of hybrids or crosses between similar animals. Thus, the books of Jasher and Jubilees concur with 1 Enoch by saying that human women and fallen angels engaged in unlawful sexual unions together. Furthermore, all three books agree that the sons of men and the wives of the fallen angels engaged in genetic engineering before the Great Flood. These books also clarify what sorts of creatures were mixed together this way.

In mythologies and legends around the world, many types of chimeras abound, and many have something in common. Though some chimeras such as manticores, griffins, centaurs and fawns appear to be connected to cherubim and thus have a symbolic Zodiac connection, have you ever noticed that the sirens, harpies, gorgons, and gargoyles of myth often had feathered wings, talons, and some even had beaks like birds? Could these be the traits of a real class of beings that no longer exists, but that displayed other bird-like characteristics, such as being bipedal and laying eggs in nests like birds? If so, is their fossil evidence that such a race of creatures existed at one time? The fact is that one does not have to look long or far to find them, for many museums around the world have prominent displays featuring them.

Are Dinosaur Fossils the Bones of the Nephilim?

After making the plausible assumption that the Titans and Gigantes of Greek myth were styled after the fallen Watchers and Nephilim (see Chapter Seven), I asked myself: "where is the fossil evidence that these giant beings and their superhuman children existed?" When I sought after this knowledge, God soon showed me that there is plentiful evidence that the Nephilim children of the fallen angels left numerous fossil remains.

Like many ancient structural ruins, it is possible that the fossilized skeletal remains of Nephilim giants have been found, but have been misidentified. For instance, there are massive deposits of coal and crude oil all over the world that are made up of mixed organic matter that was subjected to intense heat and pressure at the time of the Great Flood. Though no one knows what sort of plants or animals originally made up this fossil fuel, an enormous quantity of Nephilim bodies likely contributed to the world's reserves when they perished in the Flood. This means that modern technology is fueled, at least in part, by the blood and bodies of our fiercest spiritual enemies - the beings known as Nephilim.

Contrary to popular belief, fossil fuels did not need millions of years to form as Evolutionists claim, but could have materialized after only a relatively short period of time. As proof, scientists have developed a way to turn plant and animal wastes left over from food production into high quality fertilizers and fuels in a matter of hours using heat and pressure. In fact, this is currently being done in the United States as a method of creating relatively inexpensive alternatives to natural gas, coal and oil deposits.

There are other clues that the Nephilim existed, not the least of which are the gigantic skeletons of humanoids that have been found throughout the world. In the now out-of-print book entitled: "Giants: A Reference Guide from History, the Bible, and Recorded Legend" Charles DeLoach lists many documented cases where these skeletal remains have been found. In addition, DeLoach refers to numerous Bible passages besides Genesis 6:4 that describe Israelite encounters with the descendents of these giants that survived the Great Flood, as we will explore in Chapter Eight.

Before moving on, however, let me give a note of warning about anyone interested in reading any of Charles DeLoach's books. DeLoach had the unscriptural view that Adam and Eve were created as a lower class of angels, and were not originally human at all! Also, like the heretic Zecharia Sitchin, DeLoach erroneously postulates that the fallen angels combined animal genes with Adam and Eve's genes to make a still more subservient class of beings that became modern Homo sapiens.

Using these same erroneous conclusions, DeLoach also espouses reincarnation and Evolution - *both of which are not taught in the Bible in any form*. Instead, these are lies perpetrated by the father of all lies: Satan himself! It was, rather, *the Nephilim* that came from such unlawful genetic experiments, and not humans! Indeed, the Bible tells us that God created mankind in His image *from the beginning*, and also that *"it is appointed for men to die once, but after this judgment"* (Genesis 1:27; Hebrews 9:27).

Besides skeletons that are decidedly humanoid in appearance, but on a larger scale, the fossil bones of the original types of Nephilim may be on prominent display in Natural History museums around the world - although they have been blatantly misidentified and poorly reconstructed. In fact, it takes no large leap of faith at all to see the evidence for these creatures brazenly displayed as various types of dinosaurs. Of course, accepting most dinosaur skeletons as the bones of the Nephilim requires assuming a Creationist's worldview rather than an Evolutionary viewpoint, and this may be difficult for some Christians who have been taught Evolution in school. Sadly, since teaching Creationism can lead teachers to lose their jobs, there is an almost total lack of Creationist or Intelligent Design ideas being taught in public schools globally.

But think about it! The Bible explicitly states that God didn't create Adam and Eve to be dumb monkeys, but to be like Him:

> *"Then God (Elohim) said, 'Let Us make man in Our image, according to Our likeness; let them have dominion over the fish of the sea, over the birds of the air, and over the cattle, over all the earth and over every creeping thing that creeps on the earth.' So God (Elohim) created man in His own image; in the image of God (Elohim) He created him; male and female He created them." - Genesis 1:26-27 (NKJ)*

This Scripture makes it clear that God created the first human couple to be a physical, intellectual and spiritual reflection of Yahweh's invisible form. Therefore, the logical conclusion is that Adam and Eve must have been fully formed humans and not derived from apes, which are incapable of abstract creativity and higher reasoning. Now, if Evolution is a lie, and God created Adam and Eve as fully formed humans with God-like intellects, then it stands to follow that dinosaurs were contemporaneous with mankind at some point in history. Thankfully, there are many myths and legends that support this conclusion, not the least of which are the Greek mythological stories surrounding the Titans and Gigantes or Giants, and their defeat by the Olympian gods, which may have been none other than mortal men of high status that were honored as gods.

Due to the great size and strength attributed to the Titan gods and Giants in myth, the massive bones of some of the larger dinosaurs could have belonged to the first race of these alien beings whose fathers were fallen Watchers. However, I firmly believe that some of these fossils have been so poorly pieced together and reconstructed that they bear little resemblance to the original creatures! In fact, it is likely that there has been a deliberate attempt by world academia to hopelessly jumble, hide or destroy all of the humanoid Nephilim fossil skeletons that have been found, while dinosaur fossils that depict more reptilian or bird-like Nephilim have been more faithfully reconstructed.

The reason for this is simple. If descendents of the humanoid Nephilim are involved in controlling the world academic, economic and government circles via the Illuminati as some people claim, they would not want any conclusive proof of their existence to be found, and that is why the gods, goddesses, partly divine heroes, and mythical creatures eulogized in Greek Myth are now considered to be fantasies rather than one-time realities.

Furthermore, the reptilian and bird-like dinosaur fossils that have not been altered drastically may be the remains of the many reptilian or bird-like chimeras found in ancient myths and folklore. These chimeras may be a distinct class of Nephilim that were derived differently and had little in common with the first humanoid Nephilim race. In fact, nearly all of the skeletons labeled as dinosaurs, regardless of size, would likely fit within the three broad categories of Nephilim described by the ancients: giants, chimeras and elves.

Since the mothers of the first race of Nephilim were the human wives of the fallen Watchers, they were humanoid in appearance like the giants, ogres and elves of myth, while the races created via genetic splicing most closely resembled mammals, birds and reptiles. But if dinosaur bones are the remains of both the naturally and genetically created races of Nephilim, some of which were humanoid, is there any way we can prove it?

Unfortunately, the information that is given to us by the power elite in the world is of little use, for they have certainly doctored many fossil remains to remove as much of their humanoid characteristics as possible, and made certain that what we are told about these creatures fits into the evolutionary model of the origin of species. Nonetheless, after much prayer and study, and after closely examining the available fossil evidence, Yahweh's Spirit has led me to conclude that many diverse varieties of Nephilim can be found in dinosaur graveyards and museums throughout the world.

The Book of 1 Enoch tells us that all of the genetically abominable creatures that were destroyed in Noah's Flood had an unusual propensity to violence. In the last few sections, quotations from the Bible, the Book of 1 Enoch, the Book of Jasher, and the Book of Jubilees all help to substantiate my belief that most dinosaur remains are actually various types of Nephilim giants - and that these Nephilim fell into two broad categories: those that were the unholy offspring of the fallen angels and human women, or those that were genetically engineered monsters.

If this is true, some people may ask: "Why have modern scientists routinely mislabeled the remains of the Nephilim as various types of meat and plant-eating dinosaurs? In addition, why have they greatly over-exaggerated the age of these giant reptilian creatures - suggesting that they lived between 200 million and 65 million years ago, and long *before* men walked the Earth?"

Sadly, as already mentioned briefly, the main reason for this deception is that there are many ungodly governments that are secretly being ruled over by an elite group called the Illuminati. This group of power mongers may include Nephilim descendents and demonically possessed individuals that have great power and influence in government, banking, and religious circles. Furthermore, these diabolically powerful people appear to be working to enslave, destroy, and control all humanity under the same government and religious ideology of the coming Antichrist.

Sadly, many scientific and educational institutions were created by and are being funded by the Illuminati. As a result, the ungodly educators and scientists being employed by these institutions are being conditioned and cajoled into promulgating the Illuminati worldview, which is completely antagonistic to God and His people.

If some of the Illuminati are descended from the Nephilim who lived before the Great Flood, then they would be living representations of the demonic "seed of the Serpent" (Genesis 3:15) that God prophesied about to Adam and Eve before expelling them from the Garden of Eden. In fact, this prophecy strongly suggests that there has to be a literal seed of the Serpent on the Earth today that is warring against God and all of his human children who are the Seed of the Woman through Christ.

Sadly, those belonging to this Serpent seed line will not rest until they annihilate every last vestige of the Seed of the Woman. Her "seed" includes those who view Abraham and King David as ultimate spiritual icons of truth and righteousness (i.e. the Jews), as well as those who see Yahshua as the Seed of the "Woman" or Holy Spirit and the Inheritor of the promises made to Abraham and David (i.e. Gentile Christians).

Despite the current worldwide deception of humanity that is going on by the Illuminati though, we can gain an accurate assessment of the past by using the Bible and other Judeo-Christian literature as our guide. In addition, there is no doubt that God Almighty is leaving us plenty of clues via his holy angels and anointed servants in the world, of which there must be many millions. Let's examine some of these clues.

If we view all the fossil evidence with a biblical worldview as stated in the first chapter, we can draw a far different opinion of who and what these fossilized skeletal remains of *real giant creatures* were. In addition, using the information in 1 Enoch, the Book of Jasher, and Jubilees, we can propose a far more accurate date for when the majority of these Giants walked the Earth, which would have been from about 3350 BC to around the time of the Great Flood of Noah in 2347 BC.

In addition to ancient Judeo-Christian literature, which clearly asserts that monstrous giants and humans lived on Earth concurrently, *the fossil evidence that is available concerning dinosaurs clearly shows that many were much larger and more powerful than humans - just as the Nephilim were.* Furthermore, a number of them had gigantic mouths full of razor sharp teeth and feet armed with dagger-like claws. Coupled with their enormous strength, this made them highly efficient killing machines that could easily rip a smaller mammal or human to shreds in seconds.

As will be shown in the next section, Enoch reported that the Nephilim resorted to murder and cannibalism when the world supply of edible vegetation began to run out. If so, many supposedly plant-eating Sauropod dinosaurs eventually became carnivorous as well as cannibalistic when there weren't enough plants to feed these giant eating machines. All of them certainly had the strength and sharp teeth or beaks to be meat eaters when it was required. Besides the so-called plant-eating dinosaurs, which were fairly slow-moving due to their incredible size, the carnivorous dinosaurs were extremely fast, agile and had dagger-like claws and teeth that marked them as efficient killers. The fearsome size, strength, horns, claws and/or sharp teeth of almost all dinosaurs indicate that they were highly capable of killing other creatures to feed upon.

Unfortunately, most dinosaurs also had incredibly tiny brains in comparison to their massive physical bulk. For example, the Tyrannosaurus Rex, which stood 30 feet high at the shoulder and could cut a grown man in half with one bite of its massive jaws had a brain that was about the size of a walnut! *Coupled with these relatively small brains that indicate a lack of intellect, these gigantic creatures were likely totally remorseless killers* who did not look any farther into the future than their next meal. Nor did they spare a moment worrying about the ultimate fate of themselves or their victims! Their sole purpose and desire in life likely surrounded killing, eating, fornicating with one another, and producing young.

Scientists now believe that, because of their great size, all the giant Sauropods were voracious, non-stop eaters. This is just as the Nephilim are described in the Book of 1 Enoch. Could it be that these so-called Sauropods were really just one form of Nephilim? Could they be the "elephants" and "camels" that Enoch allegorically identified as the children of the stars or angels in his vision that was quoted on pages 248 and 249? Could it also be that some of the bipedal Carnosaurs like the Theropods and Raptors had a distinctly more human-like, upright appearance than the decidedly elephantine or moose-like bodies they are given in artist's imaginary drawings? Could it also be that many large dinosaur skeletons have been pieced together to hide their far more human-like or beautiful appearance? Could the illustrations being presented in books about dinosaurs have been purposely drawn to hide many of the human characteristics that these creatures might have had?

As far as their size, the most gigantic partial Sauropod skeleton found is estimated to have been about 180 feet long, though this is based solely on one vertebrae of the animal! How could scientists be reasonably sure of anything about an animal from only one of its vertebrae unless they were conducting genetic experiments using the DNA in these bones? In any case, the most common size cited for the Titanosaurs - as the giant Sauropods were known - is about 120 feet from snout to tail-tip, and this figure jives well with the height of the Nephilim being 30 British ells of 45 inches each (or roughly 4 feet per ell).

A Composite Dragon Displaying Possible Nephilim Traits

(Preliminary Sketch Drawn in College, finished by Author 30 years later in 2009)

Mythical
Fire-Breathing
Dragon Displaying
Composite Nephilim
Genetic Traits

Some of these creatures also had armored bodies with huge spikes along their spines and tails. Intriguingly, artistic representations of a non-armored type of Sauropod-like animal have been found in ancient Egyptian carvings and petroglyphic art in the Americas. This suggests that at least one variety of these creatures may have survived the Flood. A bit later, we will discuss the Behemoth mentioned in the book of Job and 1 Enoch as a possible Sauropod-like creature that may have been taken aboard the Ark.

Among the dinosaurs, the Sauropods were no doubt the largest land animals that ever walked the Earth. Even the Camarasaurus, which was the smallest of the Sauropods that scientists recognize, weighed about 20 tons and was about 60 feet long. This means that they were five times the size of an average adult male African Elephant, which weighs about 8,000 pounds (3,600 kilograms or 4 tons) and eats 220 to 440 pounds (100 to 200 kilograms) of vegetation daily!

Unlike elephants, Sauropod dinosaurs had long, thick necks, and long, powerful tails that they most likely used to harvest the enormous quantities of vegetation they needed to eat daily. Intriguingly, this would have been in excess of 1 ton! Considering how much even these relatively small Sauropods had to eat, a pack of a dozen or so of these creatures could strip an entire forest clean of all vegetation in a matter of days! According to Enoch, some of these creatures resorted to eating flesh when the vegetation they preferred ran out.

But even if the largest Sauropods stood upright instead of on all fours, the longest-necked Titanosaurs could not have exceeded the Sears Tower in height - especially if they actually looked the way that they are fancifully portrayed in artist's conceptual illustrations today. However, since the hind legs are decidedly longer and stronger looking than the forelegs on some Sauropods, some of these creatures could well have stood upright for short periods of time when they were foraging for food in the tree tops.

Intriguingly, if the shoulder blades of some dinosaurs in the Carnosaur and Theropod families are moved up higher and outward from the neck to give these creatures stronger-looking and broader shoulders, they would have looked much more humanoid in appearance. In fact, the bones of these especially large and fearsome creatures could be of the first race of Nephilim children descended from the fallen Watchers, which according to Greek myths had huge tails like serpents. This possibility is shown in my own hypothetical reconstruction, which is coupled with a traditional reconstruction on pages 274 and 275.

Indeed, it is entirely possible that dinosaur fossils have routinely been assembled incorrectly - in some cases with extraordinarily long necks that may have actually been the tails of other dinosaurs found in the same fossil sites. In addition, it is a little known fact that *many dinosaur fossils have conveniently been found with their heads missing, or supposedly crushed beyond recognition*. Could it be that many of these skulls were actually found but have been hidden and suppressed because they look too humanoid? In addition, could some of them have been reconstructed to look more animal-like? This is very possibly the case, just as human skulls have been reconstructed to look more primitive in appearance to support Evolution, and ape skulls have been manipulated to look more human.

Since there is so much room for scientists to mislead and deceive the public in regard to the past, no Messianic or Christian should assume that any archeologist, anthropologist, or paleontologist desires to share the truth - especially not the near-charlatans involved in reconstructing dinosaur fossils. Remember: *if the world were filled with honest people who wanted to present the whole, unadulterated truth, Yahweh would not be standing in judgment of it!*

In that regard, I am also suspicious of another scientific cover-up: the so-called Paluxy riverbed scandal. From 1969 to the present, various archeologists have uncovered fossilized dinosaur tracks in the Paluxy riverbed that run through the middle of Dinosaur Valley State Park in Texas. In addition to these dinosaur tracks found in the fossilized mud, some archeologists found footprints that were unmistakably humanoid in appearance. At times these humanoid tracks crisscrossed directly over or appeared inside dinosaur tracks in the same strata. The impressions of a heel, high-arched foot and five toes were clearly visible in some tracks.

At 11.5 inches in length, the humanoid tracks in the Paluxy riverbed are about the size of a modern human male, and may have belonged to a humanoid that was about 6 feet tall. These tracks have been used to prove that humans may have coexisted with dinosaurs, and that dinosaurs probably did not evolve millions of years before humans. To document these footprints, their discoverers took plaster casts and photos showing their clearly defined, humanoid style feet and toes.

Not long after their discovery, however, other scientists came to investigate the same tracks in the Paluxy riverbed. But the scientists who came later produced suspiciously conflicting evidence. Indeed, their photos and plaster casts showed that these supposedly humanoid tracks did not have clearly defined toes after all. Some previously identified as humanoid in appearance even looked remarkably like three-toed dinosaur tracks instead of human footprints! But the strangest part of their findings was the altered color of the tracks they found. Compared to the original photos, the new photographs showed dark discolorations around the tracks that could have been caused if they were deliberately altered with acids or solvents.

Nonetheless, the original scientific teams that discovered these fossil footprints have repeatedly asserted that the humanoid prints they found were *deliberately obscured* by people with an Evolution-based agenda in an effort to discredit their findings. They also insist that the dark or rusty discolorations that can be seen around these fossil footprints today were caused by acids used to hide the tool marks made when the prints were altered. As a whole, however, the scientific community has ignored their accusations, and the Paluxy riverbed finds are now considered to be a hoax.

This is just one example of how the scientific community is opposed to accepting any evidence that supports the existence of God, or points to a special Creation of the Universe. Though Christian scientists have found much evidence that refutes Evolution and a vastly old Earth, atheistic scientists blithely dismiss their findings.

Though the Paluxy riverbed finds have been discredited, there is little real evidence to support Darwin's claim that men evolved from apes. In fact, upon examination, all the supposed Neanderthal skulls on display in museums have jaws that have been forced forward to give the skulls a far more ape-like appearance. Another often-overlooked fact is that these Neanderthal skulls have a consistently larger cranial capacity than modern man, and a person's potential intelligence has been scientifically proven to be connected to the size of the cranium. Why, therefore, were Neanderthals considered more stupid than modern man? If Neanderthals had a larger brain than we do, then they were biologically predisposed to be smarter than us!

Nonetheless, because scientists that hate God want people to be deluded, they will never stop religiously defending the Darwinian Theory. The reason they don't want those who trust them to see the truth is found in the Bible:

> *"Whoever has will be given more, and he will have an abundance. Whoever does not have, even what he has will be taken from him. This is why I speak to them in parables: 'Though seeing, they do not see; though hearing, they do not hear or understand.' In them is fulfilled the prophecy of Isaiah: 'You will be ever hearing but never understanding; you will be ever seeing but never perceiving. **For this people's heart has become calloused; they hardly hear with their ears, and they have closed their eyes.** Otherwise they might see with their eyes, hear with their ears, understand with their hearts and turn, and I would heal them.' " - Matthew 13:12-15 (NIV)*

It is clear from this Scripture that Yahshua is condemning people who are easily deceived by the scientific community because their spiritual eyes and ears are closed. These deceived people all have several things in common. First of all, they do not have the baptism of the Holy Spirit, who gives mankind wisdom. Secondly, they deny the existence of the Creator God or the need for a special creation. The Apostle Paul spoke of these types of people in his letter to the Thessalonians. For impact, I have added my own bold-faced interpretation of Paul's wording in the pertinent section of the letter:

> "The coming of the lawless one **(the Antichrist, as well as the little antichrists in the scientific and Pagan spiritual communitie**s) will be in accordance with the work of Satan displayed in all kinds of counterfeit miracles, **(the wonders of medical science, cosmetic and other types of surgery, and false healings enacted by Pagan shamans)** signs **(false "proof" that man evolved from apes, and the lies found in "channeled" writings)** and wonders, **(how man has evolved from primitive, stupid, and superstitious savages to civilized, clever and spiritually enlightened modern man)** and in every sort of evil **(as in deliberately covering up the truth disclosed in archeological and anthropological digs)** that deceives those who are perishing. They perish because they refused to love the truth **(they flatly deny the need for a Creator or a Savior)** and so be saved. For this reason God sends them a powerful delusion so that they will believe the lie **(the Darwinian Theory and "New Age" Humanism)** and so that all will be condemned who have not believed the truth but have delighted in wickedness." - 2 Thessalonians 2:9-12 (NIV)

There it is - clearly laid out in prophetic Scripture! This is an accurate portrayal of the sorry state of our modern world, and a sure sign that we are very near to the seven-year Tribulation period culminating in the 3-1/2 year Great Tribulation. Thankfully there are a few non-deluded, godly scientists like Jack Cuozzo, who in his book "Buried Alive" convincingly asserts that the whole anthropological community has deliberately identified portions of ape skulls as primitive humanoids. In other cases, they have also falsely positioned the jaws on actual Neanderthal and other humanoid skulls seen in museums or mainstream academic books to make them look more human. Another scientist named Marvin L. Lubenow presents similar information in his book "Bones of Contention." These books are highly recommended, and should be read before formulating your own opinion.

Many intelligent, god-fearing people believe that Darwin's Theory of Evolution is a lie. Like me, they suspect that the claims that millions of years have past since the Earth was formed and life began as single-celled organisms is the biggest hoax in history. The sad truth is that ungodly scientists who want to disprove the Bible are perpetrating these lies with the full support of every major world government and institution of higher learning. In the meantime, the Creationist position that the geological strata was laid down very rapidly during the cataclysmic Flood of Noah rather than over millions of years is being ignored.

Nonetheless, Creationists are not without their own problems when interpreting the available data. In fact, nearly all scientists in support of Creation and Intelligent Design believe that dinosaurs and animals were simultaneously created by God and were contemporaneous with man. They also believe that dinosaurs were taken aboard the Ark and died out after the last Ice Age. However, this theory has some serious flaws, not the least of which is that hundreds of enormous varieties of dinosaurs have been found. So, even though Noah's Ark was likely bigger than the Titanic, it would have quickly filled up with dinosaurs that left little room for other types of animals.

Furthermore, taking younger varieties of dinosaurs that were smaller on board the ark would not have made much difference because of the huge amounts of food these animals needed to eat in order to survive. Even an average sized elephant eats over 350 pounds of vegetation a day! How much more, then, would Sauropods that were many times the size of an elephant eat? The fact remains that, unless all the Sauropods aboard the Ark were anesthetized for their entire one year incarceration on the Ark, there is no way the Ark could have contained enough food to feed them all for that length of time, and if it did, it would have been so heavy that the Ark would have likely sunk the minute that it began to roil and pitch about in the turbulent seas of the Flood.

Though men and dinosaurs likely roamed this planet at the same time, the current Christian assessment that all of these creatures were part of Yahweh's original Creation is highly unlikely. One must ask why Yah, if He truly loves mankind, would have created such fearsome and gigantic creatures like the dinosaur called Tyrannosaurus Rex, which surely would have terrified the average human being at first, even if it was supposedly friendly. Or, how would humans have reacted to seeing giant, armored Sauropods that were 120 feet long? These creatures could totally crush a human being to pulp under just one of their massive feet! Indeed, it seems far more likely that *the majority of these gigantic killing machines were creations of the evil Watchers*, and that they became extinct because they all died in the Great Flood, just as Yahweh intended them to.

Now let me raise an interesting point regarding the apparent absence of dinosaur finds near Wooly Mammoth remains. To date, many Mammoth remains have been found that appear to have been flash-frozen in the Siberian tundra. Since no dinosaur remains have been found frozen in the ice with them, however, it suggests that dinosaurs did not exist when these mammoths walked the Earth in large herds, and that they were flash-frozen some time after the dinosaurs disappeared. Otherwise one would expect to find dinosaurs with the mammoths, which surely would have presented an ideal source of food for a brood of hungry raptors or some T-Rexes on the prowl for meat. That is, unless these mammoths were frozen to death a good deal of time *after* the Flood! We will explore this possibility in the next chapter.

Genetically Engineered Monsters Hidden in Museums

Based on certain fossil evidence, many scientists believe that modern birds evolved from some of the dinosaurs that are displayed in Natural History Museums throughout the World. This is because of the many similarities between dinosaurs and birds that can't be merely coincidental. For instance, many dinosaurs built nests, laid eggs, had feathers, and walked upright on their hind legs like birds. Some, like the Pteranodon and the fully feathered and bird-like Archaeopteryx could even fly. Could it therefore be that fabled accounts of creatures like griffins and harpies have a basis in fact?

Indeed, fossil evidence and CT scans have revealed that many smaller dinosaurs were covered with fur or feathers rather than scales. In addition, *a fossilized dinosaur heart found recently disclosed that it had four chambers like a warm-blooded mammal or bird's heart.* This evidence strongly supports the idea that dinosaurs were warm-blooded like birds and mammals, and that they may have been genetically engineered by splicing the genes of the ordinary creatures that God created into a bird, human or animal embryo in a laboratory and then planting the altered embryo into the waiting womb of a surrogate animal or human female.

The idea that giant reptilian or animal beings with many bird traits once existed on Earth is fully supported by the dinosaur fossil record. Hundreds of dinosaur fossils have been found all over the world, and these have been extensively cataloged and displayed by the world's

Natural History museums. In fact, an overwhelming number of museum dinosaur reconstructions show that *countless dinosaurs had bizarre combinations of bird and animal traits, with the majority of them related to birds.*

? Hollow bones

Could the reason why even the largest dinosaurs had bird-like traits have been to keep their weight down so that they could move rapidly? If their bones were essentially hollow, these giant creatures would have been able to move fairly easily despite Earth's strong gravitational field. Indeed, many big dinosaur skulls have hollow areas all over them, suggesting that the bone mass in the largest dinosaur heads was deliberately kept down so that they could easily be lifted up against gravity.

While some dinosaurs were lizard-hipped, the ones that were this way still had many traits in common with birds such as beaks or boney protrusions on their heads. But many dinosaurs were also bird-hipped. In addition to building nests, laying eggs and walking on two legs like birds, all of the bigger dinosaurs had highly porous bones filled with hollows and large openings in their skulls just like birds. These would have made them much lighter than is often supposed. *Many dinosaurs also had bird-like postures, feathered hides, and clawed, four-toed feet like birds.*

Indeed, a small, fully feathered, two-winged dinosaur with a long beak filled with tiny, razor-sharp teeth called the Archaeopteryx was so close to being a bird that it is almost indistinguishable. In addition, a fully intact fossil specimen of a four-winged dinosaur has been found in China. Named "Microraptor Gui," this strange fossil is approximately two and a half feet long and resembles a monkey with large feathers covering its legs and arms instead of fur. This made it appear to have two sets of wings. It also had a prehensile tail tipped with long feathers and a mouth filled with tiny, razor sharp teeth.

Besides this clear evidence of a creature that was part bird and part animal, there were duck-billed dinosaurs called Hadrosaurs, which were bipedal like humans and appear to have had hand-like forepaws. These include a subspecies called Ornithopods that were also bipedal. As shown in the Iguanodon illustration on page 274, the Ornithopod family of dinosaurs had boney protrusions on their noses and also had forepaws that greatly resembled human hands with large, clawed thumbs.

Since the Iguanodon stood upright and had forepaws similar to human hands, it is possible that this dinosaur was far more humanoid in appearance than ungodly scientists are willing to reveal. In fact, they not only may have positioned this particular dinosaur's pelvis and shoulders incorrectly, but also given it a more bird-like head than it originally had. But even with the bird's head, my reconstruction of what this dinosaur may actually have looked like resembles the hawk-headed gods Ra and Horus.

Here and on the facing page are two drawings of Iguanodons - one as conventionally envisioned by scientists, and one as they may actually have looked to the ancient people that feared and worshipped them:

Conventional Drawing of an Iguanodon

Iguanodon
26.2 to 42.6 feet long,
2.5 tons

Humanoid Depiction of an Iguanodon

Humanoid
Reconstruction
of an Iguanodon

Shades of Horus?

   In addition to the bird-billed dinosaurs, there was a whole family
of bipedal Theropod dinosaurs that bore a striking resemblance in size
and shape to modern birds like the Ostrich. They even sported similar-
sized forelimbs or wings, and were most likely covered with feathers just

like the ostrich, though this traditional depiction of a small Theropod
with an ostrich gives it a reptilian look:

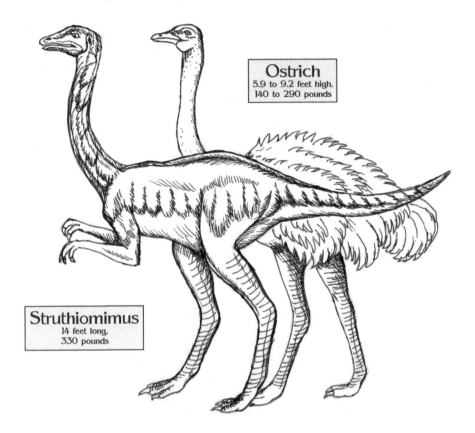

Ostrich
5.9 to 9.2 feet high,
140 to 290 pounds

Struthiomimus
14 feet long,
330 pounds

Interestingly, these smaller dinosaurs are considered to be related
to the huge carnivorous Theropods like the Tyrannosaurus Rex,
Giganotosaurus and Allosaurus, whose forelimbs were much smaller, as
shown in the illustration of the Allosaurus on page 280. However,
though smaller, could the two or three clawed appendages of these
Theropods and their much larger cousins have worked in opposition to
one another? If they could, they would function like human hands and
would have enabled these dinosaurs to carefully manipulate tools and
weapons. Of course, these dinosaur skeletons may also have been
originally found with more appendages than are now being shown - for
obvious reasons.

Besides the aforementioned dinosaurs that had many bird-like
features, whole families of strange, rhinoceros-like dinosaurs have been
discovered that had parrot-like beaks. Perhaps because their faces are so

rhinos

parrot-like, these creatures are rarely shown in museums today. Examples of parrot-faced dinosaurs include the heavily-armored Triceratops and Styracosaurus, as shown on this page:

Drawings of Styracosaurus and Triceratops

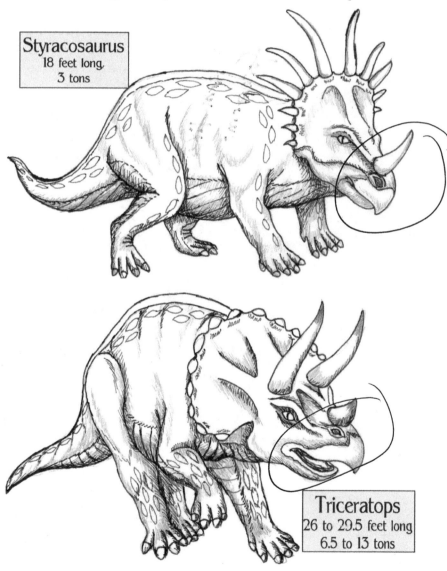

Styracosaurus
18 feet long.
3 tons

Triceratops
26 to 29.5 feet long
6.5 to 13 tons

Nearly all the Theropods labeled Carnosaurs or meat-eaters had arm-like forelimbs with two, three or four finger-like appendages. Examples of these include the Allosaurus, Tyrannosaurus, and Gigantosaurus, as well as the raptors like Velociraptor and its larger cousin known as Deinonychus. The next three pages feature drawings of a traditional and modern reconstruction of a Deinonychus, followed by a drawing of a fierce-looking Allosaurus:

Deinonychus - Traditional Reptilian Reconstruction

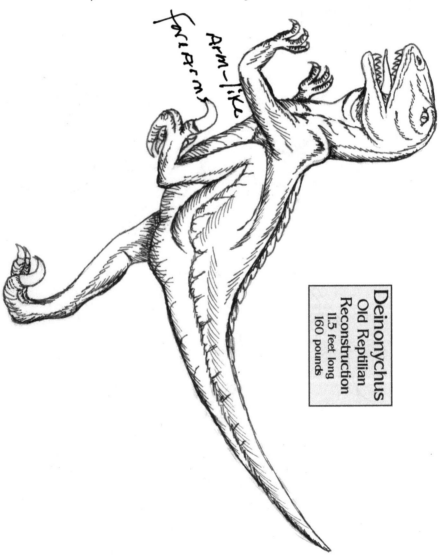

Deinonychus - Modern Bird-like Reconstruction

Thunder Bird

Bird tracks

Dino tracks

Deinonychus
Bird-like
Reconstruction
based on most
current theories

"the sons of men... took from the cattle of the earth, the beasts of the field and the fowls of the air, and taught 'the mixture of animals of one species with the other... to provoke the Lord..." - Jasher 4:18

word not used in Bible —

Drawing of Allosaurus, Smaller Cousin of Tyrannosaurus Rex

Allosaurus
30 to 42 feet long,
2 to 2.5 tons

Despite their overall alien appearance, many dinosaurs display disturbingly hand-like forepaws that have simply been drawn to look more like clawed bird feet rather than the hands that these fossilized bones far more closely resemble. If some dinosaurs did have prehensile forepaws, they could have grasped objects securely and potentially manipulated them as tools. In fact, it takes only a little stretch of the imagination to view these creatures as essentially humanoid in appearance despite the fact that their humanoid skulls were likely switched for more beastly ones.

Remarkably, many huge dinosaurs have been conceptualized from just a few scattered fossil bones - just like the spurious reconstructions of proto-humans often found in museums. For example, scientists have only found a few bones of a supposedly gigantic North African Theropod dinosaur called the Spinosaurus. They also have no fossilized examples of its skin whatsoever. This means that ninety percent of this massive creature's supposed features are purely hypothetical! In other words, they really have no idea what this fantastical creature looked like.

Scientists also have no idea how much soft tissue like cartilage each dinosaur had, and therefore they have no idea what their ears or faces actually looked like. In truth, almost all **artist's renderings of dinosaurs are simply the figment of some scientists' or artists' imagination, including my own** (though, as shown, some of my old drawings were eerily prophetic). In light of these facts, if we ignore their prominent tails that helped them maintain an upright stance despite their incredible size, some bipedal dinosaurs essentially had arms, hands and an overall humanoid appearance.

Demons: Evil Spirits of a Fallen Alien Race

Since all sorts of evil and violence came about because of the Watchers who sinned, Yahweh judged these fallen angels very harshly. For their involvement in creating their evil Nephilim offspring, Yahweh has bound the angels who were responsible in darkness until the Last Judgment:

> "And the angels who did not keep their positions of authority but abandoned their own home - these he has kept in darkness, bound with everlasting chains for judgment on the great Day." - Jude 1:6 (NIV)

This passage from the Book of Jude echoes the teachings of the Book of 1 Enoch, which tells us that - for their many sins - Satan or Azazel and the other fallen angels were thrown into a prison of darkness and torment to await judgment *"on the great Day."* Though few recognize it, the Great Day spoken of here is the Last Day, or Day of the Lord, and it is not a single 24-hour day but a thousand-year divine day! This means that the fallen angels await their final judgment over a thousand year period that begins with the Tribulation and ends with Satan's final judgment at the end of Christ's Millennial Rule - after Satan incites a massive insurrection against Yahshua's Kingdom seat in Jerusalem.

Several passages from 1 Enoch that were quoted earlier in this chapter teach about the imprisonment and punishment of the fallen angels (See 1 Enoch 18:11-14, 19:1-2 on page 216 and 1 Enoch 54:1-6 on pages 217 and 218). In addition to these, 1 Enoch also indicates that **Satan or Azazel has already been imprisoned along with the other fallen angels.** Furthermore, it states that the Nephilim children of the Watchers are condemned to destruction and will not be offered everlasting life:

"The Lord said to Raphael: 'Bind Azazel hand and foot, and cast him into the darkness: and make an opening in the desert, which is in Dudael, and cast him therein. And place upon him rough and jagged rocks, and cover him with darkness, and let him abide there for ever, and cover his face that he may not see light. And on the day of the great judgement he shall be cast into the fire. And heal the earth which the angels have corrupted, and proclaim the healing of the earth, that they may heal the plague, and that all the children of men may not perish through all the secret things that the Watchers have disclosed and have taught their sons.'

'And the whole earth has been corrupted through the works that were taught by Azazel: to him ascribe all sin.' And to Gabriel said the Lord: 'Proceed against the bastards and the reprobates, and against the children of fornication (i.e. the Nephilim): and destroy [the children of fornication and] the children of the Watchers from amongst men [and cause them to go forth]: send them one against the other that they may destroy each other in battle: for length of days shall they not have. And no request that they (i.e. their fathers) make of thee shall be granted unto their fathers on their behalf; for they hope to live an eternal life, and that each one of them will live five hundred years.'" - 1 Enoch 10:5-11

This passage makes it clear that the Nephilim were to be pitted violently against each other in battle and not given *"length of days,"* which is not just referring to mortal longevity but to immortal salvation. Meanwhile, the Watchers who sinned were imprisoned immediately after the very last Nephilim died in the Great Flood. These Watchers are to remain in prison until they are to be judged and condemned:

"And when their sons have slain one another, and they have seen the destruction of their beloved ones, bind them fast for seventy generations in the valleys of the earth, till the day of their judgement and of their consummation, till the judgement that is for ever and ever is consummated. In those days they shall be led off to the abyss of fire: and to the

torment and the prison in which they shall be confined for ever. And whosoever shall be condemned and destroyed will from thenceforth be bound together with them to the end of all generations.

And destroy all the spirits of the reprobate and the children of the Watchers, because they have wronged mankind. Destroy all wrong from the face of the earth and let every evil work come to an end: and let the plant of righteousness and truth appear: and it shall prove a blessing; the works of righteousness and truth shall be planted in truth and joy for evermore." - 1 Enoch 10:12-16

This passage is filled with utter condemnation for the fallen Watchers and their Nephilim children, yet ends with a message of hope indicating that a line of righteousness would emerge among mankind after all the wrongdoing was destroyed by the Flood. This plant of righteousness began with Noah, led to Abraham, gave birth to the Kingdom of Israel, and will ultimately lead to the establishment of the Kingdom of God without end.

In the meantime, until their time of judgment, the fallen angels are bound in prison and are not physically capable of interfering in human affairs. Not even Lucifer or Azazel is physically at loose in the world today. Nonetheless, his spirit is free to roam the Earth using astral projection, and can assume many different tangible forms in order to cause mischief while in this state. However, along with the other fallen angels and the demon spirits of their Nephilim offspring, Azazel (a.k.a. Apollyon) will be released during the Great Tribulation to torment the unrepentant people alive then:

"Then the fifth angel sounded: And I saw a star fallen from heaven to the earth. To him was given the key to the bottomless pit (a.k.a. abyss). And he opened the bottomless pit, and smoke arose out of the pit like the smoke of a great furnace... Then out of the smoke locusts came upon the earth... They were commanded not to harm the grass of the earth, or any green thing, or any tree, but only those men who do not have the seal of God on their foreheads..."

"And they had as king over them the angel of the bottomless pit, whose name in Hebrew is Abaddon (i.e. Destruction), but in Greek he has the name Apollyon (a.k.a. Lucifer or Azazel)."

"Then the sixth angel sounded: And I heard a voice from the four horns of the golden altar which is before God...

*saying 'Release the four angels who are bound at the great
river Euphrates.' So the four angels, who had been prepared...
were released to kill a third of mankind. Now the number of
the army of the horsemen was two hundred million... And
thus I saw the horses in the vision: those who sat on them
had breastplates of fiery red, hyacinth blue, and sulfur yellow;
and the heads of the horses were like the heads of lions; and
out of their mouths came fire, smoke, and brimstone. By these
three plagues a third of mankind was killed... For their power
is in their mouth and in their tails; for their tails are like
serpents, having heads; and with them they do harm." - Rev.
9:1-4, Rev. 9:11, Rev. 9:13-19 (NKJ)*

In these passages from the Book of Revelation, we are told that
the bottomless pit or abyss is inside the Earth, and that it is going to be
opened as the Fifth Trumpet is sounded during the Great Tribulation. At
that time, the demons that emerge from the pit will assume the shape of
the locust-like creatures that will torment all the people who do not have
God's seal on their foreheads. As my earlier discussion of Enoch as the
scribe of God showed, this will not be the first time people are sealed
with the "Tav" representing the Cross of Christ (Ezekiel 9:2-6, 11). These
people sealed by God are the Tribulation Saints, and they will be spared
from the torment inflicted by these demons. Then the Sixth Trumpet will
sound, and four fallen angels that are currently imprisoned near the
Euphrates River will be released to lead a demonic army of 200 million
horsemen riding on lion-faced "horses" with a second venomous head at
the end of their serpent-like tails.

Could it be that this army of horsemen will not be human, but
made up of Nephilim or Anakim? If these beings are Giants, their
"horses" could not be conventionally sized. Because no modern variety
of horse could carry a rider that massive or heavy, this suggests that
their mounts will be gigantic as well. If not elephants, could their
mounts be a strange new variety of Sauropod-type Nephilim? If so, they
would certainly be large enough to support the weight of a 9 to 13-foot
tall Anakim warrior. If so, these Sauropods will be different than the
specimens currently displayed in museums, having a head that is able to
breathe fire on the end of their necks as well as another dangerous head
at the end of their tails, as shown in the drawing on page 285.

Nephilim "Horse" with Anakim Rider

Nephilim "Horse" with Anakim Rider
Sixth Trumpet Plague

"Now the number of the army of the horsemen was two hundred million; I heard the number of them. And...I saw the horses... those who sat on them had breastplates of fiery red, hyacinth blue, and sulfur yellow; and the heads of the horses were like the heads of lions; and out of their mouths came fire, smoke, and brimstone." "For their power is in their mouth and in their tails; for their tails are like serpents, having heads; and with them they do harm." - Revelation 9:16-17, 19

If this proves to be true, will this unholy army of 200 million horsemen and horses be developed before the Great Tribulation using dinosaur DNA? Or have these Anakim and Nephilim been hidden over the centuries in an extremely remote place to take part in this final battle? Could they be hidden inside a huge underground cavern somewhere within the vast wilderness areas and deserts of Central Asia? It certainly could be possible. After all, the four fallen angels who are to summon this unholy army emerge near the Euphrates River, which - along with the Tigris River - divides the Middle East from Central Asia.

As was explored in the movie "Jurassic Park" and its sequels, growing dinosaurs from their fossil DNA may be possible with the knowledge that scientists have today of genetic splicing and cloning. Though most Bible prophecy teachers assume that this army of 200 million will consist of human soldiers, it may consist of 200 million Anakim Giants riding 200 million two-headed Sauropod-type Nephilim with lion-like heads and serpent's tails. If so, these creatures may have already been created via cloning and genetic splicing, and - in an effort to deceive the entire human race - these Nephilim may be made to appear as if they were transported to Earth via advanced spacecraft piloted by their fallen angel sires.

Could it be that the four fallen angels who will be released before this army appears will rapidly develop a new Nephilim army that is animated with the demonic Nephilim spirits of old? If so, the original seeds of the Serpent from before the Flood will be allowed to oppress and destroy those who are damned like them, while the people who are of the Seed of the Woman through Christ will be spared God's wrath.

Interestingly, the four fallen angels that are to be released from their prison by the Euphrates River are the evil counterpart to the four archangels of God that control the four corners and four winds of the world (Rev. 7:1; 1 Enoch 40:2-3, 8-11). Since the four archangels of God are so powerful, it suggests that the four evil angels of the Tribulation will have power as well - though it is not their own, but is stolen power from God. Nonetheless, no one really knows if or when the Nephilim will be resurrected to aid these four evil angels in their desire to destroy humanity. The only thing that is certain is that *the army of 200 million horses and riders will be supernaturally manifested*, and will use fire, smoke and brimstone to kill one third of the human beings on this planet that have taken the Mark of the Beast.

Thankfully, at the end of the Tribulation, Apollyon or Satan is to be cast into the abyss again to await the final battle between good and evil at the end of the Christ's Millennial Rule:

"Then I saw an angel coming down from heaven,
having the key to the bottomless pit and a great chain in his
hand. He laid hold of the dragon, that serpent of old, who is

the Devil and Satan, and bound him for a thousand years; and he cast him into the bottomless pit, and shut him up... so that he should deceive the nations no more till the thousand years were finished. But after these things he must be released for a little while." - Rev. 20:1-3 (NKJ)

At the end of the Last (thousand-year) Great Day that will be Christ's Millennial Rule, Satan is to be released from this same prison to deceive the nations:

"When the thousand years are over, Satan will be released from his prison and will go out to deceive the nations in the four corners of the earth..." - Rev. 20:7-8 (NIV)

Now, since the Book of Revelation indicates that Satan was cast down to Earth with one third of all the angels (i.e. stars) after a great angelic war in Heaven, some people think this has yet to occur. However, it is likely that this war initially occurred before the Great Flood, and that all these fallen angels are now imprisoned somewhere inside the Earth. Nonetheless, they are still at loose in the world via astral projection, through which they likely control the evil spirits of the dead Nephilim that became the demons who have plagued mankind since before the Flood. Indeed, the Book of 1 Enoch tells us that, for their crimes against humanity, the Nephilim were condemned to become demon spirits. The following excerpt from the Book of 1 Enoch has Enoch speaking to the fallen Watchers on Yahweh's behalf:

*"Fear not, **Enoch, thou righteous man and scribe of righteousness: approach hither and hear my voice. And go, say to the Watchers** of heaven, who have sent thee to intercede for them: 'You should intercede for men, and not men for you:' Wherefore have ye left the high, holy, and eternal heaven, and lain with women, and defiled yourselves with the daughters of men and taken to yourselves wives, and done like the children of earth, and begotten giants (as your) sons?"*

*"But you were formerly spiritual, living the eternal life, and immortal for all generations of the world. And therefore I have not appointed wives for you; for as for the spiritual ones of the heaven, in heaven is their dwelling. **And now, the giants** (i.e. the Nephilim)**, who are produced from the spirits and flesh, shall be called evil spirits upon the earth, and on the earth shall be their dwelling.** Evil spirits have proceeded from their bodies; because they are born from men and from the holy Watchers is their beginning and primal origin; **they***

shall be evil spirits on earth, and evil spirits shall they be called... [As for the spirits of heaven, in heaven shall be their dwelling, but as for the spirits of the earth which were born upon the earth, on the earth shall be their dwelling.]"

"And the spirits of the giants afflict, oppress, destroy, attack, do battle, and work destruction on the earth, and cause trouble: they take no food, but nevertheless hunger and thirst, and cause offences. And these spirits shall rise up against the children of men and against the women, because they have proceeded from them." - 1 Enoch 15:1-12

In the above passage, Enoch was called a righteous man and a scribe of righteousness who was called to condemn the fallen angelic Watchers on God's behalf. Because Enoch was a godly scribe for God and had been called by God's edict, he wrote down what had occurred so that later generations of mankind would know the truth about the Watchers and the Nephilim or Giants. At this time, Enoch was told that the Giants were to be denied salvation and rest. Instead, though the Nephilim offspring of the Watchers claimed to be immortal, God swore to shorten their lives to 500 years (1 Enoch 10:10-11). Furthermore, after the Giants died, God condemned them to wander the Earth without bodies - and hence to remain forever incapable of quenching their insatiable hunger and thirst for flesh and blood. *These Earth-bound evil spirits (i.e. demons) are thereby conclusively identified as the spirits of the Giants or Nephilim.*

Interestingly, this passage of Enoch emphasizes that the spirits of Heaven will remain in Heaven, while the spirits of the Earth will remain on the Earth. This is referring to the spiritual origin of the life force within each living thing. For example, the Bible makes it clear that God Almighty is the spiritual source of the breath of life that He gave to Adam and Eve and all the other life that He created (Genesis 2:7, 7:15; Rev. 11:11). For this reason, when people die, their bodies return to the Earth while their spirits return to God in Heaven - where they originated. But in the case of the Nephilim, their life force is not from God, but is connected to the fallen angels who became forever physically earthbound when they sinned (see more on this in Chapter Five). For this reason, *the spirits of the first races of Pre-Flood Nephilim can never be granted salvation* by the life-giving Spirit of Christ, who came from Heaven to save those of us whose life force originated in Heaven. We will discuss the ultimate fate of the Nephilim further in the next section.

In the meantime, the Book of 1 Enoch makes it clear that *the fallen angels who sinned with women have already been cast into an abyss in the valleys of the Earth to await judgment* (1 Enoch 10:12-14,

88:1-3). This is why there are no new habitations of the fallen angels to be found on the Earth today. Even Azazel or Satan was imprisoned, but - like his fallen comrades - Satan still roams Heaven and Earth in spirit form via astral projection as he searches for new converts to his rebellion against Yahweh.

Like Azazel, it is highly likely that all the angels that were going to join in his rebellion against Yahweh did so before the Flood. Furthermore, along with Satan, these fallen angels are now imprisoned with unbreakable bonds - though they may be released to aid the Antichrist in deceiving mankind during the Great Tribulation. In addition, like Azazel, the other fallen angels may still roam the Earth in spirit form. Though this greatly limits their destructive power, the fallen angels are still able to plague mankind with evil. ***In addition, the spirits of the Pre-Flood Nephilim also haunt mankind as demons today.*** These evil sprits masquerade as our dead loved ones, haunt houses, and possess and oppress people around the world. They are the ones who cause all mankind much grief and misery with their continual deceptions and evil schemes, and they are the false gods who are worshipped by those who practice idolatry, Paganism, shamanism and voodoo.

In 1 Enoch 15:11-12, which was quoted earlier, Enoch states that the demonic spirits of the Nephilim ***"take no food, but nevertheless hunger and thirst..."*** This means that, even after death, the spirits of the Nephilim never stop wanting to feast on human and animal flesh and blood. Yet, though these demon spirits will try to satisfy this need, their incorporeal nature will prohibit them from doing so. Therefore, could the bloody sacrificial practices of various past native people groups in the Americas and Polynesia such as the Maori, Incas, Aztecs, Mohawks, Tonkawa and many other native tribes have stemmed from the demands of their demon "gods" that still sought to satiate their lust for human flesh and blood? Is it possible that demonic forces brought about grisly human and animal sacrifices, and the occasional drinking of blood and cannibalism from these sacrifices that seemed to plague so many Pagan societies?

Due to the influence and control of the many demons that were falsely worshipped as gods by deluded people, this scenario is highly likely. In fact, it is also probable that many cold blooded murderers who sadistically mutilate and kill people and/or eat their remains are in fact possessed by one or more demon spirits of the Giants. Some of them might even be blood descendents of the Giants. This is why all people who claim to love Christ need to remain close to Him in prayer and worship, and to continually seek God the Father's protection from demonic oppression or attack. Indeed, this is why Paul warned:

*"For our struggle is not against flesh and blood, but
against the rulers, against the authorities, against the powers
of this dark world and against the spiritual forces of evil in the
heavenly realms. Therefore put on the full armor of God, so
that when the day of evil comes, you may be able to stand
your ground, and after you have done everything, to stand." -
Ephesians 6:12-13 (NIV)*

If nothing else, this book should make what Paul meant in this
Scripture abundantly clear. There are indeed both good and evil unseen
forces at work behind the scenes in our world today, and they are the
ones we should be asking God to command or condemn on our behalf.
In other words, when we are fully equipped with the spiritual armor of
God, we have the authority in Christ to ask God to command His holy
angels to aid us, and we also have the power in Christ to deliver
ourselves and others from demonic attacks and to bind and cast demons
into the abyss. I have personally done these things, and all believers in
Christ can do so as well, as is explained further in Chapter Five.

For their help in corrupting the Earth, the wives of the Watchers
were also condemned to an afterlife of great pain:

*"And the women also of the angels who went astray
shall become sirens." - 1 Enoch 19:2-3*

Condemned to exist only as "sirens," these deluded and
misguided women are now separated from Yahweh's light and love
forever. In Greek mythology, sirens were depicted as part predatory bird
and part woman. Their seductive singing was said to have lured sailors
to their deaths when their boats were shipwrecked against the rocky
coasts where the sirens lived, and may still exist today. Indeed, in
Arabian folklore, these women are considered to be the daughters of the
evil female spirit Lilith. Along with her, the spirits of the other women
who wed the Watchers are said to inhabit the desert wastelands where
they still lure people to their untimely deaths.

The punishment of these sinful women may seem harsh to us.
However, these women were the same ones who freely slept with the
fallen angels, raised their evil Nephilim children, performed genetic
experiments with their fallen husbands, and set themselves up as
goddesses. For rejecting Yahweh and polluting His Creation through
war, bloodshed and genetic corruption, the fallen angels, their human
wives, and their Nephilim children incurred Yahweh's fierce wrath and
condemnation. Tainted with the same genetic and moral corruption,
almost all of humanity was also condemned to perish with the original
Nephilim. As a result of their sinfulness, Yahweh nearly destroyed the

Earth completely through the cataclysmic events that culminated in the Great Flood.

Interestingly, the Arabs also have a rich folkloric tradition concerning spirit beings known as the Djinn, from whence came Genies. Muslims also have their own version of the Devil who is known as Iblis or Shaitan (i.e. Satan), and whom they believe is a Djinn or Genie. In the Quran (or Koran), Sura (i.e. Chapter) 72 entitled "Al Jinn" or "The Djinn" is entirely about these spirits. The Quran teaches that Shaitan would not bow to mankind when Allah created them, and this is the reason why Shaitan hates mankind and has been condemned to Hell. Incidentally, the Nephilim race name "Eljo" could be the root word that inspired the supposedly Celtic names "Elvin" or "Elgin," which can refer to Elves and may be related to the Arabic phrase "Al Jinn" or "The Djinn."

According to Arabic tradition, the world of Djinns and men are usually separate unless Black Magic is used to breech the gap between them. For this reason, many Arabs believe that Djinns can ordinarily only be contacted and cajoled to act with the use of magic spells and incantations. This belief, which is imbedded within both Western and Eastern occult traditions, is behind every religion that relies on Magic and Sorcery to gain power or achieve desired ends.

Significantly, Djinn share traits in common with both angels and demons. For example, these spirit beings are considered to be capable of shape-shifting or taking the form of other living creatures. This might be wholly possible for angels to do on a supernatural level, though demons can also mimic this ability by possessing any kind of living thing and causing it to act abominably. In fact, the common superstition that crossing paths with a black cat can cause ill fortune originated in Arabia, where many believe that black dogs and black cats are Djinns in disguise.

Djinns are considered to be less intelligent than humans but much stronger than them. This echoes my theory that most Nephilim were Dinosaurs, which invariably displayed tiny brain cases in their generally enormous skulls, yet had enormous physical strength. Among Arabs, the Djinn are also thought to have free will. Some Muslims believe that - along with the ability to choose between good and evil - the Djinn will be judged by God and sent to Heaven or Hell on the basis of their deeds. In addition, some Muslim Arabs believe that every person has been assigned an evil Djinn or Jinni called a Qareen or Kareen that whispers to people to follow their evil desires. Though demons can and do influence people to sin, however, there is good reason to believe that not just the Kareen, but all demons are evil, and they are destined to be thrown into the Lake of Fire at the Last Judgment - as will be explained in the next section.

Is Salvation Open to the Giants?

Thankfully, a few righteous and genetically untainted people still existed and found favor with God at the time of the Flood or all human life on Earth would have been extinguished forever. Indeed, if it wasn't for Noah and his family, God's promise of redemption through Yahshua Ha Mashiach would have never had a chance to be fulfilled. Thank God that Noah was a righteous man, and salvation is now offered freely to any human being who repents of their sins!

Unfortunately, some Nephilim survived the Flood. Though no Nephilim likely survived atop Noah's Ark as one ancient Jewish Midrash claims, some legends suggest that they found refuge in a large underground cavern beneath the Earth's crust. As mentioned earlier, there may even be Nephilim hiding in this same underground cavern today. After these Nephilim emerged from their secret sanctuary, they found a place to settle and wait until the time that they could again mingle their bloodlines with the purely human populace. This would have been possible as soon as a group of wayward humans that shunned Noah and Shem's teachings against mixing their blood with strange flesh accepted the Anakim descendents of the Nephilim into their ranks.

Another very real possibility is that some of the more humanoid Nephilim escaped destruction on the Earth during the Flood by using the advanced spacecraft of the fallen Watchers that were capable of interplanetary travel. If some Nephilim did so, they could have temporarily left the Earth, lived for a year or so on stored food rations somewhere in Outer Space, and then returned to Earth to establish a hidden homeland or base for themselves. After that, they would no doubt have set about to create the new generations of Nephilim called Anakim like those the Israelites destroyed. If this is so, then the supposed pyramids and half leonine and humanoid face that some people claim are visible in the Cydonia region on Mars could have been built by these Nephilim, though the most recent high resolution images of these odd structures show them to be nothing more than natural mesa-like formations on the surface of the red planet.

Now, since the Anakim were never fully exterminated by the Israelites, some believe that God may have opened a way for their genetically watered down descendents to find salvation through Christ. This is suggested by the fact that Christ - who was fully human and fully divine - took on the image of the Serpent when He became sin for us on the Cross and died a sinner's death - even though He was totally innocent of any crime or sin. In fact, Christ died and rose again to triumph over the death and condemnation now reserved for Azazel and his followers, and to prove that everyone tainted by the sin and rebellion of the Serpent, but who repent and get baptized with the Holy Spirit can be saved. This is one of the major reasons why Yahshua instituted the rite of Communion, in which we take on Christ's purely human and fully righteous flesh and blood in exchange for our own potentially Anakim tainted flesh and blood.

Nonetheless, despite the gift of salvation that is now being offered to all people, and the full redemption from sin and corruption that Christ will one day manifest in His New Creation and everyone who believes in Him, it is unlikely that many who know that they possess Anakim blood *and are proud of it* will ever readily accept the redemption that can be found through Christ and the Cross. Even though God may have opened a way for redemption to be found among the Giants who were part Nephilim, but increasingly more human genetically, *the demonic spirits of the Giants who died before the Flood show no signs of repenting*. Instead, they continue to rebel against God and hate humanity just like they did when they walked the Earth. This is evidenced in their promotion of false religion, and the violent and aggressive behavior of the people they possess, who murder, lie, manipulate, rape and pillage - and who tout atheism, pantheism, hedonism, humanism, Magic, Sorcery, fortune-telling, bloodthirsty violence, and every kind of sexual fornication.

Sadly, archeological findings prove that all of the people that the Giants had any influence over were as spiritually rebellious, polytheistic and murderous as their alien mentors were. The Hittites, Ammonites, Philistines, and other Pagan cultures in and around Canaan literally hated the God of Abraham and Abraham's descendents through Isaac, and were constantly fighting against them and each other for dominance and supremacy. *Search the Scriptures! You will not find one instance of a Giant or a demon doing good or seeking repentance,* for demons are the spirits of dead Nephilim. You will also find only a few instances where people in these cultures sided with the cause of Israel. Indeed, there were very few like the harlot Rahab, who lived in Jericho, helped the Israelite spies, and is featured in the genealogy of Christ.

Interestingly, Israel's worst enemies - the Palestinians and their radical Islamic neighbors in Syria, Iran, Jordan, Egypt, and Saudi Arabia are carrying on the same tradition of hate and violence against God's people that the Giants who once inhabited their lands did. Their evil behavior says much about the legacy of hatred and genocidal warfare that the Giants inspired and perpetuated in the people that they mingled their flesh and blood with. It also reveals the wicked agenda of the demon spirits of the Nephilim on the Earth today, who have a mostly free reign to oppress and possess people in Muslim dominated lands. Since Muslims worship a god of war and oppression that strongly resembles Satan, there is no doubt that most radical Muslims that have declared war against the nominally Christian and democratic West and the predominantly Jewish land of Israel are demonically possessed or satanically inspired, and their evil actions reflect the nature of the demonic forces controlling them.

It takes little imagination to see that the evil spirits of the Nephilim likely have possessed and deceived many outwardly righteous Muslim men and women who give alms, live humbly, promote sobriety and fidelity in marriage, do not use birth control or engage in abortion, believe in one Creator God, and engage in pilgrimages, yet who also ruthlessly engage in terrorist beheadings, bombings, mutilations, and dismemberments of Christians, Jews, and other "infidels." In fact, these otherwise godly people promote acts of terror against anyone who interferes with their totalitarian desire to rule and oppress - including fellow Muslims.

In an ironic way, it is also the Nephilim who are inadvertently funding the Jihadist aspirations of the followers of Radical Islam today. This is because many of the largest underground stores of crude oil and natural gas in the world are located in the Middle East, and - as already explained - these fossil fuels were formed when large masses of biological matter, which included countless land animals and perhaps millions of Nephilim were rapidly torn apart, buried and compressed under billions of gallons of water during the Great Flood. How sad that the sale of that same oil and gas is funding another genocidal desire to destroy humanity by the descendents of the same people that were heavily influenced by the Anakim after the Flood. Like the Nephilim and their active demonic spirits, these deluded people irrationally seek to destroy God's people Israel wherever they may be, and in the process even seek to destroy themselves if it will lead to more deaths among those whom they consider to be infidels for not worshipping their god of war and hate.

Fascinatingly, the Bible abruptly stops recording the names of the patriarchs in Cain's line after the eighth generation before the Flood. This eighth generation includes the names of Lamech the Cainites' three sons: Jabal, Jubal, and Tubal-Cain (Genesis 4:19-22). Though few have addressed possible reasons behind this, it is a glaring fact that should be analyzed. In light of the history recorded in 1 Enoch, the Book of Jasher, Jubilees, and the histories of Josephus, the fact that the line of Cain is no longer mentioned after the eighth generation suggests that the remaining generations of Cainites before the Flood ceased to be considered open to atonement when their offspring became violent and bloodthirsty, and they also ceased to be fully human.

Could it be that the Cainites were the first to mingle their bloodlines with the Watchers and Nephilim, and to intermarry with them in an effort to establish their power and supremacy over the Sethites? Due to the violent behavior of the Cainites as revealed in Chapter Five, and the fact that God rejected Cain's sacrifice, it is possible. After all, Cain's sacrifice of plants was rejected by God because it indicated his rejection of God's Blood Covenant of redemption with Adam and Eve - a belief Adam no doubt passed down to all of his descendents. The terms of this Covenant are stated in Genesis 3:15, and it was cut with Adam and Eve when God provided them with special animal skin clothes that gave miraculous protective powers to anyone who wore them (Jasher 7:24-30). Sadly, as discussed in the Book of Jasher, Nimrod acquired these garments via Cush's treachery, and they were the source of his superhuman power.

Intriguingly, Lamech the Cainite's son Tubal-Cain was a metal smith (Gen. 4:22), and this suggests his direct involvement with Azazel, who taught mankind how to work metals and make war (1 Enoch 8:1). If the Cainites did welcome the fallen Watchers and their Nephilim offspring into their communities, they would have become spiritually corrupted rapidly. In addition, when they inevitably mingled their blood with the Watchers and Nephilim, their genetically tainted offspring would have lost their classification as humans, and subsequently would have been denied the temporary redemption offered by ordinary animal sacrifices.

Though only a handful of pastors in the world today teach this truth, the Bible tells us that the Israelites invading Canaan were told to slaughter everyone and every living thing in sight because **Canaan was inhabited by the Anakim descendents of the Nephilim.** In effect, God wanted the Israelites to wipe these part-Nephilim giants out of existence in a divinely ordered attempt at genocide. In Chapter Eight, we will explore passages in the Old Testament from Deuteronomy, Joshua, 1 Kings and 1 Chronicles that confirm this.

The Book of 1 Enoch informs us that the reason for this divinely decreed slaughter is that these alien beings were totally evil. Even though they were part human, the Anakim, Rephaim and the other Giant races of Canaan were contaminated with the strange flesh of the

Nephilim. Since their flesh was automatically in rebellion against God, this practically ensured that their spirits would also be in rebellion. As a result, they were often completely bankrupt morally, and many of them were doomed to become demons whose sole purpose and desire is to shed as much blood and corrupt as many human minds and bodies as possible.

Though the first Nephilim were so gigantic that their alien origin was obvious, it is not true of the much watered down Anakim descendents of the Nephilim who have survived to this day. Though they are no longer giants with superhuman strength, it is frightening to consider that members of this part alien race who know their roots may be hidden on Earth today in positions of great authority and power. Furthermore, it is a dreadful possibility that though some of them have been truly saved by the Blood of Christ, others among them may have become even more bloodthirsty in their desire to destroy mankind because of their inability to accept their fallen natures and their need for Christ's salvation.

Indeed, as evidenced by the total depravity of all demonic spirits and the testimony of Enoch, the first Nephilim had no true sense of guilt or remorse when they sinned at all. Though they might have been able to cry or act distressed, it was not because they were hurt by real injustice, but because the selfish desires of their heart were not being met - and their greatest desire was to totally annihilate mankind! They therefore showed no ability to repent of their sins even if they could be offered salvation through Yahshua, whose pure and untainted human blood was shed for the sins of all humanity, and whose coming Millennial reign of peace and prosperity will gradually and forever liberate the whole Universe from the evil grip of sin, pain, destruction and death.

However, before this utopia on Earth and in Heaven is achieved through Yahshua, the Bible promises that there will be a time of great trouble such as has not been experienced in the world since the time of the Great Flood (Daniel 12:1). To make matters worse, the Nephilim were never fully destroyed, and so their descendents are definitely in the world today - whether or not people wish to accept this fact. Because of their desire for revenge against the descendents of the Israelites for waging a genocidal war against the Anakim in Canaan, some of these part alien beings have aimed for and acquired high level government, military and economic positions around the world, and are likely using their power to further their own destructive aims. In fact, some direct descendents of the Anakim may be the driving force behind a highly secretive and dangerous organization of extremely rich and powerful men called the Illuminati.

Over the centuries, the Nephilim who survived the Flood have inbred with humanity so much that it is difficult to tell anyone who might be part Anakim apart from pure human beings. However, those who are part Nephilim tend to display certain physical traits. For example, most part Anakim people are fairly tall - usually about 6 feet high, and sometimes even taller. However, keep in mind that - due to the greatly improved diet, health and medical care in the West in the last century, many people who likely have no Nephilim blood at all are now as tall as, or even taller than those who may be part-Nephilim.

If there are watered-down Nephilim descendents on the Earth today, those with Anakim blood would tend to be very strong without need of steroids. In addition, some people suspected of being Nephilim in the past have had six fingers and toes each on their hands and feet. Oddly, having six appendages is fairly common - one in 1000 children are born with them. Could this be a sign that various branches of humanity have been selectively polluted with Anakim blood over the centuries?

Other common traits in those with Nephilim blood may include large hands and feet, bushy eyebrows and deep-set eyes with very little space between their eyes and eyebrows. They also tend to have broad foreheads, big ears, big noses that point downward sharply, curly or wavy hair and prominent jaw lines with pointed chins.

Have you ever seen Prince Charles of Wales, or his father Prince Philip? There is good reason to believe that both of these men are part Nephilim. Both men are fairly tall (Charles 5' 10", Philip 6' 2"), and have the big ears, strong chins, deep set eyes, and the big, slanted noses of those who could be part Nephilim. See Book Four for more about these royals and their possible link to the Antichrist's kingdom and Babylon the Great.

A fully selfish and unrepentant nature is another definite sign that someone could be part Nephilim or totally beyond redemption. This is exactly the type of attitude that Prince Charles displayed toward his first wife - the beautiful, graceful, kind (and purportedly fully human) Lady Diana. Indeed, since their spirits can easily be demonically controlled, those who are part Nephilim or who are fully unrepentant are often incapable of the slightest remorse or concern - even when they murder someone in cold blood. As a result, they are often very selfish and drawn to use witchcraft and the occult to get what they want at any cost. Furthermore, they usually have no compassion for others - even their own friends or family.

Though some people with these previously listed wicked personality traits could be part Nephilim, many are simply unrepentant or demonically possessed by a Nephilim spirit. If these remorseless individuals either house or are possessed by evil spirits, they undoubtedly have the same dark agenda. In fact, in a sick act of revenge against God, the primary goal of all demons seems to be either the total destruction of all human beings who refuse to worship them, or the complete annihilation of all life fully created by God - and either goal is untenable.

Yet, even though demonically-controlled people have gained much power in the world and may be seeking to destroy a large segment of the human population of this planet using manufactured super viruses and diseases, technology-caused "natural" disasters, starvation, weapons of mass destruction, and mass beheadings, the Good News for Christians and Messianic Jews is that the Bible promises that all those who trust in Christ today will be taken in the Rapture, and those who come to a saving faith after that will ultimately win the Antichrist's war against them and will not be harmed forever by the part-alien Anakim and the wicked people that Nephilim demons have possessed.

Instead of being destroyed, those who believe in Yahshua Ha Mashiach as Savior and Lord or Adonai will go to Heaven to attend the Wedding of the Lamb during the Great Tribulation, and will rule with Him in His future Kingdom on Earth. Furthermore, those who are saved before the last half of the Great Tribulation will likely be spared from this coming showdown that will pit the physical and spiritual descendents of the Nephilim and the rest of unsaved humanity against the Tribulation Saints and the Jews. Those who are saved by the Blood of Christ shortly after the Tribulation begins will be spared God's supernatural wrath against the wicked, as well as Satan's wrath against the righteous that will result in martyrdom. As shown in Book Four, there may be two Raptures - one at the beginning and one at the end of the Great Tribulation, while the Tribulation martyrs will be resurrected into immoral life after the Battle of Armageddon and Christ's Second Coming, rather than making a trip to Heaven first.

Why Some of the Watchers Rebelled

Since unnaturally large, ravenous giants were born from the unholy unions between the sons of God or Beni Elohim and the daughters of men, these sexual relationships created a race of beings significantly unlike the women they were born to. If these unions had merely been between the Sethites and Cainites as some scholars have postulated, the offspring of these unions may have been spiritually suspect, but otherwise unremarkable - just as unions between people of different faiths and people groups today produce physically healthy but otherwise unremarkable children.

Fortunately, as quoted at the beginning of this chapter, the Book of Daniel reveals that some of the Watchers did not fall into sin and therefore still delivered and enforced God's decrees over men after the Flood. This means that not all of the Watchers became evil or rebelled against God. Furthermore, it suggests that - besides the seven holy archangels *"who watch"* (1 Enoch 20:1-8), many Watchers who love God and are obedient to Him are still involved in the affairs of men today.

The Book of Jubilees offers us the first clue as to why some of the Watchers eventually rebelled. Since the Watchers were meant to instruct people on God's behalf, these angels were specifically created to serve mankind. Furthermore, these Watchers knew that mankind was given dominion over all living things - including themselves and all the other angels. In fact, mankind was created to eventually have dominion over all Creation through Yahshua, who always has had dominion over all created things in both the spiritual and material dimensions of reality (Coloss. 1:15-17; 1 Peter 5:11-12; Rev. 1:5-6). The Bible supports this conclusion, affirming that people were Yahweh's last and best creation, and that Yah originally gave them total dominion over the Earth as a learning ground for their eventual dominion over all Creation (Genesis 1:26):

> *"For He has not put the world to come, of which we speak, in subjection to angels. But one testified in a certain place, saying: 'What is man that You are mindful of him, or the son of man that You take care of him? You have made him a little lower than the angels; you have crowned him with glory and honor, and set him over the works of Your hands.'"*
> *- Hebrews 2:5-7 (NKJ)*

This New Testament passage delineating mankind's dominion over Creation is derived from Psalm 8. There, King David spoke of mankind's superiority over the angels via a messianic prophecy, which speaks of a crown of glory being given to the only perfect Son of Man - Yahshua the Messiah - so that He could share it with His redeemed brethren:

"What is man that You are mindful of him, and the son of man that You visit him? For You have made him a little lower than the angels, and You have crowned him with glory and honor. You have made him to have dominion over the works of Your hands; you have put all things under his feet."
- Psalm 8:4-6 (NKJ)

This Scripture has two meanings. First of all, despite the fact that mankind is currently inferior to angels in glory, this Scripture tells us that people still have dominion over the Earth and the living things upon it. That is why men regularly herd cattle and sheep and not the other way around, why people can tame and ride horses, elephants and even whales, and why no animals have willfully attempted to tame men and ride on their backs (or break them) except those alien creatures with strange flesh!

Of course, sin has also horribly marred mankind's dominion over the Earth and his judgment of how to tend and keep it, just as Satan knew it would. After all, Satan's goal was to usurp mankind's place in the Universe, and to rob mankind of their authority and dominion over the Earth as well as the angels. As a result, men and animals often fear and hurt one another and people often make stupid decisions that have a negative and destructive environmental impact. But in the beginning, when the world was new, people knew how to take perfect care of their world, and animals were designed by God to interact peacefully with mankind. Furthermore, people and animals shared and ate fruit, nuts and seeds together, and animals did not eat one another to survive.

That is why Yahshua came to be our Savior. In order to restore what Satan had robbed Adam of, a new Adam that would not sin was needed to pay mankind's blood penalty for sin and make atonement for their guilt. After this, the dominion over all things that Adam once had could then be put under the last Adam Yahshua's feet. But this means that only Yahshua currently has full authority over the Earth and all Creation. This is why people need to believe in Yahshua's sacrifice for their sins and their need for His redemption before they can reclaim their lost dominion over the Earth and everything in it, including the demons that are trapped upon it. This is also why Yahshua's disciples could only cast out demons in His Name. They needed His authority!

As the Bride of Christ, a great multitude of redeemed people are destined to rule over all Creation with Christ one day. As a result, the angels will then be subject to the will of mankind as well as to Christ's Will. At that time, both God and man shall finally be in perfect accord with each other. Since this is destined to occur, the unfortunate truth is that some angels began to feel jealousy toward mankind, and their joy in

God and His Creation dissolved as their overweening pride in themselves asserted itself in rebellion against God.

How many angels fell via the sins of pride and jealousy is not known, but there are likely as many people that will rebel against God's authority and will never repent of their sins as there are fallen angels. Indeed, the Book of Revelation reveals that one third of the myriads of angels that God originally created fell with Satan, and have already suffered his fate as prisoners inside a fiery abyss (Jude 1:6; 2 Peter 2:4; Rev. 12:3-4). Likewise, one third of all the wicked, unrepentant people on the Earth will perish like the fallen angels (Rev. 9:15).

From the Book of Daniel, it can be inferred that both Nebuchadnezzar and Daniel believed in the holy angelic beings that were called Watchers. The prophet Enoch tells us that this class of angels was sent to instruct mankind shortly after the dawn of human existence. Enoch also tells us that two hundred of these Watchers eventually chose to openly rebel against God like Azazel had before them. However, unlike Azazel, who tempted Eve with promises of power and knowledge rather than lust, the fallen Watchers chose mortal human women as wives - engaging in sexual relations with them:

> "And it came to pass when the children of men had multiplied that in those days were born unto them beautiful and comely daughters. And the angels, the children of the heaven, saw and lusted after them, and said to one another: 'Come, let us choose us wives from among the children of men and beget us children.' And Semjaza, who was their leader, said unto them: 'I fear ye will not indeed agree to do this deed, and I alone shall have to pay the penalty of a great sin.' And they all answered him and said: 'Let us all swear an oath, and all bind ourselves by mutual imprecations not to abandon this plan but to do this thing.' Then swore they all together and bound themselves by mutual imprecations upon it. And they were in all two hundred; who descended in the days of Jared on the summit of Mount Hermon, and they called it Mount Hermon, because they had... bound themselves by mutual imprecations upon it." - 1 Enoch 6:1-7

Here, 1 Enoch tells us that the Watchers who sinned descended on Mount Hermon before they found wives for themselves. Looking at a map of ancient civilization centers, it becomes obvious that they chose this mountain as their new home among men because it was in the very center of the Fertile Crescent extending from Ethiopia through Egypt, and then up through Israel and Phoenicia into Mesopotamia. It is also likely that the Cainites had settled near to Mount Hermon, and the

Watchers knew these people were already heavily steeped in sin and would be easy to coerce into deeper rebellion against God. The unholy sexual unions between the Watchers and human women led to a horrible consequence: the creation of the Nephilim who eventually terrorized mankind and all other terrestrial life.

The Worthless Teachings of the Fallen Watchers

Among the most useless and dangerous types of knowledge shared with the antediluvians by the fallen angels, the concept of Magic was taught by Semyaza, the leader of the fallen angels that took human wives. Magic and Sorcery are evil because they promote gross perversions of spiritual principles, and they also *call on demonic power* to affect certain desired results. Magic is a form of manipulation focused on altering the circumstances surrounding an individual or group of individuals *without asking permission from God, and against the will of God*. Sadly, throughout history - and in many modern fantasies - magicians, witches or sorcerers often pretend to have God's authority when they do not. In addition, they perform manipulative actions on others *without having their fellow man's or their Creator God's consent.*

For this reason, there is no such thing as "White Magic" in any context. If anyone tries to supernaturally enact change in another person's life without God's permission or approval, they have entered the realm of Sorcery. All Pagan magical practices and rituals, regardless of their supposed purpose, are demonic and unquestionably evil, and are a terrible sin against Yah and mankind because they do not follow God's Will, or support His Plan of Redemption. The only real "White Magic" in the world is found in the indwelling presence of the Holy Spirit within true believers, and the powerful actions of their prayers as they make their requests known to God and trust Him to provide for them. In addition, the ministering presence of holy guardian angels has a magical element to it. Indeed, all the godly miracles that occurred in biblical times and that still regularly occur in our world today attest to the magical quality of God's direct intercession in believer's lives as a result of their sincere repentance, praise, worship and prayers.

But, as evil as Magic and Sorcery are in turning people away from a godly focus on prayer and petition before God, the fallen Watchers found even more grievous ways to thwart Yah's place in mankind's world. They did so by teaching humanity how to perform genetic splicing, and how to engage in the forbidden mixing of different kinds of living things to create monstrous abominations that are naturally in rebellion against God and His Creation.

In addition, the fallen angels taught the counterfeit of Sacred Astronomy called Astrology. Enoch tells us that several fallen angels introduced this forbidden knowledge. Furthermore, Enoch makes it clear that - in striving to foresee and control the future - many people began to perish. This is most likely because people inevitably had to be killed or enslaved for Sorcerers and Witches to manipulate history, and to gain the absolute power over others that they selfishly sought and craved:

> *"Semjaza taught **enchantments**, and **root-cuttings**, Armaros the resolving of **enchantments**, Baraqijal (taught) **astrology**, Kokabel the constellations, Ezeqeel the knowledge of the clouds, Araqiel **the signs of the earth**, Shamsiel **the signs of the sun**, and Sariel **the course of the moon**. And as men perished, they cried, and their cry went up to heaven..."* - 1 Enoch 8:3

As recorded in this passage, the knowledge and promotion of Astrology, Sorcery, war, vanity, sensuality and genetic splicing were all encouraged by the fallen angels because they served to pervert every good thing that Yahweh had created. Because this knowledge was morally wrong and spiritually and physically degrading and destructive, humanity should never have had it in the first place. Therefore, the knowledge mankind was given by the fallen angels was essentially worthless because it accomplished nothing from a godly perspective. Instead of drawing people into a righteous relationship with Yahweh and the world, it caused untold destruction and drew mankind irrevocably away from God:

> *"And now as to the watchers who have sent thee to intercede for them, who had been aforetime in heaven, (say to them): 'You have been in heaven, but all the mysteries had not yet been revealed to you, and you knew worthless ones, and these in the hardness of your hearts you have made known to the women, and through these mysteries women and men work much evil on earth.' Say to them therefore: 'You have no peace.'"* - 1 Enoch 16:2-4

In Satan's eyes, the worthless knowledge humanity received from his followers was great news for him, for this false knowledge furthered along his plan, which was to utterly ruin and enslave the entire world through sin. Indeed, it was Satan's objective to completely destroy and annihilate not just mankind, but every living thing on the Earth through violence and corruption:

> *"And the third was named Gadreel: he it is who showed the children of men all the blows of death, and he led*

> *astray Eve, and showed [the weapons of death to the sons of*
> *men] the shield and the coat of mail, and the sword for battle,*
> *and all the weapons of death to the children of men. And*
> *from his hand they have proceeded against those who dwell*
> *on the earth from that day and for evermore." - 1 Enoch 69:6-7*

Though this passage indicates that the fallen angel Gadreel led Eve astray and taught mankind how to make and use weapons and deadly force, Azazel or Satan was the first to do so (See 1 Enoch 8:1). Gadreel may therefore be just another name for Satan, who taught mankind where to hit another person to kill them, and how to make weapons and armor for war. If this wasn't bad enough, another fallen angel taught mankind how to record all the worthless knowledge that they learned from the fallen angels with pen and ink on paper, and then to rely on these misleading records:

> *"And the fourth was named Penemue: he taught the*
> *children of men the bitter and the sweet, and he taught them*
> *all the secrets of their wisdom. And he instructed mankind in*
> *writing with ink and paper, and thereby many sinned from*
> *eternity to eternity and until this day. For men were not*
> *created for such a purpose, to give confirmation to their good*
> *faith with pen and ink. For men were created exactly like the*
> *angels, to the intent that they should continue pure and*
> *righteous, and death, which destroys everything, could not*
> *have taken hold of them, but through this their knowledge*
> *they are perishing, and through this power it is consuming*
> *me." - 1 Enoch 69:8-12*

In this telling passage, Enoch sees human mortality as a consequence of wanting forbidden knowledge that warps the mind and forces the spirit to work antagonistically toward the flesh or soul of every human being. Indeed, even though Enoch is credited with the invention of writing in the Book of Jubilees, it is likely that he only pursued learning the art of writing because he saw the need to offer an alternative source of wisdom in an effort to thwart the deception of the fallen angels!

Sadly, relying on pen and ink and paper to record knowledge became a major threat to gaining true wisdom partly because paper is easily destroyed and writing can be altered by the unscrupulous. Furthermore, relying on written records made people forget that they had real intuitive abilities and could ask God to reveal the truth to them in prayer. Nonetheless, because of the sins of prevarication and deception, written records came to be considered more reliable than oral traditions or prayer. This has led to a world where no one's word is to be trusted. Despite Yahshua's admonition for us to let our yes be yes and our no be no (Matthew 5:37), many supposed Christians can't be trusted to tell the truth in today's world - to say nothing of the constant lies being voiced by non-Christians who have no true source of spiritual knowledge and no fixed moral standards!

Since all human beings are fallen sinners, Enoch knew that nothing people create is perfect. Therefore, their records will be marred by their imperfection, biased perspectives, mistakes, poor choices, and agendas. At times, written records can even reflect the author's outright stupidity or denial of God's truth. While modern works like "The Satanic Bible," "The Witch's Bible" and "The Wicca Spellbook" are obvious examples of totally malevolent and unrighteous writings, there are also countless subtle attacks on the Judeo-Christian faith to be found among New Age and Positive Thinking adherents and practitioners.

Unlike baked clay tablets and finished stone blocks, ink on paper is also a fairly flimsy medium for transmitting knowledge. As a result, records can easily be replaced with falsified documents, thereby making it relatively simple to change names, times, and dates. Indeed, history could even be re-written from the perspective of someone who hates God Almighty. Incidentally, this is exactly what the Egyptians, Babylonians, Greeks, and Romans did when they recorded their false religious myths! These myths that totally ignore the truthful, perfect, sinless and merciful Creator God in favor of relaying the sinful antics of countless false gods were written down and preserved for us on paper with pen and ink, and are now considered "classic" examples of powerful literature. Sadly, this blatant prevarication and bending of the truth is still going on today. That is why virtually every museum and school in the West has written God out of history by teaching the lies surrounding evolution, humanism, and ecumenism.

Then there is the problem that arises when truthful factual records are irrevocably lost. Despite the efforts of countless godly kings to record their own histories on stone instead of paper, many of their greatest achievements were lost to their posterity when their stone palaces and monuments were reduced to rubble and their paper records were subsequently lost or destroyed. Only records kept on clay tablets as they were in Mesopotamia or on tomb or temple walls as was frequently done in Egypt have sometimes survived intact, and therefore give us a better record of the culture, civilization, and religion they stemmed from. Unfortunately, false religious beliefs have also survived intact, causing millions to be misled today.

Though written sources of knowledge can present major problems, however, the worst sin mankind learned from the fallen angels is one that really isn't discussed much. In fact, it is still often glorified as an achievement rather than a sin, and this sin is pride. This is not the simple pride that comes from doing a job well done, but the pride that exalts people above their peers, and causes them to think they are better than others because of an accident of birth or supposedly superior genetics.

Indeed, one wonders if Eve ever fully repented of her own overweening pride that led her to take a bite of the forbidden fruit so that she could become a goddess. After all, when Eve fell, she permanently acquired a sinful nature that needed redemption and transformation through Christ - just as all of us do as children of Eve. Contrary to Judeo-Christian depictions of Eve as repentant and humble, the Pagan-riddled record of ancient history suggests that neither Eve nor Adam escaped deification or that they discouraged the view that - because they were without father or mother - they were the only true children of God. Indeed, as Chapter Seven shows, Adam, Eve and many of their descendents that filled leadership positions were often deified and worshipped as gods by fallen humanity - just as the fallen angels and Nephilim were.

Subsequently, this led to the further spiritual degradation of Adam and Eve's children at the hands of beings like Satan, who appeared as a god to Adam and Eve, and led their children to want his evil knowledge and power. Together with Satan, the other fallen angels and their inhuman Nephilim offspring incited and perpetuated the spiritual, moral, intellectual, and genetic downfall of mankind. As a result of the unsavory forbidden knowledge they gave to humanity, the world became hopelessly corrupt and violent.

Baalbek: Evidence of the Watchers Near Mount Hermon

The Book of 1 Enoch stipulates that, when some of the Watchers fell, they banded together and descended to Earth at a place called Mount Hermon (1 Enoch 6:6). Then, after descending from their new abode atop Mount Hermon, each fallen angel took as many human wives as he wished from among the local population (Genesis 6:4; 1 Enoch 6:1-2). Intriguingly, there is a mountain situated in the middle of the region known as the Fertile Crescent, which refers to the lands surrounding the Nile, Jordan, Tigris and Euphrates rivers. This is where many Semitic people groups settled after the Great Flood, and - as the incredibly ancient ruins in this region attest - it was also a central location among many of the civilizations that existed prior to the Flood.

In affirmation of the veracity of 1 Enoch, stunning archeological finds have been discovered in a high mountain valley that is located just south of Mount Hermon. This valley is called Baalbek, and located there is an ancient Roman temple complex that sits upon the ruins of still older temples that had walls made from enormous blocks of finely worked stone. Even more amazingly, these older temples were built on top of the largest level stone foundation ever made. This platform is constructed of the largest cyclopean sized blocks ever found, with several of them weighing an estimated 1500 tons, or three million pounds! Since there is no feasible way that any modern engineer could have cut and moved these gigantic blocks much less people working with Stone Age equipment, the use of these enormous stone slabs clearly suggests that evil Watchers once inhabited the area.

The only ancient stone blocks used to construct monuments that may even approach the size of those at Baalbek were used to form the ceilings over the Queen's Chamber, Grand Gallery and King's Chamber inside the Great Pyramid at Giza. Of course, this suggests that, just as Noah received some help from the Watchers when building the Ark, the Sethite builders of the Pillar of Enoch needed some divine assistance in completing it. Despite the wondrous monolithic constructions at Baalbek and elsewhere in the world, this magnificent pyramid dedicated to Yahweh in Enoch's memory is encoded with spiritual and celestial wisdom that - of all the people ever born - only Enoch the Sethite fully understood.

Three level and expertly worked monolithic stone blocks weighing an estimated 1200 tons each have been found at Baalbek that are fitted together underneath the foundations of a large ruined Temple Acropolis. These stones are approximately 63 feet long, thirteen feet high and ten feet thick. They are so immense and heavy that there is no possible way the Romans could have moved them. In addition, though the ruins atop these blocks are dated to no later than ancient Roman times, some of the monoliths at the bases of many of the walls are far larger and more finely worked than the masonry atop them.

The smaller monolithic blocks atop the three base slabs found at Baalbek would have formed part of one wall of the original structure that was atop the platform. These blocks of stone are beautifully worked and appear to be fitted together in the same precise and unusual style to those in the Valley Temple and the Great Pyramid at Giza, as well to those high in the South American Andes at Machu Picchu, Tiahuanaco and Sacsayhuaman. In addition, it has been estimated that there are more stone blocks comprising the entire 15 million square foot platform at Baalbek than there are in the Great Pyramid at Giza.

Despite the advanced construction machinery available today, modern engineers reel under the thought of having to move such huge blocks of stone. Even if they could have, how could they then have lifted these huge stones the twenty-three feet required to place them on top of the underlying stone foundation? All those who have investigated the size and layout of these stones at Baalbek are at a loss to explain how the architectural engineers of ancient times could have done so. For this reason, some have suggested that the Nephilim, the Watchers, or aliens from another world created this immense platform of huge stone blocks for some unknown purpose.

The giant stone platform that these stone blocks form a part of may have served as the foundation for a now vanished palace or temple. When standing, this temple would have dominated the entire site. In fact, the high mountain valley called Baalbek may have been the original abode of the fallen Watchers after they left their holy (i.e. set-apart) abode located elsewhere. It is interesting to note here that - along with the Israelites - many ancient Pagan cultures saw certain mountaintops as particularly sacred. This suggests that God's angelic representatives could indeed once be found atop some of the mountains of the world.

As proof of this, Greek myths clearly convey that rival sets of gods lived on different mountain peaks. In Greek accounts of the war between the Titans and Olympian gods, the Titans were said to have lived on Mount Othris, while the Olympians lived on Mount Olympus. However, there is little or no evidence that the fallen angels ever inhabited these peaks located in Greece. Despite this, both the holy and fallen Watchers likely did live atop mountains. They just weren't located in Greece!

Unlike the Grecian peaks, Mount Hermon in the Middle East and several other prominent mountain tops in South America do show evidence of having been inhabited by cultures with advanced technological knowledge and enormous architectural skill. But it is Mount Hermon that Enoch identifies as the first home base of the fallen Watchers. Despite its designation as the place of the Watcher's descent into sin, however, Mount Hermon was likely a place set aside to the worship of Yahweh long before that. In fact, this may be the exact reason why the Watchers chose that particular peak. It may already have been revered as a holy place dedicated to Yahweh by the Sethites.

Intriguingly, the borders of the Kingdom of Israel may have extended as far north as Mount Hermon, making Baalbek part of Israel at one time. This is suggested in the New Testament Gospels, where it is recorded that Yahshua went to the region of Caesarea Philippi, which is near to the foot of Mount Hermon (Matthew 16:3; Mark 8:27). Not long after entering this region, Yahshua went atop a high mountain with only Peter, James and John at His side so that they could witness His transfiguration (Matthew 17:1; Mark 9:2). The highest mountain immediately in that region is Mount Hermon, and it would be poetic justice if Yahshua chose this peak to show His divine nature. Indeed, it would have shown Yahshua's complete supremacy over any angels or demons who dared to pretend to be God! In this way, Yahshua could have reclaimed and rededicated that mountain to Yahweh for His and His Father's sake, just as my books are reclaiming the Star Gospel for them.

Long before Roman times, the Baalbek site on Mount Hermon was known as Heliopolis or On, which is identical in name to the city in ancient Egypt where the cult of the Sun god Amun-Ra was centered. There is also evidence that the Israelite Tribe of Dan may have controlled this sacred site when the kingdom of Israel still existed. The Danites built a temple somewhere in the northernmost part of Israel that was intended to replace the Temple to Yahweh in Jerusalem. This occurred when Israel split into two kingdoms: Israel in the north and Judah in the south. The Bible tells us that the Danites built their city called Dan over the ruins of the ancient city of Laish (Joshua 19:47; Judges 18:7).

Though the location of Laish is uncertain, it would have been in the northernmost part of Dan's northern land allotment in ancient Israel. This is certain, since Laish figured prominently as a trading stop on the road to the great trade city of Damascus in ancient Syria (Judges 18:27-31). Archeologists place the city of Laish near to Baalbek and outside the traditional boundaries of ancient Israel. However, if the idolatrous temple of the Danites was built in or near Laish, then the city must have been within the borders of ancient Israel at one time. Ancient Israel therefore must have covered much more land area at that time than most archeological estimates allow for. In fact, the ancient kingdom of Israel could have extended well past the northern borders of modern Israel into parts of modern-day Syria and Lebanon.

After the erection of this idolatrous temple of the Danites, King Jeroboam of the Northern Kingdom of Israel made two images of a bull calf. He placed one image at a religious shrine in Bethel and the other was placed "in Dan," the city built over the ruins of Laish (1 Kings 12:28-29). This bull calf was likely similar to the one that Moses' brother Aaron regrettably fashioned in the Sinai wilderness for the Israelites when they begged him to make idols for them (Exodus 32:2-5). Both calf idols were probably copied from Egyptian carvings of the black Apis Bull worshipped by the followers of Ptah in the city of Memphis. If the Temple of Dan was built at Baalbek, it was fashioned atop still older ruins that were likely already revered as sacred high places by the local population. The Bible calls this forbidden place of worship that the Danites built *"the sin of Israel"* (Judges 18:12-20; 1 Kings 12:30; 13:33-34; Hosea 10:81). The sin of Israel was a multifold one entailing the use of household gods, which were most likely ancestral idols (i.e. demons in disguise), bull calf idols, and a separate, mostly non-Levite priesthood that used a forbidden Oracle to foretell the future.

The Tribe of Dan is often reckoned as evil because they built a place of false worship that was abominable to Yahweh. Possibly for this very reason, the Book of Revelation omits Dan from the list of the Twelve Tribes of Israel. Instead, it replaces Dan with Manasseh, one of the two half Tribes of Joseph. As shown in Book Four, this may be because the nation allegorically connected to Manasseh is going to produce the Antichrist.

That may be why the Book of Revelation mentions Joseph in place of Ephraim. Could this be a way of identifying one Israelite tribe with the global body of believers that worship Christ? Because Joseph was a prefiguration of Christ and his father, mother and brothers bowed to him as Pharaoh's Vizier, this could definitely be a clever allegorical clue that not all those being reckoned as Dan or Manasseh in this Last Day are evil, and many people among all the literal and allegorical tribes of Israel will be saved from destruction. After all, the hoofed bull legs of Cherubim allegorically correspond to the pillars or corners of the Earth, and thereby represent all of God's Creation!

As It Was in the Days of Noah...

In an eerie echo of the past, mankind is now approaching the same level of debauchery as their antediluvian forebears. Like the evil Watchers, Nephilim and humans of the past, modern doctors and scientists are terminating pregnancies as casually as they would cut off a wart or mole, using embryonic stem cells to attempt to heal the sick and thereby murdering humans when adult stem cells would work just as well, and implanting fertilized eggs into surrogate mothers' wombs as if it were child's play. Oddly, no one seems to suspect that the scientists that create these embryos for implantation are up to no good. But how could anyone but these scientists really know if the embryos they produce via in vitro fertilization and then implant in women's wombs are fully human or not? Makes one pause to reconsider the superficially benevolent and safe label this practice currently has.

In addition to these well-documented activities that mimic the evil behavior of our antediluvian ancestors, modern scientists have successfully smashed the atom to provide nuclear power and create atomic bombs capable of wiping out all life on Earth. They have also unwisely given this knowledge to the military establishments of the world, and a few militant societies today such as North Korea and Iran are making it clear that they plan to use such destructive weapons on their heavily nuclear-armed enemies (i.e. the USA and Israel, respectively) in the very near future.

One of the worst modern abominations of God's sacred trust with mankind to remain righteous is the current scientific fascination with cloning animals and making hybrid animals from splicing the genes of various animals together. That these experiments are going on casually behind our backs is not only frightening, but inherently evil. There are also reports that ungodly hybrid plants with animal traits are already being grown and fed to both humans and livestock without our consent or permission, and without adequate studies to see what long and short term harmful affects these abominated foods may have after digesting them.

In addition, terrifying reports are being made that highly secretive experiments into recreating the Nephilim are being conducted among various governments of the world. Some report that scientists are currently mixing the genes of animals and humans in an attempt to create a new brand of Nephilim, and that these hybrid monsters may soon be used as the ultimate fighting machines in future conventional wars. Though this may not be true yet, mankind certainly has reached a knowledge threshold that makes raising the Nephilim from the dead alarmingly possible using the DNA in bones supposedly belonging to dinosaurs.

Sadly, as the above three paragraphs show, this current generation of mankind is capable of far more destruction, violence and debauchery than any previous Post-Flood generation. In fact, it is fast approaching the ability to commit violence at a comparable level to what our antediluvian ancestors engaged in before the Great Flood. This is especially true due to the unprecedented and potentially deadly technological advancements mankind has recently devised. These include multi-megaton atomic and neutron bombs, biological weapons such as genetically modified bacteria and viruses that are immune to all known drugs, the HAARP ionosphere control system built in the United States (along with smaller versions in Norway, Russia and elsewhere), and the series of CERN particle reactors in Europe and the United States.

Among the most frightening of these current potential threats to the existence of all life are the six atomic reactors created by CERN, which stands for the European Organization for Nuclear Research. Over the years since CERN began its operations in 1964, six atomic particle accelerators and one decelerator have been built deep underground somewhere between France and Switzerland. In addition, a seventh reactor called the Large Hadron Collider that some say has the potential to destroy or devastate the Earth in several terrifying ways was scheduled to begin operation in May 2008. This was the same month that a massive earthquake in China occurred, which killed thousands of people and left millions more homeless. Unsettlingly, though CERN's identifying logo is supposed to suggest the spinning of atoms, it looks like the number six being spun about. Could this logo be an allusion to the Mark of the Beast consisting of the number "666" that is spoken of in the Book of Revelation?

Though the technology behind these potentially destructive devices have beneficial applications, they all can just as easily be used to cause untold devastation and death around the world if they fall into the wrong hands - and *the Bible warns that they will fall into evil hands when the Antichrist takes control of the world in the not too distant future!* In fact, it is possible that they already have fallen into evil hands. Take, for example, the fact that many underground news sources have pinned the blame for the May 2008 earthquake that destroyed millions of buildings, killed over 80,000 people and injured as many as 300,000 individuals in central China on the US Government-controlled HAARP towers in Alaska, which may be able to control the weather by generating storms, hurricanes, and tsunamis. In addition, some say HAARP microwave technology could potentially cause earthquakes, and they suspect it of causing recent ones around the world.

Uncannily - although HAARP may indeed be capable of affecting Earth's ionosphere in a way that could cause highly destructive earthquakes - some have also pointed their fingers at CERN's Large Hadron Collider (i.e. LHC) as a potential cause of the devastating 2008 earthquake in China. If this atomic reactor, which is in a large tunnel over 328 feet (i.e. 100 meters) below the ground were to malfunction, it has such enormous power that it could cause great devastation - including earthquakes. In fact, some scientists warn that the LHC has the alarming potential to create a gaping hole in the Earth's crust by dissolving or compacting it. This in turn could trigger severe earthquakes and volcanic eruptions that might approach the destructive magnitude of those unleashed during the Great Flood. In addition, it might generate a miniature version of a phenomenon in Outer Space known as a black hole inside the Earth. If it did, this black hole might be unstoppable, and could act like a huge garbage compactor that would gradually gobble up the Earth.

In the Book of Revelation, there are descriptions of numerous plagues to be unleashed on the Earth during the Great Tribulation. Of these, many could potentially be caused by weapons of mass destruction such as those discussed in this section, which may include other even more potentially deadly top-secret weapons in undisclosed locations around the globe. Other events before and during the Tribulation are discussed in Book Four on prophecy.

After taking stock of mankind's current potential to destroy themselves and the Earth, and contemplating the enormous knowledge that the Watchers who sinned originally possessed, it is not so difficult to imagine that all fleshly creatures could have potentially been destroyed before the Great Flood if Yahweh had not put a sudden stop to their violence. Nor is it difficult to imagine that it might happen again in the very near future if God does not intervene in human affairs. In fact, Yahshua Himself warned that if He doesn't put a stop to our current love of violence with His Second Coming, no life would be able to survive it:

> "For nation will rise against nation, and kingdom against kingdom. And there will be famines, pestilences, and earthquakes in various places. All these are the beginning of sorrows..." "And unless those days were shortened, no flesh would be saved; but for the elect's sake those days will be shortened." - Matthew 24:7-8, 24:22 (NKJ)

Note that, in Matthew 24:7-8, Yahshua intimates that the initial famines, pestilences, and earthquakes before the Great Tribulation will be caused by nations and kingdoms rising up against one another. In other words, **these plagues upon mankind will not be forces of nature or Acts of God, but artificially induced** by mankind's technological tampering with natural forces, which have been secretly harnessed as weapons of war. Therefore, this passage is prophesying about this current time in history, when the CERN reactors and HAARP systems are now fully operational and capable of mass destruction.

In addition to this manmade destruction, Matthew 24:22 is alluding to the many violent and destructive Acts of God that will be poured out on mankind during the Great Tribulation. These divine acts of wrath and justice coupled with mankind's own ability to destroy will create a situation where all life could be extinguished if it were not for the mercy that God will show by prematurely ending this dire period of devastation and death.

Yes, with mankind's current knowledge of advanced technology and their constantly destructive and violent use of it, our current world is indeed becoming *"as it was in the days of Noah"* before the Flood, just as Yahshua stated:

> *"Just as it was in the days of Noah, so also will it be in the days of the Son of Man. People were eating, drinking, marrying and being given in marriage up to the day Noah entered the ark. Then the flood came and destroyed them all. It was the same in the days of Lot. People were eating and drinking, buying and selling, planting and building. But the day Lot left Sodom, fire and sulfur rained down from heaven and destroyed them all. It will be just like this on the day the Son of Man is revealed." - Luke 17:26-30 (NIV)*

This Scripture makes it clear that the terrible destructive force of God's Wrath during the Great Tribulation will come upon the people of the Earth during a time of relative peace and calm, and they will not be prepared for it. Furthermore, it makes it clear that this destruction will not end until Yahshua, who is the Son of Man and Son of God, is revealed in glory at His Second Coming.

In the section entitled "Demonic Oppression and Deliverance" in Chapter Five, it is explained that the days of Noah were marked by widespread demonic activity, and that Noah beseeched God for deliverance from the demons that were trying to destroy all mankind, especially Noah and his family. Likewise, the Tribulation Saints will be in the same position, and they will need to rely fully on God for protection from fallen angels, demons and demonically possessed people at that time if they are to survive.

The Abrahamic Covenant and the Anakim Menace

When Yahweh made His famous Blood Covenant that promised the whole land of Canaan to Abraham and his descendents, Canaan was still populated by the godly descendants of Shem, and Shem or Melchizedek was still the King of Peace, Shalom or Salem, which was another name for Jerusalem. However, not everyone who lived in adjacent lands were righteous. In fact, there is a very strong likelihood that some of the lands surrounding Canaan in Abraham's time were already populated with the descendents of the Nephilim who survived the Great Flood.

The offspring of the Nephilim Giants who mated with human women were generally known as Anakim, though there were other names for them such as Rephaim. Unlike pure Nephilim, who were only male, Anakim could be male or female, and they and their descendents may enter into the same salvation offered to the rest of humanity if they believe in and follow Christ. Nonetheless, archeological records attest to the fact that the Giants were corrupting both the bloodlines and spiritual hearts of the sinful or ignorant people they lived among. Sadly, these people either were willfully disobeying God by mingling their flesh with the Anakim, or were ignorant of the fact that it was sinful to do so.

Just as dumb animals are considered strange flesh that humans have no business fornicating with, the fleshly bodies of the Nephilim and Anakim were no less strange or forbidden. Nonetheless, some perverse people found strange flesh of all kinds sexually appealing. For example, in the following passage, the Apostle Jude refers to the propensity of the inhabitants of Sodom, Gomorrah and neighboring cities to go after strange flesh:

> *"But I want to remind you, though you once knew this, that the Lord, having saved the people out of the land of Egypt, afterward destroyed those who did not believe. And the angels who did not keep their proper domain, but left their own abode, He has reserved in everlasting chains under darkness for the judgment of the great day; as Sodom and Gomorrah, and the cities around them in a similar manner to these, having given themselves over to sexual immorality and gone after strange flesh, are set forth as an example, suffering the vengeance of eternal fire."* - Jude 1:5-7 (NKJ)

Interestingly, just before mentioning this strange flesh, Jude talks about the sexual sins of the fallen angels and then compares it to what the people of Sodom and Gomorrah were doing. It therefore infers that the people of Sodom and Gomorrah had gone after the strange flesh of another race: the Nephilim who survived the Flood. Sadly, since the Nephilim were not completely destroyed in the Great Flood, the strange flesh that these Giants possessed was still capable of infecting the human populaces they married into. As to how they survived the Flood, one legend states that some of the Nephilim heeded Noah's warning of coming destruction and built an underground shelter where they survived. *These survivors likely included all three races of Nephilim, which means that not all of them were human in appearance.*

After the Flood, the Bible records that many Anakim descendents of these Nephilim populated the land of Canaan and also re-populated other parts of the Earth. Though at first they would have been shunned and killed as evil betrayers, some of these Nephilim were skilled at deception and eventually grew in favor because of their strength and handsomeness. After that, it would not have taken long for them to intermingle with the people groups that spread out as the population of the world increased. In the Bible, the giant offspring created from humanoid Nephilim and human unions were called by various names, including Anakim, Rephaim, Zamzummim, Emim and Giants - as in the case of Goliath of Gath, and Og, the King of Bashan.

Since Yah wished to preserve a purely human bloodline from which the promised Redeemer would come, the Nephilim, their Anakim children, their Pagan religious beliefs and their rampant promiscuity were a definite threat. Therefore, when the Israelites entered Canaan, one of the divine mandates given to them by Moses was to destroy all the Anakim living in the parts of Canaan that the Israelites were to be allotted by God:

> "For it was of the LORD (Yahweh) to harden their hearts, that they should come against Israel in battle, that He might utterly destroy them, and that they might receive no mercy... as the LORD (Yahweh) had commanded Moses. **And at that time Joshua came and cut off the Anakim from... all the mountains of Judah, and from all the mountains of Israel;** Joshua utterly destroyed them with their cities. **None of the Anakim were left in the land of the children of Israel; they remained only in Gaza, in Gath, and in Ashdod.** So Joshua took the whole land, according to all that the LORD (Yahweh) had said to Moses; and Joshua gave it as an inheritance to Israel... Then the land rested from war." - Joshua 11:20-23 (NKJ)

The preceding Scriptural passage indicates that, under the leadership of Joshua, the Israelites were doing as God had instructed Moses to do when they destroyed most of the Anakim living in the land of Canaan. Interestingly, this passage also asserts that the Anakim lived in the mountains of Israel, and these mountains are still liberally peppered with caves - especially in the north where the Anakim king named Og settled. This suggests that some of the Post-Flood varieties of Nephilim were primarily cave-dwellers, and their cavernous hill cities were not to be confused with the human settlements they lived near.

Sadly, the preceding Bible passage also tells us that the Israelites failed to exterminate all of the Anakim. Some Anakim therefore remained and ruled in the neighboring cities of Gaza, Gath, and Ashdod (Joshua 11:22). Gaza is in the far south of Israel on the coast, while Gath and Ashdod are further inland between the Dead Sea and the Mediterranean coast. Eerily, due to US involvement in attempting to establish lasting peace in the Middle East, Israel recently gave up their ownership of Gaza to the Palestinians. As a result, that little strip of land was quickly overrun with Hamas Terrorist cells that are continually acting in accord with the evil spirits of the Nephilim.

In addition to these Anakim-controlled cities, there were likely some Giants that wisely left Canaan when they saw the Israelites systematically hacking their kind to pieces in city after city. These escapees fled to other parts of the world. In fact, legends everywhere are riddled with stories of Giants and tombs where the remains of Giants have reportedly been found. Many of the Giants who fled from Canaan no doubt took great pride in their skills as warriors, and they were likely regarded with fear and respect wherever they went because of their impressive size and strength. The skill of the Giants as warriors also ensured that some of them would win prestige as generals and kings. *This, in turn, allowed many Giants to intermarry with the royal bloodlines of Europe and elsewhere.* Therefore, the actual descendents of the Anakim are likely in control of the Illuminati and the Freemasons.

In Rabbinic writings such as the Zohar, legends state that the Antichrist will contain the Serpent seed or genes of the Nephilim, and will be descended from the Giants who once dwelt in Canaan. If, as legends suggest, many of the royal bloodlines of the world are tainted with Anakim blood, then the likelihood that a bonafide prince that is part Nephilim will come to power is certainly possible. In that regard, Prince Charles of Wales or his son William are the most likely royal candidates for the Antichrist position, as is discussed in Book Four.

Now, the Bible makes it clear that - before the Israelites came as conquerors - the Giants came to rule over many fortified cities in Canaan, and mingled their blood with the Philistines through intermarriage. It is therefore likely that their descendents - who are known today as the Palestinians - have some leaders with Anakim blood. However, this does **not** mean that all Palestinians are tainted with Anakim genes.

The surviving Anakim descendents among the Palestinian people are no doubt restricted to their leading families. In addition, the Anakim blood among them has been enormously watered down over the centuries by intermingling with humans. Nonetheless, this Palestinian connection to the Nephilim partly explains why they utterly hate the Jews now inhabiting Israel, as well as Christians and other so-called

Infidels. This may also explain why many Muslim Terrorists seem Hell-bent on destroying all the supposed Western democratic enemies of Allah.

Could it be that Allah is none other than another name for Azazel? Since Allah is the name of the Pagan Moon god once worshipped in Arabia, this god of war and hatred toward women certainly has a very dark, satanic connection. Of course, the rivalry between Isaac and Ishmael and Jacob and Esau are also adding to the larger hatred between Arabs, Jews and Christians today. We will further discuss Israel's God-given mandate to destroy the Anakim in Chapter Eight.

Created by Yah: Behemoth, Leviathan, and the Flying Seraph

For those who believe that dinosaurs were not contemporaneous with mankind, the Bible offers some good circumstantial evidence that dinosaur-like creatures flew in the sky, frolicked in the sea, and walked on land at the same time as mankind. The Book of Job describes these creatures.

In the remarkable discourse where Yahweh speaks to Job from out of a whirlwind, God describes the Behemoth and Leviathan that He created (Job 40:15-24, 41:1-34; Psalm 104:26). But for God's message to have any meaning, Job would have had to be familiar with these creatures. The Behemoth therefore must have been taken aboard Noah's Ark or it would not have survived the cataclysmic Flood. Being an enormous sea creature, however, the Leviathan would have survived in the ocean since Noah was not instructed to bring any sea life into the Ark. Amphibious animals like seals and otters would have been on the Ark, but not whales and other huge sea creatures!

The Book of Job tells us much about the appearance of both the Behemoth and the Leviathan. There, God tells Job to look at the Behemoth, which dwelled near the Jordan River's edge and was of an immense size and strength like a hippopotamus:

> "Look now at the behemoth, which I made along with you; he eats grass like an ox. See now, his strength is in his hips, and his power is in his stomach muscles. **He moves his tail like a cedar;** the sinews of his thighs are tightly knit. His bones are like beams of bronze, his ribs like bars of iron. He is the first of the ways of God; only He who made him can bring near His sword. Surely the mountains yield food for him, and all the beasts of the field play there... Indeed the river may

rage, yet he is not disturbed; he is confident, though the
Jordan gushes into his mouth..." - Job 40:15-23 (NKJ)

Though scholars often identify the Behemoth with the hippopotamus, the Behemoth had a cedar-like tail and a long neck reaching toward the mountains (Job 40:17, 20). In this respect, the Behemoth sounds similar in appearance to a Sauropod, which were the largest and strongest land animals that ever existed. Of the Sauropods, the Brachiosaurus was one of the largest and the Camarasaurus was one of the smallest. However, even the Camarasaurus, which weighed about 20 tons and was about 60 feet long, was nearly five times the size of an average-sized adult male African Elephant that - as already stated - weighs about 8,000 pounds (3,600 kilograms) and eats 220 to 440 pounds (100 to 200 kilograms) of vegetation daily!

As if in mockery of current science, which claims that all dinosaurs died out long ago, reports of two different creatures resembling medium-sized Sauropods have reportedly been spotted in the swamps of Zaire, the Congo, Zambia and Angola. Popular native names for these creatures are the Mokole Mbembe, which is purported to be a medium-sized Sauropod, and the one-horned Chipekwe, which may be a Ceratopsian dinosaur such as the Triceratops, only with one instead of three horns. In a recent expedition to find the Mokole Mbembe, a native eyewitness drew a depiction of this creature. This drawing showed an animal that closely resembles modern reconstructions of Sauropods that supposedly were extinct millions of years ago. In addition, the drawing showed a large air sac on the creatures' throat near to the head. This would have allowed the Behemoth to make unusually loud and piercing vocalizations.

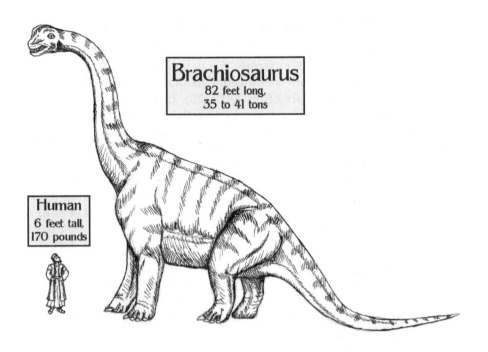

Here is a traditional drawing of one of the largest Sauropods: the Brachiosaurus. Though this creature is much larger than a Mokole Mbembe, which is purported to be closer to the size of a Camarosaurus, modern depictions of it show the air sac on the throat, which is similar to those on the neck of a turkey. If the Behemoth is a type of Sauropod that has this air sac, it would likely be used to make loud vocalizations in an attempt to attract its aquatic mate: the Leviathan. After all, sounds traveling through the air become extremely muffled in water. This is due to the greater impedance of water, which has a higher density than air. So, the Behemoth's call would have to be incredibly loud to attract a submerged Leviathan.

Now, the Leviathan mentioned in the Book of Job was a gigantic sea-dwelling creature that crawled onto shore (ostensibly to lay eggs). When it did so, the Leviathan left ridges in the mud or sand because of its heavily scaled underbelly (Job 41:30). It also had a nearly impenetrable scaled body (Job 41:15-17,) a fearsome mouth full of big teeth (Job 41:14), and such great strength it could churn up the ocean and leave huge, white-capped waves in its wake (Job 41:31-32). Though having a few points in common with the crocodile, the Leviathan was clearly far larger and more terrifying. In fact, Job makes it clear that *the Leviathan could breathe out fire and smoke:*

Reconstructions of Elasmosaurus and Kronosaurus

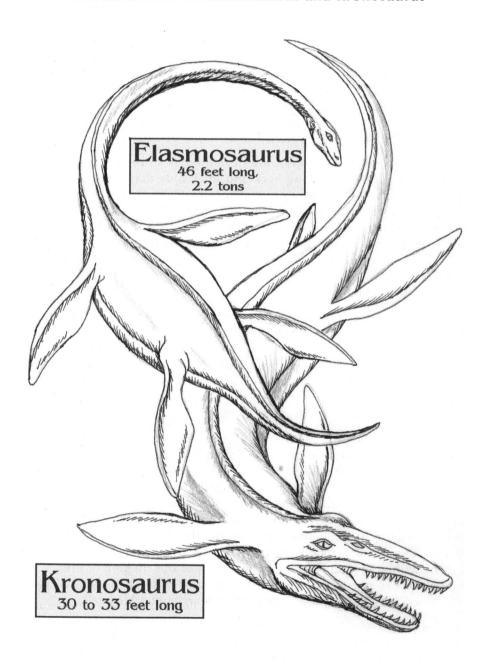

Elasmosaurus
46 feet long,
2.2 tons

Kronosaurus
30 to 33 feet long

*"His sneezings flash forth light, and his eyes are like
the eyelids of the morning. Out of his mouth go burning
lights; Sparks of fire shoot out. Smoke goes out of his nostrils,
as from a boiling pot and burning rushes. His breath kindles
coals, and a flame goes out of his mouth. Strength dwells in
his neck... The folds of his flesh are joined together; they are
firm on him and cannot be moved... When he raises himself
up, the mighty are afraid; because of his crashings they are
beside themselves. Though the sword reaches him, it cannot
avail; nor does spear, dart, or javelin. He regards iron as
straw, and bronze as rotten wood." - Job 41:18-27 (NKJ)*

The above description of the Leviathan as a fire-breathing sea
creature with a powerful, long neck and thick hide that even a spear
cannot penetrate was definitely *not* a crocodile! The closest fossil
representatives that we have for the Leviathan today would be Pliosaur-
type sea animals like Kronosaurus, Muraeonosaurus or the Macroplata.
Among these ancient sea monsters, the enormous Kronosaurus was the
largest, as shown in the illustration on page 321. The Kronosaurus had a
fierce-looking, huge mouth full of razor-sharp teeth, and would have
been very powerful.

Though the Kronosaurus was large and strong, the Megalodon,
which was the supposedly huge prehistoric cousin to the Great White
Shark, would have been even larger - *if* it existed. So far, however, only
a few teeth and vertebrae have been found that supposedly identify this
ancestor to the shark. In addition, some prehistoric whales were likely
much larger than the Kronosaurus, though they were still most likely its
prey.

Despite scientific claims that all the prehistoric species of
pterosaurs are extinct, a section of 1 Enoch indicates that both the
Behemoth and Leviathan are alive today and will play a role during
God's judgment of the Earth during the Tribulation. Intriguingly, this
section of 1 Enoch is attributed to Noah and mentions the Behemoth and
Leviathan as creations of God that have been hidden in the thickest
wilderness areas and the deepest ocean depths. There, they are being
reserved to enact judgments against the wicked at a time when the
heavens will be severely shaken. This vision of the shaking of the
heavens was so terrifying to Noah that he apparently died and had to be
resurrected into his mortal existence by the archangel Michael!

The section of 1 Enoch that mentions the Behemoth and
Leviathan opens by telling us that it is the 500th year of the life of
Enoch, so the vision was given to Noah 135 years after Enoch's
translation. It also mentions that it was the 14th day of the seventh

month. On the Jewish Calendar, the 14th day of the seventh Lunar month is the day before the Feast of Tabernacles or Sukkot, which always begins on the fifteenth day - at the time of a Full Moon. This means that this vision is likely tied to the last year of the Great Tribulation, which will be the year that Christ returns to conquer the wicked and set up His Millennial Rule on Earth. Interestingly, the Book of Revelation describes this same time that Noah saw when the heavens will be shaken:

> "I looked when He opened the sixth seal, and... there was a great earthquake; and the sun became black as sackcloth of hair, and the moon became like blood. And the stars of heaven fell to the earth, as a fig tree drops its late figs when it is shaken by a mighty wind. Then the sky receded as a scroll... and every mountain and island was moved out of its place." - Rev. 6:12-14 (NKJ)

By the placement of this quote at the opening of the Sixth Seal, it indicates that this shaking of the heavens will occur near to the beginning of the Great Tribulation. Here is the section in 1 Enoch that describes Noah's vision of this heavenly quake and God's creation and separation of the Leviathan and Behemoth:

> "In the year 500, in the seventh month, on the fourteenth day of the month in the life of Enoch... I saw how a mighty quaking made the heaven of heavens to quake, and the host of the Most High, and the angels, a thousand thousands and ten thousand times ten thousand, were disquieted with a great disquiet. And the Head of Days sat on the throne of His glory, and the angels and the righteous stood around Him:
>
> > And a great trembling seized me,
> > And fear took hold of me,
> > And my loins gave way,
> > And dissolved were my reins,
> > And I fell upon my face.
>
> And Michael sent another angel from among the holy ones and he raised me up, and when he had raised me up my spirit returned; for I had not been able to endure the look of this host, and the commotion and the quaking of the heaven. And Michael said unto me: 'Why art thou disquieted with such a vision? Until this day lasted the day of His mercy; and He hath been merciful and long-suffering towards those who dwell on the earth. And when the day, and the power, and

the punishment, and the judgement come, which the Lord of
Spirits hath prepared for those who worship not the righteous
law, and for those who deny the righteous judgement, and for
those who take His name in vain - that day is prepared, for
the elect a covenant, but for sinners an inquisition.

When the punishment of the Lord of Spirits shall rest
upon them... it shall slay the children with their mothers and
the children with their fathers. Afterwards the judgement
shall take place according to His mercy and His patience.

And on that day (i.e. on the fifth Great Day of
Creation) were two monsters parted, a female monster named
Leviathan, to dwell in the abysses of the ocean over the
fountains of the waters. But the male is named Behemoth,
who occupied with his breast a waste wilderness named
Duidain, on the east of the garden where the elect and
righteous dwell, where my grandfather was taken up, the
seventh from Adam...'" - 1 Enoch 60:1-9

Interestingly, these passages from 1 Enoch suggest that the
Leviathan is the female and the Behemoth is the male version of the
same monstrous and powerful animal species and that the males and
females oddly live in separate habitats. This passage also suggests that
the Leviathan and Behemoth have been hidden in Earth's most remote
places to be preserved so that they will be able to help bring judgment
on the wicked just before Christ's return.

There is modern-day evidence to support the supposition that the
Leviathan and its Pliosaur cousins still exist. For example, a Pliosaur
type sea-creature was fished out of the water and photographed by
Japanese fishermen in 1977. It was 32 feet long, and weighed over 4000
pounds. The skeleton of this creature was too big to be a killer whale's,
yet it had a mouth full of razor sharp teeth that larger whales of the
same size simply do not possess. In addition, though Great White Sharks
have been known to reach phenomenal sizes, the skull and side fins of
the creature that the Japanese fished out of the water was totally unlike a
shark's. The strange skeleton also had none of the bones associated with
a shark's large dorsal fin. In fact, it looked more like the immensely
oversized skeleton of some kind of seal or walrus-like sea creature with a
somewhat longer neck and snout – a similarity suggesting that this
skeleton was indeed one of a Pliosaur.

Among the prehistoric creatures created by God that may still
exist on the Earth today, the Book of Isaiah records the appearance of a
"fiery, flying serpent" or Seraph - a creature that may still be extant in

remote areas of the American Southwest, Mexico, and New Guinea. Here are two passages from Isaiah that speak of this creature:

> "Do not rejoice, all you of Philistia, because the rod that struck you is broken; for out of the serpent's roots will come... a viper, and its offspring will be a **fiery flying serpent.**" - Isaiah 14:29 (NKJ)

> "Through a land of trouble and anguish, from which came the lioness and lion, the viper and **fiery flying serpent**, they will carry their riches on the backs of young donkeys..." - Isaiah 30:6 (NKJ)

This fiery flying serpent could be any one of several winged creatures known as Pterosaurs that include the Pteranodon and the Pterodactyl. A particularly good fit for the Seraph was the Pterodactyl, which had a long, bony protrusion on the top of its long-beaked head that could have been used to hold chemicals, and may have worked somewhat like the defense mechanism of the tiny bombardier beetle. A fiery chemical reaction could have taken place in this horn, after which it might have been exhaled out of this flying reptile's big, sharply pointed beak or nostrils. This may also have been the case for the herbivorous duckbilled Hadrosaurs known as Lambeosaurus and Parasaurolophus, which had large, boney protrusions on the back of their heads. As shown on page 326, these Hadrosaurs had odd horn-like crests of bone that may have served as combustion chambers allowing these creatures to literally breathe fire. Interestingly, they also had very human-like "hands" that are suspiciously missing any trace of a thumb.

Egyptian god Set

Could it be that these Hadrosaurs were actually Nephilim? Intriguingly, depictions of the strange animal head attached to the Egyptian god Set or Seth actually resemble the Lambeosaurus shown on page 326. Could it be that the bizarre "ears" atop the animal face of the god Set are actually meant to signify the horny protrusions on top of the Lambeosaurus' head? Is it also possible that the Lambeosaurus dinosaurs were in actuality Nephilim, and one of them was so powerful that it was eventually worshipped as a god by the Egyptians? Was this Nephilim god then falsely associated with the antediluvian patriarch Seth and his descendents by the Hamites after the Flood? As will be shown in Chapters Six and Seven, this is a highly likely possibility.

Reconstructions of Lambeosaurus and Parasaurolophus

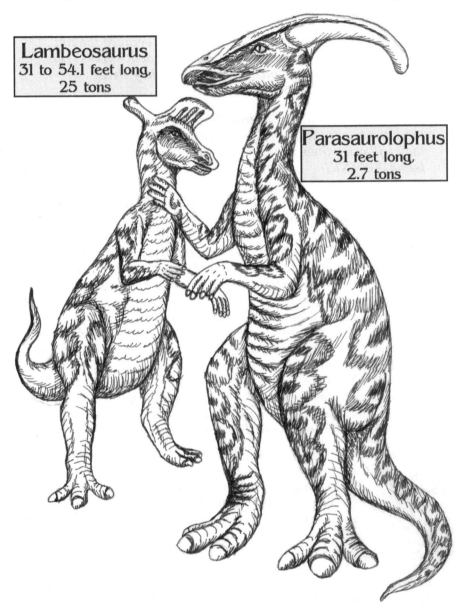

Lambeosaurus
31 to 54.1 feet long,
25 tons

Parasaurolophus
31 feet long,
2.7 tons

Unfortunately, many Creationist publications assert that all dinosaurs were creations of God, which seems highly unlikely due to the Bible's mention that: *"There were giants on the earth in those days, and also afterward..."* (Gen. 6:4). Evidently - and this is a mystery to me -

most scientists with a Christian background do not see the connection between the giants of old and dinosaurs. This is really baffling to me, especially since the Bible repeatedly mentions that God wanted the Israelites to slaughter the numerous giant inhabitants of Canaan!

Dubious Reconstructions of Pteranodon and Quetzalcoatlus

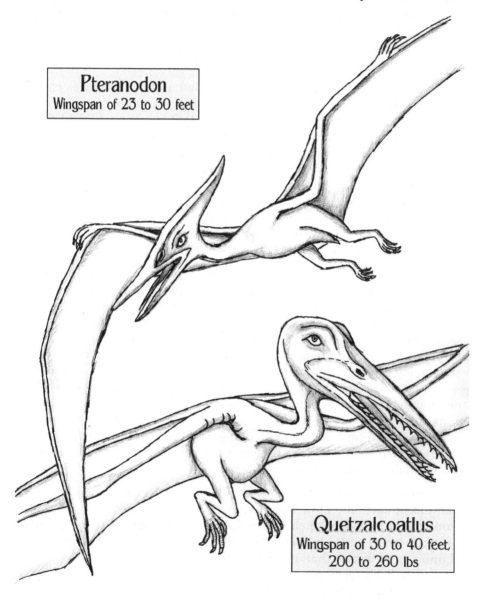

Pteranodon
Wingspan of 23 to 30 feet

Quetzalcoatlus
Wingspan of 30 to 40 feet,
200 to 260 lbs

Could it be that the thought of dinosaurs as malignant creatures that were designed by the evil intelligence of the fallen angels to destroy or corrupt mankind is just too frightening for most Creationists to contemplate? Whatever the case, their publications mimic secular dinosaur books for children, which consistently depict dinosaurs as benign, almost friendly-looking creatures that Adam and Eve and our other antediluvian ancestors would not have had reason to fear. Indeed, many of the drawings in this book that were inspired by both Creationist and secular illustrations of dinosaurs reflect this bias that they were somehow harmless, amiable, and even frail creatures. The reality, however, is that they were anything but friendly or frail.

Recently, as an example of just how lethal these creatures could have been, the fossil remains of a Pterosaur that was at least two times the size of a Pterodactyl was found in Texas that has been dubbed the Quetzalcoatlus. This fearsome-looking, bat-winged creature had a giant puffin-shaped head and could have had up to a 40 foot wingspan, which is similar to that of a modern fighter jet! Ignoring the traditional drawing of the Pterodactyl and Quetzalcoatlus on page 327 that depicts them as skimpy, frail creatures, it is likely that they had enough bulk and aerodynamic power that they could have swept down, grasped a large fish or a small mammal in their gigantic beaks or giant clawed feet, and then carried it through the air to a secluded area to feed.

Though Pterosaurs have supposedly been extinct for millions of years, there are recent scattered reports of people who have seen Pteranodon-type flying creatures in isolated North American desert areas. In any case, it is obvious that something like the Pteranodon was alive during the time of Isaiah. In addition, stone statues of griffin-like creatures that supposedly combine the traits of lions and eagles to form fearsome-looking guards at the entrances of ancient tombs have also been found that resemble Pterosaurs. Though it is possible that these fanciful creatures have a symbolic meaning much like the human-faced sphinxes with lion's bodies that can be found everywhere in Egypt and represent Zodiac signs, some depictions of griffins could depict real creatures like the Pteranodon that were not yet extinct when the tombs they originally guarded were constructed.

Some scientists believe that the flying fiery serpents spoken of by Isaiah did not actually blow fire or smoke, but may have had bioluminescent areas on their bodies like fireflies or lightning bugs - only on a much larger scale. In fact, flying Pterosaur type creatures with bioluminescent bodies that are called "Ropen" or "Indava" have purportedly been seen, filmed and photographed in the vicinity of Papua, New Guinea recently. These creatures have been described by local natives as closest in appearance to a small, long-tailed Pterosaur called a Dimorphodon. However, unlike the Dimorphodon pictured in the illustration, the Ropen may be the size of small airplanes!

Dimorphodon
3.3 feet long

These creatures have been sighted flying near to the water and just above the tropical treetops at night, when they appear to use their bioluminescent bodies to view the surrounding topography of the landscape before landing. Now, though bioluminescence is an intriguing possibility that Isaiah's fiery flying serpents could very well have possessed, the image of a flying Seraph as a fire-breathing, winged dragon being ridden by a human still holds my imagination at times.

Because of its big size, is it possible that the Quetzalcoatlus could have been mounted and ridden upon by a human being to travel through the air much like horses and camels are for land travel? Fantasy yarns aside, it is an intriguing possibility that people may actually have flown through the air on the backs of these giant creatures - provided that they could be domesticated. However, since creatures that resemble Pterosaurs have been sighted in highly remote locations on the Earth today, they likely would have been difficult to spot or capture in the past as well - and possibly even tougher to train.

Before I was saved in 1987 at the age of 30, I had a very human and sinful desire to gain power over the course of my life. Even though the only Being that has true power over anyone's life is our triune God Yahweh, I did not know this truth yet. This may be one reason why I drew many pictures of dragons when I was younger. Back then, I was a technically unsaved, troubled, and highly creative Catholic youth going to a spiritually dead church on Sundays that had not taught me anything about spiritual warfare or the Holy Spirit that gives believers Christ's triumphant power over demons. Furthermore, I was living in a dysfunctional home with my two alcoholic Catholic parents and a constantly abusive older brother that was destroying himself with his own pronounced alcohol and drug abuse - and trying to destroy me.

Sadly, I was virtually powerless to do anything about my life circumstances at the time, and - though I have since learned to forgive my family and pray for their salvation - the scars of living in that emotional hell have never fully left me. That is just one more reason why I can't wait until Yahshua returns! I want to be fully emotionally healed someday, and able to love perfectly just as Yahshua loves us.

How about you?

Chapter 5: The Causes and Affects of Noah's Flood

> *"So God said to Noah, 'I am going to put an end to all people, for the earth is filled with violence because of them. I am surely going to destroy both them and the earth. So make yourself an ark of cypress wood; make rooms in it and coat it with pitch inside and out... I am going to bring floodwaters on the earth to destroy all life under the heavens... Everything on earth will perish. But I will establish my covenant with you, and you will enter the ark -- you and your sons and your wife and your sons' wives with you.'" - Genesis 6:13-18 (NIV)*

In the above Scripture, when God made this astounding pronouncement to Noah, it probably came as no surprise since God had already warned Enoch that He planned to destroy all life on Earth, and Enoch had told Methuselah, who was the father of Lamech, Noah's father (1 Enoch 83:7-9). In addition, God sent the holy angel Uriel to Lamech to notify him that it was time to tell Noah of the coming destruction of the Earth that Lamech already knew about:

> *"The Most High... sent Uriel to the son of Lamech, and said to him: 'Go to Noah and tell him in my name "Hide thyself!" and reveal to him the end that is approaching: that the whole earth will be destroyed, and a deluge is about to come upon the whole earth, and will destroy all that is on it. And now instruct him that he may escape and his seed may be preserved for all the generations of the world.'" - 1 Enoch 10:1-4*

Per God's instructions, Uriel made sure that Lamech would give Noah plenty of advance warning about the Flood and also made it clear that Noah needed to hide by saying *"Hide thyself!"* Though no commentary is given as to why Uriel said this on God's behalf, it implies that the Nephilim or fallen angels might discover God's plan and seek a way to destroy Noah and his family unless no one knew of their existence. Therefore, Noah needed to find an extremely remote location to build the Ark that would preserve a small remnant of genetically untainted animals, plants, and people. In that regard, there is no doubt that God found such a place for Noah - a place that must have remained undiscovered until the time of the Flood.

Besides Noah and his sons, the Book of Jasher indicates that there were other good people living until Noah's 480th year of life:

> *"And Jared the son of Mahlallel died in those days, in
> the three hundred and thirty-sixth year of the life of Noah...
> **And all who followed the Lord died in those days, before they
> saw the evil which God declared to do upon earth**. And after
> the lapse of many years, in the four hundred and eightieth
> year of the life of Noah... all those men who followed the Lord
> had died away... and only Methuselah was left..." - Jasher 5:4-
> 10*

This portion of the Book of Jasher indicates that - for 150 years
before Noah's period of isolation - Noah was part of a small righteous
remnant of Sethites. In fact, Noah procured his Sethite wife from among
them (Jasher 5:14-15). Later, Noah took three of his grandfather
Methuselah's daughters from these last remaining godly people to be
wives for his sons:

> *"In his five hundred and ninety-fifth year Noah
> commenced to make the ark, and he made the ark in five
> years, as the Lord had commanded. Then Noah took the three
> daughters of Eliakim, son of Methuselah, for wives for his
> sons, as the Lord had commanded Noah." - Jasher 5:34-35*

Since most of the righteous Sethites had died by the time Noah
reached his 480th year, this passage of Jasher indicates that Methuselah
had a wife and daughters who went into hiding with Noah.
Furthermore, Noah did not procure Methuselah's daughters to be his
sons' wives until he was 595 years old - or just five years before the
Flood!

While Noah and his sons built the Ark, the Nephilim would have
virtually wiped each other out in accord with God's will, the fallen
angels would have been imprisoned, and no one would have been left
that saw Noah and his sons as anything other than totally crazy and
genetically un-enhanced humans that were deluded into thinking the
Earth was about to be destroyed by some imaginary god. This was also
true in ancient times, when the Way of Cain was reintroduced and
flourished in ancient Greece and Rome. It should also sound eerily
familiar to modern believers in Yahshua, since today's nearly global
secular humanist society often reacts with the same derision whenever
Messianic Jews and Christians talk about the Rapture, Great Tribulation,
and Second Coming of Christ.

Incidentally, Noah never stopped preaching about God's love
and mercy and coming judgment up until the time of the Flood.
According to the Book of Jasher or Upright Record, both Noah and
Methuselah boldly preached to *"the sons of men"* for 120 years,

suggesting that there were still genetically pure humans in the world whose fathers were fully human and *these two godly witnesses were meant to reach human beings with their message of judgment, sacrifice and forgiveness, but not the Nephilim who were beyond redemption:*

> *"And Noah was five hundred and two years old when Naamah bare Shem, and the boys grew up and went in the ways of the Lord, in all that Methuselah and Noah their father taught them. In that time, the Lord said to Noah and Methuselah,* ***'Stand forth and proclaim to the sons of men all the words that I spoke to you in those days, peradventure they may turn from their evil ways, and I will then repent of the evil and will not bring it.'*** *And Noah and Methuselah stood forth, and said in the ears of the sons of men all that God had spoken concerning them. But the sons of men would not hearken, neither would they incline their ears to all their declarations. And it was after this that the Lord said to Noah, 'The end of all flesh is come before me, on account of their evil deeds, and behold I will destroy the earth.'"* - Jasher 5:18-25

Despite Yahweh's mercy and the two powerful witnesses He sent to try and turn people's hearts from evil, not one human being or genetically corrupted Nephilim or Anakim humanoid at that time was even remotely willing to repent until the Ark was sealed, the heavy rain started to fall, and the doom of those unrepentant souls was forever decided by the hand of Almighty God. As a result, perhaps billions of humans and Giants perished in the Flood because they were incapable of true repentance. Again, this story of Noah and Methuselah witnessing to their own generation has an eerie future counterpart in Revelation's Two Witnesses, who will preach during the Tribulation and be resurrected just before the Great Tribulation (Rev. 11:3).

In this chapter, the evil behavior of mankind and all other life on Earth leading up to the Great Flood, the cataclysmic events of the Flood that caused vast devastation, and the preservation of a righteous remnant of humanity and other life will be explored. Then, in the next two chapters, we will discuss the re-emergence of evil that occurred by the time of Nimrod.

The Flood: Judgment against Sin and Genetic Splicing

In Chapter Four, we discussed the possibility that the fallen Watchers mixed the genes of different animals to create the Nephilim, as evidenced in the dinosaur fossil record that exists all over the Earth. This sinful genetic mixing is attested to by several ancient manuscripts. Among them, the Book of Jasher laments: *"...and God saw the whole earth and it was corrupt,* **for all flesh had corrupted its ways** *upon earth, all men and all animals"* (Jasher 4:18). Therefore, Watchers, Titans or Nephilim and humans may have mixed their genetic material in increasing amounts in various ways, and this eventually led to the mutation and degradation of the entire human race outside of the oldest generations of Sethites, who remained faithful to God until they died of natural causes.

The severity of this corruption was the catalyst that moved Yahweh to destroy all life on Earth with the Great Flood. But even before this, Yahweh promised the fallen angels that they would watch their evil children destroy one another, and then they would be cast into an abyss to await judgment. Thus, the Nephilim were instrumental in destroying one another.

Now, at some point during his life, Enoch had a very powerful dream vision that showed the entire course of human history. Below is a portion of this vision, which covers the destruction of the Nephilim prior to the Flood. In it, I have provided my own interpretations of the text in parentheses:

> *"And I saw one of those four who had come forth first (the four Archangels of God that were created before the other angels), and he seized that first star which had fallen from the heaven (Azazel or Satan), and bound it hand and foot and cast it into an abyss (so Satan was imprisoned in an Abyss long ago): now that abyss was narrow and deep, and horrible and dark.* ***And one of them*** *(one of the four archangels)* ***drew a sword, and gave it to those elephants and camels and asses: then they began to smite each other, and the whole earth quaked because of them*** *(one Archangel gave the Nephilim a supernaturally charged weapon to destroy themselves with). And as I was beholding in the vision, lo, one of those four who had come forth stoned them from heaven, and gathered and took all the great stars whose privy members were like those of horses, and bound them all hand and foot, and cast them in an abyss of the earth."* - 1 Enoch 88:1-3

This passage teaches that, probably sometime after Azazel had been imprisoned in the Abyss and Noah's father Lamech became the leading patriarch of the Sethites, Yahweh stepped in to alter human history and sent one of His archangels to equip one of the warring factions of the Nephilim with a powerful weapon that they subsequently used to destroy their enemies with. Since human beings were likely considered too weak to be of any use in combat, Nephilim rulers primarily used Nephilim warriors to fight against rival Nephilim leaders and their own Nephilim armies.

When the Nephilim destroyed one another in their horribly violent wars, the supernaturally designed weapons they used against each other were so powerful that *"the whole earth quaked."* This suggests that the weapons given to the Nephilim were similar in intensity to the highly destructive nuclear weapons devised by humanity in this last century - weapons that have since become a serious threat to all life on Earth.

Unfortunately, it is likely that many humans were often among the victims in past Nephilim instigated wars as well. This can be deduced from the vitrified remains of several ancient cities, especially Mohenjo Daro in the Indus Valley region of Pakistan. There, the burned and scorched buildings and the many bodies of dead humans found littering the streets when the city was partially excavated suggest that Mohenjo Daro's inhabitants all came to a sudden, violent and horrible end.

Now, the reason that only Noah, his wife, his children and their wives were saved from these wars and the destruction of the Flood is because Noah was *"a just man, perfect in his generations"* (Genesis 6:9). This can be interpreted to mean that, among the millions and perhaps billions of humanoids on the Earth at that time, only Noah and his immediate family were genetically untainted by Nephilim genetic material, and also spiritually untainted because they shunned the use of Sorcery and Magic to defy Yahweh. Therefore, **Noah and his kin were the only people who were still both fully human and essentially righteous due to Noah and Methuselah's guidance and leadership.** These combined factors sealed their fate as the builders of the Ark and the only fully human survivors of the Great Flood.

A section of "The Legends of the Jews" by Louis Ginzberg summarizes the sad state of affairs on Earth just before the Flood. Though Ginzberg's writings contain occasional anecdotal remarks and comments that are probably not entirely true, they do accurately reflect the legends that have been hidden away in a large body of extra-biblical Jewish Literature that is generally not available to Gentile audiences. In this section of his exhaustive compilation of these texts, Ginzberg shares some fascinating legendary information concerning antediluvian society and sin:

Excerpt from "The Legends of the Jews," Volume One,
"The Punishment of the Fallen Angels" By Louis Ginzberg:

"The fall of Azazel and Shemhazai (i.e. Semyaza) came
about in this way. When the generation of the deluge began to
practice idolatry, God was deeply grieved. The two angels
Shemhazai and Azazel arose, and said: 'O Lord of the world!
It has happened, that which we foretold at the creation of the
world and of man, saying, "What is man, that Thou art
mindful of him?"' And God said, 'And what will become of
the world now without man?' Whereupon the angels said: 'We
will occupy ourselves with it.' Then said God: 'I am well
aware of it, and I know that if you inhabit the earth, the evil
inclination will overpower you, and you will be more
iniquitous than ever men.' The angels pleaded, 'Grant us but
permission to dwell among men, and Thou shalt see how we
will sanctify Thy Name.' God yielded to their wish, saying,
'Descend and sojourn among men!'

When the angels came to earth, and beheld the
daughters of men in all their grace and beauty, they could not
restrain their passion. Shemhazai saw a maiden named
Istehar, and he lost his heart to her. She promised to
surrender herself to him, if first he taught her the Ineffable
Name, by means of which he raised himself to heaven. He
assented to her condition. But once she knew it, she
pronounced the Name, and herself ascended to heaven,
without fulfilling her promise to the angel. God said, 'Because
she kept herself aloof from sin, we will place her among the
seven stars, that men may never forget her,' and she was put
in the constellation of the Pleiades.

Shemhazai and Azazel, however, were not deterred
from entering into alliances with the daughters of men, and to
the first two sons were born. Azazel began to devise the finery
and the ornaments by means of which women allure men.
Thereupon God sent Metatron to tell Shemhazai that He had
resolved to destroy the world and bring on a deluge. The
fallen angel began to weep and grieve over the fate of the
world and the fate of his two sons. If the world went under,
what would they have to eat, they who needed daily a
thousand camels, a thousand horses, and a thousand steers?

These two sons of Shemhazai, Hiwwa and Hiyya by
name, dreamed dreams. The one saw a great stone which
covered the earth, and the earth was marked all over with

lines upon lines of writing. An angel came, and with a knife
obliterated all the lines, leaving but four letters upon the
stone. The other son saw a large pleasure grove planted with
all sorts of trees. But angels approached bearing axes, and
they felled the trees, sparing a single one with three of its
branches.

When Hiwwa and Hiyya awoke, they repaired to their
father, who interpreted the dreams for them, saying, 'God will
bring a deluge, and none will escape with his life, excepting
only Noah and his sons.' When they heard this, the two
began to cry and scream, but their father consoled them: 'Soft,
soft! Do not grieve. As often as men cut or haul stones, or
launch vessels, they shall invoke your names, Hiwwa! Hiyya!'
This prophecy soothed them.

Shemhazai then did penance. He suspended himself
between heaven and earth, and in this position of a penitent
sinner he hangs to this day. But Azazel persisted obdurately
in his sin of leading mankind astray by means of sensual
allurements. For this reason two he-goats were sacrificed in
the Temple on the Day of Atonement, the one for God, that
He pardon the sins of Israel, the other for Azazel, that he bear
the sins of Israel.

Unlike Istehar, the pious maiden, Naamah, the lovely
sister of Tubal-Cain led the angels astray with her beauty, and
from her union with Shamdon sprang the devil Asmodeus.
She was as shameless as all the other descendants of Cain,
and as prone to bestial indulgences. Cainite women and
Cainite men alike were in the habit of walking abroad naked,
and they gave themselves up to every conceivable manner of
lewd practices. Of such were the women whose beauty and
sensual charms tempted the angels from the path of virtue.
**The angels, on the other hand, no sooner had they rebelled
against God and descended to earth than they lost their
transcendental qualities, and were invested with sublunary
bodies**, so that a union with the daughters of men became
possible.

The offspring of these alliances between the angels and
the Cainite women were the giants, known for their strength
and their sinfulness; as their very name, the Emim, indicates,
they inspired fear. They have many other names. Sometimes
they go by the name Rephaim, because one glance at them
made one's heart grow weak; or by the name Gibborim,

simply giants, because their size was so enormous that their thigh measured eighteen ells; or by the name Zamzummim, because they were great masters in war; or by the name Anakim, because they touched the sun with their neck; or by the name Ivvim, because, like the snake, they could judge of the qualities of the soil; or finally, by the name Nephilim, because, bringing the world to its fall, they themselves fell."

- End of Excerpt from "The Legends of the Jews"

Though this legendary information has obviously been embellished with ideas that may sound utterly fantastic to most of us, there is a great deal of truth being shared here in the guise of an amusing and easily remembered story. This type of storytelling is found throughout the Jewish Midrash, from which Ginzberg derived much of his information. Let's examine the elements in this section of "The Legends of the Jews" that ring true.

First of all, this legend indicates that the Jews firmly believed that Yahweh initially sent the Watchers to reside on Earth to help mankind, as well as to test their faithfulness and obedience to God. This echoes Jubilees 4:15-16, where we are told that the Watchers were sent to Earth to be mankind's helpers and to act as guardians of the planet. Secondly, due to their sinful condition, the fallen angels are described as having lost their transcendental (i.e. supernatural) abilities such as being able to travel about at will. In addition, the legend says that the fallen Watchers were given *"sublunary bodies,"* meaning that they were confined and limited by terrestrial bodies of flesh. Though they may have been handsome beyond compare, the fallen Watchers no longer may have had supernatural power. They therefore would have had to rely on technology to appear as godlike as they were prior to their fall.

This is an interesting point, and if true, suggests that the fallen angels were closer to being like ordinary men than one would initially think. So, even though the fallen angels were immortal and powerful in ways mortal men could not compare, they were no longer like their holy Watcher counterparts who never sinned. As a result, they could no longer leave the Earth at will, travel about rapidly without aid, or call on God's power to enact miracles or fight God's adversaries.

As a sub-story to the fall of the Watchers in this Jewish legend, we are introduced to Hiwwa and Hiyya, the supposed Nephilim children of Semyaza (i.e. Shemhazai in the legend). These Nephilim brothers are depicted as having a huge daily appetite for flesh consisting of *"a thousand camels, a thousand horses, and a thousand steers."* Though this may be somewhat exaggerated for comic effect, it does clearly convey the idea that the Nephilim were ravenous monsters that never stopped eating meat. They are also depicted as rather dull-witted creatures that, though they could dream and cry, were not capable of true sorrow and repentance.

Another point this story makes is that the Cainites were depraved people with no moral values whatsoever. As will be shown a bit later, the historian Josephus depicted them in a similar fashion, and he had access to many ancient manuscripts such as those in the Library of Alexandria to draw this information from that are now lost to us. Furthermore, Cainite women are identified as the first to have seduced the angels with their charms, beginning with Tubal-Cain's sister Naamah. This means that Cainite women were the first to give birth to Nephilim giants, or the seed of the Serpent. The story also lists the many names that the Nephilim were called by, and what these names reveal about the different qualities found among the three races of Nephilim.

It appears that the names "Emim" and "Nephilim" applied to all these alien creatures, with Emim meaning "terror" or "fright" and Nephilim meaning "fallen." Then there were those among them that were called Rephaim meaning "faint" or "failure" because they were so terrifying to look at that they could cause fainting or heart failure by the mere sight of them. Among these, the Carnosaurs such as the Giganotosaurus, Tyrannosaurus Rex and Allosaurus could definitely inspire this kind of terror.

One of the races of Nephilim were called the Zamzummim - meaning "imagine" in an evil sense. These creatures *"were great masters in war,"* which suggests that the Zamzummim were skilled as military tacticians and fighters. The term "Zamzummim" may therefore have referred to armored dinosaurs like the Stegosaurus (pictured on page 340), Ankylosaurus or the giant Sauropod called Ampelosaurus. Whether or not this was so, the Zamzummim were no doubt prone to imagining all sorts of evil outcomes and plotting ways to achieve them.

Other Nephilim were called Gibborim meaning "Giants" because they *"were so enormous that their thigh measured eighteen ells,"* which means they had a thigh that was 36 feet around! By anyone's standards, these creatures must have been so stupendously large that they could easily have smashed anything in their paths. Among the dinosaur fossils found, the largest Sauropod Titanosaur fossils so far found measured about 200 feet from head to tail. An animal this large would have indeed needed sturdy Redwood-sized legs with thigh muscles at least 30 feet around to move its bulk.

Stegosaurus
30 feet long,
5 tons

Other types of Nephilim were known as Anakim, meaning "necklace" because they *"touched the sun with their neck."* This suggests that Anakim were very tall. In addition, the Anakim may have been fond of necklaces or neck rings to decorate their long necks just as women in the Kayan tribe of Thailand or Paduang tribe of Burma do today - perhaps in unwitting imitation of the demon spirits behind their false religions. Among the dinosaurs, the Sauropods had the longest necks and tails of them all. Therefore, when they were destroyed, the demonic spirits of the Sauropods that were legitimate Nephilim may have encouraged many destructive practices, including the artificial lengthening of women's necks. In the Bible, most of the Post Flood descendents of the Nephilim that were called by other descriptive names were also referred to as Anakim.

Finally, some Nephilim were apparently called Ivvim because *"like the snake, they could judge of the qualities of the soil."* Upon studying the nature of snakes to see what this passage might mean, I discovered that all snakes are carnivorous and constantly flick their forked tongues to test the chemical qualities of the soil and air for the presence of prey. This suggests that the Ivvim among the Nephilim had highly developed senses of smell and taste that could help them identify the chemicals in the air and soil surrounding them. This made them highly lethal killers, as it would have been almost impossible for even the most skillfully hidden or well camouflaged animals or people to escape their detection if they were close by.

Interestingly, the Bible mentions all the Nephilim mentioned by Ginzberg's "Legends of the Jews" *except the Ivvim.* This means that most types of Nephilim were represented in a much more scaled down and humanized form in and around Canaan before and during the Israelite conquest. Nonetheless, though almost all Post-Flood descendants of the Nephilim were smaller in stature and more humanoid in appearance than their Pre-Flood forebears, some of them were still far larger and stronger in comparison to humans.

Besides the fascinating recollection of what the Nephilim names describe, the previously quoted section of "The Legends of the Jews" contains the story of the virtuous woman named Istehar. This section of the narrative is a real prophetic gem both in the truths it conveys allegorically and in the insightful devices that it uses to communicate the truth. For example, Istehar's story suggests that there were virtuous antediluvian women on the Earth that did not sin with the angels, but only sought them out to discover how mankind could find salvation. In other words, there were righteous people besides Enoch who conversed with the Watchers prior to the Flood.

On the other hand, the story of Istehar also suggests that God has a secret name that allows those who know and utter it aloud to ascend to heaven like Enoch did, and to become stars in the heavens. Though this sounds fantastical, if it is viewed as a parable, it conveys the idea that there are secrets about God and salvation hidden in the Universe that the angels or "stars" are privy to, and that mankind has to seek out by communing with the angels and God and studying the stars. And though the idea that Yahweh has a secret name of power may sound false to some, **there is a Name of God that absolutely is the key to salvation, and that Name above all names is Yahshua Ha Mashiach,** i.e. Jesus the Christ!

Finally, though it is illogical to assume that Yahweh actually changed Istehar into one of the stars in the Pleiades, this delightful fantasy conveys the truth that the Pleiades represent the Seven Church Ages that have raised up an army of saints that are and will always be a part of Christ's Body, the True Church. Indeed, when one realizes that this is a Jewish legend, and the Jews have no tradition tying themselves to the Pleiades, then the true prophetic quality of this legend of Istehar becomes even more apparent. Delightfully, even the name of the heroine is prophetic, as it relates to Ishtar or Esther - the Israelite maiden who became the Queen of Persia. As shown in Book Two, Queen Esther prophetically signifies the True Church of purified saints acting as one body with Yahshua the King of kings during the Tribulation - and onward into the Millennial Rule of Christ.

Of course, there are elements of Ginzberg's story that blatantly contradict the Bible, Jasher, Jubilees, and 1 Enoch, so they should not be seriously entertained as truth. Some of these ideas include the suggestion that Semyaza was actually repentant and Azazel and Semyaza were not imprisoned like the other fallen angels, but are still free to do as they choose. Since these ideas oppose the clear teaching of 1 Enoch and Scripture, they have not been considered in the next section.

The Way of Yahweh Versus the Way of Cain

After studying humanity's past history, Solomon's prophetic statement that *"there is nothing new under the Sun"* seems totally appropriate to me now (Eccles. 1:9). This is because the spiritual and ideological divisions that have always been present in human society to some extent are drastically more pronounced now than they have been since before the Great Flood. As a result, those in spiritual darkness are becoming even darker spiritually, while those who love the light of Yahweh's truth are taking in even more of the Spirit of God's light and are becoming even brighter and truer to the Word of God and Light of the World, who is Christ (Isaiah 60:1-3; John 8:12). As a result, the clashes between these two opposing ways of life are becoming ever more heated, emotionally charged, and potentially deadly.

In antediluvian times, the clash of civilizations began the moment that Cain killed Abel and was banished from the community he had grown up in. As a result of his ostracism, Cain had to forge his own society, and he no doubt took along several of his siblings who sided with him when he did, including the sister he married. As shown in this chapter, Cain's immoral way of life did not stop when he killed Abel. Instead of repenting, ancient sources indicate that Cain rebelled against God and hated God's people even more. In fact, as a consequence of Cain's own warped view of the world and lack of good character, his society was wide open to infiltration when the fallen "Beni Elohim" decided to take wives, beget a race of monsters, and teach mankind every perverted thing that they could before Yahweh put a stop to their physical and spiritual meddling.

As a result of their acceptance of the Nephilim and literal love affair with the fallen Watchers, the lawless Cainite society was eventually ruled over by genetically corrupted humans that were part Nephilim like the mythical Hercules, the god-man who was styled after the true

Messiah revealed in the heavens, but - unlike Yahshua - Hercules in myth championed the Way of Cain rather than the Way of Yahweh. Due to the Nephilim rejection of the invisible Godhead, His Covenant with mankind, and His righteous laws, these corrupt superhuman rulers became the gods of the Cainites and anyone else that they subdued with violence. That is, until things began to go horribly wrong as a result of the sins of the fallen Watchers, whose Nephilim children became murderous tyrants that craved human flesh and blood.

Since the Cainites were already violent and lawless by the time their Nephilim kin decided to dine on humans, their natural reaction would likely have been to fight back with all the force they could muster. In consequence, the Nephilim inevitably would have sought not only to eat any humans defeated in battle, but to destroy or enslave every last human and part-Nephilim that sided with their enemies. This genocidal war would have eventually affected the Sethites - even if their land was far removed from the land of Nod.

When the Cainites rejected their superhuman overlords, they had only themselves to fill the spiritual void in their souls - especially since they had already rejected Yahweh. As a result, the essentially godless religion of Humanism filled that void. In Humanism, mankind is viewed as superior to all other forms of life because people are capable of logic and creativity, and atheists and humanists refuse to believe other living things possess these thought processes. In other words, they reject the idea that there is spirit world populated with beings that are just as logical, rational and creative as mankind.

In its most radical form, Humanism allows man to become his own god by assuming that the sentience humans possess is connected to an impersonal spiritual force that can be used for good or evil by those who master controlling it. Those who believe in this Star-Wars type New Age spirituality believe that the way to control this force is through the Universal Mind - an impersonal, non-sentient universal body of knowledge. This type of Humanism is the Way of Cain, which seeks to turn everyone into his or her own idol who is in total rebellion against Yahweh's authority.

Many cultural and religious philosophies have bought into and furthered the lies of the Way of Cain since the Flood. Modern religions such as Theosophy, Freemasonry, Rosicrucianism, Gnosticism, the New Age Movement, Wicca, traditional Paganism and Apostate Christianity all basically tout the same values and beliefs that originated with the Cainites and hold billions of people around the world captive with their vile rejection of God, sin, and judgment. Besides believing in an impersonal divine force that permeates all things and can be used for good or evil, these groups generally share a belief that there are no moral absolutes. Many also believe that all people are gods in the making, and gaining knowledge, spiritual enlightenment through self discipline, meditation and the cultivation of self esteem and self actualization are essential in order to ascend to the next intellectual and spiritual level via the process known as reincarnation.

In fact, the entire Greco-Roman style culture and civilization of the West is based on these exact same Humanistic principles. This does not mean that all aspects of civilization are evil, but that most of its institutions are tainted with false ideals and standards. Many aspects of everyday life today like Socialism and Capitalism, the monetary system, the banking industry, weights and measures, regulatory government offices, credit and usury, government-controlled military forces, prisons and mental institutions all have their roots in greed or covetousness, lawlessness, faithlessness, atheism, hatred, sadism, sensuality, lack of compassion, and criminal thinking that proliferates endlessly when there is no recognition of ultimate good or evil and no revulsion toward sin.

The wayward Way of Cain is harshly condemned in the Epistle of Jude, where it is compared to the opportunistic attitude of the prophet Balaam, who prophesied for profit, and the rebellion of the sons of Korah, who felt that all the Israelites were holy and should be able to serve as priests despite God's orders that only the descendents of Aaron could be:

> *"But even the archangel Michael, when he was disputing with the devil about the body of Moses, did not dare to bring a slanderous accusation against him, but said, 'The Lord rebuke you!' Yet these men speak abusively against whatever they do not understand; and what things they do understand by instinct, like unreasoning animals -- these are the very things that destroy them. Woe to them!* **They have taken the way of Cain***; they have rushed for profit into Balaam's error; they have been destroyed in Korah's rebellion." - Jude 1:9-11 (NIV)*

The opening portion of this passage in Jude mentions the archangel Michael contending for the body of Moses with the Devil. This story is recorded in the Pseudepigraphical book called the "Testament of Moses," where it relates that the Devil falsely claimed he had a right to take Moses' body, which he intended to turn into an idol. In the above passage, Jude squarely identifies the evil behaviors of the Devil, Balaam and Korah as the actions of those following the Way of Cain.

Sources such as Josephus and Jasher make it clear that the Sethites remained separate from the Cainites and the Way of Cain for approximately 1,500 nearly blissful years after the Fall of Adam and Eve. During that time, the Sethites were relatively righteous like Abel. They lived simple pastoral lives in the countryside as farmers and shepherds. They also dwelt in small communities that coexisted in relative peace. This lasted until about the time of Lamech - the ninth antediluvian patriarch in the line of Seth. By his time, the first generations of Sethites had all blessedly died away in peace after living a sheltered life just shy of 1000 years each. After the moral direction and character of these righteous people was lost, the ancient manuscripts suggest that Lamech and other Sethites began to sin against God and mankind by becoming as violent as the Cainites already were. In effect, Lamech the Sethite abandoned his priestly shepherd's staff and robe in order to don the armor and spear of a warrior, and many followed him into sin.

Thereafter, ancient sources indicate that the Sethites swiftly became as violent and wicked as their Cainite neighbors. Nonetheless, before that time, the historian Josephus recorded that the descendents of Adam's son Seth developed a righteous culture that the Bible calls "the Way of Yahweh" (Isaiah 40:3; Proverbs 10:29) or simply "the Way" in its connection to the followers of Christ and the New Covenant (Acts 19:9, 23; Acts 24:14, 22). The first time the Way is clearly mentioned is in relation to Abraham:

> "For I have chosen him (i.e. Abraham), so that he will direct his children and his household after him to keep **the way of the LORD (Yahweh)** by doing what is right and just..."
> - Genesis 18:19 (NIV)

In this passage, the Way of Yahweh is defined as *"doing what is right and just."* In antediluvian times, the way to be right and just was revealed in the rites of burnt sacrifice and Blood Covenanting, in the rite of Marriage, and in the Gospel in the Stars that taught about the coming Messiah or Seed of the Woman. This book series has repeatedly shown that these three bodies of Sethite knowledge about Yah and His Will teach godly principles like love, fidelity, loyalty, kindness, justice, mercy, sacrifice, redemption and forgiveness. Since the Star Gospel was a major contributor to Sethite righteousness, the patriarchal priests among them would have spent much time observing the signs in the heavens and encouraging their offspring to live in peace with nature and in harmony with each other.

Though the Sethites were very close to God's Creation and desired to live in accord with all living things, however, this does not mean that they shunned technology or creativity as is spuriously suggested in apocryphal literature like the Books of Adam and Eve. Instead, the Sethites were simply more likely to have a desire to live close to the soothing presence of the natural world that reminded them of their magnificent Creator. In addition, they were more likely to have a desire to live in peace with animals and one another as they awaited the unfolding of God's Plan of Salvation that was chronicled in the Heavenly Tablets. Therefore, since preserving their peaceful way of life necessitated less of a reliance on technology, the majority of Sethites likely lived in sheltered rural farming and herding communities that were far-removed from the bustling, technologically advanced cities being built and occupied by their repulsively sinful Cainite neighbors.

Now, since people living in cities must rely on pastoral communities for survival, this would soon have led the Cainites to prey upon their peace-loving Sethite neighbors for the produce, grains, furs and animal hides they needed for feeding and clothing themselves. This would have inevitably led the Sethites to have to defend themselves or face assimilation or annihilation.

Interestingly, when Noah's father Lamech died at 777 years old, it was just five years before the Great Flood (Genesis 5:31). It has therefore been put forward by some scholars that Lamech may have died nearly two hundred years before his time due to the violence of that time in human history. Now, since the Book of Jasher indicates that Lamech the Sethite did not follow in all the righteous ways of his forefathers, it implies that he was not a loving pacifist like Noah and Melchizedek undoubtedly were (Jasher 5:19).

Since Lamech may have made the choice to rely on his own strength instead of God's provision, it is possible that he died in combat trying to protect Noah and his sons from harm by the Nephilim or Cainites. This is a possibility because, as already revealed, the Book of 1 Enoch makes it clear that Lamech was in contact with the holy Watchers and Noah before the Great Flood. Therefore, Lamech was still concerned about his righteous loved ones and was being called to take action in their lives on God's behalf within several hundred years before the Flood.

There is no doubt that both the Cainites and the Sethites were involved in terrible acts of violence against one another and the Nephilim before the Flood, especially since it appears that the Cainite Lamech brought a horrible curse of violence down upon Cain's entire bloodline when Lamech became a murderer like Cain, as attested to in the Bible and Book of Jasher. First, let's look at what the Bible says about this curse:

"Lamech said to his wives, 'Adah and Zillah, listen to
me; wives of Lamech, hear my words. I have killed a man for
wounding me, a young man for injuring me. **If Cain is
avenged seven times, then Lamech seventy-seven times**.'" -
Gen. 4:23-24 (NIV)

The real significance of this enigmatic passage has been
overlooked by many scholars partly due to the faulty translation in all
modern Bibles. In this case, only the far older King James Version retains
the true meaning of the following phrase: *"I have slain a man **to my
wounding**, and a young man **to my hurt**"* (Gen. 4:23 KJV). Worded this
way, the passage clearly suggests that Lamech was injured because he
wounded someone else - not the other way around.

Even with the King James translation to aid our understanding,
however, this passage simply doesn't make sense without the Book of
Jasher, which gives the much-needed background behind it. Through
that book, we discover that Lamech's poetic speech to his wives in
Genesis was a lamentation uttered in sorrow because he had accidentally
murdered his forefather Cain and his son Tubal-Cain while he was out
hunting (Jasher 5:26-36). As a result, Lamech's descendents would have
to endure God's seven-generation curse upon anyone who killed Cain:

"But the LORD (Yahweh) said to him, 'Not so; if
anyone kills Cain, he will suffer vengeance seven times over.'
Then the LORD (Yahweh) put a mark on Cain so that no one
who found him would kill him." - Genesis 4:15 (NIV)

For the purposes of this discussion, it is important to note here
that Yahweh issued this conditional curse. Unfortunately, whatever
divinely given mark Cain possessed that warned people not to murder
him did not work with his descendent Lamech. The Book of Jasher
explains why by telling us that Lamech was very old and nearly blind
when he accidentally shot Cain with an arrow, and then carelessly struck
down his own son Tubal-Cain in an immediate fulfillment of God's
curse:

"And Lamech was old and advanced in years, and his
eyes were dim that he could not see, and Tubal Cain, his son,
was leading him and it was one day that Lamech went into
the field and Tubal Cain his son was with him, and whilst
they were walking in the field, Cain the son of Adam
advanced towards them; for Lamech was very old and could
not see much, and Tubal Cain his son was very young. And
Tubal Cain told his father to draw his bow... And the arrows
entered Cain's body although he was distant from them, and

*he fell to the ground and died. And the Lord requited Cain's
evil according to his wickedness, which he had done to his
brother Abel, according to the word of the Lord which he had
spoken. And it came to pass when Cain had died, that
Lamech and Tubal went to see the animal which they had
slain, and they saw, and behold Cain their grandfather was
fallen dead upon the earth. And Lamech was very much
grieved at having done this, and in clapping his hands
together he struck his son and caused his death." - Jasher
5:26-30*

As a result of Cain's murder, Lamech's descendents were to be
divinely cursed with much death and destruction for seven times or
generations. That is why Lamech's pronouncement that anyone
murdering him would receive vengeance seventy-seven times was
nothing less than an act of revenge upon himself! You see, 1 Enoch
foretold that there would be seventy generations of mankind between
the time of Enoch and the judgment of the fallen angels (1 Enoch 10:12).
Therefore, since Lamech was the seventh generation from Adam and had
killed his own son, he was basically cursing all of his descendents as
well as the other descendents of Cain! So, in an ironic twist of divine
disfavor, Cain's bloodline was doomed by Lamech's remorseful folly!

Due to this curse that Lamech the Cainite made upon himself,
Noah's father Lamech's age of 777 at his death is intriguing for several
reasons. First, the number seven is a number of completion or fullness
that is related to the seven days of the week, the seven main Jewish
feasts, and the seven Great Days of human history in this fallen creation.
Secondly, the number 777 appears to be prophetically connected to
Yahshua's pronouncement that God would extend forgiveness toward
humanity for *"seventy times seven"* or seventy specific periods of time
(Matthew 18:22). Since Enoch saw the time from the fall of Adam until
the Last Judgment as a 7,000 year period, these seventy periods of time
can bee seen as centuries. Therefore, Yahshua's mercy can be seen as
being extended for seventy centuries (70 X 100 = 7,000).

Interestingly, Yahshua's *"seventy times seven"* is also connected
to the teaching in 1 Enoch that the fallen angels would be imprisoned for
70 generations (1 Enoch 10:12). Since Enoch was the seventh generation
from Adam (Jude 1:14), and the fallen angels were imprisoned during his
generation, this means that God planned to extend forgiveness and
mercy to mankind for 70 more generations after Enoch, for a total of 77
generations. This extended period of mercy shows that God's
longsuffering is great and He does not want any of His human children
to perish. Nonetheless, God will eventually have to judge all people who

have not accepted Yahshua as their Lord and Savior. Eerily, at the end of this period of mercy, 1 Enoch suggests that God will then release the fallen angels from prison so that they and all those who follow them can be judged. These fallen angels may then stage the Great Deception that will deceive all those who are perishing into believing that the Antichrist is the Messiah (2 Thess. 2:9-12).

Now, in the third chapter of the Gospel of Luke, the names of the patriarchs for 76 generations from Yahshua to Adam are listed (Note: Adam being called the son of God at the end of this genealogy does **not** count as a human generation). However, since Yahshua had no literal children but only spiritual ones, the 77th generation is a figurative one found in the Body of Christ that is made up of all born-again Gentile and Jewish believers! Furthermore, Yahshua clearly taught that one last generation of Jews and believers is to be counted before the end of the world, as indicated in the following Scripture:

> "Now learn this parable from the fig tree: When its branch has already become tender and puts forth leaves, you know that summer is near. So you also, when you see all these things, know that it is near -- at the doors! Assuredly, I say to you, **this generation will by no means pass away till all these things take place.**" - Matthew 24:32-34 (NKJ)

This passage is known as the Parable of the Fig Tree, and it is tied to the barren fig tree that Yahshua cursed so that it immediately withered (Mat. 21:18-20). This barren fig tree was also a parable representing the beleaguered nation of Israel at the time of Christ, which was called Judea by the Romans. So, just as the barren fig tree withered away so no one could eat its unripe fruit, Yahshua was showing that the Jewish homeland would be destroyed because the Jews were not bearing good fruit in and out of season. However, not long after this fig tree was cursed, Yahshua spoke of the fig tree that is ready to bear fruit again as a sign that summer is near. When Yahshua said this, He was foreseeing a time when the withered fig tree that was Judah would come back to life. Then, when Judah began to bring forth new shoots and became ready to bear fruit again, Yahshua was indicating that His Second Coming would be near.

Applied to current events, many scholars have seen that this parabolic Parable of the Fig Tree is coming true today, and it has been since May of 1948 when the new nation of Israel became a reality, Jewish Zionism reached new heights, and Jews began flocking to their ancestral homeland from every continent on Earth. What this means is that this current generation of stiff-necked Jews born since 1948 will also be the last because they will finally repent of their hardness of heart and will accept Yahshua as their Messiah! As a result, they will become "completed Jews" that will finally love all Gentile believers as their spiritual brethren in the faith!

Miraculously, since Israel became a nation once more in 1948, the generation that saw the rebirth of Israel is also seeing many other End Time prophecies being fulfilled regarding a revival of the Roman Empire with the East and West first uniting under the banner of the United Nations, and eventually uniting under the far more tyrannical and totalitarian global government of the Antichrist. This means that the children of the Jews who survived the Holocaust are the 77th generation - and they are to be the final generation before the Second Coming of Christ.

Uncannily, since the late 90's a growing number of Jews in Israel and all around the world have begun to accept Yahshua as their Messiah. As a result, there are over 20,000 Messianic believers in Jerusalem alone, and they do not keep the old Jewish traditions like many of the increasingly more numerous messianic congregations in the West do, but have non-ritualistic, unstructured and relaxed worship services with upbeat music similar to Evangelical Christian church services in America and elsewhere. Could these Messianic Jews in Israel be the leaves of the revived parabolic fig tree that signifies Israel? Are they a sign that Israel is ready to bring forth a great harvest of good fruit among the Jews as Yahshua's Second Coming draws near? As unbelievable as it may seem, Israel's rebirth in 1948 and the fact that - after 2000 years of bitter resistance - Jews are beginning to embrace Yahshua as their Messiah is a sign that Yahshua will come again within the next 20 to 30 years. In fact, as outlined in Book Four, Yahshua is likely to return in less than a decade from the present year of 2009.

Indeed, even Lamech's age of 777 at death appears to be tied to the return of Christ. As shown in Book Four, the Hallel Psalms 110 through 118 suggest that the Tribulation will occur in the years 2011 and 2018 AD, with the Great Tribulation beginning sometime in 2014 AD and ending with the bodily return of Christ in 2017 or 2018. Fascinatingly, the year 2017 corresponds to the Hebrew year **5777** - a year that reflects the triple sevens of Lamech's age at death, which was only five years before the Flood. Since the Battle of Armageddon and Yahshua's return could occur in early 2017, this may be the year when God's mercy on the wicked will temporarily cease and all those who do not repent at that time will die in the Battle of Armageddon or perish in the Lake of Fire along with the Antichrist, Beast, and False Prophet.

Regarding the coming divine judgment of the dead, the Book of 1 Enoch has as much to say about it as the Bible, and it also contains fascinating information not found in the Bible about the state of the dead and their location after death. One of the most interesting disclosures Enoch makes about Sheol or Hades is that it has four major divisions where the dead will reside until judgment, and each of these four spaces has a specific purpose - with two spaces being reserved for the righteous who await judgment. This will include godly Jews, Israelites, and Gentiles that did their best to please God, but died outside of Christ's New Covenant of Grace. Another one is being reserved for those who have already been judged and found guilty of damnation. But it is the last of the four spaces that is the most interesting, for it is a special place reserved for Cain's murdered brother Abel. Enoch makes it clear that Abel is crying out to God as a representative of all the righteous martyrs who await the time when their murderers will be brought to justice:

> "And... I went to another place... the mountain... of hard rock. And there was in it four hollow places, deep and wide and very smooth... Then Raphael... one of the holy angels who was with me... said unto me: 'These hollow places have been created for this very purpose, that the spirits of the souls of the dead should assemble therein... And these places have been made to receive them... till the great judgement (comes) upon them.' And... I saw (the spirit of) a dead man making suit, and his voice went forth to heaven... And I asked Raphael... 'This spirit which maketh suit, whose is it, whose voice goeth forth and maketh suit to heaven?' And he answered... 'This is the spirit which went forth from Abel, whom his brother Cain slew, and he makes his suit against him till his seed is destroyed from the face of the earth, and his seed is annihilated from amongst the seed of men.'" - 1 Enoch 22:1-8

Interestingly, this passage from 1 Enoch makes it clear that Abel will stand in accusation against his brother Cain until all of Cain's "seed" or blood descendents have been *"destroyed from the face of the Earth."* Though it would be logical to assume that Cain's descendents all died in the Great Flood, Enoch makes it clear that Abel will be making suit against Cain's seed until *"the great judgement,"* and this can only be referring to the Great White Throne Judgment or Last Judgment mentioned in the Book of Revelation (Rev. 20:11-12). Therefore, some remnant of Cain's seed must have survived the Great Flood to the present time.

Though the Book of Genesis seems to be silent about Cain's seed after it mentions the Cainite Lamech's three sons in the eighth generation, it is not entirely silent because Genesis 6:4 clearly states that

the Nephilim or "men of renown" existed both before and after the Great
Flood. By this one simple statement, the author of Genesis was hinting
that Cain's seed survived via the Nephilim, whom the Cainites freely
intermarried with. As such, the seed of Cain would have become
irrevocably associated with the seed of the Serpent, which seeks to
destroy the Seed of the Woman mentioned in Genesis 3:15 and
Revelation 12:1.

Before continuing, it should be noted here that there is little
possibility that Lamech the Cainite's bloodline merged with Noah's
bloodline through Lamech's daughter Naamah, whom some believe
married Noah due to the following statement in the Book of Jasher:

> "And the Lord said unto Noah, 'Take unto thee a wife,
> and beget children, for I have seen thee righteous before me
> in this generation. And thou shalt raise up seed, and thy
> children with thee...' and Noah went and took a wife, and he
> chose Naamah the daughter of Enoch, and she was five
> hundred and eighty years old..." - Jasher 5:14-15

First of all, this Naamah is firmly identified as Enoch the
Sethite's daughter, not the daughter of the Cainite named Lamech.
Secondly, since Noah was a righteous man, and he was only marrying
because Yah had asked him to, it is simply impossible that he would
have married an unrighteous woman - especially one that was not a
fellow Sethite.

The section of "The Legends of the Jews" introduced earlier
shows that Jewish legend places the seed of the Serpent squarely in
Naamah the Cainite's seductive and evil embrace. There are also Jewish
Midrash that purportedly link Naamah to the fallen angel Azael a.k.a.
Azazel himself, thereby suggesting that the angel that possessed the
Serpent in the Garden was the same angel that cohabited with Naamah.
Incidentally, as the first woman to sleep with a fallen angel, Naamah's
spirit was condemned to become a Siren after her physical death, and
since the queen of all demoness' is the one named Lilith, it is likely that
Naamah is Lilith today, and will be forever condemned to the Lake of
Fire along with Azazel and the Antichrist one day.

In this regard, Naamah the wife of the fallen angel Azazel and
daughter of Lamech the Cainite serves as the evil opposite of Naamah
the wife of Noah the Sethite and daughter of Enoch the Scribe of
Righteousness. While Naamah the Sethite bore Noah's righteous and
fully human son Shem in her womb, Naamah the Cainite slept with the
Devil and gave birth to the first Nephilim giant. Likewise, while Noah's
wife Naamah raised Shem to be the righteous son chosen by God as heir

to the promise in Genesis 3:15, Azazel's wife Lilith raised a rebellious and evil Nephilim, who upon death became the demon Asmodeus. Now, whereas Shem's bloodline led to the birth of Yahshua as the Seed of the Woman, Naamah the Cainite's bloodline has led to the birth of the Antichrist, who is surely alive today and is simply waiting for his time to rule. When the Antichrist finally does come to power, Yahshua will return to crush the Antichrist and his minions, and the prophecy in Genesis 3:15 will at last be fulfilled!

In this regard, Naamah the Cainite and Naamah the Sethite illustrate the same duality in human nature as Enoch the Cainite and Enoch the Sethite - who were also on opposite poles spiritually. Interestingly, just as the evil Cain was born before the godly Abel, the evil counterparts to several other prominent shepherds of Yahweh's flock were born before their righteous counterparts. Take for example, the fact that Nimrod was born before Abraham, Ishmael was born before Isaac, and Esau was born before Jacob, who became Israel! This clearly suggests that Satan has anticipated and attempted to counteract many of Yahweh God's biggest moves toward mankind's redemption throughout history. It also shows that Satan will do anything to obscure Yah's truth, especially by cultivating spiritually and ideologically wicked people with totally opposing goals to God's righteous followers!

As shown in this chapter and Chapter Seven, the obvious clash and animosity between the Cainite seed of the Serpent and the Seed of the Woman via the line of Seth has set the stage for many events throughout history. Indeed, this clash will reach its height immediately preceding the establishment of Christ's Millennial Kingdom. Furthermore, as will be shown in Chapter Six, our antediluvian forebears understood this battle and also physically represented it on the Earth!

Cain – the Tyrannical Antediluvian Counterpart to Nimrod

In the Book of Genesis, there are two distinct lines of patriarchs listed. One is tied to Cain's descendents, and the other is tied to Seth's. These two lists differ markedly. The list of the ten Sethite patriarchs includes their length of life and age at the birth of their heirs. In the Cainite line, however, there are only eight patriarchs listed, and their length of life is omitted as well as their ages at the births of their heirs.

In recent times, there have been attempts made by various scholars to "mold" these two separate genealogies into one in an effort to somehow reconcile them to the antediluvian king lists of Mesopotamian origin, which generally list ten kings, though the Sumerian King list contains the names of only eight Pre-Flood rulers. It has been proposed that one reason the Sumerian list has only eight names is because the first man (Adam) and the flood hero are not listed since Noah did not die before the Flood.

Like the Genesis account, the Babylonian king lists also provide two lines of antediluvian kings. One line appears to list ten Wise Men or apkallus, beginning with Adapa or Adam. This list of ten names is therefore tied to the priests who descended from Adam. In this respect, it preserves the idea that the antediluvian patriarchs in Seth's line were priests in the order of Melchizedek. The other list of eight kings mentions five antediluvian cities that were ruled over. This mimics the Sumerian king list, which identifies five successive antediluvian cities from which eight rulers reigned. The cities on this list are Eridu (Eridug), Bad-tibira, Larsa (Larag), Sippar (Zimbur), and Shuruppak (Shuruppag). These eight kings therefore correspond to the eight patriarchs of Cain's line, which founded the first antediluvian city. Significantly, these antediluvian power centers are reminiscent of the four cities that Nimrod founded after the Flood in order to consolidate his power.

Unfortunately, the names in each Pre-Flood line listed in the Bible are similar and even identical at times - as in the case of Enoch and Lamech. Therefore, it has been suggested that these two lines were not different, and really correspond to only one line of antediluvian kings. As shown in the previous section, however, one of Satan's biggest strategies for obliterating the truth is to introduce evil leaders with the same names and sphere of influence as the major players in God's Plan of Salvation. As this book reveals, Satan is doing this in an attempt to thwart God's plans, and - during the Great Tribulation - it will even appear that Satan has succeeded at his evil plan for a short time.

In truth, the Bible never suggests that various patriarchs were common to both the bloodlines of Cain and Seth. On the contrary, it clearly lists them separately and suggests that there was great animosity between the descendents of these opposing bloodlines. As already shown, the opposition between the lines of Cain and Seth were glaringly brought to the forefront in extra-biblical Jewish literature such as the Book of Jasher and the histories of Josephus.

This is likely why the Book of 1 Enoch and the Book of Jasher were "lost" and the histories of Josephus were generally unavailable to educated people throughout the Dark and Middle Ages. Satan suppressed every truth that even remotely connected the bloodline of Cain and the seed of the Serpent with the ruling elite of nearly every era of human history - especially the dark lords and ladies who ruled over huge sections of Europe, Asia and the New World throughout the

Middle Ages. Endearing romances aside, the dark truth is that the majority of the lords and ladies whose romantic way of life is idealized and coveted by millions of fantasy and Medieval enthusiasts today was really a lifestyle that promoted selfishness, greed, cruelty, and avarice of every description as the small percentage of people in the ruling classes lived off the enslaved misery of millions of peasants that constantly worked their land without pay or reprieve.

What gave rise to the Feudal societies of the past and the emerging ones developing everywhere today with the collapse of the world's economy is set forth in the Bible as a war of ideologies that the Book of Genesis candidly describes - an ideological war that began even before Cain's murder of his brother Abel. Indeed, the first chapters of Genesis clearly differentiate between these opposing bloodlines that have been battling each other throughout history. It does so by recording that there were ten Pre-Flood generations in the line of Seth while there were only eight generations in the line of Cain.

In fact, this is probably the main reason why some Mesopotamian king lists contained the names of only eight successive kings, while others contained ten. Could it be that some kingdoms traced their roots to the rebellious line of Cain instead of the righteous line of Seth? Could it also be that Cain's line survived via the part human descendents of the Nephilim who survived the Flood? Indeed, the Bible and other Judeo-Christian manuscripts make it clear that Cain was ostracized from his original clan, forced to leave the society he had grown up in, and was obliged to start his own. Therefore, the lines of Cain and Seth were permanently separated, and there is no reason to believe that the patriarchs in these opposing lines were the same individuals.

From the time that Cain left Adam's camp and went to live in the land of Nod, Cain's and Seth's societies developed separately. Furthermore, it is obvious from Cain's rejected attempt at appealing to the true God with offerings of fruit and grain that Cain had ignored the message behind the Blood Covenant rituals that are emphasized so strongly in the Book of Genesis. It is therefore likely that Cain had totally opposing spiritual beliefs that he passed on to his children. These two rival societies were therefore openly hostile to each other until nearer to the time of the Flood - when most of the Sethites became as violent and spiritually and genetically corrupted as their Cainite and Nephilim enemies.

Interestingly, patriarchal names in the Bible suggest the roles that each ruler played in their separate societies. For example, the name Enoch means "initiated" or "teacher." Since there is an Enoch listed in the line of Cain as well as the line of Seth, this means that both of these opposing societies had a great wise man or teacher that shaped their moral direction. However, these two separate teachers called "Enoch" touted opposing philosophies that agreed with the beliefs of the people they governed. In the case of the godly Enoch, he led his fellow Sethites to a greater understanding of and love for the one true God. In the case of Cain's son Enoch, however, he embraced the Serpent or Satan as his spiritual Father and led his descendents to do so, just as the Pharisees of Yahshua's day did. Even though these Pharisees were not related to Cain or his daughter Naamah by blood, Yahshua still identified them as children of the Devil:

> "Why is my language not clear to you? Because you are unable to hear what I say. You belong to your father, the devil, and you want to carry out your father's desire. He was a murderer from the beginning, not holding to the truth, for there is no truth in him. When he lies, he speaks his native language, for he is a liar and the father of lies." - John 8:43-44 (NIV)

In this Scripture, Yahshua identifies Satan as the one who inspired Cain to be the first human murderer and liar. Yahshua also makes it clear that people who are under Satan's influence cannot correctly hear righteous people when they speak. I have come across this problem many times when trying to communicate my love for God to those who hate Him.

As a result of the ungodly influence of the fallen Archangel Azazel and the fallen Watchers who followed the angel Semyaza, the people in the line of Cain rapidly became gross idolaters, murderers, barbarians, sexual perverts, and sinners. Ancient records such as the histories of Josephus and the Book of Jasher also indicate that the Cainites were especially open to embracing the sexual sins engaged in by the fallen angels and the Nephilim.

In the following passages from "The Antiquities of the Jews," Josephus sheds some valuable light on Cain's woefully sinful behavior:

> "And when Cain had traveled over many countries, he, with his wife, built a city named Nod, which is a place so called, and there he settled his abode; where he also had children. However, he did not accept of his punishment, in order to amendment, but to increase his wickedness; for he only aimed to procure everything that was for his own bodily pleasure; though it obliged him to be injurious to his neighbors. He augmented his household substance with much wealth, by rapine and violence; he excited his acquaintance to

procure pleasures and spoils by robbery, and became a great leader of men into wicked courses.

He also introduced a change in the way of simplicity wherein men lived before; and was the author of measures and weights. And whereas they lived innocently and generously while they knew nothing of such arts, he changed the world into cunning craftiness. He first of all set boundaries about lands; he built a city, and fortified it with walls, and he compelled his family to come together to it; and called his city Enoch, after the name of his eldest son Enoch..." – Josephus, The Antiquities of the Jews, 1.2.2, Verses 60-62

In the preceding passages, Josephus tells us that Cain did as Nimrod would do centuries after the Great Flood. Cain and his progeny disobeyed God by settling in heavily fortified cities and compelling all their kin to live inside them in close proximity - thereby increasing the likelihood that sin and iniquity would spread rapidly. Unfortunately, the Cainites also developed a tyrannical culture that elevated hedonism and pleasure to high virtues. Therefore, they likely needed the protection of walled cities to repel the enemies they made in pursuing their barbaric lifestyle, which encouraged and celebrated rape, plunder, and murder.

Josephus also tells us that the Cainites made it necessary for all commodities to be weighed or measured, including setting boundaries around portions of land. As a result of the development of these so-called advancements of civilization, our antediluvian ancestors gradually abandoned their simple way of life. Whereas the Sethites lived in un-walled villages where they initiated trade by barter and an attitude of trust and co-operation prevailed between different settlements, the Cainites used coinage to establish monetary value, standardized weights to measure various liquid and solid quantities, and then set up boundary markers and walls around everyone's property. They thereby created many new methods for people to cheat one another with dishonest measurements, fake coins, and false boundary markers!

The Cainites changed the way business was done forever when they set up a standard of weights and measures that implied a lack of trust in one's trading partners. Of course, the fact that the Cainites were thieves and robbers made the need for standard weights and measures absolutely necessary! The Cainites also changed society forever by rejecting Yahweh and refusing to accept the moral constraints placed upon others by religion. They therefore took what they wanted from others, not caring who they had to subjugate, enslave, or murder in the

process. According to the Book of Jasher, the wicked inhabitants of
Sodom and Gomorrah echoed this same attitude:

> "In those days all the people of Sodom and
> Gomorrah, and of the whole five cities, were exceedingly
> wicked and sinful against the Lord and they provoked the
> Lord with their abominations... And they had in their land a
> very extensive valley, about half a day's walk, and in it there
> were fountains of water and a great deal of herbage
> surrounding the water.
>
> And all the people of Sodom and Gomorrah went there
> four times in the year, with their wives and children and all
> belonging to them, and they rejoiced there with timbrels and
> dances. And in the time of rejoicing they would all rise and
> lay hold of their neighbor's wives, and some, the virgin
> daughters of their neighbors, and they enjoyed them, and
> each man saw his wife and daughter in the hands of his
> neighbor and did not say a word. And they did so from
> morning to night, and they afterward returned home each
> man to his house and each woman to her tent; so they always
> did four times in the year.
>
> Also when a stranger came into their cities and
> brought goods which he had purchased with a view to dispose
> of there, the people of these cities would assemble, men,
> women and children, young and old, and go to the man and
> take his goods by force, giving a little to each man until there
> was an end to all the goods of the owner...
>
> And if the owner of the goods quarreled with them,
> saying, 'What is this work which you have done to me?', then
> they would approach to him one by one, and each would
> show him the little which he took and taunt him, saying, 'I
> only took that little which thou didst give me;' and when he
> heard this from them all, he would arise and go from them in
> sorrow and bitterness of soul, when they would all arise and
> go after him, and drive him out of the city with great noise
> and tumult." – Jasher 18:11-17

Interestingly, the sins ascribed to Cain and his descendents and
to the people of Sodom and Gomorrah are nearly identical to those
reportedly engaged in by the fallen angels and their Nephilim offspring.
As a result, the Book of Jasher tells us that the wickedness of
antediluvian men caused Yahweh to turn the ground against them,
thereby making it impossible to grow food crops:

"And Seth lived one hundred and five years, and he begat a son; and Seth called the name of his son Enosh, saying, Because in that time the sons of men began to multiply, and to afflict their souls and hearts by transgressing and rebelling against God. And it was in the days of Enosh that the sons of men continued to rebel and transgress against God, to increase the anger of the Lord against the sons of men. And the sons of men went and they served other gods, and they forgot the Lord who had created them in the earth: and in those days the sons of men made images of brass and iron, wood and stone, and they bowed down and served them. And every man made his god and they bowed down to them, and the sons of men forsook the Lord all the days of Enosh and his children; and the anger of the Lord was kindled on account of their works and abominations which they did in the earth.

And the Lord caused the waters of the river Gihon to overwhelm them, and he destroyed and consumed them, and he destroyed the third part of the earth, and notwithstanding this, the sons of men did not turn from their evil ways, and their hands were yet extended to do evil in the sight of the Lord. And in those days there was neither sowing nor reaping in the earth; and there was no food for the sons of men and the famine was very great in those days. And the seed which they sowed in those days in the ground became thorns, thistles and briers; for from the days of Adam was this declaration concerning the earth, of the curse of God, which he cursed the earth, on account of the sin which Adam sinned before the Lord. And it was when men continued to rebel and transgress against God, and to corrupt their ways, that the earth also became corrupt." – Jasher 2:2-9

In the preceding passages, we are told that - as a result of rampant idolatry and sinfulness - Yah cursed the ground and made it produce mostly harmful weeds rather than vegetables and grain. In addition, God caused a massive overflow along the banks of the Gihon River that caused severe flooding and overwhelmed and destroyed many of the wicked people who dwelled in the land of Nod. However, the Cainites who survived this devastating flood did not repent and were therefore unable to grow food crops due to Yah's curse that caused thorns and thistles to grow where only good seed had been sown.

Unfortunately, the preceding passages from the Book of Jasher use the phrase "sons of men" when referring to the human populace engaged in idolatry during the time of Enosh, so it can be misleading in that there appears to be no room for a righteous line of believers in Yahweh from that time onward. However, later in the Book of Jasher, this notion is countered by saying that the descendents of Seth were righteous until the latter days of Methuselah (Jasher 5:5-6). This means that the Sethites maintained a righteous branch until the age when Methuselah's son Lamech, the father of Noah ruled over the Sethites. It also means that Enosh was not a wicked man in the habit of blaspheming God's Name, as some erroneously teach. Instead Enosh called out to Yahweh for protection from the evil being perpetrated around him and his children (Gen. 4:26). As upcoming quotes from Jasher and Josephus will reveal, Josephus concurs with the Book of Jasher in this regard.

Since Cain was a farmer and Abel was a shepherd at the time Cain murdered Abel, it seems logical that their descendents would have carried on the same means of livelihood. However, since the Cainites would not repent, **Yah meted out the curse of thorns and thistles against the Cainites as punishment for their wickedness. This means that they could not grow their own food!** Inevitably, this curse compelled the Cainites to do even more acts of violence to procure what they needed to survive. Though this plague of thorns was initially a judgment against the immorality of the Cainites, the inability to grow good crops eventually plagued the Sethites in the latter days before the Flood also - when the remaining Sethites began to embrace the violent and sinful ways of the Nephilim and Cainites:

> "And when Enoch had ascended into heaven, all the kings of the earth rose and took Methuselah his son and anointed him, and they caused him to reign over them in the place of his father. And Methuselah acted uprightly in the sight of God, as his father Enoch had taught him, and he likewise during the whole of his life taught the sons of men wisdom, knowledge and the fear of God, and he did not turn from the good way either to the right or to the left.
>
> But in the latter days of Methuselah, the sons of men turned from the Lord, they corrupted the earth, they robbed and plundered each other, and they rebelled against God and they transgressed, and they corrupted their ways, and would not hearken to the voice of Methuselah, but rebelled against him. And the Lord was exceedingly wroth against them, and the Lord continued to destroy the seed in those days, so that there was neither sowing nor reaping in the earth. For when they sowed the ground in order that they might obtain food

*for their support, behold, thorns and thistles were produced...
And still the sons of men did not turn from their evil ways,
and their hands were still extended to do evil in the sight of
God, and they provoked the Lord with their evil ways, and
the Lord was very wroth, and repented that he had made
man." - Jasher 4:2-7*

Unlike the Cainites, whose leading patriarch Cain was instrumental in leading his descendents into apostasy and criminal activities soon after his exile from Eden, the descendants of Adam through Seth valiantly and persistently resisted their evil ways. This is because the Sethites had a religion centered on Sacred Astronomy, the Star Gospel, and the redemptive sacrificial system of Blood Covenanting that kept them from falling into sin. By the time Noah was an adult, though, very few righteous people remained. Most of mankind had been tainted by Nephilim genetic, intellectual and spiritual tampering, while most of those that were still fully human were tainted with a despicable love of violence and sexual perversion. Here is what the Jewish Historian Josephus had to say about this sad "prehistoric" antediluvian era:

*"Now this posterity of Seth continued to esteem God
as the Lord of the universe, and to have an entire regard for
virtue, for seven generations; but in process of time they were
perverted and forsook the practices of their forefathers, and
did neither pay those honors to God which were appointed
them, nor had they any concern to do justice towards men.*

*But for what degree of zeal they had formerly shown
for virtue, they now showed by their actions a double degree
of wickedness; whereby they made God to be their enemy, **for
many angels of God kept company with women and begat
sons that proved unjust, and despisers of all that was good,
on account of the confidence they had in their own strength;
for the tradition is that these men did what resembled the acts
of those whom the Grecians call giants**.*

*But Noah was very uneasy at what they did; and being
displeased at their conduct, persuaded them to change their
dispositions and their acts for the better; but seeing that they
did not yield to him, but were slaves to their wicked
pleasures, he was afraid they would kill him, together with his
wife and children, and those they had married; so he departed
out of that land." – Josephus, The Antiquities of the Jews,
1.3.1 - All of Section 1*

Here, Josephus clearly states that the descendents of Seth were righteous for seven generations. Since Enoch was the seventh antediluvian patriarch in the line of Seth, this means that the Sethites remained reasonably righteous until the time of the prophet Enoch's son Methuselah.

The preceding quote from Josephus also makes it clear that he truly believed that a race of giants lived on the Earth prior to the Flood. Furthermore, Josephus viewed these giants as malevolent beings who were so evil that righteous Noah rightly feared for his life and that of his family. It is also clear from Josephus' testimony that Noah tried valiantly to reach out to the wayward people who had been swayed into behaving sinfully like the Giants. In fact, Noah attempted to teach these sinners the ways of righteousness until it became too dangerous to do so. When it did, Noah had to flee his homeland and live in exile - likely in a far less inhabited part of the Earth where he could more easily protect himself and his family. As explained previously, the angel Uriel told Lamech that Noah needed to hide himself.

Since the righteous priests of that era went into hiding, there was no one left in Nephilim dominated lands that taught humanity to love God and live chastely and righteously. Furthermore, in the spiritually bankrupt and violent civilizations that reigned just prior to the Flood, both Nephilim and apostate humans soon annihilated anyone foolhardy enough to continue preaching against sin like Noah had. Consequently, the spiritual state of the world deteriorated until virtually everyone save for Methuselah, Noah and his family was engaged in full-fledged Paganism, idolatry, and unrestrained wickedness.

The beguiling but erroneous ideas given to mankind by the fallen angels and their evil Nephilim offspring became the basis for all the false ancient religions that encouraged sensuality and sexual perversion and the worshipping of created things as gods. Angels, demons, animals, men, women, stars, planets, the Earth, the Sun and Moon, and all forty-eight constellations in the ancient Zodiac became objects of worship in various Pagan cultures. Furthermore, many false spiritual beliefs sprang up surrounding this false worship. Foretelling a person's future using Astrology or seeking protection or power through demonic Magic, Sorcery or Shamanism became evil and seductive replacements for true faith and reliance in one Creator God.

The ancient Pagans had forgotten the most important truth in the Universe. This truth is that faith in Yahweh Elohim and Yah's promised full redemption from sin through the Messiah to come is what gives men the direction, courage, strength, and power they need to find salvation, righteousness, and everlasting life, and to conquer the forces of evil around them that are seeking to destroy them! All past followers of our triune God knew that there was great power in the Name of Yahweh to protect them from demonic oppression and attack. Even today, by seeing God's love for them revealed in every act of demonic deliverance, those who love Yahweh still shun the false religions that the fallen angels helped spawn. These false beliefs gelled into the Paganistic humanism that developed after the Flood - when mankind was again engaged in battle with the descendents of the Nephilim over the rulership of the material wealth and resources of the Earth.

Instead of falling into idolatrous practices, those who remained faithful to Yahweh sought God's help and protection. To receive both, they called on Elohim *by His Holy Name Yahweh* in prayer, as evidenced in the Bible's remark that men called upon the Name of Yahweh during the time of Seth's son Enosh onward (Genesis 4:26). They also sought power and protection by praying and worshipping to Yahweh by Name, and offering blood sacrifices to Yah to show their desire for forgiveness and willingness to live godly lives according to God's Laws.

By calling on the Name of Yahweh and asking for Yahweh's help via His armies of holy angels, the Sethites saw Yahweh as their benevolent Father God who was fierce in offering protection to His earthly children, and who always displayed His holy, loving, and perfect character. By the time of the Great Flood, however, Noah and his immediate family were the only people who still knew Yahweh by Name. Furthermore, because of the rampant intermarriage of humanity with the Nephilim and the likely wholesale slaughter of those who were not genetically tainted with Nephilim blood, only Noah's purely human family was chosen by God to be preserved on the Ark.

Was Advanced Technology Used Before the Flood?

Though most Creationist publications and web sites insist that Noah used nothing more than Stone-Age technology to build the Ark, it is hard to believe that any amount of primitive man power using simple technology could have sustained and cared for many thousands of animals in a cold, dark, smelly floating barn for a year, which is what most Creationists say Noah's Ark successfully accomplished. We will discuss the miraculous building of Noah's Ark in a moment, but first let's focus on the evidence for other types of sophisticated Pre-Flood technology.

Some fairly impressive technology was used before the Flood by mankind, and much of it was devised and utilized without any aid from the Watchers. After all, humanity existed without angelic intervention for nearly 600 years after Adam fell until around 3400 BC, and people were far smarter, healthier and longer-lived than we are today. Furthermore, Adam and Eve were created in the spiritual, intellectual and physiological image of the Preincarnate Yahshua. As such, they were fully grown young adults who could understand and converse with God from the beginning. Because Adam and Eve were in God's image, they had intellects that could fully explore and enjoy the miracle of God's Creation and marvel at God's infinite complexity and capacity for love. This also allowed Adam to name all the animals in the Garden as he interacted, analyzed and named them according to their unique natures (Genesis 2:19-20).

Now, since Adam and Eve were created to tend the Garden of Eden (Genesis 2:15), they would automatically have been given divine guidance on how to care for, reproduce, and perhaps even improve upon all the plants and animals in the garden through selective breeding and hybridization. This means that - from the beginning - Adam and Eve had knowledge of biology and botany and understood the rudiments of farming and shepherding. In fact, this is clear from the choice of Cain and Abel's professions.

The domestication of animals and crops would have inevitably led to other inventions to aid in cooking, storing foodstuffs, farming, and sheltering and caring for people and animals. Then, as people moved into larger farming and shepherding communities, more sophisticated dwellings like community meeting halls and structures for storing raw materials, food and grain would have become necessary. In tandem with these other activities, people would have learned how to navigate rivers and streams and eventually would have found ways to safely explore the seas. Simple rafts and canoes were fine on rivers and lakes but the seas required sturdier vessels, which eventually led to ship building.

As an example of how sophisticated these ships eventually became, the Sethites who built the Pillar of Enoch at Giza dismantled and buried several whole ships in the boat pits at the pyramid's base. One of these incredibly sophisticated and seaworthy ships was excavated, reconstructed, and housed in a museum at the base of the pyramid. This boat is an incredible 142.06 feet (43.3 meters) long, 19.36 feet (5.9 meters) wide, and had a hull constructed of small slats of wood laced together with tough flax ropes that would have absorbed water and effectively sealed off the cracks between the wood slats. This gave the boat incredible flexibility and waterproofing, and would have prevented it from being torn apart or sinking in rough seas. In fact, its design suggests that it would have undulated on rough seas somewhat like a serpent moves, and this is likely why the ancient Egyptians often pictured boats as serpents and other cultures made their ships appear to look like sea dragons.

The ship from the Giza boat pit has a wooden cabin built at its center, an elegant high prow and stern, and six sets of long, beautifully made oars - with five sets in front of the cabin at the center, and one pair at the stern for steering. Uncannily, these twelve oars and their placement suggest the Six Ages of mankind and final (rudder=guiding) Millennial Age of Christ as well as the Twelve Signs of the Zodiac. Perhaps this symbolism also had something to do with myths of various deities or heroes traveling the "Path of the Sun" or the "Highway of the Gods!"

Though no mast was found in the boat pit, the reconstructed boat could easily have been outfitted with a sturdy mast or two that would hold heavy linen sails like those seen in Egyptian tomb paintings of boats on the Nile. But though this reconstructed ship is incredibly beautiful and sea-worthy, it lacks any sign of needing technological gadgetry either for building or operating it. In short, it is a grand display of mankind's primitive ingenuity.

In keeping with the silent testimony of the boat pits, certain scholars have shown that the Pyramid builders could have used various types of cranes, pulleys, and lifts that did not require mystical powers or advanced technology to build or operate. In fact, it has been proposed that a lifting machine consisting of a wooden platform attached to four or more paired sets of multi-levered wooden lifting devices could have been used to move heavy stone blocks up one course of a pyramid's masonry at a time.

A whole chain of such lifting machines set up in a single row on one side of the pyramid could have hoisted stone blocks up each course of masonry in rapid succession. This would have made the construction of a large, well-engineered pyramid like the Pillar of Enoch by a purely human work gang entirely possible, though there is no doubt that this pyramid is encoded with divine knowledge that no human could have known without special revelation from God and a little help from the holy Watchers, which is how Enoch received his wisdom.

Scholars estimate that a trained gang of about 25,000 workers would have been capable of building the Great Pyramid using relatively ordinary construction equipment such as this levered lifting device. In

Book Four, I discuss the theory put forth in Christopher Dunn's book: "The Giza Power Plant," which hypothesizes that the Great Pyramid could have been a sound resonance power generator, which could have been used to produce electrical energy before the Flood put it out of commission.

Some ancient myths suggest that the Pillar of Enoch and other structures like it were built using some sort of levitation technique. The theories surrounding this possibility include both sound waves and electromagnetic force as potential mechanisms for levitating massive stone blocks into place. Of course, if the Watchers were involved in any of the megalithic building projects scattered across the Earth, they certainly would have been able to bend the Laws of Physics as we know them. Thus they could have performed amazing, gravity-defying tricks like effortlessly cutting, shaping, and moving 1500 ton stone blocks over any kind of terrain and placing them precisely where they needed to go.

There is also some intriguing though inconclusive evidence that our ancestors had other advanced forms of technology like powered land vehicles, dirigible-like aircraft, planes, and possibly even high-powered missiles and spacecraft. The Sanskrit religious writings of India suggest that - over 4,000 years ago - men regularly flew about in several kinds of aircraft labeled by the term "Vimana." According to the Ramayana and Mahabharata, for example, ancient airmen conducted a terrible war using destructive missiles or death rays (perhaps lasers?) that were fired from the Vimanas with devastating results.

As evidence of the use of advanced weapons, there are unexplained impact craters in India and elsewhere, and vitrified walls in the ruins of the amazingly sophisticated and very ancient city known as Mohenjo Daro in Pakistan. Vitrified ruins have also been found in other places, including the southwestern USA. In addition, large desert areas are covered with vitrified sand in India, Saudi Arabia, the Sinai and North Africa. This glass that is created from sand particles that have been fused together with intense heat is strewn over huge circular regions of barren, sandy desert that may have been verdantly green in some remote era. The vitrified glass appears as scattered surface pebbles or entire sheets of black, green or yellowish glass - some of which has been found buried under many layers of sand.

Various explanations have been put forth as to how these sheets of desert glass occurred "naturally," such as ancient lunar volcanic eruptions or meteoric impacts. However, none of these sound completely convincing. In fact, there is only one explanation that fits the available evidence perfectly, and this would be that extremely intense waves of searing heat caused by a nuclear device, plasma gun, or laser ray gun was used over big areas of the ancient world to destroy civilization centers, which also fused the sand surrounding these areas into glass.

In modern times, vitrified glass that is nearly identical to that found in the deserts of the Middle East has been produced at modern atomic test sites in desert areas such as Emu Field in Australia and various sites in the southwestern United States. It is therefore highly likely that these modern desert regions with supposedly naturally occurring desert glass were turned into deserts by technologically generated blasts of intense heat.

As to the source of the technology that allowed men to fly and conduct aerial battles using atomic, plasma, or laser weaponry, it is likely that men developed some of it completely on their own. However, as evidenced in the creation of the Nephilim via genetic splicing, the fallen Watchers certainly introduced more advanced technological and scientific knowledge later on. The fallen angels also would have given knowledge of advanced technology and weaponry to their demonic Nephilim offspring and the Cainites. This would have aided the fallen angels and Nephilim in their efforts to destroy the righteous Sethites.

Meanwhile, the godly Watchers who loved humanity and wanted to protect the Sethites would have given defensive technological knowledge to the followers of God in an effort to protect them from annihilation, but not to encourage the physical violence and bloodshed that Yahweh hates. This would have included helping people to develop sophisticated medical knowledge in order to save lives as well as to construct virtually impenetrable, easily defensible hideaways and sheltered living and farming areas on the Earth where Nephilim could not easily enter.

Interestingly, the fact that people congregated in protected areas of the Earth is clearly suggested by maps that show the locations where dinosaur fossils have been found. These maps all indicate that large dinosaur fossil finds have not been found in the locations of the oldest human civilizations on Earth. This suggests that the Nephilim and humans primarily lived in their own separate communities for a long period of time prior to the Flood because people were rightly afraid of the Nephilim and wanted to keep themselves separate to preserve their spiritual and physical purity.

Nonetheless, because the Nephilim and humans were not immortal or immaterial, they both would have benefited from using technology like telescopes, magnifying lenses, clocks, electrical and atomic power, electric lights, communication devices, land vehicles, aircraft, and spaceships. As an indication that all of these types of technology could have been permissible before the Flood, obviously machined artifacts have been found scattered all over the world. In his writings, scholar Christopher Dunn has shown that there is much physical evidence for advanced, high powered machining in stone artwork and masonry in ancient Egypt. How else could the Egyptians have carved effortlessly though diorite and granite, for example? These types of stone are among the hardest naturally occurring substances known to mankind and could not have been worked with ordinary stone, copper or bronze tools.

Though it is patently ignored by most contemporary archeologists, scientists, and scholars, the physical evidence of high powered or advanced machining that has survived to modern times has been well-documented by Christopher Dunn and others. This suggests that more benign forms of advanced technology similar to our own existed in ancient times. However, historical and archeological records around the world also suggest that only the very rich and powerful may have had the means to develop, control and utilize this technology effectively, and there is no doubt that the technology at the disposal of various rulers soon contributed to the terrible violence before the Flood.

A fragment from the Book of Noah that survives within the Book of 1 Enoch suggests that advanced technology was definitely utilized in the construction of Noah's Ark. There, Noah himself wrote that God's holy angels helped him to build the Ark:

> "And in those days the word of God came unto me, and He said unto me: 'Noah, thy lot has come Up before Me, a lot without blame, a lot of love and uprightness. **And now the angels are making a wooden (building), and when they have completed that task I will place My hand upon it and preserve it,** and there shall come forth from it the seed of life, and a change shall set in so that the earth will not remain without inhabitant. And I will make fast thy seed before me for ever and ever, and I will spread abroad those who dwell with thee.'" - 1 Enoch 67:1-3

The preceding quote is highly interesting because it suggests that the Ark was at least partly built by the holy Watchers who came to help mankind. Though Noah was certainly commissioned to build the Ark by Yahweh, he likely needed help to build the enormous hull of the Ark using the divine instructions given to him in Genesis 6:14-16. Therefore, God's holy angels may have helped design and build the outer portions of the Ark, and also possibly engineered the steering and propulsion mechanisms that the Ark would have needed to avoid obstacles at sea.

Meanwhile, Noah and his family would have worked to gather, prepare and store huge amounts of food for themselves and the many varieties of animals that would have to live on the Ark with them for an entire year. Then, when the angels were finished making the Ark's hull, Noah, his sons and their wives could have installed technology invented with human ingenuity such as the "Tsohar" or lighting source in the finished ceiling of the Ark. With the light in place, Noah, Noah's sons and the four wives belonging to them could have installed all the ducts and pipes needed for ventilation and plumbing. They likely also provided the labor needed to harvest sturdy trees, cut lumber, and build the interior rooms and pens for the animals and food.

Considering all that had to be done, the Ark would have taken many hours of human labor to build. Nonetheless, a line in the Book of Jasher that was quoted earlier (Jasher 5:34) relays that Noah was 595 years old when he started to build the Ark and it took him five years to complete it. There it says: *"In his five hundred and ninety-fifth year Noah commenced to make the ark, and he made the ark in five years..."* This means that the Ark was not finished until just before the Flood. Talk about cutting it close!

Intriguingly, it seems likely that the Rapture will occur just before the Antichrist takes control of the world, and for many of us who are alive to take part in it, we may feel that God certainly cut it close! In fact, believers are already suffering from harsh persecution, the gradual but irreversible collapse of the world's economy, and the emergence of fascist political infrastructures in Europe, America and elsewhere. Due to this, there is no doubt that Yahshua is coming soon in the Rapture to rescue those who love Him. Otherwise, if left on Earth to suffer through the Antichrist's rule, they would be faced with certain annihilation.

Concerning the types of technology that were made available to Noah and his family by the Watchers, there is speculation that the "Tsohar" that Noah installed aboard the Ark within one cubit of the ceiling may have been an electrically powered light source. See Genesis 6:16, where the word "Tsohar" meaning "light" is incorrectly translated as "window." In fact, for a ship as large as Noah's Ark was, and with so many different types of animals onboard, this ship would have needed highly sophisticated forms of ventilation and plumbing, as well as efficient cooling and heating systems that did not require large quantities of fuel to utilize. These would have had to sustain the quality of life onboard for a year, which is a very long time to do so without taking on new supplies. In fact, it would be a major challenge for a modern ocean-class cruise ship to carry enough supplies to feed a full compliment of passengers and crew for three months much less a year, and humans eat far less than most vegetarian animals.

Though the technological systems on the Ark may have included electrical power as a power source, the ventilation and plumbing could have been driven by windmills installed on top of the Ark and water-powered turbines in the Ark's submerged hull. In addition, these mills or turbines could have produced enough electricity to power the Tsohar in the ceiling of the Ark continuously. Though **Noah and his kin certainly would have had the knowledge and skill to design and install much of this sophisticated technology all on their own,** there is no doubt that they could and would have enlisted any potential supernatural aid offered by the holy Watchers when it was needed. The successful building of the Ark was, after all, a real matter of life and death!

Even before the building of the Ark was undertaken, the leaders of various antediluvian civilization centers may have had aircraft, space ships, and other types of transportation technology that were comparable to or even better than modern renditions. In fact, a strange carving found on the lintel of a temple at Abydos in Egypt that is purported to be at least 4000 years old depicts ground transportation and aircraft much like those we use today - including cars, helicopters and jet airplanes! These could have been used to chart the geographical features and shores of continents with great accuracy, and to travel about with great speed and ease.

A good introduction to the subject of ancient technology can be found in the book "Secrets of the Lost Races" by Rene' Noorbergen, who wrote his excellent examination of the evidence for high technology in the past from a refreshingly biblical perspective. When doing research into ancient technology and biblical history, web sites, videos or books by Christian researchers Jonathan Gray or Ron Wyatt may also prove helpful. Much of their research is sound and came from reliable sources, though some of their claims may be fictitious and cannot be verified.

The book "Technology of the Gods" by David Hatcher Childress is also informative. Though it is not written from a Judeo-Christian standpoint, it examines the ancient Vedic texts of India, which discuss the use of different types of aircraft called "Vimanas." In addition, Childress mentions the stone lintel carving in Egypt that depicts land and air transport vehicles. However, beware of most of the current books covering ancient mysteries since they reject the veracity of the Bible and **blatantly but falsely claim that Homo sapiens are the by-product of alien attempts to create a slave race!** Despite their lies, this book series, 1 Enoch, Jasher, Jubilees and the Bible completely disprove their assumption that aliens are our creators.

Though the fallen angels did create a new race of earthly beings called Nephilim, they were not spiritually or intrinsically superior to mankind, but only physically superior in a very gross and monstrous sense. Yet, despite their physical superiority, these evil creatures likely utilized advanced technology to kill even more people than they could have otherwise, and then showed no apparent remorse for it. This sounds eerily similar to the behavior of many Terrorists today. Furthermore, the Bible makes it clear that most of the people alive today are strictly descended from Noah and his sons, and the blood of the Nephilim that survived the Flood has been restricted to a very small group of powerful and merciless individuals bent on a course of vengeance against all humanity.

Though the antediluvians and Nephilim may have developed and utilized advanced technology with the help of the Watchers, one should never assume - like some alien enthusiasts do - that God, the holy angels, or resurrected and glorified people need aircraft or spaceships to travel! This as an occult lie based on the idea that God is not God at all, but some advanced alien that helped us evolve from some lesser life form into the smart "apes" we are today. In fact, this lie may be behind the Great Delusion that the Antichrist or *"lawless one"* may deceive the whole world with during the Great Tribulation:

"The coming of the lawless one is according to the working of Satan, with all power, signs, and lying wonders, and with all unrighteous deception among those who perish, because they did not receive the love of the truth, that they might be saved. And for this reason God will send them strong delusion, that they should believe the lie, that they all may be condemned who did not believe the truth but had pleasure in unrighteousness." - 2 Thess. 2:9-12 (NKJ)

This Scripture clearly says that Satan will bring about the deception of the unrighteous using incredible power, lying signs and wonders. This could easily include the re-emergence of the fallen angels and the Nephilim as the false alien "gods" who will claim to have created us and given us our civilization. Perhaps they will even claim to have returned to bring about world peace and prosperity, and to save us from annihilating ourselves. And when they do, there is no doubt that their amazing appearance will include a display of advanced technology and power that will far surpass anything ever created or conceived by mankind alone.

Ancient Man's Advanced Knowledge of Our Solar System

There is startling evidence that our ancestors knew much more about our Solar System than most archeologists currently think they did. Earlier, I mentioned that the Babylonians might have once known that there are nine planets plus an asteroid belt that was once a planet in our Solar System. The most conclusive evidence that the Akkadians and Babylonians understood more about our Solar System than scholars give them credit for are tiny diagrams found on ancient Akkadian cylinder seals.

Cylinder seals were usually made of stone and were used for marking dates, names, and other identifying marks onto official documents that were incised into clay tablets using cuneiform script. The cylinders were pressed and rolled into the clay tablets the Babylonians used to keep records of important transactions. The cylinders were therefore like signatures used to finalize or legitimize legal transactions or to mark ownership. Between the two human figures on the cylinder seal impression depicted on this page is what appears to be a symbol depicting the Sun surrounded by *eleven other celestial bodies:*

Cylinder Seal VA 243 with possible depiction of Solar System

In the two illustrations on page 373, the part of the cylinder seal of interest in this discussion was enlarged and placed next to a graphic diagram. The diagram shows that this seal may indeed depict the Sun at the center of our Solar System circa 3000 BC - when Enoch was the leading patriarch and prophet among the Sethites. If this seal does show our Solar System, it shows it as it was before the rebel planet Marduk destroyed the planet Tiamat and turned it into our asteroid belt. Note also that - with the exception of Mercury and Pluto - it appears to show the planets in their correct orbital position from the Sun. In addition, their great differences in mass have been noted by their relative size in relation to one another:

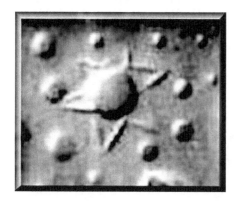 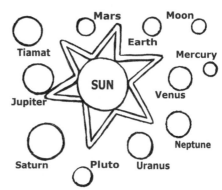

Though it is not a rendition of our Solar System as it is today, it suggests that some Mesopotamian civilizations had a far greater knowledge of Outer Space than is currently supposed. In fact, since the outermost planets Uranus, Neptune, and Pluto cannot be seen without the aid of a telescope, this cylinder seals' Solar System motif suggests that our antediluvian ancestors either had high-powered, technologically sophisticated telescopes, and/or that they acquired a superhuman knowledge of our Solar System from the Watchers, who were already on the Earth when this cylinder was created, and may have been responsible for the rapid advancement of civilization in Mesopotamia.

In addition to Seal VA 243, another cylinder seal that shows eleven wandering stars or planets associated with the Sun is pictured on the next page. This cylinder seal was dedicated to the Akkadian Sun god Shamash and can be found on display in the Louvre in France. On it, there are two depictions of eleven celestial bodies or wandering stars. The left circle surrounds the sun symbol of Shamash with seven planets above and five planets below it connected to the Sun by solar rays, while the right circle depicts the Sun with solar rays connecting to all eleven planets. This is fairly conclusive proof that the eleven celestial bodies on Seal VA-243 that were associated with a greater star signifying the god Shamash or our Sun was an Akkadian depiction of our Solar System.

It appears that the Akkadians and Babylonians were not the only ancient cultures to know the correct position and number of planetary bodies in the Solar System. The ancient Egyptians may have known that there were nine planets, though their highly figurative art and hieroglyphic method of recording information have obscured this fact. Nonetheless, if we examine Egyptian myths, there are clues. For example, at Heliopolis in the Delta region of ancient Egypt, a group of nine deities labeled the "Great Ennead" (the ancient Egyptian "Pesdjet") were worshipped. Though Egyptologists view these as nine mythical deities, the Ennead of Heliopolis' nine deities may correspond to the nine current planets in our Solar System.

Cylinder Seal of Shamash the Sun god with eleven planets connected to him, also shown as seven major and five minor planets

According to the Memphite Cosmogony taught by the priesthood of Ptah in ancient Memphis, the Creator god Ptah ruled over this group of nine deities - just as the Sun representing Yahweh God is the center of our (formerly) nine-planet Solar System. Though the deities in the Ennead changed at various times in ancient Egypt's history, it most often consisted of nine deities: Re-Atum, Shu (Air), Tefnut (Water), Geb (Earth), Nut (Sky), Osiris, Isis, Seth and Nephthys. At times the Ennead also included one other god, perhaps representing the planet Tiamat that became the asteroid belt. This tenth god was usually Horus, god of the horizon, though at times it was the scribe of the gods named Thoth.

Intriguing evidence has also been found supporting the idea that the people of ancient Central America once knew that there were at least eight planets and an asteroid belt in our Solar System. This evidence can be found at the site of the ruined temple complex at Teotihuacán in Mexico. This well-preserved series of ruins has been attributed to the Mayans, an advanced New World culture that had a highly developed civilization, built many stone monuments and pyramids that they decorated with brightly painted stone carvings and hieroglyphic texts, practiced astronomy using sophisticated mathematical calculations, and sacrificed their prisoners of war to their gods with demonic zeal - just as their descendents the Aztecs would later do.

Teotihuacán consists of a number of buildings and temples built on either side of a long, straight axis street. Though this street is ominously known today as the "Avenue of the Dead," it appears to have marked the rising and setting of the star Sirius and the Pleiades star cluster, which followed the axis of this central street around the time of Christ. Starting at the southeast side of the site, there is the imposing structure currently known as the "Citadel of Quetzalcoatl." If this is taken to represent the Sun, there are breaks along this spacious ceremonial avenue that follow the correct relative position and distance of eight planets, our Moon, and the asteroid belt from the Sun!

Going north from the Temple of Quetzalcoatl, the next feature of this temple complex is the San Juan River, which runs through the site from east to west. This river and the buildings just north of it correlate with the planet Mercury. After this, each succeeding break in the Avenue of the Dead corresponds to one of the inner terrestrial planets of our Solar System, including the Earth and the Moon.

After the break in the street for the planet Mars, the next large structure at Teotihuacán is the Pyramid of the Sun. This remarkably well preserved and ingeniously engineered step pyramid has a base that is almost as big as the Great Pyramid's. It is in the center of the temple complex at Teotihuacán, on the east side of the Avenue of the Dead.

The Pyramid of the Sun has been cited as having a correlation with the great ringed planet Saturn. However, as shown in the illustration on page 376, the Pyramid of the Sun is not in the right position to correspond to Saturn. Instead, the Sun Pyramid corresponds to the planet Jupiter, which also fits the massive size of this pyramid when compared to all the other structures at Teotihuacán.

Next in line going toward the Pyramid of the Moon is an unexcavated plaza surrounded by low walls and stepped platforms. This is immediately to the north of the Sun Pyramid on the west side of the Avenue of the Dead. This buried plaza may be meant to signify the planet Jupiter's many moons, though there is no way of knowing for certain unless more data is forthcoming from the archeological community at some point. Next in line, the Pyramid of the Moon would correspond to the planet Saturn while the wide plaza in front of it may signify Saturn's rings and moons.

Celestial Connection of the Teotihuacán Temple Complex

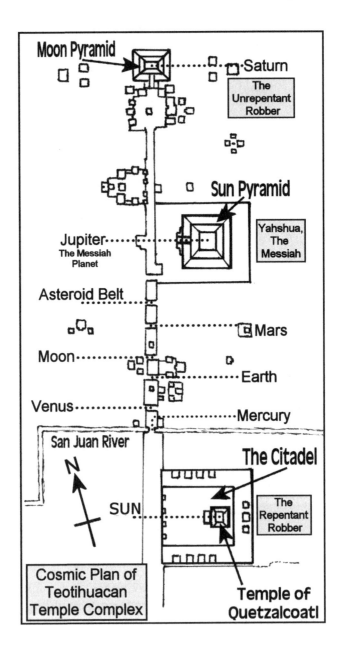

Uncannily, the agriculture and harvest god Saturn of Roman Mythology corresponds to the Greek god Kronus, who may be a deified version of the son of Noah named Ham, whose son Cush gave birth to Nimrod. Nimrod rebelled against God the Father in favor of the false deity Enlil or Cush - who usurped Yahshua's place in Heaven - and Inanna or Ishtar, who was a deified woman or demon that replaced the Holy Spirit's role. In support of the planet Saturn's currently evil connection, various occult sources state that the gods Saturn, Moloch, Baal and Shiva are spiritually identical alternative names for Satan in history. Interestingly, at certain times in its orbit around the Sun, Saturn's rings become more visible from Earth. At their best viewing angle with the naked eye, Saturn's rings resemble the giant white rim of a heavenly eye with a big white iris. This may be why Pagan cultures connected their most prominent deities or religious leaders with the symbol of an open eye such as the eye of Horus or Buddha.

Fascinatingly, the plaza in front of the Moon Pyramid is made up of a ring of twelve small pyramidal structures with stairways surrounding a central raised platform - as if in mimicry of the 12 planets that originally orbited the Sun. On a sinister note, since the planet Saturn is often associated with Satan, could the Moon Pyramid's link to Menkaure's Pyramid be tying Ishmael and his twelve sons to the unrepentant robber of Luke's Gospel (Gen. 25:12-16; Luke 23:39)?

Intriguingly, this symbolism may also reflect the idea that - just as Saturn or Satan now governs the seventh or Sabbath Day when men are supposed to refrain from doing evil works but nevertheless continue to do so - Yahshua will govern the Seventh Millennium since the Fall and take His rightful place as the true King of Heaven and Earth and Lord of the Sabbath. The 1,000-year long Great Sabbath Day that Yahshua will govern with a rod of iron will be fully dedicated to Yahweh and doing good works in keeping with His Will. For this reason, the rings around Saturn actually signify Yahshua's many symbolic crowns that indicate His kingship over the Twelve Tribes of Israel, the twelve Ishmaelite tribes, and all the Gentiles whose destinies were written in the stars before mankind was created.

Though not shown on my Teotihuacán site plan on page 376, there are two as yet unexcavated mounds quite a bit further to the northeast of the Pyramid of the Moon that apparently correlate with the planets Uranus and Neptune, whose orbits around the Sun are very distant from Saturn. Intriguingly, no ancient Old or New World culture is supposed to have known of the existence of Uranus or Neptune – planets that cannot be seen without the aid of a telescope. How, then, could the Mesopotamians and Mayans have known so much about our

Solar System? Logically, they could only have obtained this knowledge in two straightforward ways. It was either given to them via special divine revelation, or via advanced technology that we have not yet found or do not yet understand!

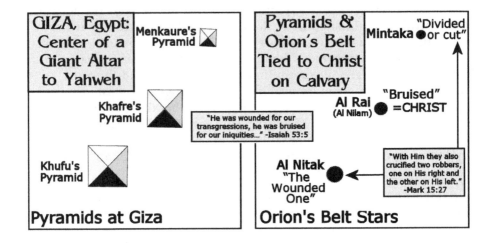

Comparison of the 3 main Giza Pyramids and Orion's belt stars

Teotihuacán's uncannily accurate representation of our Solar System is impossible to explain without some unknown source of scientific knowledge that was accessible to the ancient people who built this highly sophisticated religious site. This is also true of many other incredibly complex and scientifically thought-provoking ancient sacred sites such as the pyramid complex at Giza in Egypt. Though this knowledge could have been gained through advanced technology, it is also possible that the angelic Watchers gave this knowledge to mankind, or that Yahweh initially gave this information to mankind to incorporate into their sacred buildings through his antediluvian prophets Cainan and Enoch, who were very wise and had great spiritual knowledge.

Uncannily, as already hinted at, the three major structures at Teotihuacán - the Citadel and the Sun and Moon Pyramids - appear to mimic the belt stars of Orion just as the three biggest pyramids at Giza do. Looking at the diagram of Teotihuacán on page 376, turn it clockwise about 45 degrees. Now, compare it to the drawing showing the correlation between the belt stars of Orion and the Giza Pyramids on this page. If this is more than a coincidence, then the Temple of Quetzalcoatl represents the star Al Nitak just as the Great Pyramid does, the Pyramid of the Sun represents the middle star of Orion's Belt called Al Nilam, and the Pyramid of the Moon mimics the star Mintaka's offset alignment with the two brighter stars in Orion's Belt - just as the Pyramid of Menkaure does!

This suggests that, just as is implied at Giza, the pyramids at Teotihuacán signify the crucifixion of Christ with two robbers on either side of Him. Even more interestingly, the Pyramid of the Moon correlates with the star Mintaka in Orion's Belt, which signifies the unrepentant robber like the Pyramid of Menkaure. Amazingly, since the Pyramid of the Moon may signify the planet and god Saturn, who was also known as Kronus or Ham, it may also allegorically signify Ham's grandson Nimrod's rebellion against God - a rebellion shared by Esau, Ishmael and the robber who mocked Yahshua on the Cross.

Almost as amazing is the fact that the ancient Egyptians and Mesoamericans shared many other common cultural similarities. These include the use of hieroglyphics, mummification of the dead, leadership by lines of semi-divine kings, the use of high-prow boats made of bundled reeds, sophisticated pyramid building and architectural planning, the use of spotted leopard hides on priests and warriors, and a religion centered around star and nature worship. Yet this ancient Mesoamerican culture was supposedly separated not only by a continent and an ocean but a vast span of time from the ancient Egyptians. How then could there be such an uncanny overlap of religious and cultural ideas between the ancient Egyptians and Mesoamericans?

In Chapter Nine, we will explore the idea that the Old and New Worlds may have developed simultaneously as neighbors both before and for a few hundred years after the Great Flood. We will also discuss more about the remarkable Mayans and the pyramids at Giza in Book Four discussing Biblical and Enochian prophecies.

The Population Before The Flood

Many people wonder how there could have been a sufficient population base prior to the Great Flood to accomplish many of the technological marvels that were left behind. The immense stone and brick cities and sacred structures they left behind would have taken many thousands of skilled workers to complete. Structures like the mud-brick ziggurats of Mesopotamia and the massive stone Egyptian and American pyramids would have required many skilled people to build them in a short time using Stone Age tools. Therefore, if we believe the extremely low population estimate of less than 50,000 people per capital city or civilization center that most scholars give, it would be unlikely that these monuments could have been built prior to the Flood. However, by doing some simple math based on a biblical worldview, these low population estimates can be proven to be patently false.

Now, the Bible teaches that people lived nearly 1000 years and were usually married within their first century of life before the Great Flood. Therefore, every married couple could have had many dozens of children before they reached the end of their reproductive cycle. But for this exercise, let's assume each married couple only had eight children, which is probably well below what they actually had. But even with this low assumed birth rate, simple math proves that there were far more people living on planet Earth than there are today!

The chart on the facing page shows this amazing fact. Indeed, after only 325 years at an average birth rate, there would have been over 4.8 billion people on the Earth after Adam and Eve's Creation! Couple this low birth estimate with the extreme good health and longevity of the antediluvians, and it becomes clear that the Pre-Flood population could have been even greater by the time of the Great Flood than it is today. In fact, at the exponential rate of growth shown in the chart, there could well have been close to 100 billion people on the Earth prior to the Great Flood if it had not been for the great violence that killed so many people and Nephilim prior to it.

This is far more people than there is on the Earth today with a current world population of 6.7 billion, and a projected population of close to 7 billion by 2012 AD. Therefore, this simple math exercise clearly shows that most Evolution-touting, godless historians are very bad at estimating what the potential rate of human population growth was in the far past, especially since they are ignoring the fact that our physically and intellectually robust Pre-Flood ancestors lived in a far more environmentally idyllic climate and ate more nutrient-packed foods than we do today.

Though the heavy violence on the Earth within a hundred years of the Great Flood was responsible for killing millions of people in wars or as meals for the Nephilim, and large areas of land were ruined by wars or stripped of vegetation by voracious Nephilim giants, there were still likely many more people and animals on the planet than there is today. Sadly, however, we did not learn from our past mistakes, and many millions of people have died from violent wars and other human atrocities since the Flood. In addition, we live much shorter lives on our greatly diminished Earth than our Pre-Flood ancestors did when the Earth was much better at supporting life.

Chart: Population Growth Prior to Great Flood

Years After Creation	Human Population Growth Prior to Noah's Flood Based on a 900-Year Plus Lifespan (NOTE: 2 = 1 married couple)
Year 25	4 (4/2 = 2 couples) + 16 (2 X 8) = 20
Year 50	20 (20/2 = 10 couples) + 80 (10 X 8) = 100
Year 75	100 (100/2 = 50 couples) + 400 (50 X 8) = 500
Year 100	500 (500/2 = 250 couples) + 2,000 (250 X 8) = 2,500
Year 125	2,500 (2,500/2 = 1,250 couples) + 10,000 (1,250 X 8) = 12,500
Year 150	12,500 (12,500/2 = 6,250 couples) + 50,000 (6,250 X 8) = 62,500
Year 175	62,500 (62,500/2 = 31,250 couples) + 250,000 (31,250 X 8) = 312,500
Year 200	312,500 (312,500/2 = 156,250 couples) + 1,250,000 (156,250 X 8) = 1,562,500
Year 225	1,562,500 (1,562,500/2 = 781,250 couples) + 6,250,000 (781,250 X 8) = 7,812,500
Year 250	7,812,500 (7,812,500/2 = 3,906,250 couples) + 31,250,000 (3,906,250 X 8) = 39,062,500
Year 275	39,062,500 (39,062,500/2 = 19,531,250 couples) + 156,250,000 (19,531,250 X 8) = 195,312,500
Year 300	195,312,500 (195,312,500/2 = 97,656,250 couples) + 781,250,000 (97,656,250 X 8) = 976,562,500
Year 325	976,562,500 (976,562,500/2 = 488,281,250 couples) + 3,906,250,000 (488,281,250 X 8) = 4,882,812,500

Evidence of Earth's Catastrophic Past

In direct contrast to Uniformitarianism, which stipulates that living conditions on the Earth have changed very slowly and uniformly over long periods of time (as in Evolution), Catastrophism suggests that

periods of geological uniformity on Earth have been interrupted by one
or more catastrophic events. These events have rapidly and - at times -
drastically changed living conditions on the Earth for varying periods of
time. This was initially explored in Chapter Four of "The Language of
God in the Universe," which is the first book in the Language of God
Book Series. This chapter will re-cap the information in my first book
while adding exciting additional details.

In Chapter Nine of the Book of Job, Job tells us a bit about a past
cataclysmic event on the Earth:

> "He shakes the earth out of its place, and its pillars
> tremble." - Job 9:6 (NKJ)

Here, just as was stipulated in 1 Enoch and the Book of Jasher,
Job indicates that Yahweh shook the Earth. Indeed, Job's words suggest
that the Earth shook so violently that the "pillars" at the four corners of
the Earth trembled, suggesting that the whole world was affected. This
shaking of the Earth was likely caused by intense earthquakes and
volcanic eruptions. These could also have thrown much dust and steam
into the air, and caused torrential rain and snow to fall. In addition,
atmospheric changes could have caused a persistent darkness and
shortening of daylight hours that many ancient myths say plagued the
Earth for years.

Elsewhere, the Bible suggests that there was a tremendous
earthquake that destroyed the Tower of Babel, in which case Job may be
describing that catastrophe. In the next few sections, we will discuss
various catastrophic events that may have caused the Flood, later
destroyed Nimrod's Tower, and subsequently caused his global
totalitarian regime to end.

It has been theorized that a huge asteroid or comet impact caused
the Great Flood and the extinction of the dinosaurs or Nephilim. When
this asteroid or comet hit the Earth, our planet may have been shaken
out of its original orbit around the Sun. Some people believe that this
asteroid or comet originated when a former planet in our Solar System
collided with a large renegade planet with four moons known as Planet
X, Marduk, Nibiru or Phaeton - depending on the source.

One's definition of Planet X generally depends on one's
ideological mindset. For some, like Zecharia Sitchin's "Earth Chronicles"
book series devotees, Planet X is the code name for Nibiru or Marduk,
the home planet of the Anunnaki, the Sumerian star gods who
supposedly played a role in human evolution by altering human DNA to
make us smarter and less ape-like. For others, Planet X refers to a large
celestial body that was not necessarily the home of any alien beings, but

did play a role in the current configuration of our Solar System and may have helped to cause the Great Flood.

According to Sitchin, Marduk or Nibiru has a highly elliptical and reverse orbit to the other planets in our Solar System and may have caused the destruction of Tiamat, the primarily water planet that once existed between Mars and Jupiter and inspired Sumerian myths about the dragon goddess called Tiamat. There, the asteroid belt signifies the remains of Tiamat, and possibly the remains of one or more of Marduk's moons that may have crashed into Tiamat with deadly force in the past.

Zecharia Sitchin was the first to call Marduk the Twelfth Planet, as he believes that the eleven principle deities in the Babylonian Creation Epic known as the "Enuma Elish" are also the names of eleven planets that once existed in our Solar System. In addition to the nine previous planets in our Solar System (which has recently been reduced to eight because Pluto has been given dwarf planet status), this pantheon of planetary gods included Tiamat and Kingu, which was the primordial name for Earth's Moon, and Marduk or the Twelfth Planet that entered the scene later and usurped Tiamat's place with its moons.

The Solar System of the Antediluvians
(With Corresponding Babylonian Names Added)

In the Sumerian Solar System Sitchin sees, starting from the Sun (i.e. Shamash), there was Mercury or Mummu, Venus or Lahamu, Mars or Lahmu, Tiamat, Kingu, Jupiter or Kishar, Saturn or Anshar, Uranus or Anu, Neptune or Ea, and

Pluto or Gaga. This numbers eleven planetary bodies along with our Earth, which was known as Ki. Sitchin, however, believes that Earth did not exist before Tiamat's encounter with Marduk. Last of all in Sitchin's Cosmology was the Twelfth planet Marduk, the renegade or maverick planet that entered our Solar System after it was formed and rearranged the eleven planets already in it.

Among these planetary deities was Tiamat, a goddess that supposedly had the appearance of a great sea dragon that was associated with the primordial chaos that existed at the dawn of time. She also supposedly had a "consort" named Kingu, which Sitchin thinks became our Moon, and 11 dragon "children" or satellites. Interestingly, the sea monster Rahab that is mentioned in Job, Isaiah, and the Psalms and the fire-breathing female sea monster called Leviathan may have an allegorical connection to the Sumerian sea monster called Tiamat.

In the Enuma Elish, Tiamat is described as having given birth to many dragons and serpent beings, thereby associating Tiamat with evil. In Sumerian myth, Earth was known as Ki. However, this was also the name of a Sumerian goddess corresponding to the Greek goddess Gaia. The goddess Ki was the consort of the god Anu and supposedly gave birth to the Anunnaki (i.e. the fallen Watchers and Nephilim, who became as gods). However, the goddess Ki is most likely a primitive deification of Naamah, the daughter of the Cainite Lamech who was the first woman to beguile the vilest fallen angel of them all: Azazel.

At the time of the hypothetical impact between Marduk and Tiamat or Rahab, Tiamat and her 11 satellites were broken into pieces by one or more of Marduk's moons, though Marduk remained intact (See Isaiah 51 and Psalm 89 quoted on page 479). Tiamat's remains then formed the asteroid belt between Jupiter and Mars and many of the wandering objects in our Solar System. The other half of Tiamat was then supposedly thrown into a closer orbit around the Sun along with Kingu, which became our Moon, while a chunk of Tiamat became our Earth. This allegorically suggests that the Earth was once the literal home of Satan when it was known as Tiamat, which supposedly explains why Satan wants the Earth all to himself so badly now. However, the Bible's Creation narrative explaining how God created the Earth from a formless void negates any possibility that it is the broken remains of Tiamat.

Nonetheless, at the time of the Great Flood, it is possible that a portion of Tiamat that may have become a temporary moon of Marduk crashed into Earth, thereby causing the already existing supercontinent known as Pangaea to buckle and split apart. Interestingly, near the center of the Pacific Ocean basin, Hawaii appears to be located at the epicenter of an incredibly massive celestial impact. Such a powerful blow to one side of the Earth may have formed the Pangaea supercontinent on the other side, just as there appears to be a correlation between the mighty canyon called Valle Marinarus on one side of Mars and the Olympus Mons volcanic crater on the opposite side.

This fact seems to tie in with Sitchin's claim that Tiamat was torn in two by Marduk, with one half becoming our Earth. However, the Pacific Ocean basin looks more like an enormous impact crater than a gouge. This suggests that the Earth was smashed in on one side by the hand of God (perhaps using a portion of Tiamat when He did) in order to form dry land on the other side. Later, after mankind had fallen into sin and the Nephilim and fallen angels had corrupted everyone with violence and perversion, Yahweh sent the Flood to destroy all the wicked on the Earth. This is likely when the huge supercontinent that God had originally created broke apart.

The breakup of Pangaea can be deduced from the many impact craters and oriented lake clusters found on the Earth, as shown in the two-page illustration on pages 386 and 387. This shows superb evidence that the Earth has suffered from one or more catastrophic acts of God. In addition, *some of these impact craters may have been left by atomic-type blasts.* Remember that the Nephilim warred against one another before the Flood, and their enslaved human subjects were probably often among the victims.

The butterfly map of Earth on page 389 shows the probable direction and impact of the biggest pieces of the comet, asteroid or moon of Marduk that most likely broke up before it struck the Earth and precipitated the Flood. Furthermore, the illustration on page 388 shows how the Earth's current continents appear to fit together like the pieces of a giant jigsaw puzzle that once formed the supercontinent of Pangaea. This is clear evidence that Yahweh the Master Potter smashed the Earth and broke its one primordial landmass into pieces as easily as a man could crush a vase.

Though Tiamat is not likely to have become the Earth when it was destroyed, this now vanished planet certainly may have contributed to the Earth's current form if a Pacific Ocean-sized piece of it sank into Earth's crust and formed Pangaea! In allegorical terms, since this piece of Tiamat or Rahab would have sunk deep into a place of darkness and fire, it seems to accurately represent the coming destruction of Satan and those who follow him, and also to represent the fact that Satan and the other fallen angels are currently imprisoned inside the Earth.

Impact Crater Evidence of Earth's Catastrophic Past

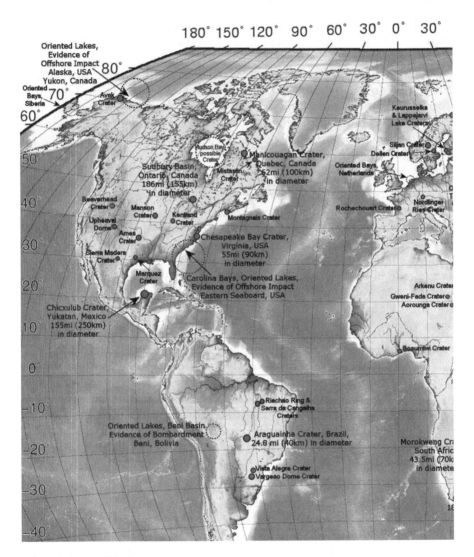

Crater Impact and Oriented Lake sites in the Western Hemisphere

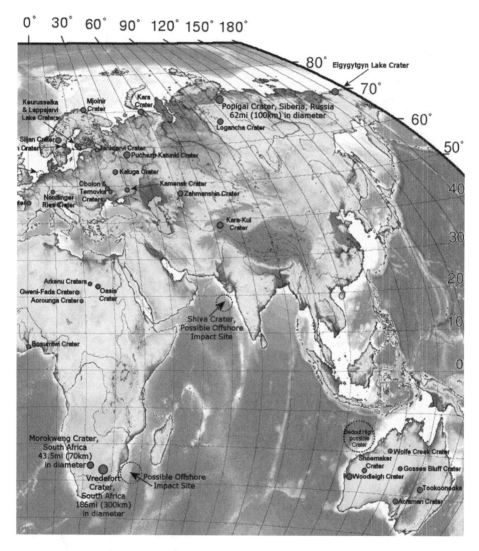

Crater Impact and Oriented Lake sites in the Eastern Hemisphere

Probable POST FLOOD Locations of Earth's Continents

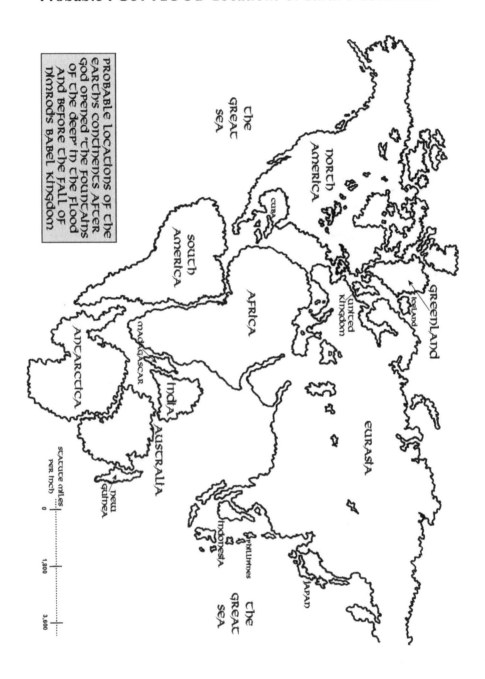

Probable Path of Celestial Bombardment Behind the Flood

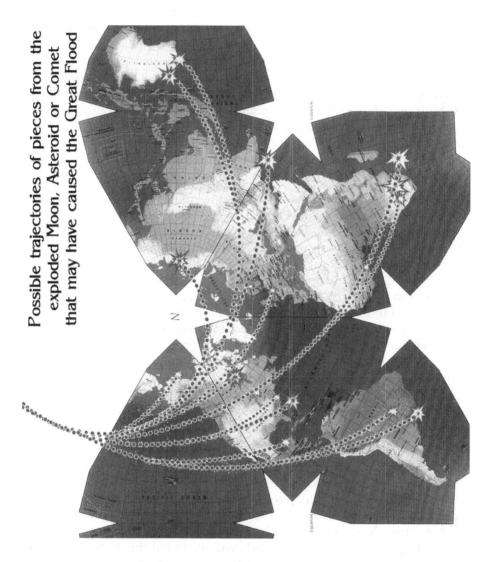

Possible trajectories of pieces from the exploded Moon, Asteroid or Comet that may have caused the Great Flood

Interestingly, the Hebrew word "rahab" means "proud" and that is what Satan is: too proud to accept mankind's dominion over him. So, just as Rahab or Tiamat was destroyed, Satan's temporary dominion over this fallen Creation will one day be completely destroyed when he is cast into the Lake of Fire with all the other fallen angels at the end of time. Thereafter, they will not be able to lead anyone into sin or roam the heavens or the Earth as astral projections ever again.

In the meantime, unlike the fallen angels who are in prison until the Great Tribulation, the holy angels who never sinned can still physically roam all of the heavenly realms, and they also have specific full-time jobs to do that preclude them spending much time in any one gathering place. They also have access to the Third Heaven where the New Jerusalem and God's symbolic Throne are located. Most ancient literature suggests that the Third Heaven was and is the primary gathering place of the angels - where they go to worship God and to fellowship with the saints and one another. Therefore, the angels do not have any other place of habitation but the Third Heaven. Nonetheless, they are so busy going about their Father's business that they currently have little time to rest - and won't until the New Heaven and New Earth are created.

Now, the Bible indicates that a supernatural war will be fought in the heavens surrounding our Earth between Satan and his angels and the archangel Michael and God's holy angels near to the beginning of the seven-year Tribulation period (Rev. 12:7-9). As a result, the fallen angels are to be kicked out of heaven and cast down to Earth, where they will setup a central command center to organize their evil activities, perhaps even in the city of Babylon located in modern-day Iraq, which was partly rebuilt by former Iraqi leader Saddam Hussein. However, it is likely that this battle between the good and evil heavenly hosts spoken of in Revelation actually occurred once in the past, after which the fallen angels were cast down to Earth and eventually imprisoned inside the Earth for their subsequent crimes against humanity. This would also explain the mythological record of a heavenly war fought between Marduk and Tiamat in the past, and why some believe that a portion of Tiamat may have sunk deep into the Earth's core.

So, though the fallen angels are currently locked in an inescapable prison beneath the surface of the Earth, they are going to be released during the Tribulation in order to face judgment. At that time, the Devil and his angels will likely attempt to conquer God's holy angels again. But they will lose and be cast down to Earth - just as they were in the past. Then, knowing that their ability to cause destruction is soon going to be stopped, the fallen angels will likely aid the Antichrist in his take over of the world by acting as if they were God's holy angels under the Antichrist's command. If so, this may be how the whole world will be deceived into thinking that the Antichrist is a cloned or reincarnated version of Yahshua that people will worship as a god.

Incidentally, much of the speculation concerning a former planet that may have been the habitation of the angels seems fairly illogical to me since the angels are supernatural beings that are able to travel between the Third Heaven where God dwells and the Earth at will. Furthermore, though angels often choose to have a distinctly human physical appearance - they can assume other fantastic shapes - as is evidenced in the biblical accounts of the Cherubim. Also, the Bible indicates that there are an *"innumerable company of angels"* (Daniel 7:10; Hebrews 12:22; Rev. 5:11). As a result, if these angels required a home outside of the Third Heaven, God would likely have given them an entire Solar System rather than a solitary planet. Therefore, it is likely that only fallen angels that have lost their transcendent qualities as a consequence of sin would need a physical planet to dwell on, and that planet has always been the Earth.

Zecharia Sitchin and those who espouse his ideas believe that the Anunnaki or fallen Watchers came to Earth from Nibiru or Marduk after the first proto humans developed by the processes of Evolution. He also believes that the Anunnaki tampered with proto human DNA to make mankind into a more intelligent and attractive slave race. The Anunnaki supposedly did this so that that humans could easily be trained to work for their angelic overlords. Sitchin also thinks the Anunnaki hoarded gold for technological and esthetic reasons and wanted humans to help them mine and extract the gold that they craved.

Some of Sitchin's followers believe that the visitation of Marduk/Nibiru into our Solar System was thousands of years after the angels fell. Others think this planet pulled the Earth slightly out of its original orbit around the Sun and caused a pole shift accompanied by many tsunamis, which the Bible records as the Flood of Noah. However, tsunamis alone were not behind the biblical account of a worldwide flood destroying all terrestrial life not in the Ark. Some also believe that another fly-by of Planet X/Marduk near to the Earth caused the destruction of the Tower of Babel and the fall of Nimrod's Babylon.

Many speculators believe that Planet X wasn't very large and it either disintegrated in Space after causing a catastrophe on Earth or that it crashed into the Sun. Others such as Immanuel Velikovsky believe that it passed very close to Earth, was slowed by its gravity and then became the planet Venus. Sitchin and others also believe that Marduk is due to return to Earth's vicinity soon and that it will cause many of the Tribulation plagues, or that it may be the catalyst for the destruction of the world predicted by the Mayan calendar, sometime on or after December 21st, 2012.

However, these theories have little likelihood of transpiring because it appears that the mysterious planet that the Babylonians named Marduk or Phaeton may recently have been discovered. Furthermore, it currently appears to be much too far away to wreak havoc in the vicinity of Earth anytime soon. As briefly discussed in Book Four, a new dwarf planet discovered in our Solar System in 2003 was named Eris after the Greek goddess of discord and strife and was subsequently inducted into our Solar System's "Hall of Fame" in late 2006. Eerily, Eris is currently visible in the constellation Cetus the Sea Monster - another symbol of Satanic strife like Rahab - and will be in Cetus for many years to come.

Now orbiting the Sun in a highly elliptical orbit beyond Pluto and the Kuiper belt, Eris is obviously not Venus - which Immanuel Velikovsky's theories suggested is Planet X. Nor has it been lost in the fiery depths of the Sun. But little else is known about Eris/Marduk except that it has at least one moon, which has ominously been named after the goddess Eris' daughter Dsnomia, a name that means "Lawlessness." The planet Eris also has a highly elliptical orbit just like Marduk supposedly had. Though Scientists have tentatively determined that Eris is not much bigger than Pluto, which is now also considered to be a dwarf planet, they are not certain of Eris' size because it is three times further out from our Sun than Pluto!

Now, due to the fact that names often have a prophetic quality, the unfortunate names given to this new dwarf planet and its moon suggests that some modern Magi or astronomers are keenly aware that the strife, discord and lawlessness prophesied about in the Bible as End Time plagues are already affecting the inhabitants of Planet Earth - and that these afflictions are bound to get worse.

In keeping with the different themes of each of the four books in my Language of God Book Series, the prophetic implications of Marduk and Tiamat as symbols in the Language of God are discussed in Book Four, "The Language of God in Prophecy." There, the most relevant aspects of the prophetic message surrounding these planets is revealed. In the meantime, the fact that these two planets have a prophetic role should be kept in mind as their potential physical affects on the Earth and our Solar System are discussed in the next section.

Earth Moved and Tilted Before the Flood

Due to the fact that the celestial bodies in our Solar System appear to be prophetic timepieces just like the stars and constellations, the suppositions made in this book concerning Marduk and Tiamat have a potential prophetic application. But to understand the explanation of their prophetic meaning that is given in Book Four, we first need to fully understand what happened to Marduk and Tiamat physically in the past.

Therefore, this section will further develop the hypothetical reconstruction of the prior effects that Marduk and Tiamat had on the Earth and our Solar System - especially as mechanisms that Yahweh may have used to cause the Great Flood.

Now, if Marduk and Tiamat encountered one another in Space on two different occasions as I and the Babylonians suppose, then at least *two successive waves of planetary fragments may have bombarded the Solar System afterward.* The first wave of impacts may have come when one or more of the supposedly seven moons of the renegade planet Marduk collided with Tiamat and broke off a massive chunk of it. Consequently, the second wave of planetary fragments may have caused much impact damage throughout our Solar System when the two planets collided - thereby destroying Tiamat and reducing Marduk in size.

During the first collision of Marduk's moons with Tiamat, a portion of Tiamat's severed rocky core - along with a large chunk of Tiamat's substantial surface water - may have been caught by Marduk's gravity as it was headed toward the Sun to make its orbit around it. It then could have been pulled through space as one of Marduk's "moons." Subsequently, God may have moved this fragment of Tiamat into a collision course with Earth. Then, when it crashed into the Earth, this enormous chunk of ice and rock may have caused the formation of the supercontinent of Pangaea.

Later, during Marduk's second approach near Earth on its orbit away from the Sun, this renegade planet may have precipitated the cataclysmic conditions necessary for the Great Flood. At that time, Marduk and its companion moons likely exerted enough of a gravitational pull on the Earth that it perturbed and tilted the planet from its original axis. This, in turn, may have caused the violent volcanic eruptions that the Book of 1 Enoch and certain legends say preceded the Flood. The highly escalated volcanism may then have created the great darkness that many mythological ancient records say preceded and followed the Great Flood. The following fragment from the Book of Noah in 1 Enoch supports these suppositions:

> *"In those days Noah saw that the earth became inclined, and that destruction approached.* Then he lifted up his feet, and went to the ends of the earth, to the dwelling of his great grandfather Enoch. And Noah cried with a bitter voice: 'Hear me; hear me; hear me;' three times. And he said: 'Tell me what is transacting upon the earth; **for the earth labors and is violently shaken. Surely I shall perish with it."** - 1 Enoch 65:1-3 (R. Laurence translation)

In this passage of 1 Enoch taken from Laurence's translation, Noah was clearly terrified by this tilting and shaking of the Earth in a major earthquake prior to the Great Flood, and this is why he sought the counsel of his great grandfather Enoch. Now let's look at a longer portion of this segment from the translation of R. H. Charles:

> *"And in those days Noah saw the earth that **it had sunk down** and its destruction was nigh. And he arose from thence and went to the ends of the earth, and cried aloud to his grandfather Enoch: and Noah said three times with an embittered voice: 'Hear me, hear me, hear me.' And I said unto him: 'Tell me what it is that is falling out on the earth that the earth is in such evil plight and shaken, lest perchance I shall perish with it?' And thereupon there was a great commotion on the earth, and a voice was heard from heaven, and I fell on my face. And Enoch my grandfather came and stood by me, and said unto me: 'Why hast thou cried unto me with a bitter cry and weeping? **And a command has gone forth from the presence of the Lord concerning those who dwell on the earth that their ruin is accomplished because they have learnt all the secrets of the angels, and all the violence of the Satans, and all their powers - the most secret ones - and all the power of those who practice Sorcery, and the power of witchcraft, and the power of those who make molten images for the whole earth."* - 1 Enoch 65:1-7*

Though worded a bit differently than Laurence's version, this section relays the same information that the Earth tilted or sank down somehow before the Flood, perhaps due to the pull of the planet Marduk's immense gravity. In addition, Marduk's gravitational pull may have precipitated a 180-degree pole shift and displacement of the Earth's crust, which would explain why what we consider the direction north today may have been considered the south prior to Noah's Flood.

The Book of 1 Enoch relays that Enoch answered Noah's cries for counsel, appeared to him, and stood beside him. By this time, Enoch had already been translated, but he may have been visiting the Garden of Eden when Noah cried out for him outside its gates. At this point, Enoch warned Noah that God was about to destroy the Earth with a worldwide flood because mankind had learned all the evil secrets of the fallen angels and Nephilim, had fallen into gross idolatry and witchcraft, and practiced the same Sorcery as the fallen angels. This sorcery may refer to genetic splicing, which means mankind may have begun to create monstrous abominations just like the fallen angels did.

It is possible that, as Marduk approached Earth, its gravitation pulled the Earth toward it, thereby tilting its axis. Furthermore, a satellite being pulled along by this planet could have entered Earth's atmosphere, where it may have broken apart into many large pieces that rapidly bombarded the supercontinent of Pangaea. If so, these collisions would have caused a massive buckling and fracturing of the Earth's crust. This, in turn, would have caused Pangaea to break apart in order to allow the fountains of the Great Deep to surge upward through the cracks. Later, this fracturing would become even more exaggerated at the time of the destruction of the Tower of Babel.

Whereas there was no Atlantic Ocean before the Flood, there was probably a narrow sea there after the Flood that would become the Atlantic Ocean during the second cataclysm that caused the Fall of Nimrod's Babel Empire. This sea may have been where the legendary island kingdom of Atlantis was located, or it may have been somewhere in the Americas, where the Atlantean civilization may really have arisen.

The impact of the fragments of this moon of Marduk or fragment of Tiamat into the Earth likely caused fountains of water to spew upward from the Great Deep. Meanwhile, a heavy rain may have begun to fall as the thick vapor and ice crystal canopy that sheltered the Earth from harsh UV radiation collapsed into Earth's lower atmosphere. How terrible it must have been for all animal life on Earth as their once perfect home was destroyed by torrents of violently surging water and flowing lava. Whatever their plans had been prior to this cataclysm, all life on Earth except that preserved on the Ark suddenly came to a terrifying, swift, and violent end. The Book of 1 Enoch adds details to this terrible time of destruction, explaining that even the fallen angels called Watchers were terrified by the cataclysm that caused the Great Flood:

> *"And all shall be smitten with fear, and the Watchers shall quake, and great fear and trembling shall seize them unto the ends of the earth. And the high mountains shall be shaken, and the high hills shall be made low, and shall melt like wax before the flame. And the earth shall be wholly rent in sunder, and all that is upon the earth shall perish, and there shall be a judgment upon all (men). But with the righteous He will make peace." - 1 Enoch 1:5-8*

Interestingly, just as the Watchers were trembling with fear in the Book of 1 Enoch, the Epic of Gilgamesh tells us that "the gods" fled the Earth in terror when the Great Flood occurred:

> **"Even the gods were afraid of the Flood weapon. They withdrew; they went up to the heaven of Anu.** *The gods*

cowered, like dogs crouched by an outside wall. Ishtar
screamed like a woman giving birth; the Mistress of the gods,
sweet of voice, was wailing." - excerpt from "Myths from
Mesopotamia," page 113, the Epic of Gilgamesh

It is highly likely that the gods or Anunnaki mentioned in the
Epic of Gilgamesh are synonymous with the fallen Watchers of the Bible.
The Epic of Gilgamesh suggests that the fallen angels were terrified and
fled into the physical heavens surrounding the Earth to watch the Flood
transpire. After this, the Book of 1 Enoch makes it clear that these
Anunnaki or fallen angels were imprisoned inside the Earth that they
witnessed being destroyed.

This mass destruction of the Earth and the annihilation of almost
all terrestrial life left the Earth forever changed. In fact, the Earth was so
badly affected that its ability to support life decreased dramatically. For
example, the first verse of 1 Enoch quoted earlier tells us *"the high hills*
shall be made low," suggesting that the mountains and valleys that
existed before the Flood would be reversed! Therefore, what were
mountaintops before the Flood became Post-Flood islands or valleys and
what were low-lying valleys or marshes at the time of the Flood may
have become hills or mountaintops. The geological topography of the
whole world was therefore drastically altered and turned topsy-turvy.
Perhaps that is partly why sea shells can be found on even the highest
mountain tops. Of course, the floodwaters that covered even the highest
mountains would have contributed to this as well.

In Enoch's prophecy about the coming flood, we are also told
"the earth shall be wholly rent in sunder." This suggests that the Earth's
surface crust would somehow be torn apart and broken up. The collision
of a massive extraterrestrial object such as a comet or asteroid with the
Earth is the only mechanism that could cause such a violent convolution
of the Earth's crust.

The Book of Jasher or Upright Record also lends support for the
idea that terrifying extraterrestrial and terrestrial events both preceded
and accompanied the Great Flood:

> *"And all the animals, and beasts, and fowls, were still*
> *there, and they surrounded the ark at every place, and the*
> *rain had not descended till seven days after. And **on that day,***
> ***the Lord caused the whole earth to shake, and the sun***
> ***darkened, and the foundations of the world raged, and the***
> ***whole earth was moved violently, and the lightning flashed,***
> ***and the thunder roared, and all the fountains in the earth***
> ***were broken up,** such as was not known to the inhabitants*

*before; and God did this mighty act, in order to terrify the
sons of men, that there might be no more evil upon earth."*

*"And still the sons of men would not return from their
evil ways, and they increased the anger of the Lord at that
time, and did not even direct their hearts to all this. And **at
the end of seven days, in the six hundredth year of the life of
Noah, the waters of the flood were upon the earth.** And all
the fountains of the deep were broken up, and the windows of
heaven were opened, and the rain was upon the earth forty
days..." - Jasher 6:10-14*

The Book of Jasher's account of the Great Flood tells us that,
**seven days prior to the arrival of the floodwaters, a terrible series of
cataclysmic convolutions of the Earth occurred**. We are told, "the Lord
caused the whole earth to shake," suggesting that terrible earthquakes
ensued. Coupled with these violent earthquakes, we are told, "the sun
darkened." This suggests that the upper atmosphere may have been
filled with smoke, dust and ash from massive volcanic eruptions. Then
we are also told that "the foundations of the world raged," and "the
whole earth was moved violently," suggesting that the Earth was
literally struck by such a massive celestial bombardment that its surface
buckled and cracked and the entire planet shifted and moved in space.
This agrees with the sinking or tilting of the Earth mentioned in the
Book of 1 Enoch that Noah saw (1 Enoch 65:1-2).

The Book of Jasher also tells us that *"the lightning flashed, and
the thunder roared,"* and *"all the fountains in the earth were broken
up,"* suggesting that this cataclysm originated in the heavens before
affecting the Earth. It therefore suggests that a massive projectile from
Outer Space could have careened into the Earth and caused the Great
Flood, lighting up the sky with lightning and filling it with a thunderous
roaring before crashing into Earth and buckling and fracturing our
planet's surface. Meanwhile, even though Noah and his kin were
sheltered inside a massive and well-equipped ship and knew God was
with them, they were as terrified by the sounds of destruction outside
the Ark as the witless animals they had preserved from destruction:

*"And the waters prevailed and they greatly increased
upon the earth, and they lifted up the ark and it was raised
from the earth. And the ark floated upon the face of the
waters, and it was tossed upon the waters so that all the living
creatures within were turned about like pottage in a cauldron.
And great anxiety seized all the living creatures that were in
the ark, and the ark was like to be broken."*

"And all the living creatures that were in the ark were terrified, and the lions roared, and the oxen lowed, and the wolves howled, and every living creature in the ark spoke and lamented in its own language, so that their voices reached to a great distance, and Noah and his sons cried and wept in their troubles; they were greatly afraid that they had reached the gates of death."

"And Noah prayed unto the Lord, and cried unto him on account of this, and he said, O Lord help us, for we have no strength to bear this evil that has encompassed us, for the waves of the waters have surrounded us, mischievous torrents have terrified us, the snares of death have come before us... And the Lord hearkened to the voice of Noah, and the Lord remembered him. And a wind passed over the earth, and the waters were still and the ark rested." - Jasher 6:27-33

In the preceding section of Jasher, we are told that the Ark *"was tossed upon the waters so that all the living creatures within were turned about like pottage in a cauldron,"* clearly indicating that the raging of the floodwaters was so severe that Noah's Ark was tossed violently about. As a result, the inhabitants of the Ark greatly feared for their lives. It is well known that flash floods can cause very violent torrents of water to surge about, destroying anything in the path of the floodwaters. As the floodwaters of this worldwide flood increased, they so violently surged about that they likely stripped the surface of the Earth utterly bare. Earth's shifting poles and buckling surface crust during the Flood, coupled with the stark barrenness of the Post-Flood Earth, are the probable mechanisms that contributed to the onset of a world Ice Age. This Ice Age possibly began immediately after the Great Flood ended, and it may have lasted one hundred years or longer.

Other evidence that there was a cosmic bombardment that severely affected Earth's climate and ability to support life at another time has been found. For example, ice core samples taken from Greenland's most ancient ice layers show that, for a geologically lengthy period in the distant past, the density of cosmic dust that settled on the Earth was over 100 times higher than it is today. **This cosmic dust in the ice was high in iridium and nickel, suggesting that it originated from the pulverized remains of a comet**. If a large comet or icy moon of Marduk once impacted the Earth at great speed and exploded into smaller bits, dust clouds would surely have formed in the upper atmosphere. These dust clouds would have taken many years to settle out, causing the prolonged period of high iridium content in the dust accumulated on the ice at the Earth's poles.

The darkened skies and colder weather resulting from this dark cloud of dust in Earth's upper atmosphere would have blocked out much sunlight. Several ancient myths and legends relay that this time of severe cold and unusual darkness lasted for a prolonged time. If it did, it would have soon caused Ice Age conditions over much of our planet. Though the dust from the comet would have settled out after several years, it is highly probable that the upper atmosphere was loaded with fine dust and ash from the massive volcanic eruptions precipitated by this proposed comet bombardment. This highly accelerated volcanic activity could feasibly have continued for many years after the Comet impact. In the Mayan Creation Myth called the Popol Vuh, the great darkness and cold that may have settled over the Earth during and/or sometime after the Flood is ominously described:

> "It was cloudy and twilight all over the world... the faces of the sun and the moon were covered." - Popol Vuh, English version by Delia Goetz and Sylvanus G. Morley

Besides this reference in the Popol Vuh, the book entitled "Maya History and Religion" by Eric J. Thompson preserves a tradition among the natives that **this period of darkness lasted twenty-six years**. If the skies were severely darkened for such a long time, this certainly could have precipitated severe Ice Age conditions all over the Earth.

Now, let me conclude this section with a note of caution. Though these tidbits of information from ancient Mayan sources offer intriguing glimpses of what may have occurred in the past, they should never be considered superior to the Bible and other Judeo-Christian accounts of past events. After reading excerpts from the Popol Vuh and the much older Babylonian Creation Epic, I discovered that they are primarily filled with fables surrounding a pantheon of bizarre deities performing inexplicable actions that seem far more human than godly. In fact, these ancient mythological treatises contain only scant references to anything historically significant, spiritually meaningful or logically truthful.

More Mythic Proof of Earth's Catastrophic Past

My search for religious writings and myths that support the concept of a cosmic catastrophe that affected the whole Earth was well rewarded. As already mentioned, the Popol Vuh and the Babylonian Epic of Creation known as the Enuma Elish are interesting source documents. But there is another mythological gem from Babylon called "The Epic of Gilgamesh" that also supports Catastrophism. It closely parallels the biblical account of the Great Flood, as seen in the following excerpt. Here, the Babylonian version of Noah named Utnapishtim gives the details of this devastating world flood to the Nephilim giant and legendary 5th King of Uruk named Gilgamesh:

> *"With everything I possessed I loaded it (i.e.: the ship)... With all that I possessed of the seed of life, I loaded it. I made to go up into the ship all of my family and kinsfolk. The cattle of the field, the beasts of the field, all handicraftsmen, I made them go up into it... I watched the approaching storm. Terror possessed me to look upon it. I went into the ship and shut the door. As soon as dawn shone in the sky, a black cloud from the foundation of heaven came up. Inside it, the god Adad thundered... En-urta went on, he made the storm to descend. The Anunnaki brandished their torches, with their glare they lighted up the land. The whirlwind of Adad swept up to heaven. Every gleam of light was turned to darkness. The land... was laid waste (or smashed like a cup)..."*

> *"Swiftly it mounted up... the water reached to the mountains (and) attacked the people like a battle. Brother saw not brother. Men could not be known (or recognized) in heaven... For six days and nights the wind, the storm raged, and the cyclone overwhelmed the land."*

> *"When the seventh day came, the cyclone ceased, the storm and battle which had fought like an army. The sea became quiet, the grievous wind went down, the cyclone ceased. I looked on the day and (all) voices were stilled, and all mankind was turned to mud."*

> *– Taken from the "Babylonian Story of the Deluge and the Epic of Gilgamesh," translated by E. A. Budge*

In the Epic of Gilgamesh, many elements of other flood myths are evident. Here we are told of the animals and people that were allowed to go onboard Utnapishtim's ship. In the Bible, only Noah, his three sons, and each man's wife are mentioned being brought onboard the Ark. The Babylonian account, however, differs in the number of people who came aboard. Not only Utnapishtim and his immediate family, but also members of his extended family and the skilled craftsmen among them were taken onboard.

Earlier, it was suggested that Noah and his family may have brought a few skilled (and spiritually and physically uncorrupted) relations, friends, and servants onboard the Ark in order to help them re-establish civilization after the Great Flood. The Babylonian Flood Epic seems to support this conclusion. Unlike the Bible, the Babylonian account also tells of the arrival of the comets that struck the land and caused countless fiery volcanic eruptions as suggested here: *"the Anunnaki brandished their torches, with their glare they lighted up the land."*

The Babylonians considered the Anunnaki to be the star gods of the night sky. The English translation of their ancient cuneiform text suggests that these "star gods" put on quite a light show in the sky before shaking up the Earth in the fiery wake of their impacts. Though they were supposedly represented by the stars and considered to be stars in their own right, however, the Anunnaki were also seen as actual deities who controlled or meddled in human affairs. As such, they correspond quite closely with the fallen angels or Watchers of Genesis 6.

We are also told of the violence and severity of the storm in the Babylonian account of the cataclysm that brought on the Flood. We are told of the cyclonic winds, the terrible darkness, the earthquakes, the water reaching to the mountaintops, and the horribly bloody deaths of countless people and animals - living things that were slaughtered as if by an army. Then, after the Flood abates, we are told of the awful silence, and the oppressive stillness of the bare and empty land - with no sign of life anywhere in the sea of mud that made up the initial Post-Flood landscape. What an awful apocalyptic scene it must have been!

Interestingly, as will be shown in Chapter Nine, various terms used to identify Noah among ancient people often meant "the far distant." This could very well be a reference to Noah as a far-seeing allegorical eagle or hawk who chose good over evil, just as eagles or hawks destroy evil when they kill and eat snakes. "The far distant" can also be a reference to the fact that Noah foresaw the Great Flood and prepared to survive it. It could also mean that Noah, as an aged wise man, was so spiritually and intellectually far ahead of other mortals that he was difficult to converse with, just like his great grandfather Enoch probably was. However, could it also refer to the place where Noah chose to reside *after* the Flood?

Let's examine the Babylonian Epic of Gilgamesh for a possible answer to that question. In this following quote from the Epic of Gilgamesh, Noah/Utnapishtim is called "the far distant:" *"Gilgamesh spoke to him, to Ut-napishtim **the far distant**..."* Now, to find Utnapishtim, Gilgamesh ventured to the mountains of Mashu, where twin mountain peaks guarded the rising and setting of the Sun. Many scholars interpret these two mountains called "Mashu" as two mountains in Lebanon. One of the two peaks is thought to be in the Lebanon Mountain range, on the western side of the fertile Beqaa Valley by the Orontes River. The other peak is considered to be a high mountain in the Anti Lebanon mountain chain, and on the eastern side of the river valley running roughly north to south through Lebanon. Gilgamesh therefore is thought to have traveled to ancient Phoenicia - the land along the eastern Mediterranean coast where modern Lebanon is located.

After arriving there, Gilgamesh befriended Urshanabi, a man who was said to be Utnapishtim's ferryman, and who ferried Utnapishtim across the sea to a distant land. With Urshanabi's help, Gilgamesh crossed the "sea" (the Mediterranean Sea?) and the "lethal waters" (the Atlantic Ocean?) by boat to a land where the Sun (identified as the Sun god Shamash) ends its transit. The place where the Sun sets is a metaphor for the Far West, which was a reference to a far distant mythical paradise where people were said to dwell after death.

Uncannily, since Noah had many ancient epithets that meant "the far distant," they suggest that he lived in the Far West. Could this be the place where Noah and his sons hid before the Flood? Furthermore, could it be the place where Noah settled after the Flood? It is possible, and the Epic of Gilgamesh lends further support for this. In it, the land far to the west of Babylonia across the "lethal waters" was called Dilmun. Though this was also the Babylonian name for Bahrain and the lands on the western shore of the Persian Gulf, many scholars equate the "lethal waters" that Gilgamesh sailed over with the Mediterranean Sea. This is because some ancient people knew the Mediterranean Sea as the Great Sea.

Now, the Great Sea was considered to be just one part of the greater world ocean surrounding all the continents on Earth. However, though it could be dangerous to traverse and many ships sank due to harsh weather over its waters, the Mediterranean Sea was generally considered safe to travel on - as long as ships hugged the shorelines. On the other hand, most ancient people considered it not only foolhardy but virtually suicidal to venture out into the very deep, cold, and unpredictable waters of the world's major oceans. Therefore, could it be possible that the body of water known as the "lethal waters" in the Gilgamesh Epic was not the Mediterranean Sea, but the Atlantic Ocean?

If the "lethal waters" meant the Atlantic Ocean, could the Dilmun that Gilgamesh visited be the lands farthest to the west of the Mediterranean Sea and across the Atlantic Ocean? In short, could Dilmun refer to the American continents? If so, the Nephilim giant **Gilgamesh may have found Utnapishtim/Noah dwelling peacefully somewhere in the Americas**. If the story of Gilgamesh is based on fact, could it be that other Nephilim giants and followers of Nimrod retraced Gilgamesh's travels to the land where Noah resided? In addition, could these Pagan invaders have eventually warred with Noah and his kin who resided in the Americas?

There is much more to this hypothesis than my own fanciful imaginings, as is clearly shown in a fascinating book called "Atlantis, the Andes Solution," by J. M. Allen. In it, he convincingly proposes that the roughly rectangular plateau high up in the Andes Mountains called the Antiplano could have been the location of Plato's Atlantis. In fact, if the Atlantic Ocean was indeed narrower in the past as stipulated in this chapter, South America would have been near to the Pillars of Hercules or Straits of Gibraltar, just as Plato said Atlantis was.

Now, though the Babylonian Flood epic gives us details about the Flood that are missing in the biblical account, this does not mean it is superior. On the contrary, the tidbits of truth found in the Babylonian account are surrounded by much larger chunks of writing about fanciful characters and events that have little basis in fact. In addition, the Babylonian account leaves out many important details that the Bible's account contains. Important examples of this include the real reasons for the Flood, the well-designed structure of the Ark that Noah built, the actual date that the Flood began, and the great length of time (one year!) that Noah, his kin, and the animals spent onboard the Ark.

The Ancient Greeks also had their own Flood myths. Finding the truth in these greatly corrupted fantasy tales, however, can be rather difficult to do unless one is familiar with the Language of God. Using God's Language, we can look behind the basic stories to find the core truths buried in each. The first of these myths concerns the stellar conflagration that may have caused the Great Flood. It is explained in the Greek myth that surrounds Phaeton. Phaeton was considered to be the son of the Sun god Helios. To give light to the world, Helios drove a golden chariot through the heavens each day. One day Phaeton made an ill-fated attempt to drive the Sun chariot. Being inexperienced, however, Phaeton drove it too close to the Earth, threatening to destroy the world with fire and terrible heat.

In order to stop Phaeton on the runaway chariot, Zeus hurled a thunderbolt at him, but this only made matters worse. Instead of ending the danger to humanity, Phaeton was killed by Zeus' thunderbolt and, with no one to guide it, the chariot of the Sun crashed into the Earth. Since Zeus is also singled out in Greek myth as causing the Great Flood, it is possible that this devastating fiery impact from Outer Space supposedly caused by Zeus may have precipitated the Great Flood.

The second Greek myth concerning the Great Flood focuses on Deucalion, the son of the Titan called Prometheus. Prometheus was supposedly a rebellious Titan who gave humanity many gifts, including the gift of fire. Zeus, however, was very angry with Prometheus and those Titans who followed him for helping humanity without Zeus' express permission. Zeus therefore plotted a horrible revenge. Forewarned by Prometheus of Zeus' plan to exterminate the Titans and all humanity with a Great Flood, Deucalion and his wife Pyrrha are said to have built a box-like ship (i.e. Ark) out of wood in an attempt to survive. Their attempt was successful, and after the rains ceased and floodwaters abated, their Ark supposedly ran aground on top of Mount Parnassus in Greece. As soon as they left the ark, Deucalion and Pyrrha offered up a sacrifice to thank the gods for their deliverance.

Like the Babylonian flood epic, this Greek flood myth has close parallels with the story of Noah in the Bible. The Titans, for example, can be equated with the Nephilim who dominated human society prior to the Flood, and who were the reason Yah wanted to destroy all life on Earth. Though in the Greek myths they are depicted as quasi-benevolent, the Titans/Nephilim were evil beings. Since the Titans/Nephilim were evil, it is certain that a Titan never fathered Noah/Deucalion. In fact, it was the genetic corruption of humanity with Nephilim blood, and the spread of their rebellion against God that Yahweh wanted to stop by bringing on the Great Flood! But, as will be shown in Chapter Seven, the Greeks demonized Noah and the Sethites by depicting them as Titans (i.e. Nephilim) in their mythology. In effect, though the Greeks saw Sethite contributions to civilization as beneficial in some respects, Sethite religious beliefs were seen as inferior to the Way of Cain that the deified human Olympian "gods" followed.

The Bible tells us that only Noah was *"perfect in his generations,"* meaning that his blood was untainted with Nephilim genes and free of the gross spiritual corruption that accompanied Nephilim influences. This genetic purity was passed down to Noah's children. Like Deucalion, Noah built an Ark and brought his family on board along with representatives of all terrestrial life (Genesis 6:18-22). Then they were sealed in to survive the most devastating flood in history. Meanwhile, outside the Ark, all life was destroyed, including genetically corrupted humans and Nephilim giants (though, as will be shown, some Nephilim survived to reek havoc on the Earth after the Flood).

After landing in the mountains of Ararat and waiting for sufficient dry land to appear, Noah left the ark and then almost immediately offered a sacrifice - just as Deucalion did. Like Deucalion, Noah did so to thank God for preserving the life of he and his family, and to ask Yah to continue to protect them (Genesis 8:18-20). Touched by his sacrifice, Yahweh blessed Noah and promised that a flood would never destroy the world again. Then Yahweh set a rainbow in the sky as a sign of His perpetual Covenant promise to Noah - a promise that also extended to all Noah's descendents forever (Genesis 9:1-17).

Another later example of a catastrophic myth that has a few points in common with the biblical account is found in the Mayan Creation Myth. Later known as the "Popol Vuh" by the Quiche' natives of Central America, the Mayan Creation Myth describes a universal flood that destroyed almost all life on Earth. The Popol Vuh tells us that great darkness accompanied this terrible flood:

> "And so a flood was brought about by the Heart of Heaven; a great flood was formed which fell on the heads of the wooden creatures... A heavy resin fell from the sky... the face of the earth was darkened and a black rain began to fall by day and by night... the wooden figures were annihilated, destroyed, broken up, and killed." - Popol Vuh, English version by Delia Goetz and Sylvanus G. Morley

Though startling in their similarity to Biblical and Babylonian flood epics, these fragments from the Popol Vuh are scattered throughout a largely fanciful account of the exploits of several Mayan gods. However, though immersed in a sea of fanciful writings, the excerpts recorded here seem to pertain to a real event: the Great Flood.

The Zoroastrians of pre-Islamic Persia/Iran also preserved recollections of similar past disasters. For example, their religious writings contain a story about a Noah-like character named Yima. In the following excerpt, the Zoroastrian Creator god Ahura Mazda instructs Yima on how to survive both the Flood and the Ice Age that occurred after the Flood in an Ark-like structure called a "var:"

> "Then said Ahura Mazda to Yima saying 'Fair Yima... **bad winters will come to the material world**, therewith the cloud will snow abundantly with snow, from the highest mountains to the depths of the Aredvi (i.e. the great "river" or world ocean)... Before that winter the land will have well cared for pasture. **Water in abundance will carry this away**. Then after the melting of the snow, O Yima, it will be a marvel for the material world if here is seen the footprint of a sheep. Then make that var with each of its four sides a stadium-length... At the same time, fetch seed of small cattle and large cattle and men and dogs and red burning fires... At the same time, fetch the seed of all men and women (and all cattle) who

are the tallest, best, and fairest upon earth... fetch the seed of
all flowers which are the most fragrant... For light, put in a
door, a window...'" – taken from "Textual Sources for the
Study of Zoroastrianism"

This Aryan account of a man's survival of the Flood and
subsequent Ice Age has many tie-ins with the story of Noah's Flood.
However, it suggests that the precipitation during the Great Flood was
as much from snow as it was from rain! Thus, a devastating flood of rain
and snow could well have been the mechanism by which God destroyed
all life on Earth. The terrible bitter cold and the ice that may have
encompassed the world following the Flood surely would have caused
drastic changes in Earth's overall climate. The coming of this Ice Age is
also remembered in the mythology of the natives of South America.
There, Toba natives still tell this story:

"Asin told a man to gather as much wood as he could
and to cover his hut with a thick layer of thatch, because a
time of great cold was coming. As soon as the hut had been
prepared, Asin and the man shut themselves inside and
waited. When the great cold set in, shivering people arrived to
beg a firebrand from them... The people were freezing, and
they cried the whole night. At midnight, they were all dead,
young and old, men and women... **this period of ice and sleet**
lasted a long time *and all the fires were put out. Frost was as*
thick as leather." - taken from "The Mythology of South
America" by John Bierhorst

Along with this short passage that supports the coming of an Ice
Age after the Flood, all the myths, religious writings and scientific
hypotheses explored in this chapter reveal that, in addition to the Great
Flood, smaller-scale cataclysmic disasters have probably occurred at
various times in Earth's history. Though, in all likelihood, an Ice Age
certainly followed the Flood, it is possible that the time of intense cold
described in these myths could have come at a later time.

Indeed, biblical and mythical evidence seems to suggest that
another cataclysm struck the Earth about 300 to 350 years after the Flood.
This would have been when Yah destroyed the Tower of Babel and
overthrew Nimrod's world dictatorship. In addition, another shorter Ice
Age lasting around 100 years may have followed the Fall of Nimrod's
Babylon. Though it isn't necessary for the Earth to have actually moved
in space for Nimrod's empire to have been destroyed, there is evidence
that a cataclysmic 180-degree pole shift occurred either at that time or the
time of the Great Flood. This shift would have flipped Earth's magnetic

poles and triggered or sped up the processes of continental drift and plate tectonics.

God's Celestial Calendar Preserved Despite Cataclysms

Though pole shifts may have occurred and Earth's orbit around the Sun may have been altered, however, it is my belief that Yahweh made sure that these deviations did not affect the meaning of the Gospel in the Stars or the way time is kept from Earth. Otherwise, God's once perfect prophetic calendar would no longer be effective. Since Yahweh created the stars to give us guidance and to show us when His plans for the future would unfold, it makes sense that He would have made sure that the deviation between the 364-day antediluvian year and the 365.242 day Post-Flood year would not affect His prophetic calendar, though human tampering with God's original celestial model for keeping time has affected it. For example, Enoch indicated that people of his era had gotten into the erroneous habit of seeing the year as only 360 days long, thereby ignoring the four crucially important intercalary days in Enoch's 364-day year:

> *"The leaders of the heads of the thousands, who are placed over the whole creation and over all the stars, have also to do with the four intercalary days, being inseparable from their office, according to the reckoning of the year, and these render service on the four days which are not reckoned in the reckoning of the year." - 1 Enoch 75:1-2*

> *"Their four leaders who divide the four parts of the year enter first; and after them the twelve leaders of the orders who divide the months; and for the three hundred and sixty (days) there are heads over thousands who divide the days; and for the four intercalary days there are the leaders which sunder the four parts of the year." - 1 Enoch 82:11-12*

These Scriptures indicate that the four intercalary days of Enoch's calendar actually helped divide up the year into four equal 90-degree parts or seasons. In addition, the intercalary days seem to have been associated with the four fixed signs of the Zodiac, the four corners and four winds of the Earth, the four seasons, and the Solar Equinoxes and Solstices that mark the changing seasons.

Besides the deviation in length between the Pre and Post Flood years, the Precessional movement or wobble of the Earth has affected the way humanity views and keeps time. However, though it is possible that the full Precessional length of time of approximately 25,800 years did not apply prior to the Flood, Enoch hinted that there was a big tilt in the Earth's orbit when he talked about the length of the daylight hours at various times in the year. As already discussed in Chapter Three, it appears that Enoch was either in a far northern or southern latitude when Uriel showed him how to construct a henge.

Nonetheless, Earth's Precessional movement may have increased somewhat in length since then as the wobble of the Earth seems to be degrading. In other words, the Earth is acting like a spinning top that is slowing down. As the spin of a top decreases, its wobble to the sides will increase. As a result, if this is the case with Earth's wobble, one Precessional Cycle of time was likely a bit shorter in the past than the 25,800 years it is today, but not appreciably so. However, this is partly why figuring the length of a year by degrees instead of days makes sense when attempting to time Yahweh's prophetic calendar.

It seems logical that, though the four intercalary days rightly figured in the length of the actual antediluvian year and seem to have been connected to the four corners of the Earth's horizon, they did not need to be counted when measuring the year because Enoch used degrees and not days to measure years. Therefore, due to Earth's cataclysmic past, a prophetic year is likely not 360 days long, but is equal to 360 degrees of celestial time. This would have made each year identical in measure to the rest - no matter how much Earth's year may have varied over the millennia.

Interestingly, according to 1 Enoch, Chapter 79, the Lunar Year was exactly 2 X 177 or 354 eighteen-part days before the Flood, which was exactly 10 days shorter than the Solar Year of 364 eighteen-part days. Though our current Solar Year is 1.242 days longer than the Pre-Flood year, the Lunar Year did not change. Perhaps that is why many ancient Post Flood societies used an inferior Lunar calendar - particularly the Israelites. Though figuring years by the 360-degree circle of the Zodiac makes each year measure the same regardless of the number of days it has, the Pre and Post-Flood Lunar Year was and still is almost exactly 354 days.

Alas, though our Solar and Lunar Years are nearly the same as they were before the Flood, the surface of the Earth and its ability to support life were drastically changed and affected by past cataclysms like the Great Flood and Fall of Nimrod's Babylon. Volcanic eruptions during these two violent upheavals could explain the unusual darkness that various myths speak of - sometimes in association with a massive flood. Volcanic eruptions may well have caused this terrible darkness that engulfed the Earth in gloom both day and night. Some scholars feel that this prolonged darkness may have been responsible for the Ice Age that preceded the Great Flood. According to some myths, this *great period of darkness lasted for as long as 25 years*. Could it be that this period of darkness also occurred three hundred years after the Great Flood during the reign of Nimrod?

Besides suggesting that the Earth has been shaken away from its original place in the Universe, Job 9:6 refers to "pillars." Some scholars feel that what Job meant by pillars were the imaginary pillars located at "the ends of the Earth," which is most likely an ancient term for the celestial equator. The ancient Babylonians, Egyptians, and Greeks believed four pillars held up the vault of heaven where the stars were located. These imaginary pillars were also said to mark the movements of the Sun, Moon, planets and certain stars along the horizon as they moved through time. In the Book of 1 Enoch, these pillars are mentioned in connection with the four winds of heaven:

> *"I saw the four winds which bear [the earth and] the firmament of the heaven. And I saw how the winds stretch out the vaults of heaven, and have their station between heaven and earth: these are the pillars of the heaven." - 1 Enoch 18:3-4*

These pillars divided the sky into four sections used in astronomical calculations. They correspond to the four fixed Zodiac signs known as Taurus, Aquarius, Scorpio and Leo. These were used to mark the positions of the thirty-six ancient decan constellations in relation to the position of the Sun. By noting the helical rising of the major star in the decan sign visible just before dawn and its proximity to one of the four Zodiac pillar signs, the heavenly locations of the other decan signs could be determined.

Having discovered the correlation of the star Sirius in the decan constellation called Canis Major with Bethlehem and Jerusalem, I find it intriguing that the ancients were especially fascinated with the helical rising of this star. The ancient Egyptians originally named this star "Seir," or "Prince." Later, when they fell into gross Paganism, the Egyptians re-named Sirius after their goddess Sothis or Sopdet.

The star Sirius is special for three major reasons. First of all, it is the brightest star in the heavens, and it is rivaled in luminosity only by the planet Venus. Secondly, it is the only one of the over two thousand visible stars that rises after a brief disappearance in the heavens every 365.25 days, a figure known as the Sothic year that is almost identical with our current Solar Year of 365.242 days, and the Sidereal Year of 365.25636 days. Third, as already discussed, Sirius is the heavenly counterpart to the terrestrial locations of Bethlehem and Jerusalem -

where God would be born as a man, would preach the Good News of Salvation by Grace to His lost sheep, and would save mankind by His righteous shed blood and His resurrection into everlasting life.

Perhaps that is initially why the ancient Egyptians marked the beginning of their years by the heliacal rising of the star Sirius, and kept track of the 1,460-year period called the Sothic Cycle. This cycle marks the astronomical point when the beginning of the Sothic Year of the Egyptians perfectly coincided with the beginning of the Solar Year. In this way, the Lunar, Solar, and Sothic Year could be reconciled every 1,460 years. Due to the significance of the Sothic Year and Sothic Cycle, many ancient people likely saw the star Sirius as the most notable of the morning stars preceding the Sun at dawn. This was especially true among the ancient Egyptians, and the Pre-Columbian indigenous people of North, Central and South America.

Since the Earth and our Moon likely shifted in space during the cataclysm that caused the Earth to shake from its place, the view of the night sky also changed. As a result, the pillars that formed the old stone henges or astronomical "clocks" had to be realigned somewhat to fit the new appearance of the heavens. There is clear evidence that many ancient sites aligned with the Sun, Moon, stars, and planets were changed to reflect different heavenly alignments. This is evident at Stonehenge and in many temples of ancient Egypt - whose entrances directly face the rising sun or a particular star at a very specific time of the year. However, none of these realignments show a big deviation in the course of the Sun along the ecliptic. They therefore preserve the knowledge that *changes in the Earth's tilt over the millennia have been very minimal at best,* and did not appreciably affect the length of our year or how we perceive the Zodiac along the plane of the ecliptic.

The ecliptic is the band of the sky that the Sun appears to pass through each day, and the moon and planets pass through at night. Since the Earth is tilted at an odd angle to the ecliptic, the Zodiac progresses in an off-center circle through our sky at night. The celestial band of the Zodiac is inclined 23-1/2 degrees to the celestial equator, which follows the Earth's equator. There is a theory that, before the Flood, the Earth's equator was aligned with the plane of the ecliptic, and this would have caused the Earth's overall climate to be far warmer and milder. This is based on the supposition that the Earth's current 23-1/2 degree tilt is the primary cause of the severe weather, storms, and blizzards that afflict the world yearly.

The theory that the Earth's off-center tilt causes bad weather is often used to explain why antediluvian people and animals lived far longer than we do today, and why - based on much fossil evidence - the world was far more lush and green back then. However, this theory has one serious flaw. As shown in Chapter Three, the chart on page 95 that was derived from Chapter 72 of the Book of 1 Enoch shows that the Earth had greatly shortened winter days and elongated days in the summer in Enoch's time just as it does today. Furthermore, prehistoric henges all over the world indicate that the Sun still rises and sets close to where it did when Enoch walked the Earth. This means that the Earth had a tilted axis before the Flood that was similar to the one it has now.

Another proof that the Earth's tilt is nearly identical to what it was prior to the Great Flood can be found by looking at the compass orientation of the Pillar of Enoch. Amazingly, the north face of this enormous pyramid is aligned almost perfectly with true north even though it was built prior to the Flood. It therefore suggests that our current view of the sky and reckoning of time was almost identical when the Great Pyramid was built.

While some scholars have used the miraculous state of preservation of the Pillar of Enoch to push its Post-Flood origin as a construction of the patriarch Joseph, it is far more probable that Yahweh made sure that the past celestial alignments necessary for Sacred Astronomy to work properly still exist today. Nonetheless, it is an intriguing thought that Joseph, whose tribe is affiliated with the sign of Taurus, would have been able to marvel at all five Old Kingdom pyramids at least a thousand years after they were built.

Since Joseph would have had ample opportunity to explore this architecture as Vizier of all Egypt, one wonders if he understood the grand spiritual message that they beckon people to find in the Star Gospel in the night sky. Did Joseph know that the belt of Orion and Taurus' horns were connected to the pyramids at Giza and Dahshur, or that they symbolized God's glorious plans for Israel to become a blessing to the whole world through the coming Messiah as well as Joseph's own two sons? Considering Joseph's education via his father Jacob who was a master Astronomer like his father Abraham per the Book of Jasher (Jasher 53:17-21), it is likely that Joseph did. Indeed, the Upright Record states that Joseph had his own star chart of the constellations in the night sky and that he and his brother Benjamin expertly knew how to read the Gospel in the Stars as it pertained to them:

> "And he ordered them to bring before him his map of the stars, whereby Joseph knew all the times, and Joseph said unto Benjamin, 'I have heard that the Hebrews are acquainted with all wisdom, dost thou know anything of this?' And Benjamin said, 'Thy servant is knowing also in all the wisdom which my father taught me,' and Joseph said unto Benjamin,

*'Look now at this instrument and understand where thy
brother Joseph is in Egypt...'* **And Benjamin beheld that
instrument with the map of the stars of heaven, and he was
wise and... divided the whole land of Egypt into four
divisions,** *and he found that he who was sitting upon the
throne before him was his brother Joseph... And Benjamin
said... 'I can see by this that Joseph my brother sitteth here
with me upon the throne,' and Joseph said unto him, 'I am
Joseph thy brother, reveal not this thing unto thy brethren;
behold I will send thee with them when they go away, and I
will command them to be brought back again into the city,
and I will take thee away from them." - Jasher 53:18-21*

Benjamin's ability to know that his brother Joseph was sitting
next to him by viewing the positions of the stars and planets on the star
chart that Joseph presented to him was based on Joseph's amazing
dream in Genesis 37:6-12. There, Joseph saw his brothers as stars, his
father as the Sun and his mother as the Moon. Thus, **Joseph's dream and
the Book of Jasher indicate that the Zodiac prophetically records the
location and destiny of the Twelve Tribes of Israel throughout time.**

The Days of Noah, Noah's Ark, and the Rapture

Since this chapter is devoted to exploring the Flood of Noah
within the context of the Language of God, the following two sections
have been included to show the inspiring message of redemption,
salvation and grace locked within the biblical Flood narrative.

Beyond the connotations given in Chapter One of an Ark as both
a tomb and a womb, Noah's Ark symbolizes the salvation we obtain
when we believe in Christ and the spiritual rebirth we obtain through
the indwelling presence of Christ's Spirit. Righteous Noah and his family
were saved in the Ark and carried to safety while the rest of humanity
perished in terror. Likewise, we who accept Yahshua as our Savior and
actively seek to know Him are protected and promised eternal life. We
too are carried away to safety by His Spirit and sheltered from harm by
His incredible love and provision for us. All believers who actively pray
and seek Yahshua's Will in their lives can and will receive miraculous
protection. That is why there will likely be a Pre-Wrath Rapture or
catching up of the Church to Heaven before the last half of the
Tribulation. This can be deduced from the Scriptures where Yahshua
alludes to Noah and the Ark:

"For as in the days before the flood, they were eating and drinking, marrying and giving in marriage, until the day that Noah entered the ark, and did not know until the flood came and took them all away, so also will the coming of the Son of Man be. Then two men will be in the field: one will be taken and the other left. Two women will be grinding at the mill: one will be taken and the other left. Watch therefore, for you do not know what hour your Lord is coming." - Matthew 24:38-42 (NKJ)

This time when some people will be taken to be with Yahshua while others are to be left behind cannot occur at the end of the Great Tribulation, since this will be the worst time of trouble that will ever befall the Earth. Rather, this Scripture suggests that it must be a relatively peaceful time. This could only be just before or at the beginning of the Tribulation period - *before* the plagues of Revelation adversely affect the Earth. At that time, those who are taken will go to Heaven to the Lamb's Wedding Supper. Those who are left behind, however, are to suffer through the Great Tribulation.

Remember that Noah and his family were separated from the ungodly and carried to safety in the Ark while the wicked perished. In a similar manner, those who are deemed righteous through Christ's shed blood will be separated and carried away to safety in Heaven while the Earth is gripped in a horrible time of trouble. As already stated, it will be the worst cataclysmic apocalypse the world has seen since the days of the Great Flood:

*"At that time Michael shall stand up, the great prince who stands watch over the sons of your people; and **there shall be a time of trouble, such as never was since there was a nation, even to that time.** And at that time your people shall be delivered, every one who is found written in the book. And many of those who sleep... shall awake, some to everlasting life, some to shame and everlasting contempt." - Daniel 12:1 (NKJ)*

Like many prophetic passages of the Bible, these verses from the Book of Daniel refer to *several sets of events* that occur in succession. First, it mentions the archangel Michael, who some believe is a reference to Christ in His Preincarnate form. However, Christ is *never* called by the name of Michael anywhere in the Bible, but rather by the phrase: *"the Angel of the LORD."* This angel is a far greater angel or messenger than Michael because He frequently identifies Himself as God (Genesis 16:7-13; 31:11-13; Judges 2:1-3, 6:11-23). This means that the Angel of the LORD is really the Preincarnate Christ and not a true angel at all.

Yahshua is also called *"the image of the invisible God"* (Col. 1:15), *"the Son of God"* (i.e. fully God: Mat. 14:33), and *"the Son of Man"* (i.e. fully human: John 6:53). Rather than being a reference to Christ, then, the reference to Michael standing up in Daniel 12:1 likely means that - when Christ orders it - the archangel Michael will lead the battle with Satan and his evil angels spoken of in the Book of Revelation:

> *"And war broke out in heaven: Michael and his angels fought with the dragon; and the dragon and his angels fought, but they did not prevail, nor was a place found for them in heaven any longer. So the great dragon was cast out, that serpent of old, called the Devil and Satan, who deceives the whole world; he was cast to the earth, and his angels were cast out with him..." "Therefore rejoice, O heavens, and... Woe to the inhabitants of the earth and the sea! For the devil has come down to you, having great wrath, because he knows that he has a short time." - Rev 12:7-9, 12 (NKJ)*

Though the Book of Revelation allegorically refers to events that occurred in the early Church due to Jewish and Roman persecution, it was primarily meant to reveal events that will happen during the Last Day or Great Day of the Lord, as is proven in Book Four. Therefore, it is likely that this war in heaven may have occurred once before but will occur a second time during the Great Tribulation, when great disturbances in the appearance and behavior of the Sun, Moon, and Earth will occur:

> *"But in those days, after that tribulation, the sun will be darkened, and the moon will not give its light; the stars of heaven will fall, and the powers in heaven will be shaken. Then they will see the Son of Man coming in the clouds with great power and glory." - Mark 13:24-26 (NKJ)*

Notice that, in the preceding Scripture, it says *"in those days, after that Tribulation."* However, upon studying the Greek root words for this phrase, it appears to be mistranslated and should instead say: *"in that day, amid this Tribulation."* This means that *"the stars of heaven will fall"* during the Tribulation on the Lord's Day, or Day of the Lord. See Book Four for the meaning of the many celestial signs that will occur during the Tribulation.

Concerning one of those celestial signs, the Book of Revelation indicates that the satanic Red Dragon's *"tail drew a third of the stars of heaven, and threw them to the earth"* (Rev. 12:4). Therefore, when these stars or angels fall from heaven, they may be physically accompanied by a very intense and destructive meteor shower. But before this,

Revelation 12:7-9 implies that the first act of these fallen angels will be to band together and make war in heaven with God's holy angels. At this time, the Archangel Michael will lead the angelic armies of God to defeat Satan and his angels, and cast them down to Earth once more. These fallen angels will then lead a third of the lost souls whose names are not written in the Book of Life into eternal damnation (Rev. 20:15).

Though it is not directly stated in Revelation 9:1-11 that these evil angels will be released with Satan (i.e. Apollyon) from the bottomless pit during the Great Tribulation, it is inferred by the release of the many locust-like creatures with the faces of men, hair of women, iron-clad bodies, and tails with scorpion-like stingers that will torment mankind for five months. In fact, the fallen angels likely will create this future army of locust-like monsters via genetic splicing - just like they did in the past. If so, then - in addition to the 200 million possibly Nephilim soldiers riding upon the two-headed Sauropod-like "horses" described in Revelation 9:17-19 - a small but deadly variety of Nephilim will appear to destroy the wicked during the Great Tribulation.

As discussed earlier in this book, the heavens are a prophetic witness to us, and when Yahshua said that *"whatever you bind on earth will be bound in heaven, and whatever you loose on earth will be loosed in heaven"* (see Matthew 16:19), He meant that - just as a disciple's actions on behalf of Christ will change the outcome of events on Earth - our heavenly Father has ensured that these heroic deeds affect the physical heavens surrounding our Earth to reflect those changes. In other words, the heavens surrounding the Earth literally mirror the spiritual destiny of mankind and God's Will as it is carried out in history. This is also why, as was shown in Book One, the Magi who believed in Sacred Astronomy could use it to pinpoint and honor the birth of our Messiah. See Book Four for more about future celestial events that may mark the times when God's Will for the End Times is to be carried to fruition on Earth.

When Satan and the evil angels who follow him are cast down to Earth again during the Great Tribulation, they will increase the wickedness perpetrated against the Tribulation Saints by all the unrepentant people who will follow the Antichrist and the False Prophet. In fact, the fallen angels may be cast down to Earth at the same time as another celestial event spoken of in Revelation:

> *"And a great star fell from heaven, burning like a torch, and it fell on a third of the rivers and on the springs of water." - Revelation 8:10 (NKJ)*

This leads back to my discussion of Daniel, Chapter 12, where the Great Tribulation is being referred to with the words: *"there shall be a time of trouble, such as never was since there was a nation, even to that time."* In the very next verse, the Rapture is being referred to. This is when Yahshua will steal away His Bride to attend the Wedding Supper of the Lamb. Therefore, rather than the Great White Throne Judgment, which will occur after the Millennial Rule of Christ, the next passage refers to the affects of the Rapture, when God's *"people shall be delivered, every one who is found written in the book. And many of those who sleep... shall awake, some to everlasting life, some to shame and everlasting contempt"* (Daniel 12:1).

The book being referred to by Daniel is likely the Book of Life mentioned in the Book of Revelation nine times. Could this Book of Life also be referring to the Mazzaroth or Zodiac, which forms the Heavenly Tablets spoken of in 1 Enoch and the Book of Jubilees? As already shown, Enoch's Heavenly Tablets refer to the Zodiacal Star Gospel, where the eternal deeds of Christ, His holy angels, and His redeemed saints are forever recorded, and where the evil deeds of Satan and his followers will one day likely be omitted or erased - just like the stars that fall from heaven in Revelation, which may occur in a literal as well as spiritual way. If this is true, then the record of the godly deeds of men and angels may be reflected in the New Heaven mentioned in Revelation, which likely refers to the physical heavens that will surround the New Earth.

The Ark of Noah was a place of safety, just as the Rapture to attend Christ's heavenly Wedding Supper will be. However, just as the Great Flood was a time of death and destruction, the Great Tribulation before the Second Coming of Christ marks a time of condemnation and death for anyone whose name is not found written in the Book of Life, or Heavenly Tablets.

Beyond the womb, prehistoric burials, and Noah's great Ark of the Flood, another Ark figures prominently in God's revealing of Himself, but this Ark did not appear until long after the Flood. As we shall see in Book Four, the Ark of the Covenant was prefigured before the Flood within the internal structure of the Great Pyramid. This direct correlation between a sacred structure built before the Flood with a sacred structure built after the Flood in honor of Yahweh God is clear evidence that our ancestors were spiritually well-informed, and likely as knowledgeable about Yahweh as biblically schooled believers are today.

The Days of Noah and the Autumn Feasts of Israel

Interestingly, as discussed in Book Two, Noah's Flood began on the seventeenth day of the second Lunar Month. Now, besides the numerous signs in the heavens on that seventeenth day that proclaimed the coming of the Flood, the first seventeen days of that month appear to be a mirror of the seventeen days between Rosh Hashanah or the Feast of Trumpets and the first day of the Feast of Tabernacles or Sukkot. Furthermore, as explained in Book Two, the prophetic nature of these autumn feasts relate to Yahshua's Second Coming and have not been fulfilled yet. To understand the connection between these autumn Feasts and the days of Noah, let's look at the Bible's account of the days just before the Flood:

> "For after seven more days I will cause it to rain on the earth forty days and forty nights, and I will destroy from the face of the earth all living things that I have made... Noah was six hundred years old when the floodwaters were on the earth. **And it came to pass after seven days that the waters of the flood were on the earth. In the six hundredth year of Noah's life, in the second month, the seventeenth day of the month,** on that day all the fountains of the great deep were broken up, and the windows of heaven were opened. And the rain was on the earth forty days and forty nights." - Genesis 7:4-7, 10-12 (NKJ)

In Book Four, which I initially finished two years before this book, I discussed a prophetic word of knowledge that the Holy Spirit gave to me concerning the autumn Feast Days of Israel. According to the word that I received, the seventeen days that fall between Rosh Hashanah or the Feast of Trumpets, and the first day of the Feast of Tabernacles or Sukkot are tied to Yahshua's words that the Tribulation would occur at a time similar to the days of Noah. As carefully explained in Book Four, the years 2000 through 2010 may be tied to the ten days between Rosh Hashanah and Yom Kippur or the Day of Atonement. This is related to the fact that Noah entered the Ark on the tenth day of the second month, and the Flood waters began to rain down upon the Earth seven days later. The fact that Noah entered the Ark on the 10th day of the month may correlate with an extra ten year period of God's mercy prior to the Tribulation. But even after that, God gave all the people outside the Ark another seven days of leniency to repent before the rains of the Flood came This seven days could be tied to the seven-year Tribulation. In Noah's Day, the people did not repent - even after the waters of the Flood came down, and they tried to break into that Ark, to

no avail. This lack of repentance will also be true of the Tribulation
Period. (See Rev. 2:21; Rev. 9:20-21; Rev. 16:9-11)

Since God rested on the seventh day or Saturday, the Sabbath is
tied to the number seven. Prophetically, therefore, the number seven
signifies completion, fullness, rest, and worship in the Bible. In addition,
the seven day week ending on Saturday is the basis of the Hebdomadal
Cycle of 52 seven-day weeks per Solar year in the Gregorian calendar.
So, the seven days between Noah's entrance into the Ark and the
beginning of the Flood are prophetically tied to a specific period of time.

Just as Noah was hidden in the Ark for seven days before the
entire world was judged, the saints taken in the Rapture will be hidden
away in Heaven with Yahshua for 1,260 days or 3-1/2 years while the
Great Tribulation rages on Earth (Rev. 12:1-5). Fascinatingly, this division
of ten days and seven days that came before the Great Flood appears to
tie in to the first seventeen years of this third millennium after
Yahshua's birth. Interestingly, the Moon appears full on the 14th and
15th days of its cycle, and on the 17th day it is beginning to noticeably
show that it is waning. Allegorically, therefore, a waning Moon signifies
a dying person, or one that chooses to ignore their full spiritual
potential. Likewise, when the Flood came, all the people outside of
Noah's Ark were destined to die, just as they were already dead on a
spiritual level.

The first year of the third millennium since Yahshua was born
began on Nissan 1 or April 6th, 2000 - the New Year on the Jewish
Sacred Calendar - and ended on Nissan 1 in 2001. As a result, ten years
will transpire before Nissan 1 on April 5th, 2011. The Jewish Sacred Year
ending on that day - and the new one beginning then - have been
prophetically signaled out as pivotal years when the Tribulation may
begin, and the Rapture, "Harpazo" or catching up of the saints in the
twinkling of an eye may be near. The First Rapture, which I believe will
be a Mid-Tribulation event just prior to the 3-1/2 years of the Great
Tribulation, will bring a time of rejoicing for the saints in Heaven, but
will trigger much destruction as the Great Tribulation unfolds on Earth.
But just as God extended mercy to Noah and his kin during the Great
Flood, God will extend mercy to anyone that repents during the seven-
year Tribulation - except those who take the Mark of the Beast. In Book
Four on Prophecy, I discuss the prophecies hidden in Hallel Psalms 110
through 118, the prophetic measurements in the Great Pyramid's interior
passages, and many amazing heavenly signs between 2008 and 2018 that
verify the period between 2011 and 2018 as a significant time in history.

Now, just as there were likely many Earth changes and
catastrophes that began before the rains of the Great Flood descended,

many plagues and catastrophes will occur all over the world during the Great Tribulation. In fact, when the bowl plagues of God's Wrath are poured out (possibly sometime between 2015 and 2018, though no one knows for sure), billions of people will die. It will be such a terrible time in human history that Yahshua may return with His army of saints before the Tribulation ends to stop the Antichrist's slaughter of the saints in hiding.

As shown in Book Four on Prophecy, this ties in with the Chanukiah Menorah that shows the reversal of history. This reversal of history can be seen in that, from the Flood to Christ, the world was being consumed by increasing wickedness and sin. However, after the ministry, death and resurrection of Christ, the world has been infiltrated by the human bearers of Yahshua's Spirit, and they are infusing the darkness of this evil word with the Light of the World, who is Christ. So, it is as if the cold-hearted mercilessness of the past is being slowly reversed in the present by Yahshua's teaching to love and forgive one another. Hence, just as a mirror image is equal but opposite to the reality it reflects, the seventeen days before the Great Flood led to the death of all life in the world, while the seventeen years of the 21st century since Christ's birth may lead to the giving of everlasting life to an army of saints as numerous as the sands of the sea. This raising up of the dead in Christ is known as the First Resurrection:

> "And I saw thrones, and they sat on them, and judgment was committed to them. Then I saw the souls of those who had been beheaded for their witness to Jesus and for the word of God, who had not worshiped the beast or his image, and had not received his mark on their foreheads or on their hands. And they lived and reigned with Christ for a thousand years. But the rest of the dead did not live again until the thousand years were finished. **This is the first resurrection. Blessed and holy is he who has part in the first resurrection. Over such the second death has no power,** but they shall be priests of God and of Christ, and shall reign with Him a thousand years." - Revelation 20:4-6 (NKJ)

Just as the preceding Scripture teaches, only the saints raised in the First Resurrection will reign and minister with Yahshua the Messiah for a thousand years. Those who take part in the First Resurrection are those who are taken up to Heaven in the Rapture as well as the Tribulation Saints, who will reject the Antichrist and refuse to take the Mark of the Beast. Unfortunately, though many will be saved during the Tribulation, some will be martyred for their faith in Christ before Yahshua returns with the armies of Heaven. Therefore, to be spared the horrors of the Tribulation, make sure that you have accepted Yahshua's sacrificial death on the Cross for your sins, have given your life to Yahshua in baptism, and are following the lead of the Holy Spirit in regard to how you conduct your earthly affairs.

Believing that Yahshua is the Messiah and the only begotten Son of God is the only way to find everlasting life forever in Yahshua's Kingdom. As Yahshua said: *"For God so loved the world that He gave His only begotten Son, that whoever believes in Him should not perish but have everlasting life"* (John 3:16). So, do not tarry when you hear God's Spirit calling you into a right relationship with Yahshua and His Father, for the time is short!

Demonic Oppression and Deliverance through Christ

Could it be possible that our righteous ancestors left monuments like the Great Pyramid to help us find the Path to Salvation in Christ, and protection from Nephilim control? After all, only Christ can offer humanity full deliverance from demonic possession or oppression.

As shown in Chapter Three, there is good reason to believe that the Sethites knew that God the Father was going to send a Messiah into the world that would conquer sin, death, demons, and the Devil forever. But first, He would have to die for our sins, and then be resurrected to everlasting life so that He could serve as humanity's only perfect and eternal God and King. Though many false dying and resurrecting gods like Osiris and Tammuz were styled after Him, however, the exact prophetic specifications for this Messiah were never perfectly met by anyone else except Yahshua our Adonai, or Lord.

Indeed, the Bible makes it clear that no would-be Messiah or Savior ever delivered more people from demons, or cured more sick people, than Christ did during His First Advent. In fact, the many eye witness accounts in the Gospels of the miracles that Christ performed and the demons He cast out can show us what we need to do to display many spiritual gifts, including the authority to miraculously deliver ourselves and others from demons and sicknesses of every kind in Yahshua's Name or character.

One of the key weapons in our spiritual arsenal against demons and demonic activity is the open and frequent invocation of the Name of Yahshua in prayer. That is likely why demonically possessed or oppressed people who may unknowingly or knowingly worship demons are often keen to attack anyone for saying the Name of Yahshua or Jesus. Indeed, the Bible tells us that demons tremble at the sound of

Yahshua's Name (James 2:1-2)! The following passages from the Gospel of Mark illustrate the great power over demons that Yahshua had, and it indicates that we can cast out even the most virulently evil and persistent demons through concerted intercessory prayer and fasting:

> *"One of the crowd... said, 'Teacher, I brought You my son, who has a mute spirit. And wherever he seizes him, he throws him down; he foams at the mouth, gnashes his teeth, and becomes rigid. So I spoke to Your disciples, that they should cast him out, but they could not.' He answered him and said, 'O faithless generation... How long shall I bear with you? Bring him to Me.' ...And when he saw Him, immediately the spirit convulsed him, and he fell on the ground and wallowed, foaming at the mouth." - Mark 9:17-20 (NKJ)*

Interestingly, though I have never heard any pastor address this passage in a sermon, doesn't it seem as if this poor boy who had suffered from demonic possession for most of his life had the classic symptoms of an epileptic? Though there is no way to know if all cases of epilepsy or seizures are caused by demons, there may be many people suffering from epilepsy today that would be fully healed if demons were exorcised out of them in the Name of Yahshua. Also interesting to note here is Yahshua's apparent disgust at his "faithless" disciples. Without true faith in God, it is impossible for people to cast out powerful demons, even if attempted in the Name of Yahshua. The next few verses of this story also inform us that we must believe in the power of Yahweh to heal us before we will see results:

> *"So He asked his father, 'How long has this been happening to him?' And he said, 'From childhood. And often he has thrown him both into the fire and into the water to destroy him. But if You can do anything, have compassion on us and help us.' Jesus said to him... 'all things are possible to him who believes.' Immediately the father of the child cried out and said with tears, 'Lord, I believe; help my unbelief!' " - Mark 9:21-24 (NKJ)*

This passage illustrates another important concept in effectively fighting demonic attacks. This is in asking Yahweh for the faith to believe in His miraculous power and in His desire to help us. Indeed, if it were not for God's desire to help us, we would never be able to exercise enough faith to achieve miraculous results. This is why, after casting the demon out of the boy, Yahshua told His disciples that they could not do so because they had not fasted and prayed. What Yahshua meant, of course, is that they had not beseeched God enough for the faith and confidence in Christ that they needed to be effective warriors in our continual battles against demonic forces (Mark 9:25-29).

Now, it is interesting to note that Yahshua delivered this man from demonically caused epileptic seizures immediately after His transfiguration, which served to reveal Yahshua's divine nature, coming kingship, and extraordinary communion with God to His closest disciples. The transfiguration of Christ also illustrated why the disciples could not cast out the most powerful demons without fasting and praying for a desired deliverance before attempting to cast it out. The truth that Yahshua could do so without any hesitation or preamble highlighted His great power and superiority to the disciples, who could only perform miracles in Yahshua's Name, and not by their own power.

Though the invocation of the Name of their Teacher was often powerful enough to cause a desired outcome, it failed in certain cases where extremely evil and powerful demons were involved. Only Yahshua could effortlessly cast out certain kinds of demons, and only He knew how to empower ordinary men to do so. By telling them that they needed to fast and pray, Yahshua was underscoring their need for the purity, love and compassion of the Holy Spirit to be with them and to aid them in their desire to deliver people from evil.

The Book of Jubilees sheds light on the nature of the evil perpetrated by the demonic spirits of the Nephilim against Noah and his family after the Flood and what defenses they had against them. It teaches that Noah prayed for protection against the demonic spirits of the Nephilim, and Yahweh granted Noah's prayer by binding all but one tenth of the demons originally let loose on the Earth when their Nephilim bodies died physically.

Interestingly, the narrator of the following passages (that I have added a few notes to in parentheses) appears to have been a holy angel that was sent to help Noah and his sons:

> *"And in the third week of this jubilee the unclean demons began to lead astray the children of the sons of Noah, and to make to err and destroy them. And the sons of Noah came to Noah their father, and they told him concerning the demons which were leading astray and blinding and slaying his sons' sons. And he prayed before the Lord his God, and said:*

>> *'God of the spirits of all flesh, who hast shown mercy unto me and hast saved me and my sons from the waters of the flood, and hast not caused me to perish as Thou didst the sons of perdition... Let Thy grace be lift up upon my sons, and*

let not wicked spirits rule over them lest they should destroy them from the earth. But do Thou bless me and my sons, that we may increase and Multiply and replenish the earth.

And Thou knowest how Thy Watchers, the fathers of these spirits, acted in my day: and as for these spirits which are living, imprison them and hold them fast in the place of condemnation, and let them not bring destruction on the sons of thy servant, my God; for these are malignant, and created in order to destroy. **And let them not rule over the spirits of the living; for Thou alone canst exercise dominion over them.** And let them not have power over the sons of the righteous from henceforth and for evermore.'

And the Lord our God bade us (His holy angels) to bind all.

And the chief of the spirits, Mastema ("Hostility" in Hebrew - the chief demon), came and said: 'Lord, Creator, let some of them remain before me, and let them harken to my voice, and do all that I shall say unto them; for if some of them are not left to me, I shall not be able to execute the power of my will on the sons of men; for these are for corruption and leading astray before my judgment, for great is the wickedness of the sons of men.' **And He (Yahweh) said: 'Let the tenth part of them remain before him, and let nine parts descend into the place of condemnation.'**

And one of us (the angels) He commanded that we should teach Noah all their medicines; for He knew that they would not walk in uprightness, nor strive in righteousness.

And we did according to all His words: all the malignant evil ones we bound in the place of condemnation and a tenth part of them we left that they might be subject before Satan on the earth. And we explained to Noah all the medicines of their diseases, together with their seductions, how he might heal them with herbs of the earth. And Noah wrote down all things in a book as we instructed him concerning every kind of medicine. Thus the evil spirits were precluded from (hurting) the sons of Noah. And he gave all that he had written to Shem, his eldest son; for he loved him exceedingly above all his sons. And Noah slept... and was buried on Mount Lubar in the land of Ararat... And in his life on earth he excelled the children of men save Enoch because of the righteousness, wherein he was perfect. For Enoch's *office was ordained for a testimony to the generations of the world, so that he should recount all the deeds of generation unto generation, till the day of judgment." - Jubilees 10:1-18*

Note here that the writer of Jubilees indicates that no other ordinary human being was as righteous as Noah except for Enoch, whose righteousness made him appear perfect. This is why Yahweh listened to Noah's pleas. Therefore, after Noah's fervent intercessory prayers, God sent His angels to bind almost all the demons on the Earth and cast them into the abyss. However, the angels let one tenth of these demons remain free in order to tempt people and to lead those who choose evil to face judgment. Also at this time, Noah was taught the science of healing with herbs by the holy Watchers. Now, if we read these passages with the eyes of our hearts (i.e. our spiritual eyes) open, we can see that Noah was taught healing as a method of counteracting illnesses caused by demonic corruption and oppression in the unrighteous. Unfortunately, these illnesses have worsened with each successive generation - especially in the spiritually unprotected physical bodies of all biological life not under Yahweh's Covenant blessings.

Thus, all sicknesses can be viewed as a byproduct of living an unrighteous lifestyle full of excesses and debauchery of the worst kind. As sin increases among those who reject Yahweh and live outside of His protection, demons are allowed to hurt our physical bodies and sickness develops and worsens if sin remains unchecked. Indeed, in the wicked environment populated by evil people that exists today, rampant sin coupled with an increase in demonic activity has begun a chain reaction of physical deterioration in plants, animals and humans, and this will lead to more frequent epidemics and plagues in the very near future.

To illustrate why anyone lost in this world of sin will perish spiritually as well as physically without Christ, we need to look into the typical unsaved person's mindset. Recently, I read the following quote on a discussion board comparing all types of spirituality: "There is no ultimate 'good' because there are cultures who disagree on what is good and what is bad. Clearly then we do not all have internal knowledge of what is right and what is wrong placed there by god." This person was arguing that good and evil are subjective, that there are many paths to god (or godhood), and no one and nothing has a monopoly on faith or righteousness. Unfortunately, this unbiblical world view that proclaims "All paths lead to God!" is fairly widespread now - even among people who still profess to be Christians. Sadly, these apostates are too blind to see that they will be judged for their rejection of the Gospel, which clearly teaches that our belief in Yahshua as the Son of God is necessary for us to be saved and promised everlasting life (John 3:16-20).

According to the Word of God in the Bible, the person that I quoted earlier was absolutely wrong when he insisted that "there is no ultimate good" and absolutely right in saying "we do not all have an internal knowledge of what is right and wrong placed there by god." Let me explain why. You see, the problem began when Eve rebelled against God and ate the forbidden fruit. Before that time, Adam and Eve enjoyed a deep and intimate personal relationship with God, could converse with Him at any time, and often sought His counsel. After Eve sinned, however, the man and woman were separated from God and His guidance by their rebellion. Since God is totally perfect and cannot tolerate any sin, He had to set Adam and Eve apart from Himself. At that time, in addition to losing the gift of eternal life, Adam and Eve lost their authority to act on God's behalf. This gave Satan authority over them and they were pawns in the hands of a fallen angel that has no mercy or love in his heart for mankind at all.

This is where Yahshua (i.e. Jesus) comes into the picture. His blood sacrifice on the Cross was the perfect act of selfless love and His resurrection from the dead set the precedent for our eventual resurrection into everlasting life, for anyone who believes that Christ died and rose from the dead receives forgiveness and redemption from sin.

No other religion offers a way to bypass doing self-directed good works to find redemption or promises more joy and happiness in the afterlife. Since we are all sinful (i.e. in rebellion against God and His righteous, eternal Laws) we cannot be set free from sin and find atonement (i.e. the action of being at-one) with God unless we find a way to perfectly pay for our sins. Christ did that for us with the sacrifice of His innocent blood. His blood covers anyone who repents of their sins and believes that Yahshua is the Son of God and the Lamb of God that takes away sin and gives the Holy Spirit as a seal guaranteeing our salvation. This is the New Covenant.

In ancient Blood Covenant rituals, the people entering into a Covenant together would often mingle their blood in some way, or alternatively would exchange their cloaks and staffs (i.e. symbols of authority) to indicate their entrance into the other's family and their promise to protect and defend the other party with their lives. When we accept Christ's sacrifice on the Cross for us and take Communion, we symbolically mingle our blood with His, and exchange our filthy, sinful bodies for His sinless, perfect one. This is the New Covenant, and it allows us to become the Body of Christ and members of His Kingdom. When we enter the Kingdom of God, in exchange for our powerlessness against demons without Christ, we receive the royal power to act with Christ's kingly authority over demons and evil.

When a person truly believes in Christ in this way, they enter into a spiritual rebirthing process that will culminate in being raised from the dead in a perfect, sinless body. But the only way one can enter this born-again state of being is through a belief in and love for Christ, and a full desire to share in His righteousness and to give up all forms of sin as delineated by His laws (like the Ten Commandments). At the moment we repent and ask Yahshua to come inside our souls through His Spirit, we enter the born-again state, are personally guided by the quiet promptings of the Holy Spirit, receive real authority over demons, and learn to make decisions and choices based on God's laws and our Spirit-led conscience rather than our physical lusts and emotional feelings.

If you do not believe in Yahshua, then you do not have the Spirit of God within you, you are spiritually unregenerated, are subject to being deceived, possessed and oppressed by demons, and will perish in sin unless you accept Christ as your Savior. Without Christ, none of us has any hope of salvation, for no one can or will choose to do good all the time without God's intervention. We are all desperately wicked, and without Yahshua we would all perish. **Yahshua is the only way to find true perfection and peace!** That is why we all need to choose the Messiah to truly be saved, and why Yahshua said: *"I AM the Way, the Truth and the Life. No one comes to the Father except through Me"* (John 14:6).

As a closing thought for this section, there is something about demon possessed people's eyes that offers a real clue to their spiritual state. Having been in the presence of demonically possessed people before, I have noted one thing that they all have in common, and this is the fact that the irises of their eyes appear totally non-reflective and pitch black when the demons are active inside them.

That's why I thought it was so very insightful when my daughter, whom I had asked to read Chapter Five of Matthew for an upcoming home Bible Study, said: "Hey mom, didn't you say once that demonically possessed people's eyes could have really black irises?" When I replied in the affirmative, she said, "Then maybe that's why Yahshua said that if our eyes are bad, our bodies will be full of darkness." I agreed and told her that was a very insightful observation. Here is the Scripture she was referring to:

> *"The lamp of the body is the eye. If therefore your eye is good, your whole body will be full of light. But if your eye is bad, your whole body will be full of darkness. If... the light*

that is in you is darkness, how great is that darkness!" -
Matthew 6:22-23 (NKJ)

The darkness in those who worship the devil or demons and are demonically oppressed or possessed is often absolute, and this darkness occasionally shows in their eyes! Though the evil in their eyes is often spiritually masked and only shows through momentarily, people who are demon-possessed can display eyes that have fathomless, intensely evil-looking, pitch-black irises. Their eyes can also have a malevolent gleam or may look reptilian in appearance. Regardless of their appearance, the evil intent coming out of demonically possessed people can be felt on an emotional and spiritual level by people who are born-again.

Thankfully, demons and demon-possessed people have much less power to hurt those who are protected by the Holy Spirit. Therefore, we need to call on the name of Yahshua for protection whenever we encounter evil people or presences. In fact, with the end of this Age so near and demonic activity so high, it would be wise for all believers to frequently pray that God the Father would give them the spiritual discernment and physical protection needed to avoid demonically possessed people and thwart their evil desires toward us even when they don't look demon-possessed, which many of them do not.

In the meantime, please join me in frequently calling out "Maranatha!" "Come, Adonai Yahshua!", for to be with Yahshua is true bliss, and all of us will be totally happy and feel completely loved, comforted, and empowered in His presence.

Vampires and Werewolves: The Nephilim Connection

For years, trend-savvy movie producers and authors who are now multi-millionaires have known that people often find a twisted form of sensual pleasure when courting death and terror in their fantasies, and many have a dark occult fascination with horror. Creatures of the night such as vampires and werewolves court people with their sinister allure, raising their blood pleasure and giving them an adrenaline high that is almost sexual and orgasmic in its intensity for some. But this sort of pleasure is sinful, and those who love Christ are called not only to reject it, but to expose it for the evil that it is:

"Have nothing to do with the fruitless deeds of
darkness, but rather expose them. For it is shameful... to
mention what the disobedient do in secret. But everything
exposed by the light becomes visible... This is why it is said:

'Wake up, O sleeper, rise from the dead, and Christ will shine on you.'" - Ephesians 5:11-14 (NIV)

Those who are truly spiritually awake and have the light of Christ within them tend to be highly sensitive, and to find no pleasure in watching people being deceived, tortured, and/or murdered in highly grotesque ways by the living dead or the damned. For someone such as myself who has always been aware of the spiritual darkness and light within the invisible spirit world around me, this is especially true. For me, there is nothing more terrifying than watching a horror movie filled with dark demonic beings that find animalistic pleasure raping or eating people, cutting or ripping them into pieces, or drinking their blood until they die or are transformed into another demonic creature of darkness.

Though few people realize it, this sort of entertainment invokes terror in me because I know that it accurately depicts the dark desires of demons that continually lust after human flesh and blood. Furthermore, I know that these unseen demonic entities are actually the spirits of the Nephilim - alien beings that hate mankind with an intense passion, that once inhabited the Earth before the Flood, and likely still do. Before the Flood, the Nephilim vied for the control of the Earth and desired to destroy every human being that was not mesmerized into submission and sexual sin by their dark, exotic and sensual allure.

Rather than be seduced into sexual promiscuity or terrified to death by these demonic spirits, I cling tightly to Yahshua my Messiah, whose love and Spirit save me from succumbing to the perverse sensuality, darkness and terror that so many foolhardy people seem to crave. I find no delight in being terrified, or in courting evil and sensuality instead of the pure and untainted intimacy with Yahweh God that we can all experience when we love the light of Yahshua more than the darkness that He alone can save us from. As the Apostle Peter said:

"But you are a chosen generation, a royal priesthood, a holy nation, His own special people, that you may proclaim the praises of Him who called you out of darkness into His marvelous light." - 1 Peter 2:9 (NKJ)

But, if Yahshua's light is so marvelous, why are many among those who profess to love Him finding pleasure in dark entertainment? What I find most alarming about this is the absolute rejection of Yahshua's light and love that these people are giving into every time they watch a horror movie or read a paranormal romance or romantic thriller. They either do not realize or do not care that they are courting Hell and the Devil when they allow their minds to be tantalized with darkness, for all of those who are saved are called to reject Satan's darkness in favor of God's light. As the Apostle Paul said:

> *"The night is far spent, the day is at hand. Therefore let us cast off the works of darkness, and let us put on the armor of light. Let us walk properly, as in the day, not in revelry and drunkenness, not in lewdness and lust, not in strife and envy. But put on the Lord Jesus Christ (Adonai Yahshua Ha Mashiach), and make no provision for the flesh, to fulfill its lusts." - Romans 13:12-14 (NKJ)*

If we desire to be citizens in Christ's Kingdom of light and love, we cannot find lustful pleasure in viewing the glorification of evil and darkness or seeing it as an acceptable form of entertainment. Nonetheless, many professing Messianics and Christians see nothing wrong with viewing horror movies or occult thrillers. They see these things as entertainment and think that there is nothing abnormal in experiencing the emotional distortions, adrenaline rush and sensory overload provided by these venues, even though they are contrary to what Christ expects from His followers. As Yahshua said:

> *"Everyone who does evil hates the light, and will not come into the light for fear that his deeds will be exposed. But whoever lives by the truth comes into the light, so that it may be seen plainly that what he has done has been done through God." - John 3:20-21 (NIV)*

What is even more alarming to me is the overwhelming popularity of modern romance novels featuring a hero or heroine that is a vampire. It boggles my mind to know that many women and teen girls (and, with the advent of the "Twilight" books and movies, men and teen boys too) are fascinated with dark romances that feature a liberated, unscrupulous, or immoral woman who is seduced into a sensual liaison with a male vampire. Even though these unlikely vampire heroes are often tormented souls who would rather perish than suck the blood out of living humans to live forever, the dictates of the dark fantasy realms these vampires inhabit insist that they are beyond redemption and - despite their tragic desire - could never be transformed into beings of light. In other words, these creatures of darkness can perish as easily in sunlight as they inevitably and irrevocably would in Yahweh God's illuminating and holy presence.

Nonetheless, with increasing frequency, even supposedly good Christian women and teens often find sick pleasure in fantasizing about falling in love with a supernaturally powerful being that is forever separated from God's love and light and could easily destroy them. But, instead of heeding the prompting of the Holy Spirit, many hapless people unwisely succumb to the dark sensuality and lust that these beings seduce them with. Then they fall even further into error when they imagine that their love might somehow miraculously transform these creatures of darkness into beings of light. They do not realize that they are toying with an impossible fantasy, for the Bible says:

> "For what fellowship has righteousness with lawlessness? And what communion has light with darkness? And what accord has Christ with Belial? Or what part has a believer with an unbeliever? ...As God has said: 'I will dwell in them and walk among them. I will be their God, and they shall be My people.' Therefore 'Come out from among them and be separate,' says the Lord. 'Do not touch what is unclean, and I will receive you. I will be a Father to you, and you shall be My sons and daughters,' says the Lord Almighty." - 2 Corinthians 6:14-18 (NKJ)

If God calls us to be like Christ, who resisted the Devil or Belial and exposed evil with God's light rather than try to love or cajole demons into the Kingdom of Heaven, how can any of us think for a moment that we can redeem the unredeemable or save the damned? There is not one instance in Scripture where Yahshua offered a demon salvation or where any demon acted even remotely interested in accepting salvation! How then can we entertain the thought that we are capable of doing what even Christ could not do? For this reason, it is absolutely foolhardy to believe that a demon can be won over to love Christ or to live in fellowship with Him or His Body, the Church.

Since we have been called to walk in the light of Christ and to flee from evil, it follows that we cannot entertain darkness or seek sensual pleasure in the dark arms of demons. Those like myself who are saved and aware of the spirit world know that **no demon spirit originating from the fallen angels, their evil wives or the first race of Nephilim they spawned ever asked to be forgiven by Christ because they are incapable of true repentance and therefore are beyond redemption**.

It's time for believers to wake up and realize that any love of paranormal paramours and the demonic divas who court them is a dangerous re-visitation of the dark sensuality that gripped the entire world before the Flood. Though few acknowledge it, this same love of physical pleasure eventually caused every human being that wasn't killed by the Nephilim to succumb to sin and to lust after their strange flesh. As a result, these people were not only physically destroyed but spiritually cursed with a fate worse than death, for this is what being totally separated from God's love and light forever will truly be.

Chapter 6: Yahweh Revealed and Concealed After the Flood

> "'It shall be, when I bring a cloud over the earth, that
> the rainbow shall be seen in the cloud; and I will remember
> My covenant... the waters shall never again become a flood to
> destroy all flesh. The rainbow shall be in the cloud, and I will
> look on it to remember the everlasting covenant between God
> and every living creature...' And God said to Noah, 'This is
> the sign of the covenant which I have established between Me
> and all flesh that is on the earth.'" - Genesis 9:14-17 (NKJ)

There is much symbolic meaning in the opening Scripture for this chapter. When Yah spoke these words about His New Covenant with all mankind, Noah was very likely looking up into a sky dotted with thinning storm clouds. As Yah spoke, the rainbow likely had just formed in the clouds above Noah and his family. While witnessing Noah's blood sacrifices of thanks to Yah, these few survivors of the Great Flood saw a colorful, gigantic celestial archer's bow overhead in the sky. It was as if God had stretched a bow of light that could shoot an imaginary arrow of light or lightning into heaven! Indeed, Yahweh was symbolically aiming an arrow at His own heart to indicate that He would die rather than break His Covenant with Noah.

In fact, 2000 years later, Yahweh did just that; He died in the person of Christ so that we could enter into an even better everlasting Covenant with Him. Yahshua died on the Cross to forever seal this more perfect Covenant, as well as to fulfill God's part in all His former Covenants made with men. Every biblical Blood Covenant is, therefore, a powerful example of Yahweh utilizing His divine Language to communicate spiritual truths to us.

When Yahweh made the first rainbow appear in the sky, He was using His powerful allegorical language to show Noah something very profound - something that could only be understood through the Gospel in the Stars. This is found in the constellation Centaurus, the Centaur - a decan sign of Virgo. A centaur is a being with a dual nature, and as such, it is a representation of the dual nature of Christ. Centaurus represents Christ at His First Advent - a mortal man who could die, yet whose Spirit was Yahweh's own. The human half of this mighty centaur in the sky is wielding a bow with an arrow aimed at the heart of Lupus the dying Wolf, which is another celestial symbol for Christ in His role as a redeeming sacrifice for sin. The magnificence of this allegorical picture in the sky lies in the fact that God the Son, our Creator and

Redeemer, is aiming an arrow at His own heart, just as He symbolically does every time a rainbow appears!

Due to great spiritual teachers like Cainan and Enoch, Noah was aware of the power of the celestial symbols in the Gospel in the Stars, and passed down this knowledge to his chosen son Shem and Shem's righteous children. They therefore understood the allegorical meaning of the Rainbow Covenant and were greatly comforted by it.

The Task of Noah – Post Flood Survival and Recovery

After the Great Flood, Noah, his sons, their wives, and their children were left with the gargantuan task of repopulating and re-civilizing a world totally stripped of every last vestige of civilization. All the civilizations these antediluvians had known were totally destroyed - buried beneath layer upon layer of sedimentation, rotting corpses, shredded plants, and other rubble. Almost all traces of their Pre-Flood world were buried or lost forever beneath submerged coastal areas. There, many once beautiful and heavily populated port cities were totally lost under greatly expanded world oceans. In addition, this new world was much more inhospitable to life. This is because the Earth's crust was stripped of vegetation, then broken and pushed up or down into new shapes during the Great Flood. This rough new terrain made the Earth much harder to travel across than it had been.

Previously unbroken stretches of verdant land - land watered everywhere from underground springs of water before the Flood - were now filled with awesome yet forbidding new mountain ranges, deserts, valleys, rivers, and seas. To further complicate things, the huge new mountain ranges certainly made Earth's weather far more violent than it had been prior to the Flood. As a result, the first Post Flood survivors huddling with Noah on a damp mountaintop in the Ararat range must have felt terribly alone and afraid when they first exited the Ark.

Indeed, they were likely terrified and hopelessly unprepared when they first experienced the terrible violence and destruction of hurricanes, thunderstorms, blizzards, tornadoes, tsunamis and cold winds. Ancient sources indicate that the entire Earth had a climate that was far more mild and uniform before the Flood, and storms hardly ever occurred. Therefore, people were not prepared to deal with the harsh weather after the Flood. But, since Yahweh had a vested interest in assuring mankind's survival, it is highly likely that He directed Noah and his kin to seek a sheltered geographical location where life would be easier. This was crucial as the first Ice Age after the Flood began to encompass the globe.

Faced with the massive devastation of the Earth surrounding them everywhere, Noah and his sons knew the great magnitude of their vulnerability. Therefore, these survivors of the Great Flood settled in the most sheltered place they could find beyond the mountains of Ararat. There, they prayed for protection, built shelters and waited for Earth's climate to stabilize. In addition, the Bible suggests that Noah introduced new methods of farming that overcame God's curse upon the ground. Indeed, Noah's name sounds like the Hebrew word for "comfort," and in order to comfort the farmers of the world, Noah likely introduced terraced farming, crop rotation, soil fertilization with dung and fish, and irrigation to produce better crops (Genesis 5:29). In addition, Noah and his sons likely utilized ancient religious symbols and ideas as they built new civilizations based on the ideas of great men of faith such as Abel, Seth, Cainan, Methuselah, Enoch, Noah and Shem.

The Restoration and Corruption of Civilization

Few people realize that Noah lived 350 years and Shem lived 500 years after the Flood. They therefore had much time to re-populate and educate a world that had been plunged into a technological Stone Age. About a hundred years after the Flood, the Ice Age caused by that cataclysm likely began to recede. When that time of bitter cold lessened enough, Noah and his immediate descendants would have obeyed the commandment of Yah to repopulate the Earth. Splitting their acquired resources, they spread out, settling in places where the climate was ideal for habitation.

Initially, people found good places to farm and tend herds in the Fertile Crescent, which stretched from the Persian Gulf west through Iran and Iraq, south through Syria, Lebanon and Israel, and into Egypt and Ethiopia along the route of the Nile River. *They also spread out around the Mediterranean coast, southern Europe, southern Russia, southern North America, Central America, and in the mountains of South America* - where it is cooler. Incidentally, these land areas still have the warmest, wettest, and most stable climates - making them ideal for settlement and cultivation.

Now, since all the people of the world at that time spoke only one language and had only one faith, there were few skirmishes and virtually no wars at first. Adding to the tranquility, communities remained fairly small and isolated, and this kept sin and aggression from spreading. So, for a short time after the Flood, people in the same regions lived in peace and harmony with one another and traded freely with each other. That is probably why there is such a tremendous cultural overlap between civilizations in Mesopotamia, the Indus Valley, Egypt, the Mediterranean, and the Americas. One example of this synchronicity is seen in the bundled reed boats used in both ancient Egypt and South America to sail on rivers and along coastlines - reed boats that are still made and used by the natives of Peru to this day.

Around the world, ancient monolithic structures made of piled earth, mud brick, or cyclopean sized stone blocks shared certain common design elements. Magnificently engineered structures with striking similarities can be found in Egypt, Mesopotamia, the Indus Valley, Mexico, Central America, and South America. In addition, on either side of the Atlantic Ocean, painstakingly well-oriented circular henges and pyramidal-shaped structures were used as focal points for veneration, worship, and following the movements of the Sun, Moon, stars, and planets. Even in the Americas, stone pyramids exist that have a striking resemblance to Mesopotamia's ziggurats and Egypt's pyramids.

Interestingly, all of the henges and pyramidal structures found worldwide can act like sundials, showing the time of day by the positions of their shadows. In addition, they can all easily be used to sight the positions of stars and planets, whether or not observers stand at their apexes, or at various points along their bases. Initially, there is no doubt that all of these monuments were inspired by the principles behind Blood Covenanting and Sacred Astronomy - principles that Noah and Shem taught that focused people's attention on their need for redemption.

All this was taught in the Gospel in the Stars. The magnificent heavens contained the written testimony of Almighty God that instructed people and angels about sin, redemption, and the coming of the Messiah that would one day restore the world to its Eden-like perfection. It therefore showed the only fool-proof way to find redemption from sin and the promise of everlasting life through the coming Messiah that God promised to send - a Messiah that would someday destroy that Serpent called Satan, his followers and his evil ways forever.

That initial Post-Flood world's religion was a star-gazing one because all the people on the Earth were endeavoring to become righteous. They sought to be worthy of God's love and salvation by reading and applying the teachings in the Heavenly Tablets to their lives like Enoch the Sethite had prior to the Flood. Like Enoch, they also wanted to read and fully understand the Star Gospel. However, because people's hearts are desperately wicked, they tend to love pleasure and fleshly fulfillment and are not usually patient enough to receive direct revelation from God or develop a relationship with Him. As a result, they grow dissatisfied. Many people eventually felt this way about the teachings of Noah and Shem and eventually rejected them in favor of other gods made in their own selfish and depraved image.

Gradually, as hedonism and self-centeredness replaced compassion and servanthood, the peacefulness, cooperation and love that characterized the Post-Flood world that Noah and Shem fostered with their leadership and ministering servant's hearts gave way to increased tension and discord. Alas, the despicable Way of Cain began to raise its ugly head once more. To make matters worse, the Anakim had grown sufficiently enough in numbers to begin attempting to take over and control human settlements and lord it over those weaker than themselves. As a result, wars and skirmishes increased and many people died in bloody outbursts.

This is when Nimrod rose up and began to destroy the Anakim and give people the liberty to govern and worship as they chose once more. Nimrod was so successful at obliterating the Anakim menace that people groups around the world loved him and eventually wanted to set him up as a king over them. One thing led to another, and soon they were venerating Nimrod as if he was equal with God. In this chapter, we will explore ancient texts that verify all of this, and show how beguiling and successful Nimrod was in leading the whole world astray.

The evidence that the Old and New Worlds were both eventually ruled over by people with the same ideological and religious agenda as Nimrod can be found when their symbols are compared. Cross, serpent, and bird imagery were prevalent in all three seats of ancient culture – Mesopotamia, Egypt, and the Americas. All three had winged guardians, demons, and deities. They also had gods and goddesses wielding or adorned with serpents, feathers, wings, and horns. In ancient Egyptian art, depictions of royalty, nobles, priests and deities were drawn wearing plumed or horned headdresses, just as the nobles and priests in the Americas and their god Quetzalcoatl did.

Another striking similarity can be found in the spotted leopard or cheetah skins that priests and the Pharaoh donned in Egypt, and the spotted jaguar skins that Mayan priests, warriors, and nobles wore in Mesoamerica. Since leopards and jaguars are nearly identical in size, nature, and appearance, their skins were likely used as symbols of strength and hunting prowess. Intriguingly, the use of these particular animal skins as symbols of power likely arose with the despotic ruler Nimrod. Nimrod's name means "subduing leopard" in Babylonian and "let us rebel" in Hebrew. This, coupled with the Bible's teaching that

Nimrod had gained worldwide fame as a "mighty hunter," suggests that Nimrod was a powerful tyrant. In addition, legends suggest that Nimrod used trained leopards to assist and protect him when he hunted game or went to battle with his armies.

Egyptian Priest Wearing Leopard Skin Robe

For this reason, leopard and jaguar skins may have begun to symbolize the ultimate power that Nimrod used to forge the first one-world dictatorship. The priests and nobles Nimrod approved of may therefore have worn leopard-skin robes as symbols of their loyalty to Nimrod and desire to enforce Nimrod's authority. Later, when his authority was unchallenged anywhere in the world and everyone had been indoctrinated with Nimrod's religion and worldview, Nimrod likely set himself and his wife up as gods and demanded to be worshipped. When this occurred, Nimrod may have ordered all priests to wear leopard skins to show that they served Nimrod and his pantheon of gods. Later in this chapter, we will focus on Nimrod's rise and fall in more detail, and explore the sad results of his infamous reign.

The Garden of Eden in the Lands Allotted to Shem

When researching this section exploring the division of the land by Noah's sons after the Flood, the Holy Spirit showed me something absolutely revolutionary. It all began with the following passages from the Book of Jubilees:

> *"And Noah rejoiced that this portion came forth for Shem and for his sons, and he remembered all that he had spoken... in prophecy; for he had said: 'Blessed be the Lord God of Shem, And may the Lord dwell in the dwelling of Shem.' And he knew that **the Garden of Eden is the holy of holies, and the dwelling of the Lord**, and **Mount Sinai the centre of the desert**, and **Mount Zion - the centre of the navel of the earth: these three were created as holy places facing each other.**" - Jubilees 8:18-20*

What this passage says is that the Lord God or Yahweh Elohim of Shem created three holy places that were all originally within Shem's territory that faced each other, meaning that **they were aligned with each other.** On page 119 in Chapter Three, Jubilees 4:25-27 reveals that there were once four holy places on the Earth, and this book has already shown that three of them were in the Middle East. This portion of the text stipulates that these four places will forever sanctify the New Earth as visible signs of God's blessing through Christ: *"For the Lord has four places on the earth, the Garden of Eden, and the Mount of the East, and... Mount Sinai, and Mount Zion (which) will be sanctified in the new creation for a sanctification of the earth."* In this section, I will show that three of these holy places can be fairly well identified. In addition, I will show the location of the fourth holy place: the Garden of Eden.

As shown earlier, Mount Zion is likely connected to the Great Pyramid or Pillar of Enoch. For further verification, 2 Samuel 7:5-6 identifies Egypt as the location of a "house" or temple of Yahweh that existed before the Israelites left Egypt during the Exodus, and the Pillar of Enoch was a magnificent temple that was built by the Sethites prior to the Flood. ·

Mount Sinai is another one of the three holy locales that was tentatively identified in Chapter Three as a mountain in Saudi Arabia known as Jabal Al-Lawz. First of all, this mountain appears to be the real Mount Sinai because its tall summit is actually charred and blackened as if it had been burned by an intense fire at one time, whereas the traditional Mount Sinai called Jabal Musa in the southern Sinai Peninsula has no such identifying feature. In addition, there is a wide desert valley near Jabal Al-Lawz where an encampment of 600,000 to 1 million Israelites could easily have been situated, whereas there is no desert area big enough to house that many tents around Jabal Musa.

Another intriguing feature of Jabal Al-Lawz is the nearby presence of a large boulder that appears to have been split in two from top to bottom, and which shows signs of having once had a vigorous spring of water flowing from its base. Could this be the rock that Moses struck with the Staff of Yahweh so that water would flow from it and quench the thirst of the Israelites?

"'Behold, I will stand before you there on the rock in Horeb; and you shall strike the rock, and water will come out of It, that the people may drink.' And Moses did so in the sight of the elders of Israel." - Exodus 17:6 (NKJ)

Probably one of the best indicators that Jabal Al-Lawz may be Mount Sinai or Horeb is the testimony of the Apostle Paul, who said that

Mount Sinai was in Arabia (Galatians 4:25). The historian Josephus also identifies Mount Sinai as a tall mountain in Arabia, and Moses first encountered God through a burning bush on the side of Mount Horeb or Sinai, which was in or near the land of Midian (Exodus 3:1-2). Traditionally, Midian has been associated with northwestern Saudi Arabia, where Jabal Al-Lawz is located.

Regarding Mount Sinai, the Bible indicates that the wayward Israelites made a golden calf idol to worship at the foot of the mountain when they tired of waiting for Moses to come down from its summit. Could this be why there is an altar of heaped up stones that is marked everywhere with glyphs of calves at the base of Jabal Al-Lawz? Furthermore, Exodus 19:12 and 19:23 indicate that the Israelites were divinely commanded to mark out the base of the mountain as a sacred place, and there are somewhat uniform piles of stones approximately 400 yards (370 meters) apart around the entire base of Jabal Al-Lawz that appear to have been man-made. An excellent book showing the amazing correlations at Jabal Al-Lawz with the Mount Sinai in Exodus is "The Exodus Case" by Dr. Lennart Moller. This heavily illustrated book also proposes a plausible Exodus Pharaoh and route for the Israelite Exodus through the Sinai wilderness and is highly recommended.

Though my identification of Mount Zion and Mount Sinai are fairly certain, however, it has proven to be difficult to positively identify the Mount of the East and the location of the now lost Garden of Eden, which will likely not exist on Earth again until the New Heaven and New Earth are created. In Chapter Three, I tentatively suggested either the Temple Mount in Jerusalem or the Mount of the Transfiguration as the Mount of the East. Now, though the Temple Mount is not really a mountain but a high hill, the Mount of the Transfiguration was a high mountain in northern Israel. In fact, it was near the town of Bethsaida, which was along the major caravan route to the East. To the Israelites, the East meant Abraham's original homeland in Mesopotamia and Chaldea.

Though Mount Carmel is usually associated with Yahshua's Transfiguration, it lies on the coast with difficult terrain lying between it and Bethsaida, whereas Mount Hermon lies north along a well-traveled trade route. As explored in Chapter Four, the snow-capped Mount Hermon is likely to have been the true Mount of the Transfiguration because of Christ's mission to reclaim and sanctify all that the Devil initially stole from mankind when Eve fell. Though Mount Hermon in modern Lebanon is the crowning symbol of Satan's initial success in deceiving mankind before the Flood, Yahshua could not have wanted it to remain so - especially since it was likely a sacred place of godly worship before the fallen angels sullied it with their lust and hate. So, though no one really knows what the writer of Jubilees meant when he referred to the Mount of the East, my guess is that it was and still is Mount Hermon, and this mountain will one day be a permanent reminder throughout eternity of Yahshua's saving Grace along with the Temple Mount, Mount Zion, and Mount Sinai.

This leaves us with attempting to identify the Garden of Eden, which was one of the three places that were holy to God in the lands allotted to Shem after the Flood. Earlier, I proposed that the Garden of Eden may have been near either Eritrea, which neighbors Ethiopia, or near Kuwait on the Persian Gulf. However, Jubilees stipulates that the Garden of Eden, Mount Sinai and Mount Zion faced or were aligned with each other and Eritrea and Kuwait cannot be simultaneously aligned with Mount Zion and Mount Sinai. Nonetheless, Eritrea is near a town called Aden in Yemen and the Gulf of Aden, and **Aden is an alternate spelling for Eden**.

Now, if we extend a straight line from the Pillar of Enoch in Egypt through Jabal Al-Lawz in Saudi Arabia to just east of the Gulf of Aden, we arrive at the modern nation of Oman - as shown in the map on page 441. Intriguingly, a coastal town in Oman named Salalah is a highly sought after resort area with a lovely tropical climate, and this is extremely unusual since the rest of the region is hot and arid desert. As such, Salalah is a rich oasis and was once the primary source of frankincense in the ancient world.

Could it be that the verdant land that was once called the Garden of Eden now lies submerged beneath the waters of the Arabian Sea just off the southern coast of the Arabian Peninsula between Salalah and the Gulf of Oman? It is possible, and the map on page 441 shows that this region does align perfectly with both Mount Zion and Mount Sinai. However, it is only an educated guess. As such, we will likely not know the true location of the Garden of Eden until Yahshua comes - when all things will be made known to those who love Him (1 Cor. 13:9-12).

Thus far, the Book of Jubilees has made it clear that Shem was the original ruler over Mount Zion, Mount Sinai and Arabia - including the original location of the Garden of Eden. Furthermore, the Book of Jasher tells us that Shem was Melchizedek, the king of Salem and Priest of God Most High of Genesis 14:18-20. So, after Noah's sons divided up the land, Shem or Melchizedek must have settled in the city of Salem (i.e. Jerusalem) in Canaan in order to be near to the Pillar of Enoch, which - as an altar to Yahweh and the Navel of the Word - was likely a sacred place to all of Noah's offspring - but was especially important to Shem as Noah's temporal and spiritual heir. As Noah's successor in the priestly line of Melchizedek, it would have also been Shem's responsibility to care for this pyramid altar complex dedicated to Yahweh and Enoch and to administer sacred rites there.

Yet history tells us that the descendents of Ham's son Mizraim took over the administration of Lower Egypt. Furthermore, Ham's grandson through his son Cush was Nimrod, who usurped Shem's authority in ancient Shinar (a.k.a. Sumer). The theory that Sumer may have been Shem's original homeland after the Flood is based on David Rohl's assumption that the name Shem was the root of the word Shumer (i.e. Shinar) or Sumer. My point is this: if Shem was a priest in the order of Melchizedek and was also the temporal heir to Noah's leadership and priestly roles, then why did Ham's descendents eventually occupy and rule over Shinar in Mesopotamia, the Promised Land, Lower Egypt and Arabia that clearly belonged to Shem? The obvious conclusion is that Noah's son Ham did not respect his eldest brother Shem's claim to Noah's spiritual or temporal authority, but felt it rightly belonged to him. Thus, Ham likely conspired with his sons and grandsons to claim Shem's authority and birthright for himself and his heirs.

As shown in Book Two, there is a stark, unembellished narrative in the Book of Jasher that proves Ham had evil intentions toward his father Noah. In this narrative, we are informed that Ham stole Adam's skin garments from Noah shortly after they left the Ark:

> "And in their going out, **Ham stole those garments from Noah his father,** and he... hid them from his brothers. And when Ham begat his first born Cush, he gave him the garments in secret, and... when Cush had begotten Nimrod, he gave him those garments through his love for him" - Jasher 7:27-29

So, though Shem was Noah's chosen heir, Noah's youngest son Ham likely refused to accept his father's choice of Shem over him. Therefore, as soon as he found an opportunity, Ham stole the garments that represented Adam's temporal and spiritual authority from Noah. Later, this stolen authority and the coveted garments symbolizing it passed down from Cush to Nimrod. Intriguingly, the Bible records a peculiar incident whereby Ham humiliated his father Noah so badly that Noah cursed Ham's son Canaan. Could this be when Ham acquired these miraculous garments? After all, we are told that Noah consumed too much wine and had apparently stripped naked in his delirium before passing out into a drunken stupor when Ham stumbled upon the scene:

Map Showing Possible Location of the Garden of Eden

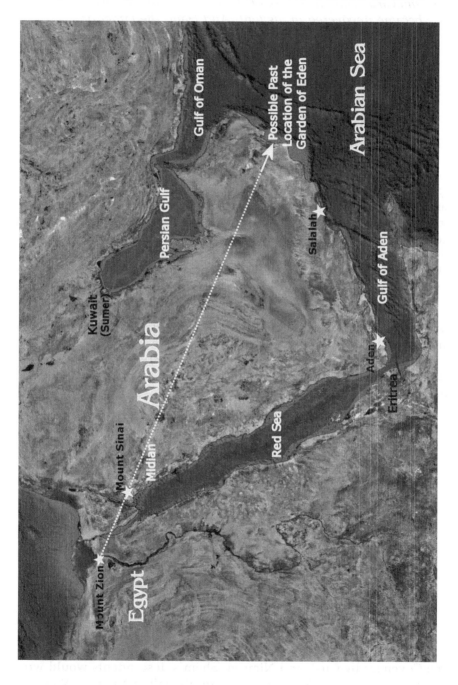

*"And Noah began to be a farmer, and he planted a
vineyard. Then he drank of the wine and was drunk, and
became uncovered in his tent. And Ham, the father of
Canaan, saw the nakedness of his father, and told his two
brothers outside. But Shem and Japheth took a garment, laid it
on... their shoulders, and went backward and covered... their
father... So Noah awoke from his wine, and knew what his
younger son had done to him. Then he said: 'Cursed be
Canaan; a servant of servants he shall be to his brethren.'" -
Genesis 9:20-25 (NKJ)*

Now, if we suppose that the garments Noah took off before
passing out was Adam's skin clothing, and Ham seized this ideal
opportunity to steal these clothes, the severity of Noah's curse on Ham's
grandson would make much more sense. If we view Ham's offense as an
affront to Noah's leadership authority, this would also explain why some
legends suggest that Ham emasculated Noah so that he could not father
more children. However, if Ham had physically maimed Noah in such an
evil way, the Bible would have recorded it. Since it does not, Ham must
have emasculated Noah by stealing his authority but not his manhood.

Oddly, instead of cursing Ham directly, Noah cursed Ham's
fourth son Canaan (Gen. 10:6). There is no doubt that this was a
symbolic gesture with a prophetic meaning. First of all, it indicated that
Canaan would soon break the Covenant made between Noah's three
sons to not infringe on one another's territory. This is, in fact, exactly
what he did, as the Book of Jubilees reveals:

*"And Canaan saw the land of Lebanon to the river of
Egypt, that it was very good, and he went not into the land of
his inheritance... and he dwelt in the land of Lebanon... And
Ham... Cush and Mizraim... said unto him: 'Thou hast settled
in a land which is not thine, and which did not fall to us by
lot: do not do so; for if thou dost do so, thou and thy sons will
fall in the land and (be) accursed... Dwell not in the dwelling
of Shem; for to Shem and to his sons did it come by their lot.
Cursed... shalt thou be beyond all the sons of Noah, by the
curse by which we bound ourselves by an oath... in the
presence of Noah our father.' But he did not harken unto
them, and dwelt in the land of Lebanon from Hamath to the
entering of Egypt, he and his sons until this day. And for this
reason that land is named Canaan." - Jubilees 10:29-34*

Despite Canaan's treachery and the subsequent breaking of the
same Covenant by Cush and Nimrod, Shem's descendents would wrestle
back their dominion of Mesopotamia with the fall of Nimrod. Now, as

Ham's grandson via Cush, Nimrod was the third generation descended from Ham. Therefore, though Noah was also prophetically indicating that the people descended from Canaan would become the servants of the Israelites, he was ensuring that Nimrod's firstborn son would be the last one to exercise Shem's authority before it returned to a descendant of Shem. But first, Nimrod would use the superhuman strength he obtained from Adam's clothes to forge a mighty kingdom for himself:

> *"And when he was twenty years old he (Nimrod) put on those garments, and...* **became strong....** *and God gave him might and strength, and he was a mighty hunter in the earth... and he hunted the animals and he built altars, and he offered upon them the animals before the Lord." - Jasher 7:30*

This narrative tells us that, when Nimrod was 20 years old, he decided to put Adam's skin garments on and discovered a marvelous secret! He found out that anyone who wore these garments obtained superhuman power. Then, seeing the potential for conquest this gave him, Nimrod soon earned the epithet of *"Mighty Hunter before the Lord." So,* rather than relying on God for his strength, Nimrod chose to use stolen power to exercise an authority he was never meant to have.

In Chapter Seven, we will explore Greek Mythology from the standpoint that it holds a record of the characters and events in Genesis as told from Cain and Nimrod's point of view. There, Cush and Nimrod's revolt against Noah and Shem's authority and religious views is not only recorded in Greek myth, but celebrated as mankind's greatest achievement. In addition, the Greek pantheon deified Eve as Hera, the great mother goddess of humanity. They also deified Adam and the Serpent who tempted her as Zeus, the upholder of the supposed superiority of the Way of Cain that is coveted by unsaved people over the Way of Yahweh.

The Worldwide Spread of Idolatry during Nimrod's Rule

The Bible and Book of Jasher tell us that Nimrod was the son of Cush, and that Cush was the son of Noah's son Ham. It is believed that Ham, as the son of Noah who populated the southern regions of the Earth, was the father of the dark-skinned races. Though Ham himself may not have been dark-skinned, some of his descendents through Cush surely were. It is therefore possible that Nimrod was dark-skinned. This, however, does not mean that all dark-skinned people are like Nimrod. It simply means that, in the far past, some people who were descended from Cush chose to reject the truth of one triune God for the lie of

Paganism - just as Nimrod and people from many other racial groups chose to.

Noah's moralizing and civilizing efforts and Nimrod's subsequent efforts to spread Astrology and Sorcery likely occurred during a three-hundred-year time span between 2250 and 1950 BC. The conflict between these opposing groups likely ended shortly after Nimrod's Empire and the Tower of Babel were destroyed. Due to their extraordinarily long lives, both Noah and Shem were contemporaries of Nimrod and his firstborn son Mardon, who are singled out as wicked and idolatrous rulers in the following portion of the Book of Jasher:

> "And they found a large valley opposite to the east, and they built him a large and extensive city, and Nimrod called the name of the city that he built Shinar... And Nimrod dwelt in Shinar, and he reigned securely, and he fought with his enemies and he subdued them, and he prospered in all his battles, and his kingdom became very great. And all nations and tongues heard of his fame, and they gathered themselves to him, and they bowed down... and they brought him offerings, and he became their lord and king, and they all dwelt with him in the city at Shinar, **and Nimrod reigned in the earth over all the sons of Noah, and they were all under his power and counsel**.
>
> And all the earth was of one tongue and words of union, but Nimrod did not go in the ways of the Lord, and he was more wicked than all the men that were before him, from the days of the flood until those days. And he made gods of wood and stone, and he bowed down to them, and he rebelled against the Lord, and taught all his subjects and the people of the earth his wicked ways; and Mardon his son was more wicked than his father.
>
> And every one that heard of the acts of Mardon the son of Nimrod would say, concerning him, 'From the wicked goeth forth wickedness;' therefore it became a proverb in the whole earth..." - Jasher 7:43-49

This section of Jasher tells us several highly important facts. First of all, it says that: *"Nimrod reigned in the earth over all the sons of Noah, and they were all under his power and counsel"* (Jasher 7:45). Since it is almost certain that Noah had other sons and daughters after he sired Shem, Ham, and Japheth, and Noah's three sons certainly endeavored to have as many children as possible, Nimrod was ruling over many more people than just Shem's and Japheth's progeny after

300 years, which is the approximate amount of time that had passed from Noah's Flood to the building of the Tower of Babel. In fact, since there were four healthy married couples after the Flood instead of the one couple after the Fall of Adam and Eve, Earth's population could easily have been anywhere from *one to six billion people* by that time according to the Population Growth Chart in Chapter Five!

Secondly, this passage of Jasher teaches us that Nimrod rebelled against God, became an idolater, and forced the people he governed to commit idolatry. This included not only the making of images used in worship, but also of the outright worship of the Sun, Moon and Stars in the heavens and the use of Astrology in Sorcery and Magic. Subsequently, Noah and Shem would have had to work tirelessly to thwart Nimrod and Mardon's evil ways and stop the spread of idolatry, immorality, and the use of Astrology. But, as history sadly shows, they were unsuccessful in abolishing these evil practices completely even after Nimrod's kingdom fell.

This passage of Jasher also tells us that Nimrod had a son named Mardon who was even more wicked than Nimrod, suggesting that he may have introduced even more serious offenses against Yahweh than idolatry and Sorcery. These may have included the abominable practices of temple prostitution, sodomy, and human and infant sacrifice. Could Nimrod's evil son Mardon's name have been the inspiration for the name of the god and planet Marduk? If so, then Mardon was likely worshipped as a living embodiment of Marduk during his lifetime. However, what the sinful Babylonians missed in this analogy was that Marduk did not signify Mardon or Nimrod, but the righteous Abraham - whose faith in Yahweh is destined to crush the worship of the Dragon or Serpent just as Marduk crushed Tiamat!

At some point, it is also likely that a fanatical group following Nimrod and his evil son Mardon migrated to other parts of the world, including Egypt, Canaan, China and South and Central America. Proof that this occurred in Egypt lies in the ties between Osiris and Cush and Horus and Nimrod. In addition, there is good reason to believe that the king named Enmerkar of Uruk in Mesopotamia was the same person as Narmer, the king of Egypt who supposedly was the first to unite Upper and Lower Egypt under one monarchy.

Startling proof that this conquest also occurred in the Americas can be found in the story of the rivalry between the opposing gods Quetzalcoatl and Tezcatlipoca in indigenous native myths. In addition, **huge stone heads of Negroes and steles depicting living or dead and mutilated Semitic men have been found at the La Venta Pre-Columbian archeological site in Mexico.** These stand as a mute but indisputable testimony to this little known time in history. In fact, they suggest that - as soon as Nimrod's followers arrived in these new lands - they forcefully drove out and killed the descendents of Noah who reigned in these regions and educated the people in the Way of Yahweh. Subsequently, Nimrod's armies subjugated the people, defiled their places of worship, installed idols, and perverted their religious rituals with abominable practices inspired by the Way of Cain.

There is also evidence in the Book of Jasher that idolatry spread rapidly in Mesopotamia at the hands of Abraham's princely father Terah, who was a very high official in Nimrod's court:

> "And Terah the son of Nahor, prince of Nimrod's host, was in those days very great in the sight of the king and his subjects, and the king and princes loved him, and they elevated him very high." - Jasher 7:43-49

> "And Terah had twelve gods of large size, made of wood and stone, after the twelve months of the year, and he served each one monthly, and every month Terah would bring his meat offering and drink offering to his gods; thus did Terah all the days. And all that generation were wicked in the sight of the Lord, and they thus made every man his god, but they forsook the Lord who had created them. **And there was not a man found in those days in the whole earth, who knew the Lord (for they served each man his own God) except Noah and his household,** and all those who were under his counsel knew the Lord..." - Jasher 9:8-10

These passages tell us that Abraham's father Terah was a high prince in Nimrod's kingdom who had great authority and was well-loved throughout the kingdom. Therefore. Terah's brand of idolatry, which appeared to center around twelve idols dedicated to the Twelve Signs of the Zodiac and the twelve months of the year - must have been equally well-loved. But, though the whole world had apparently succumbed to the idolatrous religion of Nimrod and Terah, there was one other person besides Noah and Shem who was not deceived by this gross idolatry. His name was Abraham:

> "And Abram the son of Terah was waxing great in those days in the house of Noah, and no man knew it, and the Lord was with him. And the Lord gave Abram an understanding heart, and he knew all the works of that generation were vain, and that all their gods were vain and were of no avail." - Jasher 9:11-12

To prove that Terah's idols were totally powerless and useless as deities, the Book of Jasher records - with quite a bit of refreshing mirth - that Abraham performed the following experiment:

> "And Abram took the savory meat from his mother, and brought it before his father's gods into the chamber; and he came nigh unto them that they might eat, and he placed it before them, and Abram sat before them all day, thinking perhaps they might eat. And Abram viewed them, and behold they had neither voice nor hearing, nor did one of them stretch forth his hand to the meat to eat. **And in the evening of that day in that house Abram was clothed with the spirit of God.** And he called out and said, 'Woe unto my father and this wicked generation, whose hearts are all inclined to vanity, who serve these idols of wood and stone which can neither eat, smell, hear nor speak, who have mouths without speech, eyes without sight, ears without hearing, hands without feeling, and legs which cannot move; like them are those that made them and that trust in them.'

> And when Abram saw all these things his anger was kindled against his father, and he... took a hatchet in his hand, and came unto the chamber of the gods, and he broke all his father's gods. And when he had done breaking the images, he placed the hatchet in the hand of the great god which was there before them, and he went out; and Terah his father came home, for he had heard at the door the sound of the striking of the hatchet; so Terah... ran to the room to the images, and he met Abram going out. And Terah entered the room and found all the idols fallen down and broken, and the hatchet in the hand of the largest, which was not broken, and the savory meat which Abram his son had made was still before them.

> And when Terah saw this his anger was greatly kindled, and he hastened and went from the room to Abram. And he found Abram his son still sitting in the house; and he said to him, 'What is this work thou hast done to my gods?' And Abram answered Terah his father and he said, 'Not so my lord, for I brought savory meat before them, and when I came nigh to them with the meat that they might eat, they all at once stretched forth their hands to eat before the great one had put forth his hand to eat. And the large one saw their works that they did before him, and his anger was violently kindled against them, and he went and took the hatchet that

was in the house and came to them and broke them all, and behold the hatchet is yet in his hand as thou seest.' And Terah's anger was kindled against his son Abram, when he spoke this; and Terah said to Abram his son in his anger, 'What is this tale that thou hast told? Thou speakest lies to me.'" - Jasher 11:29-41

So, while Terah was bright enough to know that his son Abraham was lying when he said that the great idol's rage at the other idols had caused it to procure a hatchet and break all the other idols into pieces, Terah seemed unwilling to see that these idols were totally powerless and therefore could not stop Abraham from destroying them. Therefore, underlying the humor in this passage is the sad commentary that idolaters are almost impossible to win over to the truth by ordinary means. Alas, it often takes a supernatural experience to awaken idolaters to their folly and show them the way to truth and righteousness. And that is just what happened to Abraham while sitting in his father's idol sanctuary (Jasher 11:31). He was invisibly clothed with the Holy Spirit and likely became as one who is born-again: filled with the knowledge of Yahweh and the desire to serve Him.

As shown in the preceding quote from the Book of Jasher and in Jasher 9:6 quoted on page 204, both Noah and Shem schooled Abraham in the Way of Yahweh. This fact underscores the fact that **the antediluvian Patriarchs were the righteous heirs to an eternal priesthood that Yahweh gave to all the patriarchal leaders in the line of Seth.** Descended from Adam's son Seth through Cainan, Jared, Enoch, Methuselah, Lamech, Noah, Shem, Arphaxad, Cainan, Selah, Eber, Peleg, Reu, Serug, Nahor, Terah, Abraham, Isaac, Jacob, on down to King David and beyond (Luke 3:31-38), Yahshua our Savior was the final inheritor and perfecter of that eternal priesthood (Hebrews 5:5-10).

But sadly, as this book shows, some of these priestly patriarchal princes like Lamech the Sethite were greatly deceived in their thinking, or else had become apostate idolaters like Terah. Indeed, Abraham's father Terah had totally lost his way and was destined for Hell, for many ignorant common people were beguiled into idolatry, deceived and corrupted into engaging in grievous sin through false teachers like him and his fellow princes under Nimrod, and many were destined to perish without ever knowing the God of Love because of their folly.

How the Earth Was Divided After the Flood

In examining the spread of people and races after the Flood, we can determine where certain people groups resided or visited based on legends and partly historical religious records such as the Bible, Jasher, and Jubilees. The Book of Jubilees tells us that, during the time of Peleg, the three sons of Noah secretly divided the Earth between themselves, and then Noah stepped in and allotted various lands to his sons by causing them to draw lots:

> *"And in the sixth year thereof, she bare him a son, and he called his name Peleg; for in the days when he was born the children of Noah began to divide the earth amongst themselves: for this reason he called his name Peleg... And it came to pass in the beginning of the thirty-third jubilee that they divided the earth into three parts, for Shem and Ham and Japheth, according to the inheritance of each, in the first year in the first week, when one of us who had been sent (i.e. a holy Watcher), was with them. And he called his sons, and they drew nigh to him, they and their children, and he divided the earth into the lots, which his three sons were to take in possession, and they reached forth their hands, and took the writing out of the bosom of Noah, their father. And there came forth on the writing as Shem's lot the middle of the earth which he should take as an inheritance for himself and for his sons for the generations of eternity..." - Jubilees 8:8-12*

The drawing of lots to make decisions rests on the biblical principle that Yahweh is active in our world, and - if we allow Him to - Yahweh will help us to make choices that conform to His Will. As a result of this, Shem and his descendents settled around Mount Ararat in what is now Afghanistan, Mesopotamia and the Middle East. Ham went south and west of there, and Japheth went north and east of there (See Genesis Chapter 10 and the Book of Jubilees, Chapter 7, 8 and 9). In the book "After the Flood," Bill Cooper performs a thorough study of ancient genealogies in order to prove that all the people of Europe descended from one man: Noah. In the process, Mr. Cooper also proves that all the kings of Europe descended from Noah's son Japheth.

In the preceding quote from Jubilees, it is interesting that Shem's allotment of the land was in the middle of the earth since it echoes J. R. R. Tolkien's Middle Earth in his famous "Lord of the Rings" book trilogy. As the one Yah chose to be a righteous ancestor of Yahshua, Shem inherited the best lands – those encompassing the most desirable regions of the Earth north of the equator. In the Lord of the Rings, this is where many different races of intelligent humanoid beings reside. In Tolkien's Middle Earth, there were ents, dwarves, elves, hobbits and humans that were locked in an epic battle against sorcerers who controlled dragons, ogres and orcs - despicable creatures who ate human flesh and one another indiscriminately.

In many respects, Tolkien's vision of Middle Earth during the rise of the wicked sorcerer Sauron matches my view of what life on Earth was like perhaps a few hundred years prior to the Great Flood. By then, there were large pockets of humanity and Nephilim that were terribly wicked and corrupt and who terrorized the people who were attempting to live in peace, follow the righteous laws of Yahweh, and uphold the teachings of His prophets. During his lifetime, Tolkien was a very learned and well-respected Catholic scholar and linguist who helped in the translation of the Jerusalem Bible. He was also a great fan of mythical lore and history who not only helped convert C. S. Lewis to Christianity but inspired Lewis in his writing of the Narnia Chronicles, a fantasy series like Tolkien's that supports Christian values and clearly defines the stark contrasts between and total incompatibility of good and evil.

Now, one day while contemplating the explanation of the land divisions given in the Book of Jubilees, I had a remarkable thought. What if the land of Giza in Egypt had been the first international religious and trade hub between the clans of Noah and his sons? What if it was not only a meeting ground between them, but a sign of the Covenant that they had agreed to keep with one another? For at the end of the explanation of the land allotments in Jubilees, it says:

> "And thus the sons of Noah divided unto their sons in the presence of Noah their father, and he bound them all by an oath (i.e. a covenant), imprecating a curse on every one that sought to seize the portion which had not fallen (to him) by his lot. And they all said, 'so be it; so be it' (i.e. Amen, Amen) for themselves and their sons for ever throughout their generations till the day of judgment, on which the Lord God shall judge them with a sword and with fire for all the unclean wickedness of their errors." - Jubilees 9:14-15

This passage clearly sets forth the terms of the Covenant agreement that Noah and his sons entered when they divided all of the Earth's continents by lots, as well as the curses that will befall anyone who breaks this Covenant. Could it therefore be that the Pillar of Enoch, which stood as a reminder of Yahweh's Covenants with Adam, Seth and Enoch before the Flood, may have been used as a pillar of witness for this Covenant over the land after the Flood? If so, this would make sense of Giza's designation as the Navel of the World.

After all, the natural border between Upper and Lower Egypt is the place known as "Giza," meaning "border" in Arabic. Since the righteous Sethites built the pyramids at Giza and Dahshur before the Flood, Seth's clan likely cared for Giza and served as priests over this sacred meeting ground up until the death of Noah, when Shem took possession of *"the middle of the earth,"* or Middle Earth (Jubilees 8:8-12). Since Giza is the Navel of the World in the natural middle of the Earth, Shem likely had control of Giza and its environs, thereby ruling over the first world center for religion and trade until Nimrod overthrew Shem's dominion.

The map of the Earth on page 452 shows a plausible way in which these land divisions were decided using the Great Pyramid's four-sided design as a guide. But first, imagine a circle drawn around the Nile Delta with the Great Pyramid as the center point of its diameter. When this is done, the Nile Delta region serves as approximately one quarter of the circle facing due north. This shows its connection with the north face of the Pillar of Enoch, whose sides face the four cardinal directions. This circular region could have served as an international sacred district belonging to Shem, who was Melchizedek the priest of El Elyon or God Most High, and whose original land allotment included Canaan up to the

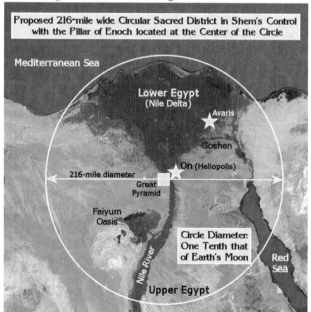

banks of the Nile River. Though the Canaanites still dominated the region at the time of Abraham, Melchizedek had won dominion over Salem, a city in Canaan that would later become Jerusalem.

As shown in the illustration on this page, this circle around the Nile Delta has a diameter of 216 miles, which is one tenth the diameter of Earth's Moon.

World Map Showing Probable Post-Flood Land Divisions

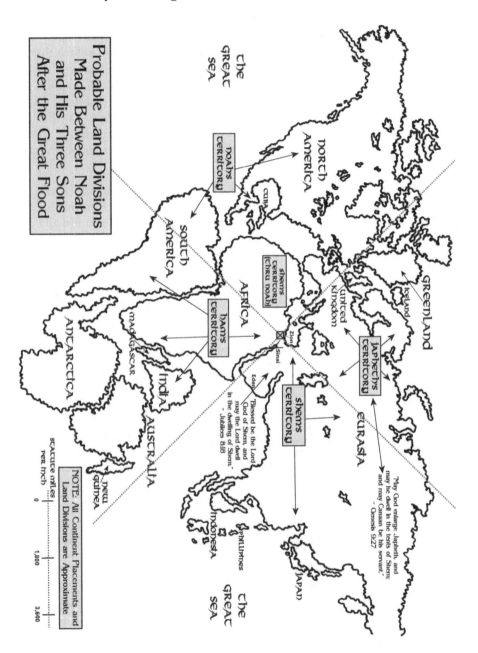

This shows another connection with the Great Pyramid, which symbolizes one hemisphere of the Earth and has an interior chamber that is symbolically tied to the Moon (See Book Four). If this circular area belonged to Shem, he would have controlled Lower Egypt and part of Upper Egypt, including the sacred districts at Giza and Dahshur, the cities of Avaris and On (a.k.a. Heliopolis) on the border marking Shem's territory, the land of Goshen, and the Faiyum Oasis. Considering how geometrically precise the Sethites were, this is an intriguing possibility.

Now, if lines are extended outward from each of the Pillar of Enoch's corners, it would have served to evenly divide the dry land areas of the Earth outside of that circle into four quarters, as shown on page 452. The two middle sections of this four-part land division spanned the whole Middle of the Earth and belonged to Shem, though I have shown a place for Noah in the "Far West" or the Americas. This is because the Americas may have been known as "Dilmun" to the Babylonians, although this term also seems to have applied to Bahrain on the west side of the Persian Gulf.

As already stated earlier, these assumptions about Noah's location after his sons divided up the land are based on the Epic of Gilgamesh, which places Noah in "Dilmun" or the "Far West," a place across the "lethal waters." This term is probably a descriptive reference for the Atlantic Ocean, which is quite stormy and highly dangerous to traverse in small wooden ships.

As shown on the map on page 452 and recorded in the Book of Jubilees, India was among Ham's land allotments (Jubilees 9:2). On the map, India is depicted as an island continent off the east coast of Africa. There is good reason for this. Geologists have discovered that India was once part of Madagascar but subsequently broke away from it and was moved to its new position in some past cataclysm, which they believe may have been caused by a massive celestial impact that left the tell-tale Shiva crater off the western coast of India.

The disaster that moved India to this new location likely occurred during the cataclysmic division of languages and the fracturing of the land that ended Nimrod's bid for world domination and made him cease building the Tower of Babel. At that time, India and Madagascar were likely broken off of Africa and then India was violently slammed into the coast of central Asia. This crushing impact probably instantly destroyed the Indus Valley civilizations and also created the massive Himalayan mountain range. In addition to India, Ham and his descendents received most of the continent of Africa with Madagascar, the southern half of South America, Australia with New Guinea, and Antarctica.

At the time of these divisions, my map shows that Japheth likely received the smallest land allotment. Perhaps this is why Noah prophesied: *"May God enlarge Japheth, and may he dwell in the tents of Shem"* (Genesis 9:27). Therefore, as Japheth's descendents moved northward into Britain, Europe, Russia and parts of Asia, Shem's descendants appropriated the lands of Southern Asia, Mesopotamia, the Middle East, and the Mediterranean regions of North Africa where they mingled with the descendents of Japheth. However, as shown on the map, Noah and Shem's descendents also likely settled and governed in a large portion of the Americas for a time. This idea will be explored further in Chapter Nine.

Idolatry, Sorcery, and Star Worship: Nimrod's Religion

For a time after the Flood on the ruined Earth, Noah and his sons likely kept their faith in Yahweh. The Book of Jasher makes it clear that Shem did so along with his father Noah. But the Nephilim who survived the Flood, the demon spirits of dead Nephilim, and the spirits of the fallen angels soon caused mankind to slip into sin.

Indeed, not long after the Flood, it is highly likely that Nimrod became known as a Mighty Hunter before Yahweh because he began to kill the Anakim descendents of the Nephilim who ruled over parts of the Earth, and caused the Anakim to fight amongst themselves in such a way that there was no hope of a centralized government or world power base. However, though Yahweh hated the Nephilim and wanted the Anakim annihilated because they stood in the way of humanity's salvation, Nimrod had an evil agenda. In short, Nimrod wanted to destroy the power of the Nephilim to further his own ambitions.

In order to unite humanity in one cause, Nimrod championed the idea of changing the way people think and what people want so that they would want to conform to a one-world system that could promise it all. He thereby sought to change the false religious doctrines of the Nephilim from the worship of demons into the worship of men, which really is no different on a spiritual level but ascribes much greater importance to men in the tangible world. With this evil agenda in mind, Nimrod and his demonically inspired followers succeeded in wiping out whole groups of Anakim and taking control of their petty kingdoms. Then, after they had succeeded in taking control of all the kingdoms on the Earth, Nimrod's minions began to completely distort the message and purpose of the Gospel in the Stars by connecting it to idolatrous Pagan worship, fortunetelling, Astrology and Sorcery.

This is why, after solidifying his power and authority with heroic deeds, Nimrod was called a Mighty Hunter *before* Yahweh:

> *"Cush begot Nimrod; he began to be a mighty one (Gibborim) on the earth. He was a mighty hunter before the LORD (Yahweh); therefore it is said, 'Like Nimrod the mighty hunter before the LORD (Yahweh).'" - Genesis 10:8-9 (NKJ)*

Here, when Nimrod is described as *"a mighty hunter before the LORD,"* it has a rather positive connotation in English, doesn't it? However, though the Hebrew word "paniym" can mean "before," and it is translated that way in English versions of Genesis 10:9, it can also mean "against," and was meant to imply that Nimrod was "before" Yahweh in the sense of an antagonist. The name "Nimrod" adds support to this supposition, since it means "subduing leopard" in Babylonian. In addition, the Hebrew verb "nimrodh" meaning "let us revolt" is the biblical meaning of Nimrod's name.

It is interesting to note here that the Jews associated the constellation of Orion, the Mighty Hunter in heaven with Nimrod, and this book series has proven that this association is mostly unwarranted. However, the bull fights that pit a torero (i.e. bull fighter in Spanish) with a toro (i.e. "bull" in Spanish, derived from the Latin "Taurus" for bull), which have been going on in Spain for centuries suggest that there is a tie. Could it be that this bullfighting ritual hearkens back to a time when mankind revolted against Yahshua, the allegorical Toro or Bull of Heaven? Because, at that time, mankind allegorically did put Yahshua to death by writing Him out of their histories and denigrating and killing those who loved the promise of His coming.

Nonetheless, these bull fights also tell us of a coming time when a heavenly Matador or Torero will come to kill the bull-like Beast and the wanton Woman or church that rides it. This Woman is signified by Europa riding the Bull called Zeus that signifies the Serpent's religion and the Way of Cain. These symbols also identify the final adversarial kingdom against Yahshua's with the European Union that will one day give rise to the Antichrist who will rule the world. Shortly after that time, Yahshua will conquer this Beast or socio-economic system and destroy the Woman or religion that rides it, thereby reversing the damage done by those like Nimrod that are leading mankind's current revolt against Yahweh and His saints.

Just like today, the past meddling of the unholy Nephilim, Anakim and fallen angels in human affairs led people to worship themselves and demons instead of the holy, perfect, and sinless Creator God. Even after the Nephilim were eradicated, they survived as the

Anakim and were permitted to encourage the sin of idolatry. As they spread their spiritual darkness, Paganism soon was touted as the truth by most of humanity.

The reason for the success of Paganistic humanism over the Star Gospel of Salvation in Yahshua is simple. It centers around the fact that some men and women always seem to want to usurp the enormous power and authority of Yahweh God and the temporal power of the Nephilim and claim it for themselves. As a result, they first tend to rewrite history to reflect their views. Then they set themselves up as god-like rulers. In the past, they also learned to use the Magic and Sorcery of the Nephilim to control the people they wished to rule over. In short, tyranny always results when the philosophy of Humanism is combined with religious and political fascism to recreate the most powerful and corrupt world government of ancient times: Nimrod's Babylon.

In the Book of Jasher, Nimrod is depicted as a man who honored Yahweh as the source of his power at first - but then fell into grievous sin later in his reign. Convinced of his own superiority, Nimrod soon deified himself and united people together in a common cause - to make a name for themselves on the Earth. They did this by establishing a powerful world government that promoted spiritual and intellectual unity while solidifying Nimrod's status as an undisputed leader and god.

Tragically, like the ancient Egyptians, the Babylonians of Nimrod's era worshipped mankind as gods alongside the one triune God Yahweh, who was faithfully represented for a short time by a trio of Sumerian gods known as Shamash (i.e. God the Father), Ea or Enki (i.e. E-Yah or Yahshua), and Anu (i.e. the Holy Spirit). As shown in the chart on pages 568 and 569, many evil or wayward biblical characters were eventually deified and worshipped as deities not only in Babylon but in Egypt, Greece and Rome. In fact, plenty of ancient sources stipulate that the whole world followed this same false, idolatrous religion at one time.

Besides creating sinful idols to represent the unseen Creator God, the Babylonians styled many of their idols to represent gods connected to the Zodiac and the planets. Now, since these constellations in heaven along with the Sun, Moon and planets represent the history of mankind, those who worshipped the heavens were really worshipping their most notable human ancestors along with various Nephilim, demons, and fallen angels. Yet, above all those who were deified stood Eve, the woman or "Isha" who had unwittingly spearheaded their mutual rebellion against God. Indeed, this first woman inspired the creation and elevation of the goddess Ishtar or Inanna, the female personification of Venus (the Morning Star) and the seductive daughter of the illuminator god "Nanna" or "Sin," the Babylonian Moon god (a.k.a. Allah!). Uncannily, this deity's very name evokes evil due to its connection to the word "sin" meaning "rebellion against God" in English.

Incidentally, the name Esther in the Bible is the Persian version of "Ishtar," and Esther was a Jewess who became the Queen of Persia and a parabolic symbol for the True Church in the Last Day. This fact stands in stark juxtaposition to Nimrod's worship of the Queen of Heaven seen in the constellation Cassiopeia, which is actually meant to represent the True Church or Bride of Christ that consists of all the saints, but that was hijacked by Satan and Nimrod to signify the Devil's followers instead! That is why people that are guided by demons love Nimrod's idea of a utopian world with one central government and religion so much, and why they are feverishly working to achieve what Nimrod did once more. These modern Pagans want to be gods like Isha or Ishtar, and they will stop at nothing until they can all claim to be god. Like the Antichrist, they wish to be perceived as gods and worshipped by those who are perishing.

Under Nimrod's tyrannical but seemingly benevolent control, people banded together to build a humanistic society unlike any there had been before. It was a society united under one language and one idolatrous Pagan faith that they all were compelled to share. At the head of this apostate government and religion stood Nimrod, who was seen as a god with a divine right to rule. Incidentally, *this is exactly what the Antichrist is going to briefly succeed in doing when he takes control.*

Nimrod built four main cities as the seat of his apostate government: Babel, Erech, Accad and Calneh in the land of Shinar, or ancient Chaldea in Mesopotamia (Genesis 10:10). The crowning achievement of Nimrod's rule was the Tower of Babel, an incomparable ziggurat that served as both a center for his government and a temple for his false astral religion. Nimrod's religion espoused the deification of human beings along with the worship of demons associated with stars, the Sun, Moon and planets and the idols created to represent them. In addition, this false religion promoted Magic and Sorcery as legitimate ways to gain power. With Magic to aid them, anyone who mastered the black art of Sorcery could act as a god. In short, Nimrod's followers began to do just as their ancestors prior to the Flood had done; *they worshipped the Creation and themselves instead of the Creator, and utilized demonic power to rebel against Yahweh and fight against His followers*.

This worship of men and celestial bodies arose from the detestable practice of Astrology. Astrology is a gross distortion of Biblical or Sacred Astronomy. Instead of seeing Astronomy as a method of

determining Yahweh's Will in order to spiritually and physically prepare
for it, Astrology is an attempt to manipulate history so that certain
prophesied events will not take place. Thus, Astrology is clearly a form
of rebellion against Yahweh. It was used to predict certain astronomically
foretold events in order to determine a way to affect a change in the
course of history, or to manipulate it to one's advantage. But any
method used to alter the divinely ordained course of history is a form of
Sorcery and is diametrically opposed to Yahweh's Will.

This false religion of human idolatry, Sorcery and star worship
originated among the fallen angels and was further practiced and
promulgated by their Nephilim offspring. Like several of the fallen
angels, some Nephilim may have claimed to be physical manifestations
of the celestial bodies that were worshipped as deities. But Nimrod and
his ilk saw stars and planets as representations of human beings who
had or would become gods. Astrology and idolatry therefore are forms of
rebellion against God's sovereignty in our lives and they both encourage
Black Magic – a manipulative form of Sorcery which the Zodiac was
never intended to foster or represent.

Indeed, though the deluded Babylonians believed it is possible to
achieve godhood through human means alone, this is only possible in a
limited sense through Yahweh God. Indeed, *there is only ONE WAY
that human beings can become like gods, and that way is found in the
Way of Yahweh that Yahshua came to fulfill and teach* - just as the
prophets before Him who were called gods did (John 10:34-36). Through
Yahshua's salvation and the resurrection to everlasting life, we become a
living cell in His Body the Church - the Body or Vessel where God will
dwell for eternity.

Nimrod's Tower and World Empire Destroyed

As discussed earlier, the Earth's one massive super-continent
may have broken up during the cataclysm that caused the Flood.
However, the continents that it fractured into may have only been
separated by narrow seas. It therefore would have been fairly easy for
men to spread out as the Earth's population increased.

After Noah and his sons' territorial dividing of the land discussed
in the last section, the Bible, Book of Jasher and Book of Jubilees tell us
that Yahweh became angry with mankind because they did not spread
out enough to keep them from uniting under one government and
religion (Genesis 11:4-9; Jasher 9:21-39; Jubilees 10:23-27). Therefore,

when Nimrod took control of the world, he earned Yahweh's wrath and judgment upon him and his evil empire.

In punishment, there is physical and written evidence supporting the fact that Yahweh caused cataclysmic earthquakes and volcanic eruptions that literally divided the Earth into the continents that we know today (See Genesis 11:8-9, Jasher 9:37-38 and Jasher 17:19-20, which pertain to this event). But just before this, Yahweh confounded the minds of all those who spoke the one world language and divided their speech just as He was about to physically divide the land. Thereafter, the world was divided into groups that spoke similar languages as well as by new physical barriers like mountains and oceans that did not exist prior to that time.

The following section from the Book of Jubilees that suggests it was recorded by a holy Watcher gives an account of this event that parallels the Bible:

> "And in the three and thirtieth jubilee... Peleg took to himself a wife... and she bare him a son... and he called his name Reu; for he said: 'Behold the children of men have become evil through the wicked purpose of building for themselves a city and a tower in the land of Shinar.'
>
> For they departed from the land of Ararat eastward to Shinar... And they began to build, and in the fourth week they made brick with fire, and the bricks served them for stone, and the clay with which they cemented them together was asphalt which comes out of the sea and out of the fountains of water in the land of Shinar. **And... forty and three years were they building it... its height amounted to 5433 cubits and 2 palms (2716.5 yards or 8,149.5 feet if the cubit is 18 inches), and (the extent of one wall was) thirteen stades (1.5 miles if the Greek Stadium Attic is used) and of the other thirty stades (3.45 miles).**
>
> And the Lord our God said unto us (the holy Watchers): 'Behold, they are one people, and (this) they begin to do, and now nothing will be withholden from them. Go to, let us go down and confound their language, that they may not understand one another's speech, and they may be dispersed into cities and nations, and one purpose will no longer abide with them till the day of judgment.'
>
> And the Lord descended, and we descended with him to see the city and the tower which the children of men had built. And he confounded their language, and they no longer

understood one another's speech, and they ceased then to
build the city and the tower. For this reason the whole land of
Shinar is called Babel, because the Lord did there confound all
the language of the children of men, and from thence they
were dispersed into their cities, each according to his language
and his nation.

And the Lord sent a mighty wind against the tower
and overthrew it upon the earth, and behold it was between
Asshur and Babylon in the land of Shinar, and they called its
name 'Overthrow.' In the... four and thirtieth jubilee, were
they dispersed from the land of Shinar." - Jubilees 10:18-28

This account from Jubilees makes it clear that the Tower of Babel
was constructed of fired bricks and had taken 43 years to build to the
height that it was at when it was destroyed. At over 8100 feet or 1.5
miles high, this tower was over 16 times that height of the Great
Pyramid, which was around 485 feet high when it was first completed.
In fact, the Tower that Nimrod built was five and half times the height of
the Sear Tower in Chicago! In addition, its rectangular base was the size
of a small town at 1.5 by 3.45 miles long. Therefore, this was no ordinary
ziggurat. In fact, it was a gigantic tower that reached so high into the sky
that people would have gotten weaker and more disoriented from
oxygen deprivation as they ascended it.

This portion of Jubilees also indicates that God first confused the
people's languages to get them to disperse and then sent a powerful
wind to destroy the Tower. Josephus also seems to have used Jubilees to
write his account of the tower's destruction and mentions a strong wind
as the destructive force used. According to the Book of Jubilees, this
happened in the 34th Jubilee, which is 34 X 50 or 1700 years after Adam
and Eve were created. However, according to my Biblical Chronology in
the Appendix, this was only 44 years after the Flood of 2347 BC. Since
Abraham was alive at the time of the Tower of Babel's destruction and
was instrumental in toppling Nimrod's Empire, the destruction of the
Tower had to have occurred after Abraham was born in 2055 BC.

After the destruction on Nimrod's Tower, Jubilees tells us that
the area where the city and tower were built was called "Overthrow."
The Hebrew word "haras" (Strong's # 2040, harac {haw-ras}) can mean
"overthrow" and appears to be related to the English word "harass,"
though dictionaries state that it is Old French. This Hebrew word bears a
resemblance to the name of the nation called Iraq, where some of the
ruins of the much later kingdom of ancient Babylon ruled over by
Nebuchadnezzar were rebuilt when Saddam Hussein was the dictator
there. However, though a small portion of this ancient city has again

risen up from the desert sands, there are reports that local workers have long refused to spend the night in the area. They won't because they say it is haunted by djinn (i.e. demons) and people have gone mad or been found dead if they attempt to spend the night there.

In this regard, it is interesting that the United States has so recently and relentlessly fought to turn Iraq into a democratic nation. Though many conspiracy theorists have said this was done in the US quest for a secure source of crude oil, one wonders if it was done for a much more prophetic purpose. Could it be that the USA has occupied Iraq to pave the way for the Antichrist or King of the North to set up a base of operations there and rule over a final world empire that will hate Yahweh and those who love Him and His Law? If so, this does not mean that the USA is Babylon the Great, as so many falsely claim. It does suggest, however, that the USA is secretly being guided to act in a manner that will ensure that God's Will regarding the Antichrist is fulfilled! Could it be that, just as the Illuminati are attempting to fight God's Will, there may be a completely secret society on the Earth today that has even greater power and authority than the Illuminati, and that exists solely to ensure that God's prophetic Will is fulfilled to the letter? I now believe that there is at least one, and that this secret organization is being guided by the disciple mentioned in John's Gospel who was to wait until Yahshua returned:

> "Then Peter, turning around, saw the disciple whom Jesus loved following, who also had leaned on His breast at the supper, and said, 'Lord, who is the one who betrays You?' Peter, seeing him, said to Jesus, 'But Lord, what about this man?' Jesus said to him, 'If I will that he (i.e. the disciple whom Jesus loved) remain till I come, what is that to you? You follow Me. Then this saying went out among the brethren that this disciple would not die. Yet Jesus did not say to him that he would not die, but, 'If I will that he remain till I come, what is that to you?'" - John 21:20-23 (NKJ)

Like many pastors and prophecy teachers, I believe that this disciple whom Yahshua loved is still alive today. Though many identify him as John, my book: "The Language of God in Humanity" reveals that it may be Lazarus, who was loved by Yahshua along with his sisters Mary and Martha of Bethany (John 11:5, 36). In addition, some of the people in this beloved disciple's secret group may be related to the Magi of old who visited Christ in Bethlehem and may be helping this disciple to know and fulfill God's timeline as it is written in the Sun, Moon, stars and planets. Though I am not worthy to be one of them, I feel privileged to have received a small measure of Enoch's spirit.

Returning to the subject of Nimrod's era, the Book of Jasher or Upright Record gives another alternative account of what Nimrod's kingdom and infamous tower was like, and what Yahweh did to judge Nimrod and bring his dominion to an end. Just as the writer of Jubilees recorded, the Upright Record indicates that the Tower of Babel was immense and built in total defiance against God. It also indicates that the people building the tower suffered from bizarre symptoms that are similar to those suffered by people undergoing oxygen deprivation and hypothermia:

> "And king Nimrod reigned securely, and all the earth was under his control, and all the earth was of one tongue and words of union. **And all the princes of Nimrod and his great men took counsel together; Phut, Mitzraim, Cush and Canaan with their families**, and they said to each other, Come let us build ourselves a city and in it a strong tower... reaching heaven... in order that the evil of our enemies may cease from us, that we may reign mightily over them, and that we may not become scattered over the earth on account of their wars.
>
> And they all went before the king, and they told the king these words, and the king agreed with them in this affair, and he did so. And all the families assembled consisting of about six hundred thousand men, and they went to seek an extensive piece of ground to build the city and the tower... and they found none like... the land of Shinar... and they... dwelt there. And they began to make bricks... to build the city and the tower that they had imagined to complete.
>
> And the building of the tower was unto them a transgression and a sin... and whilst they were building against the Lord God of heaven, they imagined in their hearts to war against him and to ascend into heaven. And all these people and all the families divided themselves in three parts; the first said We will ascend into heaven and fight against him; the second said, We will ascend to heaven and place our own gods there and serve them; and the third part said, We will ascend to heaven and smite him with bows and spears; and God knew all their works and all their evil thoughts, and he saw the city and the tower which they were building.
>
> And... they built themselves a great city and a very high and strong tower; and on account of its height the mortar and bricks did not reach the builders in their ascent to it, until those who went up had completed a full year **("a full year" - this is likely a scribal error, and should read "a full day" - see**

*underlined portions below), and after that, they reached to the builders and gave them the mortar and the bricks; **thus was it done daily. And behold these ascended and others descended the whole day; and if a brick should fall from their hands and get broken, they would all weep over it, and if a man fell and died, none of them would look at him** (this suggests the affects of oxygen deprivation and mild hypothermia).*

*And the Lord knew their thoughts, and it came to pass when they were building (that) **they cast the arrows toward the heavens, and all the arrows fell upon them filled with blood,** and when they saw them, they said to each other: 'Surely we have slain all those that are in heaven.' For this was from the Lord in order to cause them to err, and in order to destroy them... And they built the tower... until many days and years were elapsed.*

And God said to the seventy angels who stood foremost before him, to those who were near to him, saying, 'Come let us descend and confuse their tongues, that one man shall not understand the language of his neighbor,' and they did so unto them. And from that day following, they forgot each man his neighbor's tongue, and they could not understand to speak in one tongue, and when the builder took from the hands of his neighbor lime or stone which he did not order, the builder would cast it away and throw it upon his neighbor, that he would die. And they did so many days, and they killed many of them in this manner." - Jasher 9:20-34

According to this account, Nimrod's monstrous tower was actually built as an act of war against the King of the Universe and His holy angels. Those who worked on this tower wanted to wage war with Yahweh Himself. In fact, they even shot arrows or missiles of some sort into the heavens in an effort to do so. Then, to delude them, God covered the missiles that fell back down to Earth with a blood-like substance that deluded these wicked people into believing that their efforts to kill God and His angels was working.

Due to these abominable practices and the idolatrous religion that Nimrod spawned, it did not take long for Yahweh's wrath to be kindled against Babylon. However, because of His promise to Noah, God did not destroy the Nimrod's empire and tower with a worldwide flood. Instead, the Book of Jasher indicates that Yahweh sent "fire from heaven" accompanied by an earthquake:

> *"And the Lord smote the three divisions... and he punished them according to their works and designs; those who said, 'We will ascend to heaven and serve our gods,' became like apes and elephants; and those who said, 'We will smite the heaven with arrows,' the Lord killed them, one man through the hand of his neighbor; and the third division... who said, 'We will ascend to heaven and fight against him,' the Lord scattered them throughout the earth. And those who were left amongst them, when they knew and understood the evil which was coming upon them, they forsook the building, and they also became scattered upon the face of the whole earth. And they ceased building the city and the tower; therefore he (God) called that place Babel, for there the Lord confounded the Language of the whole earth; behold it was at the east of the land of Shinar. And as to the tower which the sons of men built, **the earth opened its mouth and swallowed up one third part thereof, and a fire also descended from heaven and burned another third,** and the other third is left to this day, **and it is of that part which was aloft, and its circumference is three days' walk. And many of the sons of men died in that tower, a people without number.**"* - Jasher 9:35-39*

This passage from the Book of Jasher tells us that the Tower of Babel was no ordinary Ziggurat. In fact, since so many people died within the tower and it served as their final resting place, the tower may have been like a modern skyscraper with a multitude of rooms within it that were inhabited. From this description, it appears that the Tower of Babel may have been engineered to serve as a fortress and haven from natural disasters of all sorts, not just floods. Note that, by indicating that the part of the Tower that remained was the part that was aloft, the writer of the Book of Jasher suggests that this ancient skyscraper also had a subterranean section that could have extended deep beneath the Earth. Since it took three days to walk around the remaining one-third of this ruined tower, it must have been a mountainous man-made building far bigger than the Great Pyramid at Giza or the massive earthwork pyramid found at Cholula in Mexico, which greatly exceeds the Great Pyramid in volume. It therefore would have taken a tremendously violent rain of fire and brimstone and a great earthquake to destroy this mountainous building, just as ancient writings suggest.

Like the Book of Jasher, the Bible gives us clues that the destruction of Babel was cataclysmic in nature, causing the land to break up rather than just be divided between different clans of people. The Bible says this happened during the time of the righteous ancestor of

Yahshua named Peleg, who likely was a contemporary of Nimrod. Compared to the Biblical account, the Book of Jasher agrees but also gives more detailed information:

> "To Eber were born two sons: the name of one was Peleg, for in his days **the earth was divided**; and his brother's name was Joktan." - Genesis 10:25 (NKJ)

> "These are the generations of Shem; Shem begat Arpachshad and Arpachshad begat Shelach, and Shelach begat Eber and to Eber were born two children, the name of **one was Peleg, for in his days the sons of men were divided, and in the latter days, the earth was divided**. And the name of the second was Yoktan (i.e. Joktan), meaning that **in his day the lives of the sons of men were diminished and lessened**." - Jasher 17:19-20

The agreement found in the preceding passages is just one example of the many points of similarity between the Book of Genesis and the Book of Jasher. Jasher, however, tells us that **there were two divisions at the time of Peleg - one of people by languages and religions and the other by the Earth's landmasses**. Some scholars suggest that this division of the Earth was referring to the division of the land between Noah's sons. However, Noah's sons divided Earth's landmasses between themselves long before Nimrod rose to power.

This portion of the Upright Record also tells us that men's lives were diminished and lessened (i.e.: shortened) during the lifetime of Joktan (or Yoktan). The Hebrew word "Joktan" means "to be made little" or "to diminish." Based on the meaning of Joktan's name, it suggests that the generations of humanity after him had shorter statures and life spans than they did prior to that time. One reason for their smaller stature was no doubt the shortening of their longevity. Men lived 900 years on average before the Flood and had a far longer adolescence. As a result, they would have had the opportunity to grow far bigger - just as all animals did prior to the Flood. As a result, antediluvian societies were much stronger and healthier than we are today.

Nonetheless, by the time of Abraham, men lived only around 150 years. Though this is longer compared to our own estimated life spans today, it was far shorter than the age ascribed to someone like Noah - who lived 950 years. This fact implies that **there were drastic Earth changes at the time of Peleg and Joktan that made this planet less hospitable for life.** However, judging from the feats of strength attributed to the sons of Israel in the Book of Jasher, ancient men were much stronger and possibly somewhat larger in stature than modern

humans even *after* the Earth changes that occurred during the time of
Peleg. It therefore took many generations for the robustness of ancient
men to diminish as much as it had by the time of Yahshua's First
Advent, when ancient Rome ruled the known world.

The Book of Jasher makes it clear that there were two divisions
during Peleg's lifetime. The first was the division of languages that
caused many new cultural groups to form. Secondly, there was a
division of the Earth. The word translated *"divided"* in the preceding
Bible passage is *"Peleg"* (Strong's #6385), which means "to split." The
name Peleg itself is listed as Strong's #6389, meaning "earthquake" and
suggests that the action of immense earthquakes, along with fire and
brimstone from heaven caused the fall of Babel. After the fountains of
the Great Deep were *"broken up"* and the continents formed (Gen. 7:11),
is it possible that the continents spread much further apart due to a
massive earthquake triggered by another celestial bombardment?
Furthermore, could some new and deadly forms of bacteria and viruses
have been carried to Earth from Outer Space during this cataclysm?

The Book of Jasher and many ancient myths from around the
world suggest that a rain of fire and brimstone fell over much of the
Earth's surface at the time of the destruction of Nimrod's Tower. There
is also geological evidence that this rain of fire was caused by a huge
asteroid or comet that broke up. Its largest piece may have hit in central
Canada, where the huge and craterous Hudson Bay is now located.
Another massive piece may have hit where the island of Bermuda is now
located off the Atlantic coast of the United States. This impact alone
could have caused the American continents to spread rapidly away from
Eurasia and Africa, destroying many coastland civilizations around the
world.

This rain of fire may also have led to more devastating
earthquakes and massive volcanic eruptions that speeded up the
processes of plate tectonics and continental drift. In this way, the
continents were violently separated by newly formed oceans and nearly
impassable mountains that did not exist before. This would have caused
the world's population to be forcibly divided by many physical land
barriers. The following Scripture pertains to this time in history:

> *"So the LORD (Yahweh) **scattered them abroad**... over
> the face of all the earth, and they ceased building the city.
> Therefore its name is called Babel, because there the LORD
> (Yahweh) confused the language of all the earth; and...
> **scattered them abroad** over the face of all the earth." - Genesis
> 11:8-9 (NKJ)*

The Hebrew word "puwts" (Strong's # 6327) translated as *"scattered them abroad"* in the above passage literally means "to dash to pieces." This implies the action of throwing a piece of pottery to the ground and breaking it up into many pieces. The above verses could therefore be translated: ***"So Yahweh dashed to pieces the face of all the earth and they ceased building the city. Therefore its name is called Babel, because there Yahweh confused the language of all the earth; and from there Yahweh dashed to pieces the face of all the earth."*** Regardless of Creationist arguments that this would likely have wiped out all life on planet Earth, this passage implies that a far more cataclysmic event than a simple dividing of people into different language groups occurred when Nimrod's followers ceased building the Tower of Babel.

Assuming that the Book of Jasher or Upright Record was written by a contemporary of Moses circa 1400 BC, then an immense part of this infamous Tower of Babel still stood somewhere on the Earth at one time but has subsequently been lost or misidentified. Certainly none of the ziggurats in Mesopotamia - though impressively large and tall mud-brick structures - would take *"three days walk"* to walk around! None of the stone pyramids found on the Earth could approach that size either. So, perhaps the reason why archeologists have not been able to positively identify the remains of the Tower of Babel is that they have been looking for a much smaller "tell" - those conspicuous mounds that usually mark a ruined settlement or sacred site.

Whatever the physical cause of the Tower of Babel's destruction, Yahweh ultimately caused this to occur with His all-encompassing power. By His Will also, the confusion of tongues and division of the land caused people to be immediately separated by both geography and language. Subsequently, this led to the scattering of all mankind over the face of the Earth – just as God wanted in the first place and had indicated when He told Noah and his sons to fill the Earth (Genesis 9:1).

Life must have been very hard on an Earth even more hostile than it had been after the catastrophic devastation of the Great Flood. But this did not keep people from sinning. Those first primitive burials, which showed that the earliest people had an understanding of the truth of Yahweh and His promised salvation, soon gave way to elaborate tombs meant to house the dead, their wealth, and at times even their murdered servants. Eventually, though ritual murders gave way to substituting statues of servants to labor for their masters in the afterlife, the wealthy people who commissioned these elaborate graves for themselves still believed that they would spend eternity indulging in worldly pleasures at other people's expense - just as they had done in life. There is evidence that this belief was widespread, as evidenced by the numerous grave goods found in the burials of nobles and kings in the Americas, Egypt, China, Mesopotamia and elsewhere around the world.

Esau's Murder of Nimrod - A Prophetic Event

The Book of Jasher contains one other story about Nimrod that concerns the way that he died and hints at the future revival of his failed empire by the Antichrist. According to this account, Nimrod was murdered by Jacob's brother Esau just before Esau sold his birthright to Jacob. Thus far, few scholars seem to have noted that this event has a good deal of prophetic meaning and End Time significance. As you read this story from the Book of Jasher, see if you can perceive the allegorical Language of God in this story that reveals what it means:

"Nimrod king of Babel, the same was Amraphel, also frequently went with his mighty men to hunt in the field, and to walk about with his men in the cool of the day. And Nimrod was observing Esau all the days, for a jealousy was formed in the heart of Nimrod against Esau... And on a certain day Esau went in the field to hunt, and he found Nimrod walking in the wilderness with his two men. And all his mighty men and his people were with him in the wilderness, but they removed at a distance from him, and they went from him in different directions to hunt, and Esau concealed himself for Nimrod, and he lurked for him in the wilderness...

And Nimrod and two of his men that were with him came to the place where they were, when Esau started suddenly from his lurking place, and drew his sword, and hastened and ran to Nimrod and cut off his head. And Esau fought a desperate fight with the two men that were with Nimrod, and... Esau turned to them and smote them to death with his sword. And all the mighty men of Nimrod, who had left him to go to the wilderness, heard the cry at a distance... and they ran to know the cause of it, when they found their king and the two men that were with him lying dead in the wilderness.

And when Esau saw the mighty men of Nimrod coming at a distance, he fled, and thereby escaped; and Esau took the valuable garments of Nimrod, which Nimrod's father had bequeathed to Nimrod, and with which Nimrod prevailed

*over the whole land, and he ran and concealed them in his
house. And Esau took those garments and ran into the city on
account of Nimrod's men, and he came unto his father's house
wearied and exhausted from fight, and he was ready to die
through grief when he approached his brother Jacob and sat
before him. And he said unto his brother Jacob, 'Behold I shall
die this day, and wherefore then do I want the birthright?'
And Jacob acted wisely with Esau in this matter, and Esau
sold his birthright to Jacob, for it was so brought about by the
Lord." - Jasher 27:2-12*

Now, applying the Language of God to this story, note that the
Book of Jasher tells us that Nimrod was also known as Amraphel, who
makes an appearance in the Bible as the king of Shinar who united with
three other Mesopotamian kings to conquer Sodom, Gomorrah and three
other cities upon the once fertile plain that stretched alongside the now
desert shores of the Dead Sea (Genesis 14:1,9).

At the time of this war, which occurred among the asphalt pits in
the Valley of Siddim, King Amraphel (i.e. Nimrod) and the kings who
were allied with him made the mistake of abducting Abraham's nephew
Lot and all his wealth after defeating the armies of the five kings of the
plains (Genesis 14:11-12). So, when Abraham found out about it, he went
in hot pursuit of the four Mesopotamian kings who had been so foolish.
Subsequently, Abraham defeated these kings using only 318 of his male
servants who had been specially trained by Abraham in the art of
guerilla warfare. This is suggested by the fact that Abraham attacked the
four kings' armies *by night* (Gen. 14:15). Then Abraham freed Lot and
the other people of the plains that had been taken as slaves and allowed
them to return to their homes along with all their goods (Gen. 14:14-16).
After this, Shem - who was also known as Melchizedek - blessed
Abraham after receiving a tenth of all Abraham's spoils from his victory
against Nimrod.

This is a highly significant event, for it shows that the heavenly
prophecy seen by Nimrod's court Wise Men when Abraham was born
was true - not only in this war, but on many other spiritual and physical
levels. As these wicked Magi had foretold via the signs in the heavens at
Abraham's birth (See Jasher 8:1-4 on page 574), Abraham did indeed
destroy Nimrod's power - not only through his armed servants, but by
his steadfast faith in Yahweh. Nonetheless, since Esau stole Nimrod's
magical clothing in this story, it also suggests that Esau's descendents
would inherit Nimrod's power-hungry desire to rule the world - as well
as their desire to destroy all those who follow the same faith in Yahweh

that Abraham had. It also suggests that the coming Mahdi or world leader anticipated by Muslims will be a direct descendent of Esau.

Interestingly, the animal skin clothes that Esau acquired after he sliced off Nimrod's head suggests that these skin clothes only protected Nimrod's legs, arms and torso from harm, leaving his head and neck vulnerable. Therefore, the only way Esau could kill Nimrod was to cut off his head or slit his throat. Thus, Esau beheaded Nimrod, and though Nimrod's blood must have heavily soiled the animal skin clothes that he wore, Esau took them off of the decapitated man's body and ran into the city where his dying father Isaac was residing.

Shortly thereafter, we are told that Jacob purchased Esau's birthright for a pot of stew. However, the Book of Jasher makes it clear that this was God's desire and not some trickery on the part of Jacob. Furthermore, it clearly suggests that Adam's skin clothes are still in the possession of one of Esau's blood descendents. Therefore, is it possible that these skin clothes may one day clothe and protect the Mahdi or Muslim version of the Antichrist? In addition, could these same skin clothes fall into the hands of the final Antichrist who will conquer the Mahdi and revive the Roman Empire, which once included all the now staunchly Muslim lands bordering the Mediterranean in Africa and the Middle East?

If this is so, it would make even more sense of the amazing Perseus Prophecy that is revealed in the last chapter of Book Four. This prophecy was revealed in the heavens by the crossing of three separate comets through the constellation of Perseus over a period of 20 years. These comets not only passed over Perseus, but specifically over a star in the snake-covered head of Medusa that Perseus is holding in his left hand. As will be shown in the next chapter, Medusa's head represents the hypnotizing power of the Way of Cain, also known as the Way of the Serpent.

The Knowledge of Yahweh in the Post Flood World of Job

Thus far we have looked at how the Way of Cain was perpetuated and how Nimrod's desire to destroy Abraham's seed was passed down to modern times through the descendents of Esau. Now, let's look at how the understanding of the Language of God and the Way of Yahweh is exemplified in the story of the righteous man called Job.

Several prominent Bible Scholars believe that Job lived on the Earth shortly after the Great Flood, when part of the world was gripped in a terrible Ice Age. If this is true, then the Book of Job is possibly the oldest book in the Bible. However, the Book of Jasher indicates that Job the Uzite was a contemporary of Moses' father-in-law Reuel (Jasher 67:34). If Job was alive at the same time as Reuel circa 1600 BC, this may have been about the time when that long and terrible Ice Age ended. Either way, Job's Book can tell us important things about the world *before* Moses wrote the first five books of the Old Testament. To find out what the Book of Job can reveal, let's examine what Job knew about Yahweh.

Job's story opens with the affirmation that the old sacrificial system instated during Abel's lifetime had survived and was still in use after the Flood:

> *"So it was, when the days of feasting had run their course, that Job...* **would rise early in the morning and offer burnt offerings** *according to the number of them all. For Job said, 'It may be that my sons have sinned and cursed God in their hearts.' Thus Job did regularly."* - Job 1:5 (NKJ)

The Scripture passage above reveals that Job clearly knew that no man is righteous before Yah and that burnt blood sacrifices were necessary to achieve temporary atonement for one's sins. The Book of Job also records the fact that Job had a fairly clear understanding of what the one true God is like. It portrays Job as a righteous and deeply spiritual man who loved and worshipped the Creator God. Of particular interest to note here, however, is that Job lived before most of the Bible was written. Yet Job knew that Yahweh's Son Yahshua the Redeemer was coming, as shown in the Book of Job, Chapter 19, verses 23 to 27!

Now, according to the Book of Jasher or Upright Record, the pious man Job served as an advisor to Pharaoh when the Israelites were slaves in Egypt. This places Job's lifetime to between 2000 and 1500 BC, which would have been before Moses led the Israelites out of Egypt - during the Precessional Age of Aries.

In addition to Job, the Pharaoh of the Exodus had another advisor named Reuel. Now, the Book of Jasher hints that this Reuel was none other than the Midianite Prince and priest of El known as Jethro in the Bible - the same one who was a blood descendent of Abraham and became Moses' future father-in-law. Due to further clues in the Book of Jasher, it is also clear that Job and Reuel were well acquainted and may even have been close friends. As such, these two Wise Men, or Magi may have shared many ideas, including what they knew of Yahweh and His Gospel in the Stars.

The Bible tells us that Job lived in the land of Uz (Job 1:1). Uz, however, isn't just a place name. It is also the name of a Biblical character listed in the genealogical record in Genesis 10:23. There, it is recorded that Noah's son Shem had a son named Aram, who in turn fathered Uz. Uz was therefore likely born within the first one hundred years after the Great Flood of 2347 BC. It is also certain that Uz and his descendents settled in Mesopotamia and the Middle East - the lands specifically allotted to Noah's son Shem and his descendents. It is therefore likely that Job was a Shemite or Semite, and was born to a descendent of Uz in Semite territory.

Since the advisor Reuel was a Semite descended from Abraham and Job was also a Semite, this suggests that the Pharaoh of Egypt at this time in history was at least partially Semitic like Job and Reuel. As a way of legitimizing their rule, could the Hamites who took control of Egypt and killed the Semite royalty and noblemen after Nimrod's conquest have forced the surviving Semitic princesses and noblewomen to marry them? If so, could the mother of the Pharaoh of the Exodus have been a Semite?

This is important when considering the origin and importance of the Great Pyramid. As a Covenant pillar and altar to Yahweh built before the Flood by the descendents of Seth, it is likely that - at least for a time after the Flood - the descendents of Shem presided over the Giza Pyramid Complex as its priestly caretakers. Furthermore, Shem's descendents likely ruled over all of Lower Egypt and a portion of Upper Egypt until the Hamite Nimrod conquered their territory and ousted the royal family, installing one of his own descendents on the throne instead.

Returning to our discussion of Job, the Book of Jasher tells us that Job was familiar with the plight of the Israelites as slaves in Egypt. Furthermore, the Upright Record tells us that the Pharaoh asked Job for his wise counsel in finding an effective way to cow the Israelite slaves and halt their alarmingly exponential population growth - which was apparently occurring throughout Egypt and Goshen at that time (Jasher 66:15-22). Subsequently, in a decision seemingly at total odds with the biblical view of Job as a righteous man, Job advised Pharaoh to begin killing all the males born to the Israelite slaves:

> *"And an officer, one of the king's counselors, whose name was Job, from Mesopotamia, in the land of Uz, answered the king, saying... 'Behold... the labor of the children of Israel is very good, and you must not remove from them that labor forever. But... you may lessen them, if it seems good to the king to afflict them. Behold we have feared war for a long time, and we said, When Israel becomes fruitful in the land, they will drive us from the land if a war should*

take place. If it please the king, let a royal decree go forth, and let it be written in the laws of Egypt... that every male child born to the Israelites, his blood shall be spilled upon the ground. And... when all the male children of Israel shall have died, the evil of their wars will cease; let the king... send for all the Hebrew midwives and order them in this matter to execute it... and the king did according to the word of Job." - Jasher 66:15-22

As it turned out, even though Job's seemingly wicked advice to the Pharaoh was taken, it proved useless when the Israelite midwives refused to kill the male children born to their people:

"And the king sent for the Hebrew midwives to be called... And the midwives came before the king, and stood in his presence. And the king said unto them, 'When you do the office of a midwife to the Hebrew women, and see them upon the stools, if it be a son, then you shall kill him, but if it be a daughter, then she shall live. But if you will not do this thing, then will I burn you up and all your houses with fire.' But the midwives feared God and did not hearken to the king of Egypt nor to his words, and when the Hebrew women brought forth... son or daughter, then did the midwife do all that was necessary to the child and let it live; thus did the midwives all the days.

And this thing was told to the king, and he sent and called for the midwives and he said to them, Why have you done this thing and have saved the children alive? And the midwives answered... saying, '...for many days no Hebrew woman has brought forth upon us, for all the Hebrew women are their own midwives, because they are hale.' And Pharaoh... believed them in this matter, and the midwives went away from the king, and God dealt well with them, and the people multiplied and waxed exceedingly." - Jasher 66:23-31

Does it seem impossible that a man - especially one as righteous as Job was supposed to be - would have made the evil suggestion to kill newborn Israelite males in an effort to annihilate the Israelites? Some might reason that anyone who suggested such a horrible solution to the Israelite "problem" could not be righteous like the biblical Job was supposed to be. However, what if Job's intention was not to cow the Israelites, but to make them even more bitter enemies of Pharaoh - thereby ensuring that either they or their God would rise up against Egypt one day and destroy it?

If this was so, then Job was a secret enemy of Egypt and a secret friend of the Israelites. He was not being maliciously cruel, but knowing the hardness of Pharaoh's heart would likely not be swayed by appeals for compassion, he was trying to incite the Israelites to rebellion so that they could be freed from their yoke of slavery and win the independence they needed to worship their mighty God freely. Indeed, Job may have been hoping that - if the Israelites cried out hard enough to God for deliverance - Yahweh would intercede, free His Chosen People and destroy Egypt's power forever. Therefore, Job may have been acting like certain godly men throughout history have been called to.

Has there always been a group of men like Job who have been secretly chosen by God to do His will that are working behind the scenes to see that His Will is fulfilled - despite the Devil's best efforts to thwart it even today? I believe that there always has been and Job was just one among thousands of them! If an ancient and secret organization like this still exists outside of the Freemasons, who have gone the way of Balaam and who are much too high profile to fit the clandestine nature of the organization I am envisioning here, then my prayers are with them and I wish I could be one of them! Though I have no proof of their existence, I firmly believe that such a secret organization still exists, and will succeed in its mandates! Remember, God is in control!

Now, returning to our discussion of the patriarch Job in Pharaoh's court in the Book of Jasher, the Pharaoh that Job advised has a prophetic dream that the Pagan prophet Balaam, son of Beor interprets for the king (Jasher 67:11-23). Amazingly, just as Job was probably already well aware of, Balaam tells Pharaoh that the dream is a prophecy that the Israelites will one day rise up against Egypt and destroy it:

> "And in the hundred and thirtieth year of Israel's going down to Egypt, Pharaoh dreamed that he was sitting upon his kingly throne... and saw an old man standing before him, and there were scales in the hands of the old man... And the old man took the scales and... took all the elders of Egypt and all its nobles and great men, and he tied them together and put them in one scale. And he took a milk kid and put it into the other scale, and the kid preponderated over all. And Pharaoh was astonished at this dreadful vision, why the kid should preponderate over all, and Pharaoh awoke and behold it was a dream. And Pharaoh rose up early in the morning and called all his servants and related to them the dream, and the men were greatly afraid. And the king said to all his wise men, Interpret I pray you the dream... that I may know it.

And Balaam the son of Beor answered the king, 'This means nothing else but a great evil that will spring up against Egypt in the latter days. For a son will be born to Israel who will destroy all Egypt and its inhabitants, and bring forth the Israelites from Egypt with a mighty hand. Now therefore, O king, take counsel upon this matter, that you may destroy the hope of the children of Israel and their expectation, before this evil arise against Egypt.' And the king said unto Balaam, 'And what shall we do unto Israel? Surely after a certain manner did we at first counsel against them and could not prevail over them. Now therefore give you also advice against them by which we may prevail over them.' And Balaam answered the king, saying, 'send now and call thy two counselors, and we will see what their advice is upon this matter and afterward thy servant will speak." - Jasher 67:11-23

Here, Balaam described a great evil that would one day befall Egypt at the hands of the Israelites. This was likely referring to the affects of the ten horrible, divinely sent plagues that completely devastated Egypt just before the Exodus. If Balaam, who was an enemy of Israel, could accurately foretell Israel's fate, could Job also have been divinely shown that the Israelites would one day rise up with Moses to smite Egypt and then find their freedom from slavery through the Exodus? Job's exalted place in the Old Testament and his insightful words recorded within it suggest that God enlightened Job prophetically. In addition, it suggests that Job was a secret enemy of Egypt and was looking forward to Egypt's future destruction.

Reuel, who became Moses' father-in-law, had a different approach than Job in advising the Pharaoh. Instead of using subterfuge like Job, Reuel told Pharaoh the truth from God's compassionate perspective. As such, Reuel explained that the Israelites were the beloved spiritual children of the mighty God Yahweh. He then warned Pharaoh that he would suffer Yahweh's wrath on Egypt if he refused to treat the Israelites kindly (Jasher 67:26-41). In fact, Reuel told the Pharaoh that the best way to get rid of the Israelite "threat" would be to free them from slavery and allow them to leave Egypt unhindered:

"And Reuel the Midianite answered the king and said, 'May the king live, may the king live forever. If it seems good to the king, let him desist from the Hebrews and leave them, and let him not stretch forth his hand against them. For these are they whom the Lord chose in days of old, and took as the lot of his inheritance from amongst all the nations of the earth and the kings of the earth; and who is there that stretched his

hand against them with impunity, of whom their God was not avenged?'

'surely thou knowest that when Abraham went down to Egypt, Pharaoh, the former king of Egypt, saw Sarah his wife, and took her for a wife, because Abraham said, She is my sister, for he was afraid, lest the men of Egypt should slay him on account of his wife. And when the king of Egypt had taken Sarah then God smote him and his household with heavy plagues, until he restored unto Abraham his wife Sarah, then was he healed...'

'surely Pharaoh the former, thy father's father, raised Joseph the son of Jacob above all the princes of the land of Egypt, when he saw his wisdom, for through his wisdom he rescued all the inhabitants of the land from the famine. After which he ordered Jacob and his children to come down to Egypt, in order that through their virtue, the land of Egypt and the land of Goshen might be delivered from the famine.'

*'Now therefore if it seems good in thine eyes, cease from destroying the children of Israel, but if it be not thy will that they shall dwell in Egypt, send them forth from here, that they may go to the land of Canaan, the land where their ancestors sojourned.' **And when Pharaoh heard the words of Jethro he was very angry with him, so that he rose with shame from the king's presence, and went to Midian, his land, and took Joseph's stick with him.***"

- Jasher 67:26-30, 38-41

This passage of Jasher tells us that **the Pharaoh who appointed the patriarch Joseph as Vizier of Egypt was the great grandfather of the Pharaoh that Reuel spoke to** - the same one whom Moses confronted with the will of God (Jasher 67:4, 68:2). Since Reuel told this Pharaoh to do what Yahweh later asked through Moses, it is clear that Reuel was a righteous man who listened to God's voice just like Moses did. Nonetheless, Reuel paid dearly for his advice to Pharaoh, who immediately banished Reuel from Egypt for showing his love of the Israelites and their God! As a result, Reuel was forced to return to Midian. But, before he left Egypt, Reuel obtained Joseph's Stick - the miraculous Staff of Yahweh that had been passed down from Adam to every patriarchal ruler descended from Seth and Shem.

Though it is impossible to ascertain when Reuel and Job gave their advice to Pharaoh concerning the Israelites, it could have been as much as eighty years before. This is because Moses was 80 years old when he told Pharaoh to free the Israelites, and it is likely that the advice given to Pharaoh by Balaam to destroy the baby boys born to Israel by drowning them is what prompted Moses' mother to send her newborn son adrift on the Nile River and into his destiny as a privileged Prince of Egypt and Israel's promised deliverer. In any case, it appears that Moses confronted a new Pharaoh who did not know Moses when he was a Prince of Egypt.

Incidentally, the people of Reuel and Job's era were not nearly as long-lived as Noah's son Shem. For instance, the Bible records that Abraham only lived 175 years before he died (Genesis 25:7-8). Job's lifetime could have been even shorter since he was born closer to the time of Moses, which was five hundred years after Abraham lived. Job, however, may have lived longer than many people did then because he was unusually blessed by God. In fact, the Bible records that - after his time of testing at Satan's hands - Job was highly blessed with much more wealth and prosperity than he once had:

> "And the LORD (Yahweh) restored Job's losses when he prayed for his friends. Indeed the LORD (Yahweh) gave Job twice as much as he had before. Then all his brothers, all his sisters, and all those who had been his acquaintances... ate food with him in his house; and they... comforted him for all the adversity that the LORD (Yahweh) had brought upon him. Each one gave him a piece of silver and each a ring of gold. Now the LORD (Yahweh) blessed the latter days of Job more than his beginning; for he had fourteen thousand sheep, six thousand camels, one thousand yoke of oxen, and one thousand female donkeys. He also had seven sons and three daughters. And he called the name of the first Jemimah, the name of the second Keziah, and the name of the third Keren-Happuch. In all the land were found no women so beautiful as the daughters of Job; and their father gave them an inheritance among their brothers." - Job 42:10-15 (NKJ)

Even after Yahweh allowed Satan to take away Job's privileged social standing, destroy his belongings and children (Job 1:12-22), and inflict him with sickness and misery (Job 2:3-8), Job refused to curse or blame Yahweh for his suffering. Therefore, Job was granted an extraordinarily long life as partial compensation. As a result, the Bible tells us that **Job lived for 140 years after his wealth and health was restored to him** (Job 42:16-17). Therefore, if Job were one hundred years old when he was struck with ill fortune, Job would have been over 240 years old when he died.

Due to his longevity, Job may still have been alive when the Exodus occurred and Moses wrote the first five books of the Bible known as the Pentateuch or Torah. If so, Job would likely have rejoiced to see Israel freed from slavery. Indeed, Job knew Yahweh nearly as well as Moses did and loved Him as much! Approximately six hundred years earlier than Moses, the Bible records that Abraham also stood as a pillar of faithfulness toward Yahweh God.

Like Job, Abraham knew Yahweh well - so well that he became known as *"God's friend"* (2 Chronicles 20:7; Isaiah 41:8; James 2:23) In fact, Abraham entered into a very special Blood Covenant relationship of fealty and protection with Yahweh. Yet Abraham, we are told, had no Scriptures with which to learn about Yahweh. Where then did he get his knowledge of God? As already mentioned, the Book of Jasher makes it clear that Abraham learned about Yahweh God from both Noah and Shem, as Noah was still alive during the early part of Abraham's lifetime. We will discuss this extraordinary man and his relationship with God further in Chapter Eight of this book.

Job's Knowledge of Sacred Astronomy

Through Reuel and his own descendents, the patriarch Job was likely exposed to a less corrupted version of God's metaphorical Language - both as it appears on Earth and in the Universe. Hints of his knowledge of the Star Gospel were evident when Job stated that God *"alone stretches out the heavens and treads on the waves of the sea"* (Job 9:8). In addition, Job spoke of several constellations during his discourses about Yahweh:

> *"He is the Maker of the Bear and Orion, the Pleiades and the constellations of the south. He performs wonders that cannot be fathomed, miracles that cannot be counted. When he passes me, I cannot see him; when he goes by, I cannot perceive him. If he snatches away, who can stop him? Who can say to him, 'What are you doing?' God does not restrain his anger; even the cohorts of Rahab cowered at his feet. How then can I dispute with him? How can I find words to argue with him?" - Job 9:9-14 (NIV)*

The constellations of the Bear (or Big Dipper), Orion, and the Pleiades (or Seven Sisters) all play a major role in the Gospel in the Stars. This suggests that Job was no stranger to studying the constellations and he knew the magnitude of the night sky's power to proclaim Yah's greatness. Since allegorical messages can be seen within the workings of all of Creation, an upright and wise counselor like Job may have perceived these messages and utilized them to teach others. In any case, the Bible offers sure proof that Job was a master follower of the Way of Yahweh who understood the knowledge of God hidden in the heavens:

> *"**But how can a mortal be righteous before God?** Though one wished to dispute with him, he could not answer him one time out of a thousand. **His wisdom is profound, his power is vast.** Who has resisted him and come out unscathed? He moves mountains without their knowing it and overturns them in his anger. **He shakes the Earth from its place and makes its pillars tremble. He speaks to the sun and it does not shine; he seals off the light of the stars.** He alone stretches out the heavens and treads on the waves of the sea." - Job 9:2-8 (NIV)*

In the preceding Scriptural passages, we can see that Job knew much about Yahweh's true nature. He understood that Yahweh has wisdom and power that no man or angel can match. He also mentions Rahab, which may have been a Leviathan of enormous size and strength that all men feared and that was associated with the planet Tiamat. As already discussed, Scripture tells us that the Leviathan was far bigger and fiercer than any crocodile! In fact, Job's description of the Leviathan seems to better fit the mythical descriptions of fire-breathing dragons found throughout the cultures of the world. In Job's opinion, only God Almighty could approach the dreaded sea dragon Rahab without fear since Rahab feared God alone. Isaiah and David explain why:

> *"Awake, awake, put on strength, O arm of the LORD (Yahweh)! Awake as in the ancient days, in the generations of old. **Are You not the arm that cut Rahab apart**, and wounded the serpent? Are You not the One who dried up the sea, the waters of the great deep; that made the depths of the sea a road for the redeemed to cross over?" - Isaiah 51:9-10 (NKJ)*

> *"You rule the raging of the sea; when its waves rise, You still them. **You have broken Rahab (i.e. Tiamat!) in pieces**, as one who is slain; you have scattered Your enemies with Your mighty arm." - Psalm 89:9-10 (NKJ)*

In several places, *Job also mentions a shaken and trembling Earth that clearly points to a cataclysmic event on the Earth.* From his vivid recollection of it, Job appears to be an eyewitness, or at least someone who witnessed the aftereffects of this cataclysmic event firsthand. Job may have seen all of the devastation caused by it, and knew it resulted from Yahweh's unrestrained anger. This fact would have been painfully fresh in the memory of anyone who lived through either the Ice Age that followed the Great Flood or the second Ice Age that may have followed the destruction of Babel.

A Scientist named Henry M. Morris believes Job lived during the Ice Age that occurred immediately after the Great Flood. Morris' book, "The Remarkable Record of Job" explains this theory with great eloquence. However, Mr. Morris may have the wrong Ice Age in mind since Job was apparently an advisor to the Pharaoh of the Exodus. If so, there well may have been two short Ice Ages in the past, with one immediately following the Flood, and a second Ice Age immediately after the destruction of the Tower of Babel.

Since the book by his name reveals that Job had a great knowledge of Biblical or Sacred Astronomy, it is likely that Job was aware of the cycle of Precession. It is also probable that Job and his contemporaries knew that their ancestors used these Great Ages to mark the passing of time. As a result, each succeeding generation appears to have followed this same practice. That is why there is so much bull imagery found in the religious art of the Babylonians and ancient Egyptians of the Old Kingdom - who lived in the Age of Taurus, circa 4000 BC to 2000 BC.

Not surprisingly, the bull imagery changed to ram imagery in the religious art of the later Middle and New Kingdom in ancient Egypt, which was during the Age of Aries that followed the Age of Taurus. The Age of Aries was from approximately 2000 BC to 0 BC. Since Aries falls *before* Taurus in the Zodiac, it is apparent that Precessional Ages travel in reverse of the normal clockwise course of time marked by the Zodiac that suggests that God is truly working to reverse mankind's history.

The Book of Job reveals that Job had a great knowledge of Yahweh God before Moses wrote the Pentateuch. If Job could know of Yahweh God's character and the effects of His wrath so well without the aide of the Bible, where did he get his knowledge of God? It is my belief that Job inherited the knowledge of Yahweh as a legacy from Noah and his sons, who lived before the Flood and understood the Gospel in the Stars.

Glimmers of Light in the Egyptian Book of the Dead

At the time that Job advised the Pharaoh of Egypt, the ancient Egyptians were busy creating tomb paintings for wealthy individuals.

These wall paintings almost always included scenes from the Egyptian Book of the Dead, which contained illustrations depicting the results supposedly promised by reciting the accompanying magical incantations. These were meant to aid the deceased into the star realm of Osiris (i.e. Orion), which they believed was the location of the Egyptian Duat or netherworld.

The structure of the Book of the Dead shows that, though the ancient Egyptians believed in the survival of the soul after death in a heavenly place, they nonetheless had a corrupted view of morality and seemed to believe that they could cajole or force their way into Heaven. Because of their reliance on Magic, the Egyptians made a mockery of true righteousness and wanted to be deemed worthy of eternal life even if they had not earned the right.

As a way of allegorically depicting the perfection and power derived from uttering spells and incantations, deceased individuals were always depicted as youthful in appearance, with no signs of the disfigurement or disease that may have killed them, or that are normally associated with old age. In effect, Egyptians believed that their gods could be fooled into thinking that people were always as pure and perfect as they were depicted in their tomb art.

Many texts and amulets placed in Egyptian tombs were meant to protect and guide the deceased into the afterlife, and to magically aid them in fooling the gods. Magical inscriptions were most often derived from the Pyramid Texts, which were found carved into the walls and ceilings of several tombs belonging to pharaohs who supposedly reigned during the same Old Kingdom era that produced the Great Pyramid. Due to the incredible light and truth locked into the Great Pyramid's design, however, there is no way that these pharaohs who used Magic and Sorcery to guarantee their place in a paradisiacal afterlife among the stars could have shared the ideologies and beliefs of those who built the Giza Pyramid Complex or the pyramids at Dahshur.

Later in Egypt's history, the Pyramid Texts were refined into the Coffin Texts, which were often found painted in hieroglyphics onto the interior surfaces of coffins and funerary masks. Each tomb was therefore designed to function as an elaborate road map to Heaven that was perverted with Magic and Sorcery. Still later, the incantations were written on papyrus scrolls and illustrated. Archeologists call these scrolls the Egyptian Book of the Dead. These books began to be utilized around the time of Egypt's Middle Kingdom, which fell roughly between 2040 and 1640 BC.

Instead of relying on good works alone, many ancient Egyptians hoped that the Magic in their final resting places would be powerful enough to ensure that they would pass their final judgment on the scales of Osiris, thereby allowing them to enter the heavenly afterlife. This judgment before the Throne of Osiris is one of the most common themes in tomb paintings and papyrus scrolls containing the Book of the Dead. Interestingly, a Pharaoh with a name similar to Osiris appears in the Book of Jasher. This Osiris may have been Cush, the Hamite father of Nimrod. As shown in the next chapter, it is highly possible that Cush was eventually deified and recast as the Egyptian god of the dead for some reason known only to Satan.

Now, if Osiris and the biblical Cush were one and the same person as I suspect, then there is every reason to believe that he was deified after his death to ensure that he would never be forgotten. In addition, Cush may have been deified as the god of the dead to ensure that he would always receive worship and praise. Indeed, many human and part-Nephilim rulers who were filled with overweening pride were likely deified to ensure their continued importance and authority in the demonic realms surrounding our Earth. How sad that the only claim to importance that demons and lost souls like Cush and Nimrod can attain is in being sought after to inspire, bless or aid living people in their mutual rebellion against God!

Despite the deception and Magic contained in the Book of the Dead, however, there are faint glimmers of light and truth hidden within it. In fact, as discussed in Book Four, many allegorical references to the interior passages and chambers in the Great Pyramid are found in the Book of the Dead and Pyramid Texts. This shows that whoever invented the spells in these texts was familiar with the true theology revealed within the Great Pyramid, but wanted to obscure it behind many lies and falsehoods. This insidious distortion of the truth was typical of Nimrod's infamous reign, but was certainly being practiced even before the Great Flood by followers of the Way of Cain.

Other glimmers of truth can be found in the depictions of the soul being judged in the Judgment Hall of Osiris. The art surrounding these scenes depicts a common theme in Judeo-Christian Theology, and shares many points in common with it. For example, as seen in the illustration from a papyrus scroll containing a portion of the Book of the Dead on page 483, an enthroned king serves as the judge, along with a jury of 14 other gods presiding above the scales of judgment.

Uncannily, this scene depicts two distinctly Christian concepts: the Judgment Seat of Christ and the Last Judgment. In addition, Enoch is depicted as God's Scribe in the image of the ibis-headed Thoth, and the 14 Egyptian deities presiding over the judgment hall with Osiris foreshadow the fact that the saints will rule and judge with Christ during His Millennial Kingdom. This suggests that Egypt's polytheistic religion had a righteous and monotheistic origin but was later corrupted.

The illustration below depicts several more elements found in the judgment scene above that have Christian parallels. For example, the soul is depicted as a human heart and allegorically depicts human emotions and feelings. These are being weighed against the concept of Ma'at or Truth, which is represented as a feather. The goddess of Ma'at was often depicted as a woman with outspread wings, which is reminiscent of how Christians tend to depict angels today as well as the Holy Spirit, who is often symbolized as a dove.

Ma'at represented the concept of truth as embodied in good human traits such as love, faithfulness, loyalty, mercy, justice, and kindness. Therefore, if viewed allegorically, the idea of Ma'at conforms to the Christian concept of the Holy Spirit and the spiritual gifts She gives those who possess Her in their hearts. In addition, the feather of Ma'at suggests the ability to soar above problems and sorrows with the light of Truth as a guide, and is complementary to the idea of Christ as the Way, the Truth, and the Life, as well as the Firstfruits of the Resurrection.

Ma'at, Egyptian Goddess of Truth, Justice and Goodness

In the Egyptian mind, if the heart weighed the same as Ma'at, then the soul was good at following the way of truth in life, and had earned the right to dwell with Osiris forever. But if the heart weighed more than the feather of Ma'at, it meant that the person was weighed down with bitterness, hate, sorrow, lust or greed, and had found no peace or joy in life due to their inability to let go of these negative emotions. They were therefore fit only to feed the monster of destruction and retribution known as Ammut, who is depicted as part hippopotamus, part lion or leopard, and part crocodile in the judgment scenes on page 483.

Oddly, the Egyptians transformed the demonic monster Ammut into the more benign protective goddess Tawaret, who also represented the constellation in Egyptian Cosmology that we call Draco the Dragon. This means that Ammut and Tawaret allegorically represent Satan in his most destructive guises - one as the Destroyer of Life and one that appears as an Angel of Light but only offers false security.

Tawaret, the Egyptian Goddess connected to the Constellation Draco the Dragon and the demon Ammut

In the ancient Egyptian judgment scenes on page 483, there is another major character that has a Judeo-Christian counterpart, though it is more difficult to see. This is found in the jackal or dog-headed god known as Anubis, whose job it was to protect the deceased from harm while being prepared for burial and entrance into the afterlife. One day, while studying the characteristics of this deity, it dawned on me that Anubis might be a symbol for the constellation Canis Major. At the time, however, I had not seen the connection of Canis Major with Israel, or the connection of the star Sirius with Bethlehem. In addition, none of the texts that discuss Egyptian deities in my extensive library mention a connection between Anubis and Canis Major or any star, though Sirius was tied to the goddess Isis, the wife of Osiris. So I did not know what to do with this idea. Now that I have seen the correlation of Sirius with Bethlehem, however, it appears that Anubis may have been meant to represent the Messiah of the Star Gospel in His role as the Resurrection and the Life!

Could it be that Anubis is tied to the meaning of the constellation Canis Major that includes the dog-star Sirius as its brightest star - as well as the brightest star in Earth's sky? Could Anubis in fact be an allegorical representation of the spiritual truths behind this constellation that are revealed in the Gospel in the Stars? Is it possible that many prominent

Archeologists and Egyptologists have obscured Anubis' connection to this part of the night sky because they want to hide the truth? My guess is that they are trying to hide the truth that Anubis once held the roles that Osiris and Isis stole, and that Anubis is therefore connected to Orion, Canis Major and Sirius, which - as was shown in Chapter Three - is connected to the town of Bethlehem in Israel - the place where Christ was born!

In actuality, Anubis' role was identical to that of Osiris in Egypt's earliest dynasties, and Osiris was unknown then. This means that when Osiris was added to the Egyptian pantheon and connected to the constellation of Orion and the star Sirius, he usurped Anubis' position and denigrated the canine-headed deity to a far lesser role in the afterlife. In addition, Osiris replaced Anubis as the almost universal god who dies and then is miraculously resurrected into eternal life. Nonetheless, Yahweh saw to it that Anubis still figured in the Egyptian rites of the dead, ensuring that someone like me who understands the Language of God would one day see who Anubis actually represented, and would let the world know that the tomb art of Egypt has an allegorical story to tell that is no less significant than the art of Greece and Rome!

Indeed, the tomb and temple art of Egypt tells a fascinating and tragic story of how the icons of a once relatively monotheistic people and faith were turned into idols that obscured the truth they once represented. That is why, as shown in Book One and in the chart on pages 568 and 569, so many of the deities in ancient Egypt had a Judeo-Christian counterpart and could be understood in Judeo-Christian terms. As we will see in Chapter Seven, the religious mythologies of Greece and Rome also have unmistakable Judeo-Christian parallels, though they denied the existence of a Creator god and elevated powerful people to the position of gods.

Some scholars who have seen this connection have falsely intimated that the Egyptian Book of the Dead was the closest thing to a Bible that many Egyptians had access to. What they forget, however, is that the Book of the Dead was filled with incantations, not prayers, and reciting spells and praying have completely different motivations and directions. In fact, because the artwork tells a different story than the magic texts accompanying them, the visual contents of the Book of the Dead may have a non-Egyptian origin. It is even possible that the painted illustrations in this book may have been inspired by the teachings of godly Semites like Abraham or Joseph, who were both great Wise Men in the eyes of the Egyptians. If so, their ideas could have been incorporated into the existing beliefs of the Egyptians concerning the afterlife, which were sadly mired in Magic and Sorcery long before these Judeo-Christian elements were added sometime in the Middle Kingdom.

Ancient Egypt and Asenath: Truth Mixed With Error

About a year ago, a man called me on the telephone and asked me a perplexing question that I did not have an answer to at the time. His question was this: "Why did Yahweh allow the kingdom of ancient Egypt to exist for as long as it did without punishment?" My initial reaction to his question was that Yahweh did not spare the Egyptians, but visited them with His wrath on several occasions, most notably at the time of the Israelite Exodus from Egypt.

The man who called was not satisfied with this answer, however. In fact, he grew quite irritated and hung up on me before I could offer any other explanation. His reasoning was that the kingdom of Egypt outlasted all other ancient kingdoms in length and wealth and it recovered and continued even after the Exodus, so there must have been some godly reason why it did.

At that time, I really did not have an adequate answer for him, but it would have been nice if he had left me his name and contact information in case I did find an answer! After reviewing "The Parthenon Code" and writing about the roots of Paganism, I have a precise answer for him now that I am certain would have satisfied his need. Frustratingly, however, I have no way of delivering this message to that man, and can only hope that he found the answer on his own. Or, in the off chance he might buy this book and read it someday, I will share my answer to his question here.

The answer can be found in the unique religious beliefs of the ancient Egyptians, which - despite the fanciful notions of the ancient Greeks and Romans - did not originally have a direct correlation with their own Pagan belief systems. You see, even though the Egyptians eventually had an idolatrous, polytheistic religion like the Greeks and Romans, it is highly likely that it did not start out that way. In fact, before the Flood, the reality of the Great Pyramid indicates that many righteous Sethites lived in Lower Egypt around the monuments they built until closer to the time of the Flood. In addition, it is likely that Noah's righteous son Shem initially ruled over Lower Egypt. As a result, the Egyptian religion was essentially monotheistic for centuries and only became idolatrous and polytheistic under the influence of the Way of Cain that was later promulgated by Nimrod's Babylon and the Greeks.

Nonetheless, the Egyptian religion retained certain elements that made it truly unique. First of all, it was the only Pagan religion in the entire ancient world that never ceased to acknowledge the existence of a holy Creator God who was truly separate from and above humanity. In addition, the Egyptian religion clearly taught that all people were subject to a divine moral code (i.e. Ma'at) and faced divine judgment after death in the Judgment Hall of Osiris, whose messianic overtones are legion.

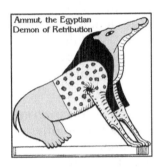

Ammut, the Egyptian Demon of Retribution

As is taught in Judeo-Christianity, the Egyptians also believed in a literal Heaven and Hell. In ancient Egypt, those who went to Heaven dwelled in a blissful abode of the dead amongst the stars that was filled with joy and merriment. Meanwhile, those who failed judgment faced the utter destruction of their body and soul for eternity via the jaws of the monster Ammut. ***No other classical religious philosophy clearly taught (or retained) these concepts, which certainly were part of Noah and Shem's religious beliefs.*** Indeed, this may be the major reason that Yahweh chose to allow His Shekinah Glory to rest within the King's Chamber of the Great Pyramid until Moses led the Israelites out of Egypt. For as long as Seth, Noah, Shem, Abraham and Joseph had influence in Egypt, Yahweh's Glory was content to rest there. But when Moses and the Israelites departed Egypt with Joseph's bones at the time of the Exodus, the Shekinah departed with them as a pillar of fire by night and a pillar of smoke by day (Exodus 13:21).

As shown in the illustrations on page 483 and above, the monster Ammut was the triple-natured dark twin of the Egyptian goddess Tawaret, which combined the appearance of a crocodile, lion and hippopotamus with a woman's breasts and belly. As Tawaret, this beast was the fierce yet loving protectress of pregnant and nursing mothers. But as Ammut, this same beast was divested of its human traits to represent the diabolical side of the constellation Draco the Dragon in the Star Gospel. This shows that, at least for a time, the Egyptians understood the prophetic duality underlying God's Word to us in the heavens - a duality that allows dragons or beasts to have either a good or evil connotation that is entirely dependant upon God's will.

As to why the Egyptian religion was profoundly different in comparison to the religions of Greece or Rome in these key areas, it likely has much to do with the fact that the legacy of Enoch and the Sethites was passed down to patriarchs like Abraham and Joseph, and these two men were allowed to greatly influence the culture of ancient

Egypt. In fact, both Abraham and Joseph likely taught the Egyptians the Gospel in the Stars and the Way of Yahweh that was reflected in the magnificent primeval monuments that the Sethites left in Egypt prior to the Flood.

As a result, despite its idolatrous veneer, the religion of ancient Egypt retained the knowledge that there was a Creator god called Ptah (or Yah) that made all things. They also believed that Osiris, who was descended from that Creator god, would judge each individual based on their merits. As a divine judge, Osiris demanded morality and righteousness as prerequisites for entering paradise. For those who did not honor and keep Ma'at and were found wanting on the day of their death and judgment, a horrible everlasting punishment awaited them in the destroying jaws of the monster Ammut.

Interestingly, while he was the vizier of all Egypt, the patriarch Joseph was married to an Egyptian noblewoman named Asenath, whose name means "belonging to Neith." Neith was an Egyptian war goddess with an interesting symbolic connection that we will examine in a moment. Asenath, who signifies the saints redeemed from Hell by their love of Christ, was the daughter of Potipherah, meaning "He whom Ra gives." Potipherah was a nobleman and priest of the Sun god Amun-Ra in the city of On or Iunu, which was Amun-Ra's cult worship center. Because the Greeks identified Amun-Ra with Helios, the Greek Sun god, they called the city of On by the Greek name Heliopolis, meaning "Helios' city."

Heliopolis is located near the Giza longitudinal meridian that is connected to the celestial meridian running between Taurus and Gemini. Currently, this meridian marks the position of the Summer Solstice Sun on the Ecliptic - a point directly above the tip of the constellation Orion's upraised sword. Furthermore, the Zodiac sign associated with Joseph is Taurus the Bull, and the decan of Taurus known as Orion signifies the patriarch Joseph himself, who was a prefiguration of Christ! Could this be why God directed the Pharaoh to give Asenath to Joseph as his wife? After all, as the daughter of the priest of the Sun god, Asenath aptly signified the sons and daughters of the Holy Spirit - God's born-again children that will one day be married to the Son of God forever.

As shown in Chapter Three, the three belt stars of Orion (which signify the three crosses erected at the crucifixion of Christ) correspond to the three biggest pyramids at Giza, with the brightest star in the belt called Al Nitak corresponding to the Great Pyramid or Pillar of Enoch. Fascinatingly, the causeway of the Pillar of Enoch points to the Summer Solstice sunrise, and this pyramid signifies the born-again saints who make up the Body of Christ and will one day dwell in the pyramid-shaped New Jerusalem, which signifies the Bride of Christ (Rev. 21:2). Meanwhile, the two pyramids at Dahshur signify Josephs' two sons named Ephraim and Manasseh, and these sons are figuratively connected to the two horns of Taurus the Bull.

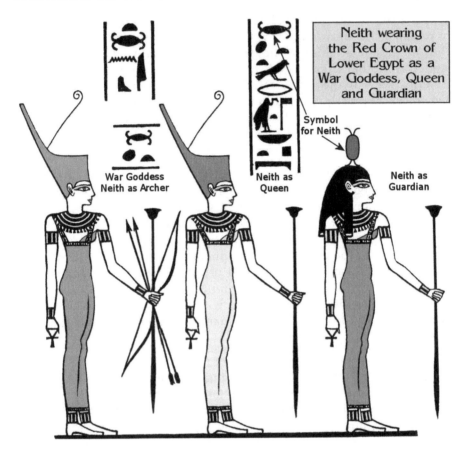

Now, since Asenath serves as a prefiguration of the True Church or Bride of Christ that is connected to the Pillar of Enoch, it is interesting that her name is connected to the war goddess Neith, whose symbol is two crossed arrows covered by a shield as seen in the illustration above. Could this symbol actually represent the Summer Solstice sunrise of our era, in which the Summer Solstice Sun now sits directly in the middle of the path of the Milky Way as seen in Earth's sky, and directly above Orion's upraised sword? Furthermore, could this symbol signify that the war of Armageddon that is to occur during the Great Tribulation will soon visit the wicked on the Earth with destruction? The next section will show that this may indeed be the case, and the climactic end of this period of grace between the Sixth and Seventh Great Day is nearly upon us!

As shown in "The Language of God in the Universe," there is a female archer depicted on the Dendera Zodiac that I identified as the Egyptian goddess Satis. She appears standing in front of the enthroned woman beneath the sign of Leo (# 12) in the illustration on page 83. This enthroned woman is the Egyptian goddess Anukis, who was considered to be the protectress of the First Cataract of Upper Egypt and the sister of Satis. In Book One, Anukis was connected to the Woman who rides the Beast in the Book of Revelation - the Harlot Queen of Evil!

Satis depicted as a War Goddess wearing the White Crown of Upper Egypt combined with divine cow horns signifying a maternal role

Fascinatingly, Satis bears an uncanny similarity to the goddess Neith that is connected to Asenath and - by extension - the True Church. For example, both of these goddesses were connected to the Nile River, which is allegorically connected to the celestial river named Eridanus (i.e. the Jordan) that runs from beneath Orion's feet into the outer darkness. In addition, both Satis and Neith were war goddesses who carried bows and arrows into battle. Both goddesses were also associated with the flooding of the Nile and were depicted as wives of the Egyptian's secondary Creator god Khnum, who was the source of the Nile River and the divine potter who fashioned all things on his potter's wheel (in an amazing parallel to Yahweh as the Potter - Isaiah 64:8). However, archeologists seem to have ignored the similarities between Neith and Satis, and have failed to ponder why the Egyptians had a need to identify and worship two nearly indistinguishable goddesses.

Perhaps the reason for this failure is that archeologists are generally unwilling to see the real spiritual battle that these two ancient goddesses appear to depict. This can be seen when noting that these goddesses were literally associated with two cities of ancient Egypt that were on opposite ends of the kingdom, with Neith connected to the completely destroyed city of Sais in the western Delta region of Lower

Egypt. Meanwhile, Satis was connected to the southern border town once called Swenet, which is known today as Aswan, Egypt. Incidentally, the First Cataract of Egypt that Anukis guarded over is also in Aswan.

Now, the city of Sais that was connected to the goddess Neith was located in ancient Sethite and Semite territory before the time of Nimrod, while the city of Swenet and the goddess Satis were in ancient Hamite territory. Likewise, just as Neith and Asenath are connected to the redeemed saints who love Yahshua, the goddesses Anukis and Satis are connected to the wicked army of people who will take the Mark of the Beast and attempt to destroy the Tribulation Saints and the Jews.

The opposition seen in Neith and Satis is also evident in the two faces of the Nile River, which can be seen as a dark twin of the Jordan River. Because of its association to the Eridanus River in the Star Gospel, the Jordan signifies the allegorical death signified by the physical act of baptism by full immersion. This immersion symbolizes both death and burial and the promise of resurrection. It also marks our receipt of the spiritual baptism or indwelling presence of the Holy Spirit that allows us to die to the lusts of the flesh and the pleasures of the world so that we can inherit everlasting life.

On the other hand, the Eridanus River signifies a fiery river of judgment for those who are not baptized with the blood and Spirit of Christ. This ties in perfectly with the meaning of Anukis and Satis, and shows that the dual war goddesses of the Nile River signify two warring groups of people. Thus, it appears that the ancient Egyptians recognized two war goddesses that believed they shared the same husband and habitation - as signified by the Nile and Jordan Rivers and the Creator god Khnum. By this analogy, then, could it be that these war goddesses were at war with one another over who was the true possessor and wielder of God's love and power on Earth?

Could it be that - to the ancient Egyptians - the goddesses Neith and Satis allegorically signified the unseen spiritual battle going on all around humanity in every age that archeologists refuse to recognize? Could it be that they also depicted the idea that - like today - two ideologies that are mutually exclusive and repulsive to each other were fighting a battle to the death over who had the superior role as the beloved of their husband and Creator? Could it be that Neith and Satis depicted the war between Shem and Ham's descendents that is still going on today between Christians, Jews, Gnostics, New Agers, Pagans, Atheists, Hindus, Buddhists and Muslims, and will end in a battle to the death one day soon? My guess is that some Egyptian priests were well aware of this war and these opposing war goddesses were just one way of depicting it.

Hawaii, Easter Island, Angkor, Tibet and the Way of Cain

In Chapter Three and an earlier section in this chapter, we discussed the spiritual legacy of the Sethites that was left for us to contemplate in the pyramids built at Dahshur and Giza in Egypt that are irrevocably and forever tied to the Star Gospel. We also explored their biblical connection and their incredible meaning for us today. But, central to all this revelation is the fact that the Sethites were identifying the physical location of Heaven on Earth - where the main command center of the Kingdom of Heaven and God's Throne will exist forever in a physical, literal way.

However, remember that the Star Gospel can be seen as circular or spherical, and on the opposite side to the glorious message of salvation and redemption hidden in Taurus and Orion is the malevolent sign of Scorpio the Scorpion with the messianic figure of Ophiuchus the Serpent Holder straining to hold Satan back. This is no accident, but contains a clear message to anyone who is proficient in the Language of God and knowledgeable about the Way of Yahweh and the Way of Cain.

Fascinatingly, the physical Gospel message that was immortalized in stone for us in Egypt and that represents the Way of Yahweh has a literal, diametrically opposed counterpart on the opposite side of the Earth. In fact, just as there is a physical location on the Earth that shows the Way of Yahweh as the one that leads to the establishment of the everlasting Kingdom of God, there is a place on Earth that depicts the transitory kingdom of *"the prince of the power of the air"* and the *"Way of Cain"* (Ephes. 2:2; Jude 1:11). In addition, just as in Egypt, the physical characteristics of and monuments in this region signify the nature and fruit of this kingdom of evil and the wicked citizens within it.

First, we need to consider where the epicenter of the kingdom identified by Scorpio is located. To do this, a physical globe of the Earth works best. Using this globe, we first need to establish where Giza is located. According to the current way the world has been mapped, Giza is about 30 degrees north of Earth's equator in latitude and 30 degrees east of Greenwich in longitude (30' N, 30' E). However, at one time, Giza was likely the Zero Meridian or epicenter that Greenwich, England is today.

By trailing one's finger along the 30th north parallel, the exact opposite location on the Earth to Giza, Egypt can be found by stopping on the longitudinal line at 150 degrees west of the Prime Meridian at Greenwich. Now, the striking thing about this exact position on the planet is that there is no land at all located there! It is, in fact, in the middle of the Pacific Ocean, which is the largest body of water in the world. This suggests a connection to Tiamat, the Babylonian dragon goddess associated with the destroyed water world where the asteroid belt now exists. As was already shown, Tiamat is also tied to Scorpio and the Tribe of Dan - from whence the Antichrist is destined to come.

Intriguingly, just southwest of this watery point is the Hawaiian Island chain. There, the Big Island of Hawaii is located in the Scorpio longitude running through the Pacific Ocean, which is exactly opposite to the Taurus longitude where Giza and Dahshur are located in Egypt. Fascinatingly, the Big Island's tallest mountain is Mauna Kea, which stands at 13,796 feet (4,205 meters) above Sea Level. However, if measured from the base of the mountain at the floor of the Pacific Ocean, it is taller than Mount Everest.

At 29,029 feet (8,840 meters) in height, Mount Everest is the highest point on dry land at the border of Nepal and Tibet. In contrast, the Big Island of Hawaii rises to about 33,500 feet (10,200 meters) from the ocean floor to the top of Mauna Kea, making it literally the highest point on Earth! How fitting, then, that the highest point on Earth and most active volcano in the world are allegorically associated with the Way of Cain, which is Satan's way. After all, Satan desired to elevate himself to godhood (i.e. the highest point), and also desired to destroy the Earth and condemn all people to Hell (like a volcano burns and destroys).

Fascinatingly, the second tallest mountain in the world is Mount McKinley in Alaska, and it actually has a larger mass and rise than Mount Everest, which gets much of its height from the fact that it rests on a high plateau. Even more fascinating, the State of Alaska is figuratively cut in half by the Scorpio-Sagittarius Longitudinal Meridian at 150 degrees west of Greenwich, and - at 151 degrees west - Mount McKinley lies one degree into the longitude tied to Scorpio! Since making this discovery, the Zodiac associations for all the longitudinal meridians were made clear to me, as shown in the map on pages 498 and 499.

On this map, it can be seen that Mauna Kea's coordinates are approximately 20 degrees north and 155 degrees west (20' N, 155' W) of Greenwich. This is fairly close to the point 30' N, 150' W that signifies the watery physical opposite to the Giza plateau. Furthermore, Kilauea - *the most active volcano in the world* - is located on the Big Island of Hawaii, and there is nothing more representative of Hell on Earth than a violently erupting volcano spewing out hot lava, ash and smoke!

However, before we explore this analogy further, it is important to keep in mind that - just as most predominantly Muslim modern Egyptians do not reflect the Way of Yahweh today - half of the modern people of Hawaii and the United States are Conservatives and believers who are not directly connected to the Way of Cain even though Hawaii is a part of the United States.

Nonetheless, anyone familiar with native Hawaiian mythology can see its connection to the Way of Cain plainly displayed. In fact, it is made crystal clear when one focuses on the legendary man who discovered the Hawaiian Islands and named them after himself: Hawaiiloa. According to Hawaiian mythology, Hawaiiloa was a great boat builder, navigator, and explorer who accidentally stumbled upon the Hawaiian Islands one day. After his discovery, Hawaiiloa returned to his homeland, which was called "Ka-aina kai mele-mele a-Kane," or "the land of the yellow sea of Kane." He then returned and colonized the islands with his three sons: Kauai, Oahu, and Maui, who subsequently settled on the islands that bear their names.

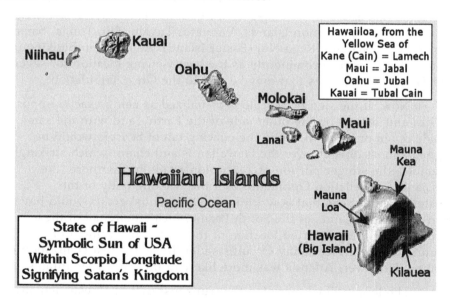

Intriguingly, Hawaiiloa heralded from a place near a sea called Kane (pronounced "Kah-Nay"), a name which bears a close connection to the name of Cain, the wayward son of Adam and Eve. Therefore, could the three sons of Hawaiiloa that are identified with three islands in the Hawaiian Island chain allegorically refer to the three sons of Lamech the Cainite, who is irrevocably connected to the Way of Cain and the seed of the Serpent through his daughter Naamah? Considering the

Scorpio connection, it is highly likely, as is shown in the illustration of the islands on page 495.

Though the human settlers of the modern Hawaiian Islands definitely did not originate before the Great Flood, there is a strong possibility that some Polynesians may be descended from the Nephilim, especially the Samoans of the South Pacific, who are one of the largest and strongest people groups on the planet, and who are often highly successful and sought after as players in many sports where size and strength are essential such as wrestling, rugby and professional football. Interestingly, American Samoa is heavily Christian, claiming over 50 percent of the population of the islands. This is heartening, as it proves that even those people who might be tainted with Nephilim blood can accept Christ and find redemption though Him!

Interestingly, the Samoan Islands are about midway between the eastern coast of Australia and French Polynesia. Looking at a map of this region, it can easily be seen that it is part of a much larger island chain of nations that extends downward from the peninsula where Thailand and Cambodia are located. These island nations are Malaysia, Indonesia, New Guinea, the Solomon Islands, Vanuatu, Tuvalu, Fiji, Tonga, Samoa, French Polynesia, and Rapa Nui (Easter Island). As noted in Book Four, Easter Island figures prominently as the best viewing location for several End Time celestial signs that may be tied to the Great Tribulation.

Now, if the sign of Scorpio is visualized as being exactly opposite to Giza and Taurus on the other side of the Earth - and with the same upside down orientation - then the curving tail of Scorpio would be aligned almost directly over the Hawaiian Island chain, which strikingly resembles the stinger portion of a scorpion's tail! Furthermore, the messianic constellation Ophiuchus and the twisting body of the constellation Serpens that is writhing in Ophiuchus' grasp would have been above the islands of the South Pacific. Incidentally, all of these islands fall in the purported location of the mythical continent of Lemuria or Mu, which many Occultists identify as the lost civilization of Atlantis. However, Atlantis was more likely in the Andes Mountains.

The longitudinal meridian that runs just east of Hawaii actually divides the 30 degree Scorpio section of the planet from the 30 degree Sagittarius section, with the Scorpio section to the west of it. This is important since Sagittarius is partly a messianic sign signifying Christ battling Satan, and one of the three decans of Sagittarius is Draco the Dragon, which is another symbol for Satan. See the drawings on pages 500 and 501 for the Star Gospel message surrounding these constellations.

Now, since the Hawaiians trace their ancestry to Tahiti in the South Pacific and people are thought to have come to Tahiti from Southeast Asia, is it possible that Hawaiiloa's ancestors' original homeland was located near to the stone temple complex built at Angkor, Cambodia, which physically represents the principle stars in the constellation of Draco the Dragon as it appeared in the sky in 10,500 BC? In addition, could this be the ancient location of Cain's kingdom called Nod, and could the first city that Cain built and then named after his son Enoch be connected to the Angkor region of Cambodia?

Could this also be why the Great Sphinx, which is a half lion and half woman chimera, is still gazing toward that region of the world associated with the Leo/Virgo longitudinal meridians shown on the map portion on page 499? Besides signifying Christ as the First and the Last, the Lion of Judah, and the Seed of the Woman, could the Sphinx at Giza be allegorically focusing its attention on the Nephilim spirit and the Way of Cain that are likely connected to the Leo and Virgo meridians over Asia? Finally, could southeast Asia be the birthplace of the pantheistic humanism and ancestor worship that Cain introduced to humanity, which is in direct opposition to the one true God who offers deliverance from sin and total transformation through Yahshua the Messiah? This is certainly an intriguing possibility, and - if it is true - it would show still another aspect of the amazing Sethite spiritual knowledge that was built into the monuments at Giza in Egypt. What an incredible undertaking it must have been when these righteous people decided to preserve Enoch's knowledge about Yahweh and His coming Messiah over 4,500 years ago!

If the Great Sphinx was partly created to point toward - and stand as a figurative guard against - the dark Tibetan spiritual center for Satan and evil's reign on Earth, there must be something about this place that makes it an ideal symbol for evil. In this regard, I found it interesting that the tallest mountain in the world is located on the border of Nepal and Tibet, China, where the Dalai Lama is from. Winner of the Nobel Peace Prize in 1989, the Dalai Lama is a Tibetan Buddhist spiritual leader who is also purportedly an Ascended Master and the current physical incarnation of the Buddha on Earth. As such, he is deeply revered by millions of Tibetan Buddhists and New Age religious practitioners worldwide. It is therefore possible that the Dalai Lama is possessed by at least one Nephilim spirit.

Ecliptic, Milky Way, & Zodiac Meridian Paths of the World

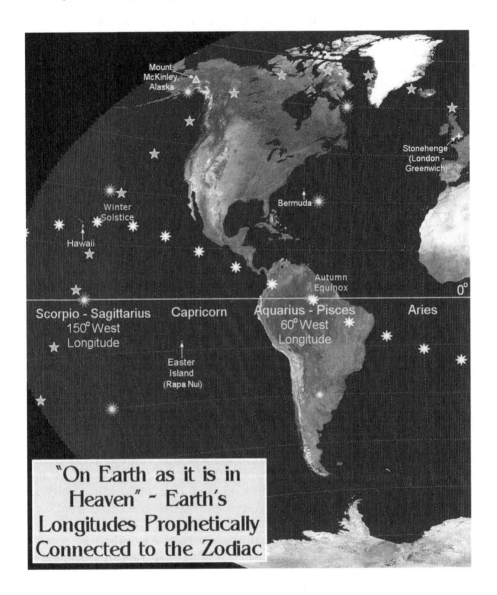

Mount McKinley, Alaska

Stonehenge (London - Greenwich)

Bermuda

Winter Solstice

Hawaii

Autumn Equinox

0°

Scorpio - Sagittarius
150° West
Longitude

Capricorn

Aquarius - Pisces
60° West
Longitude

Aries

Easter Island
(Rapa Nui)

"On Earth as it is in Heaven" ~ Earth's Longitudes Prophetically Connected to the Zodiac

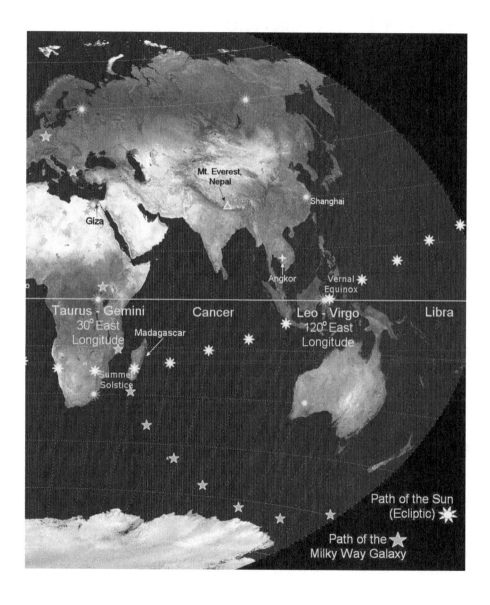

Star Gospel for Draco, Hercules, Ophiuchus & Bootes

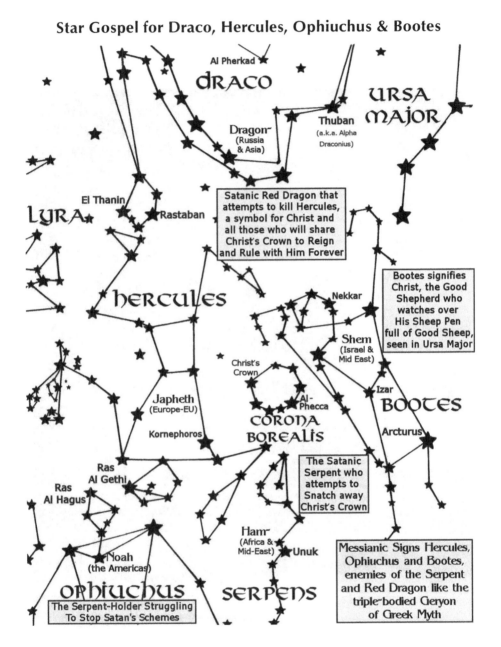

Gospel Meaning of Sagittarius, Ara, Centaurus and Scorpio

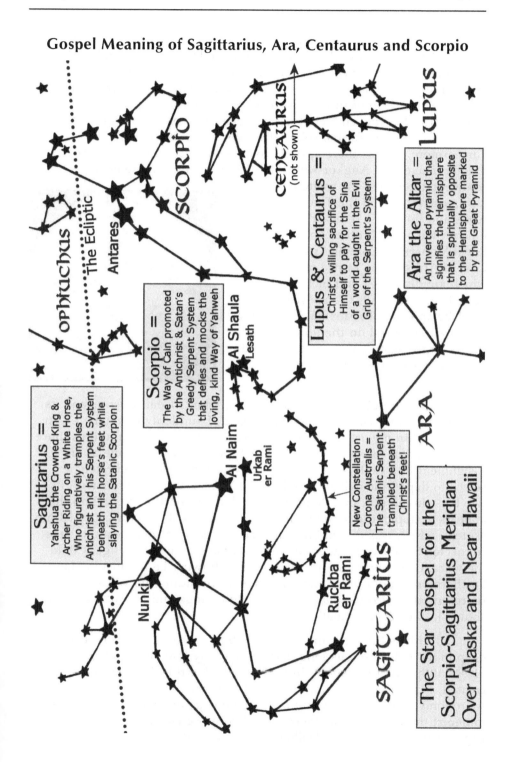

Scorpio

ophiuchus

The Ecliptic

Antares

CENTAURUS (not shown) =

LUPUS

Lupus & Centaurus =
Christ's willing sacrifice of Himself to pay for the Sins of a world caught in the Evil Grip of the Serpent's System

Ara the Altar =
An inverted pyramid that signifies the Hemisphere that is spiritually opposite to the Hemisphere marked by the Great Pyramid

Scorpio =
The Way of Cain promoted by the Antichrist & Satan's Greedy Serpent System that defies and mocks the loving, kind Way of Yahweh

Al Shaula

Lesath

Sagittarius =
Yahshua the Crowned King & Archer Riding on a White Horse, Who figuratively tramples the Antichrist and his Serpent System beneath His horse's feet while slaying the Satanic Scorpion!

Al Naim

Urkab er Rami

New Constellation Corona Australis =
The Satanic Serpent trampled beneath Christ's feet!

ARA

Ruckba er Rami

SAGITTARIUS

Nunki

The Star Gospel for the Scorpio-Sagittarius Meridian Over Alaska and Near Hawaii

Curiously, Tibet is longitudinally connected to the sign of Leo, and the Tibetan Coat of Arms created for the Dalai Lama's exiled government contains *two celestial snow lions* that are facing each other and holding up a Mandala symbol of the eight-fold path of Buddhism in front of a backdrop of three snow-covered mountains. Is it just a coincidence that this emblem features celestial lions, or does the Dalai Lama know the primordial celestial connection of his homeland? Furthermore, just as there appears to be a connection between the dragon imagery of Angkor with that of Wales, could there be a

connection between the white lions facing each other on the Tibetan Coat of Arms and the lion-like beast and white unicorn facing each other on the British Royal Monarch's Coat of Arms and the Coat of Arms of the Prince of Wales, which are discussed and pictured in Book Four? After all, the Snow Lions on the Tibetan Coat of Arms have the same four-toed feet used on the lion-like beasts on the British Coat of Arms, and these are used to signify a bear in heraldry.

Tibet's Coat of Arms - 2 Snow Lions holding Symbol of Buddhism Over the Himalayas

Fascinatingly, as I was discovering Tibet's Coat of Arms and its spiritual meaning via the Language of God, I suddenly remembered an old drawing in my art portfolio that seemed to echo these findings. Sure enough, when I located the 11 X 14 inch pencil drawing done as an assignment in a College art class, I was amazed at how accurately it seems to depict the evil signified by the Tibetan Coat of Arms with its two bat-winged (i.e. evil) lions and a coiled dragon (i.e. Nephilim) that appears to depict the Mandala for Buddhism. As shown on page 503, my sketch - which was drawn on Halloween in 1976 - also appears to have connected Satan with a volcano and a massive mountain range. Could the volcano erupting around Satan in this drawing be Kilauea in Hawaii? Furthermore, could the mountain range surrounding the volcano be a representation of the Himalayan Mountain Range and Mount Everest as shown in the Tibetan Coat of Arms?

If this is the case, then the Holy Spirit must have been at work deep in my subconscious long before I had any knowledge of these places as spiritual hot spots. In fact, at the time this drawing was created, I knew virtually nothing about the Star Gospel, Sacred Astronomy, the Great Pyramid or the Language of God. I simply wanted to depict the evil spiritual energy that I could sense surrounding the Pagan feast of Samhain or Halloween. As a result, this drawing - which I named "The Eruption of Evil" - is filled with potent allegorical symbols that seem to have been divinely inspired and show the ultimate source of the malevolence and evil in the world that seems to peak around Halloween every year.

"The Eruption of Evil" - A Sketch Tied to Tibet?

Sketch drawn by the Author in College on Halloween in 1976

Now, there are some highly interesting cities with spiritual connections that are located near to the Leo-Virgo Meridian that add spice to the designation of Tibet, India, and Cambodia as the ancestral center for the worship of humanity as gods alongside Satan and his demons. Very near to Angkor, Cambodia is a city named Ayutthaya in the Ayutthaya Province in Thailand. Furthermore, Ayutthaya is named after the city of Ayodhya in India, which is west of Nepal, and Ayodhya was the purported birthplace of Rama, the Avatar of the Hindu supreme god Vishnu.

Hanuman - Nephilim Helper of Rama, the Avatar of Vishnu the Watcher?

As mentioned earlier, what are called Ascended Masters in the Eastern and New Age religions could actually be the astral projections of the fallen angels who have been bound beneath the Earth. Meanwhile, their Avatars are real people that are most likely demon possessed so that they will carry out Satan's evil will. If so, the Neanderthal-like monkey god Hanuman who was the Hindu god Vishnu's ally was, in all probability, a humanoid Nephilim. In addition, the Avatar of Vishnu named Rama may have been an ordinary person who was possessed by a the spirit of a fallen Watcher who once called himself Vishnu, married a Cainite woman before he was bound in the abyss, and produced a Nephilim child from their forbidden sexual union that was subsequently named Hanuman. This connects Nepal and Tibet to the biblical land of Nod, where Cain settled after his exile in the land east of Eden:

> "Then Cain went out from the presence of the LORD (Yahweh) and dwelt in the land of Nod on the east of Eden." - Genesis 4:16 (NKJ)

This biblical passage tells us Nod was east of the Garden of Eden. It also contains a clue as to the location of Eden, for Adam and Eve dwelled in "the presence of the LORD (Yahweh)." Now, as mentioned in Chapter Three, the Shekinah Glory of Yahweh may have been present in the King's Chamber of the Pillar of Enoch until it led the Israelites through the desert as a pillar of smoke and fire during the Exodus. If so, the Shekinah was a manifestation of "the presence of the LORD (Yahweh)." This means that the land where Adam and Eve dwelled could have been around Lower Egypt, which may have been to the west of the Garden of Eden, or on the opposite side of Eden to Cain's settlement. If so, the Garden of Eden would have been located somewhere between Egypt and Asia - perhaps in Saudi Arabia or a lost portion of Africa that was once connected to India - which was likely situated on the eastern coast of Africa before the Flood.

Intriguingly, the most ancient forms of Hawaiian sacred hula dancing bear a striking resemblance to the ceremonial dances of India, Cambodia, and Thailand, and thus present a clear cultural connection between the two locations. What is more, Draco appears far to the northeast of Scorpio in the heavens, which means that its physical counterpart on the Earth - as per the reverse orientation of the stars associated with the pyramids at Dahshur and Giza - would be far to the southwest of Hawaii. Therefore, it should come as no surprise that the Draco-shaped temple complex known as Angkor Thom is located far to the southwest of Hawaii!

Even more fascinatingly, a prominent symbol in the heraldry of Thailand and the rest of that region of the world is a bird man named Garuda, which represents the deified mount of the god Vishnu in both Hindu and Buddhist mythology. However, though Garuda has been mythologically associated with the eagle and other birds of prey, which are the natural enemies of serpents, it is also a clear symbol of the Nephilim, who were an abominable mix of serpents, birds, people and other creatures! This may be one reason why Garuda's body is painted red in imitation of blood on Thailand's Coat of Arms.

Thailand's National Emblem ~ Garuda, Nephilim Mount of Vishnu the Watcher?

Could Thailand's Garuda figure have an allegorical connection to the Red Dragon in the Book of Revelation? If so, could it also have a connection to the Red Dragon found on the flag of Wales? Furthermore, could both the Red Dragon of Wales and the red image of Garuda be connected to the Satanic war and bloodshed associated with the twisted form of Draco, the Dragon constellation? In support of this, the Red Dragon of Wales can be allegorically connected to the pantheistic nature worship of Druidism (see Book Four and Chapter 8 in this book), whose major religious feasts were Beltane in the spring and Samhain (i.e. Halloween) in the autumn. Likewise, the Garuda Griffon is connected to Angkor, Southeast Asia and - even more specifically - to the twisted religious beliefs found in its two major religions: Hinduism, which is pantheistic polytheism, and Buddhism, which is pantheistic ancestor worship.

Significantly, fierce-looking dragons similar to those depicted in Central and South American mythology and architecture figure prominently in Chinese and Asian art and culture, and once depicted the Imperial authority of the Emperors of China. Since the Emperor was supposed to benevolently enforce law and order for the good of the people, dragons came to be viewed as benign beings that signified the rule of a just leader who cared for his subjects.

Now, as can be clearly seen in the world map shown on pages 498 and 499, the Sun and Milky Way follow serpent-like paths in the heavens surrounding our Earth that circle the globe. Furthermore, in Book One, it was shown that the winged serpent found so often in ancient Egyptian art was likely a symbol for the path of the Sun through the Zodiac on the Ecliptic. Since the Sun allegorically represents God the Father and His Preincarnate Son Yahshua, the Sun's path along the Ecliptic signifies the benevolent and righteous Way of Yahweh. Hence, winged or flying serpents signify the sunlit Way of Yahweh that is paved with the Twelve Signs of the Zodiac!

Fascinatingly, the map on pages 498 and 499 also shows that the serpentine Path of the Sun crosses the serpentine Path of the Milky Way over two spiritual hot spots: Hawaii and Madagascar. Furthermore, both of these spiritual hot spots fall at the borders of two allegorically, physically and spiritually opposite hemispheres of the Earth marked by two spiritually opposite Zodiac signs and longitudinal meridians: Taurus the Bull at 30 degrees east of Greenwich, England and Scorpio the Scorpion at 150 degrees west of Greenwich. The signs associated with the Sun and Star Path crossing over Hawaii mark the current position of the Sun in the Zodiac at the Winter Solstice, when it rises between Sagittarius and Scorpio with Scorpio rising, while the signs associated with this crossing over Madagascar mark the Summer Solstice, when the Sun rises between Gemini and Taurus with Taurus rising.

In the Western Hemisphere, the Taurus spirit of love, repentance and forgiveness of sins offered by Yahweh through Christ prevailed until recently and produced the concepts of liberty, freedom of speech and religion, democracy and equality. Meanwhile in the Eastern Hemisphere, the Scorpio spirit of inequality, slavery, worthlessness, and harsh punishment has prevailed. Despite the best efforts of Socialism and Communism to bring equality to the masses in Russia and Asia, however, the people are enslaved by political systems that are spiritually and morally bankrupt and only worship wealth, power, and human achievement.

Now, when I began to explore the Star Gospel associated with the Scorpio-Sagittarius Meridian, I found out that all of the most important aspects of the ideological war being fought today between the followers of the Way of Yahweh and the followers of the Way of Cain were mapped out in the stars by Yahshua when He created the starry Universe! The Star Gospel surrounding Sagittarius and Scorpio and their decan signs is amazingly full of spiritual knowledge that was left there by our loving Creator so that those who love Him will not be in darkness when the time for these events to unfold comes to pass. That time is now, and what Yahweh has shown me that His children need to know appears in the Star Gospel graphics on pages 500 and 501.

First, look at the star chart showing the constellations tied to the Scorpio-Sagittarius Meridian on page 501 and note how Sagittarius depicts Yahshua at His Second Coming and Scorpio signifies the Satanic System He will come to destroy. Then focus on the oft-overlooked constellation known as Ara the Altar, which is a decan of Sagittarius. To my knowledge, no other published author writing about Sacred Astronomy has seen that this upside down altar is not just an ordinary altar, but an inverted pyramid altar. And no one has likely seen what God revealed to me today: May 7, 2009!

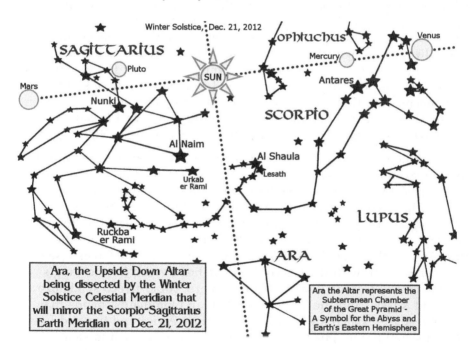

Ara, the Upside Down Altar being dissected by the Winter Solstice Celestial Meridian that will mirror the Scorpio-Sagittarius Earth Meridian on Dec. 21, 2012

Ara the Altar represents the Subterranean Chamber of the Great Pyramid - A Symbol for the Abyss and Earth's Eastern Hemisphere

By the Holy Spirit, I have just been shown that this inverted pyramid actually represents the subterranean chamber of the Great Pyramid, which is a symbol for the Abyss or Hell where Satan, the fallen angels and many demons are now imprisoned! In addition, it signifies the Eastern Hemisphere of the Earth, while the Great Pyramid signifies the Western Hemisphere. Furthermore, the Celestial Meridian marking the Winter Solstice entered the region of the sky over the sign of Ara in 1900 AD and it will remain over Ara until 2900 AD. And, most importantly, the Celestial Meridian marking the Winter Solstice today is almost an exact mirror of the Scorpio-Sagittarius Meridian on Earth! However, as shown in the smaller star chart on page 507, it will not perfectly mirror the Scorpio-Sagittarius Meridian until December 21st, 2012, the Mayan date for the end of the Fifth Sun, or the end of an Age.

In Book Four, I discuss the amazing heavenly Anti-Peace Sign that will form in the heavens on December 21st, 2012 that appears to mark the release of the Four Horsemen of the Apocalypse, which are connected to four Zodiac signs: Sagittarius, Scorpio, Libra and Taurus. Now, however, God has shown me yet another layer of importance to that date in history! It can be seen in the star chart on page 500, which shows the Star Gospel message surrounding the decan constellation of Sagittarius called Draco. Threateningly, the head of Draco the Dragon, which signifies Satan, appears to be biting the foot of Hercules just as Scorpio is pinching the foot of Ophiuchus. These heroic masculine characters being attacked under their feet by vile venomous creatures have always signified Christ as the Great Physician and Redeemer as in Ophiuchus, and as the King of kings coming to destroy His enemies as in Hercules! Incidentally, Ophiuchus and Hercules are decans of Scorpio. This means that, though Christ was wounded by the Dragon or Serpent on the Cross, He will one day crush the Dragon's head beneath His foot in the Battle of Armageddon, just as foretold in Genesis 3:15!

When viewed through the Language of God rather than Greek Mythology alone, the signs of Hercules, Ophiuchus, Bootes and Draco also appear to symbolize something even more amazing. If we view Noah, who is connected to the Americas as Ophiuchus, Noah's son Shem representing Israel and the Middle East as connected to Bootes, and Japheth as Hercules signifying the European Union, could these three signify the triple-bodied Geryon envisioned by the Greeks (see Chapter Seven!), with the Geryon's single head vying for the King's Crown seen in Corona Borealis? Furthermore, could Draco symbolize Asia and Russia, and the Serpent writhing in Ophiuchus' hands that seems ready to snatch away the crown signify Africa and the Mid-East being twisted by the Jihadists and their Mahdi, who wish to steal Christ's Crown? As shown in Book Four, if Scorpio signifies the Pale Horse of Revelation, could Serpens be riding this Pale Horse of Death?

Amazingly, this portion of the heavens may contain a revealing snapshot of the epic battle for the control of the Earth between the followers of the Way of Yahweh and the followers of the Way of Cain that is reaching its climax in this Age. Furthermore it appears to show that a President of the United States (as envisioned in Ophiuchus) may wrestle with the Mahdi signified by Serpens the Serpent for the King's Crown, but will lose that battle to the Antichrist! We will discuss this ominous scenario toward the end of the next chapter.

So, the Dragon that was and is seen as benevolent to the Chinese and the Mesoamericans is really quite a nasty character in the Star Gospel. In God's eyes, the Dragon has no true goodness at all. He signifies the antithesis of all that is right and good to Christ. In this way, the Dragon of Draco, which can be seen as a feathered serpent or Nephilim ruler, signifies the evil that comes about through corrupt kings as well as the unrepentant sinfulness of mankind that can only be obliterated through the covering of Christ's shed blood on the Cross. Yet there are times when good kings are raised up and the Feathered Serpent takes on a more benevolent connotation.

This idea that kings can do much more evil than good was reflected in the changing political situations of people in ancient Israel. Initially, the Israelites were governed only by judges and lived in a free and democratic society whose only king was God the Father. But then they desired a human king, and outside of kings like David and Josiah who were consistently righteous, the people were ruled over by many less than saintly kings and soon became enslaved and oppressed by the sinfulness, greed and debauchery of their monarchs. Perhaps that is one reason why dragons and lions have come to be associated with monarchs in the Middle East, Asia and Europe. Depending on their spiritual leanings, monarchs can be fierce protectors or violent destroyers of human life and liberty.

Now, due to the view of dragons as symbols of benevolent authority in Chinese culture, the Imperial Dragon could be connected to Draco the Dragon in its Egyptian "Tawaret" or protective aspect. In addition, Quetzalcoatl, the Feathered Serpent of Mesoamerican tradition may have a connection to Draco as well. As will be shown in the last chapter, the Feathered Serpent god of the Americas represented a benevolent figurehead who taught the natives many aspects of civilization like medicine and farming while promulgating a message of peace and brotherhood among all people. That is, until he was usurped by an evil invader who instated war and human sacrifice in place of peace and brotherhood. As will be discussed in Chapter Nine, the feathered serpent imagery pertains both to this usurper who was likely none other than Nimrod, as well as to the benevolent bringers of civilization that Nimrod conquered, who were most likely Noah and his son Shem.

Interestingly, the legendary founder of China was named Nuah or Nuwa. This name may be related to the Hebrew name Noah or to the name of his Sethite wife Naamah. Since their names are so similar, this may have led to the confusion seen in Chinese myths about Nuwa, who can be depicted as either a man or a woman depending on the source! Intriguingly, however, Nuwa was sometimes depicted as a human-headed snake goddess, and she or he may have used a feathered dragon or serpent as an identifying symbol. Therefore, the Feathered Serpent of the Americas and the Imperial Dragon of China may actually have symbolized both the wicked woman named Naamah who became the consort of Azazel, Naamah the wife of Noah and Noah himself. In addition, as already shown, Noah may have had his own separate kingdom in the Americas until Noah and his wife Naamah died and Shem's administration over China and the Americas was overthrown by Nimrod's armies.

Fascinatingly, more glimmers of mythological truth can be found in Asian lore surrounding dragons. One example of this is found in the Chinese game Mahjong, where one tile is known as the Red Dragon. This tile contains the Chinese symbol for "center" drawn in red. This symbol can also represent an arrow that has hit its assigned target. Thus, the Red Dragon tile could signify the arrow of Sagittarius the Archer that is destined to kill the Red Dragons represented by Scorpio, Serpens, and Draco!

Intriguingly, as was shown in the way the three sons of Noah divided the Earth after the Flood, Shem inherited Noah's quarter of the Earth, giving Shem the double portion that was traditionally left to a Sethite or Semite man's primary heir. In fact, the land allotted to Noah and Shem spanned the entire middle of the Earth. First, there was Noah's portion consisting of all of southern North America, Central America, northern South America and Easter Island. Then, after Noah's death, his territory was added to Shem's portion, which consisted of the Middle East, central and southern Asia, Polynesia, Micronesia, the Philippines, New Zealand, and Australia.

This is most likely why - locked into the mythology of Asia and Hawaii and placed atop its soil - there are symbols that identify the probable location of Cain's land called Nod, or "the land of the yellow sea of Kane" that is directly connected to the Way of Cain and the seed of the Serpent. Likewise, this same mythology reflects the Way of Yahweh and the bloodline of Seth as the source of the leader that will defeat the Serpent with an arrow through his malevolent heart! Thus, though most Asians are totally blind to it, the myths of India, Asia and Polynesia reflect the same truths that are hidden in the most arcane symbols for good and evil, as well as the messianic characters in the Bible and the Gospel in the Stars.

This is also why, as is shown in Book Four, Easter Island figures prominently in End Time celestial alignments that appear to be tied directly to the Gospel in the Stars and events in the Great Tribulation. Intriguingly, as found in almost all of the lands held by Shem at one time, Easter Island has its own stone memorials that are irrevocably tied to the Star Gospel, God's Plan of Salvation and the bowls of God's Wrath in Bible Prophecy.

An intriguing aspect of this Gospel map on the Earth that was left for us by the Sethites and the holy Watchers who aided them is the major differences in the physical geography and climate that these two opposing places on the Earth possess. For example, the nation of Egypt is located at the eastern end of the Sahara desert, which is the largest desert in the world. It is a bone dry and barren region of shifting sands and blistering heat that is relieved only by the occasional oasis, well, wadi or river. Yet, despite the harshness of this desert land, there is abundant life and fertility along the banks of the Nile River - life that only fresh water can provide.

How fitting then that the seemingly immortal pyramids with their spiritually charged message tied to the stars of Taurus and Orion stand in the midst of Egypt! There, the Nile flows into the fertile delta region teeming with life and the richest crop land in the world. This juxtaposition of harsh desert surrounding rich farmland shows the promise of everlasting life that comes from choosing to bear the harshness of the desert that those who follow Christ often must experience. Yet, even in the desert, those who love Christ are filled with hope and joy as they worship God and await the establishment of the physical Kingdom of God on Earth, where there will be an abundance of water, life, and greenery forever.

Secrets of the Four Corners of the Earth Revealed

In Chapter Three, it was mentioned that the four corners of the Earth that Enoch saw in visions might have a geographical counterpart on the Earth today. As has been remarkably revealed in this chapter, the

Earth's entire surface is allegorically tied to twelve 30-degree meridian bands running from pole to pole that correspond to the Twelve Signs of the Zodiac. In addition, it has been conclusively proven that the Longitudinal Meridian that is marked by the five Old Kingdom Pyramids at Giza and Dahshur in Egypt is the Taurus Meridian.

Since we know that the Great Pyramid is tied to Orion, Orion is a decan of Taurus, and Orion's upraised sword marks the point directly between Gemini and Taurus, it is clear that it marks the Taurus-Gemini Longitudinal Meridian. Since Taurus is a fixed sign and its horns are so prominently marked at Dahshur, this reveals that the Sethites considered the Taurus Meridian as a marker for one of the four corners or quarters of the Earth. Fascinatingly, the Taurus Meridian runs over a good portion of Africa and most of Europe. Could this be why the Minoans and Egyptians worshipped bulls and the Europeans seem to see themselves as the bull form of Zeus that carried Europa away? After all, as shown earlier and in the other books of "The Language of God" Series, Taurus has two horns and its right horn is tied to Gemini signifying Yahshua with His Bride the True Church, while the left horn appears to signify the Antichrist with his wicked bride, the apostate New Age church of the Tribulation period.

Utilizing the world map on pages 498 and 499, we can now find the other three corners of the Earth by locating the meridians of the other three fixed signs, which are Aquarius, Scorpio and Leo. According to the map, the Aquarius Meridian between 60 and 90 degrees west of Greenwich marks another corner of the Earth, which runs right over the US eastern seaboard, all of Central America and the mountainous regions of South America. Interestingly, Aquarius signifies both God's outpouring of the Holy Spirit over the last 2,000 years and the destruction of the Great Flood. Could this be why there is such a volatile mix of religious and political conservatives and socialistic and humanistic liberals in this part of the world that reflects both the unrepentant wicked and the redeemed in Christ?

Meanwhile, Easter Island and western North America are within the Capricorn Meridian at 90 to 120 degrees west of Greenwich, and Capricorn signifies both the salvation of Noah - who escaped certain destruction on the Ark - and the annihilation of the wicked corrupted by the Nephilim. Considering that Aquila the Eagle is a decan of Capricorn, could this be a sign of God's coming protection over the western states in the USA? Could it be a sign that the people who are left behind but convert to Christianity during the coming Tribulation will be somewhat protected in this sector of America and will live to see Yahshua's glorious return and rescue of those who remain alive until the end?

Interestingly, only eastern Alaska and the coastlands of British Columbia and the Northwestern USA fall within the neighboring Sagittarius Meridian, which is between 120 and 150 degrees west of Greenwich. The sign of Sagittarius represents Yahshua's defeat of the Serpent seed and the Way of Cain via His shed blood for our sins. Incidentally, the Way of Cain is aptly represented in this region by the lifestyles of the many homosexuals living in San Francisco - the American Sodom that lies at 122 degrees west of Greenwich.

In stark juxtaposition, the devout Christian and former Governor of Alaska named Sarah Palin grew up in Wasilla, Alaska, which is about 149 degrees west of Greenwich within the Sagittarius Meridian. This is highly significant because Sarah Palin represents a type of Esther for this unsettling time in history. Indeed, she may have been divinely chosen to serve as a messenger of hope and righteousness under fire in these dark days. In any case, Sarah Palin's morality and faith in God do serve as beacons of light guiding all who love and follow Christ and are being persecuted like Sarah has been ever since she became a national political figure and conservative Christian celebrity.

As already shown in this chapter, the corner of the Earth opposite to the one marked by the Taurus Meridian is located over Hawaii, which is within the Scorpio Meridian. Furthermore, this corner of the Earth runs over the Samoan Islands and several other island groups in the South Pacific that are associated with the curving decans called Serpens the Serpent and Draco the Dragon in the Gospel in the Stars. Ominously, the Samoans may partially descend from the Nephilim, and Barack Hussein Obama claims to have been born in Hawaii, even though he may actually have been born in Africa. Judging from what I have uncovered in this book, however, could it be that President Obama claimed to be a Hawaiian because of its sinister allegorical meaning in the Star Gospel and because he already knows his dark purpose, which appears to be aimed at the total destruction of the United States and the establishment of the wicked kingdom of the Antichrist called the New World Order?

Finally, the fourth corner of the Earth is marked by the Leo Meridian, which runs across Indonesia, Malaysia, Southeast Asia, China, Mongolia, eastern Russia and Siberia. Fascinatingly, Leo signifies Yahshua coming in wrath at the end of this age - when the Book of Revelation declares that Yahshua will return as the King of kings with a huge army of saints and angels. Indeed, since this is such a densely populated region of the world, could it be where the blood of the slain wicked will flow up to the bridle of the Messiah's heavenly white horse during the Battle of Armageddon (Rev. 14:19-20; Rev. 19:11-18)? If so, the

Sethite connection of this geographical area with Leo the conquering
Lion of Judah will clearly be prophetic.

In addition to these four corners, there are two air current
streams running opposite to each other in the Northern Hemisphere, and
two also in the Southern Hemisphere, thus showing that the four winds
spoken of in Scripture also have a real physical counterpart that has been
scientifically proven to exist. So the Earth does indeed have four corners
and four winds just as the Bible intimates, and they have a fascinating
spiritual story to tell us when we know how to read the allegorical
symbolism of the Language of God and the Gospel in the Stars.

British Occultism and the Queen's House

Before returning to a discussion of the spiritual messages locked
into the cultures around the Pacific Ocean, it is important to note here
that Giza's place as the Navel of the World was usurped by the British
Empire in its heyday, making the motives of the British Monarchy in the
United Kingdom highly suspect. Whereas Giza is the natural midpoint
between the Occident and the Orient, the world was forced, cajoled and
beguiled to accept the British Empire's creation of a new center of the
world or Prime Meridian in Greenwich - a wealthy district along the
south bank of the Thames River in London, England. Incidentally
Greenwich was once home to a royal palace, and it currently is home to
a former royal residence called the Queen's House, which was designed
and built by the architect Inigo Jones, who lived from 1573 to 1642.

Significantly, Inigo Jones was the first British architect of note. Is
it therefore possible that this architect was the author of the Indigo
Jones' Manuscript so revered by Freemasons? If so, why did the
Freemasons add the letter "d" to the middle of Inigo's first name when it
was associated with this spurious document? Could the "d" stand for
"Devil"? Unfortunately, the origin of the Indigo Jones manuscript, which
was discussed as a false historical record tied to the Way of Cain at the
end of Chapter Three, is unknown. In fact, outside of a copy of the
manuscript at a Freemasonry web site, absolutely no information on the
origin or author of this treacherous document is available anywhere on
the Internet. Curious, isn't it?

What is even more curious is the interior architecture of the
classical style home that Inigo Jones designed for royalty to dwell in. Its
most prominent and mysterious feature is an absolutely magnificent
spiral staircase that has no central supports at all and appears to defy
gravity. This bizarre yet beautiful staircase is topped by an enormous

black-framed, pale blue glass lantern that looks like a circular skylight window. Even more curious is the number of glass panes in this imposing lantern. As shown in the photo of the Tulip Staircase on this page, there are exactly 18 panes in the central lantern. This suggests that it was meant to depict the 18 parts of the Enochian day - even as the staircase spiraling upward evokes the passage of time and space through the ages.

Note the 18 panes of glass in the Lantern at the top of the spiral stairwell...

Tulip Staircase -
Queen's House,
Greenwich, England

Could it be that the Queen's House is not just the house of any ordinary queen, but was meant to invoke the Pagan Queen of Heaven that is connected to the evil Queen or Harlot who rides the Beast in the Book of Revelation? Could this queen be Queen Elizabeth II, and could her son Charles the Prince of Wales be the "Red Dragon" who seeks to devour the Messiah and His followers? See Book Four for more on this!

The very existence of this unusual staircase in Greenwich suggests that the Freemasons, the Illuminati and the Royal families they work for may already know many of the secrets in this book, and they are the evil architects of this current apostate world that is being prepared for the Antichrist's rule. Yet, despite their despicable plans that are connected to the Way of Cain and the seed of the Serpent, there is likely an even more secret organization in the world today that is connected to the Way of Yahweh.

In fact, it is likely that a modern group of righteous Wise Men or Magi are just as entrenched in the United States of America as the sinister Freemasons, and that some of these followers of the Way of Yahweh will be given immortal bodies at the Rapture and be returned to the Earth afterward to serve as part of the 144,000 Witnesses of Revelation. These Witnesses will likely consist of racially-mixed male and female Gentiles (i.e. Lost Israelites) and Messianic believers in Yahshua that will be sent to help the Tribulation Saints. By instilling hope and faith in the beleaguered saints and helping them to mount a powerful resistance against the Antichrist, these immortal Witnesses of Christ will be able to help their mortal brethren to thwart Satan's plans.

Ideological Duels in the USA Tied to Secret Societies?

The evidence that there are two groups with hidden and diametrically opposed agendas in the world today are clearly reflected in the present political leanings of the citizens of the United States, which are heavily divided into two opposing spiritual and political ideologies. These two groups are nearly equal in numbers, with one half of the USA consisting of Conservatives and believers who are trying to stem the tide of radical socialistic changes that are occurring in the United States at an unprecedented rate. Meanwhile, many Liberals despise any and all Conservatives, whom they love to call Right Wing Radicals and Terrorists. The reason for their hate? They rejoice over the US Governments' complete disregard of the US Constitution and advancement of the New World Order, while Conservatives want the nation to remain sovereign and the US Constitution to be fully upheld.

Thankfully, conservative factions in America have not been silent. They have been free to make their displeasure about immoral pro-abortion and pro-homosexual legislation and unconstitutional laws known, though this liberty is being threatened, and is continually being ignored by the media and the White House. The President of the United States since 2008, Barack Obama and his Administration have a decidedly socialistic and Antichristian agenda. In 2008, Senator Obama and Senator Joe Biden held the Democratic (Socialist ticket, while Senator John McCain and his Esther-like running mate Sarah Palin, who was the Governor of Alaska at the time, held the Republican ticket. When they lost to Obama under suspicious circumstances, there was likely a hidden agenda behind their acquiescence and graciousness that escaped the public eye. After all, remember that Yahshua told His disciples to be *"wise as serpents and harmless as doves"* (Mat. 10:16). Therefore, mature saints who follow the Way of Yahweh and hear Yah's voice through His Spirit are not going to draw attention to themselves with unkind remarks and foolish behavior. But they are going to be constantly working behind the scenes to bring about Yah's Will!

Uncannily, the 2008 US Presidential race had many other allegorical ties to the ideas being shown in this chapter. Not the least of these was the fact that the seemingly staunch Christian woman Sarah Palin was the Governor of the State of Alaska, while President Barack Hussein Obama may be a Muslim or Universalist and was a former resident of Hawaii, and both of these states are located at least partly within the Scorpio Longitudinal Meridian signifying the Way of Cain or the Serpent. In fact, President Obama also lived in Indonesia as a boy, which is near Tibet and Mount Everest. He also invites demonic help by carrying a miniature carving of Hanuman the Nephilim-inspired Hindu monkey god in his pocket as a good luck charm.

Interestingly, the Scorpio Meridian is directly opposite to the Taurus Longitudinal Meridian marked by the Great Pyramid, which signifies the Way of Yahweh. This is why the Scorpio Meridian signifies the Way of Cain. As if in confirmation of this, prominent volcanoes from Chile and Peru to Alaska that are near to the Scorpio Meridian have recently erupted, including Kilauea and the imposing Mount Redoubt volcano in Alaska, which began to erupt again in 2009. There have also been severe mega earthquakes in these same regions recently.

Because of their origins near Earth's Scorpio Meridian and their opposite spiritual paths, is it possible that Sarah Palin and Barack Obama work for two secret organizations in the world today with diametrically opposing ideologies and desires? As I have shown, one of the secrets that the guardians of the Way of Yahweh and those who guard the opposing Way of Cain have likely known since before the Flood is the mystical message hidden in the geographical location and mythology of Hawaii, which is nearly on the other side of the world to Greenwich, England. In contrast to the barren desert at Giza and the cool, mist-covered mystery of England, the Hawaiian Islands have been likened to Paradise - having one of the most ideal warm climates in the world.

Interestingly, the biggest trouble areas in the world today are centered around the epicenter marked by Mount Everest in Asia, where Iran and North Korea are being led by oppressive fascist regimes that especially hate Israel and the United States, but also threaten the security of all the Western nations. To the north and east of Mount Everest, Russia and communist China are also threatening the rest of the world, and both countries may soon seek to be dominant world powers as trouble heats up in the Middle East. In addition, there is no doubt that Russia still has a huge, hidden nuclear arsenal that could obliterate civilization centers around the world.

But Russia and China are not the West's only foes, for sandwiched between China and Japan is the tiny nation of North Korea, which has long been led by a radical communist regime with a deep-seated hatred of the United States and desire to destroy it. In fact, North Korean educators have systematically inbred the same hatred into its populace. If not now, it won't be long before one of their missiles contains a nuclear warhead. So, unless someone moves to stop them, the North Koreans could soon aim their missiles at targets in South Korea, Japan, Hawaii and/or the west coast of the USA and set off a limited nuclear exchange that could easily terrify the world enough to accept the Antichrist's one-world empire: the New World Order. Of course, as many students of Bible Prophecy know, the trouble won't end after the Antichrist takes control, but will eventually escalate into World War III.

Now, immediately southwest of the Mount Everest epicenter and North Korea are the nations of Pakistan and India - both of which have nuclear capabilities and populaces filled with Hindus and Muslims that tend to hate and persecute the devout Christians within their borders. So, despite their democratic forms of government, these nations may pose a threat to all nations with a Christian majority such as the United States, Australia, South Korea, and the Philippines. In addition, Afghanistan has long been a nearly impenetrable stronghold for Al Qaeda and other radical Muslim groups with a deep seated hatred for the West. Though it appears that these radical groups may soon be routed out of Afghanistan by American and foreign troops, the neighboring nuclear-armed government in Pakistan is unstable because of a large radical Muslim presence among their populace.

A bit further west, and adding to the volatility of the region is the nation of Iran, whose hatred is currently centered on the USA and Israel - the only democratic nation in the Middle East, and one with a populace that has been favorably disposed toward the United States for decades. Meanwhile, the predominantly Muslim countries surrounding Israel continue to foment hatred of the West and Israel. With its Jewish majority, Israel is hated by many Muslims partly because the Jews claim to have an exclusive right to the blessings of Abraham, while the Muslims believe Abraham's illegitimate son Ishmael inherited the birthright that God gave to Abraham's legitimate son Isaac.

Now, while some Christians view all Jews with contempt for their rejection of Christ, and many of the troubles facing Jews today have indeed been caused by their refusal to accept their Messiah, there are many Christians and Messianics including myself that support Israel's right to exist because it is God's will that Israel has regained the land that was promised to Abraham, Isaac and Jacob. In fact, there are countless prophecies in the Bible that foretold the regathering of the Jews in Israel in the last days. The miraculous rebirth of Israel in 1948 was a major fulfillment of End Time prophecy, and the conflict over Israel's survival in the Middle East is no accident. It was foretold in the Bible thousands of years ago - as was the ultimate outcome of this conflict, which will lead to World War III, Armageddon and the Second Coming of Christ.

I'm anxiously looking forward to Yahshua's literal and awesome return with joyful anticipation, and pray that many people will discover the truth of the Gospel of the Kingdom of Yahshua Ha Mashiach before it is too late.

Demonic Elements in Polynesian and Native Art

Since it seems that trouble around the Hawaiian Islands may lead to the rise of the Antichrist's power, and Hawaii falls within Earth's Scorpio Meridian that is associated with the celestial signs in the heavens on December 21st, 2012 that show the release of the Four Horsemen of the Apocalypse (See Book Four, "The Language of God in Prophecy"), let's see if it might have something to do with the religious beliefs of the native Polynesians who once lived life on the Hawaiian Islands in comfort and ease from birth to death - free from the moral and social constraints so prevalent in the rest of the world.

Alas, despite the seemingly idyllic nature of life on their island home, native Hawaiians once paid a terrible price for their isolation that manifested itself through genetic and spiritual corruption. In fact, their demonic-looking Tiki god carvings accurately reflect the dark spiritual nature of the religious rituals, evil spirits and oppressive taboos that controlled their lives.

Sadly, the Hawaiians were not alone in creating demonically inspired art and cultural elements. Demonic-looking statues of humanoid deities were once common to almost all of the native religions of the world, including the Polynesians. Indeed, some of the most demonically charged cultures of the Pacific were located in North America. There the Tlingit, Haida and other indigenous peoples of the Pacific Northwest created imposingly tall totem poles and large wooden masks depicting so-called nature spirits that most often resemble giant bird-like monsters. Despite their artistic beauty, these artifacts depict spirits that are physically reminiscent of, and invoke the same sense of unease as the Nephilim and the demons that they became at death.

The religious plays that the natives of the Pacific Northwest enacted using ritual wooden masks were especially frightening, as the plays were usually conducted at night in dark, smoky lodges with only flickering firelight to illuminate the masked men. These men were drugged and put into a trance-like state before they began to swirl and swoop about in bizarre pantomimes reflecting the evil nature of the false gods that their bird-like masks represented and were most-likely possessed by.

As an example of how evil these masks are, let me relay my experiences walking through a darkened section of the Field Museum of Natural History in Chicago where many varieties of these native ritual masks are on display. From the moment I entered this large room full of display cases and totem poles, I had a deep sense of foreboding. As I gazed at the frightening masks in row after row of display cases, I could actually feel the demonic presences connected to them in the room - as if they were waiting to entrap anyone not protected by the Spirit of God with their evil power. As a result, I had no desire to dwell in that place and was grateful to leave.

Incidentally, I felt a similar sense of foreboding at the same museum when looking at the actual fossil remains of Sue - the largest, most complete Tyrannosaurus Rex skeleton so far discovered. In addition, I have sensed demonic spiritual energy when viewing Hawaiian Tiki god carvings and African native carvings. In fact, almost every native-made religious artifact I have come across seems to be tainted with evil spiritual energy - regardless of what culture they originated in. This includes the "dream catchers" that are so popular in America.

As an example of this, shortly after a friend gave my daughter a beautiful Native-American made dream catcher as a gift, she started having night terrors. In addition, no amount of praying seemed to help with her constant nightmares and fear of the night until we got rid of the dream catcher. Amazingly, it was my daughter who finally sensed that the dream catcher was causing her night terrors, and as soon as I rid the house of it at her request, the night terrors stopped completely! This was a real eye-opener for me, and made me realize how vulnerable even born-again believers are to demonic attack unless we are vigilant!

So, if you have any actual native artifacts displayed in your home and you do not wish to invite demons there, I would suggest ridding yourself of them immediately. This does not pertain to cheap replicas of these artifacts, but to actual artifacts that were either used in worship, or were demonically "blessed" by the native people who made them prior to distribution. These ritual objects are magnets for demons and can bring harm to anyone without spiritual protection - even those who profess to love Christ but have no idea how to recognize channels for demonic activity. For this reason, even replicas of these artifacts should be shunned by those whose ability to seek divine protection and deliverance by performing exorcisms and healing is weak - as is the sad case among most professing believers today.

A Question Of Race - Are We All Under Grace?

In this chapter, we have discussed many intriguing areas of the world and their prophetic place in history. We also discovered that the world could once easily be divided into two opposing eastern and western hemispheres with radically different spiritual, political, religious and cultural ideologies. In addition, we spied the connection of Caucasian female Sarah Palin of Alaska and the half white and half African American Barack Obama of Hawaii with the Scorpio Meridian in the Pacific Ocean. Finally, we discerned that these two politicians that follow completely opposing spiritual ideologies and conflicting political paths have become spiritual icons for people holding their worldviews around the world.

Spurred on by my perceptions of the two opposing worldviews that have been prevalent throughout history, a news story that I wrote during the last half of the US Presidential race in the autumn of 2008 revealed how Barack Obama was raised as a Muslim in Indonesia, now professes Christianity and a love for democracy but acts like an unsaved Socialist Muslim. Furthermore, it revealed that the black American talk show hostess Oprah Winfrey is a New Age "guru" or "goddess" who endorsed Obama and called him "The One" - a epithet that may indicate that Oprah thinks Obama is the New Age Movement's Messiah called Maitreya as well as "the Messiah" that the Black Muslims of the USA see Obama as.

As a result, these two apostate black individuals with their high approval rating around the globe resemble two infamous characters in the Book of Revelation - namely the Antichrist and False Prophet. However, they may not be those particular enemies of God. They simply may be forerunners that are paving their way. In addition, even though these two people are at least partly of African descent, this does not mean that black-skinned people are any more inherently evil than the rest of humanity. It simply means that two people that happen to be black-skinned have brought and will continue to bring about much wickedness due to their perceived hatred of true Christianity and the God of the Bible. In closing this chapter, therefore, I wanted to destroy the myth that human skin coloration has anything to do with the mark of Cain or the curse of Canaan so often attributed to blacks.

For the purposes of this study, let us assume that almost all the Anakim were destroyed in the past, and nearly everyone alive today is fully human. In fact, this is likely to be absolutely true. Though there may still be some people groups who could trace their roots to the Nephilim such as the Samoans, they are so heavily watered down with human blood that they are virtually indistinguishable from the rest of humanity today. Furthermore, it is highly likely that any remaining Anakim on Earth today have remained largely isolated - either by choice or by God's design.

Now, since I believe God's account of Creation in the Bible, there is no room in my worldview for the theory of Evolution, but only the processes of adaptation and Natural Selection. The Bible teaches that all people are descendants of Adam and Eve through Noah and his three sons. This means that every racial group is related in some way, and they all share common ancestors. That is why, no matter what skin color people possess, they can intermarry and give birth to healthy, beautiful children. That is also why people the world over share many common diseases and genetic abnormalities.

Nonetheless, though all people are genetically related, they are also tainted with sinful, rebellious dispositions. Ever since Adam and Eve sinned in the Garden of Eden, there have been many conflicts between various people groups over the millennia. Undoubtedly, this is because sin and evil are interracial and cross cultural phenomena. There is no one people group on Earth today that can claim to be sinless, nor does any one people group have a monopoly on evil. As the Apostle Paul said: *"For all have sinned and fall short of the Glory of God"* (Romans 3:23).

In addition to sharing a sinful nature, every human being on this planet shares a common bloodline. Since we are all descended from Adam and Eve and Noah, and over seventy percent of humanity has black or dark brown hair, it would be wise to conclude that Adam, Eve and Noah did not have blond or red hair. Like black hair - which is a dominant genetic trait - skin color is a function of who one's ancestors were too. However, the human biological characteristic that allows skin to lighten or darken depending on where one lives and how much Sun exposure is received also plays a part in our skin color over time.

As Bill Cooper hypothesized in his book "After The Flood" (available on line at: http://www.ldolphin.org/cooper/contents.html), skin color seems to be largely determined by how close one lives near to the equator for an extended period of time. The reason for this is quite simple. Infertility can increase when people are exposed to too much or too little sunlight. Therefore, people with light skin have the lowest rates of infertility in temperate climates where exposure to the Sun is limited, and where light skin is best suited to absorb limited solar radiation. It follows then that light-skinned people who live near to the Equator will tend to be infertile. In addition, the descendents of light skinned people will tend to have darker skin over time. This is why people groups that live closer to the equator are likely to have darker skin tones.

Likewise, when people with darker skin coloration move from the equator to colder climates, they tend to be infertile and unhealthy from not getting enough sunlight. As a result, until their skin tones lighten sufficiently, dark-skinned people have a tendency to have fewer successful pregnancies and higher mortality rates than their lighter skinned neighbors.

Now, since the Bible makes it clear that all people are genetically related, the racial divisions and the cultural squabbles that humanity has experienced are really a function of ideology rather than biology. If nothing else, world history should show all of us that every culture on Earth is capable of feeling racially superior to others. In fact, many of the wars being fought today are attempts at genocide. Unlike in the past, however, the genocidal wars being fought today are more often over spiritual beliefs rather than skin color or genetic descent.

Today, regardless of where one lives, there is mistrust and hatred between various religious and ethnic communities. In most of the world outside of the West, for example, Christians are heavily persecuted with little regard for race or culture. Though the persecution of Christians is especially high in Communist or Islamic nations, however, intolerance toward Christians is on the rise even in the West. Furthermore, there is much hatred between religious factions within Islam. Hence, though Muslims all profess to worship one Supreme deity named Allah, Sunnis and Shiites find it almost impossible to live in peace with one another because they each claim doctrinal superiority.

Throughout the world today, New Age beliefs, Neo-Paganism and Wicca are also on the rise, and most of the people practicing these Pagan religions dislike and mistrust anyone who is a committed Christian. Then there are the class distinctions found within the Hindu caste system that cause mistrust, prejudice, and outright disdain and hatred between the various castes. Even those who follow the gentle spirited and non-confrontational religion of Buddhism tend to disagree over political ideologies, and none of the aforementioned religions tolerate Christians or Messianics well.

People groups are also constantly divided over moral issues. In today's world, for example, Christians are often divided over the issues of homosexuality and abortion. Regarding abortion, some Christians and Messianics believe that life begins at conception, while others believe life begins at birth, and therefore have no problem accepting abortion. However, the Bible teaches that life begins at conception, and this is supported by countless medical studies detailing human fetal development (See Psalm 139:13; Luke 1:15, Luke 1:41-42).

In regard to homosexuality, some Christians and Messianics believe that one's sexual preference is more a function of biology rather than an issue of sin. However, there are Scriptures in both the Old and New Testaments that clearly teach that homosexuality is wrong (Leviticus 20:13; Romans 1:27). Furthermore, though the Bible teaches every Christian to love one another even as Yahshua loved us, it also teaches that people who actively practice sexual immorality are not to be associated with, whether they are Christian or not (Romans 6:11-14; 1 Corinthians 6:18).

Ideally, since Christianity is a purely non violent religious ideology that teaches people to tolerate and love one another, and to love the sinner even while fleeing their sin, there should have been peace on Earth over a thousand years ago, when most of the West was heavily under the influence of Christianity. However, people were unfamiliar with the power of the Holy Spirit back then. As a result, they were far more bigoted, hypocritical, and judgmental, and this sorely affected their ability to understand and implement Scripture. As a result, many atrocities were performed against whole people groups in the name of Christ, such as genocidal style slaughters of Africans and Native peoples in the Americas, Africa, and elsewhere during the Spanish, Portuguese, French, English, and American colonial conquests of the 16th through 19th centuries.

Due to the colonial expansion era, many people who were won for Christ at the edge of a sword distrust the white Jesus they were introduced to by western missionaries. As a result, Asians want to see Yahshua as Asian, Africans want to see Him as black African, and Anglo-Saxons generally depict Yahshua with fair skin and light hair - with each culture tending to deny His Jewishness. This is partly due to each culture's misplaced feelings of superiority over others and the general resentment among people of color toward whites - who tend to harbor supremacist ideas. However, there is also an underlying prejudice toward Jews due to the misconception that they were primarily to blame for Christ's murder - even though Yahshua was a good Jew and His sacrificial death was necessary to provide everlasting salvation and complete freedom from divine judgment. Since this is true, Christians should feel a certain amount of gratitude and compassion toward Jewish people rather than resentment!

As a result of all these points of conflict, the world's current desire for global peace seems as illusory as ever. The reason for this is simple. The only way to bring about world peace is through the establishment of a global theocracy that is governed by Christ Himself, Who is all, and is in all:

> "Here there is no Greek or Jew, circumcised or uncircumcised, barbarian, Scythian, slave or free, but Christ is all, and is in all." - Colossians 3:11 (NIV)

Someday soon, the Bible tells us that Yahshua's theocracy will be miraculously established (2 Timothy 2:11-12; Revelation 20:6). However, before this happens, the Bible also warns that a time of severe judgment is coming to the whole world (Isaiah 2:12-19, 13:6-13; Joel 3:13-16; Zech. 14:1-9). During this time, mankind will be coerced into uniting under one ideology by a spiritually warped political and spiritual leader known as the Antichrist, who will appear to be good but will have evil intent.

After defeating the Mahdi or Muslim Antichrist, this pretender will vie for and temporarily sit on Christ's earthly Davidic throne, will claim to be a god, will demand worship, and will attempt to bring about a false utopian society by setting out to exterminate all the monotheists that refuse to worship him (Rev. 11:7, 13:7, 20:4). Thankfully, the Bible also tells us that the Antichrist will not succeed fully. Instead, before the Antichrist's henchmen destroy every last Christian and Jew, Yahshua will return from Heaven riding on a white horse and followed by an army of His saints riding on white horses (Revelation 19:11-21). Then the Antichrist and his followers will be defeated and the Antichrist will be cast into the Lake of Fire (Rev. 19:20).

Unfortunately, until Yahshua sets up His Kingdom on Earth, people around the world are going to be beset by evil, and life and death struggles will be common. Fueling the fire for discord are several long-standing conflicts that are adding to the volatile mix of ideologies in the world today. The very first conflict of note was between the Seed of the Woman named Eve that was found through her righteous son Seth, and the Seed of the Serpent found in the line of Cain via their ill-fated love affair with the fallen angels and their Nephilim children.

The second major world conflict began when Noah cursed Ham's son Canaan with perpetual servanthood and submission to Shem and Japheth's descendents. As per Bill Cooper's hypothesis, Japheth became the father of the fairest-skinned races due to his settlement of far northern lands, Shem became the father of the yellow, red, and light brown-skinned races living around the 30th parallel, and Ham became the father of the darker skinned races that lived nearest the equator.

Now, since the darkening of the skin caused by heavy exposure to sunlight takes hundreds of years to develop into a genetic adaptation, there is no reason to believe that Canaan was particularly dark-skinned, as he was among those born in the first generation after the Flood. In fact, he was probably light to middle brown in skin tone.

Unlike Mizraim and Cush who settled in southern Egypt and Africa and spoke Hamitic languages, the Egyptians of the Delta and the Canaanites spoke the Semitic language of the original inhabitants of Lower Egypt and Canaan, who were the offspring of the first king of Salem (i.e. Jerusalem) named Melchizedek (a.k.a. Shem). In other words, Lower Egypt and Canaan were Shemite or Semitic territories shortly after the Flood, but were later taken over by the Canaanites and their Nephilim friends through conquest. This likely occurred when the confusion of tongues and destruction of the Tower of Babylon in a worldwide cataclysm ended Nimrod's despotic reign.

Later on, the Israelites were called by God to conquer the Canaanite kingdoms that were overrun with the descendants of the Nephilim. Acting with courage and persistence, the Israelites soon killed most of the Nephilim and Canaanites who had intermarried with the Nephilim (Deut. 2:9-22, 3:1-15; 2 Samuel 21:15-22). They thereby ousted most of the Canaanites from the land that once belonged to Shem and was Abraham's inheritance. In addition, some Canaanites that were not tainted with Nephilim blood became the servants of the Israelites - in direct fulfillment of Noah's curse upon Canaan (Joshua 9:15-27).

The prevalent notion that Noah's curse was extended through Canaan to all the black African nations is erroneous since Canaan was not likely black, but light to middle brown like modern Arabs are today. Nonetheless, the false teaching that the curse upon Canaan applied to all the African nations persisted and led to the horrors of the black slave trade. Today, we can see the lingering prejudice resulting from it, as well as the sense of resentment and entitlement many blacks carry for the many precious lives that were destroyed by white men who felt they were superior to them.

Despite the legitimate cause of their bitterness, blacks and whites need to learn that slavery can take many forms - from Feudalism to Fascism - and as a result, almost every race and culture on Earth has experienced oppression and slavery at various times. Therefore, until tyranny and injustice are completely done away with, there can be no real peace in this world. Instead, the unjustly treated will go on hating their oppressors until both sides accept a better path - the Way of Yahweh exemplified in the path of love and forgiveness forged by Christ on the Cross.

Another one of these ancient conflicts is the ongoing feud between the Jews and their Arab half-brothers. Both sons of Abraham, both fiercely proud and accomplished, Ishmael and Isaac were at odds from Isaac's birth, for Isaac was Abraham's wife Sarah's child, while Ishmael was the son of Sarah's Egyptian handmaiden Hagar, who was a slave. So, though both Ishmael and Isaac wanted to be heirs to God's promises to Abraham, Yahweh picked Isaac as Abraham's heir. Indeed, Ishmael would never have been born if Sarah and Abraham had trusted God with His promise that Sarah would conceive one day, so they brought this trouble upon themselves, and their descendents have been paying for their mistake ever since.

As a result of God's choice, the tension between the two half brothers became so pronounced that Sarah finally asked Abraham to send Hagar and Ishmael away. Neither Hagar nor Ishmael ever forgot this humiliation, however. In addition, their descendents settled with the descendents of Jacob's brother Esau, who callously lost his birthright to Jacob over his desire for a pot of stew. As a result, the feud between Abraham's chosen heirs and those who felt they were unfairly ostracized became even more deep-seated. This is why the Arab descendents of Ishmael and Esau surrounding Israel often seem to be plotting that tiny nation's untimely demise. Furthermore, many Muslims hate the West due to the Crusades, and they especially hate the USA for interfering with their blood feud with Israel.

Ultimately, effectively dealing with all these conflicts in the world today will not be found in engaging in diplomacy, politics, or war, but in Christ's shed blood and finished work on the Cross. Through His sacrificial death and resurrection, Yahshua could at last send His Spirit to teach all who love Him to truly love and forgive one another. Indeed, the Holy Spirit is the only force in Heaven or on Earth that can forever transform our hearts and minds to be like Yahshua's, and that is the only way that we can achieve the future utopian society promised in the Bible. We all need a heart and a brain transplant, which is what everyone who truly has faith in Christ will receive. Through our love of

Yahshua and desire to keep His commandments, we are born again and will one day become the Body and Bride of Christ!

Through that spiritual transformation, and later through the Resurrection into everlasting life that it promises to us through Christ, we will all one day be royal heirs and priests with Yahshua - regardless of our skin color or station at birth. To that I say: "Hallelu-Yah for the coming Kingdom of God in Yahshua!" If that sounds good to you too, please join me in frequently praying *"Your Kingdom come, Your will be done"* - just like Christ did.

Chapter 7: The Pagan Corruption of the Star Gospel

> *"They served their idols, which became a snare to them.* **They even sacrificed their sons and their daughters to demons,** *and shed innocent blood, the blood of their sons and daughters, whom they sacrificed to the idols of Canaan; and the land was polluted with blood. Thus they were defiled by their own works, and played the harlot by their own deeds.* **Therefore the wrath of the LORD (Yahweh) was kindled against His people, so that He abhorred His own inheritance. And He gave them into the hand of the Gentiles,** *and those who hated them ruled over them." - Psalm 106:36-41 (NKJ)*

The stirring confession in the Psalm opening this chapter is a testimony to the wrath that Yahweh God unleashed on His chosen people Israel for their rebellion. It should have come as no surprise to Israel, however. Yahweh had warned them many times of the punishment that He would mete out if Israel broke the Blood Covenant made with them through Moses at Mount Sinai. These Blood Covenants were considered perpetually binding yet were conditional on one thing: they required all future generations to faithfully keep the Covenant. Those who broke this conditional Blood Covenant with Yahweh paid dearly for their disobedience, for Yahweh afflicted them with adversity and trouble just as He had warned them:

> *"But if you do not obey Me, and do not observe all these commandments, and if you despise My statutes, or if your soul abhors My judgments, so that you do not perform all My commandments, but break My Covenant... I will even appoint terror over you, wasting disease and fever which shall consume the eyes and cause sorrow of heart. And you shall sow your seed in vain, for your enemies shall eat it. I will set My face against you, and you shall be defeated by your enemies. Those who hate you shall reign over you, and you shall flee when no one pursues you." - Leviticus 26:14-17 (NKJ)*

In any Age, Yahweh is an awesome God who will not be mocked. He is the Creator of all things and the giver of all life and goodness. For these reasons alone He deserves our eternal allegiance and adoration. However, just as in past Ages, this isn't the case in today's world. In this so-called age of enlightenment, people the world over are again bowing down to idols of wood, stone and precious metals.

Buddhists, Catholics, Hindus, Hare Krishnas, Wiccans and many other religious groups all worship or ascribe power to various types of graven images.

As a one-time Roman Catholic, I am deeply disturbed by the idolatry so prevalent in this branch of the Church. In the Chicago-land area where I live, countless statues of Mary are found in front of various homes. This is a deplorable practice because **these statues are blatant forms of idolatry**. Many seem to overlook this because these statues supposedly represent Yahshua's holy and saintly mother. However, many Catholics view Mary as their intercessor before God and as their real Savior, thereby robbing Christ of His unique place in their salvation! Sadly, many Catholics are unaware that **Scripture does not support any intercessory role for Mary.** Instead, Scripture clearly tells us that **Yahshua and His Holy Spirit alone are our only Intercessors** before Yahweh. My initial discussion of Mary's highly esteemed but humble place in the Church is found in Book Two of the Language of God Series, Chapter Six. There, 1 Timothy 2:5 was quoted to verify that Yahshua alone is our only Mediator or Intercessor before Yah. Here are two other Scriptures that teach this:

> "Therefore He (Yahshua) is also able to save to the uttermost those who come to God through Him, **since He (Yahshua) always lives to make intercession for them**. For such a High Priest was fitting for us..." - Hebrews 7:25-26 (NKJ)

> "But if anybody does sin, we have one who speaks to the Father in our defense-- Jesus Christ (Yahshua the Anointed One), the Righteous One." - I John 2:1 (NIV)

These Scriptures show that Yahshua alone pleads our case before our heavenly Father. By extension, Yahshua's Spirit dwelling within us also intercedes for us - as the following Scripture shows:

> "In the same way, the Spirit helps us in our weakness. We do not know what we ought to pray for, but **the Spirit himself intercedes for us with groans that words cannot express**. And he who searches our hearts knows the mind of the Spirit, because **the Spirit intercedes for the saints in accordance with God's will**." - Romans 8:26-27 (NIV)

The Spirit living within believers and that intercedes for them is **Yahshua's Spirit**. We should therefore direct our intercessory prayers only to Yahshua and His Father. This is because, though Yahshua and the Spirit work as a team in our salvation, it is Yahshua alone who intercedes for us before the Father. He then graciously ministers to us through His Spirit living within us.

The Second Commandment tells us that depicting Mary, Yahshua, or any saint, angel or cherub as a graven image used in worship is a terrible sin (Exodus 20:4-5). If prayers are offered up to them, then they are idols – false substitutes for the supreme Creator God and His Son. One of the worst incidences of this form of idolatry is among Catholics who boldly display depictions of Mary wearing a crown in their homes or gardens. These deluded people are blatantly declaring their belief that Mary is their personal Savior and the Catholic Queen of Heaven. Yet they fail to realize that "the Queen of Heaven" is a title for an ancient Pagan goddess!

Since the Catholic view of Mary is so far off-kilter, **all channeled messages from any apparition purporting to be Mary must be demonic in origin**. Do not let yourself be fooled by demons! Mary is not and never was our intercessor before Yahweh, and only Yahshua can fill this role! For those who have practiced idolatry but now realize that it is a sin, it is never too late to repent. All they have to do is discard their idols of Mary, Jesus, various saints, and their crucifixes. Then they need to pray to their Heavenly Father Yahweh and His Son, ask them for forgiveness, and then turn to the true Christ to find their salvation before it is too late. Sadly, however, there are many that will never repent of their idolatry. This is because demonic spirits have seduced them into believing that idols have real power.

In many cases, **human ancestors can serve as idols - whereby people worship themselves**. Buddhists and Hindus alike bow to one another in greeting in a show of respect to the divine essence that they all assume they have. In the case of the Hindus, they bow to the spirit of Brahman that is said to permeate all living matter, while Buddhists bow to the divine spirits of their ancestors living on in them. They all therefore view themselves as little gods who have to earn their place among all the other seen and unseen deities that populate their view of the Cosmos. These people believe that the spirits of their gods or ancestors can guide them to perfection. In this way, they become open to demonic deception by evil spirits that pretend to be their gods or ancestors. In addition to being totally open to demonic influences, Pagans, humanists and atheists tend to focus on their own personal power, pleasure and needs instead of on the needs of others. They therefore can become very selfish and cruel.

Reincarnation: Saving Oneself Without Need for a Savior

This self-centered attitude is also prevalent among most people who are allied with the New Age Movement. They adore the godly essence that they imagine they can see in themselves and every created thing. They believe that all humans are potential gods that have immortal spirits and must progress upward through multiple physical reincarnations until they reach the level of avatar or ascended master, at which point they become incorporeal spirits without need for a body. Reincarnation, while not a new idea, is becoming increasingly more accepted even among nominal Christians the world over. However, there is no evidence in the Bible to suggest that the concept of reincarnation is a valid method to obtain salvation from sin and death.

Anyone who has read and believed what the Bible says would not be able to accept the concept of reincarnation. This is because one of the Bible's central themes is the Blood Covenant, which teaches that the only way to salvation is through the blood sacrifice of an innocent victim. As covered exhaustively in Book Two, **the Blood Covenant ritual that Yahshua sealed in His blood with all mankind on Calvary teaches us that we cannot find salvation without Him!** We are, in fact, powerless to save ourselves and need our sinless Savior Yahshua to help us achieve what we never could on our own.

As a further argument against reincarnation, the Bible makes it clear that we aren't meant to live many lives in an effort to find our own perfection, but only once:

> *"And as it is appointed for men **to die once**, but after this the judgment..." - Hebrews 9:27 (NKJ)*

This passage makes it clear that the writer of the Book of Hebrews knew that men die only once before being judged. Since the writer did not attempt to explain his meaning further, this belief was also likely held by his Messianic Jewish audience.

Further collaboration for the idea that we can only die once is found in the Parable of the Rich Man and Lazarus. Here, Yahshua clearly taught that the immortal spirits of men go immediately to either Heaven or Hell when they die:

> *"There was a certain rich man who was clothed in purple and fine linen and fared sumptuously every day. But there was a certain beggar named Lazarus, full of sores, who was laid at his gate, desiring to be fed with the crumbs which fell from the rich man's table. Moreover the dogs came and licked his sores. So it was that the beggar died, and was*

carried by the angels to Abraham's bosom. The rich man also
died and was buried. And being in torments in Hades, he
lifted up his eyes and saw Abraham afar off, and Lazarus in
his bosom."

"Then he cried and said, 'Father Abraham, have
mercy on me, and send Lazarus that he may dip the tip of his
finger in water and cool my tongue; for I am tormented in this
flame.' But Abraham said, 'son, remember that in your
lifetime you received your good things, and likewise Lazarus
evil things; but now he is comforted and you are tormented.
And besides all this, between us and you there is a great gulf
fixed, so that those who want to pass from here to you
cannot, nor can those from there pass to us.'" - Luke 16:19-26
(NKJ)

In the above Scripture, the bosom of Abraham is a euphemism
for a special part of Heaven. This part of Heaven is equivalent to our
notion of Paradise. The part of Paradise called Abraham's Bosom is
reserved for the spirits of those who are true believers in Yahweh and in
His promise of a Messiah. It is therefore open to all people who love Yah
- including those who died in their faith long before Yahshua's First
Advent but believed in His coming.

Saint Paul mentions that he visited the Third Heaven, which is
one of seven heavens as reckoned in Jewish Eschatology (2 Cor. 12:2-4).
The First Heaven is our own Solar System and the Second Heaven is the
Universe at large. The Third Heaven, however, is beyond the physical
Universe. In fact, it is considered to be the beginning of the five invisible
levels of Paradise where Yahweh, His angels and His saints dwell.

While in the Third Heaven, Paul mentions that he saw wondrous
and unspeakable things. From Paul's comments concerning this
experience, it is certain that Paul felt he was swept up into Paradise
without experiencing death. Interestingly, the Pre-Flood patriarch Enoch
also mentions being swept up into the First, Second and Third Heaven
often. In one of his dream visions of what lies in the Third Heaven, the
prophet Enoch describes a place very much like Abraham's Bosom:

"And there I saw another vision, the dwelling-places of
the holy, and the resting-places of the righteous. Here mine
eyes saw their dwellings with His righteous angels, and their
resting-places with the holy. And they petitioned and
interceded and prayed for the children of men, and
righteousness flowed before them as water, and mercy like
dew upon the earth..." - 1 Enoch 39:4-5

From Enoch's vision of Paradise, it is obvious that Enoch believed in a literal place called Heaven where the righteous dead dwell, just as Saint Paul did. Furthermore, from various statements in the Bible about Sheol or Hades, it is certain that **Abraham's Bosom is a place where dead souls come to dwell until the Resurrection of the Dead on the Last Day**, not just for a time before returning to live repeated earthly lives in search of some illusive state of spiritual perfection.

In addition to the preceding Scriptural passages that clearly teach that reincarnation is a lie, there are intellectual arguments against reincarnation. My favorite method of showing reincarnation's fallacy is to ask: "Why would a just and loving God make anyone suffer hundreds of lifetimes filled with pain, suffering and death before allowing them to achieve Nirvana, which is not so much a state of perfection as it is of nothingness? Furthermore, how could a loving God allow these poor people to suffer so many past lives without allowing them to easily remember what they did wrong in their previous incarnations?" The truth is that **no just or loving God would ever allow this!**

Instead, Yahweh made our Path to Salvation simple because He loves us so much. He sent His only Son to die for our sins and become a sin offering for us so that we could be counted as pure and holy by that blood covering alone. The *only* good work we need to do to enter Heaven is to fervently believe in Yahshua as God, Savior and King. Through His blood *alone*, we are sanctified for salvation. The only effort required by us to obtain that salvation is to steadfastly believe in Yahshua as our Savior. And if someone is saving you, wouldn't you cling to them with every ounce of strength you had as they pulled you out of the mess you were in?

In direct opposition to the Christian teaching that Yahshua is the only way to Heaven, however, proponents of reincarnation teach that people can achieve salvation by their own merits, albeit with the help of others who have achieved perfection prior to them. At the point when people supposedly become one with the essence of God through their own efforts, Hinduism and the New Age religions state that these truly enlightened individuals become ascended masters. These invisible, incorporeal spiritual masters are then supposedly capable of teaching others to reach the same heights through various types of meditation and occult mysticism. Unfortunately, this teaching opens the way for demons disguised as these so-called ascended masters to lead millions of people astray. This is done when those seeking to reach Nirvana more quickly contact these demons in disguise through mediums (often known today as channelers) and clairvoyants or psychics.

In effect, the New Age Movement espouses a humanistic religion completely based on self-willed works to find salvation. To make matters worse, it is also demonically inspired and promulgated. The greatest tragedy of this religion, however, is that it rejects the need for a Savior while deifying mankind. Nonetheless, this Neo-Pagan movement is growing astronomically. One day soon, it will probably be the dominant world religion and the one that the Antichrist will herald as the truth. He will likely use its points in common with all religions to unite the world in one faith, just as Nimrod did and every dictator tried to do long before the Antichrist. This is why the Book of Revelation clearly teaches that the Wrath of God will be kindled against all mankind for their idolatry and apostasy:

> "But the rest of mankind, who were not killed by these plagues, did not repent of the works of their hands, that they should not worship demons, and idols of gold, silver, brass, stone, and wood, which can neither see nor hear nor walk. And they did not repent of their murders or their sorceries or their sexual immorality or their thefts." - Rev. 9:20-21 (NKJ)

Sadly, this is nothing new. All the ancient kingdoms of the world gave in to the same temptation to deify idols and eventually themselves. They did this in the form of ancestor worship and by worshipping human, Watcher and Nephilim kings as gods. Eventually these sins also lead to gross sexual perversion and murder - when humans perform sex for or sacrifice people to demons. The preceding Scripture from the Bible tells us that Neo-Pagans will also be guilty of sexual immorality and murder. Through their adulation of idolatrous statues and demons masquerading as benevolent spirits (and eventually, the Antichrist), Neo-Pagans worship the fallen angels and their demon offspring just as our ancestors before and after the Great Flood did. Saint Paul knew this and warned his disciples not to partake in ritual meals that served food sacrificed on a Pagan altar:

> "The things which the Gentiles sacrifice they sacrifice to demons and not to God, and I do not want you to have fellowship with demons. You cannot drink the cup of the Lord and the cup of demons; you cannot partake of the Lord's table and of the table of demons." - 1 Corinthians 10:20-21 (NKJ)

In the preceding Scripture, "Gentiles" refers to any non-Jew who does not know, love, and follow Yahweh Elohim as Jews do, or His Son Yahshua as Christians and Messianics do. Anyone who shows faith in any other form of deity other than Yahweh and Yahshua is not worshipping the one triune God but a demonic counterfeit.

Prior to the Flood, the fallen angels and the Nephilim were the first to openly promulgate false religion and idolatry. In fact, ***Paganism and idolatry stemmed from the same primary source before and after the Flood. This primary source is the fallen angels and their Nephilim children***, who taught mankind to worship gods of flesh and bone rather than the one true God of Spirit. This false religion was initially wiped out when Yahweh destroyed all the Nephilim and most of humanity with the Flood. Sadly however, some Nephilim survived the Flood and slowly began to spread their false religion as the population of Anakim hybrids grew. Later, though Nimrod and his followers rejected Anakim as objects of worship, they instead erroneously adored mankind as the greatest divinities in the Universe. In addition, they worshipped the demonic spirits of the Nephilim and revived their false religion of Astrology, Sorcery and star worship.

Both before and after the Flood, the demonic Nephilim offspring of the fallen Watchers would naturally have been worshipped as gods by humans since humans likely felt physically, and at times mentally inferior to their seemingly divine and immortal overlords. All the Pagan religions of the world could easily have been inspired by folktales surrounding the fallen angels and the Nephilim. These false "gods" gave many supposed "gifts" of knowledge that led to horrible sin and ultimately served to destroy all life on Earth.

Then, for a brief time after the Flood, the Way of Yahweh reigned on Earth, and everyone worshipped God in truth. But, as will be shown in upcoming sections through the proper interpretation of Classical myths, it appears that Noah's son Ham turned his back on the worship of Yah and instead began to exalt himself and his sons as gods. After Ham's defection from the true faith, his son Cush became the high priest of a new religion that exalted mankind over all Creation. Then Nimrod stepped in to further change the status quo by leading people to shun and kill their Anakim overlords.

Like the Hercules of myth, Nimrod killed all the evil Anakim (i.e. Saurian) beasts that threatened mankind and offered people the ability to be as God once more, just as Eve and Cain did long before him. This is why Nimrod deified Eve as the Queen of Heaven by instating the worship of the false goddess Inanna/Ishtar. Under Nimrod, men and women were now equally able to pursue their desire to become "immortal" as false deities worthy of mankind's capricious worship.

The Post-Flood Revival of Pre-Flood Astrology and Magic

The Book of Jubilees explains that the Post-Flood revival and practice of Astrology originated through a descendent of Arphaxad after the Flood. Unfortunately, these Pagan teachings were recorded prior to the Flood, and later were found and promulgated by Arphaxad's son. Arphaxad was the son of Shem who is believed to have settled close to the Persian Gulf (Genesis 10:22). As such, Arphaxad likely founded the Sumerian and early Babylonian cultures of Eastern Mesopotamia. He was said to have had only one son named Shelah in the Book of Genesis (Genesis 10:24, 11:12). The Book of Jubilees, however, names Cainan (a.k.a. Kainam) as another son of Arphaxad (a.k.a. Arpachshad):

> *"In the twenty-ninth jubilee, in the first week, in the beginning thereof Arpachshad took to himself a wife and her name was Rasu'eja... the daughter of Elam, and she bare him a son... and he called his name Kainam. And the son grew, and his father taught him writing, and he went to... seize for himself a city.* **And he found a writing which former (generations) had carved on the rock, and he read what was thereon, and he transcribed it and sinned owing to it; for it contained the teaching of the Watchers in accordance with which they used to observe the omens of the sun and moon and stars in all the signs of heaven. And he wrote it down** *and said nothing regarding it; for he was afraid to speak to Noah about it lest he should be angry with him on account of it." - Jubilees 8:1-5*

According to my Biblical Chronology, Cainan would have been born around 2250 BC, which was not long after the Great Flood of 2347 BC. Interestingly, nowhere does Jubilees say that *"the omens of the Sun and Moon and stars"* found by Cainan preserved knowledge about the occult use of Astrology. All it does say concerning Cainan's discovery is that he sinned on account of them. In other words, the teachings of the Watchers that Cainan found were not necessarily evil. After all, there were good Watchers on the Earth before the Flood that taught Enoch Sacred Astronomy and how to read the Star Gospel - an art he freely shared with his Sethite descendents. Furthermore, finding an omen in the heavens does not have to involve Sorcery or desiring to change the course of history. It is strictly meant to be a way to discern the unchanging and perfect Will of God, and to live in a manner that will speed the fulfillment of God's Will.

Since the writer of Jubilees records that Cainan sinned on account of these teachings, and archeology has revealed that the Babylonians were obsessed with foretelling the future and doing horoscopes in order to apply Sorcery, it is obvious that Cainan's sin was using Astrology as a basis for Magic. In fact, of the tens of thousands of cuneiform tablets that have so far been unearthed in Mesopotamia, fully half of them contain detailed astrological horoscopes and astronomical calculations. This evidence clearly shouts that the rulers of Babylon had set their own will against Almighty God's and they wanted to control their own destiny.

Though Cainan likely found an ancient record of how to apply Sacred Astronomy in its purest and most innocent form, however, it is possible that he found, copied, and later promulgated the Pyramid Texts found in the Old Kingdom Pyramid tombs of Unas, Pepi 1, and several other pharaohs. These writings in stone may have originated not with the godly line of Seth, but with the Cainite patriarch Enoch, who may have been none other than the Pharaoh Unas of Egypt's 5th Dynasty.

Unas supposedly reigned between 2356 and 2323 BC, though these dates are not certain. Unas could have been born much earlier - especially if he lived 900 years or more like other antediluvian patriarchs. If Unas was Cain's son Enoch, he would have reigned in southern or Upper Egypt anytime between 3900 and 3000 BC, which is my estimate for his life span after reaching adulthood. The Book of 1 Enoch tells us that the fallen Watchers arrived and began to corrupt humanity during the reign of Jared. Jared was the father of the righteous Enoch, and the Watchers' teachings would have begun to be recorded sometime during Jared's reign, or shortly afterward.

Could the Post Flood descendent of Shem named Cainan have found the Pyramid Texts in the pyramid tomb of the 5th Dynasty Pharaoh Unas, whose name is similar to the name Enoch in structure? Furthermore, could Unas be Enoch, the son of the spiritually reprobate patriarch named Cain, and *not* the son of the godly Jared? If Cainan did find the Pyramid Texts, he would have found magical formulas that required a working knowledge of the celestial objects in the heavens to understand. Therefore, the perverted form of Astronomy called Astrology was definitely involved in utilizing these incantations.

Modern Egyptologists believe the Pyramid Texts were written about two hundred years after the Great Pyramid was built. Some Egyptologists see a tie-in with the five Old Kingdom tombs containing Pyramid Texts and the five-sided Great Pyramid at Giza, which also has five divisions within its internal structure. These arcane hieroglyphic texts were meant to transform the dead king of Egypt into a spiritual being who could rise effortlessly and unhindered into the heavenly abode of Osiris, god of the dead and holder of the keys to a blissful afterlife. In fact, there is no doubt that these magical texts relied on the sacred internal and external architecture of the Great Pyramid as an interface for accomplishing their magical aims. Since the Pyramid Texts rely on astronomically inspired magic rituals to override the just judgments of God, however, righteous Sethites like Jared's son Enoch could not have written the Pyramid Texts. Instead - perhaps a generation or more after the Great Pyramid was built - these incantations were probably composed by another group of individuals with a diametrically opposing spiritual and social worldview.

Upon studying various translations of the Pyramid Texts, it has become clear to me that these magic spells were written in direct contradiction to the godly message being presented in the Great Pyramid and the Gospel in the Stars. In fact, these texts are primarily aimed at making the dead pharaoh (or anyone who placed them in their tombs) a god-like being with control over all the demonic forces in the Universe. Based on his or her knowledge of the Magic in the Pyramid Texts, these little gods could supposedly then fool their demonic gods into seeing their spirits as powerful, blameless, and pure. Subsequently, this would allow them to ascend unhindered into the starry dwelling place of Osiris, and into the supposedly imperishable abode of the dead in the stars. Thus, the ancient Egyptian version of the resurrection of the dead was seen as a magical undertaking that only those initiated in Sorcery could obtain. This meant that the ancient Egyptians believed they could not find salvation by living a righteous life, but only by using Sorcery or Magic to fool the gods!

The Book of Jubilees records that the followers of Cainan found teachings about the Heavenly Tablets that were written by the Watchers and their followers prior to the Flood. I believe that the sympathetic Magic of the Pyramid Texts could be part of the teachings that Cainan found. Utilizing these false teachings, the followers of Cainan incorrectly interpreted the divinely inspired message of the Great Pyramid after the Flood. Subsequently, the Post Flood civilizations that sprang up in Egypt may have incorporated the written teachings of the Watchers into every aspect of their lives. As a result, every spiritual truth that they may have initially possessed due to the godly teachings of their ancestor Noah were corrupted almost beyond recognition.

The Pyramid of Unas may be the symbolic or literal burial chamber of the Enoch who descended from Cain. When Cainan found these writings and copied them down, he hid his knowledge of them until he could leave and establish his own kingdom. This is when he probably introduced this false knowledge as a new religion based on the teachings of the Watchers. This is also likely when Astrology was re-born after the Flood and men did their best to become gods by following the teachings of demonic angels that posed as deities representing the Sun, Moon, and various stars. Thus, the sacred knowledge of the heavens that was originally used to determine God's Will in order to keep it holy was instead used to thwart God's purposes. Instead of following God's Will, those who practiced Magic and Sorcery wished to do only their own will, and to mold outcomes to suit themselves. The Pyramid Texts strongly suggest that they did so by using Magic and calling upon demons to destroy God's Will and do their own. We will discuss the modern day promulgators of the false religion centered around Sorcery and star worship a bit later.

Since Jared was born in 3543 BC, I date the approximate time of the fallen Watchers' arrival to 3400 BC, just before the birth of the righteous son of Jared called Enoch in 3381 BC. Cain's evil son named Enoch, if he was Unas, was therefore beguiled into idolatrous sin and Sorcery by the Watchers' teachings sometime after their arrival in 3400 BC. Enough evidence is presented in this book to substantiate my claim that the Great Pyramid is a Temple to Yahweh built by the righteous descendents of Seth. Since the Sethites went to such great efforts to record their knowledge of the one true God and His Gospel in the Stars, the fact that the ungodly antediluvian ancestors of Cain may also have recorded their own beliefs should come as no surprise. I believe that what the Cainites recorded was the evil teachings of the fallen Watchers, whom they likely believed were gods.

Cain's son Enoch (who, according to Biblical Chronology, was born around 3800 BC) was possibly the first human king to be beguiled by Sorcery. If so, he and his misguided Cainite progeny could have built the five stone mastabahs filled with the earliest known record of the Pyramid Texts in Saqqara, near to Giza. However, since this is highly unlikely to have occurred while the righteous descendents of Seth controlled the Giza plateau, the Pyramid Texts must have been recorded after most of the followers of Seth had fallen into gross apostasy and wickedness. Since the whole world had fallen into grievous sin just before the Flood, Cain's son Enoch or one of his blood descendents would likely have had little trouble taking control of the abandoned sacred precincts of the Sethites. This is likely why the tombs containing the oldest Pyramid Texts are found so near to Giza.

Alternatively, the Cainites and the Nephilim may have eventually driven the godly followers of Seth out of Egypt, or at least out of the area of Giza. This would have allowed the Cainites to build and inscribe the interiors of their tombs using the same hieroglyphic notation that the godly patriarchs Cainan and Enoch likely used and perfected. Hence, the false religion of the Watchers may have survived the Flood in these tombs. Subsequently, the Post-Flood Cainan found these false religious teachings before or shortly after he and his descendents infiltrated Egypt and intermarried with the local Hamitic peoples.

Later, around 2100 BC, the descendents of Mizraim and Cainan may have founded two separate ruling dynasties early in Egypt's Middle Kingdom. Just as many pharaohs had been deified before the Flood, the new Egyptian priests of that time period would likely have deified the pharaohs who preserved and supported their newly revived false religion. To honor the new "gods," crude pyramids may have been built over the tombs of these Sorcerer Pharaohs to signify their status as gods. In this way, the true meaning of the Great Pyramid as a tribute to the one true God Yahweh and to His Son Yahshua may have been masked behind the false notion that all Pharaohs had the right to build a pyramid to proclaim their deity.

Ominously, Cainan was the thirteenth patriarch in the line of Seth. Twelve righteous men preceded Cainan (ten before the Flood and two after). But after the righteous reigns of Shem and his son Arphaxad after the Flood, the thirteenth patriarch named Cainan was beguiled by the false teachings of the Watchers to rebel against the God of his fathers. Subsequently, this second man named Cainan led the entire world into the sinful use of idolatry and Magic.

The Gospel of Luke identifies a man named Cainan (a.k.a. Kainam) as the son of Arphaxad in the genealogy of Yahshua. Since Arphaxad was the son of Shem, Cainan was Shem's grandson. Luke records this Cainan to have been the father of Shelah, not Arphaxad, who would have been Shelah's grandfather:

> "...the son of Serug, the son of Reu, the son of Peleg, the son of Eber, **the son of Shelah, the son of Cainan, the son of Arphaxad, the son of Shem,** the son of Noah, the son of Lamech..." - Luke 3:35-36 (NIV)

Due to the passages in the Book of Jubilees about the thirteenth patriarch Cainan and the mention of a patriarch named Cainan in the Gospel of Luke, it appears that the unholy writings of the once holy Watchers who sinned (i.e. fallen angels) were found by this descendent of Arphaxad. Subsequently, Cainan must have been beguiled by these false teachings and may have begun to re-introduce Astrology and Magic as part of the old false religious system of the Watchers. It is also likely that this newly revived false religion inspired the Pagan philosophies of Nimrod's Babylon as well as those that arose in ancient Egypt. These astrological and religious teachings of the fallen angels were diametrically opposed to the writings of Cainan the Sethite that were similarly carved in stone. Instead of a saving knowledge of the Star Gospel and an explanation of the allegorical Language of the one true God, the carvings found by the Cainan born **after** the Flood likely taught Astrology as the key to utilizing the demonic supernatural forces behind every form of Sorcery and Black Magic.

This occult form of Astrology sought to identify when certain God-ordained people, events or circumstances were to come about. This was so that these people or circumstances could then be thwarted or eradicated in order to alter the divinely ordained course of human history. Furthermore, this wrongful use of Astrology was centered on the worship of the stars, Sun, Moon and planets as gods. *This may be why the genealogies of Genesis, Chapter 10 omit Arphaxad's son Cainan's name from the record.* This Post-Flood Cainan was the probable source of the false spiritual knowledge that the entire Pagan world later espoused and perpetuated after the Great Flood.

If this scenario seems farfetched, it is only because the knowledge that Satan has attempted to grossly pervert every known truth of God throughout history was demonically suppressed. But why else would there have been two men named Enoch before the Flood that were diametrically opposed to one another on a spiritual level? Likewise, in the totally opposite spiritual legacies left behind by two men named Cainan - one before and one after the Flood - *it should be abundantly clear that Satan has created a powerful and confusing counterfeit for every legitimate Judeo-Christian belief.*

This demonically inspired confusion is so prevalent that it is difficult for most of us to discern the truth from the lie. Satan's perversion of spiritual truth is evident in all of the idolatrous structures built near to the Great Pyramid. Furthermore, it is also apparent in the tampering that has been done to the Great Sphinx and to the record of what the planets, stars and constellations in the heavens were meant for and why they came into being.

Paganism: Demon and Ancestor Worship

Dictionaries define the term "Pagan" as anyone who observes a pantheistic or polytheistic religion, or does not observe a monotheistic faith such as Judaism, Christianity or Islam. Atheists, hedonists, and apostates (i.e. those with a Judeo-Christian background who are decidedly irreligious or immoral) can also be considered Pagans. Though numerous agnostics and apostates would undoubtedly be offended if they were referred to as Pagans, their lack of love and adoration for the one true God defines them as such. However, in a Christian or Messianic context, a Pagan can be defined as anyone who does not worship the one true God *correctly*. To most Christians and Messianics, this means believing in one triune God defined as a Trinity of God the Father, God the Son, and God the Holy Spirit.

By this definition, Orthodox Jews and Muslims who do not accept the Son of God or the Spirit of God as separate Persons acting within the one triune Godhead could be deemed Pagans, although God Almighty has a special place in His heart for the Jews, and He has promised that the devout ones will be saved, and will have an honored place in His Kingdom (Ezek. 37:19; Zech. 12:9-10, 13:8; Rev. 1:7). In fact, there are also prophetic indications that many Muslims will finally accept Yahshua as their Savior or Mahdi, and will serve alongside their Jewish brethren during the Millennial Rule of Christ (Isaiah 19:23-25).

As has already been shown in the "Language of God" Book Series, Paganism has not always been present on the Earth. In fact, there was a time before Adam and Eve fell when they were both unswervingly monotheistic. They not only knew Yahweh from the Gospel in the Stars, but from direct interaction with the Preincarnate Yahshua in the Garden of Eden (Genesis 3:8). Unfortunately, that changed forever when the satanically inspired Serpent convinced Eve that she could be like God. In essence, Satan insinuated that Eve could be a goddess with as much power and knowledge as the almighty triune God that she had previously worshipped. But first, she had to disobey Yahweh to learn the forbidden knowledge of good and evil.

Nonetheless, since the dawn of time, there has always been one true monotheistic faith. Though it originated with Adam, who was the first priest in the line of Melchizedek, it was perpetuated and transmitted to future generations by his sons Abel and Seth. In fact, sometime during the lifetime of Seth's son Enosh, the Bible suggests that righteous people had already begun to call on the Name of Yahweh in supplication and prayer (Genesis 4:26).

Before the Flood, Paganism was likely the natural result of the adoration that ordinary people developed for, or were forced to give to various fallen angels, their wives, and their Nephilim offspring. This is likely why even the earliest false deities found in Sumer and Akkadia were recorded to be as fickle and capricious as their human subjects. In fact, many of these demonically inspired deities constantly needed to be pleased, cajoled, and adored before they would even consider granting the desires of the deceived people who sought their blessing or help.

Not long after, these false deities were also associated with the original Star Gospel created by Yahshua, revealed to the righteous Sethites by the holy Watchers, and subsequently perverted into Astrology by the fallen angels. Thus, the Gospel in the Stars was altered almost beyond recognition. However as was shown in Books One and Two, the truth can still be discerned in many Greek and Roman Myths. These next two sections reveal that this may be because these myths were not necessarily attempting to mask the truth as originally hypothesized, but were meant to reinterpret it from the perspective of those lost souls who honored and worshipped Eve and the Serpent that deceived her instead of the one triune Creator God Yahweh and the righteous patriarchs who worshipped Him.

To complicate what we know about the beliefs of our ancestors before and after the Flood, a process called syncretism soon turned the Paganism surrounding the worship of the fallen angels and the demonic spirits of the Nephilim into a strange blend of ancestor, alien, and demonic worship. Syncretism is defined as: "the attempted reconciliation or union of different or opposing principles, practices, or parties, as in philosophy or religion."

As shown earlier in this book, almost every godly monotheistic symbol was systematically perverted by being merged with opposing philosophies. The result of this syncretization of monotheistic truths with polytheistic falsehoods was the humanistic Paganism that propelled ancient Egypt, Babylon, Greece and Rome to reach new heights of cultured civilization after the Flood even while turning their backs on the one true God. As any museum full of Greek or Roman religious sculptures will attest - all their glorious achievements were dedicated to their capricious deities, who were all clearly made in mankind's own fallen, and often unashamedly (and rebelliously) nude physical image.

The second fall into polytheistic demon and ancestor worship happened rapidly over a period of several hundred years after the Flood. In that time, historical and archeological records show that the monotheism that sprang up from the correct interpretation of the Star Gospel and Sacred Astronomy soon degenerated into gross pantheism and polytheism. In fact, by the time that the Tower of Babel was being built, there are indications that the whole world was not only of one language, but of one faith that was a form of polytheistic idolatry centered on ancestor worship, making it humanistic at its core.

As a result of the formation of this unifying false religion in the far past, most Pagan philosophies are essentially humanistic and demonic - where the worship of demonic and human heroes are melded together into one. Most of these false religions promote and utilize the magical pseudo-science of Astrology, which - as a total bastardization of Sacred Astronomy - is a demonic attempt to give humanity god-like foresight and control over their destinies in rebellion against Yahweh.

The ancient form of Astrology also entailed the worship of various celestial bodies, stars, and demonic spirits as false representations of powerful but unrighteous humans, fallen angels, and Nephilim who were deified for their great deeds. As already shown in Books One and Two, Pagan religious leaders did this in rebellion against Yahweh, and in the process of rebelling they almost totally obscured the truth behind Sacred Astronomy and turned it into an abomination instead of a holy science. What the records do not tell us, however, is how this process occurred so quickly.

Interestingly, the development of Paganism could have happened rapidly at any given time if the people who controlled the recording and dispensation of knowledge began to slowly and systematically alter and pervert those records, and change the nature and meaning of the symbols, events, and people recorded therein. Could it be that the Post-Flood fall into Paganism was the result of the evil intent of demonically possessed leaders with direct access to various libraries of historical and religious records?

World leaders such as Nimrod often controlled all the world's institutions of higher learning, and therefore would have had a virtually unlimited ability to pervert the teachings of every historical and religious text to suit his own aims. In fact, Nimrod and his followers could have rewritten history with their own false religious ideas in a belief that it would better serve to control and unite the populace. By indoctrinating each generation until no one remembered the truth behind the lies, Nimrod would have succeeded in creating a one world government with a one world religion that combined humanism with gross idolatry and polytheistic ancestor worship.

Incidentally, this is just as the demonic leaders of this world are seeking to do today with the global forced teaching of Evolution as a fact that denies the existence of any all-knowing, all-perfect, and all-holy Creator God and instead exalts mankind and the Anakim over God. In fact, in a direct attempt to deny the existence of Yahweh, some Evolutionists are postulating that alien beings such as the Nephilim or fallen Watchers can be the only possible source of Intelligent Design in the Universe!

Proof that the ancients primarily worshiped their rulers and human heroes as gods can be found in "The Forgotten History of the Western People" by Mike Gascoigne. Early in the book, the author makes use of "Cory's Ancient Fragments" and other ancient historical sources to show that many of the deified characters of Greek and Roman Mythology were actually styled after historical biblical characters found in the Book of Genesis. In other words, the ancient Greeks and Romans were not true polytheists, but humanistic ancestor worshippers. This was the major factor behind the rise to the self-centered philosophies of that era, which included the glorification of the human body, sexual immorality and perversion, and the Bacchanalian celebration of every great individual and corporate human achievement.

From fragmentary ancient records, we can piece together a family tree identifying various Pagan deities with the biblical characters they partially represent, as well as their demonic associations. Before the Flood, for example, the line of Cain can be identified with the Olympian gods, while the line of Seth was associated with the Titans. In fact, the seventh Cainite patriarch named Lamech appears to be the character behind Zeus, the king of the Olympian gods who was known as Jove or Jupiter by the Romans. Like Zeus, who had numerous wives and lovers, Lamech was the Bible's first polygamist (Gen. 4:19). Through the process of syncretism, however, Zeus was eventually tied to Cush and his son Nimrod. These people were no doubt like Lamech in character, and therefore were deemed worthy to be seen as the Cainite patriarch Lamech's spiritual ancestors after the Flood.

The Cainite polygamist Lamech's connection to Zeus can also be seen in the identification of his three sons with three particular offspring of Zeus who were born to different women. Though we are not told this in the Book of Genesis, Lamech also likely had several daughters by his two wives. In addition, Lamech likely had many more children by the female slaves that waited upon his wives. Despite this, however, we are only told of Lamech's three sons: Jabal, Jubal, and Tubal-Cain, who all have a deified Greek counterpart just like their father:

Jabal, who was the father of tent-dwellers and those who keep cattle, **can be tied to the god Apollo** in his shepherd role. **Jabal can also be tied to the god Hermes (i.e. Mercury)**, a son of Zeus who was a thief and cattle driver. However, Ham's son Cush later assumed the role of Hermes.

Jubal, who was the father of those who played the harp and organ (i.e. bagpipes), **can be tied to the god Apollo** in his role as the god of art and music.

Tubal-Cain, who was an artificer of brass and iron, **can be tied to Hephaestus** (i.e. Vulcan), who was a blacksmith who could work all types of metals, and became the armorer of the gods. However, Azazel was the original Vulcan.

Despite the fact that the Paganism of classical times was a form of demonic ancestor worship, the memory of the Watchers or fallen angels and the Nephilim certainly influenced the mythology of these ancient cultures, and was always represented in their myths by the symbol of a serpent, which the Pagans saw as a benevolent being who gave mankind divine knowledge instead of death and sorrow. In particular, Greek Mythology mentions two races of giant beings - **the Titans** that were purported to be humanoids with serpent tails and who were overthrown by the Olympian gods before the Flood, **and the "Gigantes" or Giants** who later fought to overthrow the Olympian gods.

Greek Mythology therefore supports the biblical record in that the Greek Titans are directly connected to the fallen angels and Nephilim who were *"the Mighty Men"* before the Great Flood, while the Gigantes or Giants are analogous to the Anakim and the Rephaim descendents of the Nephilim who roamed the Earth after the Flood. Along with them, the Bible mentions other part-Nephilim beings such as the Zuzim, the Emim and the Horites:

> *"In the fourteenth year, Chedorlaomer and the kings that were with him came and attacked the Rephaim in Ashteroth Karnaim, the Zuzim in Ham, the Emim in Shaveh Kiriathaim, and the Horites in their mountain of Seir, as far as El Paran, which is by the wilderness." - Genesis 14:5-6 (NKJ)*

This war instigated by Chedorlaomer occurred when Abraham was residing in Canaan, and the above Scripture suggests that Chedorlaomer defeated the Giants living in that area of the Middle East surrounding Canaan at this time. Note also that these giant descendents of the Nephilim were not cited as living anywhere in Canaan. This is because Canaan was part of Noah's son Shem's kingdom at that time, and the Giants did not dare set foot in Shem's domain until that great man of God (who was also known as Melchizedek) died. The Giants had, however, surrounded Canaan in anticipation of overrunning it after Shem's death

The Giants sought to establish themselves in the vicinity of Mount Hermon in present-day Lebanon, where the Watchers who sinned likely built their first mountain home, and where the first Nephilim may have been born. At the time of Abraham, the Rephaim Giants lived around Ashteroth Karnaim or Ashteroth, meaning "Ishtar's Horns," "Ishtar's Shame," or "Cave-land," depending on which of the varying translations of "Ashter" and "roth" are used. All that remains of this place now are the ruins around Tell Ashterah in the southwestern region of Syria called Hauran. This largely treeless region - which is characterized by its conical volcanic peaks, barren lava fields, and rich soil in the south - is the location of ancient Bashan, the land once ruled over by the fearsome Rephaim King named Og - whom legends identify as a Nephilim that survived the Great Flood. The Druze Mountains are in the northeast of this region, and they contain numerous caverns that were once inhabited by the Rephaim who descended from Og.

Meanwhile, the Emim Giants lived in Shaveh Kiriathaim, which is located in west central Jordan, and the Horite Giants lived in the mountains of Seir. Seir was later known as Edom, which was a large kingdom spanning all of southern Jordan and the land south of Israel between the Dead Sea and Red Sea. Finally, the Zuzim Giants lived in "Ham," a place between Ashteroth Karnaim in Syria and Shaveh Kiriathaim in Jordan that is not to be identified with Noah's son Ham.

Interestingly, the Greeks seem to have associated the worst human enemies of their religious philosophies with the Titans and the Gigantes, who were no doubt modeled after the Pre-Flood fallen angels and Nephilim and the Post-Flood Anakim Giants. In fact, the Greeks may have tied the first twelve biblical patriarchs in the line of Seth to the twelve Titans of Greek myth, who were originally Nephilim or fallen Watchers that had been deified! Therefore, they painted the righteous followers of Yahweh as an errant and inferior race of gods that needed to be defeated so that the humanistic civilizations of mankind could unite and advance to new heights.

Just as the Sethites were falsely associated with the Titans, Noah and his wife were falsely identified with Ouranos or Uranus, the god of the heavens, and his wife Gaia, the goddess of the Earth who was depicted as the mother of many of the Titans. Furthermore, Noah's three sons Shem, Ham and Japheth were erroneously connected to three of the Titan sons of Uranus that have a place in Greek Mythology as follows:

Shem, the son of Noah who settled most of the Orient and Middle East, and who was chosen to inherit the messianic promise, and to possess the bulk of his father's wealth, **can be equated with the Titan named Titan, who was also known as Helios or Hyperion.**

Ham, who settled most of Africa, **can be tied to the Greek god Kronus or Cronos**, who was known to the Romans as the god Saturn, although Saturn/Kronus also signifies the fallen angel Azazel (i.e. Satan).

Japheth, who settled most of Europe and Russia, **can be tied to the Greek Titan Iapetus.**

Due to their similarity in names, Japheth has been tied to the Titan named Iapetus ever since ancient times, though this tie has been disputed because Iapetus was said to be the father of Prometheus, whose son was the Flood hero Deucalion. However, though Deucalion shares an obvious connection to Noah, who was actually the father of Japheth rather than his offspring, the process of syncretism effectively explains this discrepancy. It also explains how the Titan called Titan also became associated with the sun god Helios and the Titan son of Gaia and Uranus (i.e. Noah) named Hyperion, who - like Seth and Shem - was a master Astronomer:

> "Of Hyperion we are told that he was the first to understand, by diligent attention and observation, the movement of both the sun and the moon and the other stars, and the seasons as well, in that they are caused by these bodies, and to make these facts known to others; and that for this reason he was called the father of these bodies, since he had begotten, so to speak, the speculation about them and their nature." - Diodorus Siculus (5.67.1)

Due to the fact that Hyperion's father Uranus can be associated with Noah, and Shem was likely the only one of Noah's sons to be taught all the secrets of Sacred Astronomy, it is possible that Hyperion was none other than Shem or Melchizedek, the King of Salem and priest of God Most High. If this is the case, then just like Noah, Shem underwent at least two idolatrous transformations into godhood within the annals of Greek Mythology: first as Titan, and secondly as Hyperion.

Interestingly, Helios was a solar deity that can be identified with the Roman Sun god Sol, just as Noah and Shem can be allegorically identified with the Sun in that they were considered the righteous heirs of the messianic promise made by Yahweh in Genesis 3:15. In addition, Helios was often identified in Greek myths with both Titan and Hyperion. It is therefore possible that all three gods depict Noah in one aspect of his many historical roles.

According to the "Iliad," the division of the surface of the Earth by the three Titan sons of Uranus was later mimicked by the Olympian gods, who divided up the whole of creation between themselves. In this myth, Zeus received dominion over the entire region of the sky, Hades was given control over the underworld, and Poseidon received authority over the seas. Curiously, in this myth the only portion of the cosmos not allotted to the gods was the surface of the Earth itself, implying that they had no control over the surface of the Earth where mankind alone held dominion. This may be because the Greeks eventually worshipped themselves, and saw the habitation of the gods as essentially separate and far removed from the concrete world of mortals. Nonetheless, since mortal men were still dependent on the Sun, Moon and seas to grow and harvest crops and on the underworld to mine metals, they reluctantly had to honor the other gods that shared their dominion.

In the Sibylline Oracles - a collection of Greek utterances recorded in Dactylic hexameters - the gods Titan, Kronus and Iapetus purportedly received a third of the Earth as an inheritance from their father Uranus, just as the three sons of Noah divided the Earth into three separate kingdoms after the Flood. However, this record also states that Kronus was chosen to rule over all the other kingdoms. However, Kronus is the Greek rendition of Noah's son Ham, and the Bible tells us that Ham was not Noah's heir. Though Japheth was Noah's eldest son (see Genesis 10:21), Shem was divinely chosen to be the heir to Yahweh's Covenant promise to Adam and Eve, as well as the heir to Noah's kingship or authority. It is therefore logical to assume that - after Noah's death - Shem presided over all the kingdoms of the Earth until his authority was wrested away by Nimrod - that descendent of Ham who made rebellion against Yahweh his life's work.

Before Nimrod's rebellion, there is little doubt that Shem had control over his father's portion of Middle Earth to the west of the Pillar of Enoch, as well as his own territory to the east. Since Shem initially ruled over twice as much land as Japheth or Ham, this likely eventually caused rivalries to spring up between the three brothers. This may be why Ham's descendent Nimrod used an overwhelming force of arms to wrestle away Shem's vast dominion of Middle Earth, which bordered Hamite lands to the south.

Besides the Sibylline Oracles, the association between Noah's three sons and the Titans of Greek Mythology is made by one of the Chaldean fragments, which states: *"After the Flood, Titan and Prometheus lived, and Titan undertook a war against Kronus."* In this fragment, the mention of Prometheus in the place of his father Iapetus suggests that Japheth may have been dead by the time this war between the Semites and Hamites ensued. Note also that this fragment suggests that there was a fellowship between the descendents of Titan and Prometheus, just as Noah mentioned a fellowship between their biblical counterparts Shem and Japheth:

> *"Then he (Noah) said: 'Cursed be Canaan; a servant of servants he shall be to his brethren.' And he said: 'Blessed be the LORD, the God of Shem (i.e. Yahweh, the Elohim of Shem), and may Canaan be his servant. May God enlarge Japheth, and may he dwell in the tents of Shem; and may Canaan be his servant.'" - Genesis 9:25-27 (NKJ)*

When Noah uttered this prophetic curse upon Ham's son Canaan, he was foretelling that there would be trouble between Shem and Ham's descendents. This started when Ham's son Canaan forcibly inhabited a portion of the land that belonged to Shem, and would one day be promised to Abraham. It was then further exacerbated when Nimrod conquered Lower Egypt and took over the administration of the sacred Giza precinct. Based on my findings regarding the way the land was divided between Noah and his three sons at Giza using the Great Pyramid as a guide, there is no doubt that the southern half of the Promised Land that included Jerusalem and Bethlehem, and the Giza Pyramid Complex in Egypt originally were Semite strongholds, and wrestling them away from Noah and Shem would necessarily have been hostile.

Another Chaldean fragment helps to make sense of what happened at this period in history. It enigmatically says:

> "Kronus, coming into the country of the south, gave all Egypt to the god Taauthus (i.e. Thoth), that it might be his kingdom."

Among the Chaldean fragments, there is evidence that the Egyptian god Thoth that was associated with the Greek god Hermes was actually a deified version of Nimrod, the son of Cush who became the first world dictator after the Flood, and may also have been the Pre-Dynastic Egyptian Pharaoh called Narmer, whom the Egyptians identified as the king of Upper Egypt that conquered Lower Egypt and became the first ruler to unite "the Two Lands." Sadly, when Narmer became the first Pharaoh to rule over Upper and Lower Egypt simultaneously, he also may have claimed dominion over all of Shem's vast Middle Earth inheritance. Thus, Nimrod's desire to conquer and rule the whole world and to unite it under one religious ideal came that much closer to fruition.

Due to syncretism and the confusion of tongues after the destruction of the Tower of Babel, it should come as no surprise that the top deities of ancient Greece and Egypt are remarkably similar. Indeed, this is why the Greeks and Romans could so easily identify their own deities with various entities in the Egyptian pantheon, and why every Pagan religion had similar deities that were said to control various celestial bodies and forces in nature.

The Parthenon Code and the Way of Cain

In 2004, another theory concerning the origins of Greek Mythology that is complimentary to the one explored in Gascoigne's "Forgotten History" emerged. This theory was proposed by scholar Robert Bowie Johnson, Jr. in his fascinating book "The Parthenon Code." According to Mr. Johnson, Greek Mythology tells the same story found in the Book of Genesis, but from Cain's opposing perspective. As the story of mankind's revolt against Yahweh, the mythology of the ancient Greeks chronicles the humanistic rebellion of Eve and the line of Cain, its temporary demise in the Great Flood and re-emergence afterward, and its success in defeating the righteous people and the religion of submission and redemption promulgated by the lines of Seth and Shem.

Mr. Johnson carefully unravels this amazing story by connecting the myths artistically painted on Greek vases with the exquisite sculptures that once adorned the metopes on the friezes and the triangular pediments above the friezes on all four sides of the Parthenon in Greece. He does so with careful reconstructions of the gods and heroes that the sculptures on the Parthenon portrayed, detailed explanations of the mythology behind them, and excellent comparisons of how they relate to the myths portrayed on Greek pottery art and the biblical record in Genesis. Though Mr. Johnson does not acknowledge that the races of alien beings called the Watchers and Nephilim existed or played a big part in the development of the Pagan mythologies of Babylon, Egypt, Greece, and Rome, he does show how humanity rebelled against the worship and authority of both waves of alien races and set themselves up as gods in their own right.

On the east pediment of the Parthenon that is depicted on pages 554 and 555, the Greeks portrayed Athena, Zeus, Hera, and Hephaistos (a.k.a. Hephaestus) in the center. On the left of Hera, they depicted Hermes and Atlas, and on the right of Athena, they depicted Nike, Herakles, and Helios as the primary deities that played a significant role in this spiritual rebellion before and after the Flood. Since this revolt centered around Eve's desire to be like God instead of being subject to Him, there is no Creator God in the Greek Pantheon. Instead, all of the players in this rebellion were either deified humans like Eve, or fallen Watchers or Nephilim.

Fascinatingly, the Garden of Eden, Eve before her fall, the forbidden tree, and the Serpent in the tree make an appearance on the left side of the Parthenon's east pediment. There, they are depicted in the serpent-entwined tree with the golden apples in the Garden of the Hesperides. Next in the scene is Atlas holding the heavens on his shoulders, and it is Atlas who represents Adam after he chose to follow Eve into rebellion, but before he actually ate the fruit. Johnson explains that - as Atlas - Adam is allegorically pushing the heavens where the one true God dwells out of the way so that men can eat from the Tree of the Knowledge of Good and Evil and proceed to be their own gods.

East Pediment shown in this reconstruction is inaccurate, though at the correct scale

1897 Full Scale Reproduction of the Parthenon in Nashville, TN, USA

46 out of 92 of the Metopes on the Parthenon Frieze are visible here. These depict the Battle of the Centaurs and Lapiths

Next to Atlas, the Greeks chose to portray Hermes, who Mr. Johnson feels signifies Ham's son Cush. Hermes also signifies the false or evil wisdom of the Serpent, and Johnson sees Cush as the first high priest of the Zeus or Serpent religion. Mr. Johnson identifies the cloak draped over Hermes shoulders on the pediment as Noah's cloak of authority. This cloak of Sethite authority that was wrestled away from Noah and Shem by the followers of the Way of Cain likely represents the animal skin coverings that God made in Eden for Adam and Eve after they fell.

As mentioned in the Book of Jasher, these divinely tailored animal skin clothes had the magical property of making anyone who wore them virtually invincible. Noah received these sacred clothes from his father Lamech and meant to pass them down to Shem. However, the Book of Jasher records that Cush stole this covering from Noah, who was known to the Greeks as Nereus. Thereafter, Cush gave this magical clothing to his son Nimrod, just as Hermes gave the cloak of Nereus to Herakles. Just as Herakles was virtually invincible and used his great strength to do valiant deeds for the false gods he served, Nimrod used Adam and Eve's clothes as armor to make himself virtually invincible. In this way, Nimrod was able to conquer the world, elevate mankind to godhood, and become a mighty warrior against Yahweh God.

Next to Hermes on the east pediment stands Hephaistos, whom Johnson identifies as the deified Cain. Hephaistos stands to the left of his mother Hera or Eve and father Zeus or Adam. When Eve ate the forbidden fruit, she was the first false goddess to know good and evil, and to choose freely between the two without restraint or immediate consequences. Yet, as a sign of her repentance, Eve as the Hera of Greek myth stood in staunch opposition to Herakles or Nimrod, whereas the rival goddess Athena aided Heracles and later supposedly gave him immortal life.

The East Pediment of the Parthenon

NOTE: The following 3 illustrations by Holmes Bryant are derived from the book "The Parthenon Code" by Robert Bowie Johnson, Jr., and are being used here with permission. You may contact Mr. Johnson at: **www.theparthenoncode.com**

Reconstruction of the Right Side of the East Pediment

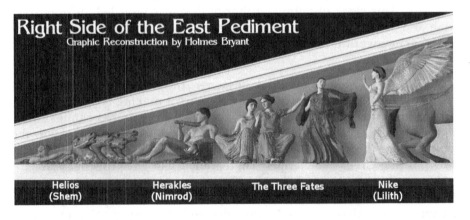

Reconstruction of the Center of the East Pediment

Reconstruction of the Left Side of the East Pediment

To the right of Zeus on the east pediment is the goddess Athena, who Mr. Johnson feels represents Eve re-born after the Flood. However, since Cush's son Nimrod is the primary warrior who fought the line of Shem for supremacy over the world, and Nimrod is represented in the figure of Herakles (i.e. Hercules) on the right side of the pediment by the three Fates, could it be that Athena also represents Nimrod's wife? Some scholars believe Nimrod's wife was named Semiramis or Shammuramat and that she may have been the real power behind Nimrod's ambitions to unite humanity and elevate mankind to godhood. As such, Shammuramat would indeed have been like Athena, who derived her power and authority from the wisdom and guidance of the Serpent.

To the right of Athena on the right side of the Parthenon's east pediment is the goddess of justice and victory called Nike. There, Nike represents Athena's triumph as the war goddess who helped defeat the line of Shem. Next to Nike are the three Fates who cannot shorten the life of the immortal Athena, but only measure it in order to share a portion of it with the mortal Herakles for his faithful service. This is why Herakles is shown on the pediment between the three Fates and the dawning light of Helios, the Sun god associated with Shem. In affect, Herakles is basking in the light of the Sun god because he was seen as the human embodiment of the Sun and therefore the victor over and replacement for Shem.

Interestingly, the Greeks often depicted Nike with huge bird-like wings such as those of the Egyptian goddess of justice called Ma'at. As shown in Books One and Two, winged depictions of deities or animals found among Pagans were likely meant to show a false connection between them and various symbols and spiritual concepts originally found in the Star Gospel. In the case of Nike, it is likely that she was styled to depict Libra as the symbol of truth, justice, judgment, and ultimate victory over evil. Since the giant statue of Athena inside the Parthenon was depicted holding a small statue of a winged Nike in her hand and Athena was supposed to be a perpetual virgin, this statue of Nike may also have been meant to signify Virgo the Virgin, who appears to be standing atop the scales of Libra along the ecliptic. On the next page is a photo of the giant gilded reproduction of an idol of Athena that once rested in the Parthenon in Greece. On this idol, note that the winged goddess Nike is in Athena's hand, the protective Serpent is beneath her shield and the severed head of Medusa is attached to the front of her Aegis - a ceremonial collar worn like a talisman:

Gilded Idol of Athena
Inside the Parthenon
Reproduced in Nashville

Nike

Head of Medusa
on Athena's Aegis

Serpent
Guardian
& Shield

Like Nike, the Egyptian goddess Isis was also depicted with the widespread wings of Ma'at and the horned crown of the mother goddess Hathor, showing Isis' eventual association with both Ma'at and Hathor. Interestingly, the goddess Ma'at represented morality and a love of truth and justice that was far closer to God's Spirit of Wisdom than Nike's wisdom, which was satanic and may actually represent the wickedness of Naamah, the consort of Azazel. If so, then Nike may depict Naamah after she was turned into a Siren or demoness at death and became known as Lilith. But it was Isis' role as a composite goddess combining the traits of Hera, Athena and Nike (and no doubt Lilith as well) that made her highly appealing to the Greeks and Romans, who eventually adopted and worshipped her because they saw Isis as more powerful than the Greek goddesses Hera, Athena, Nike and Aphrodite and their Roman counterparts Juno, Minerva, Victoria and Venus.

Though all of the Greek deities on the east pediment of the Parthenon were significant players in the formation of the two opposing ideologies that violently clashed before and after the Great Flood, there were many lesser players in this epic saga. Some were depicted in their supporting roles on the sculpted metopes on the exterior friezes above the rows of stone pillars around the Parthenon as well as on the interior friezes. For example, the war between the Centaurs (lovers of Yahweh) and Lapiths (followers of Cain) are recorded on the Parthenon's exterior metopes.

The Revenge of Cain and Glorification of Nimrod

As shown in "The Parthenon Code," the roof of the Parthenon was literally surrounded with beautifully sculpted carvings that faithfully remembered many biblical characters but completely distorted their roles in history. This is because they saw history through the filter of the Way of Cain rather the Way of Yahweh, and - in the process - they twisted every good character of the Bible into a villain! After all, the Ancient Greeks totally rebelled against Yahweh in order to follow a humanistic religion that originated with Cain and Nimrod. Therefore, the Greeks saw the Way of Cain as superior to and victorious over the Way of Yahweh.

According to Mr. Johnson, the Greeks felt their culture and religion were so superior that they even falsely associated their defeated Sethite and Semite enemies with the inhuman Titans and Kentaurs (i.e. Centaurs) who opposed the Olympian gods and Hellenistic way of life. Nonetheless, while Johnson saw this demonization of the followers of the Way of Yahweh as a result of their opposing ideology to Hellenism, he completely failed to acknowledge that there were real inhuman Giants on the Earth that were the sworn enemies of *all* humanity. As a result, he missed the point that the Greek Pantheon is riddled with demonic Nephilim-inspired gods and heroes that have been syncretized with sinful, deified versions of biblical characters.

Greek artists showed this syncretization of the Sethite and Semite Followers of Yahweh with the Nephilim by connecting identifiable biblical characters with some of the monstrous or part-animal beings in

Greek Mythology; namely the Titans, Gigantes and Kentaurs or Centaurs - though Noah was also depicted as a merman. In addition, the Greeks rejected the biblical view of the Serpent as evil and instead associated it with their top deities Zeus and Athena as a symbol of wisdom, power and authority. By doing so, the Greeks were showing their belief that the Serpent offered immortality, creative power, and god-like wisdom to Eve and her descendents instead of death and separation from God.

Though Greek Centaurs may partly depict the genetically spliced together creations of the fallen angels, the dichotomy seen in the Centaurs envisioned in the heavenly Star Gospel depictions of Sagittarius

A Centaur Fighting A Lapith
From a Metope of the Parthenon

and Centaurus primarily signify good triumphing over evil in the Person of Yahshua, who had a dual nature as both the kingly Son of God, and the sacrificial Lamb of God who was slain to atone for our sins. Therefore, the association of Centaurs with evil in Greek Mythology is a total aberration from their originally intended symbolic purpose - just as Christian scholar and visionary C. S. Lewis seemed to fully understand when he wrote the Narnia Chronicles and depicted the Centaurs as forces for good.

Unlike the Centaurs, however, the Titans and Giants in Greek myth definitely have a connection to the Nephilim and the demonic spirits of dead Nephilim, as well as to the Sethites and Semites. As a result, the triumph of the Olympian gods over the Titans and the Giants can be viewed as depicting the following two different events:

1.   The victory of the Hellenistic followers of the religion of Humanism over the Nephilim, who attempted to set themselves up as gods over all humanity before the Great Flood, and·

2.   The victory of the Hellenistic religion of humanism over the followers of Yahweh, who valiantly attempted to stop the spread of humanistic polytheism after the Flood, but failed.

Though the war of the Titans with the Olympian gods and their later battle with the Gigantes are mythical in nature, they all retain the underlying truth that there were three races of god-like beings vying for control of the Earth in ancient times, and each group sought to be universally worshipped as gods. This mythology ties three races - Titans, humans, and Giants - with three events in the biblical record:

1. **Titans:** The unlawful marriages between certain sons of God known as Watchers or angels and the daughters of men, who produced an evil race of giants known as the Nephilim before the Flood, as recorded in Genesis 6:1-6.

2. **Humans:** The rise of Nimrod's humanistic, demonically controlled empire, the elevation of mankind to godhood, and the building of the Tower of Babel after the Flood, as recorded in Genesis 10:8-10 and 11:1-9.

3. **Gigantes:** The presence of fearsome and inhuman Anakim and Rephaim giants in and around Canaan prior to and after the Israelite conquest, as primarily recorded in Gen. 14:5 and 15:20; Deuter. 2:9-12, 19-22, 3:1-15; Joshua 12:1-6; and 2 Sam. 21:15-22.

In particular, Nimrod's world empire centered in Babylon was likely forged by mounting a direct assault against the Giants and the followers of Yahweh, who both presented a threat to Nimrod's government and religion, which wanted to elevate humanity to godhood and unite them in a common cause against the one true God, the followers of Yahweh and the demonic Nephilim. Evidence that the followers of Yahweh suffered terrible losses at the hands of the Cainites and followers of Nimrod are retained in Greek myths surrounding the Titans, Gigantes, Centaurs and Amazons.

In "The Parthenon Code," Johnson shows that the mysterious Amazons or female warriors who declared a war to the death against the Greeks also have a biblical counterpart in that they symbolically signify Noah's daughters or female descendents, and - by extension - the female descendents in the line of Shem. In Greek Mythology, the Amazons are connected to Nereus' daughters, who were known as the Nereids. The Nereids were the sisters of Thetis, a daughter of Nereus/Noah who was abducted by the Greek hero Peleus to become his wife and a mother figure to those who followed the Way of Cain or the Serpent.

In retaliation for Thetis' abduction, the Nereids went against their father's wishes and sought revenge for their sister's abduction. They donned armor and then fought to free her - only to find later that Thetis had turned traitor and become a follower of the Serpent god Zeus instead of Yahweh Elohim. Despite this, the Amazons fought against the serpent system of Zeus until they were all killed and their religion and culture effectively ceased to exist in the Greek universe.

Hidden within these myths of the Nereids and Amazons, several other truths become apparent when the people involved are properly identified with their biblical counterparts. First of all, Thetis' father Nereus is Noah, and Greek mythology depicts him as having lost all his sons so that only daughters or female descendents remain to him. With no men around to protect them, Nereus' daughters were being abducted against their will by outsiders. In fact, Noah's daughter Thetis' abduction suggests that the female followers of Yahweh were being abducted, forced to marry outside their faith and culture, and compelled to learn the Way of Cain instituted by the Serpent or Satan.

If this mythical scenario surrounding Thetis' abduction is based on fact, it should lead us to ask: "What happened to Noah's other male descendents?" The logical conclusion is that they had been killed, driven into slavery, and/or brainwashed into abandoning their belief in Yahweh, which would leave only a group of unwed maidens and widows with children to perpetuate their opposing religion and culture.

If this was the case, the remaining women were no doubt further threatened by assimilation and a loss of territory. But, instead of fleeing, these female followers of Yahweh unwisely retaliated by equipping themselves for battle and waging a war to the death against their enemies. Sadly, the courageous Amazons lost that war, though the Greeks probably greatly exaggerated their victory over the Amazons as a crushing defeat. Though the Amazons were defeated, it was happily only a temporary defeat of the culture and religion of the followers of the Way of Yahweh by the followers of the Way of Cain or Serpent line of Zeus.

Intriguingly, I found an old fantasy drawing in my portfolio dated to 1975 that reflects the raw courage of the female descendents of Shem whom the Greeks depicted as Amazons. In the drawing pictured on page 562 there are two winged women wearing full Greco-Roman style battle armor and brandishing swords that one of the women had just killed a reptilian humanoid with. When I looked at this drawing again after writing this section, I knew the ideas found in "The Parthenon Code" were unmistakably and prophetically reflected in this drawing, which was done when I had absolutely no knowledge of the Watchers, Nephilim, Way of Cain, and Way of Yahweh, and little knowledge of Greek Mythology or Amazons.

Drawing: "Death of Evil"

This drawing was aptly named "Death of Evil" when it was completed, and there is no doubt that this drawing depicts a spiritual battle between good and evil - a battle where good ultimately triumphs. In that regard, note that the winged woman who killed the beast is wearing a cross and has a sword engulfed in supernatural fire that is emblazoned with the perennially Jewish Star of David symbol. Meanwhile, the other Amazon-type warrior angel has a cross-decorated helmet, is kneeling as if in prayer and is holding up a sword with a living vine growing on it. In addition, note that there is a small Grecian style temple atop a hill in the background of this drawing that appears to be an allusion to the Parthenon atop the ancient hill-top Acropolis of Athens, Greece.

Utilizing the Language of God, it also became clear to me that the two winged women in this drawing may signify the Two-House Church seen in the constellations of Andromeda and Cassiopeia that will one day be united to form the Bride of Yahshua. In addition, the winged warrior with the vine-entwined sword may signify the True Vine who is Yahshua in the hands of His loyal Christian followers, while the winged warrior wearing the cross but carrying a sword emblazoned with the Star of David signifies Messianic believers. There is also no doubt that the demonic-looking reptilian humanoid lying on the ground represents the death of evil Nephilim and Anakim beings at the hands of both ancient and modern Israelites. As such, this drawing reflects the divine commission given to the Israelites to obliterate the Nephilim and their tainted blood from history.

Since this drawing has so much prophetic significance, I firmly believe that God gave me the elements of this drawing even though I was unaware of what they meant at the time. Nor did I know that He intended to reveal what this drawing really meant when the time was right, and that time is now - when I now know how to read and understand the Star Gospel and Parthenon Code!

In "The Parthenon Code," Johnson identifies four events in Greek Mythology that show the temporary victory of the religion of the Serpent over the Way of Yahweh and the transferring of temporal authority to the followers of the Way of Cain. These are:

1.   **Athena-Minerva** taking the cloak of Noah/Nereus - an event that is carved on the Parthenon

2.   **Herakles-Hercules** taking the belt of authority belonging to the Amazon Queen Hippolyte after killing her

3.   **Poseidon-Neptune** taking the trident belonging to Nereus/Noah

4.   **Zeus-Jove** taking Nereus/Noah's scepter

Among the dozens of mythical characters that are discussed in "The Parthenon Code," Johnson describes another person who is vitally important to this study. The Greeks named him Kaineus, who was said to have hailed from the Thessalonian kingdom of Lapith, where a war between Centaurs (i.e. followers of Yahweh) and Lapiths (i.e. followers of Cain or the Serpent) once occurred.

According to Greek myth, Kaineus was once a beautiful woman named Caenus who was raped by Poseidon, the sea god. After her rape, Caenus supposedly asked Poseidon to change her into a man in order to escape being raped again. Her wish was granted, and at the time Caenus became the man named Kaineus, she/he was also given the gift of invulnerability, which helped Kaineus to become a great warrior. Eventually, however, Kaineus was defeated by being beaten into the ground and smothered to death by a group of angry Centaurs.

Interestingly, it is fairly easy to piece together from Greek myths that Poseidon is an evil replacement for the righteous patriarch Noah. In effect Poseidon combined the characteristics of the hero who survived the Great Flood blended together with Yahweh, the True God who caused the same Flood. What is not so easy to see, however, is that Poseidon also represents a perverted cross between a Nephilim and a fallen Watcher. This is because Greek myths completely obscure the reason for the Great Flood, which was to destroy the sinful and corrupted bloodline of Cain/Kaineus. After all, the Cainites who sprang from Kaineus not only fully rebelled against Yahweh on a spiritual and behavioral level, but were genetically polluted via intermarriage with the fallen angels and Nephilim.

Because of the clever Greek white-washing of evil and sin, the myth describing the rape of Caenus by Poseidon effectively serves as the Pagan explanation for the emergence of the corrupted bloodline of Cain. In the Bible, however, remember that Cain was forced to be a fugitive and was robbed of his livelihood as a farmer because he wickedly murdered his godly brother Abel (Gen. 4:12). The Greeks allegorically described this banishment and loss of profession through the act of rape, which caused women to be shunned and lose their status in society. However, the Greeks left out that this allegorical "rape" or banishment was actually invited by Kaineus' wicked actions in murdering his brother. In addition to being exiled, Kaineus or Cain was given a mark by God so that no one would kill him in revenge (Gen. 4:15). This likely explains why the Greeks depicted Kaineus as virtually invulnerable.

Remember that the very first messianic prophecy in the Bible in Genesis 3:15 states that the Seed of the Woman, who is Christ would bruise the seed of the Serpent on the head, and the Greeks depicted Kaineus being pounded on the head into the ground by the Centaurs. Is it therefore just a coincidence that - in the Zodiac - Christ and the followers of Yahweh are depicted by the two heavenly Centaurs found in Sagittarius and Centaurus, and that both of them are archers in the process of shooting bows with arrows pointed toward the satanic sign of Scorpio? Incidentally, the front hooves of the Centaur forming Sagittarius are actually trampling a celestial band of stars in the serpentine shape of the Serpent signifying Satan!

Serpent depicted beneath Athena's Shield inside the 1897 Scale Reproduction of of the Parthenon in Nashville

The re-birth of the Way of Cain inspired by the seed of the Serpent after the Flood is allegorically depicted in Greek art via the birth of Erichthonius and the story of Chiron and Achilles. First, let's discuss the birth of Erichthonius. This demigod and legendary king of Athens was supposedly conceived when a semen-soaked piece of cloth was thrown to the ground by Athena after Hephaestus attempted to rape her. Per "The Parthenon Code," Hephaestus (or Hephaistos, known in Rome as Vulcan) was the deified Cain, who appears in the center of the east pediment reconstruction on page 555. As the forger and armorer of the gods, Hephaestus is allegorically linked to Tubal-Cain, and Tubal-Cain likely learned his skills from Azazel or Satan - the original Vulcan. According to Greek myth, the cloth covered with Hephaestus' semen accidentally impregnated the Earth goddess Gaia, and the result was Erichthonius, the son of Hephaestus.

Interestingly, just like Athena and Zeus, Erichthonius' symbol was the serpent, and he was often depicted as resembling a Titan or Gigantes with a serpent's tail instead of legs. In fact, the hidden serpent shown on the underside of Athena's shield in Greek art is meant to be a depiction of Erichthonius, showing that the secret source of Athena's spiritual power is the Serpent or Satan.

This spiritual association with a serpent is tied to the worship of demons in human form, or to the deification of humanity's ancestors that were possessed by demons and thus promulgated the humanistic self-gratification, hedonism, and immorality that characterized (and still characterizes) Hellenistic culture. Incidentally, the word the Greeks used to refer to themselves was "Hellene," which means "enlightened," but by the Serpent instead of Yahweh God! Perhaps that is one reason why the word "hell" means a place of fiery torment rather than the location of Paradise. Incidentally my name is a derivative of the Greek word "Hellene," but thankfully I have been enlightened by the Holy Spirit rather than the Serpent worshipped by the Ancient Greeks!

A Titan Being Overcome, Pergamum Altar to Zeus

Another story describing the re-emergence of the Way of Cain is found in the story of Achilles and the "friendly" Centaur Chiron, who was actually a symbol for Noah's son Ham. According to Greek myths, the Kentaur Chiron was different from his drunken, unruly Kentaur peers (i.e. Noah, Japheth and Shem and family) and seen as a cultured and educated being who was sympathetic to the Way of Cain. Chiron also claimed to be the recipient of Noah's cloak of authority, which actually was to be given to Shem, but was stolen by Cush and given to Nimrod. As a traitor to Noah's cause, Chiron supposedly instructed many Greek heroes such as Hercules and Achilles in the art of war against the followers of the Way of Yahweh. In the case of Achilles, Peleus and his wife Thetis sent their son Achilles to Chiron for tutoring.

Now, remember that Thetis was a Nereid or daughter of Noah whom Peleus abducted. Therefore Achilles represents another stage in the supposed success of the Way of Cain over the Way of Yahweh. Later, all of these Greek successes in forwarding the Way of Cain and his bloodline's Serpent seed were epitomized in the illustrious career of Nimrod, who was known to the Greeks as the half god and half mortal Herakles.

Though myths surrounding Herakles suggest that he was a Nephilim, Nimrod was probably not. Therefore, Herakles or Nimrod is just one of many characters in Greek mythology that forwarded the cause of the Nephilim and was therefore unwittingly associated with them even though the Greeks saw the Nephilim as enemies of the Olympian (or human) gods and their way of life. Herakles' greatest feats against the followers of the Way of Yahweh became known as the Twelve Labors of Herakles.

Among these feats, the Tenth Labor of Herakles was to murder the Geryon, a giant with one head, three bodies, and six arms and legs. Though Johnson thinks Geryon the Giant and Cerberus the three-headed dog guarding the gates of Hell represented the three sons of Noah combined, both creatures most likely depict Noah joined with his sons Shem and Japheth in a fight to the death against the Way of Cain epitomized in the line of Ham (Chiron) via the birth of Cush (Hermes) and Nimrod (Herakles).

The Eleventh Labor of Herakles was to snatch the golden apples from the Garden of the Hesperides. But, in order to do so, Herakles had to confront Nereus (i.e. Noah) and coerce him into telling him how to find the garden first. In one depiction of Herakles threatening Nereus that Robert Johnson reproduced in his book, Nereus is pictured as a merman with a fish tail! Typical of the Greeks, here again a follower of Yahweh is connected to the genetically spliced chimeras among the Nephilim.

One thing that is really interesting about this Labor of Herakles is that these golden apples signified the fruit of the Tree of Life or immortality that was located in the Garden of Eden. Therefore, this myth suggests that the Garden of Eden was still on the Earth at the time of Nimrod, who was Herakles. It also suggests that Nimrod threatened Noah with bodily harm if he did not divulge the way there. This supports my conviction that Nimrod was a tyrant who threatened to kill Noah and all the followers of the Way of Yahweh, and since Noah and his righteous kin were peace-loving pacifists who believed in love and forgiveness, they did not fight Nimrod until they were nearly obliterated.

Table Showing the Biblical Role of Many Pagan Deities

Biblical Characters	In Babylonian & Sumerian Myth	In Egyptian Mythology	In Greek Mythology	In Roman Mythology
Yahweh	Shamash, El, Enlil	Ptah, Ra, Amun (Ya	manu) -------	-------
Yahshua	Ea (E-Yah) Enki	Anubis, Osiris	Logos (concept)	-------
Holy Spirit	Anu, Ninhursag	Ma'at	---------	-------
Azazel, Satan	Sin, Nanna, Nergal, Pazuzu	Apep, Apophis	Kronus, Hades, Hephaestus	Saturn, Pluto, Vulcan
Adam	Adapa - Adamu	Atum	Uranus, Zeus	Jupiter
Eve	Inanna - Ishtar	Iusaaset, Nekhbet	Gaia, Hera, Pandora	Juno
Abel	Dumuzi (Tammuz)	Type of Osiris	Adonis	-------
Seth	Marduk (Maverick)	Set or Seth	Ares	Mars
Sethites → (Way of	Yahweh) Enoch	Set, Neith, Thoth	Kentaurs	Kentaurs
Cain (Way of Cain)	Utu, child of Sin	Stole role of Osiris	Kaineus/Hephaistos	
Lamech (Cainite) (Way of Cain)	Anu, Stole role of Ea, Enki	Killed Cain and took role of Osiris	Erichthonius, Zeus re-born	Usurps Adam's role as Jupiter, Zeus
Naamah (Lilith) (Azazel's consort)	Tiamat, Lamashtu, Lilith, Ishtar re-born	Sekhmet, Wadjet	Nike, Athena, Aphrodite	Venus, consort of Vulcan/Azazel

Biblical Characters	In Babylonian & Sumerian Myth	In Egyptian Mythology	In Greek Mythology	In Roman Mythology
Jubal & Jabal	--------	--------	Apollo	Apollo
Tubal-Cain	Replaced Abel as Tammuz	--------	Hephaestus, Adonis re-born	Vulcan re-born
Noah (Way of Yahweh)	Enki, Utnapishtim Dagon, Oannes	Sobek, Horus	Nereus, Deucalion Dionysus, Uranus	Asclepius, Bacchus, Cerberus, Geryon
Shem, Melchizedek (Way of Yahweh)	Marduk (Maverick)	Horus (via Noah)	Titan, Helios, Satyrs Cerberus, Geryon	Fauns, Kentaurs
Ham (Way of Cain)	Stole role of Enki	Stole role of Horus	Kronus, Kentaur Chiron	Kronus & Saturn re-born
Japheth	--------	--------	Iapetus, Geryon	Fauns, Kentaurs
Cush	Stole role of Enki	Stole role of Thoth from Sethite Enoch	Hermes, giver of false wisdom	Mercury
Nimrod - who usurped roles of Abel, Seth, Shem	Tammuz, Enmerkar stole role of Marduk (Maverick), Melkart	Khnum, Narmer - Stole Noah's Horus throne & title	Herakles, Adonis, Ninus	Hercules (Way of Cain)
Semiramis (Way of Cain)	Astarte, Ashteroth, Ishtar/Lilith reborn	Isis, Satis - Minoan dove goddess	Artemis, Athena re-born	Minerva - Diana

After Herakles retrieved the golden apples from the Garden of the Hesperides, he gave them to the goddess Athena as a gift, and she eventually returned them to the Garden. As already mentioned, it is my contention that Athena was not only Eve but a representation of Nimrod's wife Semiramis, and that she was deified like her infamous husband. In this regard, though "The Parthenon Code" does not see a connection between Nimrod's wife and Athena, it does point to the fact that the Woman who rides the Beast in the Book of Revelation may be an allusion to Athena, while the Beast she rides is a symbol for the Way of Cain. In other words, the political, economic, and spiritual underpinnings of today's world follow the Way of Cain or the Serpent rather than the Way of Yahweh, and the Woman or goddess leading mankind astray atop that Beast signifies the Zeus religion of secular humanism that Athena promoted and defended, and the whole world will eventually buy into and worship.

On pages 568 and 569 is a table showing how the deities of Egypt, Babylon, Greece, and Rome can be associated with biblical characters. This table shows that Adam, Eve, Noah, Cush, Nimrod and his wife Semiramis were given prominent divine roles that only our triune God Yahweh could have fulfilled. In the table, note that only the Babylonian and Egyptian mythologies acknowledge three deities that were personifications of Yahweh. But outside of acknowledging the Logos or Word as a non-divine philosophical concept, Greek and Roman mythologies leave out any reference to Yahshua and totally ignore God the Father and the Holy Spirit. Sadly, the Greeks and Romans only worshipped fleshly beings and works. As a result, they callously rejected the Creator of all things.

Of course, as shown in Books One and Two in the Language of God series, the entire Greek, Roman, and Babylonian pantheon of gods and goddesses were false representations of the many roles that Yahshua and the Holy Spirit would play in history themselves, and via their chosen righteous representatives such as Enoch, Abraham, Job, Moses, King David, and Elijah. This could not be made plainer than when studying the meaning of the Mazzaroth or Zodiac, in which all forty-eight ancient constellations were clearly perverted to represent Pagan heroes and gods instead of Yahshua and the followers of Yahweh that anxiously awaited the fulfillment of God's messianic promises to Adam and Abraham.

Anakim and Rephaim: Teachers of Paganism and Sorcery

After the Flood, the revival of Paganism attests to the fact that the evil demon spirits of the Nephilim, and the Nephilim known as Anakim or Rephaim eventually sought to be deified as well. In fact, they were likely so good at deceiving people with their god-like powers that these false gods became more real to many ancient people than the true God. As a result, Pagans that had forgotten the true meaning of their religious images and the triune God behind them soon overran the world. The true spiritual ideas that their artistic renderings originally represented were thereby lost and many nefarious interpretations of the facts resulted in documents like the British Edda, which makes a mockery of both Yahweh and His chosen people.

Inevitably, despite the purity and beauty of their original faith, the Israelites soon forgot the greatness of Yahweh and were beguiled by the sinful ways of their neighbors. They felt deprived living lives governed by the Torah that promoted sobriety and introspection. They instead abandoned the teachings of the Torah and sought the temporary enjoyment of fleshly pursuits that the Pagans enjoyed as a part of their religious practices. This eventually led many of the Israelites into total debauchery and wickedness.

As the portion quoted from Psalm 106 at the beginning of this chapter attests, the Israelites fell into grievous sin. Instead of studying the Torah with others who loved Yah, the Israelites longed to join in numerous seasonal Pagan festivities that were always accompanied by music, dancing, excessive drinking and sexual promiscuity. Instead of being sprinkled with the blood of a bull to find sanctification, they sought a Pagan form of it in the arms of shrine prostitutes (In the NIV, see: 1 Kings 14:24; 15:12; Hosea 5:14). Instead of worshipping their spiritual Creator God who is without form but who manifests His power in all things, the Israelites made lifeless idols of gods and goddesses and worshipped them instead. Instead of sacrificing animals on the altar to Yah and asking Him for real forgiveness, they began to sacrifice their own children to appease supposedly angry Pagan deities who were only demons masquerading as gods:

> "So they left all the commandments of the LORD their God (Yahweh Elohim), made for themselves a molded image and two calves, made a wooden image and worshiped all the host of heaven, and served Baal. **And they caused their sons and daughters to pass through the fire,** practiced witchcraft and soothsaying, and sold themselves to do evil in the sight of the LORD (Yahweh), to provoke Him to anger. Therefore the

LORD (Yahweh) was very angry with Israel, and removed
them from His sight; there was none left but the tribe of Judah
alone. Also Judah did not keep the commandments of the
LORD their God (Yahweh Elohim), but walked in the statutes
of Israel which they made." - II Kings 17:16-19 (NKJ)

By doing all the detestable things that their Pagan neighbors did,
the Israelites lost their favor with Yahweh and the once glorious
kingdom of Israel gradually fell into ruin and decay. The Israelites had
forsaken the Law of God and broken their sacred Blood Covenant with
Yahweh. They therefore reaped the horrible consequences of their
actions:

"This is what the Sovereign LORD (Yahweh) says: 'I
will deal with you as you deserve, because you have despised
my oath by breaking the Covenant.' " - Ezekiel 16:59 (NIV)

This same trend is happening today. The world is full of bigoted,
promiscuous people. Lawlessness and crime are increasing. Court
systems are failing as laws are stretched and bent until they have little or
no meaning. Nothing is applicable to everyone and no absolute truth is
acceptable. In the current world scene with its emphasis on pluralism
and relativism, each person seems to be a law unto themselves. The
most popular slogan of this era seems to be "whatever works for you."
No consideration is given to whether our way of doing things hurts
others or not. Few believe in the inerrancy or truth of the Bible and the
justice of its laws. Few are willing to concede that we are all fallen
human beings and all have sin in common. ***They also refuse to accept***
that only one method for healing our bodies, minds and spirits actually
works and that they must deny their flesh in order to heal.

Nonetheless, every method of healing that works always entails
limiting the intake of chemical and spiritual pollutants into one's body,
mind and spirit. ***Real physical and spiritual healing only happens when***
people learn discipline and obedience to God. In other words, no one
can find true healing unless they get things right with God first. They
may find temporary healing, but lasting or miraculous healing only
comes when Yahweh is an active participant and guide in the healing
process.

Instead of finding true healing, however, most people reject
sound healing practices and spiritual growth to pursue more pleasurable
pastimes that are touted as being restorative and healthy. Yet they do
not realize that unscrupulous con artists are getting rich off their
foolishness and are deceiving them with fables and myths. This sad state

of affairs is a clear sign that the end of our current world system is near. Thank Yah that it cannot last!

In ancient times, this same state of affairs led to the downfall of many great civilizations such as Egypt, Greece and Rome. Back then, sound doctrine was also exchanged for myths in ever-increasing amounts. The ancient Egyptians had such a plurality of gods with animal forms that even the Pagan Greeks and Romans had difficulty with their bizarre brand of idolatry! Like the Egyptians, *the Romans and Greeks worshipped gods that looked and acted much like human men and women*. However, they couldn't understand the Egyptian propensity to worship dumb animals as gods too. In that regard, the ancient Egyptians were even further off the mark than their neighbors. They sinned greatly by assigning the attributes of God to animals that lacked both a will and a conscience.

The Hindus still do this today. The religion of the ancient and modern Hindus is nearly identical to the religion of ancient Egypt. For example, *Hindu religious teachers teach that their many deities are just another aspect of the one universal Spirit they call Brahman.* This is very similar to what those who are following a New Age version of the ancient Egyptian religion teach today. Both India and Egypt also have many human and animals gods and goddesses. They both have idolatrous statues in their temples that are fed, clothed and entertained as if they were alive. They offer their deities the fruits of their farms and then eat the feasts that their demonic gods cannot consume. Furthermore, they practice magical religious rites to secure false blessings from their evil gods.

Triads (or divine trinities) also abound in both religions. In India, the one God Brahman is said to consist of three deities. These are: Brahma, the creator of the Universe; Vishnu the preserver of all things; and Shiva the destroyer. Shiva is considered a dual god whose wife or feminine aspect is called Kali and is viewed as the goddess of destruction. This trinity in India retains vestiges of the truth, though that truth is sadly hidden behind gross lies and idolatry. This is because Satan is also a destroyer who is represented quite graphically in the dual image of Shiva/Kali. Satan has therefore replaced the healing reality of the Holy Spirit within the Hindu faith's Pagan version of the Trinity. What a tragedy this perversion of the truth is for the many millions who believe in this false religion!

Nonetheless, despite this tragedy of faith in demons, God Almighty is moving in India! Today as never before in history, millions of former Hindus and Buddhists in India and China are coming to Christ. Through the efforts of brave Christian missionaries to these countries from the USA, South Korea, the Philippines and elsewhere, many inroads have been made. Even more amazing is the apparent outpouring of God's Holy Spirit in massive quantities that is aiding them in their task! Via God's Grace, people in Asia, India and all over the Islamic strongholds of the Middle East have reportedly been having visions and dreams of the risen Christ! In addition, these fast converts to the Christian faith often report that they were divinely directed to find a Bible and a Bible teacher to teach them more about Yahshua, and then forsake their family, friends and old faith if necessary in order to follow the true Messiah Yahshua and His teachings.

Sacred Astronomy Perverted Into Pagan Astrology

Added to this propensity amongst us to make idols for ourselves is the widespread practice of turning the entire Zodiac into an idol. This is done whenever Astrology is used for fortune telling, or in magical rites. The temptation to apply the truths of Biblical Astronomy to our own individual lives - as is done in modern Astrology - isn't anything new. Every ancient Pagan king had court astrologers who tried to correctly determine the divine omens in the Zodiac sign the king was born under. They also constantly searched the night sky, looking for omens in the Zodiac that might affect the kingdom. Ostensibly they did this to help give the king an edge over his adversaries, and make him appear more god-like and omnipotent. The Bible is full of references to, *and condemnations of* this practice (See Genesis 41:8; Ester 1:13; Isaiah 19:11-12, 47:13-14; Daniel 2:12-13, 4:7, 5:7).

According to the Book of Jasher, Ancient Astrologers also warned Nimrod of Abraham's birth using such practices:

> *"And it was in the night that Abram was born, that all the servants of Terah, and all the wise men of Nimrod, and his conjurors came and ate and drank in the house of Terah, and they rejoiced with him on that night.* **And when all the wise men and conjurors went out from the house of Terah, they lifted up their eyes toward heaven that night to look at the stars, and they saw, and behold one very large star came from the east and ran in the heavens, and he swallowed up the four stars from the four sides of the heavens.** *And all the wise men of the king and his conjurors were astonished at the sight, and the sages understood this matter, and they knew its import. And they said to each other, This only betokens the child that has been born to Terah this night, who will grow up and be fruitful, and multiply, and possess all the earth, he and*

his children for ever, and he and his seed will slay great kings, and inherit their lands..."

"...and they all went to the king and bowed down to him to the ground, and they said, May the king live, may the king live. We heard that a son was born to Terah the son of Nahor, the prince of thy host, and we yesternight came to his house, and we ate and drank and rejoiced with him that night. And when thy servants went out from the house of Terah, to go to our respective homes to abide there for the night, we lifted up our eyes to heaven, and we saw a great star coming from the east, and the same star ran with great speed, and swallowed up four great stars, from the four sides of the heavens.

"And thy servants were astonished at the sight which we saw, and were greatly terrified, and we made our judgment upon the sight, and knew by our wisdom the proper interpretation thereof, that this thing applies to the child that is born to Terah, who will grow up and multiply greatly, and become powerful, and kill all the kings of the earth, and inherit all their lands, he and his seed forever. And now our lord and king, behold we have truly acquainted thee with what we have seen concerning this child. If it seemeth good to the king to give his father value for this child, we will slay him before he shall grow up and increase in the land, and his evil increase against us, that we and our children perish through his evil." - Jasher 8:1-4, 8:8-13

In the preceding passages from the Book of Jasher, these astrologers, Wise Men, and conjurers from Nimrod's era were the evil forerunners to the good Magi who saw Yahshua's star in the east and came to worship Him. Nimrod's Wise Men or Magi told Nimrod of the portents they saw in the heavens surrounding Abraham's birth. They saw that the heavens foretold that this babe would become a great and powerful man who would be against Nimrod. They also recommended that the infant Abraham be put to death so he would not fulfill his destiny! Therefore, the sin of the Astrologers of Nimrod's day was their use of the stars as an aid in Sorcery, which is a form of Magic, and open rebellion against Yahweh. Despite their ability to correctly use Sacred Astronomy, the ancient astrologers of Nimrod's court consistently applied it to evil ends.

Fortunately, the Magi mentioned in Yahshua's birth narrative indicate that Sacred Astronomy was used for good purposes by at least one righteous line of Wise Men. These Wise Men were most likely descendents of the sages who had served the Persian king through the prophet Daniel. Though the Magi who came to worship Christ may have been Zoroastrians, it is more likely that they had converted to Judaism at some point, since the Zoroastrians were not looking for a Jewish Messiah to be their Savior or King. The Magi, however, had come specifically to worship the babe who had been born *"King of the Jews"* (Mat. 2:2)!

Now, if we take this at face value without making other assumptions, the desire of these Gentile Magi to worship a foreign enemy king of the Jews makes no sense. This is because the Zoroastrians of Yahshua's day were citizens of the Parthian Empire while the Promised Land belonged to Rome, and Parthian kings and citizens viewed Rome as a potential enemy and were not on friendly terms with them. For this reason, the Parthians in general would not have cared about the birth of any Jewish King unless they felt he was a threat and wanted to annihilate him.

Another factor suggesting that the Magi may have been Jewish converts is the fact that many Jews like the prophet Daniel were exiled to Babylonia for seventy years after the fall of the Kingdom of Judah to Nebuchadnezzar. During that time, Daniel became the top-ranking leader of the Magi who served the King of Persia. During this time, it is likely that some of the Pagan Astrologers in the king's court may have learned about and accepted the truth of Yahweh from Daniel, who correctly identified Yahweh as the Creator of the Mazzaroth.

From this supposition, another interesting theory can be drawn that concerns Zoroastrianism. Iranian historians place Zoroaster's era to around 600 BC, which would have made Zoroaster a likely contemporary of the prophet Daniel! If so, is it possible that Zoroaster was a Magi in the king's court at that time and he learned about the true God Yahweh from Daniel? If so, this may explain why there are so many interesting parallels between Zoroastrianism and Judeo-Christianity.

Though there were some Magi at the time of Christ's First Advent that followed a pure form of Sethite Astronomy, however, others obviously rejected the truth and practiced Astrology, which was used solely for fortune-telling in an effort to usurp God's Will. Indeed, many ancient cultures were led terribly astray by their own brand of evil Astrologers who were really engaging in Sorcery. One such kingdom was ancient Egypt.

Yahweh vehemently condemned Egypt for their perversion of the Star Gospel and their evil use of its power to predict the future that is embodied in the pseudo science of Astrology:

> *"The officials of Zoan are nothing but fools; the wise counselors of Pharaoh give senseless advice.* **How can you say to Pharaoh, 'I am one of the wise men, a disciple of the ancient kings'?** *Where are your wise men now?* **Let them show you and make known what the LORD Almighty** *(Yahweh Tsavout)* **has planned against Egypt. The officials of Zoan have become fools, the leaders of Memphis are deceived; the cornerstones of her peoples have led Egypt astray.** *The LORD (Yahweh) has poured into them a spirit of dizziness; they make Egypt stagger in all that she does, as a drunkard staggers around in his vomit."* - Isaiah 19:11-14 (NIV)

In the 11th verse of the preceding Scripture, Yahweh said sarcastically: *"How can you say to Pharaoh, 'I am one of the wise men, a disciple of the ancient kings?'"* By saying this, Yahweh made it clear that the Magi of Pharaoh's court felt that they were the inheritors of a legacy that existed since the times of *"the ancient kings."* Could the time of these *"ancient kings"* have been before the Flood - the time known to the ancient Egyptians as "Zep Tepi" or the "First Time?" If so, the ancient kings being referred to were likely the godly antediluvian patriarchs of the line of Seth, since they were the first people to understand and correctly interpret Sacred Astronomy. Unfortunately, however, the Astrologers of Pharaoh's court had perverted the truths found in the stars and constellations tied to the Great Pyramid and Great Sphinx that the descendents of Seth left behind and Abraham had reintroduced them to. *This is why Yahweh condemned the Astrologers of ancient Egypt: they had not only made false predictions using Astrology, but perverted the once pure and holy message of God's Star Gospel of truth.*

Unfortunately, modern Astrology is still being used for the same evil ends as it was in Nimrod's day and in ancient Egypt. Many people delve into Astrology to direct their own future and obtain the best that life can offer with the least amount of pain. However, the Bible makes it clear that we are not to use Astrology to seek ungodly outcomes or to attempt to manipulate the future to our advantage. We instead need to learn to pray and rely on Yahweh God to direct our paths and bless our future endeavors. This is because *Yahweh is not subject to the influence of the Zodiac and has the power to make or break the predictions of the stars.* For the same reason, we are not to bow down and worship stars or any other created thing or use them to practice Magic or Sorcery:

> *"There shall not be found among you anyone who makes his son or his daughter pass through the fire, or one who practices witchcraft ("kaseem," i.e. lot-caster and*

interpreter, or spell-caster), or a soothsayer ("muneen," i.e. false predictor), or one who interprets omens ("nakash," i.e. "hissing one," or one who curses others for revenge), or a sorcerer ("kashaph" or "whisperer," i.e. gossiper, or one who utters falsehoods behind someone's back), or one who conjures spells ("chobeer," i.e. hypnotist, or brainwasher), or a medium ("showeel owb," i.e. one who inquires of demons), or a spiritist ("yiday onee," i.e. knower of "hollow ones," or ghosts), or one who calls up the dead ("darash el moothim," i.e. seeker (or worshipper) of the dead). For all who do these things are an abomination to the LORD (Yahweh)..." - Deut. 18:10-12 (NKJ)

When interpreted true to the original Hebrew (as seen in the parentheses), the above Scripture is a strong admonition against (1) whispering magical incantations, (2) engaging in idolatrous practices such as fortune-telling, astrology, or star worship, (3) falsely interpreting omens without God's guidance, (4) trying to manipulate the behavior of others through mind-control, (5) giving false interpretations of omens, (6) beseeching demons for help, (7) seeking or worshipping the spirits of the dead, and (8) attempting to manipulate the outcome of future events by practicing Sorcery.

However, because the people in the Northern Kingdom of Israel eventually did all these things, Yahweh allowed their kingdom to be destroyed. This left only the Southern Kingdom of Judah to remain for a time:

*"And they caused their sons and daughters to pass through the fire, **practiced witchcraft and soothsaying**, and sold themselves to do evil in the sight of the LORD (Yahweh), to provoke Him to anger. **Therefore the LORD (Yahweh) was very angry with Israel, and removed them from His sight;** there was none left but the tribe of Judah alone." - II Kings 17:17-18 (NKJ)*

As punishment for their sins, the inhabitants of the Northern Kingdom of Israel were either slaughtered or carried away to Assyria where they served as slaves. Once they were freed from there, these former captives formed bands of marauding tribes that spread throughout Europe and the Mediterranean civilizations.

The Kingdom of Judah, however, sinned grievously against Yahweh Elohim too. That is why, after the righteous king of Judah named Josiah came to power, one of the things he did during his thirty-one year reign **was abolish Baal, Zodiac, and planetary worship:**

> *"Then he removed the idolatrous priests whom the kings of Judah had ordained to burn incense on the high places in the cities of Judah and in the places all around Jerusalem, and those who burned incense to Baal, to the sun, to the moon, to the constellations, and to all the host of heaven."* - *II Kings 23:5 (NKJ)*

We must therefore heed the practice of King Josiah and **make sure we do not turn the physical heavens or the symbols and meaning of the Zodiac into an idol.** However, though we shouldn't worship the Zodiac, we need to recognize the starry expanse of heaven as a prophetic time clock created by Yahweh God. This prophetic astronomical clock is examined closely in all of the Language of God series books, especially Book One and Book Four.

Appropriate Use and Interpretation of Symbols in Religion

Through the preceding discussions about mankind's idolatrous worship of the heavens and themselves, we can see that once good symbols like the Trinity and the Zodiac can be grossly perverted. This is peculiar to almost all ancient and modern Pagan religions. The truth behind godly symbols is eventually lost and the lies associated with these symbols are believed and remembered instead. We therefore have to be careful *not* to misapply the Language of God and twist it out of proportion, thereby turning truth to fantasy. This is why Yahweh strictly prohibited any graven image to be made to depict His dealings with mankind. That is also why Yahweh was so angry at the Israelites for their fall into idolatry, and this is why the Israelites were punished - just as all mankind will be punished for their idolatry on the Day of the Lord.

However, confusion exists in the minds of some that makes all symbols potentially idolatrous. This is why the Muslims have gone to great lengths to obliterate real-life imagery of any kind from decorative elements in public places. They fear that it could be used idolatrously. As a result, they use only abstract designs in their art and architecture. There is, however, a vast difference between using symbols to teach others and blatant idolatry. The Muslims have therefore gone too far in their interpretation of God's Will.

There is nothing wrong with symbols. As this book has shown, metaphorical symbols are what Yahweh uses to teach us about Himself. He made these symbols inherent in all Creation to teach us much about His greatness and our own nature. He has also revealed the past, present and future to us in the prophetic symbolism of the Zodiac and in the annual Jewish High Sabbaths such as Passover, the Feast of Unleavened Bread, Rosh Hashanah, Yom Kippur and the Feast of Sukkot or Tabernacles. As I have shown previously, all these Jewish holidays have prophetic applications. That is why it is so important for Christians to study their symbolic meanings. In fact, people who ignore the allegorical, spiritual, and prophetic messages behind these Biblically ordained Jewish holidays do so at their own spiritual peril.

The Jews were not the first to receive divine revelations from God in the symbolism of tangible things, however. As was shown previously throughout this book, Yahweh gave Enoch and his Sethite descendants the knowledge of the Universe that they recorded for us in the complex symbolism of the Great Pyramid and the symbolism of the Mazzaroth. The incredible handiwork of massive stone monuments such as the Great Pyramid complex and Great Sphinx, the pyramids at Dahshur and the circular Zodiac stone found at Dendera in Egypt shows us that they clearly understood Yahweh's symbolic Language. By putting *no writing of any kind* within their pyramids, they also showed that God's Language is based on pure symbolism. The symbolic images of this Language are defined using principles in geometry, science, astronomy and mathematics - not sounds that can have altered meanings over time.

Symbols have been shown throughout this book as being excellent teaching tools. The symbolism in Judeo-Christian rituals and in created things teaches us about ourselves and Yahweh God and His plans for us. That is why we were created with an ability to understand and apply this divine Language. But **without the Spirit of God, our ability to correctly discern symbolic truth is nonexistent.** Instead we see what we want to see, leading others and ourselves into error and sin. Even with the Holy Spirit within us, we are still at times susceptible to placing too much stock in the importance of symbols.

Examples of this are very common. Some Christians, for instance, assume that symbols of crosses or statues/pictures of saints can have divine protective powers. In the old vampire movies of the past, the only way to fend off a vampire's attack was with a crucifix. This odd belief stems from actual religious beliefs found among various groups of Roman Catholics around the world. In some cultures, crucifixes and statues of Mary, Jesus or recognized Saints are actually used as good luck charms said to offer protection from evil. Even Bibles are similarly ranked among items that ward off evil – whether or not the Bible is ever opened and actually read by those who cling to the book as a talisman.

Orthodox and Messianic Jews are also guilty of idolizing symbols with their insistence that Christians should doggedly follow regular

Jewish Sabbath and High Sabbath holiday traditions. In doing so, they deny the teachings of the Apostle Paul, who taught that Christians only need to follow the Law that Yahshua taught and that they are guided to keep by the Holy Spirit. This is *not* the Law prescribed by Moses that is a curse that calls for physical adherence without transformation, but the Law kept via a transformation of the heart as is required by Christ (See Galatians 2:16-21, 3:6-14; Romans 3:19-23, 27-28).

These misguided Jews are often guilty of turning symbolic articles of their faith into idols. For example, when the Jewish "tallit" (i.e.: prayer shawl) or phylactery or Menorah become paramount in their religious traditions - when they *must be used* to broadcast their faith to others - then they have become idols to the Orthodox or Messianic Jews who use them. That is why it is never good to become too attached to symbols. If we find our faith caught up in using one or more symbols, we are in danger of idolatry.

At Easter among devout Polish Catholics in the past, some wouldn't eat their beautifully decorated Easter eggs until the priest had blessed them - as if the eggs were some sort of holy offering! At Christmastime today, many Christians place great importance in displaying Advent wreaths and Nativity scenes. Catholics in some cultures burn candles before Nativity scenes or statues of Jesus or the saints and attempt to worship God through them. Others wear crosses routinely as talismans or decorations rather than using their actions to quietly broadcast their faith or piety.

Sadly, some people find it impossible to pray unless they use a prayer shawl, rosary or prayer beads or look at a crucifix. Many know nothing about having real intimacy in their relationship with Yahweh. Instead they pray automatically by following a prescribed formula and think this blind recitation has some magical ability to win God's favor even though Yahshua condemned it as evil (Mat. 6:7). These practices are all idolatrous and abominations unto Yahweh. **Yah hates anything that we have transformed into an idol, even if its original symbolic purpose was good.**

If we think idolatry can't affect us because we don't believe in the power of idols, we need to think again. Idolatry is an ever-present threat in this dark world and we need to be on guard and pray against it continually. This is as true today as it was thousands of years ago, when ancient Israel was judged with destruction for the same sins. In the Kingdom of Judah, for example, only one in dozens of kings of Judah was truly righteous before Yahweh. Though all of them sinned, some Israelite kings fell into varying degrees of apostasy and idolatry. As they sinned, so did the people. But when a righteous ruler arose and abolished the evil ways of his predecessors, he was proclaimed as a godsend and hailed as a great king. As an example of this, we will examine the righteous King Josiah of Judah in the next chapter, which explores God's purpose for His chosen people Israel and the warning message that the failed Kingdom of Israel has for us today.

The Ancient Origin of the 21st Century Ideological War

Many reading this book are probably familiar with the idea that the plan of Washington DC, the capital of the United States of America is supposedly designed around several different Zodiac signs. Many also know that there are many interesting Zodiacs incorporated into sculptures or monuments within important buildings there that leaders in the US Government with a background in Freemasonry commissioned. It is also widely believed that these contain hidden messages encoded with a secret Masonic alphabet of occult symbols. However, though some of these Zodiacs could contain sinister messages, there may be hidden godly motives behind some of them as well!

Indeed, most of the monuments erected in Washington DC reflect the knowledge and imaginations of men that were better educated in Classical subject-matter than most people are today. Two centuries ago, the teachings of Freemasonry were fully grounded in Christianity, and the men who joined this organization were unswervingly Christian in their worldview. In addition, they were generally much better educated with Classical literature than we are today. Those who aspired to political offices were generally college-educated in a broad range of subjects like the Renaissance men who preceded them. As a result, they were well versed in many different subjects, including Biology, Science, Math, Geometry, Astronomy, Astrology, and Classical Mythology.

Due to their extensive educations and their strong religious background, the American statesmen who penned the Declaration of Independence and the US Constitution thought differently than modern politicians and statesmen and most Americans do today. Since so many Americans are unfamiliar with America's Christian roots and the Classical knowledge of its first statesmen, many of them are easily led to believe that some secret sinister society with a dark hidden agenda has always been shaping America's destiny, though this is certainly not true in every case.

Though the Freemasons have put Zodiac designs in their own lodges and temples in modern times, and they seem to enjoy more power and popularity now than they have at any other time in history, they have not always been so well-known or influential. Therefore, it is just as likely that ordinary, well-educated men of past eras could have designed the American Capital with many Classical ideas in mind, including Astronomy, Astrology and Mythology. This would have especially been the case back in the 1800s. At that time, several prominent scholars in England and America deciphered the Gospel in the Stars using biblical knowledge, star names, Classical Mythology, and the symbolic pictures associated with each constellation to show how amazingly faithful to the Bible these stories depicted in the heavens are.

Since that time, over a dozen scholars have acknowledged that the Star Gospel is much more than a fantasy concocted by men to reflect ideas in the Bible. For proof of this, the Bible itself states that God numbered (i.e. created) and named all the stars! Now, one may ask, why did God name the stars? The answer is that He did so to give them meaning! In fact, the ancient Zodiac with its 48 constellations tells a Gospel story that is identical to the Bible's stories. Why? Because God wrote this Gospel in the heavens Himself, just as He inspired every word of the Bible.

In my book: "The Language of God in the Universe", I went much farther than any of these past authors did in deciphering the messages in the stars. This is why I am so excited about the knowledge hidden in the Great Pyramid. As already shown, this pyramid and the other two big pyramids at Giza and the Red and Bent Pyramids at Dahshur are tied to the Zodiac signs of Taurus and Orion in absolutely amazing ways. To my knowledge, no current author outside of me has ever seen these connections, and I have found no exact record of it in any existing book that I've had access to. However, there may be some dusty old tome or more current publication that carries this knowledge hidden in a library or institution of higher learning. Therefore, I welcome anyone who has access to such a book that would be willing to let me know the author and title. I'd be delighted to know that another ancient or modern seer saw the same connection and shared its details.

From studying the past and the Star Gospel, I have learned a very important secret that explains the reason why most Western Democratic cultures are rapidly becoming more socialistic and intellectually and spiritually promiscuous. This secret is that one's choice of religious ideology will determine one's choice of political ideology, and also the moral direction of a country. This is why, when Judeo-Christian monotheism is removed from the thought processes of well-educated men, something sinister inevitably begins to happen.

In fact, the big difference between the Renaissance thinkers and the Masons of yesterday and the members of the Illuminati and

Freemasonry today is the fact that most of our Christian forefathers would never have presumed that all paths lead to God, mankind is the measure of all things, or morality is relative. Nor would they ever have imagined that mankind could achieve lasting peace and prosperity without God Almighty presiding over humanity's affairs in every area of life, and they therefore tempered their choices with divinely-inspired love, mercy, compassion and justice. But, sadly, Christian temperance has almost vanished in the world today.

Indeed, the world is moving swiftly toward a rejection of faith in God in favor of seeing humanity as one all-encompassing deity that can do anything when they put their collective minds to the task. In other words, many now believe the lie that Azazel beguiled Eve with - that people can become god and successfully exercise divine authority and power without any need for one omnipotent, invisible, sentient, just and loving God in control. But the Bible teaches just the opposite:

> *"Do not be deceived, my beloved brethren. Every good gift and every perfect gift is from above, and comes down from the Father of lights, with whom there is no variation or shadow..." - James 1:16-17 (NKJ)*

After reading this book, little doubt should remain in anyone's mind that the one world religious system that will dominate just before and during the Great Tribulation will be centered around the religion of Secular Humanism, which is a philosophy that emphasizes reason, scientific inquiry, and human fulfillment and physical satisfaction in the natural world, but rejects the spiritual and moral importance of a belief in one just, loving, and completely perfect Creator God.

Don't be fooled! The materially fulfilling ideologies surrounding Positive Thinking, New Age beliefs, Wiccan Magic, Earth worship, and the Emergent Church that is in league with the Pope in their desire to unite all Christians under one banner will be part of this humanistic religious system, and many apostates who falsely call themselves Christians, Muslims and Jews will be comfortable with this false religion because they will believe, or will want to believe that all spiritual paths lead to God. Nonetheless, this is a lie that contradicts both the Bible and the Star Gospel, which teach that Yahshua alone is the Author and Finisher of mankind's salvation, and no one will attain everlasting life without believing in His finished work on the Cross or desiring His Spirit to lead them (Hebrews 12:2; Roman 8:9-17).

I pray we will be in Heaven when this evil humanistic religious system completely takes over the world via a totalitarian one-world government. In the meantime, however, *Christians and Messianics need to be especially vigilant that they are not deceived by seemingly sincere religious teachers that either deny that Christ came in the flesh, and/or that He is NOT coming again in the same glorified body that He attained at His resurrection from the dead.* Among these false teachers are supposedly Christian preachers that promote Amillennial Dominion theology, or Kingdom Now theology. Both of these supposedly Christian doctrinal teachings stress each believer's royal inheritance through Christ and His need for our help in establishing His kingdom on Earth, which has some positive truth in it. But then they destroy it all by claiming that the Kingdom of God will be brought forth without a need for Yahshua to return in the flesh!

These apostate believers are highly likely to be left behind in the Rapture and deceived by Satan, the Antichrist, the fallen angels and the demonic spirits of the Nephilim during the Great Tribulation because they have not tempered their desire to usher in the Kingdom of God on Earth with a full desire to become a prisoner or bondservant of Christ. These misguided soldiers that are promoting the Social Gospel of Rick Warren that stresses community service and communal aid without loving evangelization are falling dangerously close to Eve and Cain's humanistic desire for godhood and physical and sensual fulfillment.

Also, many seemingly sincere Christians believe that God is not actively judging the world because of sin. They no longer see natural disasters and bad turns of events as the same acts of God that our forefathers saw them as. Instead they think that God is no longer a God of wrath, and that the world is not going to be judged because it supposedly will bring in God's Kingdom of Righteousness without the bodily return of the Son of God, whom they believe will forever rule only from Heaven, and never on Earth in a literal kingdom.

These same people hold to the Neo-Platonist view that all religious paths lead to God no matter how different they may appear on the surface, and that the Universe has essentially one spirit that is manifested in multiple ways (as in Polytheism and/or Pantheism). Therefore, they think no one should be judged or evangelized because it is not necessary for salvation, as all paths lead to unity with the Universal All or One. Sadly, *some apostate Christians share these views and expect Christ to rule invisibly while His disciples win over the tangible world with their unconditional love of wickedness and total tolerance of sin!* This is why the Apostle Paul wrote the following Scriptures in warning:

> *"But know this, that in the last days perilous times will come: For men will be lovers of themselves, lovers of money, boasters, proud, blasphemers, disobedient to parents,*

*unthankful, unholy, unloving, unforgiving, slanderers,
without self-control, brutal, despisers of good, traitors,
headstrong, haughty, lovers of pleasure rather than lovers of
God, having a form of godliness but denying its power. And
from such people turn away!" - 2 Timothy 3:1-5 (NKJ)*

*"Do you not know that the unrighteous will not inherit
the kingdom of God? **Do not be deceived.** Neither fornicators,
nor idolaters, nor adulterers, nor homosexuals, nor sodomites,
nor thieves, nor covetous, nor drunkards, nor revilers, nor
extortioners will inherit the kingdom of God." - 1 Cor. 6:9-10
(NKJ)*

Even though the current world economy and political scene is failing miserably at achieving global peace and prosperity, some deluded people think that humanity will learn to beat their weapons into plowshares after they all unite under the essentially godless and immoral ideologies of Humanism and Neo-Platonism.

Neo-Platonism and atheistic Humanism are essentially identical religions that place mankind and the Earth in the center of the Universe instead of the one triune God Yahweh and His Son, which are allegorically signified by our Sun. Indeed, Humanism is well on its way to taking over the thinking of a large percentage of the nearly 7 billion people in this world because they have already rejected worshipping the One True God in favor of worshipping everything as godlike even while becoming their own gods. Sadly, these same individuals believe the lie that they can achieve anything without the blessing of any god other than themselves! This is why Paul admonished believers to sow truth and reap everlasting life by following the Spirit of God rather than the doctrines of demons disguised as men:

*"**Do not be deceived, God is not mocked; for whatever
a man sows, that he will also reap.** For he who sows to his
flesh will of the flesh reap corruption, but he who sows to the
Spirit will of the Spirit reap everlasting life. And let us not
grow weary while doing good, for in due season **we shall reap
if we do not lose heart.**" - Galatians 6:7-9 (NKJ)*

*"Now the Spirit expressly says that **in latter times
some will depart from the faith, giving heed to deceiving
spirits and doctrines of demons**, speaking lies in hypocrisy..."
- 1 Timothy 4:1-2 (NKJ)*

Because I have seen the dire direction that this current world is going in, I am issuing this stern warning to all those who believe they are in the Body of Christ. If you truly love Yahshua, then you will **not** be fooled into thinking that the world will become perfect as soon as everyone starts thinking positively, claims their royal status as children of God, and begins exercising authority over demons, sickness and evil by commanding them all away with positive thoughts and the supposedly "loving" tolerance of sin.

If anyone believes in this patently demonic doctrinal stance, they are buying into the Great Deception that Christ does not need to return to build the Kingdom of God on Earth. Therefore, they will naively accept a fallen angel or demon as their Anti-Messiah. Even now, those being prepared for great spiritual deception are being conditioned to believe that - through their unconditional love and tolerance of sin and evil - they will bring God's Kingdom of Righteousness into existence and evil will cease to exist. Sadly, it appears that most of humanity is ready to believe the lie that they can and will bring in a global kingdom of peace and prosperity without any need for the bodily, supernatural return of Yahshua Ha Mashiach, the glorified, immortal Son of God.

Though there is no doubt that people can achieve much when they are united under one ideology, history has shown repeatedly that even the most idealistic and free societies on Earth like the United States was in its heyday have never brought lasting happiness or stability. Just as ancient Babylon, Greece, and Rome failed to achieve everlasting peace and prosperity, all of the modern nations of this world will never be able to stay united under one banner in order to achieve a perfect humanistic utopia without God.

The simple truth is that this world will never become a paradise unless Yahshua the Messiah returns in the flesh, conquers the humanistic and fascist enemies of God, establishes law and order, and appoints only resurrected saints to hold key positions in the government and educational systems of the world. Only they can truly help Yahshua establish His everlasting Kingdom on Earth. These resurrected saints will not tell the world what their itching ears want to hear, but will deliver the truth in love because they have been spiritually born-again, perfected, glorified, and given incorruptible spiritual and physical bodies:

> *"For we ourselves were also once foolish, disobedient, deceived, serving various lusts and pleasures, living in malice and envy, hateful and hating one another. But when the kindness and the love of God our Savior toward man appeared, not by works of righteousness which we have done, but according to His mercy, He saved us through the washing of regeneration and renewing of the Holy Spirit, whom He poured out on us abundantly through Jesus Christ (Yahshua*

*Ha Mashiach) our Savior, that having been justified by His
grace we should become heirs according to the hope of eternal
life. - Titus 3:3-7 (NKJ)*

*"There is one glory of the sun, another glory of the
moon, and another glory of the stars; for one star differs from
another star in glory. So also is the resurrection of the dead.
The body is sown in corruption, it is raised in incorruption. It
is sown in dishonor, it is raised in glory. It is sown in
weakness, it is raised in power. It is sown a natural body, it is
raised a spiritual body. There is a natural body, and there is a
spiritual body. And so it is written, 'The first man Adam
became a living being.' The last Adam became a life-giving
spirit." - 1 Corinthians 15:41-45 (NKJ)*

This resurrection from the dead will give all believers in Yahshua
incorruptible bodies like His that are infused with God's perfect Spirit
and melded to perfect flesh and bone.

Sadly, however, a time is coming when a great pretender known
as the Antichrist will come and attempt to deceive the whole world. He
will pretend to be the loving image of Christ, and he will do it so
effectively that the majority of humanity will believe that he is a god. In
fact, he may appear on the world scene with whole legions of angels and
demons to back his claim. In addition, he may raise up an army of
Nephilim, claim that they are his resurrected saints, and put them in
positions of power just as Christ will legitimately do with His purely
human saints one day:

*"Who is a liar but he who denies that Jesus (Yahshua)
is the Christ (Messiah)? He is antichrist who denies the Father
and the Son." - 1 John 2:22 (NKJ)*

Will the Antichrist delude the world into thinking he is Christ by
either coming to Earth in a spaceship filled with fallen angels and
Nephilim, or commanding evil armies filled with them? Only time will
tell. ***But the evidence in this book is definitely pointing in that direction.***
Because of this, we should be thanking our Heavenly Father that He has
provided a way of escape for those who love Him through Christ. As
shown in Book Four, the Rapture has been foretold repeatedly in both
Scripture and the Star Gospel.

Someday soon, the Rapture or catching up of all Christ's true
disciples on the Earth today will occur. At that time, God's elect saints
will be taken to Heaven for a number of years while the rest of the world
is being deceived and destroyed by the Seed of the Serpent that idolizes
Cain and worships the Devil. In fact, it is the Rapture that will likely

allow Satan to set the stage for the Antichrist to reveal himself with all of his lying signs and wonders, and his unholy angelic and demonic army (2 Thess. 2:9-12). Be careful that you are not deceived when the Antichrist rises to power in this world! As Yahshua said:

> *"Take heed that you not be deceived. For many will come in My name, saying, 'I am He,' and, 'The time has drawn near.' Therefore do not go after them." - Luke 21:8 (NKJ)*

Yes, take heed that you correctly identify those whom you should not follow, for Yahshua clearly says that these people will say *"I am He!"* This means that they will claim to be God or to be like God, having power over good and evil. In addition to believing this, these wicked people will also be teaching that *"the time has drawn near"* in the sense of a great spiritual awakening. Many supposedly Christian and occult spiritual leaders have been promising that this awakening or revival is near or happening right now. But everywhere one looks the opposite seems to be true from a Biblical standpoint!

Instead of any great revival over the past thirty years, the Church has been infiltrated by occultism and magic masquerading as gifts of the Spirit. In addition, the Church as a whole is succumbing to Amillennialism, which denies that Christ will return bodily and teaches instead that Christians must unite under one banner and change the world by praying the kingdom into existence as Christ's representatives, and with His power and authority. Sadly, though Christians do have real power and authority over angels and demons through Christ in prayer, they do not realize that - in denying Christ's coming in the flesh - their Amillennialism reflects the spirit of the Antichrist:

> *"and **every spirit that does not confess that Jesus Christ (Yahshua Ha Mashiach) has come (or is coming!) in the flesh is not of God.** And this is the spirit of the Antichrist, which you have heard was coming, and is now already in the world." - 1 John 4:3 (NKJ)*

> *"For many deceivers have gone out into the world who do not confess Jesus Christ (Yahshua Ha Mashiach) as coming in the flesh. This is a deceiver and an antichrist." - 2 John 1:7 (NKJ)*

It is extremely important to note here that these passages are referring not only to Christ's coming in the flesh in the past, but also of His coming in the future to set up His Millennial Rule! Whether these naysayers are outside or inside the Body of Christ, *those who deny Christ's future coming in the flesh are antichrists, and they will be*

deceived by the Antichrist of antichrists when he makes his astonishing and seemingly miraculous appearance on the world scene in the near future!

In the meantime, don't make the mistake of assuming that the Antichrist is or must be a Muslim. It's not that the Muslims aren't antichrists. That is a given because - even though Muslims do acknowledge that Yahshua came in the flesh - they deny that He is the Son of God and should be worshipped, and they deny that He is the Messiah that will be returning in the flesh, and these are the beliefs of all the antichrists in the world (1 John 2:22; 2 John 1:7).

Unfortunately, all of this false labeling of the Muslims as the only "antichrists" is leading many people to believe that all Muslims are evil and no one else qualifies as an antichrist, and that is simply not true! For example, many so-called Christians are now saying that Yahshua either was not born in the flesh from a virgin, never rose from the dead, or is not coming again in the flesh in the future. This makes all the Christians that believe these doctrines antichrists! In addition to this, because many Christians now believe that there will not be a specific person (or possibly two persons) who will be the final Antichrist, they will not be paying attention when he rises to power, and they will not be prepared when Yahshua returns for His disciples at the Rapture.

Take heed that you are not deceived! Though some of the greatest Christian spiritual leaders of the past decade have highlighted learning how to exercise spiritual gifts and authority in Christ, they have ignored the Bible's teaching that God's Son - Yahshua Ha Mashiach - is the only one who can restore the Kingdom of God in our hearts as well as on the Earth. In light of this, take a cold, hard look at the world around you to find the real culprits that are fiercely working to build the Antichrist's one-world religious and political system.

If you are born-again, you should clearly be able to discern that nearly every pusher of ecumenism - including, but not limited to many Roman Catholics, Evangelicals, Emergent Church members, Kingdom Now disciples, Muslims, Positive Thinkers, New Agers, Wiccans, Atheists and Pantheists - are working toward establishing a global spiritual kingdom or theocracy with a fully ecumenical leader at the helm. That is why **many recent presidents, princes, pastors, and preachers have been caught telling believers that there is more than one way to God or that all paths lead to salvation.** Could it be any clearer that the Great Deception and falling away spoken of in Scripture is already well underway?

"Let no one deceive you by any means; for **that Day will not come unless the falling away comes first, and the man of sin is revealed, the son of perdition,** *who opposes and exalts himself above all that is called God or that is worshiped, so that he sits as God in the temple of God, showing himself that he is God." - 2 Thess. 2:3-4 (NKJ)*

Though (as of the time of my writing this text in late 2008 and early 2009) "the son of perdition" has not yet been fully revealed, he will be soon. As shown in Book Four, there are many clues that appear to identify the Antichrist or King of the North (the North in ancient times was Assyria but can now be identified with Europe, or a future (or secret) alliance between Europe and Russia united. The activities of this king are detailed in the Book of Daniel (Dan. 11:6-40). Elsewhere in Scripture, the Antichrist is also identified as a bonafide prince (Antichrist as prince: Daniel 9:26; Ephesians 2:2). I believe this refers to Prince Charles of Wales, whose number is 666 based on the number of his name (Rev. 13:18; also see Ch. 10 in Book Four). However, it could also refer to Charles' son Prince William.

In the meantime, there is reason to suspect that the Muslim Mahdi, King of the South, or New Age Messiah called "Maitreya" may be the current President of the United States: Barack Hussein Obama (See Daniel 11:5-40). Intriguingly, the King of the South was an Egyptian king in the past, and Barack Obama was depicted in the kingly regalia of King Tutankhamen of Egypt's 18th dynasty early in his presidency. Even more ominously, King Tut may have been the firstborn son of the most likely Pharaoh of the Exodus: Amenhotep III, and his bloodline may be of Nephilim origin. If so, the Pharaoh Tutankhamen would have been an Anakim and would have died when the Death Angel passed over Egypt at the time of the first Passover!

One reason why President Obama could be the Muslim Mahdi or King of the South (or a forerunner to him) is the fact that he may not have been born Hawaii but in Kenya, which is due south of Israel. In addition, Scripture warns that one of the two coming Antichrists will confirm a false peace treaty (i.e. covenant) between the Islamic nations in the Middle East and Israel, and every recent US President has taken an active role in attempting to resolve the Middle East Crisis. The Book of Daniel and Book of Revelation stipulate that the Antichrist will orchestrate the signing of a seven-year peace agreement between Israel and many other nations that he will subsequently break after 3-1/2 years (Daniel 9:27). Indeed, with many US troops fighting terror in Afghanistan and Iraq and the USA's strange alliance with Saudi Arabia (which is a modern-day kingdom that also lies south of Israel) the United

States has been acting as the reigning "king" of the South since it invaded Iraq in 2003, whether anyone cares to acknowledge it or not. As such, the USA may soon find itself pitted against the future King of the North or Antichrist, who is described as a prince by the prophet Daniel:

> "And... the people of **the prince who is to come** shall destroy the city and the sanctuary. The end of it shall be with a flood, and till the end of the war desolations are determined. Then he shall confirm a covenant with many for one week; but in the middle of the week he shall bring an end to sacrifice and offering." - Daniel 9:26-27 (NKJ)

As shown in "The Language of God in Prophecy" I carefully identify *"the prince who is to come"* in Daniel's prophecy with Prince Charles or his son William. This would identify *"the people"* of that prince as the white, English speaking people of the world today, *including those in America*. Next, the prophecy says that the coming prince or Antichrist *"will confirm a covenant with many."* Traditionally, this covenant has been viewed as a peace treaty signed between Israel, the leaders of the West, and the Middle Eastern nations. However, I believe this is referring to a covenant that the Antichrist will establish with the world, and it may not have anything to do with getting the entire Middle East to acknowledge Israel as a nation, but with establishing world peace. I addition, I believe that the leader that signs this "covenant with many" is positively one of the two Antichrists revealed in Daniel's prophecies of the Kings of the North and the South.

Another reason Barack Hussein Obama may be the Mahdi or a forerunner to the Mahdi is the fact that his birth certificate says he was born in Hawaii, which is within the sinister Scorpio Meridian of the Earth. Furthermore, Obama's first and middle name are Arabic, he was raised as a Muslim during his childhood in Indonesia and he may secretly still be a Muslim. Sadly, Indonesia is a Muslim nation, a suspected Terrorist stronghold and a known hotbed of organized crime and sexual sin - so it is not a good place to be from. Finally, Obama's high popularity is legend and several prominent politicians, Black Muslim religious leaders and the TV celebrity Oprah have either identified Obama as a Messiah-figure or singled him out as a potential candidate to lead the New World Order.

Regardless of what role Barack Obama will play in the End Times, however, it is highly disturbing that Israel is not being allowed to act on its own initiative in protecting itself. Instead, it is being coerced by the USA, the UK, the EU and the United Nations to ignore Iran and Syria's threats and to give up land to achieve a dubious state of peace with the Palestinian under Hamas terrorist control. In addition, as attested to by the Gulf War in Kuwait in 1991, the long and heavy US Military presence in Iraq, and the US Military's ongoing war against terrorist cells in Afghanistan, Pakistan, and Iraq, the USA seems to be the primary aggressor in the Middle East, and they also seem to have an inordinate amount of control over Israel's military forces - even openly telling the Israeli Military what they can and cannot do. In short, the US Military seems to be acting as the King of the South's army should.

But this is not totally the case, for the United States appears to be playing on both sides of the War on Terror to what they may feel is to their own advantage. Could this be a sign that the USA is secretly acting on God's behalf? As shown in "The Language of God in Prophecy," Psalm 108 is tied to the year 2008 and contains a prophecy about the current state of affairs in Israel. In this prophecy, the nations of Europe, the United Kingdom and her commonwealth nations, and the United States are identified as allies with Israel who join forces with her against her enemies in Russia, Turkey, Syria, Iran, Iraq, Egypt and Saudi Arabia.

When these Muslim nations join forces and attempt to invade Israel, the King of the South (which may or may not be President Obama) will likely turn against Israel and join the nations it formed secret alliances with in the Middle East in an effort to destroy Israel. Before the Mahdi can carry out his plot, however, Israel may strike first. If so, this will likely be when the city of Damascus in Syria will be utterly destroyed (Isaiah 17:1). Later, however, the USA may be invaded by the armies of the princely Antichrist or King of the North when they resist his rule. See Book Four "The Language of God in Prophecy", where Scriptures that show the USA being attacked are identified.

Now, some might wonder why I don't identify Russia, with its current alliances with Iran and Syria (i.e. Damascus), as the King of the North. To this, I would say that, though Russia is in the far north, Russia, Iran and Syria are likely to be fighting against both the King of the South and the King of the North, who will control Europe and the United Kingdom, which are also far North of Israel. In other words, **Russia, Iran and Syria will likely align themselves against Israel and both of the Kings vying to control Israel and the Middle East.** Nonetheless, these nations are destined to lose their bid for power in the Middle East, for Scripture indicates that the King of the North will be victorious over the King of the South, and Russia and the Middle Eastern nations will be assimilated into the King of the North's one world empire, also known as the New World Order (Daniel 11:4-43; Ezekiel 38:2-21 & 39:1-11).

In the meantime, though the Antichrist has not yet been fully unmasked, *the great falling away or deception that Scripture warns us about is well underway right now.* That is why this entire section of the book has been liberally sprinkled with Scriptures that admonish us not to be deceived! Sadly, however, those who are not born again will no doubt reject my hypothesis altogether and believe Satan's lies (2 Thess. 2:9-12).

In light of these Scriptures warning us not to be deceived, and in view of the part that the United States is playing in the Middle East today, let me clarify my feelings regarding America in the End Times. Though this section opened with an appeal to view the past history of the United States as being firmly in the hands of godly men who worshipped God the Father and His Son, this is no longer the case in America today or in the rest of the world at large - at least not on the surface. This is why Islam is becoming so militant and dangerous in the USA and all over the world. As the light of God's truth grows dimmer in the USA and the world daily, the darkness of Satan's lies will engulf what light is left and will seek to smother and destroy it all.

In Book Four it was shown that, though America does have a big part to play in the Great Tribulation, it will be primarily at a Grass Roots level unless the US Military performs a revolutionary coup, and this seems unlikely. Nonetheless, many Americans have and will continue to work in direct opposition to Satan and the current ungodly direction of the US Government. This will also likely be true after the Rapture, when many currently apostate Americans will likely turn to Christ and be saved, and will fight the Antichrist during the Great Tribulation.

Though many currently think the Islamic nations are the Beast out of the Sea in the Book of Revelation, they are wrong! This is because they do not realize that **Humanism will soon be the nemesis of both Islam and Apostate Christianity.** The reasons for this centers around the fact that modern Christianity and Islam have serious flaws that make them undesirable spiritual ideologies for controlling a world empire.

For example, Islam demands allegiance to a demonic god of war and darkness that seeks totalitarian control over every aspect of life. Furthermore, those who are allied with Allah have no hope of everlasting life in Heaven outside of Jihad and martyrdom, so those who are serious about getting into Heaven will readily join in Jihadist activities bent on overthrowing the West. However, religion of any kind tends to get in the way of Satan's objective, which is to puff mankind up and cause humanity to sin so badly that God will have no choice but to condemn everyone to Hell - and Islamic "Sharia" Law definitely would interfere with the free expansion of immorality.

Likewise, if it were practiced in its purest form, Christianity could put a stop to all of Satan's plans for the foreseeable future. This is because Yahshua offers people freedom from legalism, power over and freedom from demonic activity, and the power to reverse sickness and be miraculously healed. Furthermore, Yahshua promises everlasting life to all who believe in Him, repent of their sins and ask His Holy Spirit to help them become as loving and just as He is.

Nonetheless, many believers have never really embraced Christ's totally pacifist and loving ideology. Instead, as in the days of Noah, they are trying to fight violence with violence, and are therefore reaping what they are sowing (Luke 16:25; Gal. 6:7-9). This is why New Age tainted Humanism is on the rise, and these ideologies will likely soon be the guiding principle behind the Antichrist's global empire. Those embracing Humanism are totally weary of war and terrorism and their hatred of religion is a natural result of living in a modern world governed by warring religious ideologies.

Meanwhile, millions of believers in the Middle East, Africa, and Asia have already died at the hands of Muslim extremists in the past thirty years, and the Muslim terrorists perpetrating this violence are waiting for the perfect opportunity to exterminate countless more in the free West. This will undoubtedly happen as the Western powers let their guard down too far and attempt to embrace all Muslims as their intellectual and spiritual equals.

When this backfires, as it surely will, then the humanists are going to have their heyday. At that time, anybody with a firm religious faith in one God will be persecuted and exterminated when they attempt to overthrow or reject the ruling authorities that will outlaw a belief in any god other than mankind or the fallen angels. Therefore, the escalating hatred of Christians, Muslims and Jews in America and around the world is only going to get worse.

Since this will inevitably be the case, how should those who profess to be believers begin to live life now? Thankfully, in no uncertain terms, Scripture tells us exactly how we should be living:

> *"When He (Yahshua) had called the people to Himself, with His disciples also, He said to them, 'Whoever desires to come after Me, let him deny himself, and take up his cross, and follow Me. For whoever desires to save his life will lose it, but whoever loses his life for My sake and the gospel's will save it. For what will it profit a man if he gains the whole world, and loses his own soul? Or what will a man give in exchange for his soul? For whoever is ashamed of Me and My words in this adulterous and sinful generation, of him the Son of Man also will be ashamed when He comes in the glory of His Father with the holy angels." - Mark 8:34-38 (NKJ)*

With this Scripture as provocation, shouldn't Christian and Messianic pastors be teaching all believers to shun the pleasures of this world and deny their sinful flesh in favor of the everlasting rewards that are promised to all those who love and serve Christ and preach His Gospel of love, forgiveness and peace no matter how unpopular it is right now? The answer is "Yes!" However, many pastors are not teaching the true Gospel to their congregations. As a result, many supposed Christians and Messianics are allegorically shaking hands with the Devil!

In order to follow Yahweh in truth, true disciples of Yahshua need to get out of Babylon by ending all fellowship with corrupt churches and other religious and political organizations. They also need to lose faith in the humanistic "man as god" world system and Health and Wealth gospel of the Antichrist before it's too late! Seek instead the Kingdom of Heaven and the Spirit of God within you, pray fervently to God, read the Bible, and - if you are sincere in your faith - everything will eventually be made clear to you, for *"He who has begun a good work in you will complete it until the day of Jesus Christ (Yahshua Ha Mashiach)"* (Philippians 1:6).

Pagan Lies Obscuring the Truth of the Rapture

The Rapture is a nickname taken from the Latin word "raptus" found in 1 Thessalonians 4:17 of the Latin Vulgate, where it is translated in Koine Greek as "harpazo" and in English as "caught up:"

> *"Then we who are alive and remain shall be* **caught up** *(i.e. raptus or harpazo) together with them in the clouds to meet the Lord in the air. And thus we shall always be with the Lord."* - 1 Thess. 4:17

This Rapture is the promised snatching away or catching up into Heaven of millions of believers worldwide in order to be with Christ. In the Rapture, all devout believers in Yahshua who shun the world's sinful pleasures and attractions, who love God and each other with their whole hearts, and who live in the world but are not of it will instantly be transported to Heaven. This is so they can be spared from God's vengeful wrath upon the unrepentant wicked during the Great Tribulation, as well as to become the Bride of Christ at the Wedding of the Lamb of God, who is Christ.

There are clues in Scripture that the Rapture event may happen in several stages before the terrible plagues unleashed by the Seven Bowls of God's Wrath are unleashed on an unsuspecting world (Rev.

15:7-8, 16:1-20). Meanwhile, the wicked will be oblivious to their doom because they will be deluded and lulled into thinking the Antichrist is the true Christ, and they will firmly believe that his false kingdom will usher in the greatest Age of peace and prosperity in history. What those so deceived will not accept, however, is that their supposed human savior is the Antichrist, whose promises of peace will ultimately be false. As a result, they will live through the Great Tribulation.

Bible prophecies of the world's coming doom are coming true before our very eyes in this generation, which is highly likely to see the rise of the Antichrist, the Rapture, the massive death and suffering of the Great Tribulation, the glory and promise of the Second Coming of Christ, the setting up of His righteous Kingdom on Earth, and the gradual restoration of the Earth to its Pre-Flood splendor under Christ's wise leadership. Nonetheless, it seems most believers are sleeping as these events unfold and are unaware of how many End Time biblical prophecies are being fulfilled - just as Yahshua warned that His disciples would be sleeping (Matthew 26:40-46; Luke 9:32).

Though the biblical promises of the Rapture and Christ's return to rule the world with justice and peace for a thousand years should be the hope that believers hold fast to in these unsettling times of wars and rumors of wars, pestilences, and earthquakes, many supposedly Christian Americans either have no knowledge of, or no respect for these prophesied events. As a result, a few of them believe that their only hope of survival is to prepare for a revolutionary war and the deprivation it will entail by stockpiling survival gear and weapons. Rather than allowing God to be the world's judge and the almighty Protector of His saints, these misguided people will be fighting against the Antichrist's world system because they most likely will be left behind in the Rapture.

As hard as it is for people to understand today with the glorification of violence as a form of entertainment, any show of violence is inherently evil according to Yahshua, who preached a Gospel of love, brotherhood, and complete nonviolence toward any human being (Mat. 5:38-48; Acts 7:59-60; Rom. 12:10-21; 1 Cor. 4:12-14, 13:4-7; 1 Peter 2:23, 3:9). Furthermore, the truly righteous among the antediluvians were also likely totally nonviolent until the last generations before the Flood. However, despite the fact that many of these misguided End-Time lovers of justice and freedom are planning to fight the Antichrist, many of them will likely be fully transformed and saved by the love of Christ someday, and will lay down their weapons and join the ranks of the many nonviolent Tribulation Saints that may be martyred, but may also find a safe refuge or hideaway in the wilderness until Yahshua returns.

At the moment, however, large groups of New Agers and apostate believers are under the mistaken impression that they are going to bring about a global utopia of peace and prosperity gradually on their own, but without any need for the physical return of Christ or any divine intervention whatsoever other than some nefarious energy called the Christ (or Krishna) consciousness that the false messiah or Antichrist will be a master at wielding. This Anti-Messiah will preach a false gospel combining humanism, ecumenism, and tolerance that will make it illegal to preach the Word of God as it is recorded in the Bible, and will label the Bible as hate literature intended to harm homosexuals, pedophiles, child molesters, adulterers and other unrepentant sinners.

Among Christians, this idea that the Church is going to advance the Kingdom of God on Earth until everyone is willingly living a Christian life is called Amillennialism, Dominion Theology or Kingdom Now Theology, and all of these doctrines directly oppose the idea of Christ's bodily presence on Earth and leadership of the world in His coming Millennial Kingdom, which will feature Jerusalem as its Capital.

New Agers call this coming global utopia or awakening of the "Christ consciousness" within all humanity the Great Awakening or Enlightenment. This event will supposedly be brought about by a messiah figure they call Maitreya, who is supposedly an Avatar or human incarnation of an Ascended Master or Buddha. Found in both Hinduism and Buddhism, Ascended Masters and Buddha incarnations (of which the Dalai Lama is considered to be the fifth and last) are spiritual adepts that are supposedly fully connected to the impersonal intelligence that created our Universe. These Ascended Masters are soon supposedly going to forcibly remove all the evil people on the Earth who are holding back the full spiritual expression of this Great Awakening.

The forced removal of these supposedly lost souls who resist the New World Order and the Antichrist is slated to occur sometime on or after December 21st, 2012 - when occultists and Pagans expect major world events to occur that will usher in a New Age of enlightenment and spiritual power. Around that time, those whom New Agers and apostate believers would deem spiritually asleep (but who are totally awake!) will supposedly be taken out of the way, thus allowing everyone left on the Earth to become one in thought, spirit and deed.

Sadly, the apostasy in the Church today is only serving to feed those who believe in this twisted New Age interpretation of the Rapture and Tribulation. But the fact that so many New Agers and Pagans are voicing the same lies concerning these events strongly suggests that the Rapture is indeed going to transpire, and that Satan has had to find an alternative and believable explanation for it to be used when necessary.

Thankfully, after the Rapture occurs, some people who are left behind will see this New Age lie about the Rapture as the Great Deception that it is, and they will be saved. Meanwhile, others will be fully deceived by the Antichrist's and False Prophet's mesmerizing words, deceptive signs and lying wonders, and they will ultimately perish.

In Book Four, I discuss many Scriptures concerning the truth of the Rapture and the fact that it may be a two-part event. However, I initially thought that the First Rapture would be sometime near to the beginning of the Tribulation, and the Second Rapture would be Mid-Tribulation. I also explore the timing of the First and Second Rapture, which may be sometime between 2010 and 2018. As shown in my Revelation Timeline revealed in Book Four, 2011 through 2017 might be the seven years of the Tribulation. This Timeline centers around the prophetic messages in the Hallel Psalms, in the prophetic inches measuring the interior passages in the Great Pyramid at Giza that lead upward from the entrance to the Antechamber, and in prophecies hidden in the Biblical Autumn Feast Days of Rosh Hashanah or the Feast of Trumpets, Yom Kippur or the Day of Atonement, and the Feast of Sukkot or Tabernacles.

According to the Jewish Sacred Calendar, 2010 will not end until April 5th, 2011, or Nissan 1. This is also the date that marks the beginning of 2011. Fascinatingly, April 5th is a date tied to the discovery of Easter Island in 1722 - and Easter Island figures prominently as a prime location for viewing several End Time Signs in the Heavens discussed in Book Four focusing on prophecy.

Also, as revealed in Book Four, and in several articles at my POEM Blog at http://pillarofenoch.blogspot.com and at my ministry web site at http://pillar-of-enoch.com, I no longer feel that the First Rapture will be a Pre-Tribulation event, but a Mid-Tribulation event occurring sometime on or after the Mayan date for doomsday on December 21st, 2012. It is also possible that the First Rapture will be a Pre-Wrath event during the Great Tribulation, and the Second Rapture may occur just before the Battle of Armageddon at the end of the Great Tribulation. However, since no one knows the exact day or hour of the Rapture except our heavenly Father, keep in mind that these are predictions, NOT prophecies.

Chapter 8: The Legacy of the Kingdom of Israel

> *"And in the days of these kings the God of heaven will set up a kingdom which shall never be destroyed; and the kingdom shall not be left to other people; it shall break in pieces and consume all these kingdoms, and it shall stand forever." - Daniel 2:44 (NKJ)*

Though this chapter contains a summary of Israel's initial triumph and ultimate past failure, it is also a herald of things to come, for it shows that Yahweh has plans to set up a righteous kingdom upon the Earth that will far surpass the ancient Kingdom if Israel in glory - a kingdom that will never end. This is clearly intimated in the prophecy quoted from the Book of Daniel above, as well as from the following passage, which was given during the Babylonian Captivity of the Jews:

> *"Then the kingdom and dominion, and the greatness of the kingdoms under the whole heaven, shall be given to... the saints of the Most High. His kingdom is... everlasting... and all dominions shall serve and obey Him." - Daniel 7:27 (NKJ)*

This Scripture clearly tells us that the Kingdom of Israel was a prototype for the everlasting Kingdom that Christ will one day establish on the Earth. This kingdom will fulfill the promise of the spiritual kingdom that was established in people's hearts with Yahshua's First Advent. However, before we explore this coming literal Kingdom of God on Earth, let's examine the failed earthly prototype from its inception with Abraham to its destruction at the hands of the Assyrians, Babylonians and Romans.

Though the idea of the Kingdom of God was planted in the hearts of Adam and Eve with the prophecy about the Seed of the Woman in Genesis 3:15, they and their descendents refused to accept the fact that no ordinary man would be able to become the Messiah prophesied about in the Star Gospel or to reign on God's throne in His stead unless he was perfect. Therefore, all of their attempts to establish an everlasting throne, kingdom, and priesthood on Earth for this coming Messiah to inherit have failed, from ancient Egypt's pharaohs, temples and palaces, to the Roman Catholic Church's popes ensconced in Vatican City. In addition, no Pope in Vatican City, Monarch reigning from Buckingham Palace or President inhabiting the White House has ever succeeded in bringing peace and prosperity to the world.

Nonetheless, Yahweh God had a plan to establish peace on Earth one day and He established a secret line of priests and kings of his own choosing that were in the order of Melchizedek. Sometimes those who filled this role were no more than desert princes living in tents and reigning over a nomadic people with flocks of sheep, goats and cattle, while at other times they ruled as kings and lived in real palaces of brick and stone. But in every case, each preserver of the Messiah's ultimate heritage carried the Staff of Yahweh, from Adam down to Moses. God therefore established and preserved this line of shepherds and kings against all odds to survive until the One who could inherit their legacy was born humbly in Bethlehem around the time of Sukkot in 3 BC.

The establishment of God's literal everlasting Kingdom and throne on Earth began to see its first major fulfillment when Yahweh first spoke to Abraham, establishing an unconditional Blood Covenant with him and his kin that was based on faith and did not require circumcision or any other human work to be fulfilled. This meant that God would fulfill this initial Covenant regardless of the ability or inability of Abraham's descendents to keep it. In fact, in addition to blessing Abraham and his immediate descendents, **Yahweh promised Abraham that all the nations of the Earth would be blessed through Abraham and his seed or offspring:**

> *"Now the LORD (Yahweh) had said to Abram: 'Get out of your country, from your family and from your father's house, to a land that I will show you. I will make you a great nation; I will bless you and make your name great; and...* **in you all the families of the earth shall be blessed.'** *" - Genesis 12:1-3 (NKJ)*

> *"'I swear by myself,' declares the LORD (Yahweh), 'that because you have done this and have not withheld... your only son,* **I will surely bless you and make your descendants as numerous as the stars in the sky...** *Your descendants will take possession of the cities of their enemies,* **and through your offspring all nations on earth will be blessed,** *because you have obeyed me.'" - Gen. 22:16-18 (NIV)*

When Yahweh called Abraham out of Ur, He made His initial unconditional Covenant promise to Abraham, who was still called Abram at that time. The reason for Yah's beneficence toward Abraham is that Abraham pleased Yah with his faith and obedience, despite the fact that Abraham was an uncircumcised Gentile at the time. Nevertheless, this Gentile had departed from Nimrod's Babylonian Empire and fled into the wilderness to follow Yahweh Elohim - and Him only. Because of Abraham's faith and obedience, Yah knew that Abraham would always do his best to believe and follow what Yah told him. Yah therefore made a Covenant promise to Abraham:

> *"He took him outside and said, '**Look up at the heavens and count the stars** - if indeed you can count them.' Then he said to him, 'So shall your offspring be.' **Abram believed the LORD (Yahweh), and he credited it to him as righteousness.**" - Genesis 15:5-6 (NIV)*

Here, Yahweh took Abram outside at night. In the Mesopotamian wilderness on a cloudless night, there would have been an ocean of bright stars in the dark sky. These were the same stars that Nimrod worshipped and had turned into idols through the practices of Astrology and Sorcery. Yet Abram knew the truth behind the meaning of the stars because he had learned of the Gospel in the Stars and Sacred Astronomy firsthand through Noah and Shem. He therefore must have been in awe when Yahweh pointed to His sacred heavenly Gospel and told Abram that his descendents would be like the stars. The double meaning must not have been lost to Abram, for **Yahweh was unconditionally promising Abram that his descendents would be both too numerous to count and a beacon through the darkness of sin - just like the Gospel in the Stars!** How filled with joy Abram must have been as he envisioned a whole army of descendents who would become symbolic "stars" of righteousness and great spiritual blessings to the world.

The prophet Daniel and the Apostle Paul also spoke of the righteous spiritual children of Abram as stars of righteousness who would rise up one day to everlasting life:

> *"Multitudes who sleep in the dust of the earth will awake: some to everlasting life, others to shame and everlasting contempt. **Those who are wise will shine like the brightness of the heavens, and those who lead many to righteousness, like the stars** for ever and ever." - Daniel 12:2-3 (NIV)*

> *"Do everything without complaining or arguing, so that you may become blameless and pure, children of God without fault... **in which you shine like stars in the universe** as you hold out the word of life..." - Phillip. 2:14-16 (NIV)*

Abram's faith in Yah's unconditional promise of a great army of righteous witnesses that would spring from his loins was especially remarkable since Abram once lived in a large city of Nimrod's empire called Ur. There, the lies of Paganism and many practicing Pagans surrounded Abram. As a result, the cultural and social pressure on Abram to conform to their ways would have been great. It also would have been quite difficult for anyone in Abram's position to be a faithful and devout monotheist. Despite the tremendous opposition he faced, however, Abram's clear devotion and obedience to Yah showed the exemplary character of his faith. It was this single-minded commitment to Yah that earned Abram the great honor of being called *Abraham,* as well as God's *friend.* This was especially true since no ordinary man in the Bible outside of Abraham ever received that honor:

> *"But you, Israel, are My servant, Jacob whom I have chosen, the descendants of Abraham My friend." - Isaiah 41:8 (NKJ)*

What a wonderful blessing to be called a "friend" by Yah Himself! Abraham was considered Yah's friend because he kept his faith in Yah despite tremendous opposition. Yahweh's Blood Covenant with Abraham was therefore established on the basis of Abraham's faith and friendship with God, rather than on his good works alone.

In return for Yah's protection and blessing, Abraham kept his faith in Yahweh and served Him only. As a reward for the faithfulness of Abraham and his descendents, Yahweh blessed Abraham's offspring even more by deepening His Covenant promises with them. In fact, when Yahweh renewed His Covenant with Isaac's son Jacob, Yahweh changed Jacob's name - just as he had changed Abraham's. But this time, Yah did not put a phonetic sound from His Name into Jacob's. Instead, Yah completely changed Jacob's name to Israel, or "Yisray-EL," meaning "God will prevail" or "God's strength:"

> *"And God said to him, 'Your name... shall not be called Jacob anymore, but Israel shall be your name.' ...Also God said to him: 'I am God Almighty (El Shaddai)... a nation and a company of nations shall proceed from you, and kings shall come from your body. The land which I gave Abraham and Isaac I give to you; and to your descendants...'" - Genesis 35:10-12 (NKJ)*

In the preceding Scripture, Yahweh changed Jacob's name as a sign of His Covenant promise. In addition, Yah promised Jacob/Israel that his descendents would become *"a nation and a company of nations."* This meant that the Twelve Tribes of Israel that would spring from Jacob's twelve sons would become not only one nation called "Israel" or two nations called "Judah" and "Israel," but *a company* of nations. **This can only mean that Jacob's children would one day establish many other nations besides Judah and Israel.**

This blessing on the nations was an unconditional promise that Yah guaranteed to fulfill. As mentioned in the opening quotes cited in this chapter, the New Covenant that Yahshua sealed in His own blood was the fulfillment of the spiritual blessings promised to the nations in Yah's Old Covenant with Abraham. Nonetheless, Yahweh also meant to literally fulfill these promises of material blessings to mankind through Abraham's son Isaac's blood descendents. Since Abraham was to be the father of a company of nations, these nations must have been represented somewhere on the Earth throughout history.

But where, if Yahweh's promises to Abraham and Jacob were *unconditional,* did this company of nations spring up? Is it possible that these many nations exist today, but are hidden to those who do not understand both world history and the Bible prophecies made to Israel? If so, could it be that modern Israel, the nations of Europe and the nations that sprang from Great Britain represent these nations that sprang from Jacob? Many people in today's English-speaking countries believe this due to certain prophecies in Scripture, historical and genealogical evidence, and recorded English legends that support this hypothesis. But is it true?

In this chapter, we will explore God's promises to Abraham and Israel as well as the facts surrounding the belief that there is a company of nations that are literally descended from Abraham on the Earth today. Many biblical, historical, and spiritual facts suggesting that there is a company of nations that can be seen as Abraham's literal offspring and heirs to the material promises made to Jacob's descendents will be disclosed here. Then, in Book Four of "The Language of God" series, we will engage in a final exploration of these kingdoms or nations and their role in End Time prophecy.

Please note, however, that these explorations do not support the traditional teachings surrounding British-Israelism, Preterism, or Replacement Theology. Instead, they teach that - though there is a literal group of nations that represent the physical blessings of Israel upon the world - there is a far greater spiritual nation of Israel that is formed by the company of believers that share Abraham's faith in God from every nation and culture on Earth! Furthermore, spiritual Israel will share the land inheritance made to the literal Israelites that inhabited the old kingdom of Israel. In addition, all believers that form spiritual Israel will one day serve as royal priests in the Kingdom of God on Earth.

Abraham: A Wealthy, Traveling Magian Prince

There are several events recorded in the Book of Jasher that parallel happenings in the lives of different biblical characters. For example, the Book of Jasher states that Moses was unjustly imprisoned by Jethro for ten years, just as Joseph served as a slave in Potiphar's house for ten years and then languished for three years in prison before becoming Pharaoh's Vizier (Jasher 76:23; Jubilees 46:3-4). As another example, after the Wise Men followed the miraculous star to Bethlehem, Yahshua's stepfather Joseph was warned to flee to Egypt in order to avoid Herod's slaughter. Likewise, Abram's birth was announced in the heavens at his birth and he had to be hidden in a cave for many years to avoid being murdered by Nimrod (Mat. 2:9-13; Jasher 8:2-7).

The Book of Jasher supports the idea that Abram and Sarai were nobles via a fascinating story about them. Interestingly, this story has close parallels to that of the three friends of the prophet Daniel named Hananiah, Mishael and Azariah. These men were cast into a furnace by the Babylonian king Nebuchadnezzar nearly fifteen hundred years after Abram had suffered this fate and miraculously survived (Daniel 3:17-27).

Now, regarding the fiery furnace event in Abram's life, the Book of Jasher relates that Abram was imprisoned and then thrown into a fiery furnace after destroying the idols dedicated to false gods that were in his father Terah's household temple (Jasher 11:53-12:6). Nonetheless, due to his righteousness, Abram miraculously survived three days in the heat and flames of the intensely hot furnace that the king had ordered kindled, and he was finally released.

Because Abram survived, all those who witnessed this miracle were convinced that Abram was innocent of any wrong-doing. Furthermore, those who witnessed this spectacle realized that a very powerful god was protecting Abram. In fact, Nimrod's own awe and fear of Abram's god caused him to honor Abram after his deliverance from the fire. At this time, King Nimrod and his court officials gave Abram many riches - including Nimrod's head palace servant named Eliezer. Consequently, several hundred men who witnessed Abram's miraculous rescue also willingly chose to serve Abram instead of Nimrod. Here is the excerpt from the Book of Jasher telling us how this came about:

> *"And this thing seemed very wonderful in the eyes of the king and princes, that Abram was saved from the fire and that Haran was burned; and the king (i.e.: Nimrod) gave Abram many presents and he gave him his two head servants from the king's house; the name of one was Oni and the name of the other was Eliezer. And* **all the kings, princes and servants gave Abram many gifts of silver and gold and pearl,** *and the king and his princes sent him away, and he went in peace. And Abram went forth from the king in peace,* **and**

many of the king's servants followed him, and about three hundred men joined him."

> *"And Abram returned on that day and went to his father's house, he and the men that followed him, and Abram served the Lord his God all the days of his life, and he walked in his ways and followed his law. And from that day forward Abram inclined the hearts of the sons of men to serve the Lord.* **And at that time Nahor and Abram took unto themselves wives, the daughters of their brother Haran; the wife of Nahor was Milca and the name of Abram's wife was Sarai.** *And Sarai, wife of Abram, was barren; she had no offspring in those days." - Jasher 12:39-44*

The above passage indicates that Abram's wife Sarai was the daughter of his brother Haran, who, in turn, was the son of a high-standing prince in Nimrod's court. This made Sarai both a legitimate princess as well as Abram's cousin. Interestingly, the name "Sarai" as well as Sarai's future name "Sarah" can also mean "princess." In addition, as revealed earlier in this book, Abram's father Terah was a high-ranking, idolatrous prince in Nimrod's court. This means that both Abram and Sarai were the children of highly placed nobles in Babylon. Furthermore, Abram obtained riches from Noah and Shem, from his father Terah and brother Haran's estates, and from Nimrod after he survived being thrown into the fiery furnace at Nimrod's hands. This ensured that Abram never suffered materially, and became a fabulously wealthy man long before his death.

In addition to these sources of wealth, Abram would have been blessed by the dowry of his princess wife Sarai. He also acquired wealth when, like Pharaoh had earlier, the Philistine king Abimelech gave Abraham many gifts in compensation for attempting to steal Sarah away from him (Jasher 20:24-25). It is therefore highly likely that Abraham could afford to live in high style despite his status as a semi-nomadic wanderer, and that his robes were finely woven and richly embroidered rather than the dull rags that movie producers and religious artists invariably envision both him and Moses in. Indeed, as a former Prince of Egypt and King of Cush, Moses certainly would have had some wealth accrued by the time he made his way to Midian and got thrown in prison by Reuel, who was an advisor to Pharaoh and likely saw Moses as a fugitive from both Egyptian and Cushite justice (Jasher 67:24, 72:1-42, 73:1-48, 76:12, 76:22-23).

Based on these facts, Abraham was no mere shepherd when he left Ur. Instead, he would have lived much like the fabulously wealthy

Bedouin desert princes of Arabia did in medieval times and still do today. In addition, as a way to increase his wealth, Abram may have acted as a traveling merchant, and likely trained his male servants that were acquired in Nimrod's Babylon to be businessmen and craftsmen as well as warriors who protected Abram's household caravan on its travels. As indicated in the Bible, the several hundred well-armed and powerful men that Abraham had in his household helped him to rescue Lot (Genesis 14:14).

Abraham and Melchizedek Against Nimrod and the Giants

Early in the Bible record of Abraham's life story, a special event occurred that marked a great turning point in his life. The Bible records that Abraham met with a remarkable priest and king named Melchizedek, which means "King of Righteousness" (Genesis 14:18-19). Note that, in the following excerpt from the Book of Jasher that records this same allegorically and prophetically charged meeting, **Melchizedek is called Adonizedek, and is identified as the patriarch Shem, the son of Noah:**

> "And Abram recovered all the property of Sodom, and he also recovered Lot and his property, his wives and little ones and all belonging to him, so that Lot lacked nothing. And when he returned from smiting these kings, he and his men passed the valley of Siddim where the kings had made war together. And Bera king of Sodom, and the rest of his men that were with him, went out from the lime pits into which they had fallen, to meet Abram and his men.

> **And Adonizedek king of Jerusalem, the same was Shem,** went out with his men to meet Abram and his people, with bread and wine, and they remained together in the valley of Melech. And Adonizedek blessed Abram, and Abram gave him a tenth from all... the spoil of his enemies, for Adonizedek was a priest before God." - Jasher 16:8-12.

From this, it is clear that the title Adonizedek, which means "Lord of Righteousness," meant almost the same thing as Melchizedek and referred to the same person. Incidentally, the term "Adoni" or "Adonai" means "Lord" and was used to refer to Yahshua in His First Advent role as the Son of God. Interestingly, Noah's son Shem's name means "named" and "renowned" and the term "Ha Shem" or "The Name" is used to obliquely refer to God's personal Name "Yahweh" by the Jews to this day. In addition, "Melchizedek" and "Adonizedek" were not personal names but titles for kings - particularly for one king named Shem. It is therefore likely that Shem's name and titles were prophetic of his role in spreading, upholding and preserving the knowledge of Yahweh Elohim. As such, Melchizedek/Shem was a prefiguration of Christ, who will be the everlasting Priest and King over the New Jerusalem and its Temple to Yahweh (Hebrews 7:1-21).

Now, Melchizedek was the king of the fortified city called Salem, which means "peace" in Hebrew. This ancient city was also known as "Jerusalem," which means "Shower (or Rain) of Peace." Now, the Bible tells us that King Melchizedek was a priest of *"God Most High, Creator of Heaven and Earth"* (Genesis 14:18-19). God Most High (i.e. El Elyon in Hebrew) means nearly the same thing as Elohim, and was another title for Yahweh. Shem therefore worshipped and served Yahweh, just as Abraham did. It is also likely that the local inhabitants of the area surrounding *Salem* worshipped the same God as Shem, and were his direct descendents.

Now, when speaking to the King of Sodom during his visit with Melchizedek, Abraham addressed El Elyon as Yahweh (Gen. 14:22), thereby indicating that the Sodomites initially worshipped Yahweh as well. However, the Sodomites eventually perverted their religion by adopting many false gods and acting inhospitably to their neighbors, raping and/or robbing any travelers unfortunate enough to visit there (See Jasher 18:11-17 on pages 358). Despite the wickedness of the Sodomites and other peoples of the plains surrounding Sodom, however, Melchizedek remained a king of righteousness who loved Yahweh and worshipped Him alone. For this reason, it is certain that something extraordinary was going on when the priest-king Melchizedek went out to meet Abraham in the Valley of Melech and blessed the patriarch after his great victory against the four kings who attacked Sodom and Gomorrah (Genesis 14:17-20).

As we learned in Chapter Seven, one of those kings was Amraphel, who was none other than Nimrod. Remember also that Noah and Shem had mentored and protected Abraham while he was in hiding from Nimrod, who sought to put him to death after Nimrod's wicked court Magi told him to (See Jasher 9:6 on page 204 and Jasher 8:1-4, 8:8-13 on pages 574 and 575). So, when Abraham (who was still called Abram at that time) paid a tenth of all the booty that he had taken from Nimrod's armies and gave them to this great king and priest who prefigured Christ, Abram was not only giving a tithe to Yahweh and showing great respect and admiration for this priest and king whom he viewed as a superior, but he was also allegorically giving back a portion of what Nimrod had unlawfully stolen from Shem and Noah many years before! Indeed, in Chapter Seven, we learned that Greek Mythology records that Nimrod's armies waged war against Shem and Noah, and either put their descendents to the sword, enslaved them, or subjected them to Nimrod's authority, forcing them to worship strange gods and follow the Way of Cain or the Serpent.

Also, as we discovered in Chapter Six, though the land that came to be called Canaan was originally allotted to Shem and his descendants after the Flood, Canaan decided to settle there rather than go further south into Hamite territory with Ham, Cush, Mizraim and Put. However, it is likely that Shem had already settled in the area of Salem with his household when Canaan arrived there. From archeological data, we know that the city of Jerusalem was fortified with thick stone walls from very early in its history, and it is likely that Shem fortified it to withstand the constant skirmishes that erupted in the region with the Canaanites, who no doubt constantly tried to encroach on Shem's territory. Therefore, the land of Canaan was probably only partly inhabited by Canaanites until after Shem died. Then, by the time of the Exodus, the king of Jerusalem was an Amorite named Adoni-Zedek in mimicry and mockery of Shem's kingly title.

This explains why Yahweh promised the land of Canaan to Abraham. Yahweh was not giving Abraham land that rightfully belonged to another people at all! Instead, God was promising that, as direct descendents of Shem, Abraham's descendants through Isaac would one day regain ownership of a land that was rightfully theirs all along!

Now, though the Amorites were originally descended from Canaan (Genesis 10:15-16), large portions of their territory were being ruled over by the Anakim at the time of the Exodus. For example, the following Scripture chronicling the Israelite conquest of Canaan mentions the Anakim Giant named Og, who was the king of the city called Bashan in Amorite territory:

> "And at that time we took the land from the hand of the two kings of the Amorites who were on this side of the Jordan, from the River Arnon to Mount Hermon... all the cities of the plain, all Gilead, and all Bashan, as far as Salcah and Edrei, cities of the kingdom of Og in Bashan. **For only Og king of Bashan remained of the remnant of the giants.** Indeed his bedstead was an iron bedstead. (Is it not in Rabbah of the people of Ammon?) Nine cubits is its length and four cubits its width, according to the standard cubit." - Deuteronomy 3:8, 10-11 (NKJ)

Most biblical scholars believe that a standard Israelite cubit was about 20 inches, five inches shorter than the cubit used by the Sethites prior to the Flood. But even at this shorter measure, Og's bed would have been 15 feet long! This passage in Deuteronomy also says that Og was the last remaining Anakim alive at that time. However, before that time, Og was not the only Giant ruling in Amorite territory. In fact, the earlier Amorite king Adoni-Zedek was likely part Nephilim. Furthermore, since **Adoni-Zedek was an usurper of Melchizedek's throne, and his ancestors had unlawfully settled in Shem's territory and possibly intermarried with the Anakim, Joshua and his Israelite armies won back what had always rightfully belonged to Abraham and his descendents.** This also explains why Yahweh told Joshua to leave no survivors when they conquered the Canaanites. Joshua was not only killing practitioners of a false, demonically inspired religion, but destroying people and animals that were likely tainted with Anakim genes.

In fact, as recorded in Genesis, Nimrod and the three other kings who attacked Sodom and Gomorrah had earlier gone into the heart of Anakim-held territory and apparently won a resounding victory against the Giants living there (See Genesis 14:5-6 quoted on page 547). This shows that the record of the defeat of the Giants or Gigantes in Greek Myth agrees quite faithfully with Scripture, where it records that these four Mesopotamian kings led a successful war against the Giants called Rephaim, Zuzim, Emim and Horites. But later, when they decided to conquer the cities of the plains that still contained Yahweh-believing descendents of Shem including Lot, Abram took action and won a resounding victory against them with less than 400 soldiers! Tellingly, the Greeks obviously didn't want to acknowledge or record Abram's victory over Nimrod because it showed that the Way of Cain is foolishness, and Yahweh is infinitely greater than man and far stronger than the Serpent or Satan!

Indeed, it was not truly Abram who won the war, but Yahweh Elohim who fought for Abraham and his Yahweh-believing servants trained for war. And it was Yahweh that made Abram and his small band of mighty men a more formidable force than the many thousands of strong men following Nimrod and the Way of Cain that came against them! Now, in acknowledgement of Abram's great faith and heroism in the face of overwhelmingly bad odds...

> "...the word of the LORD (Yahweh) came to Abram in a vision, saying, 'Do not be afraid, Abram. **I am your shield, your exceedingly great reward'**... On the same day the LORD (Yahweh) made a covenant with Abram, saying: 'To your

*descendants I have given this land, from the river of Egypt to
the great river, the River Euphrates-- (the land of) the Kenites,
the Kenezzites, and the Kadmonites, the Hittites, the
Perizzites, and the Rephaim, the Amorites, the Canaanites,
the Girgashites, and the Jebusites.'" - Genesis 15:1, 18-21
(NKJ)*

In this promise made to Abram, Yahweh was saying that all the
lands that were currently held by Canaan's descendents and the part
Nephilim Giants such as the Rephaim and Amorites that stretched from
Egypt to Mesopotamia would one day belong to Abram's spiritual and
literal descendents. Then Yahweh told Abram that, even though he had
not yet had a son of his own, he would one day have literal
descendents that would be as numerous as the stars in the heavens.
Afterward, Yahweh asked Abram to make a bloody path between several
killed and halved animals for a Blood Covenant sacrifice:

*"Then He said to him, 'I am the LORD (Yahweh), who
brought you out of Ur of the Chaldeans, to give you this land
to inherit it. And he (Abram) said, 'Lord GOD, how shall I
know that I will inherit it?' So He said to him, 'Bring Me a
three-year-old heifer, a three-year-old female goat, a three-
year-old ram, a turtledove, and a young pigeon.' Then he
brought all these to Him and cut them in two, down the
middle, and placed each piece opposite the other..." - Genesis
15:5-10 (NKJ)*

Eventually, however, Yahweh passed through the halved animals
alone (Genesis 15:8-21). Abram was not accompanying Yahweh as two
people entering a Covenant usually do because this Covenant was not
dependent on Abram's faithfulness to God. It was an unconditional
divine Blood Covenant dependant on God's faithfulness to Abram alone,
and it showed that God alone would fulfill the Covenant by sacrificing
Himself to pay for any breach in it made by Abram and his spiritual and
literal descendents. This is why, when Abraham was asked to sacrifice
Isaac later on, he did not hesitate to act. Abram likely already knew that
God would one day sacrifice His own Son for the sins of the world, and
God was just testing Abraham to see if he would do the same to pay for
his own sins against God.

Interestingly, just before God passed through the animals, Abram
fell asleep and had a dream vision in which Yahweh said to him:

*"Know certainly that your descendants will be
strangers in a land that is not theirs... and they will afflict
them four hundred years. And also the nation whom they*

serve I will judge; afterward they shall come out with great possessions. Now as for you, you shall go to your fathers in peace... But in the fourth generation they shall return here, for the iniquity of the Amorites is not yet complete.'" - Genesis 15:13-16 (NKJ)

Just as Yahweh prophesied, the twelve sons of Jacob, who were the fourth generation from Abraham, went to live in a strange land that was not their own (Egypt), where they resided and eventually were enslaved over a four hundred year period. Then, after their forty year sojourn in the wilderness, the Israelites destroyed all of the Amorites, just as God foretold:

"Then Israel sent messengers to Sihon king of the Amorites, saying, 'Let me pass through your land. We will not turn aside into fields or vineyards; we will not drink water from wells... until we have passed through your territory.' But Sihon would not allow Israel to pass through his territory. So Sihon... went out against Israel in the wilderness... and fought against Israel. Then Israel defeated him with the edge of the sword, and took possession of his land... So Israel... dwelt in all the cities of the Amorites..." - Numbers 21:21-25 (NKJ)

In this way, Yahweh made the Israelites His right arm of wrath and vengeance against all those who love the Way of Cain over the Way of Yahweh.

Coveters of the Abrahamic Land Covenant

Abraham probably left Ur around 2000 BC, which would have been shortly before Yahweh destroyed Nimrod's Empire by the confusion of tongues and the destruction of the Tower of Babel. After Abram left Ur by divine order, Yahweh God approached Abram at different times to form two Covenants with him, and on both occasions God promised the land stretching from the Nile River through Canaan to the Euphrates River to Abraham's posterity as an everlasting possession. However, these Covenants were not the same. The first of these Covenants was unconditional and applied to anyone who shared Abraham's love for and faith in Yahweh, but especially pertained to Abraham's blood descendents (Genesis 15:1-21). However, the second Covenant was conditional and was based on obedience to the Law of God that is self-evident through the Language of God in nature, the Cosmos, and the rite of blood sacrifice for sin. In addition, this conditional Covenant required the rite of circumcision as the first act of obedience (Genesis 17:1-16).

At that time of the second Covenant marked by circumcision, Abram's name changed to Abraham to reflect his new Covenant relationship with the Creator of the Universe. As part of that Covenant ceremony, each party entering the Covenant took on part of the name of the other party. At this time God changed Abram's name to Abraham, taking the letters "ah" from the first syllable of the name Yahweh and making them the middle syllable of Abram's new name (Genesis 17:4-5). Likewise, Abraham's wife Sarah was originally named Sarai until her name was changed to Sarah to reflect her entrance into the same binding Blood Covenant with Yahweh Elohim (Genesis 17:15). At the same time, Yahweh became known forevermore as Yahweh Elohim, the God of Abraham (Genesis 31:42, 53).

Yahweh God's first Covenant with Abram ascribed the land of Israel to Abram's literal descendants as well as Gentile believers in Yahweh who are grafted into Israel through their faith in Christ, while the second Covenant ascribed the same land to the Israelites for as long as they remained faithful to God's Law and showed love to their neighbors by sharing their faith in Yahweh with them, which they repeatedly failed to do. Therefore, *the land of Israel is not the possession of Jews alone. It was always meant to be shared with all people who love Yahweh regardless of sex, race, or culture*, and this includes any and all Egyptians, Arabs, and Persians that become Christians.

Unfortunately, however, Abraham had many descendents, and nearly all of them eventually thought they were the only heirs of the promises God made to Abraham. In other words, they ignored the fact that God promised that the land of Canaan would become the everlasting habitation of all the righteous, not just Abraham's son Isaac's descendants. They also forgot the promise that Abraham's descendents through Isaac would become a blessing to all people. This was accomplished through a suffering Messiah who offered salvation to the world by the shedding of His innocent blood.

The following account of an aged Abraham instructing his children and grandchildren in the ways of righteousness is taken from the Book of Jubilees. It lists all the immediate descendents of Abraham, gives an idea of what they inherited and where they settled, and records Abraham's final religious instructions and prophetic words to his descendents, which mentions the judgment of the Giants:

> *"And in the forty-second jubilee, in the first year of the seventh week, Abraham called Ishmael, and his twelve*

sons, and Isaac and his two sons, and the six sons of Keturah, and their sons. And he commanded them that they should observe the way of YHWH; that they should work righteousness, and love each his neighbour, and act on this manner amongst all men... **'and let them not take to themselves wives from the daughters of Canaan; for the seed of Canaan will be rooted out of the land.'**

And he told them of the judgment of the giants, and the judgment of the Sodomites, how they had been judged on account of their wickedness, and had died on account of their fornication, and uncleanness, and mutual corruption through fornication. 'And guard yourselves from all fornication and uncleanness, And from all pollution of sin, Lest ye make our name a curse... And ye become accursed like Sodom, And all your remnant as the sons of Gomorrah.'

'I implore you, my sons, love the Elohim of heaven And cleave ye to all His commandments. And walk not after their idols, and after their uncleannesses... For they are vanity, And there is no spirit in them; For they are work of (men's) hands, And all who trust in them, trust in nothing.'

'Serve them not, nor worship them, but serve ye the most high Elohim, and worship Him continually: And hope for His countenance always, And work uprightness and righteousness before Him, That He may have pleasure in you and grant you His mercy... and bless all your works which ye have wrought upon the earth... And bless the fruit of your womb and the fruit of your land... **And ye will be for a blessing on the earth, And all nations of the earth will desire you,** And bless your sons in my name, That they may be blessed as I am.'

And he gave to Ishmael and to his sons, and to the sons of Keturah, gifts, and sent them away from Isaac his son, and he gave everything to Isaac his son. And Ishmael and his sons, and the sons of Keturah and their sons, went together and dwelt from Paran to the entering in of Babylon in all the land which is towards the East facing the desert. And these mingled with each other, and their names are called Arabs, and Ishmaelites." - Jubilees 20:1-13

Interestingly, the final verses in Chapter 20 of Jubilees tell us that the sons of Ishmael and Keturah settled throughout ancient Arabia, which stretched from the borders of Babylon (i.e. Iraq) to the lands east of the Gulf of Aqaba and north of the Indian Ocean. Therefore, the territory where they initially settled and interbred was south of the Dead Sea and included a portion of the Sinai and all of the Arabian Peninsula. In these lands, the Ishmaelites settled and intermarried with Keturah's sons, and together they became the ancestors of the Yahweh-believing Midianites of Moses' day as well as many other people groups. How sad that most of them now identify themselves as Arabs that follow a strange god of terror and darkness instead of Yahweh. And how terribly warped it is that they seek to exterminate not only unsaved Jews who will all one day love Yahshua too, but all Messianic Jews and Christians - the true inheritors of God's promises to Abraham together with the Jews.

Perhaps one of the major catalysts that led the Midianites and other non-Israelite descendants of Abraham into idolatry and Paganism was Esau, who married idol-worshipping, sexually perverse Canaanite women, and then eventually ruled over a large swath of Arabian lands. Indeed, because Yahweh knew Esau would rebel against Yahweh and would not respect his father Isaac and grandfather Abraham's wishes to not marry Canaanite women because they were to be rooted out of the Promised Land one day, God chose Jacob over Esau. Had Esau truly believed in Yahweh and desired to live in the Promised Land, he would have married one of his remote cousins' daughters instead of several Pagan women from among Israel's enemies like the Hivites and Hittites, who lived in Canaan, and the Ishmaelites who lived in neighboring Arabia (in what is now modern Saudi Arabia):

> *"Now this is the genealogy of Esau, who is Edom.*
> *Esau took his wives from the daughters of Canaan: Adah the*
> *daughter of Elon the Hittite; Aholibamah the daughter of*
> *Anah, the daughter of Zibeon the Hivite; and Basemath,*
> *Ishmael's daughter, sister of Nebajoth."   "Then Esau took his*
> *wives, his sons, his daughters, and all... his household, his*
> *cattle and all his animals, and all his goods... gained in the*
> *land of Canaan, and went to a country away from the*
> *presence of his brother Jacob. For their possessions were too*
> *great for them to dwell together... So Esau dwelt in Mount*
> *Seir. Esau is Edom." - Genesis 36:1-3, 6-8 (NKJ)*

Sadly, when Esau's descendants married into the families of Canaan and the Ishmaelites, the enmity between them and Israel grew exponentially. The following portion of Jasher explains what happened between Jacob and Esau just before the famine that led to the reunion of Jacob and his sons with Joseph in Egypt and the settling of Jacob's entire clan in Goshen. It indicates that Esau took all of Isaac's material wealth from Jacob and thereby reaffirmed Jacob's right to claim the land of

Canaan that was promised to Abraham's seed as an everlasting inheritance:

> "And Jacob and Esau buried their father Isaac in the cave of Machpelah, which is in Kireath-arba in Hebron, and they buried him with very great honor, as at the funeral of kings. And Jacob and his sons, and Esau and his sons, and all the kings of Canaan made a great and heavy mourning, and they buried him and mourned for him many days. And at the death of Isaac, he left his cattle and his possessions and all belonging to him to his sons; and Esau said unto Jacob, Behold I pray thee, all that our father has left we will divide it in two parts, and I will have the choice, and Jacob said, We will do so...
>
> And Jacob said unto Esau, 'Hear thou I pray thee what I will speak unto thee, saying, The Lord God of heaven and earth spoke unto our fathers Abraham and Isaac, saying, Unto thy seed will I give this land for an inheritance forever. **Now therefore all that our father has left is before thee, and behold all the land is before thee; choose thou from them what thou desirest.** If thou desirest the whole land take it for thee and thy children forever, and I will take this riches, and it thou desirest the riches take it unto thee, and I will take this land for me and for my children to inherit it forever.'
>
> And Nebayoth, the son of Ishmael, was then in the land with his children, and Esau went on that day and consulted with him... And Nebayoth said... 'behold all the children of Canaan are dwelling securely in their land, and Jacob sayeth he will inherit it with his seed all the days. Go now therefore and take all thy father's riches and leave Jacob thy brother in the land, as he has spoken.' And Esau rose up and returned to Jacob, and did all that Nebayoth the son of Ishmael had advised; and **Esau took all the riches that Isaac had left,** the souls, the beasts, the cattle and the property, and all the riches; he gave nothing to his brother Jacob; and **Jacob took all the land of Canaan, from the brook of Egypt unto the river Euphrates,** and he took it for an everlasting possession, and for his children and for his seed after him forever. Jacob also took from his brother Esau the cave of Machpelah... in Hebron, which Abraham had bought from Ephron for a possession of a burial place for him and his seed forever." - Jasher 47:13-25

Of course, nothing was ever really settled between Esau and Jacob's descendents because some relatives on both sides must have remained bitter over the outcome of this supposedly final exchange between Jacob and Esau in settling their father Isaac's estate. Consequently, the old wounds between these different bloodlines kept being re-opened and were never allowed to heal. In fact, as a direct result of the antagonism felt by Esau's descendants toward the Israelites, God eventually destroyed Esau's kingdom under Saul and David, for both kings fought the Edomites and David's military commander Joab eventually conquered Edom for David (1 Samuel 14:47; 2 Samuel 8:13-14; 1 Kings 11:15-16). This added the Sinai Peninsula and part of the Arabian Peninsula to Israelite held territory and opened the strategically and economically important ports of the Red Sea to Israel's armies and merchants. Not long after, Solomon dramatically exploited these Red Sea ports in order to make Israel one of the richest and most peaceful kingdoms of the Middle East during his reign.

After God's initial judgment against Edom, the prophet Malachi was inspired to express Yahweh's continuing disgust with Edom's choices and the reason for His perpetual wrath against Esau's descendents:

> "'I have loved you,' says the LORD (Yahweh). 'Yet you say, "In what way have You loved us?" Was not Esau Jacob's brother?' Says the LORD (Yahweh). 'Yet Jacob I have loved; But Esau I have hated, and laid waste his mountains and his heritage for the jackals of the wilderness. Even though Edom has said, "We have been impoverished, but we will return and build the desolate places,"' Thus says the LORD of hosts (Yahweh Tsavout): 'They may build, but I will throw down; they shall be called the Territory of Wickedness, and the people against whom the LORD (Yahweh) will have indignation forever.'" - Malachi 1:2-4 (NKJ)

Interestingly, Malachi's prophecy against Edom has no expiration date. This means that God's declaration that He would never allow any Edomite controlled kingdom or nation to reign securely and that He would hold these people in contempt forever is still in effect, and will be until the people of Edom willingly repent and accept Yahshua as their Lord and Savior. However, this is not likely to happen until Yahshua's return, for the people of Edom can now be identified as the Arab Muslims that are the primary inhabitants of many Middle-Eastern nations. Sadly, these Muslim-controlled nations are antagonistic toward anyone who worships Yahweh and Yahshua, so Yahweh's animosity toward the Arab descendents of Esau remains to this day. These Arab nations include Jordan, Syria, Saudi Arabia, Egypt and Iraq, and God will soon exact His ultimate judgment against these nations. In fact, as shown in Book Four, God promises that the final destruction of these Arab nations will occur during the wars that will be fought just before and during the Tribulation period (See Ezekiel, Chapters 38 and 39).

The Palestinian and Davidic Covenants

God's promises to Israel concerning the Promised Land did not end with Jacob. In fact, it was clearly re-affirmed to the Israelites just before they entered Canaan to take the land for Yahweh by force: *"These are the words of the covenant which the LORD (Yahweh) commanded Moses to make with the children of Israel in the land of Moab, besides the covenant which He made with them in Horeb..."* (Deut. 29:1; Also see Deut. 29:12-13). This Covenant promise is commonly and unfortunately known as the Palestinian Covenant. However, the Promised Land was not known as Palestine at that time, but was called Canaan after the wayward son of Cush who unlawfully inhabited this land that rightfully belonged to Shem and his descendants.

At the time of this Covenant that was partly meant to restore the Promised Land to Shem's descendants, God made it clear that the Israelite claim to the land was conditional upon their faithfulness to Yahweh and desire to follow His righteous laws. If any of them failed to love and worship Yahweh and keep His Law, God promised instead to curse them, uproot them and exile them to foreign lands where they would be persecuted and despised (Deut. 29:24-29). Nonetheless, even if they rejected Him for false gods, Yahweh promised that He would never forget His Covenant promises to Abraham and Israel. Indeed, instead of forgetting them forever, Yahweh promised that He would eventually gather the Israelites out of exile and back into the Promised Land. In addition, God promised that they would then acknowledge Him as their God and King forever:

> *"Now it shall come to pass, when all these things come upon you, the blessing and the curse which I have set before you, and you call them to mind among all the nations where the LORD your God (Yahweh your Elohim) drives you, and you return to the LORD your God (Yahweh your Elohim) and obey His voice, according to all that I command you today... that the LORD your God (Yahweh your Elohim) will bring you back from captivity, and have compassion on you, and gather you again from all the nations where the LORD your God (Yahweh your Elohim) has scattered you... Then the LORD*

*your God (Yahweh your Elohim) will bring you to the land
which your fathers possessed, and... He will prosper you and
multiply you more than your fathers.*

*And the LORD your God (Yahweh your Elohim) will
circumcise your heart... to love the LORD your God (Yahweh
you Elohim) with all your heart and with all your soul, that
you may live. Also the LORD your God (Yahweh your Elohim)
will put all these curses on your enemies... who persecuted
you. And you will again obey the voice of the LORD (Yahweh)
and do all His commandments... The LORD (Yahweh)... will
then make you abound in all the work of your hand, in the
fruit of your body, in the increase of your livestock, and in the
produce of your land for good. For the LORD (Yahweh) will
again rejoice over you..." - Deut. 30:1-9 (NKJ)*

This promise to Israel that Yahweh would restore them to the
Promised Land after a period of exile and greatly bless them while
cursing their enemies is repeated many times in the prophetic literature
of the Old Testament. See Jeremiah Chapter 29, verses 11 thru 14 for
another powerful example of this promise. Now, though this prophecy
was initially fulfilled when a portion of Israel returned to rebuild
Jerusalem and the Temple to Yahweh after their 70-year Babylonian
Captivity, it has also been miraculously repeated in the last century
despite the unbelief of many of the Jews living in Israel today. Indeed,
even that will soon change, for Yahweh has vowed to bring all of their
hearts back to Him forever:

*"Thus says the Lord GOD (Yahweh Elohim): "I will
gather you from the... countries where you have been
scattered, and I will give you the land of Israel. And they will
go there, and they will take away all its detestable things and
all its abominations from there. Then I will give them one
heart, and I will put a new spirit within them... that they may
walk in My statutes and keep My judgments and do them;
and they shall be My people, and I will be their God." -
Ezekiel 11:17-20 (NKJ)*

Note that this prophecy indicates that the Jews living in modern
Israel will cleanse the Promised Land of the detestable things that are
there, and then they will be given the Holy Spirit and be saved. Could
this mean that the Al Aqsa Mosque, which is dedicated to a detestable,
demonic god named Allah, will be destroyed before Yahshua's return?

In addition to the Covenant over the Promised Land, Yahweh
made a specific promise to King David of Israel concerning the

establishment and preservation of David's Throne and reign over Israel and Judah through his son Solomon. This promise is known as the Davidic Covenant and was delivered to David by Nathan the prophet shortly after David brought the Ark of the Covenant to Jerusalem to rest in the new Tabernacle that David had built for it:

> "And it shall be... when you must go to be with your fathers, that I will set up your seed after you, who will be of your sons; and I will establish his kingdom. **He shall build Me a house, and I will establish his throne forever.** I will be his Father, and he shall be My son; and I will not take My mercy away from him, as I took it from him who was before you. And I will establish him in My house and in My kingdom forever; and his throne shall be established forever. According to all these words and according to all this vision, so Nathan spoke to David." - 1 Chronicles 17:11-15 (NKJ)

Though many have attempted to discredit the Davidic Covenant by saying that the Davidic line of kings ended when Nebuchadnezzar conquered the Kingdom of Judah and killed all of the king's sons, God never promised that the Davidic royal bloodline would reign in an unbroken chain forever, or that Solomon's throne would be established forever. In fact, God spoke to Solomon and told him that his house or throne and his kingdom would be destroyed if they broke their Covenant with God:

> "But if you or your sons at all turn from following Me, and do not keep My commandments and My statutes which I have set before you, but go and serve other gods and worship them, then I will cut off Israel from the land which I have given them; and this house which I have consecrated for My name I will cast out of My sight. Israel will be a proverb and a byword among all peoples." - I Kings 9:6-7 (NKJ)

Sadly, though the Kingdom of Israel was a glorious land at its richest and most powerful under Solomon's reign, Solomon was unfaithful to God later in life because he let his heart be swayed by the many foreign women with Pagan beliefs that he married. As it says in Scripture:

> "But King Solomon loved many foreign women, as well as the daughter of Pharaoh: women of the Moabites, Ammonites, Edomites, Sidonians, and Hittites - from the nations of whom the LORD (Yahweh) had said... 'You shall not intermarry with them, nor they with you. Surely they will turn away your hearts after their gods.' Solomon clung to

these in love. And he had seven hundred wives... and his wives turned away his heart... and his heart was not loyal to the LORD his God (Yahweh his Elohim), as was the heart of his father David... **Solomon did evil in the sight of the LORD (Yahweh)...** *" - I Kings 11:1-6 (NKJ)*

In short, despite all his wisdom, King Solomon was a fool for women! That is why Solomon allowed his lust and love of sensuality to lead him into the perverted worship of deities that encouraged and condoned such behavior! This shows that even great human wisdom is not enough to ensure a person's ability to be righteous by God's uncompromisingly perfect standards. And, as a direct consequence of his sin, King Solomon brought down the curse of Yahweh, which stated that God would send Israel into exile and destroy Solomon's royal house if Solomon or his sons worshipped other gods.

In light of this, isn't it interesting that the Freemasons are constantly referring to King Solomon and his half Tyrian and half Danite architect Hiram in their Masonic rites and rituals? Isn't it curious that they honor and admire a king of Israel who allowed his love of sensuality to dominate his spiritual course and sway him to worship demons and do evil in the sight of Almighty God? Isn't it sad that **they also uplift a half Pagan and half Danite architect** that helped to build the first Temple to Yahweh in Jerusalem and they ascribe all sorts of occult and magical meaning to the two bronze pillars Hiram cast for either side of the Temple entrance? How telling that this once top secret organization is now so openly hostile about their contempt of God, those who love God, and the Bible today! Perhaps it is a reflection of their belief that the forces of darkness have won, and their true god Satan is now about to regain Solomon's Throne through a direct descendent of Solomon and Christ! Could that be Barack Obama - perhaps through Solomon's Ethiopian lineage descended from the Queen of Sheba? Or is it Prince Charles of Wales - who may be descended from King Zedekiah's daughters? Only time will tell.

So, though British-Israelists claim that the last reigning king of Judah's daughters escaped to England with Jeremiah the prophet and established the Throne of Judah there by marrying into the ruling families of the British Isles (which may or may not be true), the real fulfillment of the Davidic Covenant was never meant to be fulfilled on a fallible earthly throne, but on a perfect heavenly one. As Psalm 110, which was written by King David, says:

"The LORD (Yahweh) said to my Lord (Adonai or Yahshua!), 'Sit at My right hand, till I make Your enemies Your footstool.'" - Psalm 110:1 (NKJ)

This was nothing less than a prophecy that David's Messiah and Lord would one day reign in his stead at God's right hand, and it is reiterated many times in the New Testament in regard to Yahshua alone. Indeed, one of the most succinct explanations of the meaning of this Psalm was offering by Yahshua Himself:

> *"While the Pharisees were... together, Jesus asked them, saying, 'What do you think about the Christ? Whose Son is He?' They said to Him, 'The Son of David.' He said to them, 'How then does David in the Spirit call Him "Lord," saying: 'The Lord said to my Lord, "Sit at My right hand, till I make Your enemies Your footstool" '? If David... calls Him "Lord," how is He his Son?'" - Matthew 22:41-45 (NKJ)*

See Mark 16:19, Ephesians 1:20 and Hebrews 12:2 for a few examples where Yahshua's place at the right hand of God the Father's throne is reaffirmed. Incidentally, Psalm 110 correlates to the year 2010, and this is one of the years that the Great Pyramid interior passages targeted as significant. Though I am uncertain, I strongly believe that it may be tied to the year before the seven-year Tribulation period, which will end with Yahshua defeating His enemies at the Battle of Armageddon in order to make way for His Millennial Reign on the Earth.

Besides Psalm 110, where David acknowledges his coming Messiah as the King of Israel, the genealogies of Christ listed in the New Testament indicate that God fulfilled His Covenant with David through his son Nathan on Yahshua's father Joseph's side (2 Samuel 5:14; Luke 3:31) and through Jeconiah, one of King Josiah of Judah's sons that never sat on the Throne of Israel on Yahshua's mother Miriam's side (Mat. 1:10-12). Since King Josiah was a direct descendent of King Solomon and also was one of the most righteous kings of Israel, his princely son Jeconiah's descendents were certainly capable of helping to fulfill God's promise to David. Therefore, Yahshua's parental lineage shows that He was fully capable of establishing David's Throne forever.

Besides his royal pedigree on both parental sides, Yahshua's mother Miriam was told by an angel that she would conceive and bear a Son who was the promised Messiah and King that would reign on David's throne forever:

> *"And behold, you will conceive in your womb and bring forth a Son, and shall call His name Jesus (Yahshua). He will be great, and will be called the Son of the Highest; and the Lord God will give Him the throne of His father David. And He will reign over the house of Jacob forever, and of His kingdom there will be no end." - Luke 1:31-33 (NKJ)*

This prophecy told Miriam that she had been chosen to bear the Messiah and King of all Israel in her womb, and she was overjoyed by the prospect despite the danger it placed her in. However, this prophecy also eventually caused Miriam and her other children much grief. This is because Yahshua refused to stand up to His adversaries in Jerusalem, announce plainly who He was, and provide the necessary miracles to convince one and all that their longed-for Messiah had come. But later, this same prophecy was recalled for the comfort it offered to them when they realized that Yahshua had not come to serve as their King on Earth yet. Instead, Yahshua had come to redeem Israel from sin and to serve as their King on a heavenly throne and within their hearts. But Yahshua also promised to return one day, at which time they knew He would save Israel from tyranny and set up the Throne of David on Earth just as it has already been set up in Heaven.

Indeed, since the Throne of David and Solomon was to be established forever, this prophecy could not have been fulfilled by anyone else! This is because - in order to reign forever - a Prince of Judah would have had to cheat death and live forever! That feat has so far only been accomplished by one man in the history of Israel and when Yahshua takes His rightful place on Israel's Throne here on Earth, He will reign upon it through eternity. Hallelu-Yah for our coming King of kings, whose heavenly Father is, was and always will be the King of the Universe!

Ominously, however, not everyone who calls themselves a Christian believes that Yahshua died, rose from the dead, ascended to Heaven, sits at the Father's right hand, and will return to Earth someday soon to save humanity from themselves and establish His kingdom on Earth forever. Instead, they think Yahshua gave birth to children through Mary Magdalene and then died an ordinary death. They also think that His bloodline has been preserved and a future Messiah will be born from this bloodline. But what these deceived people do not realize is that this whole story is a prefabricated lie meant to hide the identity of the true bloodline it preserves, which is the Serpent seed line that Azazel established through his human consort Naamah!

Israel - Destroyer of the Anakim That Survived the Flood

As already mentioned, there is much biblical evidence that some Nephilim survived the Flood. Indeed, Moses made this clear when he wrote: *"There were giants on the earth in those days, and also afterward"* (Genesis 6:4). Ancient legends maintain that, though forbidden entrance onto Noah's Ark, some of the Nephilim survived the

Flood below ground in an underground cavern that must have been well-stocked with food and other provisions. This means that some of the Nephilim must have taken Noah's dire warnings of imminent destruction by flood seriously. At the time of the Exodus, the Bible records that the descendents of these Nephilim populated many regions in and around the land of Canaan. As previously stated, these giants were called Emim, Rephaim and Anakim (Genesis 14:5, 15:20; Deuteronomy 1:28, 2:10-11; Joshua 11:21-22, 18:16).

The Amorites, Horites, and Hivites were biblically depicted as giants in stature and strength and were considered to be descendents of the Anakim/Nephilim who survived the Flood and intermarried with humans (Genesis 14:5,6; Amos 2:1,9). Before the Flood, the Nephilim and fallen angels demanded that men either worship them or perish. Therefore, they became the false gods of many different Pagan mythologies. According to 1 Enoch, the Nephilim offspring of the fallen angels were violent and bloodthirsty monsters that sought to destroy humanity. That is why God destroyed most of them in the Great Flood. Sadly, however, they were not completely exterminated and - just as they did before the Flood - the Anakim descendants of the Nephilim and their demonic spirits have successfully led many people to worship the Nephilim, fallen angels, and demons as gods once more. But, for a short time, there was a very blessed ancient people group that was especially chosen to worship and serve the one true God Yahweh alone. These were the Israelites, who left Egypt as faithless slaves but arrived at the borders of Canaan forty years later as a faith-filled and battle-hardened nation of conquerors.

As the Israelites infiltrated the land of Canaan, their faith in Yahweh gave them a supreme military advantage, for it was Yahweh's angelic armies that went before the Israelites and helped them conquer all the Anakim and Rephaim-held territory in Canaan. In the Book of Deuteronomy, Moses gives an account of how he directed Joshua to lead the Israelites to do battle in Canaan. In several places where Lot's descendents settled, Moses instructed Joshua not to invade these lands. Moses also noted that the giant descendents of the Nephilim called Emim and Zamzummim once lived in these places before Lot and his clan destroyed them and inhibited the land in their stead:

> "Then the LORD (Yahweh) said to me, 'Do not harass Moab, nor contend with them in battle, for I will not give you any of their land as a possession, because I have given Ar to the descendants of Lot...' (The Emim had dwelt there in times past, a people as great and numerous and tall as the Anakim. They were also regarded as giants, like the Anakim, but the

*Moabites call them Emim. The Horites formerly dwelt in Seir,
but the descendants of Esau... destroyed them... and dwelt in
their place, just as Israel did to the land... which the LORD
(Yahweh) gave them.)" - Deuteronomy 2:9-12 (NKJ)*

*"'And when you come near the people of Ammon, do
not harass them or meddle with them, for I will not give you
any of the land of the people of Ammon... because I have
given it to the descendants of Lot as a possession.' (That was
also regarded as a land of giants... ...the Ammonites call them
Zamzummim, a people as great and numerous and tall as the
Anakim. But the LORD (Yahweh) destroyed them... and they
(i.e. Lot's descendents) dispossessed them and dwelt in their
place, just as He had done for the descendants of Esau, who
dwelt in Seir, when He destroyed the Horites from before
them...)." - Deuteronomy 2:19-22 (NKJ)*

Though God spared the Ammonites from invasion during
Joshua's day, He did not do so when David was King in Israel, for
Israel's armies eventually were provoked by the Ammonites and
defeated them in battle (1 Chronicles 20:1-3). But at the time of Joshua,
instead of entering the lands of the Ammonites, the Israelites focused
their attention on the lands that were east of the Jordan River - from
Mount Hermon in the north to the cities of the plain in the south where
Sodom and Gomorrah once had been. At this time, Joshua also
destroyed the Anakim stronghold of Bashan in the hill country of the
north. Here are two detailed biblical accounts of Israel's conquest of this
of area around Canaan:

*"Then we turned and went up the road to Bashan; and
Og king of Bashan came out against us, he and all his people,
to battle at Edrei. And the LORD (Yahweh) said to me, 'Do
not fear him, for I have delivered him and all his people and
his land into your hand; you shall do to him as you did to
Sihon king of the Amorites, who dwelt at Heshbon.' So the
LORD our God (Yahweh our Elohim) also delivered into our
hands Og king of Bashan, with all his people, and we attacked
him until he had no survivors remaining.*

*And we took all his cities at that time... sixty cities, all
the... kingdom of Og in Bashan. All these cities were fortified
with high walls.. besides a great many rural towns. **And we
utterly destroyed them, as we did to Sihon king of Heshbon,
utterly destroying the men, women, and children of every
city. But all the livestock and the spoil of the cities we took as
booty for ourselves. And at that time we took the land from***

the hand of the two kings of the Amorites who were on this side of the Jordan, from the River Arnon to Mount Hermon... all the cities of the plain, all Gilead, and all Bashan, as far as Salcah and Edrei, cities of the kingdom of Og in Bashan.

For only Og king of Bashan remained of the remnant of the giants. Indeed his bedstead was an iron bedstead. (Is it not in Rabbah of the people of Ammon?) Nine cubits is its length and four cubits its width, according to the standard cubit. And this land, which we possessed at that time... I gave to the Reubenites and the Gadites. The rest of Gilead, and all Bashan, the kingdom of Og, I gave to half the tribe of Manasseh. (All the region of Argob, with all Bashan, was called the land of the giants. Jair the son of Manasseh took all the region of Argob... and called Bashan after his own name, Havoth Jair, to this day.) And I gave Gilead to Machir." - Deut. 3:1-15 (NKJ)

"These are the kings of the land whom the children of Israel defeated, and whose land they possessed on the other side of the Jordan toward the rising of the sun, from the River Arnon to Mount Hermon, and all the eastern Jordan plain: One king was Sihon king of the Amorites, who dwelt in Heshbon and ruled half of Gilead, from Aroer, which is on the bank of the River Arnon, from the middle of that river, even as far as the River Jabbok, which is the border of the Ammonites, and the eastern Jordan plain from the Sea of Chinneroth (i.e. Gennesaret, another name for the Sea of Galilee) as far as the Sea of the Arabah (the Salt Sea - i.e. the Dead Sea), the road to Beth Jeshimoth, and southward...

The other king was Og king of Bashan... who was of the remnant of the giants, who dwelt at Ashtaroth and at Edrei, and reigned over Mount Hermon, over Salcah, over all Bashan, as far as the border of the Geshurites and the Maachathites, and over half of Gilead to the border of Sihon king of Heshbon. These Moses... and the children of Israel had conquered; and Moses the servant of the LORD (Yahweh) had given it as a possession to the Reubenites, the Gadites, and half the tribe of Manasseh." - Joshua 12:1-6 (NKJ)

Though the Israelites under Joshua utterly destroyed many of the Anakim and the people groups their strange flesh had contaminated, they either did not annihilate all of the Anakim or Rephaim that inhabited Canaan or a few of those Giants fled and eventually returned to the area. Therefore, the descendents of these Giants continued to be

Israel's enemies. During the time of David, for example, a few descendents of the Rephaim Giants inhabited the coastal lands still controlled by the Philistines. In fact, Goliath - the Giant that David slew with a stone flung from a slingshot - was one of these Rephaim. Later, David and his mighty men had to contend with several more of the offspring of Goliath of Gath. But by this time, David had gotten older and was not as strong and quick as he once had been, so one of the Giants they fought almost killed him one day. This frightened David's mighty men so much that they demanded that he retire from combat. This story is recorded in the following Scripture:

> "When the Philistines were at war again with Israel, David and his servants... went down and fought against the Philistines; and David grew faint. **Then Ishbi-Benob... one of the sons of the giant, the weight of whose bronze spear was three hundred shekels... thought he could kill David.** But Abishai the son of Zeruiah came to his aid, and struck the Philistine and killed him. **Then the men of David swore to him, saying, 'You shall go out no more with us to battle, lest you quench the lamp of Israel.'**
>
> Now it happened afterward that there was again a battle with the Philistines at Gob. **Then Sibbechai the Hushathite killed Saph, who was one of the sons of the giant.** Again there was war at Gob with the Philistines, where **Elhanan the son of Jaare-Oregim the Bethlehemite killed the brother of Goliath** the Gittite, the shaft of whose spear was like a weaver's beam. **Yet again there was war at Gath, where there was a man of great stature, who had six fingers on each hand and... foot, twenty-four in number; and he also was born to the giant.** So when he defied Israel, Jonathan the son of Shimea, David's brother, killed him. These four were born to the giant in Gath, and fell by the hand of David and... his servants." - 2 Samuel 21:15-22 (NKJ)

There is a parallel record of this same period in history in 1 Chronicles 20:1-8, which offers some tantalizing details missing in the earlier account:

> "It happened in the spring of the year... that Joab led out the armed forces and ravaged the country of the people of Ammon, and... Joab defeated Rabbah and overthrew it. **Then David took their king's crown from his head, and found it to weigh a talent of gold, and there were precious stones in it. And it was set on David's head.** Also he brought out the spoil of the city in great abundance. And he brought out the people

who were in it, and put them to work with saws, with iron picks, and with axes. So David did to all the cities of the people of Ammon. Then David and all the people returned to Jerusalem.

*Now it happened afterward that war broke out at Gezer with the Philistines, at which time **Sibbechai the Hushathite killed Sippai, who was one of the sons of the giant...** Again there was war with the Philistines, and **Elhanan the son of Jair killed Lahmi the brother of Goliath the Gittite, the shaft of whose spear was like a weaver's beam.** Yet again there was war at Gath, where **there was a man of great stature, with twenty-four fingers and toes, six on each hand and... foot; and he also was born to the giant.** So when he defied Israel, Jonathan the son of Shimea, David's brother, killed him." - 1 Chron. 20:1-8 (NKJ)*

This passage from 1 Chronicles shows the partial fulfillment of Noah's curse against Canaan yet again as the people of Ammon were defeated and put to work for the Israelites as their servants. Incidentally, the enforced servitude of all the non-Israelite inhabitants of the Promised Land was fully carried out during the reign of King Solomon, who needed much forced labor to build his palace and the Temple to Yahweh. He also used these laborers to build up Israel's defenses and to build his storehouse cities in Judah (1 Kings 9:15-21).

The preceding passage in 1 Chronicles that records the demise of Goliath's Rephaim children at the hand's of David's mighty men also mentions a magnificent solid gold crown weighing one talent that David claimed as booty. This crown had belonged to the defeated King of Rabbah in Ammon, who most likely was an Anakim or Rephaim Giant. Now, according to the International Standard Bible Dictionary notation for the monetary unit called a "talent," one talent is equal to about 120 pounds troy or 96 pounds avoirdupois, and one "avoirdupois" pound is the current weight of one US pound. As such, this crown that David wore weighed nearly one hundred pounds or about 46 kilograms!

With all the heavy gold and precious stones in it, this crown must have been positively spectacular. Yet one wonders how David could have worn it without having super-human power due to its heaviness, or if successive kings of Judah ever wore it. In addition, it raises the question of where this magnificent crown ended up. Was it taken as plunder in ancient times and dismantled to make other trinkets, or was it buried with David's remains when he died? All we do know for certain is this: no solid gold crown weighing over 90 pounds has ever surfaced in modern times. Even the spectacular Imperial State Crown of

England with its huge diamond called the Cullinan II only weighs 910 grams, or a little over 2 pounds! Therefore, the whereabouts of David's crown that was acquired as spoils in war remains a mystery.

In addition to his missing crown, the massive sword that David acquired after killing Goliath has never turned up anywhere. Of course, just as God made sure that Moses' tomb was never found, no one knows where David's tomb is located either. So one is left to wonder if David's magnificent possessions still exist and if Yahshua will find and display these items during the Millennium as a testimony of the Kingdom of Israel's existence and King David's greatness. One also may wonder if the Antichrist covets these priceless items and if he knows where to find them or has acquired them. But if he has or will, it is likely that Yahshua will reacquire these symbols of David's success as a warrior and king of Israel at the appointed time.

Interestingly, there is another priceless item that may turn up in Yahshua's right hand during the Millennial Kingdom: the Staff of Yahweh, which was otherwise known as Joseph's Stick. We will explore the lore surrounding this amazing symbol of Yahweh's authority and power in the next two sections.

What Moses, King David, and King Arthur Had In Common

Besides the fact that both the Patriarch Joseph and Moses were hailed as Princes of Egypt, another little-known connection between them exists, and it is found in the Staff of Yahweh. This is the same staff that Moses used to show the Israelites many miraculous signs from Yahweh. As mentioned earlier and in Book Two, this supernaturally forged staff marked Moses and Aaron as Yahweh's choice of leader and high priest. At the same time, this staff served as a physical manifestation of God's power. As such, it represented Yahweh's love and desire to protect His people, as well as the rod of correction Yah allegorically wields to shape people into useful disciples. The Book of Jasher teaches that each Patriarch who led the righteous descendants of Seth once carried the Staff of Yahweh as a mark of authority:

> "And when God had driven Adam from the Garden of Eden, he took the stick in his hand and went and tilled the ground... And the stick came down to Noah and was given to Shem and his descendants, until it came into the hand of Abraham the Hebrew. And when Abraham had given all he had to his son Isaac, he also gave to him this stick. And when Jacob had fled to Padan-aram, he took it into his hand... Also

when he went down to Egypt he took it into his hand and
gave it to Joseph, one portion above his brethren, for Jacob
had taken it by force from his brother Esau." - Jasher 77:43-48

Interestingly, we are told that Jacob fought with Esau to acquire
Joseph's Stick, which means that Isaac may have given the stick to Esau
before Jacob became Isaac's primary heir. But since Jacob was now the
ruling patriarch over God's people and he was the heir to God's
Covenant promise over the land, Joseph's Stick also belonged to him as a
symbol of Jacob's leadership and authority. The Book of Jasher also
records that Moses obtained the stick by being the only man deemed
worthy enough to pull it from the ground. You see, Reuel (a.k.a. Jethro,
prince and priest of Midian and, later, Moses' father-in-law) had taken
the staff after the patriarch Joseph died, and planted the staff in the
ground - probably as a result of God's revealing His will to Reuel. In
"The Legends of the Jews," compiler Louis Ginzberg recorded that Reuel
or Jethro stole this staff from Pharaoh, who took it from Joseph's
apartments after he died. This legend was probably derived from the
Book of Jasher, where the rod is called *"Joseph's Stick:"*

> *"And when Pharaoh heard the words of Jethro he was*
> *very angry with him, so that he rose with shame from the*
> *king's presence, and went to Midian... **and took Joseph's stick***
> ***with him**." - Jasher 67:41*

As shown in the following quote taken from the Book of Jasher,
Jethro or Reuel planted the rod or stick that once belonged to Joseph
deep into the ground so that only the top and inscribed crook of the staff
was visible:

> *"And after the death of Joseph, the nobles of Egypt*
> *came into the house of Joseph, and the stick came into the*
> *hand of Reuel the Midianite, and when he went out of Egypt,*
> *he took it in his hand and planted it in his garden." - Jasher*
> *77:48*

Reuel then offered his daughter Zipporah's hand in marriage to
anyone who could retrieve Joseph's Stick from the ground:

> *"And all the mighty men of the Kinites tried to pluck*
> *it when they endeavored to get Zipporah his daughter, but*
> *they were unsuccessful. **So that stick remained planted in the***
> ***garden of Reuel**, until he came who had a right to it." - Jasher*
> *77:49-50*

Though many strong men tried, the staff was immovable until
Moses came and miraculously pulled it out of the ground:

*"And... Moses went into the garden of Reuel which
was behind the house, and he there prayed to the Lord his
God, who had done mighty wonders for him. And... whilst he
prayed he looked opposite to him, and behold - a sapphire
stick was... planted in the midst of the garden. And he
approached the stick and he looked, and behold the name of
the Lord God of hosts was engraved thereon, written and
developed upon the stick. And **he read it and stretched forth
his hand and he plucked it** like a forest tree from the thicket,
and the stick was in his hand..." "And **when Reuel saw the
stick in the hand of Moses... he gave him his daughter
Zipporah** for a wife." - Jasher 77:38-41, 77:51.*

Amazed that Moses had claimed the stick, Reuel did as he had
sworn and gave Zipporah's hand in marriage to Moses. This made
Moses not only a renegade Prince of Egypt and former adopted King of
Cush (read part of this story in Chapter Nine), but a desert Prince of
Midian, and - by virtue of his possession of the Staff of Yahweh - the
chosen leader of the Israelites as well. In fact, the Book of Jasher and the
Bible concur in reporting that Moses and Aaron both used this
mysterious and wondrous Sapphire Stick or Staff to perform wonderful
miracles during the Exodus, and for a time during the Israelites'
subsequent forty-year sojourn in the Sinai and Arabian wilderness. Here
are some passages mentioning this stick, which was also called a staff or
rod:

*"**And this is the stick with which all the works of our
God were performed**, after he had created heaven and earth,
and all the host of them, seas, rivers and all their fishes." -
Jasher 77:42*

*"Then Moses took his wife and his sons and set them
on a donkey, and he returned to the land of Egypt. **And
Moses took the rod of God in his hand**." - Exodus 4:20 (NKJ -
[staff of God, NIV])*

*"Moses said to Joshua, 'Choose some of our men and
go out to fight the Amalekites. Tomorrow **I will stand on top
of the hill with the staff of God in my hands**.'" - Exodus 17:9
(NIV)*

In regard to prophecy, it is important to note that these passages
alternatively call Moses' staff a stick like a shepherd would hold, a rod
like a judge would wield, and a staff like a king would display as a sign
of his authority. Did you also note that the story of Moses' retrieval of
the staff is very similar to the legend of King Arthur and his acquisition

of the mighty, magical sword Excalibur? Is it possible that the story of how Moses acquired the Staff of Yahweh and used it to shepherd and protect the Twelve Tribes of Israel was available to medieval scholars, and - in conjunction with the tales in the British Edda - were the inspiration for the beloved legends of King Arthur?

Since the copy of the Book of Jasher available to us today has been traced to the medieval period, it is possible that Arthurian legends were heavily influenced by the Book of Jasher. Along with many other biblical and extra-biblical manuscripts, the Book of Jasher may have been procured and preserved by a few select people among the European and English nobility, who twisted its contents to serve and support their own nefarious desires. Nonetheless, as a work likely deemed uncanonical by the Church, the Upright Record was not available to study in most monasteries, and this may be why it was virtually unknown until a copy of it resurfaced and was made available to scholars in more recent times.

What Happened to the Staff of Yahweh?

The story of the Sapphire Stick or Staff of Yahweh that is found in the Book of Jasher is incomplete as it does not tell us what happened to the Staff after Moses plucked it out of the ground. However, that is not all we know of the Staff, since it is also mentioned dozens of times in the Bible. As shown in Chapter Ten of Book Two and in the Bible quotes found in the preceding section of this chapter, the Staff's history is connected to Moses and Aaron, who both used this staff to lead and protect the people of Israel during their forty years of desert wandering. In the Bible, Joseph's Stick was called the rod or staff of God as well as Aaron's staff. This is the same rod that turned into a serpent and gobbled up the serpents that came from Pharaoh's magician's staffs (Exodus 7:11-12). It was also used by Moses to part the Red Sea so that the Israelites could escape from Pharaoh's chariots (Exodus 14:16).

During the Israelite's desert sojourn, the miraculous Staff of Yahweh was eventually given to Aaron as a symbol of his authority over the Levite clan and the special line of priests that came from Aaron's lineage. In fact, this staff that was made by God at the dawn of human history and had served as a powerful tool in the hands of many generations of patriarchs miraculously sprouted overnight with an almond branch complete with leaves and ripe almonds to show God's approval of the Levite priesthood (Numbers 17:5-11). This put a stop to the rebellion against Moses and Aaron by the Levite named Korah, who felt that the priesthood should be extended to include all the tribes of Israel (Numbers 16:1-3). After it sprouted, the rod was set before the Ark of the Covenant in the Most Holy Place inside the Desert Tabernacle. Then, eventually, it found its way inside the Ark along with a golden jar of Manna and the stone tablets of the Law (Hebrews 9:4).

Not long after this, God called Moses to retrieve the rod from the Most Holy Place and use it to split a rock from which a pure spring of water gushed out in the desert (Numbers 20:7-11). This was done to end the bitter complaining of the Israelites, who were weak and dehydrated from a lack of water. However, it was also a symbol of the Messiah to come, who would become the *"Rock of our Salvation"* and the *"Living Water."* After this, the Staff of Yahweh is not cited again until David mentioned it as bringing him comfort during his exile in the wilderness as he hid from King Saul's wrath:

> *"Yea, though I walk through the valley of the shadow of death, I will fear no evil; for You are with me;* **your rod and Your staff, they comfort me.**" - Psalm 23:4 (NKJ)

There, in the beautiful passages of the Shepherd's Psalm, David poetically revealed that he was in possession of that mighty rod of power! It therefore likely continued to serve as David's rod of authority when he became king over all Israel. As if in confirmation of this, the writer of Chronicles recorded that Aaron's rod was no longer inside the Ark when King Solomon finally retrieved it from the Tabernacle of David and had it transported into the magnificent Temple of Solomon on the shoulders of the Levite priests:

> *"Then they brought up the ark, the tabernacle of meeting, and all the holy furnishings that were in the tabernacle. The priests and the Levites brought them up."* *"Nothing was in the ark except the two tablets which Moses put there at Horeb, when the LORD (Yahweh) made a covenant with the children of Israel, when they had come out of Egypt."* - 2 Chronicles 5:5, 10 (NKJ)

After this final clue is given that the Staff of Yahweh was no longer inside the Ark, that rod that was once in Joseph's possession in Egypt is not mentioned again until this prophetic passage in the Book of Ezekiel:

> *"Thus says the Lord GOD (Yahweh Elohim): 'surely I will take the stick of Joseph, which is in the hand of Ephraim, and the tribes of Israel, his companions; and I will join them... with the stick of Judah, and make them one stick, and they will be one in My hand.'"* - Ezekiel 37:19 (NKJ)

Here, the Stick of Joseph is a definite allusion to the Staff of Yahweh that Reuel took from Joseph's palace, and Moses later obtained from Reuel's garden. This time, however, the Staff of Yahweh is described as being in the hands of Ephraim and the Tribes of Israel. As shown in Books Two and Four, Ephraim partly refers to believers who fled to the USA to escape religious persecution. However, Ephraim also figuratively refers to the global community of believers in Yahshua that are an intimate part of Yahshua's Two-House Church. As explained earlier, this church consists of Judah (Jewish believers in Yahshua) and Ephraim (Gentile believers), who are united in marriage to their Messiah. In addition, the expression "Tribes of Israel" is referring to the Ten Lost Tribes of Israel that were scattered across Europe during the Diaspora that occurred in three waves when the northern Kingdom of Israel fell to the Assyrian King Shalmaneser the Fifth, when the southern Kingdom of Judah fell to King Nebuchadnezzar of Babylon 150 years later, and when Jerusalem fell to the Romans.

In Ezekiel 37:19, Yahweh is stating that He will allegorically twist Joseph's stick (i.e. the Gentile Church) together with the stick of Judah (Messianic Jews) during the Millennial Rule of Yahshua on the Earth. At that time, the lion will lay down with the lamb, and these currently warring congregations will love and nurture each other - something that has never occurred before. Incidentally, David was the King of Judah as well as Israel, so he would have been in possession of these two staffs of authority - the staff that the leading patriarchs of Judah carried, *and the Staff of Yahweh!* However, no one knows for certain what happened to the Staff of Yahweh after this. In fact, there is no further mention of the Staff except in conjunction with Bible prophecies concerning the coming of Yahshua the Messiah as King of kings.

In this regard, Ezekiel 37:19 clearly suggests that ***Joseph's Stick is being secretly held by a person or society within Gentile Christianity that has been entrusted with its care.*** Nonetheless, this stick does not belong solely to the Gentile Church. In fact it will one day be returned to its rightful owner, our Mehlek and Adonai Yahweh Yahshua Ha Mashiach (or, in English: our King and Lord God Joshua the Messiah). This is why Yahshua is identified as *"a Rod from the stem of Jesse,"* who has a *"rod of iron"* in His hands. His rod of iron is no doubt an allusion to the "rod of God," which is another name for the Staff of Yahweh:

> ***"There shall come forth a Rod from the stem of Jesse,***
> *and a Branch shall grow out of his roots. The Spirit of the*
> *LORD (Yahweh) shall rest upon Him, the Spirit of wisdom*
> *and understanding, the Spirit of counsel and might, the Spirit*

*of knowledge and of the fear of the LORD (Yahweh)." - Isaiah
11:1-2 (NKJ)*

*"Listen! The LORD (Yahweh) is calling to the city-- and
to fear your name is wisdom-- **Heed the rod and the One who
appointed it."** - Micah 6:9 (NIV)*

*"She bore **a male Child who was to rule all nations
with a rod of iron**. And her Child was caught up to God and
His throne." - Revelation 12:5 (NKJ)*

*"Now out of His mouth goes a sharp sword, that with
it He should strike the nations. **And He Himself will rule them
with a rod of iron.** He Himself treads the winepress of the
fierceness and wrath of Almighty God. And He has on His
robe and on His thigh a name written: KING OF KINGS AND
LORD OF LORDS." - Revelation 19:15-16 (NKJ)*

From these passages of Scripture, it is fairly clear that the last
possessor of this mighty Staff of Yahweh will be none other than
Yahshua, the Rod of Jesse, the Son of David, the Branch, the True Vine,
and the Lion of Judah:

*"But one of the elders said to me, 'Do not weep.
Behold, the Lion of the tribe of Judah, the Root of David, has
prevailed to open the scroll and to loose its seven seals.'" -
Revelation 5:5 (NKJ)*

So, until the time that Yahshua comes again to reclaim that Rod
that He gave to Adam long ago - and lastly gave to Ephraim - its location
will remain hidden. Indeed, no one but Yahshua now has a right to hold
that miraculous Staff in His merciful and powerful right hand. Therefore,
God will see to it that no one else has the power to touch the Staff of
Yahweh - not even the Antichrist - who surely would covet the idea of
holding that Staff in mockery of God's authority.

The Kingdom of Israel Disguised as Camelot

With the miraculous help of Joseph's Stick, the Hebrew slaves
that Moses led out of bondage finally entered the land that Yahweh
promised to Abraham's righteous descendants. Once there, they
conquered the wicked Canaanites under Joshua's expert leadership.
Then they set up an earthly kingdom that shined very brightly for a brief
time under the leadership of Samuel, David, and Solomon. Under King
David, the Twelve Tribes of Israel formed an undefeatable army that
conquered every neighboring kingdom and made them subject to David

as their overlord. Even the might of Phoenicia bent under the threat of David's superior fighting forces.

Seeing their might, the Phoenician kings wisely formed a strategic alliance with Israel during David and Solomon's glorious reigns. As a result of their close alliance with Phoenicia, Israel's wealth from trade and tribute increased dramatically, and its citizens dwelt in absolute peace and safety for nearly a hundred years. Sadly, the true extent of the Kingdom of Israel's splendor during the reigns of David and Solomon is largely overlooked in today's history books.

Though few people realize it, Israel's Golden Age carries clear connections to the myth of King Arthur and his fabled kingdom called Camelot. For example, the twelve Knights of the Round Table are found in the Twelve Patriarchs who led each of the Tribes of Israel. Similarly, the righteous and just King Arthur embodies the godly traits of many of Israel's leaders such as Moses, Joshua, Samuel, King David, and Solomon. Likewise, Arthur's beautiful though fickle Queen Guinevere represents Israel, whose citizens became adulterers when they began worshipping false gods instead of Yahweh. Even King Arthur's sword had its ancient counterpart in the mystical Staff of Yahweh that Moses retrieved and he and his brother Aaron carried. Just like Excalibur was lost to Arthur, the Staff of Yahweh was also lost to Israel long before the Ark of the Covenant disappeared or their remaining temple treasures were taken as plunder by the conquering Babylonians (2 Kings 24:13).

Because the Israelites stopped worshipping Yahweh, their glorious and powerful kingdom was destined to fall. Just like the fabled Camelot, the kingdom of God on Earth that Israel represented was slowly conquered and destroyed. This happened so that Yahweh could prove a twofold point. First, it shows that *only a perfect man who is without sin could rule the Earth perfectly and justly*. Secondly, it shows that *only perfect people can perfectly keep Yahweh's righteous laws as set forth in the Torah*. Without the perfect King giving us the ability to become His perfect subjects, the fabled glory of Camelot will never last forever in any nation or kingdom on Earth. Adonai Yahshua alone is that perfect King!

Despite their flaws, King David - and to some extent King Solomon - had points in common with the longed-for Messiah who would be their descendent. King David in particular makes a good allegory for the mythical King Arthur. King David's life has many parallels to Yahshua's. The most striking parallels between them are in the roles they both played. For example, David served as a shepherd boy before he became a warrior king. Likewise, at His First Advent, Yahshua was the Good Shepherd who came to save His sheep (John 10:11).

Someday, like David was to a smaller degree, Yahshua will be the conquering King of kings when He comes again. Indeed, with so many points in common, no one resembles King Arthur better than Yahshua!

Based on these striking comparisons, it is highly possible that the stories of Moses, Joshua, Samuel, David, Solomon, and the Twelve Tribes of Israel are the real basis behind much of the mythology surrounding King Arthur and the supposed Knights of the Round Table. These great leaders of Israel were all embodied in the fabled goodness, wisdom, and valor of King Arthur. In addition, the patriarchs of each of the Twelve Tribes of Israel very well could have served as the inspiration for the fabled Knights of the Round Table. In the further transformation of truth into myth, the powerful and seemingly magical Staff that Moses wielded but that was eventually lost became the sword Excalibur that was destined for Arthur, the rightful king. Later, like the Staff of Yahweh and the Ark of the Covenant it was stored in, the mystical sword Excalibur mysteriously vanished.

As I mentioned earlier, the rightful king who wields the Staff of Yahweh will ultimately be Yahshua, the Anointed One. Furthermore, there is no question that His future Millennial Rule on Earth will be the ultimate Camelot. It is also possible that the ancestors of Israel's son Judah who were in the genealogy of Yahshua were the inspiration for the myth of the Holy Grail. This is even more plausible when we note that the mythology of the Grail includes references to it being the chalice that once held the actual spilled blood of the Messiah. It is also believed that the Grail may have been the actual wine cup that Yahshua drank from at the Last Supper, whose contents symbolized His sacred blood.

Moses' miraculous leadership of the Tribes of Israel is very much a part of Judeo-Christian history. However, this does not mean that the fables surrounding King Arthur actually occurred as exact parallels of the biblical stories, or that the United Kingdom is in possession of the Staff of Yahweh or the Holy Grail, which some heretically believe refers to Yahshua's bloodline or lineage through the children that He supposedly sired with Mary Magdalene.

Nonetheless, King Arthur's leadership of the Knights of the Round Table has become so much a part of Medieval and English history that many might balk at the thought that King Arthur and Camelot never existed, or that the sword Excalibur and the Holy Grail are figments of the collective imagination of the English nobility. Though there is little doubt that some actual ruler of England is tied to the Arthurian legends, many of the legends surrounding him were obviously greatly embellished with events from factual stories in the Book of Jasher and the Bible!

As addressed in Book Four on prophecy, the obvious tie-ins between the main characters of the Arthurian Legends or Grail Romances and biblical characters may have a sinister motive. This is because some people believe that the Holy Grail is a symbol for Mary Magdalene and the children that resulted from her supposed marriage to Christ. In Book Four, the origins of this heretical legend and its evil purpose will be fully examined in relation to the End Times and the possible identity of the Antichrist.

King Josiah: Champion of Religious Reform in Judah

Of all the kings of Israel, only two were consistently righteous and both of these kings ruled over the Kingdom of Judah. The first of these was King David, and though there were several other kings after David who were righteous at times like Solomon, none were as constantly righteous as David - with one lone exception. This was found in King Josiah, who ruled shortly before the Kingdom of Judah fell to King Nebuchadnezzar. Before Josiah came to power, Yahweh had grown tired of the sinfulness of the remaining Israelites in Judah. Starting with King Solomon, successive kings of Israel and Judah either built and worshipped at sacred shrines and altars to many false gods on top of the high places in the land or freely allowed the Israelites to do so. Others defiled Yahweh's temple in Jerusalem with altars or idols dedicated to Pagan deities. Still others sacrificed children in the sacred fires dedicated to the god Molech. In short, Judah was ripe for judgment and Yahweh would soon unleash His wrath unless the king and the people of Judah repented.

When Josiah took the throne in Judah, he was only eight years old, but he had a noble character and ruled well and authoritatively enough to be considered righteous before Yahweh. Then at the age of eighteen, Josiah's scribe read to the king from the book of the Law that the High Priest in the Temple had loaned to him. When Josiah heard the Word of the Law of God, he understood how lax and sinful Israel truly had become and he was deeply grieved. As a result, he tore his clothes in lamentation. Later, Josiah was even more terribly distraught when he heard of the horrible judgments that were going to befall Judah because of the breaking of their Covenant with Yahweh. Josiah was so horrified by the sins that his predecessors had allowed to be perpetrated that he decided to go on a campaign to cleanse his kingdom of all the abominations and idols that were an affront to Yahweh God:

> "Moreover Josiah put away those who consulted
> mediums... and idols, all the abominations that were seen in

the land of Judah and in Jerusalem, that he might perform the
words of the law which were written in the book... found in
the house of the LORD (Yahweh). **Now before him there was**
no king like him, who turned to the LORD (Yahweh) with all
his heart, with all his soul, and with all his might, according
to all the Law of Moses; nor after him did any arise like him.
Nevertheless the LORD (Yahweh) did not turn from the
fierceness of His great wrath... against Judah, because...
Manasseh had provoked Him." - II Kings 23:24-26 (NKJ)

In the preceding Scripture, note that King Josiah is singled out in this Scripture in a highly unusual way. He is touted as the *greatest king* not only of Judah, but also of all Israel throughout their history - up until the Babylonian captivity of the Jews. This means King Josiah was even more highly esteemed by Yahweh than King David, and had earned this distinction due to the greatness of the righteous works he performed for Yahweh. Let's examine why this one man was given such high praise.

This Scripture also mentions that the prior King of Israel named Manasseh had provoked Yahweh to anger at His chosen people. The reason for this is recorded in the following Scripture:

"For he rebuilt the high places which Hezekiah his
father had destroyed; he raised up altars for Baal, and made a
wooden image, as Ahab king of Israel had done; and he
worshiped all the host of heaven and served them. He also...
built altars for all the host of heaven in the two courts of the
house of the LORD (Yahweh). Also he made his son pass
through the fire, practiced soothsaying, used witchcraft, and
consulted spiritists and mediums..." "And the LORD
(Yahweh) spoke by His servants the prophets, saying,
'Because Manasseh king of Judah has... acted more wickedly
than all the Amorites ... I am bringing such calamity upon
Jerusalem and Judah...'" - II Kings 21:3-6, 10-12 (NKJ)

Sadly, after the evil King Manasseh died, his son Amon turned out to be as wicked as his father. Perhaps that is why Amon was soon murdered by his own servants, after which the people put Amon's young son Josiah on the throne. Amazingly, though his father Amon was in total rebellion against Yahweh, King Josiah grew to be just as zealous in obeying the will of God, and he displayed his fervor for the Law and love for God by destroying all the idols and abominations that could be found throughout Israel at that time:

*"They broke down the altars of the Baals in his
presence, and the incense altars which were above them he
cut down; and the wooden images, the carved images, and the
molded images he broke in pieces, and made dust of them and
scattered it on the graves of those who had sacrificed to them.
He also burned the bones of the priests on their altars, and
cleansed Judah and Jerusalem. And so he did in the cities of
Manasseh, Ephraim, and Simeon, as far as Naphtali and all
around, with axes." - 2 Chronicles 34:4-6 (NKJ)*

Josiah's campaign against apostasy began when the King rallied
the people around him at a Covenant pillar of stone. This Covenant
Pillar was either a new one Josiah had ordered constructed of undressed
stones, or one erected by some righteous patriarch of the past. At this
pillar, Josiah promised to keep the Covenant with Yahweh that his
forefathers had made. Then he asked the people to renew this same
Covenant:

***"Now the king sent them to gather all the elders of
Judah and Jerusalem to him.*** *The king went up to the house of
the LORD (Yahweh) with all the men of Judah, and... the
inhabitants of Jerusalem - the priests and the prophets and all
the people... And he read in their hearing all the words of the
Book of the Covenant....* ***Then the king stood by a pillar and
made a Covenant before the LORD (Yahweh),*** *to follow the
LORD (Yahweh) and to keep His commandments... with all
his heart and all his soul, to perform the words of this
Covenant that were written in this book.* ***And all the people
took a stand for the Covenant."*** *- II Kings 23:1-3 (NKJ)*

After this, as shown in the Scripture quoted earlier, King Josiah
went on a campaign to rid the Kingdom of Judah of the idolatrous
images and sacred places that had been made by the previously
backslidden and apostate kings and people of Israel. He destroyed many
idolatrous Pagan images, not the least of which were the statues that at
one time flanked either side of the entrance to Solomon's Temple in
Jerusalem:

*"Then **he removed the horses** that the kings of Judah
had dedicated to the sun, at the entrance to the house of the
LORD (Yahweh)...* ***and he burned the chariots of the sun with
fire****." - II Kings 23:11 (NKJ)*

These horses and chariots at the entrance to the Temple courts
represented the chariots of a Pagan Sun god such as Helios or Apollo.
Previous Kings of Judah had therefore begun to identify Yahweh with

these false gods. Though, as shown in Book One, the Sun is indeed an allegorical symbol that represents the attributes of Yahweh God, it is not a god in itself and was never intended to be an idolatrous object of worship. The Sun is merely a symbol for the Almighty, invisible Creator God of the Universe. Furthermore, the Greek myths surrounding their Sun god Apollo are tied to the sons of Lamech the Cainite that were named Jubal and Jabal. King Josiah was therefore rightly incensed by the presence of these idols near the Temple to Yahweh, and his order to have the statues destroyed must have pleased Yahweh greatly.

Interestingly, there is some evidence that the Jews or Samaritans living in Israel after the destruction of the Temple still used the symbolism of the Pagan Sun god to identify Yahweh or a past King of

Israel like David. This was found in the remains of an approximately Sixth Century mosaic synagogue floor that was excavated recently in northern Israel. There, surrounded by Zodiac symbols that some Jews knew were tied to the Twelve Tribes of Israel, is a man with the rays of the Sun surrounding his head riding in a chariot that is being pulled by four horses. Alongside the Zodiac depictions were the names of the constellations in Hebrew, but the center motif is strangely lacking a similar identifying word.

From its location on the floor, this mosaic was obviously not an object of worship and was done in a simplistic, whimsical style completely unlike the graven images that Josiah destroyed inside the Temple court hundreds of years before. Therefore, there is a possibility that this synagogue was used either by the Samaritans, who used Pagan symbolism and had some Pagan beliefs mixed in with their Judaic practices, or by some of the first Jewish believers in Yahshua. If so, the man in the chariot could actually represent Christ, which would be appropriate since Yahshua created the Universe and all the twinkling stars, including the Sun. Or could the man in the chariot be Enoch or Elijah, who were taken up to Heaven with chariots and horses of fire? Enoch, after all, was the first man to fully read and understand the

Heavenly Tablets or Star Gospel. So the archeological insistence that this heavenly charioteer signifies the Sun god Helios is simply an assumption, and it may be an incorrect one.

Like the overlooked but exceptional King of Judah named Josiah, our Savior Yahshua is a righteous king. Yet Yahshua has the added distinction of being perfectly righteous and without sin. Nonetheless, despite Josiah's failure to be perfect, this good king served as a prefiguration of Christ. Just as Josiah did before Christ's First Advent, Yahshua called all of God's people to renew their Blood Covenant with Yahweh. Believers in Yahshua do this through the symbolic partaking of Yahshua's own blood and body in Communion. In an act that foretold the need for Christ's sacrifice, Josiah likely sacrificed animals and poured blood from the sacrifices on the stone Covenant pillar that marked the renewal of Israel's Covenant with Yahweh. Then, to show their participation in the Covenant, Josiah may have sprinkled some of the blood on the people - just as had traditionally been done once a year by the High Priest on the Day of Atonement.

Though the Bible says that those who represented the people solemnly renewed their Covenant vows to Yahweh along with Josiah, too many of the people in the kingdom refused to follow their leaders and repent of their sins. Therefore, despite Josiah's tremendous efforts to right the religious wrongs of his predecessors, the people of Judah failed to keep the Covenant that was renewed at that sacred Covenant Pillar. As a result, the kingdom of Judah was allowed to fall into the hands of King Nebuchadnezzar of Babylon only a dozen years later.

Consequently, the spiritual oasis of truth and light that Israel was vanished from view, its greatest achievements were forgotten, and its wonderful religious relics were lost in the mists of time. But, in God's mercy, the holy religious relics and rituals of the Kingdom of Israel are not destined to be lost forever! As Ezekiel envisioned, a magnificent new Temple to Yahweh will be built during the Millennial Rule of Christ, and all Twelve Tribes of Israel will have a place there - even the infamous Tribe of Dan. In addition, one of King Josiah's own sons named Jeconiah was reckoned in the genealogy of Christ (Luke 3:31) as a testament to God's love for Josiah of Judah and in fulfillment of God's promises to David and Solomon!

The Lost Tribes of Israel and the Serpent Seed of Dan

In his book "The British Edda," scholar L.A. Waddell performs a great service to humanity by pointing out the fact that the Pagan religion and language of the supposedly mythic Edda is not Norse at all, even with characters named Thor and Loki. Though Waddell's thesis that the Edda is a truer telling of what really went on in Eden and that the Bible is a copy of much older literature is both heretical and untrue, Waddell makes a convincing case that the Edda is British and Gothic in origin. Furthermore, Waddell shows that the mythology of the Edda came out of Troy and was adopted from Mesopotamian sources. Finally, Waddell gives concrete examples showing that the people mentioned in the Edda like Thor and Baldur may be biblical characters like Adam and Abel.

Sadly, however, Waddell completely misses the point that the biblical characters mentioned in the Edda have been hidden beneath a twisted misinterpretation of history. This same twisted Babylonian theology that memorializes the success of the Way of Cain over the Way of Yahweh was adopted in Greece and Phoenicia for the most part - *and the Danites may have borrowed their religion from the Phoenicians and Samaritans, who often combined biblical truths with pagan ideas.* Like the Danites, the Phoenicians were a great seafaring people that traded goods and slaves with many kingdoms, and this may be one reason why the Danites had such an affinity with them and their demonically inspired religion.

If Waddell is correct that the Edda has Trojan, Mesopotamian and Semitic roots, is it possible that it found its way into European history by way of the Lost Tribes of Israel? Though this subject is highly controversial, there may be some truth behind the claims that the Ten Lost Tribes were scattered throughout Europe and England, where they eventually settled down. If so, descendents from the Tribe of Dan also likely settled there and brought their heretical religious ideas with them. Like Cain and his line, the Danites rejected Yahweh so totally that some scholars believe that their evil progeny are one day to be completely eradicated. In this regard, though there may well be some direct descendants of the Tribe of Dan scattered throughout the world today, anyone who rejects God's authority and rebels against His laws without remorse or repentance is a spiritual member of that tribe.

Nonetheless, there is evidence that people descended from the Lost Tribes of Israel including the Tribe of Dan settled throughout Europe. As they did, some of these Lost Israelites brought Pagan ideas with them, which they had learned from their Canaanite and Phoenician neighbors. Some of these displaced Israelites also absorbed Pagan ideas while held captive in Assyria and Babylon and during their wanderings across the lands around the Mediterranean and upward into Europe. As they wandered, some of the Israelites were assimilated into the local populations where they settled, while others maintained their unique identity and became known as the Jews.

In particular, the Tribe of Dan seems to have settled in many different places over time, eventually finding a permanent home in Scandinavia and Great Britain. Interestingly, their territory in Europe is in the far north, just as it was in ancient Israel! Could it be that their exposure to Pagan ideas led them to write the Edda as a denial of their true history as revealed in Scripture? As was shown in Chapter Seven, this is exactly what the ancient Egyptians, Babylonians, Greeks and Romans did, and the religion of Greece was quite similar to that of the Trojans. In fact, ancient Greek myths and the Norse myths in the Edda may have both originated in Troy.

When giving his death-bed blessings to his sons, Jacob/Israel said this as a prophecy and blessing for Dan:

> "Dan will be **a serpent by the roadside, a viper along the path**, that bites the horse's heels so that its rider tumbles backward." - Genesis 49:17 (NIV)

The term translated as "viper" in the preceding prophetic Scripture about Dan can just as readily apply to an adder or scorpion, whose stings can be equally deadly. This implies that some of the descendents of Dan would be cruel and hostile with many of the people they came into contact with. Many Bible scholars also believe that Dan's association with a serpent trail "by the roadside" partly means that the Tribe of Dan would leave some sign of where they traveled. After being taken captive out of Israel the Danites were transplanted, along with the rest of the Lost Ten Tribes of Israel, to the lands south of the Black Sea by the ancient Assyrians.

To hide their true identity as the source of the Seed of the Serpent throughout history, the Tribe of Dan used an eagle and a young lion cub as symbols.

> "And of Dan he said: 'Dan is a lion's whelp; he shall leap from Bashan.'" Deut. 33:22 (NKJ)

Note here that Dan is a lion's whelp that leaps from Bashan, and Bashan was the ancient stronghold of the Anakim and Rephaim ruled over by the Giant named Og. Could this be a reference not only to the far northern location of Danite territory around Mount Hermon, but a prophecy that some of the Danites would do what the Cainites did before them by mingling their seed with the strange flesh of the Nephilim? Could this also be what provoked God to anger toward the Tribe of Manasseh in King Josiah's time?

Once displaced into Europe, the people of Dan left telltale names in many of the geographical locations where they wandered. Since the Danites were a seafaring people and they associated their Tribal name with the places where they traveled and settled, **many rivers in Europe and around the Black Sea in Russia contain the two letters in the Hebrew name "Dan," which are "D-N."** Examples of rivers that were likely named after the Tribe of Dan around the Black Sea are the "Dnieper," "Dniester," "Don," and the great river "Danube" that winds its way through most of Europe.

The Danites left many other marks of where they traveled such as those found in ancient tribal and clan names. Hence, the Danites can be identified with the *Danish* people of *Denmark* since "Danish" means "Dan's men" in Hebrew and "Denmark" is derived from the expression "Dan's Mark," or "Dan's Seed." In addition, the people of Denmark, Sweden, Finland, Iceland and part of Germany are Scandinavians, a term that again clearly recalls the Israelitish ancestry of these people since the "din" in the middle of this word can just as easily be written "dan." The Scandinavians are descended from the Vikings, those barbaric raiders who wore horned headdresses as an emblem of their race *and religion*.

Interestingly, Mr. Waddell's interpretation of the Edda lends credence to the idea that the true identity of the people he calls the "followers of Abel" were the Vikings. Waddell sees Abel as an evil villain in the Edda named Baldur, who supposedly raped his mother Eve and tried to kill Cain. But, as anyone familiar with the Bible's book of Genesis knows, Abel was the godly son of Adam and Eve that was replaced by Seth after Abel was murdered by Cain, while Cain was in open rebellion against God. In the Edda, however, the nature of Cain and Seth/Abel are reversed, just as they are in Greek Mythology.

Sadly, some British-Israelists think Waddell is correct, and this is just one reason why British-Israelism - a variant of Replacement Theology - is condemned as a heresy by many Christian denominations. Contrary to Waddell's hypothesis, the Vikings were not the followers of "Abel" at all, but the followers of the Serpent's wisdom and the Way of Cain just as the Greeks were! One sign of this can be seen in the fact that Viking warriors wore identical horned headdresses to those described in the Edda, and ancient Babylonian deities like Ishtar and Shamash were often depicted wearing similar horned headdresses as a symbol of their authority. As an example of this, look at the cylinder seal depicted on page 372. There, the enthroned Sun god Shamash is wearing a horned headdress just like the one on the king standing before him.

Now, if the Danites did infiltrate all of Europe and settle in Denmark, Scandinavia, and the British Isles, these people groups may indeed be able to trace their lineage back to Cain and Abel through the Tribe of Dan. The serpent imagery and black-horned headdresses of ancient Scandinavian artistry are readily traced to Dan through the symbology of the Zodiac-linked Danite battle standard and the fact that a temple dedicated to *an idol in the form of a bull calf* was located in their part of Israel (1 Kings 12:28-29). As discussed in Chapter Four, this Pagan temple at one time rivaled the Temple to Yahweh in Jerusalem in popularity.

Another very clear linguistic example marking where the Tribe of Dan settled is found in the tribal name of the ancient people that settled in Ireland. In their Gaelic language, the Irish people called themselves the "Tuatha de Danaan," or literally in English: "The Tribe of Dan!" This is something that is overlooked by many that entertain the idea that Britain and America can be identified with the dual Tribe of Joseph. Though their thinking is correct, they fail to focus on the fact that **the Tribe of Dan extensively intermingled with all the people of Europe, as well as Anglo-Saxon England and America.** The Vikings, for example, were seafaring Scandinavians who raided England and the rest of neighboring Europe for booty and wives. The Irish did their share of looting and wenching in Scotland and England as well. In fact, the modern day Welsh people of Wales in England have been conclusively traced to the Tribe of Dan.

Ominously, since the Tribe of Dan is not listed among the Tribes in the Book of Revelation but is replaced with the half tribe of Manasseh, some Bible scholars believe that the Antichrist will spring from the Tribe of Dan (Revelation 7:3-8). However, it could just as easily mean that the tribe of Dan was absorbed into the tribe if Manasseh and that the Antichrist will spring from that half tribe of Joseph. As is shown in Book Four, there is good reason to believe Great Britain can be directly associated with both the Tribes of Manasseh and Dan, and that one of their reigning princes will soon assume the role of the Antichrist during the Tribulation.

Due to a prophecy that Jacob uttered to Dan from his deathbed, it is believed that the Antichrist will spring from the Tribe of Dan. This is because Jacob associated Dan with serpents and the sting of an adder or scorpion, thereby irrevocably connecting the Tribe of Dan to the serpent and scorpion symbols attached to the sign of Scorpio, which symbolizes God's adversary: Satan. The symbols associated with Scorpio would therefore have been on the banners or battle standards for the Tribe of Dan, and likely would have been emblazoned on the possessions of Danite tribal leaders. Ominously, this symbology also connects Dan to the Serpent seed of the Nephilim and the Way of Cain.

Could this be why the flag of Wales contains *one large red dragon* on a white and green background? This red dragon is a composite heraldic "Beast" that mixes the features of several creatures, including the serpent and eagle associated with the Tribe of Dan, as well as the bat and scorpion. Eerily, as was

Red Dragon on the Flag of Wales

shown in Chapter Four, the first race of Nephilim were human in appearance though on a gigantic scale, while the second race of Nephilim may have been genetically engineered monsters manufactured from the combined DNA of birds, reptiles, bats, and other creatures, thus forming the chimeras so often found in myth. It therefore may well be that the Flag of Wales is a flag inspired by the Nephilim and signifies their blood descendents in some way.

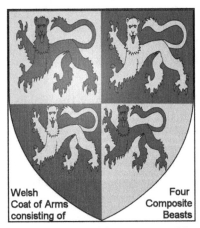

Welsh Coat of Arms consisting of   Four Composite Beasts

Interestingly, the Welsh Coat of Arms consists of four composite "beasts" representing the blending of three animals: the lion, the leopard, and the bear. As discussed in Book Four on prophecy, this symbol is attached to the ruling monarchs of the United Kingdom, which was formerly known as England or Great Britain. Furthermore, this heraldic beast shares uncanny similarities with the *"Beast out of the Sea"* and the *"four great beasts"* spoken of in Daniel and Revelation (Daniel 7:3-8; Rev. 12:3, 13:1-4).

Therefore, could it be possible that the Antichrist will be part Welshman, as well as part Nephilim? See Book Four to find out more abut this possibility.

Thankfully, the Tribe of Dan isn't the only Tribe of Israel represented in England. Historical, genealogical, and linguistic evidence also shows that some of Issac's Sons (i.e. Israel's Sons or members from the Twelve Tribes of Israel) were also the ancestors of the Saxons, which would make them Lost Israelites. Indeed, because of their part Anglo-Saxon heritage, most of Europe and England may actually be Lost Israelites by blood, as well as by spiritual baptism. If so, they collectively would be the "many nations" that sprang from Abraham's "seed" Isaac (Genesis 17:4-5). In addition, they would be the "company of nations" that sprang from Jacob's seed - the Twelve Tribes of Israel (Genesis 35:11).

What if Europe, England, and the many nations that sprang from England can be identified with the Twelve Tribes of Israel just as the Nation of Israel and modern day Jews can be? If so, then these many nations would fulfill the physical Covenant promises made to the literal seed of Abraham and Isaac. They would also fulfill the Covenant promises made to King David and his future "Seed," the Messiah Yahshua, for Christianity was the dominant faith of the West for nearly two thousand years.

Since the initial Covenant promise that God made to Abram when his name was changed to Abraham was unconditional, Yahweh meant to fulfill it regardless of the spiritual or moral condition of Abraham's descendents. Furthermore, Yahweh swore an oath to Abraham that made the fulfillment of this Covenant promise a matter of divine integrity for which Yahweh alone accepted responsibility and promised fulfillment (Genesis 22:16). Therefore, Yah's promises to make Abraham's seed as numerous "as the stars of heaven" (Gen. 26:4), and to make Abraham "the father of many nations" (Gen. 17:5) had to be both spiritually and physically fulfilled. Otherwise, these failed promises would show Yahweh to be a liar.

Spiritually, the promises made to Abraham were fulfilled through Yahshua and those who love Him after His First Advent. Since Abraham loved Yahweh and the promise of His future Messiah, Yahweh meant to multiply Abraham's faith as well as his physical progeny. Yahweh therefore meant to make Abraham "the father of many nations" both literally *and spiritually*. This is why all those who have accepted Yahshua's sacrifice on the Cross for their sins are called the spiritual "seed" of Abraham (Romans 8:14-16, 9:6-8; Galatians 4:22-29; Ephesians 1:4-7).

However, the promises made to Abraham also pertained literally to his son Isaac's blood kin and their inheritance of both a literal kingdom and the physical land of Canaan. **Yah's Covenant promises therefore have a physical, earthly fulfillment as well as a spiritual one.** Though the material aspect of these promises were only partially fulfilled through the ancient Kingdom of Israel and they will be completely fulfilled during the Millennial Rule of Christ, the material blessings promised to Abraham did not end when ancient Israel ceased to exist! Indeed, since Yahweh is *never* a liar, *He meant to fulfill these everlastingly binding Covenant Promises to Abraham's future descendents throughout time*, and not just for a short time. The key to understanding this is found in Jacob's death-bed promises to his twelve

sons that links them to the Twelve Signs of the Zodiac as well as to the
End Times:

> *"And Jacob called his sons and said,* **'Gather together,**
> **that I may tell you what shall befall you in the last days:**
> *Gather together and hear, you sons of Jacob, and listen to*
> *Israel your father.'" - Genesis 49:1-2 (NKJ)*

In this Scripture, Jacob makes it clear that these prophetic
blessings over each of his sons pertain to the End Times or Last Days. In
other words, at that time, Jacob knew that descendents of each of his
sons would survive and thrive until the End Times and be represented
among the nations of the world. After this, Jacob blessed each of his
sons using symbolic imagery that is tied to the Language of God. This
imagery identified each Tribe of Israel with a specific Zodiac sign and
also gave them an idea of their fate and the types of material blessings
they would obtain from God (See Genesis 49:3-27).

During this discourse, Jacob made a major prophecy concerning
the Tribe of Judah that British Israelists insist means that the Throne of
Judah would survive until Christ's return:

> *"The scepter shall not depart from Judah, nor a*
> *lawgiver from between his feet, until Shiloh comes; and to*
> *Him shall be the obedience of the people." - Gen. 49:10 (NKJ)*

Of course, what many British Israelists fail to tell others is that
they believe Yahshua will not return in the flesh from Heaven, but will
be reincarnated in the body of a prince born to the British monarchy.
They base their belief partly on the preceding prophecy, which they
claim was not fulfilled at Christ's First Advent because it pertains to the
literal Throne of Judah, and Christ did not come to occupy that literal
throne at His first coming. They therefore insist that the Throne of Judah
was preserved on Earth elsewhere, which they believe is in England (but
Ethiopia is a more likely place!). Though some of them believe that
Yahshua Himself will claim this throne at His Second Coming, most of
them believe that one of Yahshua's supposed descendents through Mary
Magdalene will occupy that throne as the promised End-Time Messiah,
and this is how the Antichrist may obtain his power.

In Jacob's prophecy for Judah, the term "Shiloh" is used as if it
were a proper name or title referring to Christ. However, though it
specifically refers to a place in Israel called *"the House of the Lord
(Yahweh)"* where the Ark of the Covenant was kept (1 Samuel 1:24), it
also may refer to Christ in that "Shiloh" is a reference to the Hebrew
phrase "asher loh" meaning "whose (it is)" or "to whom it belongs."

That this is the intended meaning is inferred in Ezekiel, where the prophet speaks of the termination of the Throne of Judah in this way:

"Now to you, O profane, wicked prince of Israel, whose day has come, whose iniquity shall end, thus says the Lord GOD (Yahweh Elohim): 'Remove the turban, and take off the crown; nothing shall remain the same. Exalt the humble, and humble the exalted. Overthrown, overthrown, **I will make it overthrown! It shall be no longer, until He comes whose right it is, and I will give it to Him.'"** *- Ezekiel 21:27 (NKJ)*

Therefore, despite the claims of British Israelists, no prophecy in Scripture specifically states that the Throne of Judah would exist or be established in an unbroken line of rulers until the messiah whom it belongs to appears on the scene to claim it! Nonetheless, British Israelists still misinterpret Genesis 49:10 and Ezekiel 21:27 in order to support their notion that the literal descendents of the Tribe of Judah will perpetually rule over a material kingdom just as King David did until the messiah called Shiloh arrives. But according to the Word of God, that literal kingdom ended over 500 years before Christ was born when the Kingdom of Judah fell to Nebuchadnezzar. Furthermore, this kingdom is only destined to be established again at the literal Second Coming of Christ from Heaven - and not with Him arriving in a space ship but riding upon a literal white horse that will miraculously descend through the clouds of Earth's atmosphere (Rev. 19:11).

Coronation Chair with Stone of Scone in Westminster Abbey

According to English historians who support the spurious claims of British Israelism, the Throne of David was not overthrown but overturned and transplanted from Israel to Ireland, then to Scotland, then to England, and then to Scotland again (in modern times) via Jacob's Pillow, a.k.a. the Stone of Destiny or Stone of Scone. This stone was supposedly used as a pillow by the patriarch Jacob when he had his dream about the ladder reaching up to Heaven at Bethel (Genesis 28:11-19). At this time God promised the land of Canaan to Jacob and his descendents and also told

Jacob that his descendents would be as the dust of the Earth, which they literally became through the Lost Tribes of Israel. Nonetheless, the mysterious stone that once rested beneath the chair used at coronations of British royalty up to Queen Elizabeth II was recently scientifically proven to bear no resemblance to any type of stone that is naturally found in Israel. Therefore, it likely did not originate in Israel at all! Perhaps this is why the stone was recently returned to Scotland and is no longer beneath England's coronation chair in Westminster Abbey.

Also according to British Israelists, the old Irish royalty and the Welsh descended from the "Tuatha de Danaan," or the Tribe of Dan. To support their connection to the Tribe of Judah, they also claim that the harp on the old Irish royal crest is an allusion to the great harpist and Psalmist of the Bible: King David. Indeed, even the Scots supposedly descended from the Danites and other Tribes of Israel. So British Israelists believe that the Throne of Judah supposedly passed to the Lost Tribes of Israel (and specifically to the Tribe of Dan) through the intermarriage of the last King of Judah's daughters to the ruling classes in the British Isles, who descended from a mixture of Lost Israelite and Danite ancestors. In addition, since the Welsh are supposedly the most closely tied to Dan and Judah, this may be why every future King of England is given the title "Prince of Wales."

Most of this royal stone swapping in Great Britain supposedly took place before the time of Christ. However, according to the British Israelist interpretation of prophecy, the Scepter had to stay in the possession of the Jewish ancestors of Christ until He was born. After His Bar Mitzvah at the age of 13, Yahshua would have been considered a man, and could have left for England to pass His Scepter on to the English Kings with their part Davidic bloodline and their connection to the Lost Tribes of Israel. Of course, though most people aren't aware of it, there is a literal Scepter and it is none other than the Staff of Yahweh or Joseph's Stick and it begs the question: "Is this miraculous staff in the possession of the British monarchy?" My answer to this is "No!", since Scripture tells us this staff is in the hands of Ephraim, and Great Britain does not represent Ephraim, but Manasseh.

Along with all the prefabricated lies in the legends of King Arthur and the Holy Grail, there are other British legends spuriously claiming that Yahshua went to England with Joseph of Arimathea before He began His ministry in Galilee and Judea. They also say that, in order for the prophecy about Shiloh to be literally true, Yahshua would have had to be in possession of the actual Scepter of His kingship *before* He even arrived in England! But, they say that because Christ likely knew He was going to have to die then go to Heaven for a long time, He may have given the literal Scepter of His kingship to the royalty of England descended from King Zedekiah's daughters to keep it for Him until His Second Advent. However, British Israelists fail to reason that there is a literal Antichrist who will one day lay claim to Christ's kingship. In fact, they often deny the coming of the Millennial Kingdom of Christ altogether and believe in a form of Amillennial Dominion Theology, which states that believers will ultimately usher in the Kingdom of God on Earth on their own, without any direct divine intervention.

Despite British Israelite claims, however, the throne in Scotland and the scepter in England have no connection to Christ at all, and the Throne of David and Scepter of Judah literally belong to Him today. As it says in Isaiah:

> "For unto us a Child is born, unto us a Son is given; and the government will be upon His shoulder. And His name will be called wonderful, Counselor, Mighty God, everlasting Father, Prince of Peace. Of the increase of His government and peace there will be no end, upon the throne of David and over His kingdom, to order it and establish it with judgment and justice from that time forward, even forever. The zeal of the LORD of hosts (Yahweh Tsavout) will perform this." - Isaiah 9:6-7 (NKJ)

Nonetheless, the patriarch Jacob did make quite a few promises to his sons that were not to be fulfilled until "the last days." It is these promises that have a real modern-day application that is undeniable - especially those made to the patriarch Joseph and his two sons Ephraim and Manasseh, which became the two Half Tribes of Joseph that were supposed to be counted as one tribe in ancient times, but were nonetheless reckoned separately in every way and given their own unique land allotments. This is also true in Bible prophecies relating to these two tribes descending from Joseph.

The Half Tribes of Joseph are symbolized by the horns of Taurus the Bull, which symbolizes Joseph in the heavens, just as Moses prophesied on his death bed:

> "His glory is like a firstborn bull, and his horns are like the horns of the wild ox; together with them he shall push the peoples to the ends of the earth; they are the ten thousands of Ephraim, and they are the thousands of Manasseh." - Deuteronomy 33:17 (NKJ)

Of these two horns or sons, the horn that supposedly signified Ephraim is symbolized as a white unicorn on both the Scottish and English Royal Coat of Arms. This unicorn is a symbol of Joseph's glory or his royalty, which Manasseh - as the firstborn - was supposed to inherit. However, Joseph placed his younger son Ephraim over Manasseh as the heir to God's promises to Joseph. Therefore, despite their claims that Manasseh was numbered as the thirteenth Tribe, Ephraim was the younger son of Joseph and the progenitor of the thirteenth Tribe of Israel by virtue of his birth, if not his inheritance. Interestingly, the ten thousands of Ephraim are symbolized as a much bigger tribe than Manasseh with her thousands in the Scripture above, and at last count, the United Kingdom - even with all her commonwealth nations added in - is still only about one third the population of the United States.

The prophecies concerning Joseph given by Jacob are different than those of Moses and do not mention a bull, but call Joseph a fruitful bough associated with archery (i.e. warfare):

> *"Joseph is a fruitful bough, a fruitful bough by a well; his branches run over the wall. The archers have bitterly grieved him, shot at him and hated him. But his bow remained in strength, and the arms of his hands were made strong by the hands of the Mighty God of Jacob (From there is the Shepherd, the Stone of Israel)." - Gen. 49:22-24 (NKJ)*

Oddly enough the fruitful bough (as an olive branch with 13 leaves and fruits) and the arrows of the archer are held in the claws of an eagle on the Great Seal of the United States, but appear nowhere in the iconography of the Irish, English, or Scottish Monarchy. In addition, the United States was founded from thirteen original colonies, which allegorically alludes to Ephraim in prophecy. Furthermore, the USA has the most efficient and powerful military in the world.

The symbols of Joseph, whose son Ephraim inherited the lion's share of the blessings listed above, are connected to both the USA and the UK. But the blessings given to each nation are as different as the symbols they both hold dear. From these symbols, it can be discerned that the glory of Joseph's heritage as a Prince of Egypt belongs to the constitutional monarchy of the United Kingdom via Manasseh, the older, firstborn son, but the blessings of prosperity given to Joseph belong to the United States via Ephraim, the younger son who possesses the blessing of the firstborn.

Since these prophecies concerning Joseph were uttered, no nation on Earth has ever been as greatly blessed economically as the United States. Despite its current economic woes, American citizens still enjoy the finest standard of living compared to any other nation on Earth. Nor has any other modern country been as greatly blessed with technological and military might as the United States.

Nonetheless, the United States now stands to be eclipsed by an even greater political power: the United Kingdom. Though few people consider it, the United Kingdom is the only modern nation to have successfully controlled a world empire within the last two hundred years, and it appears to be achieving this distinction yet again through its control of the British Commonwealth, which contains 54 member states, and its power within the European Union, which contains 28 member states. As a result, the glory of the 50 United States is now fading, while the United Kingdom is set to become the revived Roman Empire prophesied about in the Book of Daniel and Revelation. Meanwhile, the Middle East is uniting under the banner of radical Islam to set up a modern Caliphate or Babylon the Great, which may set up its headquarters in Iraq near the runs of ancient Babylon one day.

Though the UK does look like it may eclipse the USA one day soon, however, the Language of God found in symbols has a big part to play in correctly interpreting Scripture, and the tribal affiliations for Ephraim and Manasseh given by other scholars are likely wrong because they have consistently misapplied the symbols belonging exclusively to Ephraim to the British Empire. More about the Covenant promises made to the Tribe of Joseph and their fulfillment through the Ten Lost Tribes are shared in "The Language of God in Prophecy," especially in regard to Great Britain's connection to the Tribes of Judah, Dan and the half-tribe of Manasseh, the US connection to the half-tribe of Ephraim, and the role of these half tribes of Joseph in Bible Prophecy.

For now, I wanted to point out that the USA also has a direct connection to the Tribe of Dan, but its eagle emblem suggests that it may act as a destroyer of and godly replacement for the Tribe of Dan in prophecy. In fact, the eagle that replaced the evil serpent imagery originally associated with Dan became the symbol for the USA, which also originally had an association with serpent imagery before it was assigned the bald eagle as its symbol. This serpent imagery was first alluded to in 1751, when Benjamin Franklin wrote a satire in the

J O I N, or D I E.

Pennsylvania Gazette suggesting that the American colonists should send rattlesnakes to England as a way to thank them for their policy of sending convicted felons to America. It appeared a second time in a political cartoon drawn by Ben Franklin in 1754 that was meant to urge the eight English colonies existing at the time to unite during the French and Indian War. This cartoon wood cut showed a snake cut into eight sections that signified the colonies.

Later, serpent imagery was often adopted by the American colonies and their militias to represent their defiance against injustice. That is also why the snake appeared again in the Gadsden Flag with its warning statement: "Don't Tread on Me." This flag was created from the rattlesnake symbol and motto painted on the drum heads used by the first company of Marines formed to protect the American colonies against the British. Soon after, the first US Navy flag depicted a stretched-out version of the rattlesnake with the same motto on a background of seven red and six white stripes like that used on the original national flag of the United States. Interestingly, the rattlesnake on the Gadsden Flag has thirteen rattles at the end of its tail to reflect the number of colonies in America at that time. The rattlesnake was

considered a good symbol for the American military partly because rattlesnakes are unique to North America, have sharp, vigilant eyes, give due notice before they attack, and only strike in self-defense when they are provoked, which is seen as honorable. Over the years, this flag has been popular  among US political dissidents who disagree with the government's direction. As a result, the US Government has come to view the display of this flag or its motto as extremist and a hostile act of rebellion.

Now, despite the displeasure of Ben Franklin, who preferred the wild turkey, the bald eagle was adopted as a national symbol on the Great Seal of the United States along with thirteen stars, thirteen stripes, thirteen arrows, an olive branch, and a thirteen tiered pyramid with the Eye of Providence over it signifying the blessings of God on America. Though this Great Seal is discussed in depth in Book Four, three things concerning it are important to this discussion. First of all, the constant allusions to the number 13 show that the USA is connected to Ephraim. Secondly, there is absolutely no serpent imagery of any kind on either side of the Great Seal. This allegorically indicates that ***this nation did and will again reject the evil connotations of the Tribe of Dan that it initially*** *inherited from England* and will instead live up to its aspirations to become a force for good in the world that is symbolized by the white-headed bald eagle and its celestial counterpart called Aquila, a decan of the messianic Zodiac sign Capricorn. Though the future for America currently looks bleaker and darker than it ever has, I take heart in knowing that there still are great servants of God in America who are working behind the scenes to do God's will in eternity and who will likely have the last say in determining what part the USA will play during the Tribulation.

Finally, the pyramid found on the reverse side of the Great Seal is not only an allusion to God's power and sovereignty, but is tied to the patriarch Joseph. This can be seen from the fact that Joseph was an Israelite that became a Prince of Egypt like Moses and had two half Egyptian sons that inherited a permanent allotment of blessings in Israel. It also may be an allusion to the piety of Enoch, who designed the Great Pyramid as a symbol of God's love for mankind. Finally, it may be connected to the wisdom of Solomon, who married an Egyptian princess and designed a Temple for Yahweh that is connected to the design of the Desert Tabernacle and the Great Pyramid.

Despite the fact that much of this truth has been twisted by many secret societies working against the will of God and used by many conspiracy theorists to connect the USA with the nefarious plans of the Freemasons and the Illuminati, the fact remains that these symbols all originally had good connotations. They have simply been distorted over time by those who hate God to mean something evil and contrary to what God originally intended.

Coupled with the pyramid on the Great Seal, the use of the bald eagle and rattlesnake as symbols for America seem to suggest more than just a casual connection with ancient Egypt. In fact, the United States is the only country that sprang from Great Britain that still uses the Imperial Unit standard of measurement, and the British Inch appears to have been based on the Pyramid Inch, which is 1.001 British Inches in length. Interestingly, the vulture and cobra symbols used on the Uraeus worn on the foreheads of Egyptian pharaohs signified two protective warrior goddesses of Egypt. The rearing cobra signified Wadjet, the protective goddess of Lower Egypt, which was Shem's territory, while the white vulture signified the goddess Nekhbet, who protected Upper Egypt in Ham's territory. These symbols were joined together when ancient Egypt was unified into one kingdom under Narmer or Nimrod, who joined the serpent symbol of Lower Egypt with the vulture symbol of Upper Egypt to indicate his dominion over both.

Could it be that the feathered serpent symbol of the Mesoamerican god Quetzalcoatl also indicated the joining of two different lands, cultures and/or religions into one? Could this be why the United States uses the symbols of a poisonous serpent and powerful bird of prey to represent itself that are almost identical to those used in ancient Egypt? After all, the USA is a union or joining of 50 states into one, though each state retains its own individual legislatures, laws and symbols. Finally, could this use of serpent and bird imagery in the USA be divinely inspired to show America's connection to the Scorpio-Sagittarius Longitudinal Meridian via the states of Hawaii and Alaska? After all, the Zodiac Sign of Sagittarius has a decan named Aquila the Eagle, and Scorpio features Serpens the Serpent as one of its decans. We will discuss this intriguing possibility in the last chapter.

More on the subject of British Israelism can be found in the book "Judah's Sceptre and Joseph's Birthright" by J. H. Allen. The serpentine trail that the Tribe of Dan left throughout Europe is particularly easy to trace. See Part 3, Chapter IV in J. H. Allen's book, called "Dan – the Serpent's Trail" to find out more. In addition, evidence tying the Throne and Monarchy of England to the Throne and Tribe of Judah can be found in E. Raymond Capt's book "Jacob's Pillar." A newer book that covers more on this subject than any other is called "The 'Lost' Ten Tribes of Israel... Found!" by Steven M. Collins.

Though I absolutely do not agree with these authors concerning the Throne of David/Judah's literal survival in the British Isles, some of their ideas are very helpful when attempting to interpret End-Time Scriptures. But keep in mind that all their arguments tying the Throne of Judah to the Throne of England or the Scottish Throne are erroneously based on the idea that Yahshua did not fulfill God's promises to David regarding his throne, and they are therefore a clever deception that will likely be utilized to legitimatize the Antichrist's claim to be the rightful messiah and king over the Lost Ten Tribes of Israel that settled in the Western Hemisphere. The nations tied to these displaced Israelites are the United Kingdom and its Commonwealth nations, the United States, Mexico and Latin America, all of Europe, and Russia. Deceitful historians and Hollywood have been working together for years to set the stage for this coming false Messiah, especially through the quasi-historical book "Holy Blood, Holy Grail", the novel based on it called "The DaVinci Code", and the movie based on those books called "The DaVinci Code".

As a final note concerning the destiny of the United States as the fulfillment of God's blessings upon Joseph, let's take a look at the US Pledge of Allegiance. One line of this pledge states that the United States is "one nation under God, with liberty and justice for all." This line upholds the idea that the United States was founded on Judeo-Christian principles that can only be found in the Bible. As explained in Book Two, God Almighty invented true democracy - the kind where God is Sovereign, but lovingly allows men who love and honor God and keep His Law to govern themselves. This kind of democracy was established for the first time in history in ancient Israel before it became a kingdom. This is when there were only Judges over Israel, not false messiahs like many of the kings of Israel became, and like Barack Obama has become for many Americans today.

Despite the beauty of the freedom that their religion offered them, the Israelites began to feel oppressed by God's Law! As a result, they rejected Yahweh as their Sovereign, lost their monotheistic faith, and desired to have a human king (i.e. dictator) over them like the other nations around them had. This is exactly what America has done over the last fifty years. They have gradually taken God out of their government policies, schools and courts and are aspiring to create the New World Order.

This proposed one-world empire will be like that of ancient Rome, and it will eventually give one man the absolute authority to rule over the United States, Mexico, the European Union, the United Kingdom, the British Commonwealth, Russia, North Africa and most of the Middle East. After the Arabs are subdued, the Antichrist will likely proclaim another false "Pax Romana" or Roman Peace. However, this false peace will only last a short time before it dissolves, and the coming antichristian dictator known as the "man of sin" and "son of perdition" in 2 Thessalonians 2:3 begins to persecute and kill Jews and Christians - just as the ancient Roman emperors did.

Due to the godlessness of Western culture today, is it any wonder why there has been an exponential increase in violence, abuse and decay in this country and the world since then? Indeed, it is likely that God has allowed the threat of radical Islam to rage out of control due to the near total lack of righteousness in secularized Western society with its promotion of atheistic humanism and moral relativity and its ever-increasing persecution of Christians worldwide.

Fortunately, the only righteous and perfect Messiah and King of this world is Yahshua Ha Mashiach, a.k.a. Jesus the Christ and the Bible repeatedly promises that He is coming soon from Heaven to dethrone men like Barack Obama, Prince Charles, Tony Blair, Javier Solana, the reigning Pope in Rome and many others who have designs on His crown. I'm looking forward to that day.

The Spiritual Allegory in the Horns of Jacob's Sheep

Thus far, it has been shown that British Israelist claims that the

Used with permission:
www.oregonwool.com

Jacob's Sheep Ram
with two distinct
sets of horns

Throne of England and the Throne of Scotland are the literal Throne of Judah by virtue of the fact that King Zedekiah's daughters married into the Irish, Scottish and British royal lines is erroneous. In addition, though British Israelists claim that the Stone of Scone is Jacob's pillow that he rested his head upon at Bethel, it has been scientifically proven to not resemble any type of stone that is native to Israel. Nonetheless, there are many signs that God indeed blessed England above any other nation before the advent of the United States, and that God has also blessed the United States above any other nation. One of these comes by way of a common beast that is referred to constantly in Scripture as a symbol for the people that the Good Shepherd Yahshua loves (Gen. 49:24; Psalm 80:1; Hebrews 13:20; 1 Peter 2:24, 5:4). These are described as sheep: both redeemed sheep and the lost sheep of Israel (redeemed sheep: Matthew 25:32-33; lost or scattered sheep: Ezekiel 34:12, 22-23; Jeremiah 50:6; Mat. 10:6, 15:24). That is why, of all the mysteries surrounding England's religious and historical heritage, one of the most intriguing comes by way of Jacob's Sheep, a unique breed of primitive sheep that were only found in England until the early 1900's. At that time, some of these extremely mysterious multi-horned and speckled sheep were imported into the United States in limited quantities in an effort to preserve the breed.

Consequently, there are now many more breeders of Jacob's Sheep all over the United States (and a few in Canada) than there probably ever was in Great Britain. In addition, there are several associations in the United States that are solely dedicated to preserving this unique and fascinating breed of sheep, whereas in Great Britain too much crossbreeding has been done so that most of the Jacob's Sheep varieties there no longer have many primitive characteristics such as small size and speckled coats. Since I am a big believer in the power of symbols to convey truth, it caught my imagination when I discovered that these uniquely colored sheep are only bred in the USA, Canada, and the UK today (with the majority of breeders in the USA), and they are the only primitive sheep breed in the world that truly resembles the sheep that Jacob acquired from his deceitful uncle Laban in Canaan, which had speckled and spotted coats (See Genesis 30:32-39).

Jacob's Sheep are also unique because they often possess at least two sets of distinctly different horns, which allegorically suggest several things. First of all, since a horn can represent a specific nation, the two sets of horns on Jacob's Sheep may signify two different people groups or congregations, just as the left and right horns of Taurus do. As shown earlier, Taurus and Aries serve as a heavenly Altar of Sacrifice, with Taurus signifying the burnt sacrifices for sin offered outside the camp or city where the Gentiles dwell, while Aries signified the offerings burnt inside the Tabernacle or Temple court of the city or camp where the Israelites dwell. Therefore, is it possible that - in addition to signifying the horns of a bull and a ram - the four horns on the corners of the Altar of Sacrifice represented the horns of a four-horned ram like the Jacob? Furthermore, could the two sets of horns on a Jacob's Sheep ram also personify the two different congregations that love Yahshua - namely

Used with permission:
www.oregonwool.com

Jacob's Sheep Spotted Lamb

Messianic Jews and Gentile Christians? Finally, could it also signify the fact that God will unite these two currently warring congregations into one someday soon? Based on my interpretation of the Language of God, this is undoubtedly possible!

The unique coloring of Jacob's Sheep also serves as an allegorical spiritual illustration in that, though Jacob's Sheep appear to be white sheep with black, brown, and/or beige patches of wool, they are, in fact, black sheep with white patches. This can be seen in that the lambs sired by Jacob's Sheep rams with purely white ewes from another breed will always yield mostly black sheep with only a white spot or two. When breeding among themselves, Jacob's Sheep ewes almost always produce adorable spotted lambs like the one pictured on this page from Windy Acres Jacob's Sheep Farm in Heppner, Oregon.

In 2003, when writing the section in "The Language of God in the Universe" about the sign of Aries in the chapter covering the Judeo-Christian meaning of the Zodiac signs, I noted that - according to the books I used for research - it looked as though the Ram drawn by the Egyptians in the rectangular Dendera wall zodiac to depict the sign of Aries had three horns. In actuality, as already shown, the ancient Egyptians were likely depicting a unique type of ram with two distinct sets of horns in the rectangular zodiacs at the Dendera Temple to Hathor and the Esna Temple to Khnum. On the sides of their heads were the typical corkscrew type of horns seen on many kinds of rams, but between them was another straighter set of horns, as shown in the drawing of the signs of Pisces, Aries and Taurus on the rectangular Esna Ceiling Zodiac shown on page 663, along with a depiction of the Egyptian Creator god Khnum.

Interestingly, the Egyptian Creator god Khnum served as the husband of the opposing twin goddesses Neith and Satis, and he was depicted with this same type of double-horned ram's head. In Khnum's case, though, the upper set of horns was often accompanied by the sacred cobra symbol that represents the goddess Wadjet, and which often appeared next to the vulture symbol for the goddess Nekhbet on the Uraeus attached to the crown of the Pharaoh above his brow. Could it be that Khnum's double set of horns signified the two distinctly different attitudes that people can have towards the divine that is also found in the contrasting beliefs of the people groups represented by the war goddesses Neith and Satis and by the protective goddesses Wadjet and Nekhbet? Here again may be a record in ancient Egyptian art of the spiritual battle that some Egyptian priests must have known was being fought in the invisible spirit world all around them.

Egyptian Creator god Khnum with two distinct sets of horns

Esna Zodiac

Pisces

Aries

Taurus

Ancient Egyptian Art Showing a Type of Ram with Two Sets of Horns

Taken allegorically, the corkscrew horns on Jacob's Sheep rams and their black patches of wool signify unbelieving Jews who will eventually believe in Yahshua as well as some Messianic Jews, whose Shofar or trumpet is made from just such a spiraling ram's horn and whose reliance on Salvation by Works shows that they correspond to the black or colored part of the sheep signifying rebellion to Yahshua's free gift of Salvation by Grace. In contrast, the wavy or slightly curved horns of Jacob's Sheep and their white wool patches signify many Gentile and Messianic believers in the Messiah who embrace Salvation by Grace and are not subject to judgment. Instead, they rely on the Holy Spirit to help them keep the Law. Because of these strikingly true analogies, Jacob's Sheep are an ideal symbol for Yahshua's Two-House Church. This divided congregation of Jews and Gentiles will soon be united at the Wedding Supper of the Lamb in Heaven after the Rapture, and thereafter, they will keep the Feasts of the Lord together forever!

In addition to being a symbol for Judah and Ephraim, the horns of Jacob's Sheep also appear to be connected specifically to the United States and the United Kingdom by virtue of the fact that this specific type of sheep is found mostly in these two countries today. Now, in associating these two nations with certain sheep in prophecy, there are some prophetic passages in the Bible that specifically identify the Good Shepherd Yahshua with the Tribe of Joseph and the half tribes or flocks of sheep that sprang from him named Ephraim and Manasseh. In the last section, it was shown how Genesis 49:22-24 identified the United States with Joseph. There is also the following Scripture:

> "Give ear, O Shepherd of Israel, you who lead Joseph like a flock; you who dwell between the cherubim, shine forth! Before Ephraim, Benjamin, and Manasseh, stir up Your strength, and come and save us! Restore us, O God; cause Your face to shine, and we shall be saved!" - Psalm 80:1-3 (NKJ)

Both Genesis 49:22-24 and this prophecy in the Psalms are applicable to this last generation that will see the rise of the Antichrist and the Great Tribulation. For example, as explained earlier, the Scripture from Genesis is identifying the United States as Joseph by way of the fruitful bough and the arrows of a bow, which are grasped in the talons of the bald eagle on the Great Seal of the United States. The symbols also contain a prophetic message in that, though the USA will be grievously attacked by foreign nations in the End Times (as is clearly shown via Washington's vision and my analysis of Ezekiel Chapters 38 and 39 in Book Four), it will prevail against its enemies because God will defend it - just as He will defend Israel!

As explained in Book Two, the color black was associated with Joseph due to the assignation of the onyx stone to that tribe on the High Priest's breastplate. However, the type of onyx mentioned in the Bible is probably a type of banded chalcedony with black, brown and white bands swirled together. Amazingly, these match the colors of the people that have sought safe harbor in America, as well as the bald eagle on the Great Seal of the United States and the coloring of Jacob's Sheep!

Furthermore, the prophecy hidden in Psalm 80 gives a glimpse into the current political scene in the USA.

First of all, Psalm 80 states that God is the Shepherd of Israel and leads Joseph like a flock. In other words, the true believers in the USA and the UK are doing God's will by being the allies of Israel, although there are other strong hints in Scripture that the UK's and the USA's political and military support of Israel will end abruptly. This is covered in Book Four: "The Language of God in Prophecy", where my research suggests that the USA will defend Israel until the Battle of Gog and Magog begins. At that time, the USA will suffer the same fate as Ancient Israel in the End Times, and will be invaded by enemy armies until that great war known as the Battle of Armageddon puts a stop to it.

Alas, what the governing powers in Washington DC seem to be unaware of is that, by trying to force Israel to give up land for peace and to divide Israel in two, they are bringing about the same division in America. Indeed, America's fate appears to be tied to Israel in prophecy and eternity! This may be why about half the States are using their legislative authority to attempt to peaceably secede from the Union on ideological grounds. If they succeed, these States could form an independent nation with their own military - one that might back Israel against the New World Order upheld by the other half of the divided country. Such a division of America along State and ideological lines would change the United States forever, and cause the rest of the world to hate those that revolt against the liberals who follow men like President Barack Obama. Unless they repent and are saved by the Blood of Christ, all liberals will suffer horrible divine judgment.

Though the chances are slim ever since President Obama placed new liberal military leaders in all branches of the US Armed Forces that are loyal to his New World Order agenda, a full or partial US Military coup could also keep the country united. It might also allow the new government of the USA to reject the New World Order that it helped to form. If this happened, America might continue to defend Israel.

The prophecy in Genesis 49:22-24 suggests this possibility, as does George Washington's prophecy for America (See Book Four). For now, as Psalm 80 proclaims, the nation of Israel has repeatedly called on the USA and UK to save them from destruction at the hands of their enemies over the past sixty years. However, the USA and UK will not ultimately save Israel from tyranny. Instead, the Good Shepherd Yahshua will save them from oppression, damnation and hellfire!

Indeed, Psalm 80 suggests that many Jews will find Yahshua as their Messiah partly due to the loving influence of people from the Tribe of Joseph (i.e. Ephraim as the USA and Manasseh as the UK) and Benjamin (which signifies the nation of Norway and northern Europe in general) that will witness to the Jews in the Last Days! As proof of this, the number of Messianic Jews and Jews converted fully to Christianity has recently begun to grow exponentially worldwide due to the love, acceptance, forgiveness and compassion that truly born-again Christians and Messianic Jews have shown to their unsaved Jewish brethren.

Modern Pagans and Idolaters Will Be Severely Judged!

Just as Judah fell to Nebuchadnezzar in judgment, so too will this current New World Order fall to ruin when Yahshua comes again as a conquering King. The prophet Isaiah foresaw that day as a time when all the idols of men would be shown to be the frauds they are:

> "The loftiness of man shall be bowed down, and the haughtiness of men shall be brought low; the LORD (Yahweh) alone will be exalted in that day, But the idols He shall utterly abolish. They shall go into... the caves of the earth, from the terror of the LORD (Yahweh)... when He arises to shake the earth mightily. **In that day a man will cast away his idols of silver and his idols of gold...** to go into the clefts of the rocks... from the terror of the LORD (Yahweh)... when He arises to shake the earth mightily." – Isaiah 2:17-21 (NKJ)

Yahweh God will not be mocked forever! As He did from Israel and Judah, Yahweh will exact the same judgments from all the nations of the world. One day soon, our Heavenly Father will send Yahshua to conquer the armies of the Earth. At the end of the Tribulation, Yahshua will come to destroy all of the devil's strongholds and kill all the sinful people who have rejected and scorned both Yahshua and His Spirit-filled followers. In this way, Yahweh will come to judge all the people that the Bible describes like this:

> "But mark this: **There will be terrible times in the last days**. People will be lovers of themselves, lovers of money, boastful, proud, abusive, disobedient to their parents, ungrateful, unholy, without love, unforgiving, slanderous, without self-control, brutal... **lovers of pleasure rather than lovers of God - having a form of godliness but denying its power**. Have nothing to do with them. They are the kind who... gain control over weak-willed women, who are loaded down with sins and... evil desires, **always learning but never able to acknowledge the truth**. Just as Jannes and Jambres

opposed Moses, so also these men oppose the truth - men of depraved minds, who... will not get very far because... their folly will be clear to everyone." - 2 Tim. 3:1-9 (NIV)

These types of unrighteous and unrepentant people can be found in great numbers all over our world today. Many of them have seen that important national and international figures aren't punished for their sins and then think that they can ignore national laws and do what they want. They scoff at authority and hate the truth. They plan and plot and feel no remorse when their schemes to get rich, gain power or become famous bring others suffering and ruin. They arrogantly reject the need for a Savior and claim that they are already righteous and without sin. Those who do fall into the evil snares of pride and self-righteousness will be severely punished. Those among them who scoff at the need for a Savior and who are still openly hostile to the Gospel of Redemption when Yahshua comes again will perish. In the comparison chart between Enoch and the Bible in Chapter Two, I quoted a graphic passage from Enoch about the Last Judgment. Here is a portion of it that shows just how terrible the punishment of those who will not repent will be:

"And the judgement was held first over the stars, and they were judged and found guilty, and went to the place of condemnation, and they were cast into an abyss, full of fire and flaming, and full of pillars of fire. And those seventy shepherds were judged and found guilty, and they were cast into that fiery abyss. And I saw at that time how a like abyss was opened in the midst of the earth, full of fire, and they brought those blinded sheep, and they were all judged and found guilty and cast into this fiery abyss, and they burned; now this abyss was to the right of that house. And I saw those sheep burning and their bones burning." - 1 Enoch 89:24-27

This passage begins by stating that the "stars" or fallen angels will be judged, found to be unrepentant and guilty, and cast into the Lake of Fire. In addition, the seventy unrighteous leaders over Israel will be judged and cast into Hell. Finally, all the blind and unrepentant sheep will be judged and condemned to burn in Hell forever even after their bodies are consumed in the fire. This passage confirms what the Bible says about Hell and shows how real it is, and I can't think of a more horrible way to spend eternity or a more compelling reason to beg God for forgiveness now before it's too late!

Though judgment and punishment are coming to the wicked, a time of great peace and joy is coming for the many redeemed among the people of the Earth, and it will be an especially blessed time for the people of Israel. As it says in Scripture:

> *"Thus says the Lord GOD (Yahweh Adonai): 'Surely I will take the children of Israel... and will gather them from every side and bring them into their own land; and I will make them one nation... on the mountains of Israel;* **and one king shall be king over them all**... *They shall not defile themselves anymore with their idols... but I will deliver them...* **Then they shall be My people, and I will be their God. David My servant shall be king over them, and they shall all have one shepherd...** *Then they shall dwell in the land that I have given to Jacob My servant... they, their children, and their children's children...* **Moreover I will make a Covenant of peace with them... an everlasting Covenant**... *and I will set My sanctuary in their midst forevermore.* **My tabernacle also shall be with them; indeed I will be their God, and they shall be My people.** *The nations also will know that I, the LORD (Yahweh), sanctify Israel, when My sanctuary is in their midst forevermore.'" - Ezekiel 37:21-28 (NKJ)*

During Christ's Millennial Rule, all the Israelites who were lost among the nations will be gathered into the Promised Land and reunited with their Jewish brethren already gathered there. **The Tribes of Judah and Levi and the Ten Lost Tribes will be gathered together to become the Nation of Israel.** Then all of the land of Israel from the Euphrates to the Nile will be restored and it will never be divided or brought to ruin again. At that time, the above Scripture indicates that Yahweh will again cut a Covenant with Israel - an everlasting Covenant of peace. At that time, the blood that will sanctify this Covenant will be the already shed blood of our glorified Savior and Lord: Yahshua, the Son of Yahweh. Nonetheless, as a witness to the Gentile nations and unsaved or mortal people outside of Israel, the rituals and sacrifices surrounding the new Temple to Yahweh in Jerusalem will be a focal point of every Feast of the Lord throughout the Millennial period.

For reference, the chart on the next page shows the probable Zodiac and modern National affiliations of Israel's Twelve Tribes. This is partly based on Steven Collins' book: "The Ten Lost Tribes of Israel - Found!" which contains a detailed analysis of how these nations fit Israel's tribal affiliations. However, due to my own research on the identity of the Lost Tribes, I disagree with him and all other British Israelists of note in that the USA should be seen as Ephraim, not Manasseh. I also see Wales, Denmark and the USA associated with Dan, while Steven Collins does not.

Modern Nations and Zodiac Signs Tied to the 12 Tribes

(Partly Based on Genesis 49:3-27 and Deuteronomy 33:6-25)

Tribe of Israel	Modern National Association	Zodiac Sign
Born to Leah:		
Reuben	France	Aquarius
Simeon	Greece, Italy	Pisces
Levi	Throughout Europe	Libra
Judah	Israel	Leo
Issachar	Finland	Cancer
Zebulon	Holland, Netherlands	Virgo
Born to Leah's Handmaid Zilpah:		
Gad	Germany	Capricorn
Asher	South Africa	Sagittarius
Born to Rachel's Handmaid Bilhah:		
Dan	Denmark, Ireland, Wales, USA	Scorpio and Draco the Dragon
Naphtali	Sweden	Aries
Born to Rachel:		
Joseph = 2 sons **Ephraim** & **Manasseh**	**Ephraim** = United States, **Manasseh** = The United Kingdom	Taurus: **Ephraim** = right horn, **Manasseh** = left horn
Benjamin	Norway	Gemini

As Yahweh foresaw, the Israelites have been scattered all over the world and many nations can still be identified with the original Twelve Tribes that they sprang from or mingled with. In this way, the whole world has been blessed with a share in the promises that Yahweh made to Abraham and the Israelites. However, despite the inclusion of the Gentiles into God's promises of blessing and hope in the First Resurrection for those who are saved by the Blood of Christ, the modern nation of Israel is still beloved of God and was destined to be repopulated by the Jews, as was explained in this book on pages 349 and 350. There, we discussed Yahshua's Parable of the Fig Tree signifying the kingdom or nation of Israel being destroyed and then miraculously resurrected or reborn - just as it was in 1948.

Though the modern Israelites represented by Americans, Asians, Africans, Hispanics, Europeans, Russians and most of the world's Jews are largely trapped in unbelief and are ripe for judgment, God has promised that those who now faithfully follow the Way of Yahweh that promises them a place in the Kingdom of God through Christ will be spared from God's Wrath that will be poured out on mankind during the Great Tribulation. In addition, many modern Israelites that are currently lost sheep will be saved during the dire events of the Tribulation period.

So, though the glory that was the Kingdom of Israel in King Solomon's time is now lost, a glimmer of it remains in every follower of the God of Abraham. In addition, as shown in Book Four, the United States of America serves as a type of Israel in modern times. Like the Israel of old, the USA was deeply blessed with great power and prosperity - but only for as long as it followed and honored Yahweh and truly acted as "One Nation Under God." Likewise, the USA is now suffering from all of the curses associated with disobeying Yahweh and ignoring His laws such as economic collapse, severe weather, natural disasters, environmental plagues and diseases, and constant military threats from all sides. In addition, for every one of America's political actions that is against God's Will for modern Israel, the United States has suffered economically, financially, and physically. This has been well-documented by many recent books.

In summary, this chapter has served to highlight why the knowledge of the metaphorical Language of God and the Gospel in the Stars is desperately needed when interpreting Scripture in Christian churches and homes today. This is because Satan is currently working overtime to lead as many people astray as possible in these last days before the onset of the Tribulation. Many people have already been deceived into accepting ideas that are antagonistic to essential Christian doctrines like the Trinity and salvation by Christ's blood sacrifice. If the knowledge of the Language of God, Sacred Astronomy and the rite of the Blood Covenant aren't made more readily known, many more believers are going to be led astray.

Understanding the allegorical meaning of the Blood Covenant we cut with the Father through Yahshua is essential to understanding the entire Gospel of Salvation, which was written in the stars before it was written in the Bible! It is almost impossible to understand the depth of the heart and mind of Yahweh God that is revealed in Scripture unless we have knowledge of His incredible metaphorical picture Language found in every word of prophecy as well as the Gospel in the Stars. Similarly, it is very difficult to understand the depth and scope of our salvation from sin through Yahshua without the powerful symbolism of Blood Covenant ceremonies to sharpen our understanding.

We cannot know how to truly please Yahweh unless we master understanding the differences between good and evil and right and wrong. A thorough knowledge of the hidden metaphorical Language of God in the Heavenly Tablets of the Zodiac, in the Bible and in other sacred books like the Book of 1 Enoch can give us this mastery. This however, is only possible if the Holy Spirit is present within the individual seeking enlightenment. Without the Holy Spirit acting as a Guide and Mentor, any initiate into these deeper mysteries of our complex and beautiful faith might be led astray and fall into the sins outlined in this chapter.

My hope is that this book will lead many people to a deeper and fuller understanding of the only way to salvation from sin and death: Yahshua our Adonai and Messiah. May this book be a beacon in the darkness, showing sinners the way to Yahshua - our only real ladder or stairway to Heaven. May the knowledge of Yah's holy symbolic Language revealed in this book, in every Parable, and in every prophetic vision and dream help all people to draw nearer to Yahshua. As the Word of God and the Creator, Yahshua was instrumental in weaving the Language of God into the fabric of the Universe. It is therefore also fitting that we must all look to Yahshua for our salvation. He alone can save us all from our sins and give us eternal life. Making an effort to understand Yah's sacred allegorical Language is just one way of approaching Him in love and faith. By whatever means it takes, all people need to learn to approach Yah with love and humility before it is too late.

The time is coming soon when it will be too late. "The Language of God in Prophecy" deals with that time - the time when the Day of the Lord will arrive as prophesied. That book shows that the Lord's Day has already come in secret and many events leading up to the Tribulation have already come to pass. That is why it is so important to know that our only salvation from sin, and our only sure protection from the worldwide plagues of the Great Tribulation can be found in Yahshua the Messiah.

Though this study of the importance of Sethite Astronomy in understanding biblical history and End Times prophecy is nearly complete, it has not fully addressed the place of Latin America, the USA and Canada in history. In the final chapter, we will explore the place of the New World within the Bible's historical and prophetic narratives. In addition, we will explore the deeper meanings behind their association with the Sagittarius Longitudinal Meridian and the constellations Ophiuchus and Serpens, as delineated in Chapter Six.

Chapter 9: The New World Connection To Israel

"I lay down My life for the sheep. **And other sheep I have which are not of this fold;** *them also I must bring, and they will hear My voice; and there will be one flock and one shepherd.'" - John 10:15-16 (NKJ)*

The Scripture opening this chapter is from the Gospel of John, which has a depth of spiritual knowledge about Yahshua and an anointed view of His sheep that is more mystical than the other three Gospels. In this Scripture, Yahshua boldly declared that He already had other sheep that were not among the Jews and Gentiles that He was speaking to at that time. In this case, Yahshua was referring to Gentiles and Lost Israelites scattered in other lands who would become His sheep, but who did not know Him yet and were awaiting His Gospel message of redemption, peace and deliverance from sin, death and sorrow in the Kingdom of God.

In this chapter, we will explore the possibility mentioned in Chapter Six that Noah and Shem may have civilized the Americas and also lived there at one time until Nimrod overthrew their reign and either he or his evil son Mardon introduced Paganism, idolatry, and human sacrifice. In addition, we will examine the evidence that some of the Lost Sheep of Israel may have immigrated to the Americas in several stages before the time of Christ, bringing the idea of monotheism with them as well as some of the Pagan religious ideas they had learned from their neighbors.

Thus far, we have discussed world history with a focus on those kingdoms, cultures and threads of spiritual knowledge that have directly had a bearing on the formation and destruction of the Kingdom of Israel. Since all of these ancient cultures were in the Old World, nothing has been said about the New World except for the place of the United States as one of the Lost Tribes of Israel and the possibility that Noah settled in the Americas after the Flood. In this chapter, much evidence will be shown that gives feasibility to my hypothesis that the New World was visited and populated by ancient Semitic peoples that arrived in several waves beginning with descendents of Noah and Shem and ending with the Israelite tribes of Judah and Benjamin who fled the armies of Nebuchadnezzar.

In an effort to prove this, Steven M. Collins has amassed much compelling evidence in his book "The 'Lost' Ten Tribes of Israel... Found!" Though this book is no longer available at Amazon.com and other Internet outlets or regular bookstores, it can still be purchased from the author's web site: http://www.stevenmcollins.com. I highly recommend it, with one strong admonition that those reading it remember that Collins' view of the USA as Manasseh and the UK as Ephraim is incorrect for all the reasons given in this book and "The Language of God in Prophecy."

Hinting that the Lost Tribes of Israel likely spread throughout the world after their initial dispersion and settlement in Europe and Great Britain, two key Scriptures declare that Yahshua was sent to save and regather these heathenized outcasts of Israel:

> "These twelve Jesus sent out and commanded them, saying: 'Do not go into the way of the Gentiles, and do not enter a city of the Samaritans. **But go rather to the lost sheep of the house of Israel.**" - Matthew 10:5-6 (NKJ)

> "But He (Yahshua) answered and said, 'I was not sent except to the lost sheep of the house of Israel.'" - Matthew 15:24 (NKJ)

These Lost Sheep of the House of Israel were those Israelites that had been scattered throughout Asia Minor where Turkey is now located, Scythia in southern Russia, and Parthia, which was once located where modern Iran is today - making it the southern neighbor of the Scythians. In fact, it is estimated that over half the populations of Scythia and Parthia were of Israelite descent around the time of Christ. In addition to these, the powerful maritime kingdom of Carthage was also strengthened by a large influx of Israelites fleeing the drought brought on by the prophet Ezekiel (See 1 Kings 17:1, 7; 1 Kings 18:1) as well as the subsequent invasion and destruction of the Northern Kingdom of Israel by the Assyrians in two waves eight centuries before the time of Christ (2 Kings 17:4-7; 2 Kings 18:9-12).

Around 730 BC, a major portion of the population of the Northern Kingdom of Israel was taken into captivity by the Assyrians. Then, not long after, the mountainous regions of Samaria were defeated after another Assyrian siege. In his previous invasion, the King of Assyria had accepted the King of Israel's massive tribute of gold and sliver and let the Israelites in Samaria remain. This time, however, many of its elderly and weak inhabitants were slaughtered and the rest were carried away into captivity. Both waves of Israelite captives were resettled in the Assyrian Empire's less populated northern regions and they and their descendents served as laborers in the Assyrian king's building projects. It is from these resettled Israelites that the kingdoms of Parthia and Scythia emerged when Assyria fell to the Babylonians. Meanwhile, those that escaped Assyrian captivity and resettlement mostly fled to other lands like Carthage, which had an Israelite heritage and a similar language and customs.

Though it is not widely known, the kingdom of Parthia (which was at one time allied with Scythia) and the Carthaginian Empire were two of the Roman Republic's biggest rivals and both nearly succeeded in conquering Rome before they were pushed back by its legions. When they did finally fall, the Lost Israelites in these kingdoms migrated throughout the world. Though the Israelites mostly fled into what is now Russia and Europe, it is a little known fact that some of these Lost Israelites also found their way into Asia, Africa, and the Americas. In this chapter, we will discuss on how these Israelites influenced native peoples such as those living in the Mayan Civilization of Central America and the Algonquins and other native peoples living in North America. However, the primary focus of this chapter concerns the fate of Noah and Shem during the Emperor Nimrod's worldwide reign of terror and how they greatly influenced the culture and religious beliefs of the original native inhabitants of the Americas.

Now, the Bible tells us that these Lost Israelites will one day be divinely gathered from everywhere that they have settled and be returned to the Promised Land, just as God has already regathered the Jews. In fact, **people from all the nations of the world will gather together in Jerusalem to praise and worship Adonai Yahweh (a.k.a. Yahshua) one day soon:**

> "The Lord GOD (Adonai Yahweh), who gathers the outcasts of Israel, says, 'Yet **I will gather to him others besides those who are gathered to him.**'" - Isaiah 56:8 (NKJ)

> "**All nations whom You have made shall come and worship before You,** O Lord (Adonai), and shall glorify Your name. For You are great, and do wondrous things; you alone are God." - Psalm 86:9-10 (NKJ)

This gathering of believers and Lost Israelites from all the nations of the world to worship and praise Adonai Yahshua in His glorified state will occur during His Millennial Rule. At that time, believers from the Arab nations surrounding Israel will be invited to worship and praise God and live in the Promised Land as well. This is attested to in the following Scripture, which refers to Ishmael's second son Kedar, who settled in Arabia and to Sela, the Capital city of the Edomite Kingdom south of Israel that belonged to the descendents of Esau:

> "Sing to the LORD (Yahweh) a new song, and His praise from the ends of the earth, you who go down to the sea, and all that is in it, you coastlands and you inhabitants of them! **Let the wilderness and its cities lift up their voice, the villages that Kedar inhabits. Let the inhabitants of Sela sing,** let them shout from the top of the mountains. Let them give glory to the LORD (Yahweh), and declare His praise in the coastlands." - Isaiah 42:10-12 (NKJ)

Besides the Arabs, note also that "the coastlands" mentioned in the preceding Scripture is more correctly translated as "isles of the sea." These lands that were completely or mostly surrounded by bodies of water included the many peninsulas and islands of the northern Mediterranean and Europe such as Tyre, Cypress, Greece, Italy, Spain, the Netherlands, and the British Isles. Some scholars also think these coastlands may have been referring to the coasts and peninsulas in Asia and the American continents, which may have been considered to be nothing more than very large islands by the Egyptian, Phoenician, Israelite and Carthaginian merchants and miners that roamed their shores looking for marketable resources to trade in the Old World at one time. Thus, Israel and Jerusalem will be home to an international cast of believers during the Millennial Rule of Christ, all of whom will live and work together in abiding peace for the first time in history! There are references to these currently divided and fractured groups of believers in the New Testament. In the following Scripture, they are referred to as the children of God:

> "Now this he did not say on his own authority; but being high priest that year he prophesied that Jesus (Yahshua) would die for the nation, and not for that nation only, but also that **He would gather together in one the children of God who were scattered abroad.**" - John 11:51-52 (NKJ)

This passage records the words of the High Priest Caiaphas, who sought to put Yahshua to death when he realized that Yahshua was winning over the people with His miracles. Caiaphas assumed that, if Yahshua were to die, it would put a stop to any kind of rebellion, allow Caiaphas and his colleagues to retain their positions of authority in Jerusalem, and that it would appease the Romans so that the people of Judea would be spared from annihilation. He also fancied that the act of fighting and resisting the followers of this would-be messiah figure might unite the Israelites scattered abroad with the Judean leadership and they would have greater power within the Roman Empire that way. Little did Caiaphas know, however, that - though his ideas proved initially true - just the opposite would result a few short years later! Nonetheless, the High Priest's words proved prophetic in the sense that Yahshua did die for the sins of all people everywhere, not just the Jews. In addition, the amazing message of Salvation by Grace behind the blood that Yahshua shed for all mankind eventually would bring Gentiles from every nation together into one loving family.

Medicine Wheels: Their Hidden Message

More subtle Pagan perversions of the truth can be found in another ancient Native American mystical spiritual ritual. This is found in what is called a Medicine Wheel today. From its similarities with the circular Zodiac, this circular symbol for finding one's spiritual path to fulfillment appears to have once been fully linked with the Gospel in the Stars. For example, a small ceremonial Medicine Wheel that is in widespread use today among Native Americans is made up of thirty-six stones - the same number of stones as decans in the ancient Zodiac and one tenth the full number of degrees in the circle of the Zodiac.

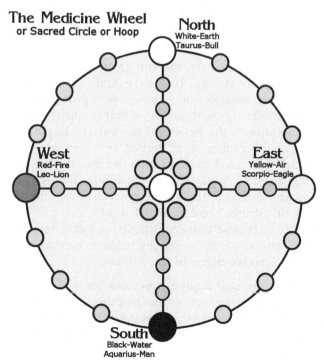

Typically, each of the stones in the Medicine Wheel is associated with a different totem animal spirit and direction on the horizon. As such they are reminiscent of the henges of Europe and Great Britain, whose pillared portals were used to keep track of star and planetary movements.

The stones of the Medicine Wheel are sub-divided into three groups. Four stones represent the cardinal directions. In Native American thought today, these stones are often associated with the four races of mankind and the four elements. The stone pointing east is associated with the yellow races and the element of air, the stone pointing south is connected to the black races and the element of water, the stone directed west signifies the red races and the element of fire, and the stone pointing north represents the white races and the element of earth. Another twelve stones represent points along the circular rim of the Medicine Wheel. These stones may represent the Twelve Signs of the Zodiac and the Sun's movement throughout the day. In addition to these stones, there are twelve stones that mark the cross-shaped "spokes" of the Medicine Wheel that connect the four directions with a central "axle."

Seven stones surround this symbolic "axle," with one last stone at the center. This is the largest stone in the wheel and - to many Native Americans - it represents the all-reaching power of the Creator God. For this reason, it is fitting that the other stones seem to circle around this stone and it is at the center of a symbolic cross signifying the totality of God's Creation. This also suggests that the stones marking the four directions of the Medicine Wheel were likely originally connected to the four Zodiac signs and four elements that are represented by the four faces of the Cherubim, with the Bull of Taurus signifying the element Earth, the Eagle of Capricorn called Aquila signifying Scorpio and the element Air, the Lion of Leo signifying the element Fire, and the Man of Aquarius the Water-bearer signifying the element Water.

Added together (4 + 12 + 12 + 7 + 1), the sub groups of stones in the Medicine Wheel equal thirty-six stones. To Native Americans, these thirty-six stones represent animal totems often known as "spirit guides" that reflect various stages in human growth and spiritual maturity. In this respect it bears a resemblance to the beliefs of the ancient Egyptians, where the thirty-six decans of the Zodiac were deified and seen as divisions of the year that could be used to determine the month, the day and the divisions of the day used to mark religious festivals. Though, in essence, the Native Americans and Egyptians were correct in assuming that these thirty-six decans or "stones" had spiritual significance, however, they were wrong in ascribing demonic spirits and erroneous meanings to these symbols - thereby corrupting the original message of the 36 decan signs within the Twelve Signs of the Zodiac.

Fascinatingly, the most popular Native American view of the Medicine Wheel today is found in the Hopi Native tradition. Their view of the Medicine Wheel is that it represents the harmony that could result if all four major races on the Earth today - white, yellow, red, and black - worked together in a spirit of love and harmony. This belief of the Hopi

Indians is highly suggestive of the way the Great Pyramid may have been utilized to divide the Earth into four quarters signifying the patriarchs Noah, Shem, Ham, and Japheth - whose descendants are likely signified by these four major races. However, the four-toned Medicine Wheel of the Hopi has become a universal symbol of peace and harmony among proponents of the New Age Movement and Wicca, which shows just one more way that Satan has twisted an originally good symbol into something evil that is tied to the world ecumenical movement.

Along with smaller Medicine Wheels, Native Americans also made much larger ceremonial Medicine Wheels or Sacred Hoops. In this case, large circles of unhewn stones with a center hub marked by a pile of similar stones were made on the ground. Many also contain a number of "spokes" radiating from the center stone "axle" in mimicry of a spoked wheel. Scattered across the Great Plains region of North America are many dozens of such Medicine Wheels - some of them surrounded by much smaller stone circles called tipi rings. The stones of these smaller rings once held down the sides of the conical animal skin tipis used by various Plains Indian tribes.

Two of the most notable Medicine Wheels are the Bighorn Medicine Wheel in Wyoming and the Majorville Medicine Wheel in Alberta, Canada. The Big Horn Medicine Wheel is the most southernmost of these sacred circles. It is 75 feet in diameter, has 28 spokes radiating from a central cairn, and five prominent cairns along the rim of the circle, as shown in the photo on page 680. Also shown on this photo are the findings of a study done by Astronomer Dr. John Eddy of Colorado. Dr. Eddy has proven that this sacred circle could have been used to track the movements of the Sun, Moon, and certain stars that still have sacred meaning to the Native Americans living in the area.

Dr. Eddy found that this sacred circle marked the time of the Summer Solstice sunrise and sunset as well as the paths of four brilliant stars. The first of these stars was Al Debaran. This Red Giant star is tied to the Red Pyramid at Dahshur, which marks the bright reddish eye of Taurus the Bull. The Zodiac sign of Taurus is tied to the patriarch Joseph, whose bull symbol prophetically replaced Reuben's sign Aquarius that is tied to mankind and water in the Star Gospel. The other three stars that the Big Horn Medicine Wheel was likely designed to track are Rigel in the right foot of the messianic constellation Orion; Sirius or the Star of Bethlehem in the decan of Gemini called Canis Major; and the bright star Fomalhaut or Fom Al Haut in the constellation Piscis Australis, which is a decan of Aquarius signifying Noah's Ark and the those under the New Covenant that are sealed with the Holy Spirit.

Bighorn Medicine Wheel Stellar Alignment Diagram

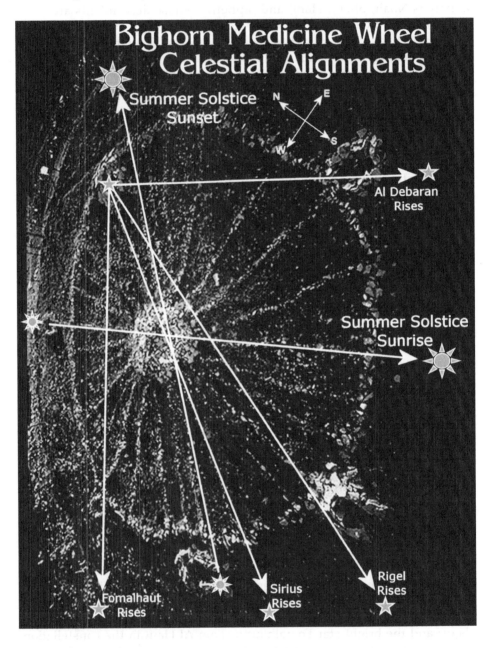

Fascinatingly, the 1000-year Great Day of the Lord is to unfold during the current Precessional Age of Aquarius, and one wonders if the makers of this Medicine Wheel knew this. In addition, three of the stars targeted by the Bighorn Medicine Wheel are located in constellations that figure prominently in Chapter Three, where their relationship to the Temple of Yahweh and two Altars of Sacrifice marked out in the heavens are shown. Could the ancient builders of the Bighorn Medicine Wheel have known of the amazing significance of these constellations in the Gospel in the Stars? Or were they preserving an ancient knowledge of their sacredness without remembering the real meaning behind them? Though there is no way of knowing for sure until Yahshua comes, this is an intriguing possibility.

The less well known Majorville Medicine Wheel is in a remote location in northern Alberta and is similar to the Bighorn Medicine Wheel in that it covers a large area of land and also has 28 spokes, which are equal to the number of astronomical Mansions of the Moon and the approximate number of days in a lunar cycle. An interesting fact tying Native American Astronomy to China is that the 28 Mansions of the Moon figure prominently in Chinese Astronomy. These Mansions were used in Asia and India to measure the length of the year following the Moon's cycles rather than the movements of the Sun through the Zodiac.

Another sacred circle more closely resembling a henge was found at Cahokia Mounds in Southern Illinois near St. Louis, Missouri. Cahokia was once one of the largest cosmopolitan centers north of the Mesoamerican cities in Mexico, at one time housing as many as 20,000 year-round residents. Cahokia is one of only eight World Heritage Sites in the United States, and it has been an ongoing site for archeological research into the customs and religious beliefs of several Native American tribes known as Mississippians that are associated with mound building. At Cahokia, archeologists have identified a large manmade earthwork platform now called Monk's Mound that is the largest so far found in North America. This earthen platform served as the central hub for ceremonial activities surrounding this ancient native community.

To get an idea of just how big it is, Monks Mound covers 13 acres, faces south and is 92 feet (28 meters) high, 951 feet (290 meters) long and 836 feet (255 meters) wide. Once believed to have been topped with a large ceremonial building, Monk's Mound is on the edge of a huge ceremonial plaza that covers 19 hectares of land. This plaza is topped with and is surrounded by many other smaller ceremonial mounds, 69 of which are located on the Cahokia Mounds park grounds.

Another intriguing feature of Cahokia Mounds is the presence of a sacred circle that once featured five rings of wooden posts around a central post. This sacred circle has been dubbed North America's Woodhenge in mimicry of the one in England, though the one in the United States is much more elaborate and was once connected to a magnificent ceremonial center - the likes of which has thus far not been found in the United Kingdom.

America's Woodhenge contained posts that were made of sacred red cedar wood, several of which were aligned with the four cardinal directions and the solstices and equinoxes. In addition, Woodhenge contained five rings of red cedar posts. The first circle, which is only partially excavated, would have had 24 posts; the second circle had 36 posts; the third had 48 posts; the fourth had 60 posts; and the last circle contained 12 posts along the eastern sunrise arc - though it would have had 72 posts if it had been made into a complete circle. Interestingly, each circle is a multiple of 12 and the number 12 is intimately connected to the solar and lunar cycles associated with our planet.

What intrigues me the most about the Medicine Wheels of North America is that they seem to contain a primitive record of Sacred Astronomy and the Gospel in the Stars. Another link between Medicine Wheels and the ancient Sethites and Israelites is the fact that these sacred circles were mostly constructed of unhewn white stones - just as the sacred pillars erected by the Patriarchs and Israelites were, and Woodhenge was made from reddish wood pillars that are just as suggestive of the rite of blood sacrifice as the pinkish-toned red granite used at the base and in the most sacred interior rooms and spaces of the Great Pyramid. These similarities add to the feasibility of my hypothesis placing Noah and his son Shem as the Post-Flood civilizers of North and Central America. Furthermore, these common points suggest that Native Americans once had a familiarity with both Sethite and Israelite religious ideas and customs.

Blood Covenant Rites in the Americas

Besides the Native American understanding of the Language of God and Gospel in the Stars in the Medicine Wheels that we explored in the last section, there is another definite clue that Noah may have lived in the Americas and taught his wisdom there at one time. Many Native Americans seem to have understood the concepts behind the biblical rite of Blood Covenanting. This biblically sanctioned practice was memorialized through the Native American concept of Blood Brotherhood. In the most common form of this native rite, two unrelated people who wished to be considered blood kin did so by cutting each others palms and clasping or rubbing their hands tightly together. This was done so that the two types of blood would mingle in each person's wound and form a scar that would forever commemorate their mutual adoption into each other's family.

In other cases, an animal's flesh would be shared with the person who was entering into a Native American familial alliance. As they sat down to eat, all the people entering into the Blood Covenant agreement together shared the cooked meat and acknowledged that the meat was a substitutionary sacrifice that allegorically represented their own flesh. In this way, they symbolically became one flesh or one family. This is why any person who was given the privilege to sit and eat at a Native American meal gathering would henceforward be treated as a beloved member of that family. In fact, **at one time in the far past, allowing a stranger to eat while seated at the family hearth was seen as an adoption ceremony in almost every culture on Earth**. Being invited to eat a meal with a native family was an invitation to become a member of their tribe and to share far more than their hospitality alone!

Interesting to note here is that similar versions of **the two basic forms of Blood Covenanting just outlined were practiced in primitive cultures everywhere on Earth**, including many found in Africa in the early part of the Twentieth Century. If nothing else, the prevalence of these rituals suggests that all the cultures of the world descended from Noah, who as a Sethite would have taught his children the rite of Blood Covenanting. Indeed, Noah's sons would have known of and practiced Blood Covenant rites whenever a marriage or adoption took place or a treaty was made. To find out more about the history and forms of Blood Covenanting found throughout the world at one time, see Book Two, "The Language of God in Humanity." In addition, please refer to the book: "The Blood Covenant" by Clay H. Trumbull, and "The Covenants" by Kevin Konner and Ken Malmin, as listed in the Bibliography.

Another more sinister religiously inspired behavior of Native Americans was the practice of ritual human bloodletting to pay for transgressions against God, show grief in mourning for the dead, and - at times - to torture enemies. Though this bloodletting was outlawed by Yahweh God in Israel, it was readily practiced by the Pagans surrounding Israel, especially by the followers and priests of Moloch and Baal, as evidenced in this Scripture concerning the showdown between Elijah and the 450 priests of Baal during the time of King Ahaz and his wicked Queen Jezebel:

> *"So they cried aloud, and cut themselves, as was their custom, with knives and lances, until the blood gushed out on them."* - I Kings 18:28 (NKJ)

This bloodletting of the priests of Baal was a demonically inspired counterfeit to the act of blood sacrifice as witnessed among godly people from the time of Cain and Abel throughout Bible times, in which an innocent animal's blood and flesh was used as a replacement for the repentant yet still desperately wicked human individuals asking for God's forgiveness and favor. This grisly practice of bloodletting eventually led to human sacrifice, which was prescribed when the Pagan priests felt that their bloodletting wasn't enough to appease or manipulate their gods to capitulate. By this fact alone, we can see that the gods of all the Pagan religions were demons in disguise that continued to lust after human flesh and blood even in their incorporeal state.

Remember that the Nephilim - whose spirits became demons - were guilty of the worst sort of violence toward humanity. In fact, these inhuman Giants devoured people alive and probably drank the blood squirting out of their freshly decapitated bodies like children sip Kool-Aid through straws. So, is it any wonder that human torture and sacrifice were a prevalent part of virtually every Pagan religion outside of Judeo-Christianity, as it is in Islam today with their killing of Jews and Christians as infidels and swine and the frequent murder of Christians in Paganistic India and Asia?

The practice of both the more godly form of Blood Covenanting and the Pagan practice of bloodletting among the Natives of the Americas suggests that they could have been influenced by both Old World religious groups at one time. This fact becomes even more provocative when coupled with many recent archeological finds that prove that there was an Old World Phoenician and Egyptian presence in the Americas as early as 1000 BC or earlier. In addition, several remarkable archeological sites have been found that clearly suggest that there was an Israelite presence in the Americas even before that time.

Old World Peoples in the New World Long Before Columbus!

Though few people are aware of it today, there is much hard evidence that Old World people visited, exploited and possibly settled in various parts of the Americas long before Christopher Columbus of Spain supposedly discovered the New World. In fact, America had already been settled by native people with varying degrees of cultural sophistication - some of which could rival any in the Old World. Furthermore, the indigenous people of the Americas could very well represent a mixture of people groups from several Old World cultures.

Truth be told, it is likely that Columbus merely rediscovered America, and Imperial Spain and England never had any real claim to the New World. For example, artifacts such as swords, coins, tools, ornaments, buildings and inscriptions have been found in various locations around the United States that appear to indicate that voyagers from ancient Egypt, Europe, Libya, Iberia, Carthage, Phoenicia, Israel, Rome, and Asia may have visited and traded with various Native American peoples. In fact, some Native Americans may actually descend from people that arrived in the Americas from the Old World.

There are several very clear examples of this that are virtually ignored by the archeological community. The first one that is extremely relevant to our discussion is known as the Los Lunas inscription, which was found in what appears to have been an Israelite defensive encampment located on top of Hidden Mountain near Albuquerque, New Mexico. On the pathway to this mountaintop encampment, carved into the rock face, is a simplified version of the 10 Commandments written in proto-Hebrew. This is called the Los Lunas Inscription, and it may date back to 1000 BC, which was the time of Solomon's kingdom in ancient Israel. Incidentally, this is the exact time period when the Israelites were involved in many seafaring voyages with their Phoenician allies in search of raw materials to build Solomon's Temple and palaces, and to enrich his kingdom through trade.

Also of enormous interest to this discussion is the alphabet that the Micmac Indians who lived in the eastern provinces of Canada utilized to communicate ideas with. These Algonquin Indians are closely related to the Wabanaki Indians living in Maine, and it is a curious fact that the Micmac word "Wabanaki" means "men of the east." Though these natives certainly lived on the Eastern Seaboard of the United States, could their name actually be referring to a land of the east across the Atlantic?

The missionaries attempting to educate the Micmacs with the Gospel message utilized an existing hieroglyphic alphabet in use by the natives to write their Scripture lessons. These lessons were recorded in a book written by a priest called Father Maillard before his death in 1762. Now, the most amazing thing about this alphabet besides the fact that the Micmacs actually had a written language is that some of its symbols are very similar in appearance and meaning to ancient Egyptian hieroglyphic and hieratic writing. Furthermore, though the priests who utilized this alphabet to teach the natives were unaware that it might have been partially related to ancient Egyptian, they nonetheless decoded and understood symbols from this ancient written language long before 1822 - when Champollion was touted as doing the same thing using the Rosetta Stone.

There also have been several interesting artifacts found in the Americas that contain Iberian-Punic writing, which is a form of writing combining the Semitic languages spoken in North Africa with the written language used in ancient Iberia or Portugal. In other words, Iberian-Punic writing combines the Semitic-derived Punic language of the Carthaginians with the pre-Latin Paleohispanic language of the Iberians. According to scholar Steven M. Collins, what these artifacts may suggest is that ancient Phoenicians and Israelites that understood Semitic and Punic languages may have visited the Americas and left traces of their visits behind long before Columbus or Cortez arrived on the scene.

Though there is no conclusive evidence, these visits by Old World people to the New World could have stimulated or encouraged the flowering of various new civilization centers throughout the Americas in the intervening years that followed some of these cultural contacts. They could even have been behind the emergence of the Inca and Aztec Civilizations so long after the Maya Civilization had come and gone. Nonetheless, though it is interesting to speculate, we will not know for certain until Yahshua returns and makes all things plain.

The Esna Zodiac Winged Serpent, the Uraeus and Noah

In Book One, readers were introduced to the Esna Zodiac panel, which has been reproduced here on the facing page. Via the symbol of a sphinx (i.e. lion) with a woman's head, this panel shows that Virgo begins the Zodiac story and Leo ends it. This panel is found far from the New World - in a temple in Egypt. There, beneath the composite sphinx on the panel and alongside the symbol of the crowned woman representing Virgo are two serpent symbols. The first is a long, slightly wavy snake that is stretched beneath the paws of the sphinx. This is a symbol for the constellation Hydra the Sea Serpent, which begins at the tip of Cancer and stretches through Leo and Virgo. Secondly, below this symbol for Hydra is the zigzagging form of a snake or serpent that has wings and a Scarab beetle symbol on either end of its body.

Fascinatingly, the Egyptians envisioned the Zodiac sign of Cancer as a Scarab beetle, which is an artistic representation of a dung beetle. In Book One, we learned that the sign of Cancer represents God's heavenly sheep pen - where God is gathering His righteous sheep among the human inhabitants of Earth. However, for the ancient Egyptians, this same Scarab beetle also symbolized the Sun - and the Sun can represent

God the Father and His glorified Son. This beetle may therefore signify Yahweh's Holy Spirit, and His Shekinah Glory shining upon His children, or faithful sheep.

Now, since the Scarab is meant to represent the Sun, the sign of Cancer, and God the Father, the winding, winged serpent so prominent in Egyptian art and in the Esna Zodiac likely signifies the path that the Sun takes through the sky along the ecliptic, as well as the paths of righteous people! Since the winged Scarab likely refers to the Sun and the godly people who symbolically follow the path or Way of the Sun by living righteously, the winding serpent that begins and ends with a Scarab most likely represents the godly path that righteous people follow in a sin-filled world currently governed by the way of the Serpent or Satan. Therefore, the winged Scarab following the Sun's serpentine path may have originally been a symbol for the people descended from Seth, Shem, and Abraham. Indeed, the symbolism of a winged serpent could also be applied to the descendents of the Twelve Tribes of Israel who initially rejected the Way of Cain or the Serpent, but later succumbed to its seductiveness and lost their identity as Israelites.

This suggests that a winged serpent can represent the Twelve Houses of the Zodiac, the first twelve patriarchs descended from Adam and Seth, and the destiny of three separate groups: the Twelve Tribes of Israel; the Twelve Tribes of Ishmael; and the followers of the Twelve Apostles who followed Christ. As explained in Chapter Two, the mysterious Heavenly Tablets that Enoch could read may have been the forty-eight constellations of the Twelve-House Zodiac. In the Book of 1 Enoch, the Heavenly Tablets were said to contain *"all the deeds of men and angels,"* and it was shown in Book One how the Zodiac tells that amazing story. Therefore, **could the feathered, zigzagging serpent symbol of Egypt and the Americas also be a symbol of the history and**

destiny of mankind as revealed in the Zodiac? Based on the fact that people in ancient times understood the Language of God, this conclusion is not only logical, but also probable.

Based on this conclusion, we can make another fascinating connection between a feathered serpent signifying the Path or Way of the Sun or the Way of Yahweh and the patriarch Noah. Now, in the Bible, it is recorded that the first farmer was named Cain, and Cain lost his ability to farm when God cursed the Earth against him and all his future generations. In addition, as this book has shown, Cain's bloodline became accursed through Lamech the Cainite as the source of the "seed of the Serpent" or the Nephilim, who were half human and half angel. So, if you are not blessed with the proverbial "green thumb," it might be wise to check your spiritual condition, because there could be an allegorical and literal correlation between those who aren't equipped with an ability to tend and keep relatively healthy plants and those who are following the Way of Cain.

Thankfully, Noah the son of Lamech the Sethite was also a farmer who likely revolutionized farming from its most primitive forms and turned it into a highly sophisticated science. This new philosophy toward farming likely incorporated advanced concepts such as superior seed selection and storage, tilling and sowing soil using rakes, hoes and plows hitched to domesticated animals, irrigation using mountain terracing, aqueducts, watermills, and canals to channel fresh water to fields and utilize water as a source of energy to power the mechanical processing of grain, fertilization and soil conditioning using fish, manure, composted plant matter, powdered minerals, natural forms of pest and disease control, and advanced harvesting methods using sickles, ropes and winnowing baskets. In fact, this is likely why the Book of Genesis proclaimed that Noah would bring comfort to farmers:

> "And he (i.e. Lamech) called his name Noah, saying, 'This one will comfort us concerning our work and the toil of our hands, because of the ground which the LORD (Yahweh) has cursed.'" - Genesis 5:29 (NKJ)

Fascinatingly, the name "Noah" is thought to derive from the Hebrew word "noach," meaning "quiet" or "rest." However, Strong's Concordance reveals other possible Hebrew root words for Noah's name that actually denote feathers or plumes. One of these words is "notsah," which means "feathers" or "plumage" (See Leviticus 1:16, Ezekiel 17:3; Strong's # 5133). Intriguingly, the first and last Hebrew letters of the word "notsah" phonetically form the name "Noah." Furthermore, the Hebrew letter in the middle of this word meaning "feathers" is Tsadek (TS), a letter that combines the sounds of Tau (T) and Shin (S). Now, the archaic symbol for the Hebrew letter Tau was a cross-shaped symbol. As was shown earlier, this symbol directly refers to God's Grace that was given to mankind by the Cross of Christ. In silent affirmation of God's Grace, the constellation Cygnus the Swan is often called the Northern Cross, and it shows a direct heavenly correlation between a beautiful white-feathered bird with a long, serpent-like neck and the Cross of Christ!

In addition, the letter Tsadek is related to the Hebrew letter Shin, and both letters were once symbolized as a wavy line like the English letter "W" in their archaic forms. Interestingly, a brilliant 20th Century American Bible scholar and archeologist named William F. Albright believed that the Hebrew letter Shin was connected to the Hebrew word "Shamash," which is the Hebrew name for the Sun. Furthermore, Albright believed that the letter Shin may have been derived from the Uraeus used on Egyptian crowns as a symbol of power and authority. As shown earlier, the Uraeus serpent signified Lower Egypt, which was the domain of Shem before Nimrod (a.k.a. the Egyptian Archaic Period Pharaoh called Narmer) took control of Lower Egypt and ousted Shem and his descendents from their hereditary lands.

The hieroglyphic symbol for the Uraeus was a serpent in the form of a hooded cobra, whose body was curved in an upside down "U" shape. In ancient Egypt, this cobra symbol was often shown draped over a celestial disk representing either the Sun or the Moon. Therefore, could the Uraeus be identical in meaning to the winged serpent used on the Esna Zodiac that depicts the Path or Way of the Sun? Furthermore, could the Way of the Sun be synonymous with the Way of Yahweh followed by Noah and Shem? If so, then the Hebrew word "notsah" and depictions of white feathers, white-feathered wings and white birds may have secretly symbolized the Path of the Sun or the Way of Yahweh to Shem and his descendents. This intriguing possibility will be explored in the next section.

Now, before exploring the connection of feathers to the righteous in the next section, let me digress a moment to focus attention on the planet Saturn. Earlier in this book, it was shown that the Roman god Saturn had a connection to Noah's son Ham and Ham's grandson Nimrod. The god Saturn was also considered to be an agricultural god connected to the harvest and was depicted with a sickle in his hand. To honor Saturn, the Romans engaged in a week-long harvest festival called Saturnalia, which encouraged raucous behavior, role reversals, drunkenness, and sexual promiscuity. In occult circles, the planet Saturn has been associated with a six-pointed star as well as with Azazel or

Satan, thus giving the Star of David a false cursed application as a symbol for the Devil himself.

Despite all these evil connotations, however, there is an underlying good and messianic side to the planet Saturn. In my Zodiac Chart in the Appendix, for example, the planet Saturn is connected to the sign of Capricorn the Goat-Fish. As was shown in Book One, Capricorn is actually connected to Noah as a symbol of his righteousness - as seen in the vigorous fish tail of the goat-fish - a fish that is being saved from the watery destruction of the unrighteous that are seen in the dying goat. It was also shown that Noah - as "the righteous fish" - later was deified via Pagan gods such as Dagon and Oannes, which were depicted as half fish and half goat or man.

Interestingly, like the god Saturn, Dagon and Oannes were agricultural gods associated with water, and - besides being a very good farmer - Noah was a ship-builder and sailor of sorts that acted on Yahweh's promptings to save mankind from utter annihilation by building the Ark to God's specifications and sailing that huge boat upon a vast world ocean to a high place of safety in the mountains of Ararat. Hence, there is also a connection between Noah and such gods as Neptune and Poseidon.

Despite his deification, Noah was not a Pagan and he never sought to be worshipped. Nonetheless, Noah was a messianic figurehead that prefigured Christ - our one and only true Messiah who will deliver all of His saints from the coming Wrath of God that will be poured out in the Great Tribulation. Hence, like the winged dragon symbols used in the Far East and the Phoenix bird and Quetzalcoatl or feathered serpent used in the Americas, the planet Saturn can be tied to the righteous followers of Yahweh. Indeed, in its highest aspect, the seventh planet Saturn is connected to Saturday, or the Sabbath. As such, instead of signifying Satan pretending to wear Christ's Crown as it does now, Saturn will one day be restored as a pure symbol of Christ reigning as the King of kings during the Millennial Kingdom, which will be a 1,000-year Sabbath Rest for God and the Universe!

Feathers and Wings - Symbols for Noah and His Kin

Since Noah likely spoke an early form of Hebrew, he would likely have known the phonetic connection of the word "notsah" to his name. Could it be, then, that Noah adopted the symbol of a brightly plumed bird like the Quetzal (possibly with a dead snake in its claws) as his own symbol since his name was linked to a word meaning "feathered" or "plumed?" Amazingly, there is a biblical reason to believe this hypothesis, which is found in a peculiar phonetic similarity between two other Hebrew words: "ebrah" and "eber." Now, **"ebrah" is the Hebrew root word for "feather," and it sounds very similar to the name "Eber,"** who was a direct descendant of Noah's son Shem. In fact, Eber was the celebrated ancestor of the Hebrews - from whom the Israelites originated (See Genesis 10:22-25). Therefore, though the name Eber is derived from the Hebrew word "eber" meaning "eastward region," it sounds like the word for "feathers," as shown in this Scripture:

> "He shall cover you with His feathers (Hebrew: "ebrah"), and under His wings (Hebrew: "kanaph") you shall take refuge; his truth shall be your shield and buckler." - Psalm 91:4 (NKJ)

Could the Hebrew word for feathers - "ebrah" - be one of the root words used to derive the name "Eber?" Is it possible that "eastward" or "of the east" was the primary meaning of Shem's great grandson Eber's name, with "feathered" or "winged" being its secondary meaning? If so, then the word "eber" could mean "Bird of the East." Supporting this theory, there is an uncanny similarity between the root

word "ebrah" and the name Abram or Abraham, who was a direct descendent of Eber. Now, suppose Noah - as an inhabitant of the Mesoamerican part of Middle Earth - had adopted a brightly plumed bird that killed and ate frogs and lizards like the Quetzal as his symbol. If he did, wouldn't it make sense for the early Hebrews, whose ancestor Eber's name could mean "feathered" or "eastward," to do the same? This may be exactly what they did. In fact, it would make sense for the ancient followers of Yahweh - who knew the Gospel in the Stars - to use a lizard or snake-killing bird like the eagle, hawk, Ibis or Quetzal as a symbol for their religion and culture.

The Resplendent Quetzal Bird Native To Mesoamerica

There are some peculiar behaviors associated with the Resplendent Quetzal that is native to Mesoamerica that would have made them an ideal symbol for Noah and his kin. First of all, Quetzals love their privacy and independence, often living alone until mating season, when they seek out their mates. As a result, Quetzals often do very poorly in captivity, usually starving themselves to death if not set free. They therefore have become a symbol of liberty and freedom in countries like Mexico where they are native. In addition, Quetzal birds often mate for life and the male and female both share in the task of incubating eggs and raising their young. As a result, they are a symbol of family strength and unity. Quetzals also have crested heads (like Mesoamerican royalty with their feathered headdresses), thick, gorgeous green and red plumage, and large eyes with excellent vision in dimly lit situations. They therefore represent physical beauty. Interestingly, eagles also share many of these traits.

Besides all these aforementioned connecting traits to Noah, Quetzals eat damaging insects, lizards, frogs and scorpions as well as whole fruits like avocados and the fruits of the laurel tree family. However, these birds regurgitate the pits afterward, thus helping to propagate these species of trees in imitation of Noah, who surely was the Post-Flood world's first expert astronomer, botanist, herbal pharmacist, farmer and conservationist.

According to most archeologists, the Quetzal was deeply revered by Mesoamerican (i.e. Central American) cultures like the Maya, where it was a crime to kill a Quetzal. However, since the tail feathers of the Quetzal were used ceremonially to link Mesoamerican kings to their civilizing and agricultural god Quetzalcoatl, Quetzals were often captured and their tail-feathers plucked before they were released back into the wild. The Quetzal's two-foot long iridescent green tail feathers were then used to decorate the headdresses of kings and head priests.

It is my contention that the Mayan civilization and culture may have developed from Noah's other descendents besides Shem, Ham and Japheth that settled in North America, Mesoamerica, and the northernmost portion of South America. In addition, Noah himself may have dwelled in Mesoamerica with his own kin. It is also possible that Shem and his clan were frequent visitors in Noah's domain until Nimrod and his armies invaded, and ousted them all. There is also evidence that the native civilizations that arose afterward were influenced by Israelite, Phoenician and Carthaginian sailors - as well as sailors from other diverse places such as Rome and China.

Many diverse adventurers from the Old World likely sailed along the shores of the Americas, traded and warred with, and sometimes settled among the local native populace. In fact, long before this, the fabled city of Atlantis may have been just to the south of Noah's domain in South America - where some of the descendents of Ham may have settled after the Flood and built an amazingly sophisticated civilization that eventually succumbed to the Way of Cain. Therefore, when

Nimrod's empire was supernaturally destroyed by fire and brimstone from heaven, the city of Atlantis may also have been destroyed - sinking into oblivion due to massive earthquakes and tsunamis.

Now, since Noah likely knew about the Longitudinal Meridian connections of the Earth as shown in Chapter Six, he would have known that his region of the Earth in the Americas was tied to Aquarius and Capricorn, which signify Noah's salvation in the Ark through the waters of the Flood in the Gospel in the Stars. In addition, Noah would have known that Shem's lands and his own adjoined at the Scorpio-Sagittarius Meridian over Hawaii that signified the great spiritual battle that would take place before the coming of the expected Messiah Yahshua as King of kings! In essence then, the Feathered Serpent "god" known as Quetzalcoatl or Kukulcan in the Americas may have originally been a symbol for Noah and Shem that was later bastardized to signify the usurping power of Nimrod and the Way of Cain! In fact, the name Kukulcan could be phonetically connected to the name "Cain," who was probably known as Kane to the Hawaiians and Kukulcan to various Mesoamerican tribes.

In Psalm 91:4, which was quoted earlier, the word "kanaph," meaning "wings," is pronounced "kau-nowf." Therefore, this word has a connection to both Cain's name and Noah's Hebrew name: "Noach." However, in Psalm 68:13, the word "ebrah" is linked to the symbolism of a sheep pen and a dove, in which the sheep are a symbol for Christ's followers, while the dove is a winged and feathered symbol for the Holy Spirit:

> *"Though you lie down among the sheepfolds, yet you will be like the wings (i.e. "kanaph") of a dove (i.e. "yownah") covered with silver, and her feathers (i.e. "ebrah") with yellow gold." - Psalm 68:13 (NKJ)*

Interestingly, the last two letters of the Hebrew word for dove are the Hebrew letters "Nun" or "N" and "Hey" or "H," which - when placed alone - spell the name Noah in Hebrew! This is likely one reason why Father Yahweh chose to represent the Holy Spirit as a dove coming down out of heaven onto Yahshua when He was baptized by John in the Jordan River:

> *"And **the Holy Spirit descended in bodily form like a dove upon Him,** and a voice came from heaven which said, 'You are My beloved Son; in You I am well pleased.'" - Luke 3:22 (NKJ)*

This passage shows that **the symbol of a sheepfold, feathers, wings, and a dove or white bird are tied to the followers of Yahweh like**

Noah! In addition, note the verse numbers of the last two Scriptures quoted showing the connection of the name "Noah" with the Hebrew words for feathers and wings. The first is verse 13, while the second is verse 22, and - as shown in Book 4 - both of these numbers are associated with the end of this world system and the Millennial Rule of Christ.

To show the interchangeability of these words "ebrah" and "kanaph," the following Scripture illustrates that both Hebrew words can be translated as "wings:"

> *"The wings (Hebrew: "kanaph") of the ostrich wave proudly, but are her wings (Hebrew: "ebrah") and pinions like the kindly stork's?" - Job 39:13 (NKJ)*

In this Scripture, Job was relaying the fact that the stork, which is a mostly white-plumed bird, is a more noble bird in the sense that it has a more pleasant disposition than the grey and black-plumed ostrich and the stork's wings enable it to fly unlike the ostrich! Now, since a winged dove is a symbol for Judeo-Christianity, and feathers and wings may have served as symbols for our righteous ancestors, could this be the reason God created the Cherubim with feathered wings, and why one of the Cherubim's four faces is an eagle symbolizing God's protection of His chosen saints? This possibility and the phonetic ties between "Abram" and "ebrah" undeniably suggest an allegorical connection between feathers and Yahweh's earthly children.

From these examples, it seems apparent that Yahweh used these symbols of His Language to convey the truth that the people symbolized by feathers, wings, or birds like the eagle and the dove will destroy the evil in the world represented by lizards, scorpions and serpents. In this way, the dove and the eagle mark those who long to see Yahshua's final triumph over evil and the Serpent Way of Cain at the end of the world. The dove and eagle are therefore symbols of hope and protection, and this is why the Bible describes Yahweh as sheltering His righteous children under His symbolic feathers and wings, and protecting them with powerful wings like an eagle's:

> *"You have seen what I did to the Egyptians, and how I bore you on eagles' wings and brought you to Myself." - Exodus 19:4 (NKJ)*

> *"But those who wait on the LORD (Yahweh) shall renew their strength; they shall mount up with wings like eagles, they shall run and not be weary, they shall walk and not faint." - Isaiah 40:31 (NKJ)*

"He shall cover you with His feathers, and under His wings you shall take refuge; his truth shall be your shield and buckler." - Psalm 91:4 (NKJ)

As mentioned in Book One, the snake-killing falcon originally may have symbolized the Spirit of the coming Son of God to the followers of Seth. Though the initial followers of Seth would not have deified this falcon symbol, subsequent generations sadly did when they tied it to the Nephilim and the worship of Nimrod. However, the falcon symbol may have remained a godly one to certain people who knew

Northern Goshawks - Juvenile (left) and Adult

the original truth behind it. In fact, Noah and his kin may have used symbols of birds such as hawks or Quetzal birds to identify themselves wherever they went. This is suggested by the fact that the word for falcon or hawk in Arabic is "Huru," a word that also means "the far distant." Uncannily, the "sudra" portion of the name of the Sumerian Flood hero Ziusudra also means "the far distant." In addition, the other early name of Noah, Atrahasis, is usually followed by the word "ruku," and it too means "far distant." This means that the mysterious Followers of Horus that came from Mesopotamia to Egypt mentioned by David Rohl could have been the righteous followers of Yahweh like Noah rather than the followers of the Way of Cain like Nimrod.

The expression "far distant" may have applied to the longed for Messiah Yahshua that the followers of Noah knew was to come, but sadly *in a far distant era from their own*. Furthermore, they may have depicted this "Far Distant One" in art as a hawk or hawk-headed man whom they called "Heru" or "Hor" (i.e. Horus). The phonetic connection of the name "Heru" to the Arabic word "Huru" is obvious, and it is likely that the ancient Egyptian word Heru or Horus also originally meant "the far distant" at one time. Later, however, this symbol and title was erroneously applied to the deified human Nimrod instead of the coming Son of God awaited by the descendents of Noah and Abraham. From the meanings of the names attached to Noah, the expression "the far distant" may also have been used to describe anyone who appeared as a savior or messiah, and Noah was certainly a prefiguration of the one perfect Messiah to come.

Since bird imagery was likely used to identify the followers of Seth and the righteous descendents of Eber and Abraham, there is much spiritual significance to the fact that the majestic bald eagle is the national bird and a prominent emblem of the United States. There is also likely much spiritual significance in the fact that - along with the snake-killing bald eagle - the stars and stripes of the first official US Flag replaced the serpent emblazoned Gadsden Flag. Its defiant slogan "DON'T TREAD ON ME" under the image of a coiled rattlesnake represented America's original thirteen colonies during the Revolutionary War, and hearkens back to the dismembered serpent symbol of Benjamin Franklin's political cartoon that sported the slogan "Join, or Die."

Unfortunately, the Gadsden Flag represents a new, more radical United States patriotism that became especially evident after the 2001 Terrorist attack on the World Trade Center in New York. For this reason, some people erroneously see the United States of America as symbolic of the Tribe of Dan, and link it to Babylon the Great. However, as shown in Book Four, this association is wrong for many reasons, especially the fact that **Scripture calls Babylon the Great a city, not a nation**.

The choice of a snake-killing, white-headed and white-tailed bald eagle (as opposed to *the purely black eagle* of Nazi Germany and Ancient Rome) as a national symbol also seems to allegorically link the United States with the descendents of Noah and Shem through Eber. This symbolic link further strengthens my reasons for connecting the United States with Ephraim as well as Assyria or Asshur - as Asshur was also a descendent of Noah, Shem and Eber.

The ancient Assyrians called their land "Asshur" - most likely in honor of their founding father and first king. If so, Shem's son Asshur was likely the first king of the people who formed the Assyrian Empire. During their heyday, the Assyrians conquered the northern Kingdom of Israel, though they did not succeed in conquering the Kingdom of Judah to the south. The Assyrian conquerors then claimed many captured Israelites as slaves and led them as captives to Assyria. This Assyrian captivity of the ten northern Tribes of Israelites likely led to their eventual dispersal throughout Europe and the British Isles.

Uncannily, when doing research about Noah for my "Pillar of Enoch Trilogy" fiction books, I found out that Noah may have been an albino, due to a description of Noah found in the Book of 1 Enoch (1 Enoch 106:1-3). 1 Enoch describes baby Noah as white as snow, and red as a rose - with hair as white as wool. Noah's coloration at birth recalls the fact that true albinos have pure white hair, and white, pigment-free skin that tends to be reddish in color from the aerated blood visible beneath it. Since Noah was likely a colorless albino, I thought it would be an interesting juxtaposition to give him a brightly plumed Macaw as a beloved pet when writing a novel centered around the life of Noah (which I have sadly not had the opportunity to finish yet). Could this have been the Holy Spirit leading me to the truth about the meaning of Noah's name? I believe it could have been!

The Bible tells us that there were only eight human survivors of the Great Flood on Noah's Ark. However, after the Flood, the Earth's human population grew rapidly and many people groups began to spread out over the known parts of the world. At this time, it is my supposition that the man who was later deified as the god Quetzalcoatl or Kukulcan in the Americas came to these disparate people groups to re-educate them. He did so primarily by reintroducing the belief in one Creator God and His religious moral code that was memorialized in Noahide Law, the rituals of Blood Covenanting, and the science and religion surrounding Sacred Astronomy and the Gospel in the Stars.

Incidentally, all the native people of the Americas had similar religious beliefs. All Native Americans, for example, observed the behavior of animals and the forces of nature in order to understand the underlying allegorical meanings in their attributes. ***Native Americans therefore understood and utilized the allegorical Language of God, and had learned to seek it in all aspects of God's Creation!*** Though all natives seem to have succumbed to the worship of demons as various nature spirits, most of them also believed that these spirits were controlled by and ruled over by a supreme deity who created all life.

Throughout the Americas, Native Americans also held the symbol of the eagle in high regard. To them, eagles symbolized freedom, majesty, power, strength, stealth, and beauty (somewhat like the Quetzal did in Mesoamerica). Like the Quetzal, the eagle was also noted for its ability to see far into the distance and to perceive things that are invisible to other creatures with lesser vision. In Native American culture, people who were gifted with great foresight and wisdom were often thought to have the eagle or owl as their totem spirit. Like owls, eagles are birds of prey with great strength. However unlike owls, eagles are associated with the godly light of day rather than the sinister darkness of night. This may be why eagle and Quetzal feathers became highly prized decorative devices in the daily dress of native priests, leaders and warriors throughout the Americas.

The history and mythology of the Quetzal bird has been presented in this chapter to identify a plausible and biblically inspired source for the "god" Quetzalcoatl and the ancient calendar system of the Mayans, Incas, and Aztecs. This candidate for Quetzalcoatl is the tenth and final antediluvian patriarch Noah. According to native legends, Quetzalcoatl came to visit them at the dawn of the Fifth Age or shortly *after* the destruction of the Earth by water (i.e. after the Great Flood). He came to people whose lives had been plunged back into the Stone Age by the loss of technology, learning, and culture caused by the Flood.

As already mentioned, the Nahuatl word for "plumed serpent" was Quetzalcoatl. However, since the "Quetzal" is a brightly colored tropical bird and "atl" means "waters," is it possible that - besides "Feathered Serpent" - the word "Quetzalcoatl" could have meant "bird of the water" or "water bird?" If so, the feathered serpent was simply an allegorical device used to depict water birds like the Ibis, and may also have been a euphemism for a lightweight type of long boat or canoe. Uncannily, the first portion of the Aztec word "Nahuatl," which means "four waters" sounds like "Noah," who is attributed with re-establishing civilization with his three sons after the Flood just as Quetzalcoatl did. Could the phonetic connection between these two disparate words be intentional? If so, *"nahu" may have been a native reference to Noah's name as well as to Noah and his three sons as the four "waters" or bringers of knowledge.* It is also possible that the native word "Quetzalcoatl" was derived from symbols that Noah may have used to identify himself until Nimrod stole that symbol and applied it to his twisted empire.

Nonetheless, the true meaning of the feathered serpent has been preserved in the Gospel in the Stars, where the Scorpio-Sagittarius Meridian converges. There, the constellation Aquila the Eagle and Serpens the Serpent are juxtaposed beside each other in opposing Zodiac signs - with Capricorn and neighboring Sagittarius signifying the Salvation of the Son of God and His offering as a sacrifice for sin, and with Aquila symbolizing Christ's Spirit. Meanwhile, Scorpio signifies the *"son of perdition"* spoken of in Scripture that attempted to destroy the Son of God before He could perform His transforming act of love and mercy for all humanity (John 17:12; 2 Thess. 2:3-4).

As shown in the Star Charts on pages 500 and 501 and the Star Chart on page 699, the great battle between good and evil that is divinely memorialized by the heavenly Scorpio-Sagittarius Meridian and Aquila the Eagle shows that the Tribulation Saints living in the Americas will provide unflinching resistance against the New World Order. These rebels will consequently receive a great amount of persecution from

Star Chart: Sagittarius and Scorpio in a Cosmic Battle

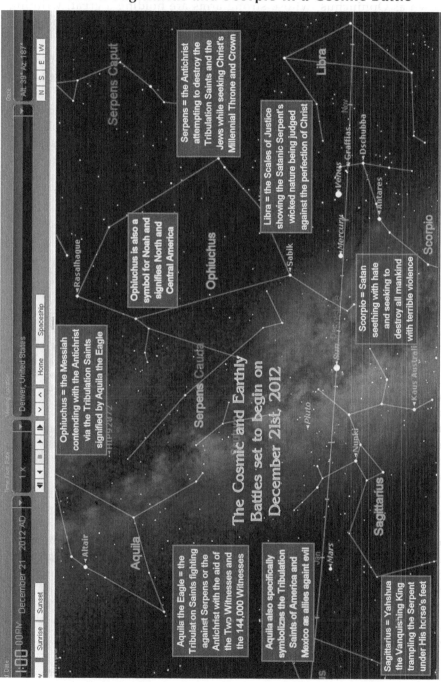

the Antichrist and his armies. This is seen in the massive constellation known as Ophiuchus, whose strong arms are holding a great, writhing serpent at bay so it can't get its hold onto the messianic crown it so desperately wants to possess.

Could Ophiuchus and Aquila signify the people of the USA and Mexico that will fight the designs of the Antichrist - and could it be that this hater of the Judeo-Christian God will rise from among their ranks? In addition, as Ophiuchus clearly implies, will they prevail against that cunning Serpent man and win? Both George Washington's prophetic vision of the destiny of America that is examined in Book Four and the stone from Heaven that crushed Nebuchadnezzar's statue's feet of iron and clay in his dream suggest that these Tribulation Saints will not win the war that they must fight by any human means - but **only** by divine aid when Yahshua returns with His army of angels and saints!

Mexico's Coat of Arms -
An Earthly Reflection of
the Scorpio-Sagittarius
Celestial Meridian

An Allegorical Key to
Understanding Quetzalcoatl

Uncannily, as if in silent agreement with my hypothesis about the meaning of the feathered serpent, the Mexican Coat of Arms features a golden eagle standing atop an edible blooming Prickly Pear Cactus with a rattlesnake being held in one of its talons and its beak! Could the use of these symbols in this Coat of Arms that are supposedly derived from Aztec mythology be a sign that Mexico will be divided like the Americans in the United States? Will a large portion of Mexico's population resist the New World Order along with the many American rebels across their northern border while the other segment blindly follows the Antichrist into perdition? Based on the Gospel in the Stars, that does appear to be what the Coat of Arms of Mexico suggests!

Moses and the Legend of the Storks and Serpents

Fascinatingly, the Book of Jasher records many incidences in the life of Moses that are not recorded in the Bible. Though no one can be sure, one likely reason that these incidents in Moses' life were left out is because they had nothing to do with the Gospel message. Therefore, Moses may have felt they were better omitted from his record of Yahweh God's dealings with the Israelites and mankind in general.

Nonetheless, Yahweh God made sure these events in Moses' life were recorded elsewhere for an important reason. Though some of these incidents may have been embarrassing to Moses or may have seemed trivial to him, they can aid diligent seekers in understanding Moses as well as the allegorical messages hidden in the prophetic books of the Bible. One of the incidents in the Book of Jasher that can aid in our understanding of the Language of God occurred after Moses left Egypt and found himself aiding the Cushite king Kikianus and his armies against Balaam, who is described as a magician in the Book of Jasher. However, this is the same wicked non-Israelite prophet and magician spoken of in the Bible who was called upon to curse the Israelites but who uncomfortably found out that he could only bless them. This was because God's power via the Holy Spirit was being exerted over Balaam and caused his demon helper to be silent while the Holy Spirit spoke blessings through Balaam instead of curses (Numbers 23:7-10, 23:18-24, 24:3-9).

According to the Book of Jasher, Balaam and his two sons were left to watch over the city of the king of Cush. Unfortunately, however, the three of them decided to rebel against the king and to bar him from entering the gates of his own city after he returned from a campaign against Aram - a subject kingdom that was rebelling against the king's authority. At this time, Moses arrived in the king's camp and - because he was already a seasoned warrior that had led Pharaoh's armies for years - he offered to aid the Cushites in their siege against the city.

In order to retake the city, a supernaturally generated legion of deadly serpents that had been conjured up by Balaam had to be destroyed. These serpents were killing the soldiers before they could get near to the walls of the city. Therefore, Moses devised a plan and shared it with the King of Cush, who then shared it with his army as follows:

> "Thus says the king, 'Go into the forest and bring with you of the young ones of the stork, each man a young one in his hand. And any person transgressing the word of the king, who shall not bring his young one, he shall die, and the king will take all belonging to him. And when you shall bring them they shall be in your keeping, you shall rear them until they grow up, and you shall teach them to dart upon, as is the way of the young ones of the hawk.' ...And all the people did so, and they went out to the wood and they climbed the fir trees

*and caught, each man a young one in his hand, all the young
of the storks, and they brought them into the desert and
reared them by order of the king, and they taught them to
dart upon, similar to the young hawks.*

*And after the young storks were reared, the king
ordered them to be hungered for three days, and all the
people did so. And on the third day, the king said unto them,
'Strengthen yourselves and become valiant men, and put on
each man his armor and gird on his sword upon him, and ride
each man his horse and take each his young stork in his hand.
And we will rise up and fight against the city at the place
where the serpents are;' and all the people did as the king had
ordered.*

*And they took each man his young one in his hand,
and they went away, and when they came to the place of the
serpents the king said to them, 'Send forth each man his
young stork upon the serpents.' And they sent forth each man
his young stork at the king's order, and the young storks ran
upon the serpents and they devoured them all and destroyed
them out of that place.*

*And when the king and people had seen that all the
serpents were destroyed in that place, all the people set up a
great shout. And they approached and fought against the city
and took it and subdued it, and they entered the city. And
there died on that day one thousand and one hundred men of
the people of the city, all that inhabited the city, but of the
people besieging not one died. So all the children of Cush
went each to his home, to his wife and children and to all
belonging to him.*

*And Balaam the magician, when he saw that the city
was taken, he opened the gate and he and his two sons and
eight brothers fled and returned to Egypt to Pharaoh king of
Egypt.* **They are the sorcerers and magicians who are
mentioned in the book of the law, standing against Moses**
*when the Lord brought the plagues upon Egypt. So Moses
took the city by his wisdom, and the children of Cush placed
him on the throne instead of Kikianus king of Cush." - Jasher
73:12-30*

Here, the Book of Jasher explains that Balaam had two sons and
eight brothers that escaped certain death by fleeing to Egypt - where
they began to serve Pharaoh instead of the king of Cush. There, Jasher

tells us that they became the evil sorcerers and magicians of Pharaoh's court spoken of in the Bible (Exodus 7:11, 7:22, 8:7, 8:18-19, 9:11) Eerily, as I wrote the preceding Scriptures references down, I became aware of the fact that the chapter and verse numbers 7-22 and 7-11 are specific dates for two Solar Eclipses in 2009 and 2010 that fell on the 1st of Av, eight days before the 9th of Av - a date of great mourning among Jews all over the world because the First and Second Temples were destroyed on the 9th of Av. Furthermore, 9-11 corresponds with the date of Yahshua's birth and the date of the 2001 World Trade Center Terrorist Attack in New York City. See the last chapter in "The Language of God in Prophecy" to read about the prophetic meaning of End Times events and the signs in the heavens such as these ominous eclipses, which indicate that there will soon be much trouble for the Jews in Israel around the time between these two eclipses, and also afterward.

Returning to our discussion, the Book of Jasher makes it clear that Balaam was not a true prophet of Yahweh at any time. Instead, Balaam was likely possessed by demons that performed magic and sorcery on his behalf. However, the Bible tells us that Yahweh God could and did control Balaam's prophetic words, behavior and actions. This shows us that Yahweh Elohim is always in control - even when He allows Satan to act powerfully and maliciously in the world at times.

Fascinatingly, the Book of Jasher also records that Moses actually served as the King of Cush for 40 years after he helped take the city. While serving as king, Moses reigned justly and defended the Cushites against their enemies (See Jasher, Chapters 73 thru 75). After this, it is recorded that Moses was asked to leave Cush but was treated honorably and given many gifts, which most likely included gold, silver, trained soldiers, slaves, pack animals, and livestock. Taking this wealth with him, Moses found his way to Midian, where he aided Reuel's daughters, suffered as a prisoner for 10 years, but eventually found a new home there until God called Moses to come to the aid of his enslaved brethren in Egypt (See Jasher, Chapter 76).

My point in relaying this interesting information about Moses and his use of storks as weapons of war is that Yahweh provided us with this incident in Moses' life to illustrate that many birds are the natural enemies of serpents, and how birds of prey can allegorically and literally be used as symbols of good fighting the forces of evil. This story therefore reinforces my supposition that birds - and specifically birds of prey that are pictured swooping down on their prey - are symbols of righteousness. This is true specifically because Quetzals and other birds such as ibises, eagles, hawks and storks (as shown in Moses' case) can kill serpents, lizards, scorpions, and other poisonous creatures that often serve no purpose other than to destroy innocent life.

This is undoubtedly why God chose to place the constellation Aquila the Eagle and the Eagle Nebula near to the rebelling serpent being wrestled by the messianic figure Ophiuchus and the malevolent Scorpion that Ophiuchus is subduing under his feet. In the remaining sections of this chapter, we will discuss what this symbolism in the Star Gospel reveals - not only about the nature of good and evil, but about the original godly purpose and destiny of the United States of America, and its subsequent oppression and takeover by the forces of evil.

Quetzalcoatl: The Truth Revealed

Quetzalcoatl and Tezcatlipoca were two New World gods who some scholars think may have been Nephilim or who used Nephilim-inspired symbols. In the next two sections, we will explore the possibility that the gods Quetzalcoatl and Tezcatlipoca were not originally false Nephilim gods at all, but deified and corrupted versions of the biblical characters Noah and Nimrod. These two diametrically opposed spiritual and temporal leaders both may have sought to rule over the people of the New World hundreds of years after the Great Flood. In addition, we will explore the possibility that Anakim fleeing the slaughter of their kind during the Israelite conquest of Canaan may have come to the Americas and introduced the rites of human sacrifice and ritual cannibalism that were mercilessly practiced by the bloodthirsty priests of various New World cultures.

First, let's examine the proof that Quetzalcoatl may be a deified version of Noah. According to New World myths, the benevolent god Quetzalcoatl and the evil god Tezcatlipoca clashed and fought against each other over the rule of the kingdom, with the evil god Tezcatlipoca being the apparent victor after a long series of battles. As a result, the Mayan and subsequent Aztec religious systems were filled with strange contrasts. For instance, though they murdered countless innocent people in the name of their gods, the Maya and Aztecs taught that there was once a benevolent god named Quetzalcoatl who did not desire human blood but forbade the natives to sacrifice people or to ritually eat them. A temple complex where the ancient followers of the god Quetzalcoatl worshiped and lived was located at Cholula in Mexico. Despite their status as part of the Aztec Empire, the followers of Quetzalcoatl lived in a way that their god would have approved of - in relative peace and without much bloodshed.

The temple dedicated to Quetzalcoatl once rested atop a giant earthwork step-pyramid. The ruins of this earthwork step-pyramid (a.k.a. ziggurat) can still be seen in Cholula, Mexico. However, it looks more like a big hill than a pyramid today. Instead of the temple to Quetzalcoatl that once rested at its summit, there is a Catholic Church that was quickly built over the temple's burned ruins by the Spanish missionaries who came in the conquistadors' wake.

The manmade hill beneath that church is the largest ancient earthwork pyramid ever found, which suggests some connection to the culture that built the brick-constructed Tower of Babel. Is it possible that this huge earthwork step pyramid in Cholula that was originally three times more massive than the Great Pyramid at Giza was contemporary to the Tower of Babel and also built by Nimrod? Though this earthwork ziggurat was supposedly dedicated to Quetzalcoatl alone, could it have once been associated with the evil god Tezcatlipoca, but then re-dedicated to Quetzalcoatl? In addition, could this have occurred when Nimrod's world dictatorship ended with Yah's smashing of the Tower of Babel and the divine confusion of languages?

Quetzalcoatl was known and deeply revered throughout Mexico, Central and South America. For the Mayans and their Toltec forebears, this god whose symbol was a feathered serpent was known as Kukulcan. To the Incas who were native to what is now Peru, he was known as Viracocha. Much later in history, the Aztecs called him Quetzalcoatl. The name Quetzalcoatl was derived from the Quetzal bird, a brightly plumed exotic bird that ate fruit, insects, *lizards, and small snakes* - and whose feathers were used extensively in making ceremonial robes. Significantly, the Aztec word meaning "feathered serpent" is "Quetzalcoatl," where "Quetzal" means feathered or plumed, and *"coatl" means serpent or water - since a wavy or zigzag line could depict both*.

Though this theory is being heavily disputed by historical revisionists with an unsavory agenda today, it was once widely taught that native legends depicted the god Quetzalcoatl as a benevolent white "god" with a beard who came to the New World by boat, sailing from the east across the ocean sometime after a devastating worldwide flood. Moreover, his ship was purportedly made from serpent skins, though other myths say the boat was made of bundles of reeds. Incidentally bundled reed boats are still in use in South America, and they purportedly writhe and move like serpents when they are in the water!

According to legend, Quetzalcoatl came to the Americas to educate the barbarous natives, giving them knowledge of religion, agriculture, science, astronomy, mathematics and writing. Quetzalcoatl is also credited with inventing the circular calendar system in common use throughout Mesoamerica. This sophisticated calendar was used for dating agricultural events and religious observances. Quetzalcoatl is also attributed with introducing a highly moral and ethical system of laws to the people that forbade the cannibalism and human sacrifice common among the natives before his arrival and, sadly, after his departure.

In these respects, Quetzalcoatl sounds as if he was a composite figure combining the traits of Enoch the Sethite and Noah. After all, this book has shown that Enoch was a great religious teacher and astronomer who introduced the utilization of henges as giant astronomical time clocks and invented at least one form of writing to record a godly record of Pre-Flood history, astronomy, and prophecy that he gave to Noah. In addition, Noah's name sounds like the Hebrew word for "comfort" because he was destined to become a successful farmer prior to and after the Flood, and he likely introduced concepts like terraced farming, crop rotation, soil fertilization, and irrigation to produce bountiful crops. Later, through the process of syncretism, it is possible that Enoch the architect and prophet and Noah the farmer became one. However, it is also just as likely that Quetzalcoatl could have been Noah alone.

Native legends depict Quetzalcoatl as the bringer of agriculture and civilization and the inventor of their astronomical calendar, and - as this book as shown - Noah was taught advanced ship-building techniques and herbal medicine by the holy angels. In addition, Noah was the preserver of the Book of Enoch, which he added to before he died and which held the knowledge of building a henge and keeping track of celestial time. In addition, Noah had to have been a skilled astronomer to know and apply the Gospel in the Stars and a farmer who likely developed revolutionary agricultural skills and made farming a much more scientific and bountiful process. It therefore takes little stretch of the imagination to see that Noah and Quetzalcoatl had much in common.

According to various native myths, the god king Quetzalcoatl was deposed and forced to leave the Americas when he was defeated at the hands of an enemy "god." Then, after Quetzalcoatl left, the new "god" who ruled over the natives coerced them to return to their old, barbaric religious customs, which included human sacrifice and cannibalism. The toll in human life this created over the intervening centuries is terribly tragic - especially since these natives practiced human sacrifice in a false effort to stave off the cataclysmic end of the world, which was an end no mere mortal could possibly stop or delay.

Even more tragically, the conquistadors apparently resembled the recorded descriptions of Quetzalcoatl and his compatriots that were preserved in native legends all too well. With their light skins, bearded faces, big ships, and shining armor, the conquistadors met little opposition when they arrived in the Americas but were treated with the utmost respect and deference. In fact, the conquistadors were welcomed as gods. Now, since the native people of Cholula did not know the conquistadors' true motives, which was to claim territory for the Spanish Crown and to search for gold and other riches to exploit for the glory of Imperial Spain, the Cholulan Aztecs did nothing to protect themselves. Instead, the natives joyfully welcomed the conquistadors and showed them all their gold and riches. Consequently, a massacre of the natives occurred during a major celebration in Quetzalcoatl's temple.

Invited as representatives of the god in the year 1519, the Spanish Commander **Hernando Cortez and his fellow conquistadors killed over 6,000 unarmed and unsuspecting natives in one single day!** In their mad lust for riches, the conquistadors then quickly slaughtered most of the remaining Cholulan natives in the vicinity and looted their temples and homes. Massacres of the natives even worse than this followed in Tenochtitlan, the seat of Montezuma's Aztec government and the location of the Teotihuacán pyramid complex. Fascinatingly the ancient name for what is now the city of Mexico - Tenochtitlan - appears to contain a clear reference to the antediluvian prophet Enoch in its name, which can be rendered as T-**enoch**-titlan. Could this be a mere coincidence, or were Tenochtitlan and neighboring Teotihuacán other Sethite repositories of Enochian knowledge like Giza before the Flood?

As previously mentioned, archeologists have identified Quetzalcoatl's symbol as a plumed serpent. Like the cross, which represents the four fixed signs of the Zodiac, the four Ages of men, equinoxes, solstices, precession, and ultimately Christ, many of the symbols used by the Mayans had both astronomical as well as spiritual meaning. As was shown in Book One on the Mazzaroth, the symbol for the allegorically malevolent Zodiac sign Scorpio is a *scorpion or serpent*. Its replacement, however, is *the eagle* - the natural enemy of the serpent.

In the case of the Mayans and Aztecs, the bird that replaced the eagle in their mythology was a Quetzal bird, a brightly colored exotic bird *that eats snakes*, other reptiles, insects, and fruit. Could Quetzalcoatl's emblem therefore be an allegorical representation of the concept of the Scorpio-Sagittarius Meridian, which with their bird and serpent imagery could signify evil being covered over or replaced with good?

Since eagles and other birds eat snakes, the symbol for Quetzalcoatl may have had a similar meaning to the number thirteen, which suggests that apostasy can be erased by righteousness (Please see

Book Four on Prophecy for more clarification on the meaning of the number thirteen in prophecy). Finally, the substitutionary sacrifice of Christ on the Cross for our sins was symbolized in Blood Covenant rituals with an exchange of cloaks. In essence, when we become believers by accepting Yahshua as our Savior, we are covered over with Christ's pure white mantle of purity even though we are still black sheep (or sinful serpents) underneath. In essence, Noah and Shem may have allegorically depicted the coming Messiah's sacrifice for our sins with the light and airy feathers of a bird covering over the heavy darkness of the serpent signifying all of Adam and Eve's sinful descendents.

Due to the preceding facts, *it appears possible that Quetzalcoatl was none other than Noah or his son Shem.* These two extraordinary righteous men lived such long lives and had such great knowledge that they would have seemed god-like to the initially primitive natives whom they ministered to. The wondrous knowledge of agriculture, science, mathematics and astronomy that these two seemingly ageless Wise Men or Magi gave to the natives of the Americas made them appear as gods. Through the knowledge of these godlike sages, native legends tell us that the once cannibalistic savages of the Americas became highly civilized and educated, developing a culture that rivaled the complexity and intelligence of any in the Old World. Archeological evidence also tells us that American natives were highly creative in adapting what they had learned. As a result, they developed advanced societies that were unique from Old World cultures, and instead reflected the cultures and values of New World people.

As previously shown, Noah and Shem likely taught others the knowledge of the Gospel in the Stars and the secrets of Sacred Astronomy used to predict the events prophesied about in the ancient Zodiac. As evidenced by the sophisticated astronomical abilities of the Maya, Inca, and Aztecs and their complex religion related to the stars, Noah and Shem likely taught the Star Gospel's moral and religious teachings and its associated astronomical principles to the natives. In doing so, Noah and Shem hoped to lead the natives into living pure and virtuous lives. If the hypothesis that Noah is embodied in the god Quetzalcoatl is correct, then Noah and/or Shem were later deified. There are some basic reasons why this may have occurred. For example, since Noah and/or Shem were so long-lived, intelligent, compassionate, and righteous, the natives may have seen these men as far superior to themselves. They therefore made the mistake of deifying them.

In Book One, "The Language of God in the Universe", I discuss how the Zodiac sign Capricorn represented Noah as well as a host of Pagan deities who were considered part man and either part goat or fish.

Like some of the ancient Old World deities such as Osiris, Oannes, and Dagon, Quetzalcoatl was the New World's patron god of agriculture. Quetzalcoatl, like Noah, was also a great teacher and righteous lawgiver who promoted peace among the natives and brotherhood among all living creatures. The Feathered Serpent god's connection to Noah as the foremost scientist, astronomer, doctor, preacher and farmer after the Flood is therefore obvious.

Besides being great farmers, it is likely that Noah and his sons knew the secrets of the Great Pyramid that was built before the Flood. Furthermore, they and their descendents were likely prolific builders and encouraged astronomical observatories with religious significance to be built wherever they went. Could this be why pyramids have been found connected to every ancient culture on Earth? Could this also be why the builders of the Pyramid of the Sun at Teotihuacán incorporated similar measurements and the same compass orientation as the Great Pyramid? I believe it is. The similarities in agricultural methods and astronomical knowledge that was extant in many diverse cultures in ancient times lend strength to the idea that these cultures shared a common knowledge base or a common ancestor who affected the beliefs of people all over the world at one time.

The Bible tells us that Noah was the one common ancestor shared by all the people who inhabited the Earth after the Flood. Due to their knowledge of the Gospel in the Stars, Noah and his son Shem could have taught people all over Middle Earth the principles of Sacred Astronomy as well as the science of agriculture. Noah, after all, was signaled out in the Bible as the one who would give men rest from their toil of working the ground to yield food. This means that Noah was the likely inventor of the principles of modern agriculture. Noah is also attributed with inventing (or re-inventing) the process of fermenting grape juice to make wine after the Flood (Genesis 9:20-21).

Quetzalcoatl VS Tezcatlipoca: Noah and Nimrod at War!

Sadly, Noah's plan to tell the world about Yahweh and His Star Gospel seems to have backfired in the Americas when the mad and malevolent "god" known to the natives as Tezcatlipoca appeared on the scene. According to native legend, Tezcatlipoca was Quetzalcoatl's archrival, and he brutally thwarted Quetzalcoatl's civilizing and moralizing efforts in the Americas. In an effort to destroy Quetzalcoatl's power, Tezcatlipoca was said to have followed after Quetzalcoatl and fought continually with him and his attendants and followers. Then, after one massive and unrelenting battle, Tezcatlipoca finally defeated

Quetzalcoatl and his followers. Quetzalcoatl was therefore forced to abandon his good works among the natives, and he and his attendants fled back to their homeland across the sea.

After Quetzalcoatl left the Americas in his ship purportedly hulled with serpent skins, the legends state that the evil god Tezcatlipoca forcibly re-introduced cannibalism and human sacrifice to the religious rites of many Native American tribes. Native legends also tell us that, sometime after his take over, Tezcatlipoca forced the once peaceful native people to make war and to obtain captives to be used in grisly human sacrifices and cannibalistic rites.

Now, is it possible that Tezcatlipoca actually craved human flesh and blood as food for himself? Just as Quetzalcoatl may depict more than one individual, could Tezcatlipoca represent at syncretism between Nimrod and the Nephilim who survived the Flood? Based on the legends about Tezcatlipoca's evil and bloodthirsty nature, this is a plausible assumption. As a result of this evil "god's" take-over, the peaceful and benevolent rule of Noah and his son Shem came to a sad end in the Americas. Soon the natives again practiced barbaric sacrificial blood rites that were gross perversions of godly blood sacrifices and the true Blood Covenant rites used among the followers of Yahweh.

In light of these myths about Quetzalcoatl and Tezcatlipoca, could the serpent skin boat covering that supposedly hulled Quetzalcoatl's boat have been made from feathered serpent skins such as those that the Nephilim sported in life? Furthermore, could this use of feathered serpent skins trace the boat's origin to Mesopotamia, where Noah and Shem likely still lived in isolation and where Nimrod had successfully waged war against the Anakim living in that region before his takeover of the world? If so, then the mere site of this serpent skin covered boat surely would have outraged any Anakim who lived on the Earth after the Flood.

After defeating Quetzalcoatl, Tezcatlipoca could do as he wished in the New World and it appears that he wasted no time in defining himself as the new and dominant god. Through the malicious meddling of the persons and Anakim that were signified by the god Tezcatlipoca, the true Star Gospel, the concept of substitutionary blood sacrifice for the redemption of sin, and the rite of Blood Covenanting were perverted into detestable crimes against God and humanity. *This happened not only in Mesoamerica but all over the world - in every ancient culture.* Evidence has been found that verifies that ancient people groups around the world practiced some form of star worship as well as human sacrifice.

To the natives in the Americas, the moral and upright man Noah became Quetzalcoatl, the god of learning and agriculture - and his symbol was a plumed serpent. However, Noah's moralizing and civilizing efforts around the world backfired because of the evil counterculture that his enemies fostered and forced people to follow. The natives knew the malevolent god known as Tezcatlipoca as the god of death and darkness. Tezcatlipoca's name meant "smoking mirror" and he was associated with the night-foraging jaguar. Since Quetzalcoatl can be identified with Noah, could it be that the "god" known to the natives as Tezcatlipoca was also a man or Nephilim/human hybrid like the Babylonian hero Gilgamesh? Could it be that Tezcatlipoca and his evil followers pursued Noah and his assistants throughout the world with an opposing mission?

I would like to propose a possibly human candidate for Tezcatlipoca, one who is mentioned briefly in the Bible. It is my contention that this evil "god" called Tezcatlipoca was not a true "god" at all but a man who wished to be a god and that **he can be identified as the biblical ruler named Nimrod.** This is not just an assumption because there is evidence to substantiate this connection. As in many other cases throughout my analysis of ancient history in this book series, it can be found in allegorical symbolism. History tells us, for example, that Tezcatlipoca and Nimrod both shared an association with a night foraging big cat. In the case of Nimrod, it is said that he used black leopards to aid him when he hunted. In addition the name "Nimrod" was probably derived from two Babylonian words: "nimr," which meant "leopard" coupled with "rod," which meant "to subdue," and meaning "subduing leopard" when combined. Similarly, Tezcatlipoca was always associated with the jaguar, a big cat like the leopard that forages for live game at night. In behavior and appearance, the jaguar is therefore the closest equivalent to a leopard in the New World.

At La Venta in the Tabasco Province of Mexico's Gulf Coast, archeological strata associated with the Olmec culture has been excavated that lends credence to my hypothesis. There, huge stone Negroid heads have been found along with carved steles depicting men with hooked noses, full facial beards and conical caps like those worn in ancient Israel and Phoenicia. Both of these racial groups were supposedly common only to Africa and the Middle East at one time. The Caucasian men carved on the steles exhibit characteristics associated with Semitic people - a race very different in appearance from the indigenous native population of the Americas. I partly base my assumption that Noah or his predecessors were once in the Americas on the existence of these telltale artifacts. Why would the natives have carved depictions of

Semitic and Negro men into stone unless they were familiar with these obvious Old World racial types in some way?

If the natives did carve these representations of Semitic and Negro men into stone, they must have been important to the natives in some highly significant way. Based on this assumption, *could the steles at La Venta actually depict the white, bearded Quetzalcoatl and his attendants? I believe they did.* Furthermore, since some of these steles show these Semitic men as badly beaten or brutally murdered, they may also show the defeat of Quetzalcoatl and his followers by the evil, bloodthirsty Tezcatlipoca. Furthermore, could it be that the huge stone Negroid heads found associated with the steles at La Venta depict the fierce enemies of these Semitic people? The Book of Jasher certainly gives credence to the assumption that Nimrod could be represented by Tezcatlipoca, for it states that Nimrod was a world dictator who was very evil, as was his son Mardon (Jasher 7:44-48). Furthermore, this book has established that Nimrod may have been a dark-skinned Negro in appearance, and this black racial type fits the appellation "smoking mirror," which is the translation of Tezcatlipoca's name from Nahuatl into English. This also may be a descriptive term for the black volcanic glass called obsidian, which was used to make weapons in Mesoamerica. In addition, the term "smoking mirror" also appears to refer to the spiritual darkness Nimrod and his son plunged the world into when they altered the Star Gospel, introduced idolatry, encouraged human sacrifice and star worship, and taught men to worship their ancestors instead of the one true God.

Ancient Attempts to Hide the Truth Resurfacing Today

Unfortunately, many archeologists that are in the business of revising history to suit the aims of evil men are now proposing that there is a big hole in the various hypotheses being presented here. Though in the past, many well-respected scholars insisted that the natives saw Quetzalcoatl as a white man with a beard, they are now insisting that depictions of Quetzalcoatl as a bearded white fellow sprang up because the Spanish missionaries and Christianized Indians depicted Quetzalcoatl this way.

Nonetheless, there is every indication that this supposedly more accurate teaching is just another attempt by archeologists and other people in power to squelch the truth. The carved figures at La Venta of Semitic-looking men and the Olmec Negroid heads found in the New World *speak for themselves*. Furthermore, the musings of archeologists don't negate other reputable reports done by natives confirming that

Quetzalcoatl was a white man with a beard - just as the men at La Venta are depicted. Therefore, it is best if we do not believe everything archeologists and scholars are trying to tell us. If all of us did, we would still see the Pillar of Enoch is a tomb and tomb only. That's all archeologists will give it credit for.

Sadly, many learned but ungodly men and women in the archeological and political world have an agenda that is diametrically opposed to supporting the truths of the Bible and the clear evidence of history and myth. As startling evidence of this, it was reported recently that Zahi Hawass, the self-proclaimed "Indiana Jones" of Egypt's archeological world is touting that he has discovered a sealed door beneath the floor of the Queen's Chamber of the Great Pyramid, and that he believes that it will lead to the hidden tomb of the pharaoh Khufu, who supposedly built the pyramid. The date for this tomb opening was to be July 26th, 2009, but it never occurred.

Intriguingly, July 26th, 2009 coincided with the completion date for this final book in the Language of God Book Series, which shows the remarkable godly purpose of the Pillar of Enoch. This date also occurred four days after the ominous Solar Eclipse on the 1st of Av that was best viewed from the Philippines, the coast of China, Japan, and the numerous small islands of Micronesia in the Pacific Ocean that are tied to the Virgo Longitudinal Meridian, but also have a connection to the Scorpio Meridian and the constellation Draco. Ominously, could there be a connection with this eclipse and the idolatrous statues of the Virgin Mary with a dead serpent under her feet that I once saw in the lobby of the Roman Catholic Church I frequented as a child? Could the leaders of the Roman Catholic Church be using these idolatrous statues to tout Mary as the Mother Goddess who will supposedly save the world from evil, just as Nimrod promoted the false worship of Ishtar the deified Eve who sought the wisdom of the Serpent?

Returning to our discussion about the possibility that there is a Pharaoh's tomb hidden in the Great Pyramid, could it be that Zahi Hawass will suddenly find a tomb with a mummy and a few unusual artifacts and treasures inside the pyramid in the near future? If he does, it is my contention that it will be an artfully manufactured one filled with real tomb goods pilfered from other tombs and hidden in the Great Pyramid. Anyone who loves Yahweh and has read this book should be able to see the obvious reason for such a stunt. It would no doubt be used to attempt to destroy any faith people might have in the Great Pyramid as a holy altar and monument dedicated to the one true God and His coming Messiah, and also would be used to point ridicule in the direction of anyone like me who is willing to challenge the status quo with accusations that their tomb might be nothing more than a clever forgery meant to obscure the truth.

This scenario is highly probable - considering the fact that there have been several researchers that have gone inside the Great Pyramid in recent years and have reported seeing large cemented-over patches in the walls of various chambers in the pyramid, especially in the King's and Queen's Chambers. These eye-witness accounts provide damning evidence that the Egyptians have been doing secret excavation projects within the Great Pyramid without telling the world about it, and they have attempted to cover up the fact by claiming they had to make repairs within the structure to make it safe for tourists.

In the past, such things were also likely done to hide the truth in Egypt. In fact, the face currently depicted on the Great Sphinx in Egypt was likely carved over its original face - a lost face that we will never see. The reason that this current face is likely not the original face of the Sphinx is because it is far too small in proportion to the full crouching form of the Sphinx. Any photographs showing the entire body of the Sphinx either from the air or from a direct side view at ground level will show this apparent discrepancy between the size of the Sphinx's body and its much tinier head. This discrepancy is further brought to fore in that the ancient artists who carved other Sphinx-shaped statues in Egypt usually always did so with the proper proportions used between face and body. The Great Sphinx is the only exception to this rule found in Egypt.

The ancient Egyptians supposedly viewed the Great Sphinx as a depiction of the Sun God Amun-Ra. However, as shown in each book of the Language of God Book Series, the Sphinx actually represents the Son of God named Yahshua. Since the Sphinx was purported to signify the Sun god, someone who wanted to be deified probably had a likeness of his or her face carved over the original face of the Sphinx. A plausible candidate for this ugly sort of puffed-up pride would have been Nimrod, his evil and enterprising wife Semiramis, or their equally evil son Mardon. Adding strength to this theory is the fact that - as a descendant of Ham from Cush, Nimrod was likely a dark-skinned man with some Negroid facial characteristics. Furthermore, the face that is now carved on the Great Sphinx is unmistakably that of a person of Negroid racial type. In addition, a forensic scientist who studied the face of the Sphinx contends that its face is not only Negroid, but may also be the face of a **black female**. This lends credence to the idea that the face of the Sphinx is either Nimrod's wife Semiramis' face or that of someone like her that had immense power and authority in some distant era.

Tezcatlipoca's Close Connection to Nimrod

When translated into English, the name "Tezcatlipoca" literally means "smoking mirror." Therefore, could this name be a symbolic designation denoting a person whose skin was extremely dark like the color of smoke? If so, *the name Tezcatlipoca may have been a descriptive word for highly polished ebony or obsidian.* In fact, this is exactly what Tezcatlipoca's name was meant to convey, since *"tezcatl" - the Aztec word for mirror - was also their word for obsidian, which is a highly shiny type of black volcanic glass!*

Chillingly, black obsidian was used by Mesoamerican priests to make both divinatory mirrors as well as the sacrificial knives they used to offer humans to Tezcatlipoca on the altar. Furthermore, as this book has shown, volcanoes can serve as apt symbols for Hell, judgment, the Lake of Fire and the first armorers among the gods who were none other than the fallen angel Azazel and his human counterpart Tubal-Cain, the son of Lamech the Cainite. *Perhaps that is why many of the first arrowheads, spear points and knife blades manufactured my mankind were chipped from pieces of black obsidian!* In addition, the first primitive mirrors used by mankind were fashioned from slabs of polished obsidian, and 1 Enoch tells us that it was Azazel himself who first taught mankind to adorn themselves to inspire lust as well as how make weapons and wage war.

Regardless of Tezcatlipoca's skin color, there is no doubt that he was a cruel and despotic ruler who forced everyone in the Americas to conform to his new false religion or suffer execution. Likewise, Nimrod was also a tyrant who forced people to worship him and do as he ordered them to do. As previously stated, due to Nimrod's desire to conquer and rule the world, this same scenario happened to some degree throughout the world.

As mentioned earlier, the Bible and Book of Jasher tell us that all the civilized people in the world spoke one language and were united in ideology at the time when Nimrod ruled:

> *"Now the whole world had one language and a common speech." - Genesis 11:1 (NIV)*

> *"And all the earth was of one tongue and words of union..." - Jasher 7:46*

In his book "Legend," David Rohl convincingly argues that the Bible passage that says everyone on Earth *"had one language"* was meant to allude to spiritual beliefs instead of *"common speech,"* which is mentioned separately. The statement in Jasher suggests this as well, saying that the people of that era not only spoke *"one tongue"* but the same *"words of union,"* with these words of union having a spiritual dimension in the words of the prayers that were offered to their gods. This could mean that - **all over the Earth** - people could not only freely communicate to each other but followed the same perverted form of Paganism that Nimrod had devised and promulgated at spear point, just as Jihadists today are using violence in a mad attempt to convert the world to their tyrannical religion called Islam.

Fortunately, Nimrod's despotic world rulership ended cataclysmically (Genesis 11:6-9). Therefore, the one unified Post-Flood culture that Nimrod devised by indoctrination and force of arms was divided into many different kingdoms that were forced to develop separately. These new cultures rapidly grew apart due to the emergence of so many new languages instead of the one language that was once known to all the people throughout the world. In addition, the dividing of the Earth into smaller continents separated by vast distances also contributed to this new religious and cultural divergence.

This unity followed by division is also what may have caused the amazing cultural and religious overlap we can see in such disparate cultures in time and place as the Mesopotamian ziggurat builders and the pyramid builders of Egypt and the Americas. As already stated, the commonality between ancient Egyptian culture and a large portion of the Americas manifested itself in that both locales had star-worshipping religions centered on observing the heavens. In addition, both societies built pyramids, mummified their dead, navigated bodies of water in reed boats, viewed their kings as representations of the divine, and used a hieroglyphic form of writing that combined glyphs for whole words with symbols for phonetic sounds.

The Startling Truth Hidden in Mesoamerican Culture

My main point in sharing all this is not just to give a revolutionary view of the history of the New World, though I certainly have done that! Rather, it is ultimately to show that the Mayan calendar may not have originated with the Maya or their predecessors the Toltecs or Olmecs. Instead, this date for the so-called end of the world - December 21st, 2012 - was really meant to mark the end of an Age that the Mayans knew as "the Fifth Sun". This date may have been calculated by, and known to the righteous antediluvian descendents of Seth. In fact, since Enoch professed to be able to read the Heavenly Tablets, and knew all the secrets hidden in the Mazzaroth regarding the fate of men, angels and demons, it is likely that the calendar attributed to the Mayans was created by Enoch the Sethite. After all, the ancient texts reveal that Enoch was guided by the godly Watchers, who were his mentors and guides into the greatest mysteries surrounding our awesome and powerful Creator God, and that he was shown the purpose and future of mankind in the stars.

After the Flood, Noah and Shem may have used Enoch's findings to devise the calendar used in the New World. If they did, it is also likely that the New World wasn't new at all, but was merely hidden after the Flood so that Enoch's knowledge would not be readily available to those who were unworthy of these secrets. This is likely why Noah's withdrawal to the Americas after the Flood was hidden, and only the lands allotted to his sons Shem, Ham and Japheth were mentioned in the divisions of land that occurred after the Flood.

It is even possible that Noah and the other righteous Sethites that were hidden away from the rest of the world prior to the Flood found refuge in Mesoamerica. Even though the Americas were attached to the African continent prior to the Flood, God could easily have hidden them all away in the secluded, roughly rectangular Antiplano region of the Andes Mountains in Peru, where Atlantis may have been located. Indeed, the fabled city of Atlantis could have existed in that location both before and after the Great Flood, but would have inevitably been destroyed both times - once by the Great Flood, and again when God sent fire and brimstone to destroy Nimrod's ill-fated Tower of Babel as well as his Pagan empire.

Through the divine science of Sacred Astronomy, the Hamite inhabitants of South America and the Shemites living in Mesoamerica obviously knew that the wicked world governed by demons and men would one day come to an ignoble end, and that the beginning of that end would occur sometime around December 21st, 2012. This is the date of the Winter Solstice and - besides being only four days before Christmas - it falls around the time of Chanukah as well. Unfortunately, the Pagan Feast of Saturnalia was also held in Ancient Rome around that time. In addition, the Winter Solstice was the supposed day of the birth of the Sun god Apollo, whose attributes as a guardian over shepherds and flocks, and as the first player of the lyre or harp connects him with the sons of Lamech the Cainite named Jabal and Jubal.

Could the righteous men who taught the native people that populated the New World after the Flood higher forms of science and religion also have taught them that the world as we know it would one day come to a final and cataclysmic end? Could this be why the Olmecs, Toltecs, Inca, Maya, and Aztecs remembered this amazing date by ensuring it remained the end of the calendar that they adapted and used themselves? Could they have known that this date may mark the end of the passage of time in the sinful world we know today? Considering that Enoch and Noah knew that the sinful world would end cataclysmically and be made new, and that a heavenly kingdom would exist on Earth someday that would never end, it seems likely that the Post-Flood inhabitants of Shem's lands in Middle Earth would have known this.

If so, this date may have been memorialized to show every initiate into Sacred Astronomy that the arrival of the world's time of judgment, and the subsequent end of the world, had been calculated before the Universe was created and set into motion! Knowing this, the godly masters of Sacred Astronomy called Magi, who served as advisers to the ancient kings, were meant to teach them about the importance of living righteous lives so that they would be counted worthy of everlasting life. Therefore, the Magi were much more than glorified Astronomers. They were meant to be the righteous guardians of God's heavenly record books, and were entrusted with seeing that Yahweh's Will would be done in every Age until the end of the world!

Noah and Shem were likely the greatest of the Magi after the Flood. As such, they would have diligently made sure that the sacred astronomical knowledge that they were entrusted with by Enoch would not be forgotten. That is why they memorialized that knowledge in stone both prior to and after the Flood. As was previously shown, this is evident in so many massive stone constructions like the Great Pyramid, Great Sphinx, Stonehenge, and the pyramid complex at Teotihuacán - which may have been constructed by Noah and Shem after the Flood to follow the celestial path of the Pleiades star cluster in Taurus at the time of Christ to symbolize the birth of the Messiah and the Church, which they also foreknew through the Star Gospel!

In many respects, the same knowledge encoded into the Pillar of Enoch in Egypt was also encoded into the less ancient but no less impressive Pyramid of the Sun at Teotihuacán shown on the facing page. This step-pyramid shaped temple is likely falsely attributed to the Aztecs. Instead, it was probably built by Noah's descendents long before the arrival of the Maya and Aztecs on the world scene. After Noah and Shem died or were driven out of the New World, however, the monuments at Teotihuacán were re-appropriated and extensively built around – just as is the case at other sacred sites all over the world such as Giza in Egypt. Consequently, those who re-appropriated the Pyramid of the Sun and all the other structures at Teotihuacán for their Pagan worship rites did all they could to hide its true connection to Yahshua the Messiah. As the photos on pages 719 and 725 show, however, they could not hide the truth forever!

The legends of the Maya and Aztecs tell us that, before the white-skinned, bearded Quetzalcoatl left the Americas, he promised the natives that he would come back one day. At the time, however, he couldn't know that the natives would mistake the white-skinned, bearded Imperialist military commander Hernando Cortez as Quetzalcoatl and the equally ignorant conquistadors he led as Quetzalcoatl's legendary attendants. Tragically, despite their advanced astronomical skills, the natives didn't know or remember that the heavens proclaim that someone like Quetzalcoatl would one day come to Earth, conquer the evil god symbolized by Nimrod/Tezcatlipoca and usher in a New Age of righteousness where the Way of Yahweh will be exalted rather than the Way of Cain.

The Pyramid of the Sun - Teotihuacán, Mexico:
Symbol for the Messiah Planet Jupiter
and Christ as a Triumphant Messiah

The natives of Mesoamerica did not know that - long before Cortez set foot in the Americas - *the promised one had already come in the Person of Yahshua our Messiah! He is the allegorical eagle of light that will completely destroy the serpent of darkness someday soon.* In the sense that Hernando Cortez' destruction of the Aztec empire began to open the way for Catholic priests to introduce the Gospel to the natives of the Americas, the prophecy of the great Wise Man named Noah that led the distant ancestors of the Aztecs came true. One like Noah did come to Earth to usher in a New Age. This was Yahshua, whose invisible reign over mankind began when the Kingdom power of God on Earth was manifested in those that are born-again by His Spirit.

But this is not the end of the story! Though many deluded people believe mankind will usher in God's Kingdom without the bodily return of Christ, the Scriptures constantly allude to the visible, earthly reign of Yahshua the Messiah on Earth. Furthermore, the Book of Revelation tells us that Yahshua will visibly return to judge His enemies. Though many End Time events may come about beginning in 2010 or 2011, the biggest events ushering in the Great Tribulation may begin on December 21st, 2012, when the Winter Solstice Sun will rise directly on the heavenly Scorpio-Sagittarius Meridian. There will also be an amazing alignment of planets and constellations that day, which may be meant to announce the release of the Four Horsemen of the Apocalypse. See Book Four "The Language of God in Prophecy" for more about these amazing heavenly signs may coincide with major End Time prophetic events.

The Amazing Angkor - Teotihuacán Connection

Thus far, we have explored the connection between Giza in Egypt and Hawaii in the Pacific Ocean and come to the conclusion that they are literally and spiritually opposite to one another. We have also seen the incredible knowledge that these locations on the Earth can communicate to us when our spiritual eyes are open. But all this knowledge is just a small piece of the whole allegorical picture, and there is so much more that can be revealed when we know where to look! For just as there is a correlation between Giza and Hawaii, there is a similar connection between Easter Island and Madagascar, a point like Hawaii where the Path of the Sun and the Path of the Milky Way cross - but on the opposite side of the Earth. Likewise, *there is an amazing connection between the sacred precinct known as Teotihuacán near modern Mexico City and those known as Angkor Thom and Angkor Wat in Cambodia!*

The startling truth about Teotihuacán is that it not only serves as an accurate map of our Solar System and a symbol for Orion's Belt stars on a giant scale, but marks the beginning of the first Great Day of God's Six Great Days of Creation on the Spring Equinox in 10,500 BC. At Noon on the day of that Equinox, Orion would have been at its *lowest* culmination in the sky due to Precession, though it would still have been positioned fully above the horizon and at midpoint in the heavens. Meanwhile, the constellation Draco would have been exactly opposite to Orion above the horizon and at its *highest* culmination. In our current Age, however, the exact opposite is true, and this is a symbol that the

Messiah Yahshua signified by Orion will complete His triumph over the Dragon that signifies Satan forever and achieve a full victory!

As discussed in Books One and Four, the see-saw motion of the constellations in the sky over great periods of time is due to the slow backward rotation of the Earth's axis known as the Precession of the Equinoxes. Indeed, it is apparent from the location of many ancient sacred architectural remains that the Sethites and their descendents in the lines of Noah and Shem were fully aware of the affects and allegorical and prophetic implications of Precession. Now, though Orion was at its lowest culmination in 10,500 AD, it has slowly crept upward in the sky over the last 12,500 years, which is a bit less than one half of a 26,000-year Precessional Cycle. Orion therefore reached its highest culmination in our sky in 2000 AD, which means that the constellation Draco the Dragon is now at its *lowest* culmination. This fact has many allegorical and prophetic implications, some of which are revealed in the following ground map of Angkor that is tied to the constellation Draco as well as in the Star Gospel charts following it:

Illustration of Angkor Temple Complex Correlation to Draco

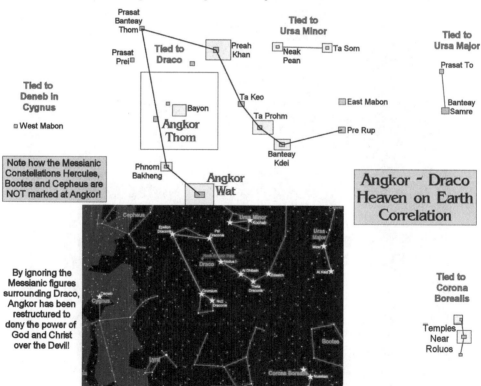

Star Chart of Orion on the Spring Equinox in 10,500 BC

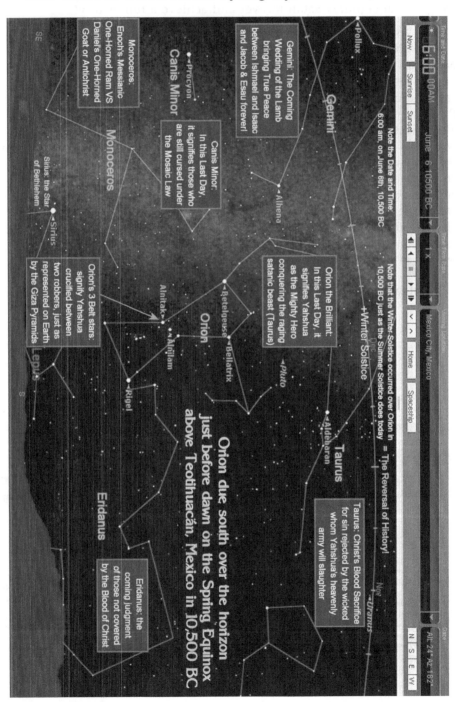

Star Chart of Draco on the Spring Equinox in 10,500 BC

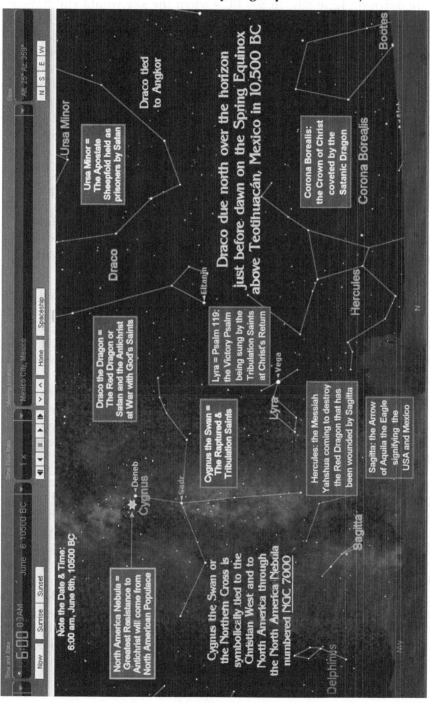

These star charts depict the northern and southern horizons just before dawn on June 6th, 10,500 BC - when the sky would still have been dark enough for many of the stars to be visible if they existed. At that time, Orion would have been due south and Draco would appear due north above the horizon. This is fascinating because - just as Orion was marked on the Earth by the Sethites at Giza - the constellation called Draco was marked on the ground at Angkor in Cambodia, as shown on page 721. Though this fact is now known and accepted among occultists, however, none have any idea that it is tied to Teotihuacán. But with the knowledge of the Star Gospel and the Holy Spirit within me, God has graciously shown me this connection so that I could reveal it!

Amazingly, Teotihuacán's Orion symbolism is directly connected to Angkor's Draco symbolism just as Egypt's Taurus symbolism is connected to Hawaii's Scorpio symbolism! Furthermore, just as Giza marks Orion's position high above the horizon when Draco is fully below the horizon at dawn on June 6th, 10,500 BC and at dawn on September 20th, 2017, Teotihuacán marks Orion and Angkor marks Draco just before dawn on the same past and future days!

Due to these amazing correlations, the three major sacred stone structures at both Teotihuacán and Giza signify the unrepentant and repentant robbers that died on either side of Christ on Calvary, which I believe occurred on Wednesday, April 25th in 31 AD (See Book Two for a detailed analysis of Christ's death and resurrection). This means that the Pyramid of the Moon at Teotihuacán shows those allegorically unrepentant robbers that mimic the behavior of the wicked that will suffer through the Great Tribulation just as the Pyramid of Menkaure does. Meanwhile, the Citadel dedicated to Quetzalcoatl and the Great Pyramid signify all the righteous saints like the repentant robber that will be spared from the Wrath of God.

Significantly, just as the Pyramid of the Sun at Teotihuacán signifies the planet Jupiter and therefore represents Yahshua when He died on the Cross for our sins between two robbers, the middle Pyramid of Khafre at Giza signifies Yahshua at that same moment in time. Therefore, though the original structures at these locations may have later been built up more or repaired and elaborated upon by subsequent rulers that must have been at least partly familiar with the celestial message of ancient Sethite and Shemite architecture, their hidden Gospel message certainly hasn't changed much. On the Angkor map on page 721, note how the stars in the triumphant Messianic figures of Bootes, Hercules and Cepheus surrounding Draco are not shown at Angkor, though the death of Christ is acknowledged through the structure marking the star Deneb. In addition, Christ's crown that Satan or the Red Dragon covets is shown by the structures marking Corona Borealis.

Alas, though Satan thought he had defeated God when Christ was crucified, Christ's crucifixion actually signified the moment when Satan was defeated, for it is by Yahshua's shed blood on the Cross that believers find redemption! Furthermore, by accepting Christ's sacrifice for our sins, all born-again believers with an active prayer life receive authority from the Holy Spirit over the Devil and his demons. This is why the Sethites took such care in showing Orion as triumphant over Draco here on Earth just as it was already ordained in Heaven before time began. Indeed, the stars were created to stand as an indelible testimony to God's awesome power and greatness!

As mentioned in Chapter Five, the long ceremonial street or plaza connecting the sacred buildings at Teotihuacán may have marked the rising and setting of the star Sirius and the Pleiades star cluster at the time of Yahshua's First Advent. Could this have been Noah's way of showing us that he knew the time period when the Messiah signified by the Pyramid of the Sun and the Pyramid of Khafre would be born?

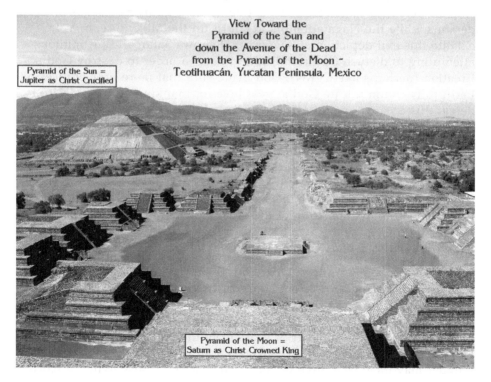

View Toward the
Pyramid of the Sun and
down the Avenue of the Dead
from the Pyramid of the Moon ~
Teotihuacán, Yucatan Peninsula, Mexico

Pyramid of the Sun =
Jupiter as Christ Crucified

Pyramid of the Moon =
Saturn as Christ Crowned King

Could Noah have also used this alignment to show when this blood feud between the Messiah and the Dragon began and will end? After all, in tandem with Angkor, Teotihuacán shows us the two opposing signs of Orion and Draco just before dawn on the Spring Equinox on June 6th, 10,500 BC - as if it were marking the beginning of Azazel's contention with Christ over the fate of mankind and the Earth! In fact, the seven-degree offset from true north and south followed by the street called the "Avenue of the Dead" at Teotihuacán may also mark the seven-degree offset from due south of the star Al Nitak in the constellation of Orion at 6 o'clock a.m. on the Spring Equinox in 10,500 BC, for that star is connected to both the Great Pyramid at Giza and the Citadel Temple of Quetzalcoatl at Teotihuacán.

Due to what God has shown me here, it seems likely that Noah and Shem and their godly descendents built the pyramids at Teotihuacán and placed standing stones or pillars where the Pagan temples of Angkor Thom and Angkor Wat now stand to allegorically announce Satan's war with Yahshua the Messiah and the spiritual battle between good and evil that will one day bring about a major harvest of saints as well as a major judgment of the wicked. Tied to Satan, a prominent wall carving at Angkor depicts a huge Naga serpent being held up by 54 Asanas or demons while the Naga attempts to churn up the Milky Ocean. Yet, despite this evil depiction at Angkor that shows Satan and his minions attempting to disturb Outer and Inner Space in order to destroy God's Creation (perhaps like CERN), God made sure that more holy edifices on Earth fully communicate God's great love for mankind and His desire to defeat this great source of evil on our behalf.

God's amazing grace and mercy as well as His wrath and judgment are clearly shown in the two pyramids and temple to Quetzalcoatl at Teotihuacán because they mimic the three crosses on Calvary just like Giza's pyramids do. In addition, as shown in the star chart on page 723, the war between good and evil can be seen in the heavens via the juxtaposition of the great Northern Cross found in the constellation Cygnus the Swan - a beautiful white bird like the dove - next to the twisted body of the Dragon of Draco.

As explained in Book One, and as shown in the illustration on the facing page from Book Four, the North America Nebula appears near to the head of the giant cross formed by Cygnus the Swan. This nebula is numbered NGC 7000, and it may be more than a coincidence that this number is tied to the number of years from the creation of Adam and Eve until the creation of the New Heaven and New Earth. In fact, this number may have been divinely inspired to assure those living in North

America that the people and nations of North America will remain throughout the Millennial Rule of Christ.

Another fascinating point about the North America Nebula is not only its striking shape but its position at the top of the Northern Cross, which is analogous to Yahshua's head and His crown of thorns. As shown in Book Four, this bird imagery is repeated again in the adjacent constellation Aquila the Eagle, which is a wounded eagle holding Sagitta the Arrow in its talons in order to deliver a death blow to the serpent writhing in Ophiuchus' strong arms.

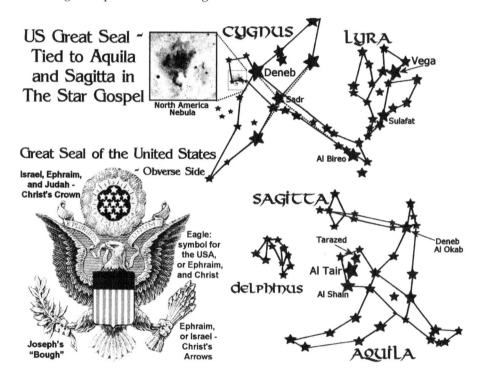

The illustration on this page and the star chart on page 699 show that all of this Star Gospel symbolism is indelibly connected not only to Mexico's Coat of Arms, but to the Great Seal of the United States - a nation whose miraculous formation, enduring constitution, remarkable productivity, Christian evangelization of the world, and rise to military and economic power suggest that it was a divinely blessed and prophetically planned attempt to reintroduce mankind to the democracy and freedom enjoyed by the ancient Israelites before they had a king. In essence, America was founded on Christian principles to re-establish the God-given Bill of Rights that belonged to Adam and Eve before they fell, and that the Devil continually seeks to rob us of by enslaving us to sin and evil. To learn more about the amazing place of the United States of America in Bible Prophecy, see "The Language of God in Prophecy."

The star charts on pages 722 and 723 also reveal bits of the Star Gospel locked into the heavens surrounding Orion and Draco. For example, Orion signifies Christ as the Redeemer while Taurus signifies that Yahshua's blood sacrifice was sufficient to pay for all the sins of the redeemed that are seen as righteous (seen in Taurus' right horn) and the unredeemed that are seen as unrighteous (seen in Taurus' left horn). Orion also signifies Christ's Second Coming as a Conquering King or Prince - when He will defeat the Red Dragon and the Beast out of the Sea signified by Taurus' left horn and Draco the Dragon.

Ominously, as indicated in the star charts, these signs in the heavens would have been visible at the 6th hour of the 6th day during the 6th month. Since the number of the Antichrist's name will equal six hundred and sixty-six or 666, this date correlation with that number shows that the signs in the heavens were given to men and angels to show them that the rise of Satan or Azazel as the great enemy of God was known to God long before it occurred. Furthermore, the Star Gospel shows us that God also has an amazing plan of action that was fulfilled through the coming of Yahshua our Messiah, the Author of our Salvation. Therefore, though the heavens declare that the wicked angel Azazel (Draco) will give all his power to the Antichrist (Serpens) before the great battle between Yahshua and His saints and Azazel and his wicked followers at the end of this Age, it also declares Yahshua's ultimate triumph over Azazel at the end of this Age.

To celebrate Yahshua's triumph over the Devil, the Sethites also built the Great Pyramid and Great Sphinx to mark the Spring Equinox on June 6th, 10,500 BC - when the sign of Leo was due east on the eastern horizon and Orion was high in the southern sky at the exact beginning of God's first Great Creation Day. Furthermore, as shown in the last chapter of Book Four, the Great Pyramid and Great Sphinx also appear to mark Yahshua's Second Coming via the signs in the heavens at sunrise on September 20th, 2017 AD, which is two days before the Autumn Equinox that year and only hours before Rosh Hashanah, which begins at dusk on the same day. Tying all of these amazing facts together, the large stone calendar that was preserved underneath the ancient main plaza of Tenochtitlan (which is now the main plaza of Mexico City) is an artifact that mathematically calculates the end of the Fifth Sun or Age on the date 13 Baktun, or December 21st, 2012 on the Gregorian Calendar. This is when the Winter Solstice Sun will rise directly on top of the Scorpio-Sagittarius Meridian in the sky.

Though this Calendar Stone is attributed to the Aztecs, it may not be Aztec at all, and it is certain that the calculations it employs to find dates originated long before the Aztecs. In fact, it likely originated long before any of the New World people who used it including the Olmecs, Toltecs, Inca, and Maya. Since the starting date for this calendar system is 3114 BC, it coincides with the 267th year in the life of Enoch the Sethite, and may have originated with him. This was easily determined using my Biblical Chronological Time Chart in the Appendix.

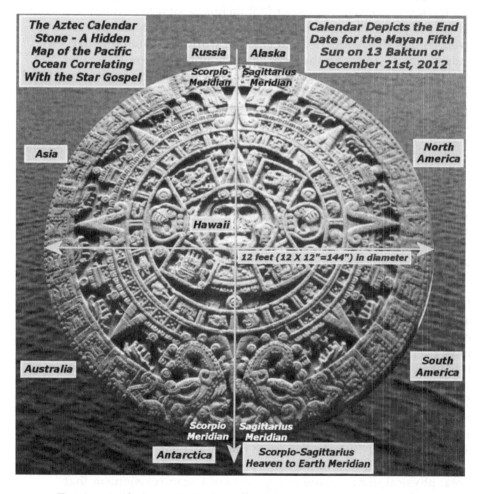

The Aztec Calendar Stone - A Hidden Map of the Pacific Ocean Correlating With the Star Gospel

Russia | Alaska

Calendar Depicts the End Date for the Mayan Fifth Sun on 13 Baktun or December 21st, 2012

Scorpio Meridian | *Sagittarius Meridian*

Asia

North America

Hawaii

12 feet (12 X 12"=144") in diameter

Australia

South America

Scorpio Meridian | *Sagittarius Meridian*

Antarctica | **Scorpio-Sagittarius Heaven to Earth Meridian**

Fascinatingly, one Baktun is equal to the passing of 144,000 days or degrees on the Zodiacal Wheel, and this Calendar Stone is 12 feet in diameter or almost exactly 144 Pyramid Inches wide! This ties this ancient stone calendar to the time when Yahshua will choose 144,000 Witnesses to minister to the lost during the Great Tribulation, and - as shown in Book Four - the Tribulation may have started around the beginning of the Jewish Sacred Year 5771 on Nissan 1 or April 5th, 2011. If this is so, the sunrise on the Winter Solstice in 2012 may be near to the end of the second year into the Tribulation period.

At dawn on December 21st, 2012, Sagittarius the Archer and Aquila the Eagle signifying Yahshua and His saints will be below the horizon and Scorpio the Scorpion and Serpens the Serpent signifying Azazel or Lucifer and his followers will be above the horizon, along with the looming messianic figure of Ophiuchus, a sign that announces that Satan will never have the upper hand over the true Messiah Yahshua, even though the Antichrist will rule the world for Satan one day soon. Indeed, that is why, on the opposite side of the sky on December 21st, 2012, the planet Jupiter signifying the Messiah Yahshua will be centered over the Red Giant star Al Debaran in Taurus - and this star depicts the great red eye of that raging celestial bull that symbolizes the unleashing of God's Wrath on the wicked during the Tribulation period!

Fascinatingly, at this current time in history, the Summer Solstice Sun now rises over the tip of Orion's upraised sword on the ecliptic. Furthermore, both the causeway of the Great Pyramid at Giza and the central axis of Stonehenge point to the Summer Solstice, and both Giza and Stonehenge also have alignments with the Winter Solstice. These alignments suggest that the builders of these sites were attempting to direct our attention to the opening of what we call the 21st Century, but what the ancient people of Mesoamerica called 13 Baktun.

Since the Calendar Stone found at Tenochtitlan that is attributed to the Aztecs appears to be the main key that interrelates the sacred sites at Giza, Teotihuacán and Angkor to the end of the world, it is my contention that this stone was not carved by the Aztecs at all, but may have been carved by Noah or his righteous ancestor Enoch. Furthermore, it is likely that the Calendar Stone was on prominent display within a temple, but then hidden underneath the plaza of the city before Noah, Shem and their descendents were forced to flee Tenochtitlan for their lives. In any case, just as Egypt has the Dendera Zodiac and the Giza Pyramid connection to Orion as a major key to the Star Gospel, Teotihuacán and Tenochtitlan have their Calendar Stone and sacred pyramid complex tied to the same constellation. Therefore - despite the great physical distance and many years of Pagan revisionism that attempted to separate them spiritually - there is no doubt in my mind that these two ancient archeological sites are connected spiritually and designed to project the same Star Gospel message.

Sadly, the Aztecs ritually murdered and buried dozens of human beings in the Citadel dedicated to Quetzalcoatl and some of these bodies were beheaded before burial. Archeologists see these sacrificial additions to the site as having occurred long after the site was built. They also believe these blood offerings were made to consecrate this sacred space as a symbolic dwelling place for the feathered serpent god, whom the natives believed craved human flesh and blood. This shows that whoever Quetzalcoatl started out as, he was either replaced by a living Anakim or the spirit of a dead one long after he left the Americas.

Tragically, by the time of the Aztecs, Quetzalcoatl had degenerated into a demonic imitation of the godly hero that was Noah and bore little resemblance to the benevolent Quetzalcoatl of myth. Undeniably, the grisly Aztec practice of burying murdered sacrificial victims in the floors of their temples was not in keeping with the behavior of the servant of God named Noah - who saved humanity from annihilation multiple times when he built the Ark, created advanced farming and calendar techniques, developed the science of herbal medicine, and beseeched God to consign many demons to Hell.

Instead, by burying these human sacrifices on the Citadel, the Aztecs were honoring the evil imitator of God named Satan, whose Antichristian End Time leader will martyr many innocent men, women and children in his vain attempt to completely annihilate those who love Yahweh from the face of the Earth. Sadly, what the Maya and later Aztecs were doing when they killed people to appease their gods was simply feeding the never-ending bloodlust of the demonic Nephilim spirits that governed their religious views. Those views were drastically changed for the worse when an evil "god" named Nimrod chased the followers of the Way of Yahweh that had governed Mesoamerica away, and reinstated the Way of Cain or the Serpent over the lives of the unfortunate natives that lived in the region. Sadly, just as the Aztecs decapitated some of their victims, believers that follow the Way of Yahweh today are dying this way at the hands of radical Muslims and Pagans, and Revelation 20:4 concurs that people will be martyred by beheading during the Tribulation, which may have already begun.

Is the Mount Olympus of Greek Myth in Peru?

Though the possibility that Noah and Shem may have civilized and lived in the Americas at one time is an intriguing enough prospect on its own, there are many other unexplained mysteries in the Americas that have only been touched upon here. One of them centers around the ruins of four amazing cities high up on several jagged and remote mountaintops in the Peruvian Andes. These four mysterious cities are now called Machu Picchu, Cuzco, Sacsayhuaman, and Tiahuanaco near

Lake Titicaca, and they are all highly inaccessible and have an altogether otherworldly aura to them - as if gods built them instead of men. In addition, all four cities were at least partly built with cyclopean-sized blocks comparable to those found at Baalbek near Mount Hermon in Lebanon. Like the ruins at Baalbek and in Egypt, these ruined cities contain buildings and walls with layers of smaller, more crudely shaped stones *on top of* a distinct layer of older and far larger stone blocks that are precisely fitted together without mortar. In stark contrast to the uppermost layers, the lower, older layers are constructed of huge, finely hewn megalithic blocks that display far greater skill and precision in their construction than the smaller blocks on top.

Although these cities are attributed to the ancient Inca civilization, which came after the Mayan civilization and was followed by the Aztec civilization, some archeologists suspect the Incas merely repaired and re-inhabited these cities long after their original construction and abandonment. Therefore, like the ruins at Baalbek, no one is sure who built and inhabited these cities when they were new. However, there is a clear explanation for these mountaintop cities that is not found in Peru, but in Greek and Roman myths, which insist that their many gods lived atop a high mountain named Mount Olympus.

Though there is a peak in Greece named Mount Olympus that is 9,570 feet (2,919 meters) tall, there are no prominent ruins atop it to suggest that anyone ever lived there. In fact, this mount is completely barren, jagged, and inhospitable. Therefore, it never appears to have served as a habitation for the fallen Watchers who took human women as wives. In contrast, the Baalbek ruins atop Mount Hermon in Lebanon contain architecture made from finely carved, cyclopean-sized blocks, and the Book of 1 Enoch explicitly states that the Watchers who sinned descended to Earth at this very location, which was situated in the middle of the region known as the Fertile Crescent. This crescent follows the paths of the Nile, Jordan, Tigris and Euphrates rivers. But was this the only place where the Watchers dwelled on Earth before the Flood? The mountaintop ruins in Peru suggest otherwise.

In addition to the telltale evidence of an earlier, far more advanced civilization that was supplanted by a much more primitive one, these impressive ruins are all built at impossibly high elevations. Machu Picchu, for example, was built at nearly 8,000 feet above sea level. Tiahuanaco, which is about 15 miles from the high mountain lake called Lake Titicaca in modern day Bolivia was built even higher up - at the incredibly high elevation of 13,000 feet above sea level. At this elevation, the air is so thin it is almost impossible to breathe without soon gasping for air unless one has been gradually acclimated to the high altitude.

This raises the question of how anyone could survive breathing air so low in oxygen while doing the hard physical labor of moving the massive stone blocks seen in the constructions at Tiahuanaco. Yet we are told the ancient architects built these massive edifices using Stone Age techniques without the benefit of the wheel or pulley! They also supposedly carved out stone blocks weighing many tons and then hauled them from quarries many miles away over impossibly rugged terrain. Finally, they allegedly moved these massive stones carefully into place and expertly cut and fit them together. But how could this have been possible within their essentially Stone Age civilization? Indeed, no architectural or structural engineer today can possibly explain how the ancients could have done it since it would even be impossible today using modern building methods and machines like trucks and cranes.

These cities built of massive stonework couldn't have been conceived, let alone constructed unless the people who built these edifices were far more intelligent, robust and powerful than we are today. In addition, they would have needed great scientific and technological knowledge to accomplish such amazing feats. In short, if these high-elevation stone constructions were the works of purely human hands, our remotest ancestors should be considered far more intelligent and resourceful than any modern archeologist believes.

Though this book is filled with evidence that human beings were capable of such remarkable stone constructions at elevations closer to sea level, the impossible heights of these temple and city ruins in the Andes mountain range strongly suggest that they were built by beings that didn't rely on oxygen for survival or strength. In short, these structures may have been built by the Watchers. However, remember that there were two groups of Watchers on Earth before the Flood, and those who sinned had settled in a separate place from their former comrades. Furthermore, the place where the fallen angels settled has already been identified as Mount Hermon.

Could it be that these cities high in the Andes Mountains were the domain of the Watchers who never sinned prior to the Great Flood? In addition, could these citadels of the angels have been taken over by the demonic Nephilim and the spirits of the fallen angels in prison after the Flood? Finally, could the same Nephilim descendents and fallen angelic and demonic spirits that congregated there have infected the native civilizations of the Americas with the demonic human bloodlust and cannibalism that they displayed in tandem with Nimrod's evil influence? It is an intriguing possibility.

In light of all these revelations, is it merely an interesting coincidence that these amazing mountain top cities were built within the massive, nearly continuous mountain ranges running all along South America's western coast, and that these mountains as a whole resemble the wavy spine or body of a serpent? Furthermore, is it possible that the mountains running all along the west coasts of Mexico, the United States and Canada may depict another even bigger serpent with its symbolic tail in Alaska - with the Scorpio-Sagittarius Longitudinal Meridian dissecting that tail? In addition, could these physical features of the Americas be behind the two serpents on the border of the Calendar Stone pictured on page 729? Could these serpents actually depict the undulating coastlines of Asia and the Americas and the southern islands of the Pacific Ocean? Could this Calendar Stone be a hidden map of sorts that indicates the coastlines of two opposing continents or hemispheres of the Earth?

The tails of the feathered serpents on the Calendar Stone meet at the top, while the heads that meet at the bottom feature the feathered headdresses worn by Mesoamerican priests and kings. In the allegorical Language of God, could the heads mark Samoa and Tahiti as the origin or hideout of the Post-Flood Nephilim who ruled the world while the tails of the serpents signify the peninsulas where Russia and Alaska nearly meet as well as the end of time? Intriguingly, all of these locations meet within the Scorpio Meridian, including Hawaii. Furthermore, the skeletal face in the center of the Calendar Stone may depict the Hawaiian volcanoes and the serpents ringing the calendar may depict the many active volcanoes or "ring of fire" on each side of the Pacific Ocean. Since volcanism and the forging of metals to make weapons of war and bodily adornments originated with Azazel of Satan, could this also be a map indicating where Azazel or Satan's spirit of evil rests in the world today, and who might possibly be connected to that evil? Could it mean that the 44th President of the United States, Barack Hussein Obama - who supposedly hails from Hawaii and is definitely a descendent of Ham and Cush - is the Antichrist or a forerunner to him?

Could this Calendar Stone also be allegorically showing that the evil perpetrated by the Nephilim and Antichrist during the Tribulation, which may occur between 2011 and 2018 AD, will reach a critical juncture sometime near to December 21st, 2012? Will 2013 mark the beginning of the end of this world that will lead to the divinely sanctioned judgment and destruction of the part-Anakim rulers, political leaders, bankers, entertainment celebrities, trend-setters, and their human followers hidden within international governments, banks, educational institutions, and in the cities of the world? Will they be destroyed during the apocalyptic battles over the souls of billions of human beings at the end of the Great Tribulation? All that Yahweh God has shown me in the heavens and on the Earth points to this conclusion!

In summary, though the fallen angelic Watchers and some of the Nephilim and Post-Flood Giants or Anakim that were part-Nephilim were intelligent enough to build their own cities, it is likely that the Nephilim did not build most of the archeological wonders on Earth that are tied to Sacred Astronomy and the Gospel in the Stars. Though both good and bad angels and Nephilim certainly may have constructed cities and sacred monuments like those in Peru and Bolivia, keep in mind that other sites share a spiritual message with mankind that is despised by demons and fallen angels alike. As a result, they would never have sought to preserve such a message, but would have done everything they could to prevent its promulgation. For this reason, many ancient ruins should not be attributed to the Watchers or Nephilim.

As already shown, many purely human cultures show evidence of having the knowledge and technology necessary to build many of the magnificent ruins that have been uncovered by archeologists worldwide. Also, despite the incredible construction difficulties that builders of monolithic stonework had to deal with - ruins similar to those found high in the Andes are located all over the world *at lower elevations*.

Indeed, there are powerful allegorical Judeo-Christian messages encoded into the Great Pyramid and Giza Complex as a whole, and the same messages are being conveyed at Teotihuacán! This, coupled with the fallen angelic and Nephilim propensity to hate and disobey God, indicates that **the Great Pyramid and Pyramid of the Sun were certainly not the handiwork of the Nephilim or fallen angels.** Furthermore, though the builders could have been godly angels, Josephus and 2 Enoch identify the antediluvian Sethites as the builders of the Great Pyramid.

So, though the Great Pyramid (and to a lesser extant the Pyramid of the Sun) displays advanced architectural design and quality stonework similar to the massive constructions at Machu Picchu and Tiahuanaco that may have been built by the holy Watchers and inhabited by the evil Anakim after the Flood, the Great Pyramid was primarily made by godly human beings - though the antediluvian Sethites may have invited some assistance from holy angels, and - together with them - created one of the most enduring and spiritually timely structures on Earth at Giza.

The last remaining of the Seven Wonders of the Ancient World, the Pillar of Enoch is certainly the most spectacular existing monolithic ruin to be found anywhere in the world. Yet the available archeological evidence suggests that **this incredible mountain of stone was almost entirely built by humans.** Nonetheless, a few holy Watchers who received their directions only from Yahweh certainly helped Enoch and Methuselah in the design and planning stages. Yet the incredible scientific and mathematical knowledge locked into the design of this pyramid is largely overlooked because archeologists insist that it was built in "the Stone Age." Thus, they imply that the people who built this sophisticated structure were little more than primitive savages that somehow acquired a rather impressive veneer of culture and civilization.

Despite the enormous evidence to the contrary, our history books teach that the Stone Age was supposedly governed by our intellectually inferior ancestors who were Paganistic and governed by myth, superstition and fantasy. In short, they were supposedly incapable of knowing the advanced spiritual, scientific and technological knowledge displayed in the Great Pyramid and four other pyramids attributed to Old Kingdom pharaohs at Giza and Dahshur as well as at Teotihuacán in Mexico. Nonetheless, the advanced scientific design and precise geometric and mathematical measurements of the Pillar of Enoch and the Pyramid of the Sun attest to the fact that sophisticated levels of science and technology were divinely given to their human builders for the purpose of instructing this last generation that will witness Christ's Second Coming. Furthermore, Giza and Teotihuacán encapsulate much relevant godly spiritual and prophetic information for our own era that is hidden in the Gospel in the Stars - a Gospel that this book demonstrates is desperately needed by every Messianic and Christian seeking to interpret End Times signs correctly.

Among the seekers or wisdom and truth in this final generation, some will take part in the Rapture or the secret snatching away of believers by Christ to Heaven - while far more will likely be left behind to live through the seven years of the Tribulation. Among those left behind, some will find salvation in Christ through that ordeal and will be purified by sacrifice and suffering. Meanwhile, many wicked people will die from an unprecedented amount of Acts of God, pestilences, economic disasters, technological catastrophes and wars. Nonetheless, many saints and all 144,000 Witnesses will miraculously live through that horrible time of judgment to see the Second Coming of Christ, and the mortal saints will be raised to everlasting life at that time. Hallelu-Yah for our Salvation in Yahshua!

If you do not know Yahshua as your Messiah or Savior and Adonai, and you want to be forgiven for your sins and given the Holy Spirit as a seal on your heart that guarantees the gifts of everlasting life and joy with Christ, ask Yahshua into your heart and life today by saying this simple prayer:

"**Heavenly Father Yahweh**, I realize my utter sinfulness and inability to do good and humbly ask for your forgiveness for all my sins. I also realize that, because of my utter wickedness, I can't make amends to You for my wrongdoing or earn my way into Heaven by doing good works. I therefore ask for your mercy and I claim the redeeming blood of Yahshua my Kinsmen Redeemer for the remission of my sins. I surrender my flesh to you as a living sacrifice, and pray that You will help me to conform to the image of my Redeemer Yahshua, who is perfect and never sinned.

Thank you for so graciously offering salvation to an unworthy sinner like me. Please help me to follow Yahshua's perfect example in all I say and do, and make me worthy of everlasting life by setting Your Holy Spirit seal within my heart and teaching me wisdom and discernment by that same Spirit. Finally, please keep me from stumbling into sin again, and protect me from all evil. **In the holy Name of Yahshua Ha Mashiach I pray, Amen!**"

~ Appendix ~

The charts provided in this Appendix were taken from Book One, "The Language of God in the Universe." These are the "Biblical Chronological Time Chart;" "A Summary of the Mazzaroth, or Zodiac;" "Jewish Civil and Sacred Years and Feast Days;" and the "Chart Showing 13,000 Years From Creation to Eternity." Since the information in these charts is referred to throughout this book series, they have been provided as a quick reference on the following pages:

The biblically based chronological chart was derived using information found almost entirely in the Bible. Following this time chart are three other handy charts full of information to aid you in understanding the vast amount of knowledge presented in this book series. The first is a summary of the Gospel in the Stars that was fully explored in Book One. The second is chart recording the Jewish sacred and civil years, and the biblical feast days associated with them. The final chart summarizes the hypothesis that there are 7 millenniums for the unfolding of Bible prophecy, and 13 millenniums from Creation to the New Creation – topics discussed throughout this book series.

Biblical Chronological Time Chart

Jewish Years	Chronology of Biblical Events - Partly Derived From Genesis, Ch. 5, 10, & 11	Julian Year
1	Creation of Adam and Eve (Birthdays of Cain, Abel, and Adam & Eve's other sons and daughters not recorded, save for Seth)	4003 BC
to 130	From Creation of Adam to birth of Seth (130 years)	3873 BC
to 235	From birth of Seth to birth of Enosh (105 years)	3768 BC
to 325	From birth of Enosh to birth of Cainan (90 years)	3678 BC
to 395	Fr. birth of Cainan to birth of Mahalalel (70 years)	3608 BC
to 460	From birth of Mahalalel to birth of Jared (65 yrs)	3543 BC
to 622	From birth of Jared to birth of Enoch (162 years)	3381 BC
to 687	Fr. birth of Enoch to birth of Methuselah (65 yrs)	3316 BC
to 874	From birth of Methuselah to birth of Lamech (187 years)	3129 BC
to 987	From birth of Enoch to Enoch's Translation at age 365	3016 BC
to 1056	From birth of Lamech to birth of Noah (182 years)	2947 BC
to 1558	From birth of Noah to birth of Shem (500 years)	2447 BC
to 1656	The Great Flood occurs - Noah is 600 years old	2347 BC
to 1658	From birth of Shem to birth of Arphaxad (102 yrs)	2345 BC
to 1693	From birth of Arphaxad to birth of Shelah (35 yrs)	2310 BC
to 1723	From birth of Shelah to birth of Eber (30 years)	2280 BC

to 1757	From birth of Eber to birth of Peleg (34 years)	2246 BC
to 1787	From birth of Peleg to birth of Reu (30 years)	2216 BC
to 1819	From birth of Reu to birth of Serug (32 years)	2184 BC
to 1849	From birth of Serug to birth of Nahor (30 years)	2154 BC
to 1878	From birth of Nahor to birth of Terah (29 years)	2125 BC
to 1948	From birth of Terah to birth of Abraham (70 yrs)	2055 BC
1958	Birth of Abraham's wife Sarah	2045 BC
1966	Peleg dies at age 209	2037 BC
2006	Noah dies at age 950	1997 BC
to 2047	From birth of Abraham to birth of Isaac (99 years)	1956 BC
2047	Covenant of Abraham at age 99 with God	1956 BC
to 2107	From birth of Isaac to birth of Jacob (60 years)	1896 BC
2123	Death of Abraham at age 175	1880 BC
2158	Noah's son Shem dies at age 600, when Isaac is 111 & Jacob is 51 years old	1845 BC
to 2537	From birth of Jacob to Israelite Exodus from Egypt 430 years later	1466 BC
to 3017	480 years from Exodus to 4th Year of King Solomon's Reign	986 BC
to 3447	430 years from 4th Year of Solomon's Reign to last year of King Zedekiah's Reign: Babylon conquers Israel, destroys Jerusalem and Solomon's Temple	556 BC
to 3517	70 years from destruction of Jerusalem to prophesied end of Israel's Babylonian Exile	486 BC
to 4000	483 years from end of Babylonian Exile to birth of Yahshua based on Daniel's 69 weeks (69 X 7=483)	3 BC

A Summary of the Mazzaroth - Gospel in the Stars

Zodiac/ Latin Mazzaroth/ Hebrew	Archetypal - Allegorical Image	Tribal and Planetary Relationship	Spiritual and Prophetic Meaning of Zodiac Signs
Virgo Bethulah	Virgin holding Branch	Zebulon, Venus	Eve & Eden before sin; Righteous Branch; Miriam, Yahshua's mother; Promised Seed of the Virgin; Eve weeping for Abel-Miriam weeping for Christ
Libra Mozanaim	Two Scales/ Round Altar	Levi Moses, Earth	Cain's Murder of Abel; Sin's Punishment = Death; Final Judgment; God's Law; Blood Sacrifice and Redemption through Christ
Scorpio Akrav	Scorpion/ Serpent Enemy: Eagle	Dan - Manasseh, Tiamat - Asteroid belt	Satan's Temptation; Knowledge of Good and Evil; War; Deceit; Rebellion and Wickedness; Greed; Pride; Destruction
Sagittarius Keshet	Archer With Body of Centaur	Asher, Pluto/Charon	Hope in a Messiah who will crush the Serpent in Scorpio; Yahshua, the God/Man and Desire of Ages; the Avenger of Blood
Capricorn Gedi	Goat Dying - Lively Fish	Gad, Saturn	Age of the Nephilim; Noah's Escape of Destruction and Death; Punishment for Earth's Corruption; Salvation from Evil
Aquarius Deli	Water-Bearer Pouring Water	Reuben, Neptune	Noah's Flood; Destruction leading to rebirth of Baptism; New Life; Ritual Purification; Holiness; gifts of the Spirit

Zodiac/ Latin Mazzaroth/ Hebrew	Archetypal - Allegorical Image	Tribal and Planetary Relationship	Spiritual and Prophetic Meaning of Zodiac Signs
Pisces Dagim	Two Fish Swimming Apart	Simeon/Israel as a Nation, Uranus & its Five Moons	Two Churches from 10 Lost Tribes & Tribe of Judah - one Apostate and one the True Church; Uranus = Bride and/or Bridegroom and 5 Moons = 5 Virgins with oil in their lamps
Aries Taleh	Crouching Ram	Naphtali Isaac, Mars	Sacrifice; the Cross of Christ; Blood Atonement for Sin; Salvation promised through the Blood Covenant/ Communion
Taurus Shor; Reem	Bull charging (& bull's horns)	Joseph as Ephraim - symbolized by an Eagle, Marduk - Eris	Mercy & Judgment toward the Gentile Nations; Avengers of Blood; Deliverers of Punishment and Retribution; Agents of God's Wrath; The Great Tribulation
Gemini Te'omim	Twin Brothers: Bride & Groom	Benjamin - Isaac/Ishmael Jacob/Esau James/John, Mercury	Adoption by Blood Covenant; Christ's Dual Nature as God/Man and Dual Role as Priest/King; Wedding of the Lamb to the Church
Cancer Sartan	Crab/ Sheepfold	Issachar, Moon	Scattering of God's spiritual Sheep; Ingathering of the Redeemed; The Rapture; Spiritual Harvest; Separate Good Sheep from Evil Goats
Leo Aryeh	Leaping or Crouching Lion	Judah, David, Christ, Jupiter	The Lion of Judah; Yahshua as Conquering King; Pouring out of God's Wrath; Divine Judgment; Ushering in of Millennial Rule of Christ.

Jewish Civil and Sacred Years and Feast Days

The Jewish Civil Calendar Year as followed from Adam's Creation	The Jewish Sacred Year in Effect After the Exodus	The Biblically Ordained Mosaic Feast Days and Their Prophetic Import
7 – Tishri (Sept.-Oct.) Virgo-Libra	1 –Abib/Nisan (Mar.-Apr.) Pisces-Aries	1st month – 14th of Abib: Passover (Pesach) followed by six day **Feast of Unleavened Bread** & **Firstfruits** Wave Sheaf Offering on the 15th to 21st of Abib. **Fulfilled at Yahshua's First Advent** when He served as the Lamb of God (Passover), Bread of Life (Unleavened Bread), and Firstfruits of the Resurrection (Wave Sheaf Offering).
8 – Heshven (Oct.-Nov.) Libra-Scorpio	2 – Iyar (Apr.-May) Aries-Taurus	
9 – Chislev (Nov.-Dec.) Scorpio-Sagittarius	3 – Sivan (May-June) Taurus-Gemini	3rd month – 6th-7th of Sivan: **Pentecost** - a.k.a. **Feast of Weeks,** Feast of Harvest, Feast of Firstfruits (Shavuot) – 49 days/seven weeks from the wave sheaf offering at Passover, counted as the 50th (Jubilee) day. Giving of the Ten Commandments and Book of the Covenant on Mount Sinai. **Fulfilled at Christ's First Advent** with the Giving of the Holy Spirit after Christ's Resurrection.
10 – Tevet (Dec.-Jan.) Sagittarius-Capricorn	4 – Tammuz (June-July) Gemini-Cancer	
11 – Shevat (Jan.-Feb.) Capricorn-Aquarius	5 – Av (July-Aug.) Cancer-Leo	
12 – Adar (Feb.-Mar.) Aquarius-Pisces	6 – Elul (Aug.-Sept.) Leo-Virgo	

The Jewish Civil Calendar Year as followed from Adam's Creation	The Jewish Sacred Year in Effect After the Exodus	The Biblically Ordained Mosaic Feast Days and Their Prophetic Import
1 – Abib/Nisan (Mar.-Apr.) Pisces-Aries	7 – Tishri (Sept.-Oct.) Virgo-Libra	7th month – 1st of Tishri: New Year's Day – Feast of Trumpets (Rosh Hashanah), to be fulfilled in the Rapture. 10th of Tishri: Day of Atonement (Yom Kippur), to be fulfilled by the Wedding Feast/Great Tribulation. 15th of Tishri: Feast of Tabernacles or Booths (Sukkot), fulfilled partly by Christ's birth, but fully fulfilled by Christ Return and the Millennial Kingdom. The 7th
2 – Iyar (Apr.-May) Aries-Taurus	8 – Heshven (Oct.-Nov.) Libra-Scorpio	Jewish month heralds the arrival of the Seventh Day of the Lord and Yahshua's Second Advent roles as King of kings & Great High Priest.
3 – Sivan (May-June) Taurus-Gemini	9 – Chislev (Nov.-Dec.) Scorpio-Sagittarius	9th month – 25th of Chislev to 3rd of Tevet, Feast of Dedication - Festival of Lights (Chanukah) - Commemorates the miracle of the Temple Menorah burning for eight days without needing to be refilled with oil just
4 – Tammuz (June-July) Gemini-Cancer	10 – Tevet (Dec.-Jan.) Sagittarius-Capricorn	after the Temple was rededicated to Yahweh. Later, the Wise men visit Christ, the Light of the World and giver of the Holy Spirit, as a toddler and present Him with costly royal
5 – Av (July-Aug.) Cancer-Leo	11 – Shevat (Jan.-Feb.) Capricorn - Aquarius	gifts.
6 – Elul (Aug.-Sept.) Leo-Virgo	12 – Adar (Feb.-Mar.) Aquarius-Pisces	12th month - 14th – 15th of Adar, Feast of Esther, Feast of Lots (Pur; Purim) - Jews saved from slaughter in Babylon due to Queen Esther's daring intervention.

Chart Showing 13,000 Years from Creation to Eternity

13,000 years - 6 Precessional Ages (approximate)	Six 1,000-Year Days of Creation, Six 1,000-Year Days of Men's Works Final Millennial Day of the Lord
Age of Leo: 10,000 BC to 8000 BC 1st and 2nd Millenniums	**1st Creation Day:** Yah creates Light and separates the light from the darkness. (Gen. 1:1-5) **2nd Creation Day:** Yah creates the sky to divide the waters above the Earth from the waters below. (Gen. 1:6-8)
Age of Cancer: 7999 BC to 6000 BC 3rd and 4th Millenniums	**Third Creation Day:** Yah gathers the water in one place, calling them seas, and makes dry land appear on the surface of the Earth to support all kinds of vegetation: trees, shrubs, flowers, vegetables, and fruit. (Gen. 1:9-13) **Forth Creation Day:** Yah creates the Sun, Moon, and stars to shed light (i.e. give both physical light and spiritual knowledge or enlightenment) on Earth. (Gen. 1:1-5)
Age of Gemini: 5999 BC to 4000 BC 5th and 6th Millenniums	**Fifth Creation Day:** Aquatic life of all kinds and birds of every kind are created. The Jews see this as the Day when Earth was now fully formed and ready to support life. It was therefore Earth's "birthday." **Sixth Creation Day:** Yah creates all mammals and other kinds of terrestrial life, with His final creation being mankind.
Age of Taurus: 3999 BC to 2000 BC	**God's Seventh Day Rest:** Adam and Eve in the Garden of Eden, **a perfect world** without sin or death for seven years. **Eve sins** followed by Adam. *Paradise lost.* God's Seventh Day Rest Ends prematurely.

Age of Taurus - continued 7th and 8th Millenniums: 1st and 2nd Days of Men's Works	**Beginning of 1st Day of Men's Works: 1000-year Golden Age of Peace**. Domestication of animals, shepherding, agriculture develops, first cities built. **2nd Day of Men's Works: Arrival of fallen angels.** Sin and war escalate. The Nephilim are created, further increasing wickedness and evil. **The Great Flood occurs**, destroying most of the Nephilim and temporarily ending mankind's moral and genetic spiral downward. Then war and conquest forge **Nimrod's world dictatorship** and full-blown Paganism is revived along with Earth Goddess worship, Magic, and Sorcery. Yah's **destruction of Babel, and the confusion of tongues** ends Nimrod's despotic rule of the world.
Age of Aries: 1999 BC to 0 BC 9th and 10th Millenniums: 3rd and 4th Days of Men's Works - **Daniel's Kingdoms of Gold, Silver, Bronze, and Iron** (Daniel 2:38-39)	**3rd Day of Men's Works:** Begins with **the time of Abraham** and mankind's dispersion throughout the Earth after **the Fall of Babel**. Rise of civilization in China, the Americas. Egypt's Middle and New Kingdoms, Rise of Babylon, Assyria, then Persia. **Greece** rises to world power and encourages the interest and resurgence in culture, philosophy, art, and science. **4th Day of Men's Works: The Roman Republic** emerges as a world power and becomes the world leader in art, science, literature, and the making of war. **Christ is born in Bethlehem at the end of the 4th Day, in 3 BC.**
Age of Pisces: 1 AD to 2000 AD 11th and 12th Millenniums: 5th and 6th Days of Men's Works - Daniel's Kingdom of Iron and those of Iron mixed with Clay (Daniel 2:33,41-43)	**5th Day of Men's Works: The Christian Age.** The Roman Empire rises then falls. The Church surges to prominence in the West while Buddhism, Hinduism, and other Pagan religions flourish in the East. **6th Day of Men's Works: Islam rises to prominence** in the Middle East. The Crusades launched in the West during the Middle Ages against the Middle East causes Muslim Arabs to find a deep-seated hatred of the predominantly Christian West.

13,000 years - 6 Precessional Ages (approximate)	Six 1,000-Year Days of Creation, Six 1,000-Year Days of Men's Works Final Millennial Day of the Lord
Age of Pisces, continued:	**6th Day of Men's Works, continued:** Islamic leaders launch a Holy War or Jihad against the West. Modern times: **Terrorism** begins to affect the whole world, giving rise to more government control in the West and a loss of freedom.
Age of Aquarius: 2001 AD to 4000 AD 13th and Final Millennium: Yah leading Men's Works, followed by the Eighth Great Day lasting all eternity **Daniel's "Stone from Heaven"** that crushes the kingdoms of the Earth and becomes a far greater kingdom, Christ's 1,000-year Kingdom of Peace on Earth (Daniel 2:34-35,44).	**Yah's 7th Great Day Sabbath Rest - The Day of the Lord.** According to Biblical chronology, the Final Great Day of the Lord already began on Rosh Hashanah, Sept. 11, 1999 AD! This is the 13th Millennium since Creation began and the 7th Millennium since the Fall of mankind. This is the Age when the war on terrorism has become critical as Muslim terrorists increase their attacks in the West. Eventually, a world government may be created to eradicate the terrorist threat, giving the Antichrist the opportunity he needs to take over the world. After this, **the Rapture** will come followed by **the Great Tribulation.** This terrible time will end with **the Millennial Rule of Christ and the reinstatement of the Seventh Day Rest** that Yah began at the end of the Creation Week. At the end of this final millennium of peace, evil and sin will be eradicated forever to usher in eternity, incorruptible bodies, no sin, a New Heaven and a New Earth. **Eighth Great Day:** *Paradise Regained!* Life and perfection without end! Time, as we know it, ceases to exist since Eternity cannot be measured. **The eternal Golden Age of Peace.**

~ Bibliography By Subject ~

This 16-page bibliography covering all four books in "The Language of God" Book Series is extensive, but partial. Many other magazine articles, books, pamphlets, religious reference works, and web sites were included in my research for "The Language of God" and "The Pillar of Enoch Trilogy" that are not recorded here.

Books are arranged by subject and author. See the Table of Contents on introductory page xiii for the nine subject headings and the pages they appear on in this bibliography.

Pre and Post Flood History, Ancient and Recent

Adkins, Lesley and Roy; Introduction to the Romans, The History, Culture and Art of the Roman Empire, 1996, Quantum Books Ltd., 6 Blundell Street, London N7 9BH, England.

Ancient Egypt, Myth and History - the religion, myths and gods explained against the background of its history, 1997, Geddes & Grosset Ltd., David Dale House, New Lanark, ML11 9DJ. Scotland.

Beechick, Ruth; Adam and His Kin - The Lost History of Their Lives and Times, 1990, Arrow Press, California, USA.

Bennett, W. H.; Symbols of Our Celto-Saxon Heritage, 1995, Herald Press Ltd, Windsor, Ontario, Canada. (The Heraldry of Israel)

Bray, Warwick; Everyday Life of the Aztecs, 1987, Dorset Press, New York, NY, USA.

Capt, E. Raymond; Abrahamic Covenant, Artisan Sales, P.O. Box 1529, Muskogee, OK 74402, USA.

Capt, E. Raymond; Jacob's Pillar, 1977, Artisan Sales, P.O. Box 1529, Muskogee, OK 74402, USA.

Capt, E. Raymond; Missing Links Discovered in Assyrian Tablets, 1985, Artisan Sales, P.O. Box 1529, Muskogee, OK 74402, USA.

Capt, Raymond E.; The Traditions of Glastonbury, 2004 Reprint, Artisan Publishers, P.O. Box 1529, Muskogee, Oklahoma 74402, USA.

Collins, Steven M; The "Lost" Ten Tribes of Israel... Found!, 1992, CPA Book Publisher, P.O. Box 596, Boring, Oregon, 97009, USA.

Cooper, Bill, B.A. Hons.; After The Flood - The Early Post Flood History of Europe, 1995, New Wine Press, Sussex, England.

Custance, Arthur C.; Noah's Three Sons - The Doorway Papers, Published online at: *http://www.custance.org/old/noah/index.html*

Deal, David Allen; Discovery of Ancient America, 1984, Kherem La Yah Press, Irvine, CA, USA.

Evans, Lorraine; Kingdom of the Ark, 2000, Simon & Schuster UK. Ltd., Africa House, 64-78 Kingsway, London WC2B 6AH England.

Fell, Barry; America B.C., 2004 reprint of 1976 Edition, Artisan Sales, P.O. Box 1529, Muskogee, OK 74402, USA.

Fox-Davies, Arthur Charles; The Wordsworth Complete Guide to Heraldry, 1996, Wordsworth Editions, Ltd., Cumberland House, Crib Street, Ware, Hertfordshire, SG12 9ET, England.

Gascoigne, Mike; The Forgotten History of the Western People – From the Earliest Origins, 2002, Anno Mundi Books, P. O. Box 752, Camberley, England. *http://www.annomundi.co.uk*

Harris, Reader, K.C.; The Lost Tribes of Israel, 2004 Reprint of the 1907 Edition, Artisan Sales, P.O. Box 1529, Muskogee, OK 74402, USA.

Hancock, Graham, & Bauval, Robert; Talisman - Sacred Cities, Secret Faith, 2004, Element Press, 77-85 Fulham Palace Road, Hammersmith, London UK.

Haywood, John, Ph.D.; Atlas of World History, 1997, published by Metro Books, an imprint of Freidman/Fairfax Publishers by arrangement with Andromeda Oxford Ltd., Abingdon, Oxfordshire, OX14 3PX, England.

Hoffmeier, James K.; Israel in Egypt – The Evidence for the Authenticity of the Exodus Tradition, 1996, Oxford University Press, 198 Madison Avenue, New York, NY 10016, USA.
Kendall, Ann; Everyday Life of the Incas, 1989, Dorset Press, New York, NY, USA.

Kenyon, Douglas, Editor; Forbidden History, 2005, Bear & Company, One Park Street, Rochester, VT 05767, USA.

Kimball, Charles Scott; The Genesis Chronicles - A Proposed History of the Morning of the World., Published online at http://xenohistorian.faithweb.com/

Long, James D.; Riddle of the Exodus, 2006 Reprint, Lightcatcher Books, 842 Kissinger Ave., Springdale, Arkansas 72762, USA.

Moller, Dr. Lennart; The Exodus Case - New Discoveries Confirm the Historical Exodus, 2002, Scandinavia Publishing House, Drejervej 11-21, DK 2400 Copenhagen NV, Denmark.

Nienhuis, James I.; Ice Age Civilizations, 2006, Genesis Veracity, P.O. Box 850, 5773 Woodway Drive, Houston, TX, 77057, USA.

Reagan, David R.; America the Beautiful? - The United States in Bible Prophecy, 2003, Lamb & Lion Ministries, P.O. Box 919, McKinney, TX 75070, USA.

Roaf, Michael; Cultural Atlas of Mesopotamia and the Ancient Near East, 1999, Facts On File, Inc., 11 Penn Plaza, New York, NY 10001, USA.

Rohl, David M.; Legend, The Genesis of Civilization, 1998, Random House, London, England.

Rohl, David M.; Pharaohs and Kings, A Biblical Quest (Published in Great Britain as: A Test of Time, The Bible From Myth to History), 1995, Crown Publishers, Inc., New York, USA.

Rohl, David M.; The Lost Testament - From Eden to Exile: The Five Thousand Year History of the People of the Bible, Century, 2002, Random House UK Ltd., 20 Vauxhall Bridge Road, London, SW1V 2SA.

Rosenberg, Joel C.; Epicenter - Why the Current Rumblings in the Middle-East Will Change Your Future, Tyndale House Publishers, Inc., Carol Stream, IL 60188, USA.

Schobinger, Juan; The First Americans, 1994 English Translation, William B. Eerdmans Publishing Co., 255 Jefferson Avenue S.E., Grand Rapids, Michigan, 49503, USA.

Waddell, L.A., LL.D.; Egyptian Civilization, Its Sumerian Origin & Real Chronology and Sumerian Origin of Egyptian Hieroglyphs, CPA Book Publisher, P.O. Box 596, Boring, OR 97009-0596, USA.

Woods, Jr. PhD., Thomas E.; The Politically Incorrect Guide to American History, 2004, Regnery Publishing, Inc., One Massachusetts Ave. NW, Washington, DC 20001, USA.

Ancient Judeo-Christian Manuscripts and Commentaries

Charles, R. H., DD.; The Book of Jubilees, 1902, Adam and Charles Black, London, England.

Charles, R. H., DD.; The Book of Enoch (from the Ethiopic), 1900? Sheldon Press, London, England. (I refer to this as the Book of 1 Enoch to distinguish it from the Book of the Secrets of Enoch, or the Book of 2 Enoch.)

Charles, R. H., DD.; The Book of the Secrets of Enoch (from Slavonic), 1896, Clarendon Press, Oxford University Press, London, England.

The NIV Study Bible, New International Version, 1985, Zondervan Bible Publishers, Grand Rapids, Michigan, USA.

The Forgotten Books of Eden, Lost Books of the Old Testament, The First and Second Books of Adam and Eve, 1980, Bell Publishing Company, USA.

The Book of Jasher - referred to in Joshua and II Samuel, 1997 reprint of the 1887 edition by J. H. Parry Publishers, Kessinger Publishing, Whitefish, MT 59937, USA.

The Epistle of Barnabus, The Lost Books of the Bible, 1979, Bell Publishing Company, New York, NY, USA.

Laurence, Richard, LL. D.; The Book of Enoch (from Ethiopic), 1980 Reprint of the 1882 Edition Published by John Thompson, Glasgow. Reprinted by Artisan Sales, Thousand Oaks, California, USA.

Mordechai, Avi Ben; Messiah, Understanding His Life and Teaching in Hebraic Context, Volumes 1, 2 & 3, 2000 edition, Millennium 7000 Communications, USA.

Morris, Henry M.; The Remarkable Record of Job, 1996, Baker Book House, Grand Rapids, Michigan, USA.

Stedman, Ray C.; Expository Studies In Genesis, Published online at: http://pbc.org/dp/stedman/genesis/index.html

Trumbull, H. Clay; The Blood Covenant, Sixth Printing, 1998
Trumbull, H. Clay; The Salt Covenant, 1999 reprint of 1899 edition,
Impact Christian Books, Inc. 332 Leffingwell, Suite 101, Kirkwood, MO, 63122, USA.

Vanderkam, James C.; Enoch – A Man For All Generations, 1995, University of South Carolina Press, USA.

Pre-Flood Wisdom: Sacred Astronomy/Gospel in the Stars

Aveni, Anthony; Skywatchers of Ancient Mexico, 1980, University of Texas Press, Box 7819, Austin, TX 78712, USA.

Banks, William D.; The Heavens Declare..., 1985, Impact Books, Inc, USA.

Bauval, Robert & Gilbert, Adrian; The Orion Mystery, Unlocking the Secrets of the Pyramids, 1995, Random House, Inc., New York, NY, USA.

Bullinger, E. W.; The Witness of the Stars, (reprint of the 1893 edition) 2000, Kregel Publications, USA.

Byrd, Gary Alexander; Keys to the Kingdom - The Year 2012 - Countdown to the Apocalypse, 2007, Author House, 166 Liberty Drive, Suite 200, Bloomington, IN 47403, USA.

Davidson, D. and Aldersmith, H.; The Great Pyramid – Its Divine Message, Reprint of 1925 edition, Kessinger Publishing, Whitefish, MT 59937, USA.

DeYoung, Donald B.; Astronomy and the Bible - Questions and Answers, 1989, Baker Book House, Grand Rapids, Michigan, USA.

Gaunt, Bonnie; Stonehenge... A Closer Look, 1987 reprint, Bonnie Gaunt, 510 Golf Avenue, Jackson, MI 49203, USA.

Gaunt, Bonnie; The Coming of Jesus - The Real Message of the Bible Codes, 1999, Adventures Unlimited Press, P.O. Box 174, Kempton, IL 60946, USA.

Gaunt, Bonnie; The Magnificent Numbers of the Great Pyramid and Stonehenge, 1988, Bonnie Gaunt, 510 Golf Avenue, Jackson, MI 49203, USA.

Gaunt, Bonnie; The Stones and the Scarlet Thread, 2001, Adventures Unlimited Press, P.O. Box 174, Kempton, IL 60946, USA.

Hancock, Graham & Bauval, Robert; The Message of the Sphinx, 1996, Doubleday Canada, Toronto, Canada.

Hunkler, Tim G.; Symbolism and Coincidences of the Great Pyramid, 1998, Published online at http://www.hunkler.com/pyramids/pyramid_symbolism.html

Hutchings, Noah W.; The Great Pyramid - Prophecy In Stone, 1996, Hearthstone Publishing, P.O. Box 815, Oklahoma City, OK 73101, USA.

Kitt Chappell, Sally A.; Cahokia - Mirror of the Cosmos, 2002, The University of Chicago Press, Chicago, IL, USA.

Lockyer, J. Norman; The Dawn of Astronomy, A Study of the Temple Worship and Mythology of the Ancient Egyptians, 1997 Reprint, Kessinger Publishing, P.O. Box 1404, Whitefish, MT 59937, USA.

LaViolette, Paul, Earth Under Fire, Humanity's Survival of the Apocalypse, 1997, Starline Publications, 1176 Hedgewood Lane, Schenectady, NY 12309, USA.

Martin, Ernest L.; The Star of Bethlehem - The Star That Astonished the World, 1998, ASK Publications, P.O. Box 25000, Portland, OR 97225, USA.

Mulfinger, Jr., George; Designs and Origins in Astronomy, 1983, Creation Research Society, USA.

Mordechai, Avi Ben; Signs In The Heavens, 1999 edition, A Jewish Messianic Perspective of the Last Days and Coming Millennium, Millennium 7000 Communications, USA.

Raymo, Chet; 365 Starry Nights, an introduction to astronomy for every night of the year, 1982, Prentice-Hall, Inc., Englewood Cliffs, NJ 07632, USA.

Rolleston, Frances; The Mazzaroth; or the Constellations. Online at: http://philologos.org/__eb-mazzaroth/

Schoch, Robert M., Phd.; Voyages of the Pyramid Builders, 2003, Jeremy P. Tarcher-Penguin Group, Inc., 575 Hudson Street, New York, NY 10014, USA.

Schoch, Robert M., Phd.; Pyramid Quest - Secrets of the Great Pyramid and the Dawn of Civilization, 2005, Jeremy P. Tarcher-Penguin Group, Inc., 575 Hudson Street, New York, NY 10014, USA.

Seiss, Joseph A.; The Gospel in the Stars, 1972 Reprint of the 1882 Edition, Kregel Publications, P.O. Box 2607, Grand Rapids, MI 49501, USA.

Smyth, Piazzi; The Great Pyramid, It's Secrets and Mysteries Revealed, 1978, Gramercy Books, a division of Random House Value Publishing; Avenel, New Jersey, USA.

Tennant, Catherine; The Lost Zodiac - 22 Ancient Star Signs, What They Mean and the Legends Behind Them, 1995, Bulfinch Press - Little, Brown and Co. USA & Canada.

The Great Pyramid - Ancient Wonder, Modern Mystery, A pamphlet by Pyramid Productions, P.O. Box 1359, Westerville, Ohio, 43086 USA.

Tompkins, Peter; Secrets of the Great Pyramid, 1978, Harper & Row Publishers, Inc., 10 East 53rd Street, New York, NY 10022, USA.

Judeo-Christian Religious Eschatology and Exegesis

Allen, J. H., Judah's Sceptre and Joseph's Birthright, 1943, A. A. Beauchamp, Publisher, Boston, Mass., USA.

Church, J. R.; Guardians of the Grail, 1989
Church, J. R.; Hidden Prophecies in the Psalms, 1990 Revised Edition
Church, J. R.; Hidden Prophecies in the Song of Moses, 1991
Prophecy Publications, P.O. Box 7000, Oklahoma City, OK, 73153, USA.

Church, J. R. & Stearman, Gary; The Mystery of the Menorah and the Hebrew Alphabet, 1989, Prophecy Publications, P.O. Box 7000, Oklahoma City, OK, 73153, USA.

Cohen, Tim; The Antichrist and a Cup of Tea, 1998, Prophecy House, Inc., P.O. Box 461104, Aurora, CO 80046-1104, USA.

Conner, Kevin L.; The Temple of Solomon - The Glory of God as Displayed Through the Temple, 1988, City Bible Publishing, 9200 NE Fremont, Portland, Oregon, 97220, USA

Conner, Kevin L., & Malmin, Ken; The Covenants, 1997 Revision of original 1983 edition, City Bible Publishing, 9200 NE Fremont, Portland, Oregon, 97220, USA
DeHaan, M. R., M.D.; The Tabernacle, 1983, Lamplighter Books, a division of Zondervan Publishing House, 1415 Lake Drive, S.E., Grand Rapids, MI 49506, USA.

DeWitt, Roy Lee; Teachings From The Tabernacle, 1988, Baker Book House, Grand Rapids, MI 49516, USA.

Drosnin, Michael; The Bible Code, 1998, Touchstone Books, Rockefeller Center, 1230 Avenue of the Americas, New York, NY 10020, USA.

Drosnin, Michael; Bible Code II - The Countdown, 2002, Penguin Group (USA) Inc., 375 Hudson Street, New York, NY 10014, USA.

Evans, Michael D.; The American Prophecies - Ancient Scriptures Reveal Our Nation's Future, 2004, Warner Faith - Time Warner Book Group, 1271 Avenue of the Americas, New York, NY 10020, USA.

Gaunt, Bonnie; Jesus Christ - The Number of His Name, 1998, Adventures Unlimited Press, P.O. Box 174, Kempton, IL 60946, USA.

Hitchcock, Mark; The Complete Book of Bible Prophecy, 1999, Tyndale House Publishers, Inc. Wheaton, IL, 60189 USA.

Hunt, Dave; A Woman Rides The Beast – The Roman Catholic Church and the Last Days, 1994, Harvest House Publishers, Eugene, Oregon 97402, USA.

Hunt, Dave; Global Peace, and the Rise of the Antichrist, 1990, Harvest House Publishers, Eugene, Oregon 97402, USA.

Hutchings, Noah W.; 25 Messianic Signs in Israel Today, 1999, Hearthstone Publishing, P.O. Box 815, Oklahoma City, OK 73101, USA.

Jeffrey, Grant R.; Heaven, The Last Frontier, 1990, Frontier Research Publications, P.O. Box 129, Station "U", Toronto, Ontario, M8Z 5M4 Canada.

Jones, Dr. Stephen R.; The Seven Churches, 2004, God's Kingdom Ministries, 6201 University Ave. NE, Fridley, MN 55432, USA.

Judah, Monte; The Prince Who Is To Come, article from Yavoh Newsletter, Nov. 2001 Issue, Lion and Lamb Ministries, P.O. Box 720968, Norman, OK 73070, USA.

Kasdan, Barney; God's Appointed Times, A Practical Guide to Understanding and Celebrating the Biblical Holidays, 1993, Messianic Jewish Publishers, Lederer/Messianic Jewish Communications, 6204 Park Heights Avenue, Baltimore, MD 21215, USA.

Levy, David M.; The Tabernacle, Shadows of the Messiah: Its Sacrifices, Services, and Priesthood, 1993, The Friends of Israel Gospel Ministry, P.O. Box 908, Bellmawr, NJ 08099, USA.

LaHaye, Tim & Jenkins, Jerry B.; Are We Living In The End Times?, 1999, Tyndale House Publishers, Inc., Wheaton, IL, USA.

LaHaye, Tim & Ice, Thomas; Charting The End Times; 1999, Harvest House Publishers, Eugene, OR 97402, USA.

Lindsey, Hal; Apocalypse Code, 1997, Western Front, Ltd., Palos Verdes, California, USA.

Manty, Jeffrey A., Prophecy Code - A New Revelation For the Last Days, 2007, Wheatmark, 610 East Delano Street, Suite 104, Tucson, AZ 85705, USA.

Matson, Daniel W.; Signs of the End - A Discovery of Biblical Timelines, 2006, Inspirational Press, P.O. Box 9901, Fountain Valley, CA 92708, USA.

Martin, Dr. Walter; Essential Christianity, 1980, Regal Books, Venture, CA USA.

Rambsel, Yacov; His Name is Jesus – The Mysterious Yeshua Codes, 1997, Frontier Research Publications, Inc., P.O. Box 129, Station "U", Toronto, Ontario, M8Z 5M4, Canada.

Sherman, R. Edwin; Bible Code Bombshell, 2005, New Leaf Press, P.O. Box 726, Green Forest, AR 72638, USA.

Van Impe, Jack; 11:59 - The Countdown, 1987, Jack Van Impe Ministries, P.O. Box 7004, Troy, MI 48007, USA.

Van Impe, Jack, & Campbell, Roger F.; Israel's Final Holocaust, 1979, Jack Van Impe Ministries, P.O. Box 7004, Troy, MI 48007, USA.

Walvoord, John F.; The Rapture Question, Academic Books, Imprint of Zondervan Publishing House, 1415 Lake Drive. S. E., Grand Rapids, MI 49506, USA.

Wouk, Herman; This Is My God, The Jewish Way of Life, Little, Brown and Co., New York, NY, USA.

Christian Apologetics – Defending the Bible

Albrecht, Mark; Reincarnation – A Christian Appraisal, 1982, Inter-Varsity Press, Downers Grove, IL 60515, USA.

Barnett, Paul, Is The New Testament History? 1986, Hodder & Stouton, Ltd., 47 Bedford Square, London WC1B 3DP, England.

Barton, David; Original Intent - The Courts, the Constitution, & Religion, 2000, WallBuilders Press, P.O. Box 397, Aledo, TX 76008, USA.

Barton, David; The Question of Freemasonry and the Founding Fathers, 2005, WallBuilders Press, P.O. Box 397, Aledo, TX 76008, USA.

Bowman, Jr., Robert M.; Why You Should Believe in the Trinity: An Answer to Jehovah's Witnesses, 1989, Baker Book House, Grand Rapids, MI 49516, USA.

Bruce, F. F.; The New Testament Documents - Are They Reliable?, 1985 Reprint, Intervarsity Press, Wm. B. Eerdmans Publishing Co., 255 Jefferson S.E., Grand Rapids, MI, USA.

Caner, Emir Fethi; The Costly Call - Muslims Who Found Jesus, 2005, Kregel Publications, P.O. Box 2607, Grand Rapids, MI 49501, USA.

Caner, Ergun Mehmet, & Caner, Emir Fethi; Unveiling Islam, 2002, Kregel Publications, P.O. Box 2607, Grand Rapids, MI 49501, USA.

Gabriel, Mark A. Phd.; Islam and Terrorism, 2002, Frontline, A Strang Company, 600 Rinehart Road, Lake Mary, FL 32746, USA.

Groothuis, Douglas R.; Confronting the New Age - How to Resist a Growing Religious Movement, 1988, Inter-Varsity Press, Downers Grove, IL 60515, USA.

Groothuis, Douglas R.; Unmasking the New Age - Is There A New Religious Movement Trying to Transform Society?, 1986, Inter-Varsity Press, Downers Grove, IL 60515, USA.

Lewis, C. S.; Mere Christianity, 1952, Macmillan Publishing Company, 866 Third Avenue, New York, N. Y. 10022, USA.

Lewis, C. S.; The Screwtape Letters, 1963, Macmillan Publishing Company, 866 Third Avenue, New York, N. Y. 10022, USA.

Lewis, C. S.; The Great Divorce, 1987 Reprint, William Collins Sons and Co, Ltd., Glasgow, England.

McDowell, Josh; The New Evidence That Demands A Verdict, 1999, Thomas Nelson Publishers, Nashville, TN USA.

Sire, James W.; Scripture Twisting - 20 Ways the Cults Misread the Bible, 1980, Intervarsity Press, P.O. Box 1400, Downers Grove, IL 60515 USA.

Spencer, Robert; Religion of Peace? Why Christianity Is and Islam Isn't, 2007, Regnery Publishing, Inc., One Massachusetts Ave. NW, Washington, DC 20001, USA.

Spencer, Robert - Editor; The Myth of Islamic Tolerance, 2005, Prometheus Books, 59 John Glenn Drive, Amherst, NY 14228, USA.

Spencer, Robert; The Politically Incorrect Guide to Islam, 2005, Regnery Publishing, Inc., One Massachusetts Ave. NW, Washington, DC 20001, USA.

Antediluvian/Ancient Technology and Civilization

Allen, J. M.; Atlantis – The Andes Solution, 1998, St. Martin's Press, Scholarly and Reference Division 175 Fifth Avenue, New York, NY 10010, USA.

Baines, John & Malek, Jaromir; Atlas of Ancient Egypt, 1994, Facts on File, Inc., 460 Park Avenue South, New York, NY 10016, USA.

Capt, Raymond E.; A Study In Pyramidology, 2002, Artisan Publishers, P.O. Box 1529, Muskogee, Oklahoma 74402, USA.

Childress, David Hatcher; Lost Cities of North and Central America, 1998 reprint, Adventures Unlimited Press, One Adventure Place, Kempton (Stelle), IL 60946, USA.

Childress, David Hatcher; Technology of the Gods - The Incredible Sciences of the Ancients, 2000, Adventures Unlimited Press, One Adventure Place, Kempton, IL 60946, USA.

Childress, David Hatcher; Vimana - Aircraft of Ancient India & Atlantis, 2004, Adventures Unlimited Press, One Adventure Place, Kempton, IL 60946, USA.

Chittick, Donald E.; The Puzzle of Ancient Man, 1997, Creation Compass, Newberg, Oregon, USA.

Collins, Andrew; Gateway to Atlantis - The Search For A Lost Civilization, 2002, Carroll & Graf Publishers, Avalon Publishing, 161 William Street, 16th Floor, New York, NY 10038, USA.

Dunn, Christopher, The Giza Power Plant – Technologies of Ancient Egypt, 1998, Bear & Company, Inc. Santa Fe, NM 87504-2860, USA.

Jacq, Christian; The Wisdom of Ptah-hotep - Spiritual Treasures from the Age of the Pyramids, 2004, Constable & Robinson Ltd., 3 The Lanchesters, 162 Fulham Palace Road, London, UK, W69ER

Joseph, Frank; The Destruction of Atlantis, Compelling Evidence of the Sudden Fall of a Legendary Civilization, 2002, Bear & Company, Rochester, Vermont 05767, USA.

Hancock, Graham and Faiia, Santha; Heaven's Mirror - Quest for the Lost Civilization, 1998, Doubleday Canada, Toronto, Canada.

Hancock, Graham; Underworld, 2002, Crown Publishers, New York, NY, USA.

Hapgood, Charles H.; Maps of the Ancient Sea Kings - Evidence of Advanced Civilization in the Ice Age, 1996 reprint, Adventures Unlimited Press, One Adventure Place, Kempton, IL 60946, USA.

Hodges, Henry; Technology in the Ancient World, 1992, Marboro Books Corp., a division of Barnes & Noble, Inc., USA.

Knight, Christopher R., and Lomas, Robert; Uriel's Machine, Uncovering the Secrets of Stonehenge, Noah's Flood, and the Dawn of Civilization, 2004, Barnes and Noble Books, Inc., USA.

Lehner, Mark; The Complete Pyramids - Solving the Ancient Mysteries, 1997, Thames and Hudson, Inc., 500 Fifth Avenue, New York, NY 10110, USA.

Noorbergen, Rene'; Secrets of the Lost Races, 1977, The Bobbs - Merrill Co, Inc., USA.

Silverman, David P., General Editor; Ancient Egypt, 1997, Duncan Baird Publishers, Sixth Floor, Castle House, 73-76 Wells Street, London, W1P 3RE, England.

Wilson, Colin and Flem-Ath, Rand; The Atlantis Blueprint - Unlocking the Ancient Mysteries of a Long-Lost Civilization, 2000, Delacorte Press, USA.

Zapp, Ivar & Erikson, George; Atlantis in America – Navigators of the Ancient World, 1998, Adventures Unlimited Press, One Adventure Place, Kempton, IL 60946, USA.

Creation – Catastrophism – Refuting Evolution

Ackerman, Paul D.; It's A Young World After All - Exciting Evidence for a Recent Creation, 1986, Baker Book House, Grand Rapids, Michigan, USA.

Allan, D. S. & Delair, J. B.; Cataclysm! - Compelling Evidence of a Cosmic Catastrophe in 9500 BC, 1997, Bear & Company, Santé Fe, New Mexico, USA.

Cuozzo, Jack; Buried Alive - The Startling Truth About Neanderthal Man, 1998, Master Books, Arkansas, USA.

Custance, Arthur C.; Evolution or Creation? - The Doorway Papers, Published online at: http://www.custance.org/old/evol/index.html

Dillow, Joseph C.; The Waters Above - Earth's Pre-Flood Water Canopy, Revised Edition, 1982, Moody Press, Chicago, Illinois, USA.

Dolphin, Lambert; On The Great Flood of Noah, Published online at: http://www.ldolphin.org/flood.shtml

Gascoigne, Mike; Impossible Theology, The Christian Evolutionist Dilemma, 2004, Anno Mundi Books. P.O. Box 752, Camberley, GU17 0XJ, England. http://www.annomundi.co.uk

Gish, Duane T., Ph.D.; The Amazing Story of Creation from Science and the Bible, 1990, Institute for Creation Research, El Cajon, California, USA.

Hancock, Graham; Fingerprints of the Gods, 1995, Doubleday Canada, Toronto, Canada.

Hapgood, Charles H.; Paths of the Poles, 1999 Reprint, Adventures Unlimited Press, One Adventure Place, Kempton, IL 60946, USA.

Lubenow, Marvin L.; Bones of Contention, A Creationist Assessment of Human Fossils, 1992, Baker Books, P.O. Box 6287, Grand Rapids, Michigan, 49516-6287, USA.

Morris, Henry M. And Parker, Gary E.; What is Creation Science?, Revised Edition, 1987, Master Books, El Cajon, California, USA.

Morris, Henry M., and Whitcomb, John C.; The Genesis Flood, The Biblical Record and It's Scientific Implications, 42nd Printing, 1998, P & R Publishing Company, Phillipsburg, New Jersey, USA.

Oard, Michael J.; An Ice Age Caused by The Genesis Flood, 1990, Institute for Creation Research, El Cajon, California, USA.

Patterson, Roger; Evolution Exposed, 2006, Answers in Genesis, P.O. Box 510, Hebron, KY 41048, USA.

Pember, G. H.; Earth's Earliest Ages, 1998 Reprint, Kregel Publications, USA.

Sarfati, Jonathan, Ph.D.; Refuting Evolution, October 1999, Seventh Printing, Master Books, Inc., P.O. Box 727, Green Forest, AR, 72638, USA.

Woodmorappe, John; Noah's Ark, A Feasibility Study, 1996, Institute for Creation Research, El Cajon, California, USA.

Velikovsky, Immanuel; Earth In Upheaval, 1955 – 11th Printing, Doubleday & Company, Inc. Garden City, New York, USA.

Velikovsky, Immanuel; Worlds In Collision, 1977, Pocket Books, New York, NY, USA.

Dinosaurs, Fallen Angels, Giants, and the Nephilim

Alford, Alan F., Gods of the New Millennium; 1996, Hodder & Stoughton, London, England.

Collins, Andrew; Gods of Eden - Egypt's Lost Legacy and the Genesis of Civilization, 2002, Bear & Co., One Park Street, Rochester, VT, 05767, USA.

Collins, Andrew; From the Ashes of Angels, The Forbidden Legacy of a Fallen Race, 2001, Bear & Company, One Park Street, Rochester, VT, 05767, USA.

Davidson, Gustav; A Dictionary of Angels, Including the Fallen Angels, Free Press, Div. of MacMillan, Inc., 866 Third Avenue, New York, NY 10022, USA.

DeLoach, Charles; Giants – A Reference Guide from History, the Bible, and Recorded Legend, 1995, The Scarecrow Press, Inc., Metuchen, NJ, USA.

Dinosaur Dictionary, An A to Z of Dinosaurs and Prehistoric Reptiles, 2001, Tangerine Press, an imprint of Scholastic, Inc., 555 Broadway, New York, NY 10012, USA.

Gish, Duane T., Ph.D.; Dinosaurs by Design, 9th printing - 1998, Master Books, Green Forest, Arkansas, USA.

Hapgood, Charles H.; Mystery in Acambaro, 2000 reprint with forward by David Hatcher Childress, Adventures Unlimited Press, One Adventure Place, Kempton, IL 60946, USA.

Lindsay, William - Text Writer, Fornari, Giuliano - Illustrator; The Great Dinosaur Atlas, 1999, DK Publishing Inc., 95 Madison Avenue, New York, NY, 10016, USA.

Missler, Chuck; As The Days of Noah Were - Return of the Aliens?, Published online at: http://www.ldolphin.org/noahdays.html.

Tanaka, Shelley; New Dinos, the Latest Finds! The Coolest Discoveries!, 2003, Madison Press Books, 1000 Yonge Street, Suite 200, Toronto, Ontario, M4W 2K2, Canada.

Taylor, Paul S.; The Great Dinosaur Mystery and the Bible, 1989, Chariot Victor Publishing, Colorado Springs, Colorado, USA.

Sitchin, Zecharia; The 12th Planet; Book One of "The Earth Chronicles," 1978, Avon Books, New York, NY, USA

Sitchin, Zecharia; The Stairway to Heaven; Book Two of "The Earth Chronicles," 1980, St. Martin's Press, New York, NY, USA.

Sitchin, Zecharia;
The Wars of Gods and Men; Book Three of "The Earth Chronicles," 1985, The Lost Realms; Book Four of "The Earth Chronicles," 1990,
When Time Began; Book Five of "The Earth Chronicles," 1993,
The Cosmic Code; Book Six of "The Earth Chronicles," 1998,
Avon Books, New York, NY, USA.

Sitchin, Zecharia; Genesis Revisited, 1991, Bear & Company, Inc., Santa Fe, New Mexico, USA.

Paganism: False Religious Mythology

NOTE: For books about Radical Islam and Terrorism, look under "Christian Apologetics - Defending the Bible"

Baigent, Michael; From the Omens of Babylon: Astrology and Ancient Mesopotamia, 1994, Penguin - Arkana Books, 375 Hudson St., New York, NY 10014, USA.

Baigent, Michael; Leigh, Richard, & Lincoln, Henry; Holy Blood, Holy Grail, 1982, Delacorte Press, 1 Dag Hammarskjold Plaza, New York, NY 10017, USA.

Bierhorst, John; The Mythology of South America, With A New Afterword, 2002, Oxford University Press, 198 Madison Ave., New York, NY 10016-4314, USA.

Barnett, Mary; Gods and Myths of the Romans – The Archeology and Mythology of Ancient Peoples, 1996, Brockhampton Press, 20 Bloomsbury Street, London, WC1B 3QA, England.

Black, Jeremy and Green, Anthony; Gods, Demons, and Symbols of Ancient Mesopotamia – an Illustrated Dictionary, 2003, University of Texas Press, Austin, Texas, USA.

Boyce, Mary, translator and editor; Textual Sources for the Study of Zoroastrianism, 1990, University of Chicago Press, Chicago, Illinois, USA.

Bunson, Margaret; A Dictionary of Ancient Egypt, 1991, Oxford University Press, 198 Madison Ave., New York, NY 10016-4314, USA.

Classical Mythology – A dictionary of the tales, characters, and traditions of Classical Mythology, 1997, Geddes & Grosset Ltd., David Dale House, New Lanark, ML11 9DJ, Scotland,

Cotterell, Arthur; The Encyclopedia of Mythology - Norse, Classical and Celtic, Acropolis Books, imprint of Anness Publishing Ltd., Hermes House, 88-89 Blackfriars Road, London, SE1 8HA, England.

Dailey, Stephanie; Myths From Mesopotamia – Creation, The Flood, Gilgamesh, and Others, 2000, Revised Edition, Oxford University Press, Great Clarendon Street, Oxford, New York, USA.

Faulkner, R. O.; Andrews, Carol - Editor; The Ancient Egyptian Book of the Dead, 1999, University of Texas Press, Box 7819, Austin, TX 78713, USA.

Finegan, Jack; Myth & Mystery, An Introduction to the Pagan Religions of the Biblical World, 1997, Baker Book House, P.O. Box 6287, Grand Rapids, MI 49516-6287, USA.

Gardner, Laurence, Bloodline of the Holy Grail, 1996, Element Books, Ltd, Shaftesbury, Dorset SP7 8BP, England.

Gilbert, Adrian; Magi, the Quest for a Secret Tradition, 1996, Bloomsbury Publishing, 2 Soho Square, London W1B 6HB, England.

Goetz, Delia and Morley, Sylvanus G.; Popol Vuh: The Sacred Book of the Ancient Quiche Maya, 1991, University of Oklahoma Press, USA.

Heron, Patrick C.; The Nephilim and the Pyramid of the Apocalypse, 2004, Xulon Press, USA.

Hinnells, John R.; Persian Mythology; 1997, Chancellor Press, imprint of Reed International Books Ltd., Michelin House, 81 Fulham Road, London SW3 6RB, England.

Hislop, Alexander; The Two Babylons or the Papal Worship, 1959, Second American Edition of the 1916 original. The Loizeaux Brothers, Inc., USA.

Horn, Thomas R.; The Gods Who Walk Among Us, 1999, Huntington House Publishers, P.O. Box 53788, Lafayette, LA 70505, USA.

Jenkins, John Major; Maya Cosmogenesis 2012, The True Meaning of the Maya Calendar End-Date, 1998, Bear & Company, Rochester, Vermont, 05767, USA.

Johnson Jr., Robert Bowie; The Parthenon Code: Mankind's History in Marble, 2004, Solving Light Books, 727 Mount Alban Drive, Annapolis, MD 21401, USA.

Lemesurier, Peter; Decoding the Great Pyramid, 1999, Elements Books, Ltd. (Barnes and Noble Book Reprint), England.

Naydler, Jeremy; Temple of the Cosmos - The Ancient Egyptian Experience of the Sacred, 1996, Inner Traditions International, One Park Street, Rochester, Vermont, 05767, USA.

New Larousse Encyclopedia of Mythology, 1989, Paul Hamlyn, London, England.

Nicholson, Paul & Shaw, Ian; The Dictionary of Ancient Egypt, in Association with the British Museum, 1995, Harry N. Abrams, Inc., New York, NY, USA.

Oakes, Lorna & Gahlin, Lucia; Ancient Egypt, An Illustrated Reference to the Myths, Religions, Pyramids, and Temples of the Land of the Pharaohs, 2002, Hermes House, a Div. of Anness Publishing Ltd., Hermes House, 88-89 Blackfriars Road, London, SE1 8HA, England.

Parker, Julia & Derek; Parkers' Astrology – The Definitive Guide to Using Astrology in Every Aspect of Your Life, 1994, Elan press – an imprint of General Publishing Co., Ltd., 30 Lesmill Rd., Toronto, M3B 2T6, Canada.

Samma, Jamie & Carson, David; Medicine Cards – The Discovery of Power Through The Ways of Animals, 1988, Bear & Company, P.O. Drawer 2860 Santa Fe, NM 87504, USA.

Sanders, Catherine Edwards; Wicca's Charm - Understanding the Spiritual Hunger Behind the Rise of Modern Witchcraft, and Pagan Spirituality, 2005, Shaw Books - WaterBrook Press, 12265 Oracle Blvd., Ste. 200, Colorado Springs, CO 80921, USA.

Waddell, L. A.; The British Edda, 1930, Christian Book Club, P.O. Box 216, Hawthorne, California, 90250, USA.

Waterson, Barbara; Gods of Ancient Egypt, 1999, Bramley Books, Ltd., Godalming Business Centre, Wooksack Way, Godalming, Surrey, GU7 1XW, England.

~ Index ~

~ *About the Author* ~

Bible scholar, historian, and astronomer Helena Lehman is the author of, and artist for the non-fiction "Language of God" Book Series, and the upcoming fictional Pillar of Enoch Trilogy. She is an avid student of the Bible and ancient history, and an expert on the connection between the Gospel in the Stars, the Tabernacle, and the Great Pyramid. Her writings explore the ancient and divine roots of the Star Gospel, and their place as the cornerstone of the Language of God - a divine allegorical language of parables and symbols that permeates every book of the Bible, and all Creation.

Helena's premiere work is the four-volume "Language of God" Book Series, originally written between 2000 and 2009. Its 2,500 plus cumulative pages reflect the accumulated knowledge of a lifetime, and challenge many traditional views of the past. It offers compelling evidence about what our righteous ancestors actually knew and believed, and how they perceived God - in light of their advanced knowledge of their world, and the Universe that God created for them. The allegorical Language of God, and the messages that God locked into the Ancient Zodiac ties the separate topics covered in each book together, and offers a feast of new ideas for every inquiring mind.

Helena has spent many years in intense research, becoming a self-made scholar in diverse areas such as ancient history, astronomy, comparative religion, and theology. In addition, her books touch on many topics of faith and evangelism, including apologetics, eschatology, exegesis, and hermeneutics. She has many writing projects underway, and is available to speak at special events. For further information about Helena, her writing and speaking endeavors, or to purchase her books, visit her web site at http://pillar-of-enoch.com, or write her at helena@pillar-of-enoch.com.

Helena currently lives with her husband Steve in the Chicago area. Steve and Helena were once childhood sweethearts, and despite thirty years of separation, they never forgot each other. When Steve found her again in 2002, Helena found an unbounded faith in miracles - a faith she holds fast to with joy as she awaits Yahshua's return.

Pillar of Enoch Ministry Book Order Form

Name:_____

Address:_____

City:_____ State/Prov._____ Postal Code_____

E-Mail Address:_____(required)

Note: All Prices include shipping in the USA. International Customers, call Customer Service at 708-977-0115 to get rates.

Paperback Titles at 33% OFF Autographed by Author	*Price:*	*Qty:*
"The Language of God in the Universe"	$24.00	_____
"The Language of God in Humanity"	$28.00	_____
"The Language of God in History"	$30.00	_____
"The Language of God in Prophecy"	$28.00	_____
"The Language of God" Series 4 Book Set	$94.00	_____

Specially Priced PDF Books on CD	*Price:*	*Qty:*
"The Language of God in the Universe"	$14.00	_____
"The Language of God in Humanity"	$16.00	_____
"The Language of God in History"	$18.00	_____
"The Language of God in Prophecy"	$16.00	_____
"The Language of God" Series 4 CD Set	$50.00	_____

Order on the Internet at pillar-of-enoch.com for special web-only discounts and extras on all book orders, or mail orders to:

**Pillar of Enoch Ministry Books, 1708 N. 77th Avenue
Elmwood Park, Illinois 60707-4107 USA**

Questions? E-mail: helena@pillar-of-enoch.com
Phone: 708-977-0115

CPSIA information can be obtained at www.ICGtesting.com
Printed in the USA
LVOW01s0807030814

397268LV00001B/3/P